EVERYMAN, I will go with thee,

and be thy guide,

In thy most need to go by thy side

WILLIAM COBBETT

Born in 1762, the self-taught son of a labourer from Farnham, Surrey. Served as a soldier, but withdrew to Philadelphia to avoid persecution. Prosecuted for libel, 1797, and returned to London, 1800, where he edited a Radical paper. Imprisoned, and went to America again, 1817–19. M.P. for Oldham, 1832. Died in 1835.

WILLIAM COBBETT

Rural Rides

INTRODUCTION BY
ASA BRIGGS

*Vice-Chancellor and Professor of History
in the University of Sussex*

DENT: LONDON
EVERYMAN'S LIBRARY
DUTTON: NEW YORK

209508

No. 638   Hardback ISBN o 460 00638 x
No. 1638 Paperback ISBN o 460 01638 5

914.1
Cob

CONTENTS

Contents

The following chapters of the book were originally printed in a second volume in Everyman's Library.

Contents

INTRODUCTION

THERE is no better way of rediscovering a lost but still not forgotten England than to turn to the colourful pages of William Cobbett's *Rural Rides*. Already when Cobbett began to write the accounts of his journeys in 1821, the England which he had known as a boy was beginning to look and to feel different. The landscape was changing as a result of the double impact of agricultural enclosure and the growth of towns: society too was changing as a result of the combined influences of industry, finance, and war. To many of Cobbett's contemporaries the changes were good, visible signs of the 'march of improvement': to Cobbett and his followers they were bad, but it still seemed that there was time enough to reverse them. 'Events are working together,' Cobbett wrote in 1825, 'to make the country worth living in which, for the great body of people, is at present hardly the case.' In order to restore the best in the past it was necessary to root out the causes of decay, causes which were all interrelated in what Cobbett came to believe was one great 'system,' 'the Thing.' In the name of true conservatism, therefore, he appealed for a radical reform of the House of Commons.

It was for the sake of discovering the true state of affairs and appealing to others to help promote the proper remedies that Cobbett began to travel round England. He rode on relentlessly, even after Whig parliamentary reform in 1832 seemed merely to parody his expectations. The account of the last ride printed in these two volumes was penned on the eve of the first elections for the reformed Parliament. Although Cobbett himself was elected a member, the new 'collective wisdom,' as he always called the House of Commons, proved no wiser than the old. The system went on, and the Thing continued to grow. What has happened between 1832 and the present day gives a certain sturdy pathos to the main themes of *Rural Rides*.

The sturdiness, however, is stronger than the pathos. There are few books in the English language which are as robust as this. When in 1830 Cobbett first assembled in book form the descriptions of his journeys which had already appeared at regular intervals in his *Political Register*, he was presenting his readers with a portrait as well as a landscape. He had put the whole of himself into *Rural Rides*, not merely his impressions or his opinions, and the modern reader learns from his book as much about the personality and development of England's greatest radical as about towns and fields or politics and economics. On an August evening in 1826, in a Wiltshire inn, as the sun was setting, and the rooks were 'skimming and curving over the tops of the trees' and a flock of sheep were 'nibbling their way in from the down and going to their fold,' he mused about the shape of his 'life of adventure, of toil, of pleasure, of peril, of ardent friendship and not less ardent enmity.' 'After filling me with wonder,' he went on, 'that a heart and mind so wrapped up in everything belonging to the gardens, the fields, and the woods should have been condemned to waste themselves away amidst the stench, the noise, and the strife of cities, it brought me to the present moment.' 'Nothing is *so swift as thought*: it runs over a life-time in a moment.' The form of *Rural Rides* was just as suited for such long-term contemplation as it was for the statement of grievances, and the author was free to trace connections or to digress into asides according to his mood. Cobbett's digressions—about the formation of clouds, the pretty faces of the local girls, the history of parish churches—are often both vivid and charming: the connections, however, were what interested him most. Just as he came to discern one great 'system' in all the separate signs of national corruption—paper money, the national debt, patronage and sinecures, the 'wen' of London, the economic power of the Jews and the religious appeal of the Methodists, Malthus and Pitt, machinery and utilitarian education—so he came to see one great unifying purpose in his life. Even his enforced flight from England to the United States in 1817 to escape from the 'Gagging Bills' of Lord Sidmouth seemed in retrospect to have been part of one grand design. 'The trip which Old Sidmouth and crew gave me to America,' he wrote in August 1823, 'was attended with some interesting consequences; amongst which were the introducing of the Sussex pigs into the American farm yards; the introduction of the Swedish turnip into the American fields; the introduction of American apple-trees into England; and the introduction of the making, in England, of the straw plat, to supplant the Italian. One thing more, and that is of more importance than all the rest, Peel's Bill arose out of the "puff-out" Registers; these arose out of the trip to Long Island; and out of Peel's Bill has arisen the best bothering that the wigs of the boroughmongers ever received, which bothering will end in the destruction of the boroughmongering. It is curious, and very *useful*, thus to trace events to their causes.'

Curious and useful though Cobbett's discovering of connections in his own and in national experience proved to be, it presents certain difficulties for the modern reader of *Rural Rides*. Cobbett's direct style, his devastating power of denunciation, his careful and detailed observation of nature, his unrestrained prejudices, his neat descriptions of places, speak for themselves and need no introduction. His quest for connections, however, will not be intelligible to a reader who is ignorant of the outlines of two basic chronologies—first, Cobbett's own biography, and second, the social and political biography of England from 1797 to 1832. Acquaintance with the two chronologies makes passages about Sidmouth, turnips, Long Island, and Peel's Bill meaningful and even exciting instead of elusive and unrewarding.

Cobbett was born at Farnham in Surrey in 1762 of farming stock. He was restless enough to read Swift's *Tale of a Tub* under a haystack at the age of 11, to try to run away to sea, and in 1782 to enlist as a private soldier. He served in Nova Scotia from 1784 to 1791, and soon became a sergeant. This was the summit of his military career, however, for he found himself in difficulties after denouncing the conditions of soldiers' pay. He withdrew to France in 1792 and later to the United States, where he remained until 1800. Within six months of arriving in America he had begun his career as a writer and a politician: eventually choosing the pen-name Peter Porcupine, he spent his time defending the old order and the English system of government and bitterly attacking the French revolution and republicanism. When he returned to England in 1800, he was the idol of the authorities, a protégé of the politician William Windham, and even on one occasion the dinner-companion of William Pitt himself.

Between 1800 and 1805 Cobbett moved in the middle of a world of ministerial writers, although he steadfastly refused to sell his independence. It was a sign of his traditionalist inclinations when he bought a farm at Botley in Hampshire in 1805, where he was to live for twelve years. His life was not 'designed' to peter out, however, in rural domesticity.

He began to feel increasingly dissatisfied with the stock-jobbing, money-making society which seemed to be taking the place of the old social order, and such dissatisfaction always goaded him to action. When in 1806 the new government, the 'Ministry of All the Talents,' of which his old patron Windham was a member, failed to attack what he regarded as political corruption, he turned—with some misgivings—from Toryism to Radicalism. In 1809 he made an indignant protest against the flogging of English militiamen by German mercenaries, which earned him two years in Newgate jail. He emerged an unflinching radical, and after the end of the Napoleonic Wars in 1815, he became the natural leader of a national movement for parliamentary reform. His *Political Register*, which had first appeared in 1802 as a Tory periodical, became the most influential radical newspaper in the country, particularly after its publication in 1816 in a special twopenny edition designed to appeal to journeymen and labourers.

The repressive measures of the post-war government, of which Lord Liverpool was prime minister and Lord Sidmouth home secretary, forced Cobbett to flee to the United States in 1817. On this occasion the New World seemed very different to him from what it had been in 1792. It was transformed into a paradise—a country without a standing army, with no 'tithe-eating tribe of parson-justices' and no national debt. When he returned to England in 1819, he held up the American example to his English audiences just as he had held up the English example to his American audiences during the 1790's. His English audiences were growing rapidly, however, and the severe agricultural distress of the early 1820's gave him an opportunity for the first time to appeal to countrymen as well as to journeymen and labourers. The country tours, 'rustic harangues,' county meetings, and local dinners, which all played a part in his 'agitation,' were to make up the contents of *Rural Rides*. If the final book seems to lack a plan, it must be remembered that behind it was the bigger plan of Cobbett's own political campaigning during the 1820's.

The first ride was from London to Newbury on a foggy day in October 1821. The fog prevented Cobbett from seeing much of the fields, but it did not make him lose his way or confuse his thoughts and feelings. No fog ever could do. However easily his contemporaries got lost in the foggy England of the 1820's, he was always sure of his direction, although it was frequently his prejudices rather than his experience which served as a beacon light. The journeys of his fellow radicals gave him little sense of a common pilgrimage, and by 1830, when long-awaited parliamentary reform was round the corner, he was as bitter in denouncing rival leaders as he was the supporters of the old 'system.' When he died in 1835, his personal independence was still intact, but he was as disillusioned with the 'reformed' world as he had been with the Ministry of All the Talents. He had expected changes in the political system to reverse changes in the social and economic system: instead they consolidated them. A new generation of radicals was even prepared to take for granted forces which he had always resisted to the limits of his power. The high hopes of certain passages of *Rural Rides* were dashed.

It is clear from this brief outline how Cobbett's own bio-graphy is inextricably bound up with the social and political biography of his country, but certain details of the national chronology are important. The key dates for Cobbett were not 1793—the year when war with France broke out—or 1815 —the year when the Napoleonic Wars came to an end, but 1797 and 1819. It was in 1797 that Pitt, driven by the needs of war finance, resorted to the issue of paper money. It was in 1819 that Peel's Act, violently opposed by Cobbett, authorized the return to gold and the resumption of cash payments. Cobbett was all in favour of gold and loathed 'rag money,' but he objected to the terms on which the return had been made. There had been no reduction in the national debt, no fall in taxation, and no sharing of burdens. The fundholders continued to profit from the peace just as they had profited from the war, and their parasitic hold on the community— expressed as much in the growth of the size of London as in the size of their own private fortunes—was actually increased. Cobbett believed that the grievances of farmers, who were heavily hit by the fall in prices and the greater burden of debt, and the distress of labourers, who were driven to starvation, could only be remedied by measures which a reformed parlia-ment would pass. He did not object to the 'rotten boroughs' on grounds of abstract principles so much as on practical and moral grounds, and he disliked the political economists and 'beastly Scotch feelosophers,' who defended the financial system, as much as the boroughmongers and placemen who upheld the political system. He was not looking for Utopia but for Old England, for a land 'with room for us all, and plenty for us to eat and to drink,' a land fit for bees and not for

drones. It needs no introductory gloss to explain the last
sentence of this edition of *Rural Rides*—'be the consequences
to individuals what they may, the greatness, the freedom, and
the happiness of England must be restored.'

ASA BRIGGS.

1956.

SELECT BIBLIOGRAPHY

WORKS. *The Soldier's Friend*, 1792: *Observations on the Emigration of Dr Joseph Priestley*, 1794; *Le Tuteur Anglais*, 1795; trans. Martens's *Law of Nations*, 1795; *The Works of Peter Porcupine, D.D.*, 1795; *The Life and Adventures of Peter Porcupine*, 1796; *The Life of Thomas Paine*, 1796; *Porcupine's Works*, 1797; *Porcupine's Works*, 1801; *A Treatise on the Culture and Management of Fruit Trees*, 1802; *Important Considerations for the People of this Kingdom*, 1803; *The Political Proteus*, 1804; *Cobbett's Parliamentary History of England*, 1804; *Cobbett's Complete Collection of State Trials*, 1809; *The Life of William Cobbett, by Himself*, 1809; *Letters on the Late War between the United States and Great Britain*, 1815; *Paper Against Gold*, 1815; *A Year's Residence in the United States of America*, 1818; *A Grammar of the English Language*, 1818; *Thomas Paine, A Sketch of his Life and Character*, 1819; *The American Gardener*, 1821; *Cottage Economy*, 1821; *The Farmer's Friend*, 1821: introduction to Jethro Tull's *The Horse-hoeing Husbandry*, 1822; *Cobbett's Collective Commentaries*, 1822; *A French Grammar*, 1824; *A History of the Protestant Reformation in England and Ireland*, 1824; *Big O. and Sir Glory, A Comedy in Three Acts*, 1825; *Cobbett's Poor Man's Friend*, 1826; *The Woodlands*, 1828; *The English Gardener*, 1828; *A Treatise on Cobbett's Corn*, 1828; *The Emigrant's Guide*, 1829; *Rural Rides*, 1830; *Advice to Young Men*, 1830; *Eleven Lectures on the French and Belgian Revolutions*, 1830; *History of the Regency and Reign of King George the Fourth*, 1830; *Cobbett's Plan of Parliamentary Reform*, 1830; *Surplus Population, A Comedy in Three Acts*, 1831; *A Spelling Book, with Appropriate Lessons in Reading*, 1831; *A Geographical Dictionary of England and Wales*, 1832; *Cobbett's Tour in Scotland*, 1832; *A New French and English Dictionary*, 1833; *Life of Andrew Jackson*, 1834; *Three Lectures on the Political State of Ireland*, 1834; *Cobbett's Legacy to Labourers*, 1835; *Cobbett's Legacy to Parsons*, 1835.

Among the most important newspapers and periodicals edited by Cobbett were *The Political Censor*, 1796–7; *Porcupine's Gazette*, 1797–1800; *The Rush-light*, 1800; *The Porcupine*, 1800–1; *Cobbett's Political Register* (with various titles), 1802–35; *Le Mercure Anglois*, 1803; *Cobbett's Parliamentary Debates*, 1804 onwards; *Cobbett's American Political Register*, 1816–18; *Cobbett's Evening Post*, 1820; *Cobbett's Parliamentary Register*, 1820; *The Statesman*, 1822–3; *Cobbett's Twopenny Trash*, 1831–2.

BIOGRAPHY AND CRITICISM. W. H. Hazlitt: *The Character of William Cobbett*, 1835; R. Huish: *Memoirs of the late William Cobbett*, 1836; J. E. Thorold Rogers: *Historical Gleanings*, 1869; E. Smith: *William Cobbett; A Biography*, 2 vols., 1878; E. I. Carlyle: *William Cobbett, A Study of His Life as shown in His Writings*, 1904; L. Melville: *The Life and Letters of William Cobbett*, 2 vols., 1913; G. D. H. Cole: *The Life of William Cobbett*, 1924 (3rd ed., 1947); G. K. Chesterton: *William Cobbett*, 1926; G. D. H. and Margaret Cole: *Index of Persons* mentioned in *Rural Rides*, a separately and privately printed appendix to their edition of *Rural Rides*, 1930; W. Reitzel (ed.): *The Progress of a Plough-boy to a Seat in Parliament*, 1933; W. B. Pemberton: *William Cobbett*, 1949; M. L. Pearl: *William Cobbett, A Bibliographical Account of His Life and Times*, 1953.

RURAL RIDES

IN THE COUNTIES OF

Surrey, Kent, Sussex, Hants, Berks, Oxford, Bucks,
Wilts, Somerset, Gloucester, Hereford, Salop, Worcester,
Stafford, Leicester, Hertford, Essex, Suffolk, Norfolk,
Cambridge, Huntingdon, Nottingham, Lincoln, York, Lancaster, Durham, and Northumberland, in the years
1821, 1822, 1823, 1825, 1826, 1829, 1830, and 1832:

WITH

Economical and Political Observations relative to
Matters Applicable to, and Illustrated by, the State
of those Counties respectively.

BY

WILLIAM COBBETT

A New Edition, with Notes,
By JAMES PAUL COBBETT, Barrister-at-Law.

LONDON
PUBLISHED BY A. COBBETT, 137, STRAND.
1853.

PREFACE

THE reader will perceive that there are, in the course of these Rides, some instances in which the Author has gone over the same part of the country on more than one occasion: and it may, also, be considered that there are certain repetitions in the writing, of statements of fact, or of remarks, which might with propriety have been omitted.

That omission, however, it was not easy to effect, without such alterations as would perhaps seem objectionable; and it has therefore been thought best to reprint the several passages in their original form.

MANCHESTER, *June* 1853.

JOURNAL

FROM LONDON, THROUGH NEWBURY, TO BURGH-CLERE, HURSTBOURN TARRANT, MARLBOROUGH, AND CIRENCESTER, TO GLOUCESTER

BURGHCLERE, NEAR NEWBURY, HANTS,
October 30, 1821, *Tuesday (Evening)*.

FOG that you might cut with a knife all the way from London to Newbury. This fog does not *wet* things. It is rather a *smoke* than a fog. There are no two things in *this world ;* and, were it not for fear of *Six-Acts* (the " wholesome restraint " of which I continually feel) I might be tempted to carry my comparison further; but, certainly, there are no two things in *this world* so dissimilar as an English and a Long Island autumn. —These fogs are certainly the *white clouds* that we sometimes see aloft. I was once upon the Hampshire Hills, going from Soberton Down to Petersfield, where the hills are high and steep, not very wide at their base, very irregular in their form and direction, and have, of course, deep and narrow valleys winding about between them. In one place that I had to pass, two of these valleys were cut asunder by a piece of hill that went across them and formed a sort of bridge from one long hill to another. A little before I came to this sort of bridge I saw a smoke flying across it; and, not knowing the way by experience, I said to the person who was with me, " there is the turnpike road (which we were expecting to come to); for, don't you see the dust? " The day was very fine, the sun clear, and the weather dry. When we came to the pass, however, we found ourselves, not in dust, but in a fog. After getting over the pass, we looked down into the valleys, and there we saw the fog going along the valleys to the north, in detached parcels, that is to say, in clouds, and, as they came to the pass, they rose,

3

went over it, then descended again, keeping constantly along just above the ground. And, to-day, the fog came by *spells*. It was sometimes thinner than at other times; and these changes were very sudden too. So that I am convinced that these fogs are *dry clouds*, such as those that I saw on the Hampshire-Downs. Those did not *wet* me at all; nor do these fogs wet anything; and I do not think that they are by any means injurious to health.—It is the fogs that rise out of swamps, and other places, full of putrid vegetable matter, that kill people. These are the fogs that sweep off the new settlers in the American Woods. I remember a valley in Pennsylvania, in a part called *Wysihicken*. In looking from a hill, over this valley, early in the morning, in November, it presented one of the most beautiful sights that my eyes ever beheld. It was a sea bordered with beautifully formed trees of endless variety of colours. As the hills formed the outsides of the sea, some of the trees showed only their tops; and, every now-and-then, a lofty tree growing in the sea itself, raised its head above the apparent waters. Except the setting-sun sending his horizontal beams through all the variety of reds and yellows of the branches of the trees in Long Island, and giving, at the same time, a sort of silver cast to the verdure beneath them, I have never seen anything so beautiful as the foggy valley of the Wysihicken. But, I was told, that it was very fatal to the people; and that whole families were frequently swept off by the "*fall-fever*."—Thus the *smell* has a great deal to do with health. There can be no doubt that butchers and their wives fatten upon the smell of meat. And this accounts for the precept of my grandmother, who used to tell me to *bite my bread and smell to my cheese;* talk much more wise than that of certain *old grannies*, who go about England crying up " the *blessings* " of paper-money, taxes, and national debts.

The fog prevented me from seeing much of the fields as I came along yesterday; but the fields of swedish turnips that I did see were good; pretty good; though not clean and neat like those in Norfolk. The farmers here, as everywhere else, complain most bitterly; but they hang on, like sailors to the masts or hull of a wreck. They read, you will observe, nothing but the country newspapers; they, of course, know nothing of the *cause* of their " bad times." They hope " the times will mend." If they quit business, they must sell their stock; and, having thought this worth so much money, they cannot endure the thought of selling for a third of the sum. Thus they hang on; thus the landlords will first turn the farmers' pockets inside out; and then their turn comes. To finish the present farmers will not take long. There has been stout fight going on all this morning (it is now 9 o'clock) between the *sun* and the *fog*. I have backed the former, and he appears to have gained the day; for he is now shining most delightfully.

Came through a place called "a park" belonging to a Mr. Montague, who is now *abroad*; for the purpose, I suppose, of generously assisting to compensate the French people for what they lost by the entrance of the Holy Alliance Armies into their country. Of all the ridiculous things I ever saw in my life this place is the most ridiculous. The house looks like a sort of church, in somewhat of a gothic style of building, with *crosses* on the tops of different parts of the pile. There is a sort of swamp, at the foot of a wood, at no great distance from the front of the house. This swamp has been dug out in the middle to show the water to the eye; so that there is a sort of river, or chain of diminutive lakes, going down a little valley, about 500 yards long, the water proceeding from the *soak* of the higher ground on both sides. By the sides of these lakes there are little flower gardens, laid out in the Dutch manner; that is to say, cut out into all manner of superficial geometrical figures. Here is the *grand en petit*, or mock magnificence, more complete than I ever beheld it before. Here is a *fountain*, the basin of which is not four feet over, and the water spout not exceeding the pour from a tea-pot. Here is a *bridge* over a *river* of which a child four years old would clear the banks at a jump. I could not have trusted myself on the bridge for fear of the consequences to Mr. Montague; but I very conveniently stepped over the river, in imitation of the *Colossus*. In another part there was a *lion's mouth* spouting out water into the lake, which was so much like the vomiting of a dog, that I could almost have pitied the poor Lion. In short, such fooleries I never before beheld; but what I disliked most was the apparent impiety of a part of these works of refined taste. I did not like the crosses on the dwelling house; but, in one of the gravel walks, we had to pass under a gothic arch, with a cross on the top of it, and in the point of the arch a niche for a saint or a virgin, the figure being gone through the lapse of centuries, and the pedestal only remaining as we so frequently see on the outsides of Cathedrals and of old churches and chapels. But the good of it was, this gothic arch, disfigured by the hand of old Father Time, was composed of Scotch fir wood, as rotten as a pear; nailed together in such a way as to make the thing appear, from a distance, like the remnant of a ruin! I wonder how long this sickly, this childish, taste is to remain? I do not know who this gentleman is. I suppose he is some honest person from the 'Change or its neighbourhood; and that these *gothic arches* are to denote the *antiquity of his origin!* Not a bad plan; and, indeed, it is one that I once took the liberty to recommend to those Fundlords who retire to be country-'squires. But I never recommended the *Crucifixes!* To be sure the Roman Catholic religion may, in England, be considered as a *gentleman's religion*, it being the most *ancient* in the country; and, therefore, it is fortunate for a Fundlord when he happens (if he ever do happen) to be of that faith.

This gentleman may, for anything that I know, be a *Catholic*; in which case I applaud his piety and pity his taste. At the end of this scene of mock grandeur and mock antiquity I found something more rational; namely, some hare hounds, and, in half-an-hour after, we found, and I had the first hare-hunt that I had had since I wore a smock-frock! We killed our hare after good sport, and got to Burghclere in the evening to a nice farm-house in a dell, sheltered from every wind, and with plenty of good living; though with no gothic arches made of Scotch-fir!

October 31. *Wednesday.*

A fine day. Too many hares here; but, our hunting was not bad; or, at least, it was a great treat to me, who used, when a boy, to have my legs and thighs so often filled with thorns in running after the hounds, anticipating with pretty great certainty, a "*waling*" of the back at night. We had grey-hounds a part of the day; but the ground on the hills is so *flinty*, that I do not like the country for coursing. The dogs' legs are presently cut to pieces.

Nov. 1. *Thursday.*

Mr. Budd has swedish turnips, mangel-wurzel, and cabbages of various kinds, transplanted. All are very fine indeed. It is impossible to make more satisfactory experiments in *transplanting* than have been made here. But this is not a proper place to give a particular account of them. I went to see the best cultivated parts round Newbury; but I saw no spot with half the "feed" that I see here, upon a spot of similar extent.

have no form, and their colour is a ground of white with black
or red spots, each spot being, from the size of a plate to that
of a crown-piece, and some of them have no small spots. These

HURSTBOURN TARRANT, HANTS,
Nov. 2. Friday.

This place is commonly called *Uphusband*, which is, I think,
as decent a corruption of names as one would wish to meet with.
However, Uphusband the people will have it, and Uphusband
it shall be for me. I came from Berghclere this morning, and
through the park of Lord Caernarvon, at Highclere. It is a fine
season to look at woods. The oaks are still covered, the
beeches in their best dress, the elms yet pretty green, and the
beautiful ashes only beginning to turn off. This is, according
to my fancy, the prettiest park that I have ever seen. A great
variety of hill and dell. A good deal of water, and this, in one
part, only wants the *colours* of American trees to make it look
like a " *creek ;* " for the water runs along at the foot of a steepish
hill, thickly covered with trees, and the branches of the lower-
most trees hang down into the water and hide the bank completely. I like this place better than *Fonthill, Blenheim, Stowe*,
or any other gentleman's grounds that I have seen. The *house*
I did not care about, though it appears to be large enough to
hold half a village. The trees are very good, and the woods
would be handsomer if the larches and firs were *burnt,* for which
only they are fit. The great beauty of the place is, the *lofty
downs,* as steep, in some places, as the roof of a house, which
form a sort of boundary, in the form of a part of a crescent, to
about a third part of the park, and then slope off and get more
distant, for about half another third part. A part of these downs
is covered with trees, chiefly beech, the colour of which, at this
season, forms a most beautiful contrast with that of the down
itself, which is so green and so smooth! From the vale in the
park, along which we rode, we looked apparently almost perpendicularly up at the downs, where the trees have extended
themselves by seed more in some places than others, and thereby
formed numerous salient parts of various forms, and, of course,
as many and as variously formed glades. These, which are always
so beautiful in forests and parks, are peculiarly beautiful in this
lofty situation and with verdure so smooth as that of these
chalky downs. Our horses beat up a score or two of hares as
we crossed the park; and, though we met with no *gothic arches*
made of Scotch-fir, we saw something a great deal better;
namely, about forty cows, the most beautiful that I ever saw,
as to colour at least. They appear to be of the Galway-breed.
They are called, in this country, *Lord Caernarvon's breed*. They

have no horns, and their colour is a ground of white with black or red spots, these spots being from the size of a plate to that of a crown-piece; and some of them have no small spots. These cattle were lying down together in the space of about an acre of ground: they were in excellent condition, and so fine a sight of the kind I never saw. Upon leaving the park, and coming over the hills to this pretty vale of Uphusband, I could not help calculating how long it might be before some Jew would begin to fix his eye upon Highclere, and talk of putting out the present owner, who, though a *Whig*, is one of the best of that set of politicians, and who acted a manly part in the case of our deeply injured and deeply lamented queen. Perhaps his lordship thinks that there is no fear of the Jews as to *him*. But does he think that his tenants can sell fat hogs at 7s. 6d. a score, and pay him more than a third of the rent that they have paid him while the debt was contracting? I know that such a man does not lose his estate at once; but, without rents, what is the estate? And that the Jews will receive the far greater part of his rents is certain, unless the interest of the debt be reduced. Lord Caernarvon told a man, in 1820, that *he did not like my politics.* But what did he mean by my *politics ?* I have no politics but such as he *ought* to like. I want to do away with that infernal *system,* which, after having beggared and pauperised the labouring classes, has now, according to the report, made by the ministers themselves to the House of Commons, plunged the owners of the land themselves into a state of distress, for which those ministers themselves can hold out no remedy! To be sure I labour most assiduously to destroy a system of distress and misery; but is that any reason why a *lord* should dislike my politics? However, dislike, or like them, to them, to those very politics, the lords themselves *must come at last.* And that I should exult in this thought, and take little pains to disguise my exultation, can surprise nobody who reflects on what has passed within these last twelve years. If the landlords be well; if things be going right with them; if they have fair prospects of happy days; then what need they care about me and *my politics ;* but if they find themselves in " *distress,*" and do not know how to get out of it; and if they have been plunged into this distress by those who " dislike my politics; " is there not *some reason* for men of sense to hesitate a little before they *condemn* those politics? If no great change be wanted; if things could remain even; then men may, with some show of reason, say that I am disturbing that which ought to be let alone. But if things cannot remain as they are; if there must be a *great change ;* is it not folly, and, indeed, is it not a species of idiotic perverseness, for men to set their faces, without rhyme or reason, against what is said as to this change by *me*, who have, for nearly twenty years, been warning the country of its danger, and foretelling that which has now come to pass and is coming to pass? However, I make no complaint on this score. People disliking my politics "neither picks my pocket, nor breaks my leg," as Jefferson said by the writings of the Atheists. If they be pleased in disliking my politics, I am pleased in liking them; and so we are both enjoying ourselves. If the country want no assistance from me, I am quite sure that I want none from it.

Nov. 3. Saturday.

Fat hogs have lately sold, in this village, at 7s. 6d. a score (but would hardly bring that now), that is to say, at 4½d. a pound. The hog is weighed whole, when killed and dressed. The head and feet are included; but, so is the lard. Hogs fatted on peas or barley-meal may be called the very best meat that England contains. At Salisbury (only about 20 miles off) fat hogs sell for 5s. to 4s. 6d. a score. But, then, observe, these are *dairy hogs*, which are not nearly so good in quality as the corn-fed hogs. But I shall probably hear more about these prices as I get further towards the West. Some wheat has been sold at Newbury-market for £6 a load (40 bushels); that is at 3s. a bushel. A considerable part of the crop is wholly unfit for bread flour, and is not equal in value to good barley. In not a few instances the wheat has been carried into the gate, or yard, and thrown down to be made dung of. So that, if we were to take the average, it would not exceed, I am convinced, 5s. a bushel in this part of the country; and the average of all England would not, perhaps, exceed 4s. or 3s. 6d. a bushel. However, Lord Liverpool has got a *bad harvest* at last! That *remedy* has been applied! Somebody sent me some time ago, that stupid newspaper, called the *Morning Herald*, in which its readers were reminded of my *"false prophecies,"* I having (as this paper said) foretold that wheat would be at *two shillings a bushel before Christmas.* These gentlemen of the *"respectable part of the press"* do not mind lying a little upon a pinch. [See Walter's *Times* of Tuesday last, for the following: "*Mr. Cobbett has thrown open the front of his house at Kensington, where he proposes to sell meat at a reduced price.*"] What I said was this:

that, if the crop were good and the harvest fine, and gold
continued to be paid at the Bank, we should see wheat at four,
not two, shillings a bushel before Christmas. Now, the crop
was, in many parts, very much blighted, and the harvest was
very bad indeed; and yet the average of England, including
that which is destroyed, or not brought to market at all, will
not exceed 4s. a bushel. A farmer told me, the other day, that
he got *so little* offered for some of his wheat, that he was resolved
not to take any more of it to market; but to give it to hogs.
Therefore, in speaking of the price of wheat, you are to take in
the unsold as well as the sold; that which fetches nothing as
well as that which is sold at high price.—I see, in the Irish
papers, which have overtaken me on my way, that the system
is working the Agriculturasses in " the sister-kingdom " too!
The following paragraph will show that the *remedy* of a *bad
harvest* has not done our dear sister much good. " A very
numerous meeting of the Kildare Farming Society met at Naas
on the 24th inst., the Duke of Leinster in the chair; Robert
de la Touche, Esq., M.P., vice-president. Nothing can more
strongly prove the BADNESS OF THE TIMES, and very *unfortunate
state of the country*, than the necessity in which the Society
finds itself of *discontinuing its premiums, from its present want
of funds*. The best members of the farming classes have got
so much in arrear in their subscriptions that they have declined
to appear or to dine with their neighbours, and general depression
damps the spirit of the most industrious and *hitherto prosperous*
cultivators." You are mistaken, Pat; it is not the *times* any
more than it is the *stars*. Bobadil, you know, imputed his
beating to the *planets :* " planet-stricken, by the foot of
Pharaoh!"—" No, Captain," says Welldon, " indeed it was a
stick." It is not the *times*, dear Patrick: it is *the government*,
who having first contracted a great debt in depreciated money,
are now compelling you to pay the interest at the rate of three
for one. Whether this be *right*, or *wrong*, the Agriculturasses
best know: it is much more their affair than it is mine; but be
you well assured that they are only at the beginning of their
sorrows. Ah! Patrick, whoever shall live only a few years will
see a *grand change* in your state! Something a *little more
rational* than " Catholic Emancipation" will take place, or I
am the most deceived of all mankind. This *debt* is your best,
and, indeed, your *only friend*. It must, at last, give the THING
a *shake*, such as it never had before. — The accounts which
my country newspapers give of the failure of farmers are

perfectly dismal. In many, many instances they have put an end to their existence, as the poor deluded creatures did who had been ruined by the South Sea Bubble! I cannot help feeling for these people, for whom my birth, education, taste, and habits give me so strong a partiality. Who can help feeling for their wives and children, hurled down headlong from affluence to misery in the space of a few months! Become all of a sudden the mockery of those whom they compelled, perhaps, to cringe before them! If the labourers exult, one cannot say that it is unnatural. If *Reason* have her fair sway, I am exempted from all pain upon this occasion. I have done my best to prevent these calamities. Those farmers who have attended to me are safe while the storm rages. My endeavours to stop the evil in time cost me the earnings of twenty long years! I did not sink, no, nor *bend*, beneath the heavy and reiterated blows of the accursed system, which I have dealt back blow for blow; and, blessed be God, I now see it *reel !* It is staggering about like a sheep with water in the head: turning its pate up on one side: seeming to listen, but has no hearing: seeming to look, but has no sight: one day it capers and dances: the next it mopes and seems ready to die.

Nov. 4. Sunday.

This, to my fancy, is a very nice country. It is continual hill and dell. Now and then a *chain* of hills higher than the rest, and these are downs or woods. To stand upon any of the hills and look around you, you almost think you see the ups and downs of sea in a *heavy swell* (as the sailors call it) after what they call a gale of wind. The undulations are endless, and the great variety in the height, breadth, length, and form of the little hills, has a very delightful effect.—The soil, which, to look *on* it, appears to be more than half flint stones, is very good in quality, and, in general, better on the tops of the lesser hills than in the valleys. It has great tenacity; does not *wash away* like sand, or light loam. It is a stiff, tenacious loam, mixed with flint stones. Bears saint-foin well, and all sorts of grass, which make the fields on the hills as green as meadows, even at this season; and the grass does not burn up in summer.—In a country so full of hills one would expect endless runs of water and springs. There are none: absolutely none. No water-furrow is ever made in the land. No ditches round the fields. And, even in the *deep valleys*, such as that in which this village is situated, though it winds round for ten or fifteen miles, there is no run of water even now. There is the *bed* of a brook, which will run before spring, and it continues running with more or less water for about half the year, though, some years, it never runs at all. It rained all Friday night; pretty nearly all day yesterday; and to-day the ground is as dry as a bone, except just along the street of the village, which has been kept in a sort of stabble by the flocks of sheep passing along to and from Appleshaw fair. In the deep and long and narrows valleys, such as this, there are meadows with very fine herbage and very productive. The grass very fine and excellent in its quality. It is very curious, that the soil is much *shallower* in the vales than on the hills. In the vales it is a sort of hazle-mould on a bed of something approaching to gravel; but, on the hills, it is stiff loam, with apparently half flints, on a bed of something like clay first (reddish, not yellow) and then comes the chalk, which they often take up by digging a sort of wells; and then they spread it on the surface, as they do the clay in some countries, where they sometimes fetch it many miles and at an immense expense. It was very common, near Botley, to chalk land at an expense of sixteen pounds an acre.—The land here is excellent in quality generally, unless you get upon the highest chains of hills. They have frequently 40 bushels of wheat to the acre. Their barley is very fine; and their saint-foin abundant. The turnips are, in general, very good at this time; and the land appears as capable of carrying fine crops of them as any land that I have seen. A fine country for sheep: always dry: they never injure the land when feeding off turnips in wet weather; and they can lie down on the dry; for the ground is, in fact, never wet except while the rain is actually falling. Sometimes, in spring-thaws and thunder-showers, the rain runs down the hills in torrents; but is gone directly. The flocks of sheep, some in fold and some at large, feeding on the sides of the hills, give great additional beauty to the scenery.— The woods, which consist chiefly of oak thinly intermixed with ash, and well set with underwood of ash and hazel, but mostly the latter, are very beautiful. They sometimes stretch along the top and sides of hills for miles together; and, as their edges, or outsides, joining the fields and the downs, go winding and twisting about, and as the fields and downs are naked of trees, the sight altogether is very pretty.—The trees in the deep and long valleys, especially the elm and the ash, are very fine and very lofty; and, from distance to distance, the rooks have made them their habitation.—This sort of country, which, in irregular shape, is of great extent, has many and great advantages. Dry under foot. Good roads, winter as well as summer, and little, very little expense. Saint-foin flourishes. Fences cost little. Wood, hurdles, and hedging-stuff cheap. No shade in wet harvests. The water in the wells excellent. Good sporting country, except for coursing, and too many flints for that.— What becomes of all the *water* ? There is a spring, in one of the cross valleys that runs into this, having a basin about thirty feet over, and about eight feet deep, which they say sends up water once in about 30 or 40 years; and boils up so as to make a large current of water.—Not far from Uphusband the *Wansdike* (I think it is called) crosses the country. Sir Richard Colt Hoare has written a great deal about this ancient boundary, which is, indeed, something very curious. In the ploughed fields the traces of it are quite gone; but they remain in the *woods* as well as on the downs.

Nov. 5. Monday.

A *white frost* this morning. The hills round about beautiful at sun-rise, the rooks making that noise which they always make in winter mornings. The starlings are come in large flocks; and, which is deemed a sign of a hard winter, the fieldfares are come at an early season. The haws are very abundant; which, they say, is another sign of a hard winter. The wheat is high enough here, in some fields, " to hide a hare," which is, indeed, not saying much for it, as a hare knows how to hide herself upon the bare ground. But it is, in some fields, four inches high, and is green and gay, the colour being finer than that of any grass.—The fuel here is wood. Little coal is brought from Andover. A load of faggots does not cost above 10s. So that, in this respect, the labourers are pretty well off. The wages here and in Berkshire, about 8s. a week; but the farmers talk of lowering them.—The poor-rates heavy, and heavy they must be, till taxes and rents come down greatly.—Saturday and to-day Appleshaw sheep-fair. The sheep, which had taken a rise at Weyhill-fair, have fallen again even below the Norfolk and Sussex mark. Some South-Down lambs were sold at Appleshaw so low as 8s. and some even lower. Some Dorsetshire ewes brought no more than a pound; and, perhaps, the average did not exceed 28s. I have seen a farmer here who can get (or could a few days ago) 28s. round for a lot of fat South-Down wethers, which cost him just that money, when they were lambs, *two years ago !* It is impossible that they can have

cost him less than 24s. each during the two years, having to be
fed on turnips or hay in winter, and to be fatted on good grass.
Here (upon one hundred sheep) is a loss of £120 and £14 in
addition at five per cent. interest on the sum expended in the
purchase; even suppose not a sheep has been lost by death or
otherwise.—I mentioned before, I believe, that fat hogs are
sold at Salisbury at from 5s. to 4s. 6d. the *score* pounds, dead
weight.—Cheese has come down in the same proportion. A
correspondent informs me that one hundred and fifty Welsh
sheep were, on the 18th of October, offered for 4s. 6d. a head,
and that they went away unsold! The skin was worth a
shilling of the money! The following I take from the *Tyne
Mercury* of the 30th of October. " Last week, at Northawton
fair, Mr. Thomas Cooper, of Bow, purchased three milch cows
and forty sheep, for £18 16s. 6d.!" The skins, four years ago,
would have sold for more than the money. The *Hampshire
Journal* says, that, on 1 November (Thursday) at Newbury
Market, wheat sold from 88s. to 24s. the quarter. This would
make an average of 56s. But very little indeed was sold at 88s.,
only the prime of the old wheat. The best of the new for about
48s. and, then, if we take into view the great proportion that
cannot go to market at all, we shall not find the average, even
in this rather dear part of England, to exceed 32s., or 4s. a
bushel. And, if we take all England through, it does not come
up to that, nor anything like it. A farmer very sensibly
observed to me yesterday, that, " if we had had such a crop and
such a harvest a few years ago, good wheat would have been £50
a load; " that is to say, 25s. a bushel! Nothing can be truer than
this. And nothing can be clearer than that the present race
of farmers, generally speaking, must be swept away by bankruptcy, if they do not, in time, make their bow, and retire.
There are two descriptions of farmers, very distinct as to the
effects which this change must naturally have on them. The
word *farmer* comes from the French, *fermier*, and signifies *renter*.
Those only who rent, therefore, are, properly speaking, *farmers*.
Those who till their own land are *yeomen ;* and, when I was a
boy, it was the common practice to call the former *farmers* and
the latter *yeoman-farmers*. These yeomen have, for the greater
part, been swallowed up by the paper-system which has drawn
such masses of money together. They have, by degrees, been
bought out. Still there are some few left; and these, if not in
debt, will stand their ground. But all the present race of mere
renters must give way, in one manner or another. They must

break, or drop their style greatly; even in the latter case, their rent must, very shortly, be diminished more than two-thirds. Then comes the *landlord's turn;* and the sooner the better.— In the *Maidstone Gazette* I find the following: "Prime beef was sold in Salisbury market, on Tuesday last, at 4*d*. per lb., and good joints of mutton at 3½*d*.; butter, 11*d*. and 12*d*. per lb.—In the west of Cornwall, during the summer, pork has often been sold at 2½*d*. per lb."—This is very true; and what can be better? How can Peel's Bill work in a more delightful manner? What nice "*general working of events!*" The country rag-merchants have now very little to do. They have *no discounts.* What they have out they *owe:* it is so much *debt:* and, of course, they become poorer and poorer, because they must, like a mortgager, have more and more to pay as prices fall. This is very good; for it will make them disgorge a part, at least, of what they have swallowed, during the years of high prices and depreciation. They are worked in this sort of way: the tax-collectors, the excise-fellows, for instance, hold their sittings every six weeks, in certain towns about the country. They will receive the country rags, if the rag man can find, and will give, security for the due payment of his rags, when they arrive in London. For want of such security, or of some formality of the kind, there was a great bustle in a town in this county not many days ago. The excise-fellow demanded sovereigns, or Bank of England notes. Precisely how the matter was finally settled I know not; but the reader will see that the exciseman was only taking a proper precaution; for, if the rags were not paid in London, the loss was his!

MARLBOROUGH,
Tuesday noon, Nov. 6.

I left Uphusband this morning at 9, and came across to this place (20 miles) in a post-chaise. Came up the valley of Uphusband, which ends at about 6 miles from the village, and puts one out upon the Wiltshire downs, which stretch away towards the west and south-west, towards Devizes and towards Salisbury. After about half a mile of down we came down into a level country; the flints cease, and the chalk comes nearer the top of the ground. The labourers along here seem very poor indeed. Farm houses with twenty ricks round each, besides those standing in the fields; pieces of wheat, 50, 60, or 100 acres in a piece; but a group of women labourers, who were attending the measurers to measure their reaping work, presented such an assemblage of rags as I never before saw even amongst the hoppers at Farnham, many of whom are common beggars. I never before saw *country* people, and reapers too, observe, so miserable in appearance as these. There were some very pretty girls, but ragged as colts and as pale as ashes. The day was cold too, and frost hardly off the ground; and their blue arms and lips would have made any heart ache but that of a seat-seller or a loan-jobber. A little after passing by these poor things, whom I left, cursing, as I went, those who had brought them to this state, I came to a group of shabby houses upon a hill. While a boy was watering his horses, I asked the ostler the *name* of the place; and, as the old women say, " you might have knocked me down with a feather," when he said, " *Great Bedwin.*" The whole of the houses are not intrinsically worth a thousand pounds. There stood a thing out in the middle of the place, about 25 feet long and 15 wide, being a room stuck up on unhewed stone pillars about 10 feet high. It was the Town Hall, where the ceremony of choosing the *two members* is performed. " This place sends members to parliament, don't it? " said I to the ostler. " Yes, sir." " Who are members *now* ? " " I *don't know*, indeed, sir."—I have not read the *Henriade* of Voltaire for these 30 years; but in ruminating upon the ostler's answer; and in thinking how the world, yes, *the whole world*, has been deceived as to this matter, two lines of that poem came across my memory.

Représentans du peuple, les Grands et le Roi:
Spectacle magnifique! Source sacrée des lois! [1]

The Frenchman, for want of understanding the THING as well as I do, left the eulogium incomplete. I therefore here add four lines, which I request those who publish future editions of the *Henriade* to insert in continuation of the above eulogium of Voltaire.

Représentans du peuple, que celui-ci gnore,
Sont fait à miracle pour garder son Or!
Peuple trop heureux, que le bonheur inonde!
L'envie de vos voisins, admiré du monde! [2]

[1] I will not swear to the very *words ;* but this is the meaning of Voltaire: " Representatives of the people, the Lords and the King: " *Magnificent* spectacle! *Sacred* source of the Laws! "

[2] " Representatives of the people, of whom the people know nothing, must be miraculously well calculated to have the care of their money! Oh! people too happy! overwhelmed with blessings! The *envy* of *your neighbours*, and *admired* by the *whole world* ! "

The first line was suggested by the ostler; the last by the words which we so very often hear from the bar, the bench, the *seats*, the pulpit, and the throne. Doubtless my poetry is not equal to that of Voltaire; but my rhyme is as good as his, and my *reason* is a great deal better.—In quitting this villainous place we see the extensive and uncommonly ugly park and domain of Lord Aylesbury, who seems to have tacked park on to park, like so many outworks of a fortified city. I suppose here are 50 or 100 farms of former days swallowed up. They have been bought, I dare say, from time to time; and it would be a labour very well worthy of reward by the public, to trace to its source, the money by which these immense domains, in different parts of the country, have been formed!— Marlborough, which is an ill-looking place enough, is succeeded, on my road to Swindon, by an extensive and very beautiful down about 4 miles over. Here nature has flung the earth about in a great variety of shapes. The fine short smooth grass has about 9 inches of mould under it, and then comes the chalk. The water that runs down the narrow side-hill valleys is caught, in different parts of the down, in basins made on purpose, and lined with clay apparently. This is for watering the sheep in summer; sure sign of a really dry soil; and yet the grass never *parches* upon these downs. The chalk holds the moisture, and the grass is fed by the dews in hot and dry weather.—At the end of this down the high-country ends. The hill is high and steep, and from it you look immediately down into a level farming country; a little further on into the dairy-country, whence the North-Wilts cheese comes; and, beyond that, into the vale of Berkshire, and even to Oxford, which lies away to the northeast from this hill.—The land continues good, flat and rather wet to Swindon, which is a plain country town, built of the stone which is found at about 6 feet under ground about here.—I come on now towards Cirencester, through the dairy country of North Wilts.

CIRENCESTER,
Wednesday (noon), 7 Nov.

I slept at a dairy-farm house at Hannington, about eight miles from Swindon, and five on one side of my road. I passed through that villainous hole, Cricklade, about two hours ago; and, certainly, a more rascally looking place I never set my eyes on. I wished to avoid it, but could get along no other way. All along here the land is a whitish stiff loam upon a bed of soft stone, which is found at various distances from the surface, sometimes two feet and sometimes ten. Here and there a field is fenced with this stone, laid together in walls without mortar or earth. All the houses and out-houses are made of it, and even covered with the thinnest of it formed into tiles. The stiles in the fields are made of large flags of this stone, and the gaps in the hedges are stopped with them.—There is very little wood all along here. The labourers seems miserably poor. Their dwellings are little better than pig-beds, and their looks indicate that their food is not nearly equal to that of a pig. Their wretched hovels are stuck upon little bits of ground *on the road side*, where the space has been wider than the road demanded. In many places they have not two rods to a hovel, It seems as if they had been swept off the fields by a hurricane, and had dropped and found shelter under the banks on the road side! Yesterday morning was a sharp frost; and this had set the poor creatures to digging up their little plats of potatoes. In my whole life I never saw human wretchedness equal to this: no, not even amongst the free negroes in America, who, on an average, do not work one day out of four. And this is " *prosperity*," is it? These, O Pitt! are the fruits of thy hellish system! However, this *Wiltshire* is a horrible county. This is the county that the *Gallon-loaf* man belongs to. The land all along here is good. Fine fields and pastures all around; and yet the cultivators of those fields so miserable! This is particularly the case on both sides of Cricklade, and in it too, where everything had the air of the most deplorable want.—They are sowing wheat all the way from the Wiltshire downs to Cirencester; though there is some wheat up. Winter vetches are up in some places, and look very well.—The turnips of both kinds are good all along here.—I met a farmer going with porkers to Highworth market. They would weigh, he said, four score and a half, and he expected to get 7s. 6d. a score. I expect he will not. He said they had been fed on barley-meal; but I did not believe him. I put it to his honour, whether whey and beans had not been their food. He looked surly, and pushed on.— On this stiff ground, they grow a good many beans, and give them to the pigs with whey; which makes excellent pork for the *Londoners ;* but which must meet with a pretty hungry stomach to swallow it in Hampshire. The hogs, all the way that I have come, from Buckinghamshire, are without a single exception that I have seen, the old-fashioned black-spotted hogs. Mr. Blount at Uphusband has one, which now weighs

about thirty score, and will possibly weigh forty, for she moves
about very easily yet. This is the weight of a good ox; and yet,
what a little thing it is compared to an ox! Between Cricklade
and this place (Cirencester) I met, in separate droves, about
two thousand Welsh cattle, on their way from Pembrokeshire
to the fairs in Sussex. The greater part of them were heifers
in calf. They were purchased in Wales at from £3 to £4 10s.
each! None of them, the drovers told me reached £5. These
heifers used to fetch, at home, from £6 to £8, and sometimes
more. Many of the things that I saw in these droves did not
fetch, in Wales, 25s. And they go to no *rising* market! Now,
is there a man in his senses who believes that this THING can go
on in the present way? However, a fine thing, indeed, is this
fall of prices! My " cottager " will easily get his cow, and a
young cow too, for less than the £5 that I talked of. These
Welsh heifers will calve about May; and they are just the very
thing for a cottager.

GLOUCESTER,
Thursday (morning), Nov. 8.

In leaving Cirencester, which is a pretty large town, a pretty
nice town, and which the people call *Cititer,* I came up hill into
a country, apparently formerly a down or common, but now
divided into large fields by stone walls. Anything so ugly I
have never seen before. The stone, which, on the other side
of Cirencester, lay a good way under ground, here lies very near
to the surface. The plough is continually bringing it up, and
thus, in general, come the means of making the walls that serve
as fences. Anything quite so cheerless as this I do not recollect
to have seen; for the Bagshot country, and the commons
between Farnham and Haselemere, have *heath* at any rate;
but these stones are quite abominable. The turnips are not a
fiftieth of a crop like those of Mr. Clarke at Bergh-Apton in
Norfolk, or Mr. Pym at Reygate in Surrey, or of Mr. Brazier at
Worth in Sussex. I see thirty acres here that have less *food*
upon them than I saw the other day, upon half an acre at Mr.
Budd's at Berghclere. *Can* it be good farming to plough and
sow and hoe thirty acres to get what *may* be got upon half an
acre? Can that half acre cost more than a tenth part as much
as the thirty acres? But, if I were to go to this thirty-acre
farmer, and tell him what to do to the half acre, would he not
exclaim with the farmer at Botley: " What! *drow* away all
that 'ere ground between the *lains!* Jod's blood!" — With

the exception of a little dell about eight miles from Cititer, this miserable country continued to the distance of ten miles, when, all of a sudden, I looked down from the top of a high hill into *the vale of Gloucester !* Never was there, surely, such a contrast in this world! This hill is called *Burlip Hill ;* it is much about a mile down it, and the descent so steep as to require the wheel of the chaise to be locked; and, even with that precaution, I did not think it over and above safe to sit in the chaise; so, upon Sir Robert Wilson's principle of taking care of *Number One,* I got out and walked down. From this hill you see the Morvan Hills in Wales. You look down into a sort of *dish* with a flat bottom, the Hills are the sides of the dish, and the City of Gloucester, which you plainly see, at seven miles distance from Burlip Hill, appears to be not far from the centre of the dish. All here is fine; fine farms; fine pastures; all inclosed fields; all divided by hedges; orchards a plenty; and I had scarcely seen one apple since I left Berkshire.—Gloucester is a fine, clean, beautiful place; and, which is of a vast deal more importance, the labourer's dwellings, as I came along, looked good, and the labourers themselves pretty well as to dress and healthiness. The girls at work in the fields (always my standard) are not in rags, with bits of shoes tied on their feet and rags tied round their ankles, as they had in Wiltshire.

JOURNAL

FROM GLOUCESTER, TO BOLLITREE IN HEREFORD-SHIRE, ROSS, HEREFORD, ABINGDON, OXFORD, CHELTENHAM, BURGHCLERE, WHITCHURCH, UPHURSTBOURN, AND THENCE TO KENSINGTON

BOLLITREE CASTLE, HEREFORDSHIRE,
Friday, 9 Nov. 1821.

I GOT to this beautiful place (Mr. William Palmer's) yesterday, from Gloucester. This is in the parish of *Weston*, two miles on the Gloucester side of Ross, and, if not the first, nearly the first, parish in Herefordshire upon leaving Gloucester to go on through Ross to Hereford.—On quitting Gloucester I crossed the Severne, which had overflowed its banks and covered the meadows with water.—The soil good but stiff. The coppices and woods very much like those upon the clays in the south of Hampshire and in Sussex; but the land better for corn and grass. The goodness of the land is shown by the apple-trees, and by the sort of sheep and cattle fed here. The sheep are a cross between the Ryland and Leicester, and the cattle of the Herefordshire kind. These would starve in the pastures of any part of Hampshire or Sussex that I have ever seen.—At about seven miles from Gloucester I came to hills, and the land changed from the whitish soil, which I had hitherto seen, to a red brown, with layers of flat stone of a reddish cast under it. Thus it continued to Bollitree. The trees of all kinds are very fine on the hills as well as in the bottoms.—The spot where I now am is peculiarly well situated in all respects. The land very rich, the pastures the finest I ever saw, the trees of all kinds surpassing upon an average any that I have before seen in England. From the house, you see, in front and winding round to the left, a lofty hill, called *Penyard Hill*, at about a mile and a half distance, covered with oaks of the finest growth; along at the foot of this wood are fields and orchards continuing the slope of the hill down for a considerable distance, and, as the ground lies in a sort of *ridges* from the wood to the foot of the slope, the hill-and-dell is very beautiful. One of these dells with the two adjoining sides of hills is an orchard belonging to Mr. Palmer, and the trees, the ground, and everything belonging to it, put me in mind of the most beautiful of the spots in the North of Long Island. Sheltered by a lofty wood; the grass fine beneath the fruit trees; the soil dry under foot though the rain had scarcely ceased to fall; no moss on the trees; the leaves of many of them yet green; everything brought my mind to the beautiful orchards near Bayside, Little Neck, Mosquito Cove, and Oyster Bay, in Long Island. No wonder that this is a country of *cider* and *perry;* but what a shame it is, that here, at any rate, the owners and cultivators of the soil, not content with these, should, for mere fashion's sake, waste their substance on *wine* and *spirits!* They really deserve the contempt of mankind and the curses of their children.—The woody hill mentioned before, winds away to the left, and carries the eye on to the *Forest of Dean,* from which it is divided by a narrow and very deep valley. Away to the right of Penyard Hill lies, in the bottom, at two miles distance, and on the bank of the river Wye, the town of Ross, over which we look down the vale to Monmouth and see the Welsh hills beyond it. Beneath Penyard Hill, and on one of the *ridges* before mentioned, is the parish church of Weston, with some pretty white cottages near it, peeping through the orchard and other trees; and coming to the paddock before the house, are some of the largest and loftiest trees in the country, standing singly here and there, amongst which is the very largest and loftiest walnut-tree that I believe I ever saw, either in America or in England. In short, there wants nothing but the autumnal *colours* of the American trees to make this the most beautiful spot I ever beheld.—I was much amused for an hour after daylight this morning in looking at the *clouds*, rising, at intervals, from the dells on the side of Penyard Hill, and flying to the top, and then over the hill. Some of the clouds went up in a roundish and compact form. Others rose in a sort of string or stream, the tops of them going over the hill before the bottoms were clear of the place whence they had arisen. Sometimes the clouds gathered themselves together along the top of the hill, and seemed to connect the topmost trees with the sky.—I have been to-day to look at Mr. Palmer's fine crops of *swedish turnips*, which are, in general, called "*swedes.*" These crops having been raised according to *my plan,* I feel, of course, great interest in the matter. The swedes occupy two fields: one of thirteen, and one of seventeen acres. The main part of the seventeen acre field was *drilled,* on ridges, four feet apart, a single row on a ridge, at different times, between 16th April and 29th May. An acre and a half of this piece was *transplanted* on four-feet ridges 30th July. About half an acre across the middle of the field was sown *broad-cast* 14th April.—In the thirteen-acre field there is about half an acre sown *broad-cast* on the 1st of June; the rest of the field was *transplanted;* part in the first week of June, part in the last week of June, part from the 12th to 18th of July, and the rest (about three acres) from 21st to 23rd July. The drilled swedes in the seventeen-acre field, contain full 23 tons to the acre; the transplanted ones in *that* field, 15 tons, and the broad-cast not exceeding 10 tons. Those in the thirteen-acre field which were transplanted before the 21st July, contain 27 if not 30 tons; and the rest of *that* field about 17 tons to the acre. The broad-cast piece here (half an acre) may contain 7 tons. The shortness of my time will prevent us from ascertaining the weight by actual weighings; but, such is the crop, according to the best of my judgment, after a very minute survey of it in every part of each field.—Now, here is a little short of 800 tons of food, about the fifth part of which consists of *tops;* and, of course, there is about 640 tons of *bulb.* As to the *value* and *uses* of this prodigious crop I need say nothing; and as to the time and manner of sowing and raising the plants for transplanting, the act of transplanting, and the after cultivation, Mr. Palmer has followed the directions contained in my *Year's Residence in America;* and, indeed, he is forward to acknowledge, that he had never thought of this mode of culture, which he has followed now for three years, and which he has found so advantageous, until he read that work, a work which the *Farmer's Journal* thought proper to treat as a *romance.*—Mr. Palmer has had some *cabbages* of the large, drum-head, kind. He had about three acres, in rows at four feet apart, and at little less than three feet apart in the rows, making *ten thousand* cabbages on the three acres. He kept ninety-five wethers and ninety-six ewes (large fatting sheep) upon them for *five weeks* all but two days, ending in the first week of November. The sheep, which are now feeding off yellow turnips in an adjoining part of the same field, come back over the cabbage-ground and *scoop out the stumps* almost to the ground in many cases. This ground is going to be ploughed for wheat immediately. Cabbages are a very fine *autumn crop;* but it is the *swedes* on which you must rely for the spring, and on *housed* or *stacked* swedes too; for they will *rot* in many of our winters, if left in the ground. I have had them rot myself, and I saw, in March 1820, hundreds of acres rotten in Warwickshire and Northamptonshire. Mr. Palmer greatly prefers the *transplanting* to the drilling. It has numerous advantages over the drilling; greater regularity of crop, greater certainty, the only *sure* way of avoiding the *fly*, greater crop, admitting of two months later preparation of land, can come *after vetches* cut up for horses (as, indeed, a part of Mr. Palmer's transplanted swedes did), and requiring less labour and expense. I asserted this in my *Year's Residence;* and Mr. Palmer, who has been very particular in ascertaining the fact, states positively, that the expense of transplanting is not so great as the hoeing and setting out of the drilled crops, and not so great as the common hoeings of broad-cast. This, I think, settles the question. But the advantages of the wide-row culture by no means confine themselves to the green and root crop; for Mr. Palmer drills his wheat upon the same ridges, without ploughing, after he has taken off the swedes. He drills it at *eight inches*, and puts in from eight to ten gallons to the acre. His crop of 1820, drilled in this way, averaged 40 bushels to the acre; part drilled in November, and part so late as February. It was the common Lammas wheat. His last crop of wheat is not yet ascertained; but it was better after the swedes than in any other of his land. His manner of taking off the crop is excellent. He first cuts off and carries away the *tops*. Then he has an implement, drawn by two oxen, walking on each side of the ridge, with which he cuts off the *tap root* of the swedes without disturbing the land of the ridge. Any child can then pull up the bulb. Thus the ground, clean as a garden, and in that compact state which the wheat is well known to like, is ready, at once, for drilling with wheat. As to the *uses* to which he applies the crop, tops as well as bulbs, I must speak of these hereafter, and in a work of a description different from this. I have been thus particular here, because the *Farmer's Journal* treated my book as a pack of lies. I know that my (for it is *mine*) system of cattle-food husbandry will finally be that of *all England*, as it already is that of America; but what I am doing here is merely in self-defence against the slanders, the malignant slanders, of the *Farmer's Journal*. Where is a *Whig lord*, who, some years ago, wrote to a gentleman, that " *he* would have *nothing to do* with any *reform* that *Cobbett* was engaged in? " But, in spite of the brutal *Journal*, farmers are not such fools as this lord was: they will not reject a good crop, because they can have it only by acting upon my plan; and this lord will, I imagine, yet see the day when he will be less averse from having to do with a reform in which " Cobbett " shall be engaged.

OLD HALL,
Saturday night, Nov. 10.

Went to Hereford this morning. It was market-day. My arrival became known, and, I am sure, I cannot tell how. A sort of *buz* got about. I could perceive here, as I always have elsewhere, very ardent friends and very bitter enemies; but all full of curiosity. One thing could not fail to please me exceedingly; my friends were *gay* and my enemies *gloomy :* the former smiled, and the latter, in endeavouring to screw their features into a sneer, could get them no further than the half sour and half sad: the former seemed, in their looks to say, " Here he is," and the latter to respond, " Yes, G— d—— him ! "—I went into the market-place, amongst the farmers, with whom, in general, I was very much pleased. If I were to live in the county two months, I should be acquainted with every man of them. The country is very fine all the way from Ross to Hereford. The soil is always a red loam upon a bed of stone. The trees are very fine, and certainly winter comes later here than in Middlesex. Some of the oak trees are still perfectly green, and many of the ashes as green as in September.—In coming from Hereford to this place, which is the residence of Mrs. Palmer and that of her two younger sons, Messrs. Philip and Walter Palmer, who, with their brother, had accompanied me to Hereford; in coming to this place, which lies at about two miles distance from the great road, and at about an equal distance from Hereford and from Ross, we met with something, the sight of which pleased me exceedingly: it was that of a very pretty pleasant-looking lady (and *young* too) with two beautiful children, riding in a little sort of chaise-cart, drawn by *an ass*, which she was driving in reins. She appeared to be well known to my friends, who drew up and spoke to her, calling her Mrs. *Lock*, or *Locky* (I hope it was not *Lockart*) or some such name. Her husband, who is, I suppose, some young farmer of the neighbourhood, may well call himself Mr. *Lucky ;* for to have such a wife, and for such a wife to have the good sense to put up with an ass-cart, in order to avoid, as much as possible, feeding those cormorants who gorge on the taxes, is a blessing that falls, I am afraid, to the lot of very few rich farmers. Mrs. *Lock* (if that be her name) is a real *practical radical.* Others of us resort to radical coffee and radical tea; and she has a radical carriage. This is a very effectual way of assailing the THING, and peculiarly well suited ior the practice of the female sex.

*B 638

But the self-denial ought not to be imposed on the wife only: the husband ought to set the example: and, let me hope, that *Mr. Lock* does not indulge in the use of wine and spirits, while Mrs. Lock and her children ride in a jack-ass gig; for, if he do, he wastes, in this way, the means of keeping her a chariot and pair. If there be to be any expense not absolutely necessary; if there be to be anything bordering on extravagance, surely it ought to be for the pleasure of that part of the family, who have the least number of objects of enjoyment; and for a husband to indulge himself in the guzzling of expensive, unnecessary, and really injurious drink, to the tune, perhaps, of 50 or 100 pounds a year, while he preaches economy to his wife, and, with a face as long as my arm, talks of the low price of corn, and wheedles her out of a curricle into a jack-ass cart, is not only unjust but *unmanly*.

OLD HALL,
Sunday night, 11 November.

We have ridden to-day, though in the rain for a great part of the time, over the fine farm of Mr. Philip Palmer, at this place, and that of Mr. Walter Palmer, in the adjoining parish of Pencoyd. Everything here is good, arable land, pastures, orchards, coppices, and timber trees, especially the elms, many scores of which approach nearly to a hundred feet in height. Mr. Philip Palmer has four acres of swedes on four-feet ridges, drilled on the 11th and 14th of May. The plants were very much injured by the *fly ;* so much, that it was a question, whether the whole piece ought not to be ploughed up. However, the gaps in the rows were filled up by transplanting; and the ground was twice ploughed between the ridges. The crop here is very fine; and I should think that its weight could not be less than 17 tons to the acre.—Of Mr. Walter Palmer's swedes, five acres were drilled, on ridges nearly four feet apart, on the 3rd of June; four acres on the 15th of June; and an acre and a half transplanted (after vetches) on the fifteenth of August. The weight of the first is about twenty tons to the acre; that of the second not much less; and that of the last even, five or six tons. The first two pieces were mauled to pieces by the *fly :* but the gaps were filled up by transplanting, the ground being digged on the tops of the ridges to receive the plants. So that, perhaps, a third part, or more of the crop is due to the *transplanting*. As to the last piece, that transplanted on the 15th of August, after vetches, it is clear, that there could have been no crop without transplanting; and, after all, the crop is by no means a bad one.—It is clear enough to me, that this system will finally prevail all over England. The " loyal," indeed, may be afraid to adopt it, lest it should contain something of " radicalism." Sap-headed fools! They will find something to do, I believe, soon, besides railing against *radicals*. We will din "*radical*" and "*national faith*" in their ears, till they shall dread the din as much as a dog does the sound of the bell that is tied to the whip.

BOLLITREE,
Monday, 12 *Nov.*

Returned this morning and rode about the farm, and also about that of Mr. Winnal, where I saw, for the first time, a plough going *without being held*. The man drove the three horses that drew the plough, and carried the plough round at the ends; but left it to itself the rest of the time. There was a skim coulter that turned the sward in under the furrow; and the work was done very neatly. This gentleman has six acres of *cabbages*, on ridges four feet apart, with a distance of thirty inches between the plants on the ridge. He has weighed one of what he deemed an average weight, and found it to weigh fifteen pounds without the stump. Now, as there are 4320 upon an acre, the weight of the acres is *thirty tons* all but 400 pounds! This is a prodigious crop, and it is peculiarly well suited for food for sheep at this season of the year. Indeed it is good for any farm-stock, oxen, cows, pigs: all like these loaved cabbages. For hogs in yard, after the stubbles are gone; and before the tops of the swedes come in. What masses of manure may be created by this means! But, above all things, for *sheep* to feed off upon the ground. Common turnips have not half the substance in them weight for weight. Then they are in the ground; they are *dirty*, and, in wet weather, the sheep must starve, or eat a great deal of dirt. This very day, for instance, what a sorry sight is a flock of fatting sheep upon turnips; what a mess of dirt and stubble! The cabbage stands boldly up above the ground, and the sheep eats it all up without treading a morsel in the dirt. Mr. Winnal has a large flock of sheep feeding on his cabbages, which they will have finished, perhaps, by January. This gentleman also has some "*radical swedes*," as they call them in Norfolk. A part of his crop is on ridges *five* feet apart with *two rows* on the ridge, a part on *four* feet ridges with *one* row on the ridge. I cannot see that

anything is gained in weight by the double rows. I think that
there may be nearly twenty tons to the acre. Another piece
Mr. Winnal transplanted after vetches. They are very fine;
and, altogether, he has a crop that any one but a " loyal " farmer
might envy him.—This is really the *radical* system of husbandry.
Radical means, *belonging to the root ; going to the root.* And the
main principle of this system (first taught by *Tull*) is, that the
root of the plant is to be fed by *deep tillage*, while it is growing; and to do this we must have our *wide distances.* Our
system of husbandry is happily illustrative of our system of
politics. Our lines of movement are fair and straightforward.
We destroy all weeds, which, like tax-eaters, do nothing but
devour the sustenance that ought to feed the valuable plants.
Our plants are all *well fed ;* and our nations of swedes and of
cabbages present a happy uniformity of enjoyments and of bulk,
and not, as in the broad-cast system of Corruption, here and
there one of enormous size, surrounded by thousands of poor
little starveling things, scarcely distinguishable by the keenest
eye, or, if seen, seen only to inspire a contempt of the husbandman. The Norfolk boys are, therefore, right in calling their
swedes *Radical Swedes.*

BOLLITREE,
Tuesday, 13 *Nov.*

Rode to-day to see a *grove* belonging to Mrs. Westphalin,
which contains the very finest trees, *oaks, chestnuts,* and *ashes,*
that I ever saw in England. This grove is worth going from
London to Weston to see. The lady, who is very much beloved
in her neighbourhood, is, apparently, of the *old school ;* and her
house and gardens, situated in a beautiful dell, form, I think,
the most comfortable looking thing of the kind that I ever saw.
If she had known that I was in her grove, I dare say she would
have expected it to blaze up in flames; or, at least, that I was
come to view the premises previous to confiscation! I can
forgive persons like her; but I cannot forgive the parsons and
others who have misled them! Mrs. Westphalin, if she live
many years, will find, that the best friends of the owners of the
land are those who have endeavoured to produce such *a reform
of the Parliament* as would have prevented the ruin of tenants.
—This parish of Weston is remarkable for having a rector,
who has constantly resided for twenty years ! I do not believe
that there is an instance to match this in the whole kingdom.
However, the *" reverend "* gentlemen may be assured, that,

before many years have passed over their heads, they will be very glad to reside in their parsonage houses.

Rode to the Forest of Dean, up a very steep hill. The lanes here are between high banks, and, on the sides of the hills, the road is a rock, the water having, long ago, washed all the earth away. Pretty works are, I find, carried on here, as is the case in all the other *public forests !* Are these things *always* to be carried on in this way? Here is a domain of thirty thousand acres of the finest ,timber-land in the world, and with coal-mines endless! Is this *worth nothing ?* Cannot each acre yield ten trees a year? Are not these trees worth a pound a piece? Is not the estate worth three or four hundred thousand pounds a year? And does it yield *anything to the public*, to whom it belongs? But it is useless to waste one's breath in this way. We must have a *reform of the Parliament :* without it the whole thing will fall to pieces.—The only good purpose that these forests answer is that of furnishing a place of being to labourers' families on their skirts; and here their cottages are very neat, and the people look hearty and well, just as they do round the forests in Hampshire. Every cottage has a pig, or two. These graze in the forest, and, in the fall, eat acorns and beech-nuts and the seed of the ash; for, these last, as well as the others, are very full of oil, and a pig that is put to his shifts will pick the seed very nicely out from the husks. Some of these foresters keep cows, and all of them have bits of ground, cribbed, of course, at different times, from the forest: and to what better use can the ground be put? I saw several wheat stubbles from 40 rods to 10 rods. I asked one man how much wheat he had from about 10 rods. He said more than two bushels. Here is bread for three weeks, or more, perhaps; and a winter's straw for the pig besides. Are these things nothing? The dead limbs and old roots of the forest give *fuel ;* and how happy are these people, compared with the poor creatures about Great Bedwin and Cricklade, where they have neither land nor shelter, and where I saw the girls carrying home bean and wheat stubble for fuel! Those countries, always but badly furnished with fuel, the desolating and damnable system of paper-money, by sweeping away small homesteads, and laying ten farms into one, has literally *stripped* of all shelter for the labourer. A farmer, in such cases, has a whole domain in his hands, and this, not only to the manifest injury of the public at large, but in *open violation of positive law*. The poor forger is hanged; but where is the prosecutor of the monopolising farmer, though the *law* is as clear in the one case as in the other? But it required this infernal system to render every wholesome regulation nugatory; and to reduce to such abject misery a people famed in all ages for the goodness of their food and their dress. There is one farmer, in the North of Hampshire, who has nearly eight thousand acres of land in his hands; who grows fourteen hundred acres of wheat and two thousand acres of barley! He occupies what was formerly 40 farms! Is it any wonder that *paupers increase*? And is there not here cause enough for the increase of *poor*, without resorting to the doctrine of the barbarous and impious Malthus and his assistants, the *feelosofers* of the *Edinburgh Review*, those eulogists and understrappers of the Whig-Oligarchy? "This farmer has done nothing *unlawful*," some one will say. I say he has; for there is a law to forbid him thus to monopolise land. But no matter; the laws, the management of the affairs of a nation, *ought to be such as to prevent the existence of the temptation to such monopoly*. And, even now, the evil ought to be remedied, and could be remedied, in the space of half a dozen years. The disappearance of the paper-money would do the thing in time; but this might be assisted by legislative measures.—In returning from the forest we were overtaken by my son, whom I had begged to come from London to see this beautiful country. On the road-side we saw two lazy-looking fellows, in long great coats and bundles in their hands, going into a cottage. "What do you deal in?" said I, to one of them, who had not yet entered the house. "In the *medical way*," said he. And, I find, that vagabonds of this description are seen all over the country with *tea-licences* in their pockets. They vend *tea*, *drugs*, and *religious tracts*. The first to bring the body into a debilitated state; the second to finish the corporeal part of the business; and the third to prepare the spirit for its separation from the clay! Never was a system so well calculated as the present to degrade, debase, and enslave a people! Law, and, as if that were not sufficient, enormous subscriptions are made; everything that can be done is done to favour these perambulatory impostors in their depredations on the ignorant. While everything that can be done is done, to prevent them from reading, or from hearing of, anything that has a tendency to give them rational notions, or to better their lot. However, all is not buried in ignorance. Down the deep and beautiful valley between Penyard Hill and the hills on the side of the Forest of Dean, there runs a stream of water. On that stream of water there is a *paper-mill*. In that paper-mill there is a set of workmen. That set of workmen do, I am told, *take the Register*, and have taken it for years! It was to these good and sensible men, it is supposed, that the *ringing of the bells* of Weston church, upon my arrival, was to be ascribed; for nobody that I visited had any knowledge of the cause. What a subject for lamentation with corrupt hypocrites! That even on this secluded spot there should be a leaven of common sense! No: *all* is not enveloped in brute ignorance yet, in spite of every artifice that hellish Corruption has been able to employ; in spite of all her menaces and all her brutalities and cruelties.

OLD HALL,
Thursday, 15 Nov.

We came this morning from Bollitree to *Ross-Market*, and, thence, to this place. Ross is an old-fashioned town; but it is very beautifully situated, and if there is little of *finery* in the appearance of the inhabitants, there is also little of *misery*. It is a good, plain country town, or settlement of tradesmen, whose business is that of supplying the wants of the cultivators of the soil. It presents to us nothing of rascality and roguishness of look, which you see on almost every visage in the *borough-towns*, not excepting the visages of the women. I can tell a borough-town from another upon my entrance into it by the nasty, cunning, leering, designing look of the people; a look between that of a bad (for *some* are good) Methodist parson and that of a pickpocket. I remember, and I never shall forget, the horrid looks of the villains in Devonshire and Cornwall. Some people say, " O, *poor fellows!* It is not *their* fault." No? Whose fault is it, then? The miscreants who bribe them? True, that these deserve the halter (and some of them may have it yet); but are not the takers of the bribes *equally* guilty? If we be so very lenient here, pray let us ascribe to the *Devil* all the acts of thieves and robbers: so we do; but we *hang* the thieves and robbers, nevertheless. It is no very unprovoking reflection, that from these sinks of atrocious villainy come a very considerable part of the men to fill places of emolument and trust. What a clog upon a minister to have people, bred in such scenes, forced upon him! And why does this curse continue? However, its natural consequences are before us; and are coming on pretty fast upon each other's heels. There are the landlords and farmers in a state of absolute ruin: there is the debt, pulling the nation down like as a stone pulls a dog under water. The system seems to have fairly wound itself up; to have tied itself hand and foot with cords of its own spinning! —This is the town to which Pope has given an interest in our minds by his eulogium on the " *Man of Ross* " a portrait of whom is hanging up in the house in which I now am.—The market at Ross was very *dull*. No wheat in demand. No buyers. It must *come down*. Lord Liverpool's *remedy*, a bad harvest, has assuredly failed. Fowls 2s. a couple; a goose from 2s. 6d. to 3s.; a turkey from 3s. to 3s. 6d. Let a turkey come down to *a shilling*, as in France, and then we shall soon be to rights.

Friday, 16 *Nov.*

A whole day most delightfully passed a hare-hunting, with a pretty pack of hounds kept here by Messrs. Palmer. They put me upon a horse that seemed to have been made on purpose for me, strong, tall, gentle and bold; and that carried me either over or through everything. I, who am just the weight of a four-bushel sack of good wheat, actually sat on his back from daylight in the morning to dusk (about nine hours), without once setting my foot on the ground. Our ground was at Orcop, a place about four miles distance from this place. We found a hare in a few minutes after throwing off; and in the course of the day, we had to find four, and were never more than ten minutes in finding. A steep and naked ridge, lying between two flat valleys, having a mixture of pretty large fields and small woods, formed our ground. The hares crossed the ridge forward and backward, and gave us numerous views and very fine sport. —I never rode on such steep ground before; and, really, in going up and down some of the craggy places, where the rains had washed the earth from the rocks, I did think, once or twice, of my neck, and how Sidmouth would like to see me.—As to the *cruelty*, as some pretend, of this sport, that point I have, I think, settled, in one of the chapters of my *Year's Residence in America*. As to the expense, a pack, even a full pack of harriers, like this, costs less than two bottles of wine a day with their inseparable concomitants. And as to the *time* thus spent, hunting is inseparable from *early rising* ; and with habits of early rising, who ever wanted time for any business?

We left Old Hall (where we always breakfasted by candle-light) this morning after breakfast; returned to Bollitree; took the Hereford coach as it passed about noon; and came in it through Gloucester, Cheltenham, Northleach, Burford, Whitney, and on to this city, where we arrived about ten o'clock. I could not leave *Herefordshire* without bringing with me the most pleasing impressions. It is not for one to descend to particulars in characterising one's personal friends; and, therefore, I will content myself with saying, that the treatment I met with in this beautiful county, where I saw not one single face that I had, to my knowledge, ever seen before, was much more than sufficient to compensate to me, personally, for all the atrocious calumnies, which, for twenty years, I have had to endure; but where is my country, a great part of the present hideous sufferings of which, will, by every reflecting mind, be easily traced to these calumnies, which have been made the ground, or pretext, for rejecting that counsel by listening to which those sufferings would have been prevented; where is my country to find a compensation!—At *Gloucester* (as there were no meals on the road) we furnished ourselves with nuts and apples, which, first a handful of nuts and then an apple, are, I can assure the reader, excellent and most wholesome fare. They say that nuts of all sorts are unwholesome; if they had been, I should never have written Registers, and if they were now, I should have ceased to write ere this; for, upon an average, I have eaten a pint a day since I left home. In short, I could be very well content to live on nuts, milk, and home-baked bread.—From *Gloucester* to *Cheltenham* the country is level, and the land rich and good. The fields along here are ploughed in ridges about 20 feet wide, and the angle of this species of *roof* is pretty nearly as sharp as that of some slated roofs of houses. There is no wet under; it is the top wet only that they aim at keeping from doing mischief.—*Cheltenham* is a nasty, ill-looking place, half clown and half cockney. The town is one street about a mile long; but then, at some distance from this street, there are rows of white tenements, with green balconies, like those inhabited by the tax-eaters round London. Indeed, this place appears to be the residence of an assemblage of tax-eaters. These vermin shift about between London, Cheltenham, Bath, Bognor, Brighton, Tunbridge, Ramsgate,

Margate, Worthing, and other spots in England, while some of them get over to France and Italy: just like those body-vermin of different sorts, that are found in different parts of the tormented carcasses at different hours of the day and night, and in different degrees of heat and cold.

Cheltenham is at the foot of a part of that chain of hills, which form the sides of that *dish* which I described as resembling the vale of Gloucester. Soon after quitting this resort of the lame and the lazy, the gormandising and guzzling, the bilious and the nervous, we proceeded on, between stone walls, over a country little better than that from Cirencester to Burlip-hill.— A very poor, dull, and uninteresting country all the way to Oxford.

BURGHCLERE (HANTS),
Sunday, 18 Nov.

We left Oxford early, and went on, through *Abingdon* (Berks) to *Market-Ilsley*. It is a saying, hereabouts, that, at Oxford, they make the living pay for the dead, which is precisely according to the Pitt-System. Having smarted on this account, we were afraid to eat again at an inn; so we pushed on through Ilsley towards Newbury, breakfasting upon the residue of the nuts, aided by a new supply of apples bought from a poor man, who exhibited them in his window. Inspired, like Don Quixote, by the *sight of the nuts*, and recollecting the last night's bill, I exclaimed: "Happy! thrice happy and blessed, that golden age, when men lived on the simple fruits of the earth and slaked their thirst at the pure and limpid brook! when the trees shed their leaves to form a couch for their repose, and cast their bark to furnish them with a canopy! Happy age; when no Oxford landlord charged two men, who had dropped into a common coach-passenger room, and who had swallowed three penny-worths of food, 'four shillings for *teas*,' and 'eighteen pence for *cold meat*,' 'two shillings for *moulds and fire*' in this common coach-room, and 'five shillings for *beds !*'" This was a sort of grace before meat to the nuts and apples; and it had much more merit than the harangue of Don Quixote; for he, before he began upon the nuts, had stuffed himself well with goat's flesh and wine, whereas we had absolutely *fled* from the breakfast-table and blazing fire at Oxford.—Upon beholding the masses of buildings, at Oxford, devoted to what they call "*learning*," I could not help reflecting on the drones that they contain and the wasps they send forth! However, malignant as some are, the great and prevalent characteristic is *folly :* emptiness of head; want of talent; and one half of the fellows who are what they call *educated* here, are unfit to be clerks in a grocer's or mercer's shop.—As I looked up at what they call *University Hall,* I could not help reflecting that what I had written, even since I left Kensington on the 29th of October, would produce more effect, and do more good in the world, than all that had, for a hundred years, been written by all the members of this University, who devour, perhaps, not less than *a million pounds a year,* arising from property, completely at the disposal of the " Great Council of the Nation; " and I could not help exclaiming to myself: " Stand forth, ye big-wigged, ye gloriously feeding Doctors! Stand forth, ye *rich* of that church whose *poor* have had given them *a hundred thousand pounds a year,* not out of your riches, but out of the *taxes,* raised, in part, from the *salt* of the labouring man! Stand forth and face me, who have, from the pen of my leisure hours, sent, amongst your flocks, a hundred thousand sermons in ten months! More than you have all done for the last half century!" I exclaimed in vain. I dare say (for it was at peep of day) that not a man of them had yet endeavoured to unclose his eyes.—In coming through Abingdon (Berks) I could not help thinking of that great financier, Mr. John Maberly, by whom this place has, I believe, the honour to be represented in the Collective Wisdom of the Nation.—In the way to Ilsley we came across a part of that fine tract of land, called the *Vale of Berkshire,* where they grow *wheat* and *beans,* one after another, for many years together. About three miles before we reached Ilsley we came to *downs,* with, as is always the case, chalk under. Between Ilsley and Newbury the country is enclosed; the land middling, a stony loam; the woods and coppices frequent, and neither very good till we came within a short distance of Newbury. In going along we saw a piece of wheat with cabbage-leaves laid all over it at the distance, perhaps, of eight or ten feet from each other. It was to catch the *slugs.* The slugs, which commit their depredations in the *night,* creep under the leaves in the morning, and by turning up the leaves you come at the slugs, and crush them, or carry them away. But besides the immense daily labour attending this, the slug, in a field sowed with wheat, has a *clod* to creep under at every foot, and will not go five feet to get under a cabbage-leaf. Then again, if the day be *wet,* the slug works by day as well as by night. It is the sun and drought that he shuns, and not the light. Therefore the only effectual way to destroy slugs is, to sow lime, in dust, and *not slaked*. The slug is wet, he has hardly any skin, his *slime* is his covering; the smallest dust of hot lime kills him; and a few bushels to the acre are sufficient. You must sow the lime at *dusk;* for then the slugs are sure to be out. Slugs come after a crop that has long afforded a great deal of shelter from the sun; such as peas and vetches. In gardens they are nursed up by strawberry beds, and by weeds; by asparagus beds; or by any thing that remains for a long time to keep the summer-sun from the earth. We got about three o'clock to this nice, snug little farm-house, and found our host, Mr. Budd, at home.

BURGHCLERE,
Monday, 19 Nov.

A thorough wet day, the only day the greater part of which I have not spent out of doors, since I left home.

BURGHCLERE,
Tuesday, 20 Nov.

With Mr. Budd, we rode to-day to see the *Farm of Tull*, at *Shalborne*, in Berkshire. Mr. Budd did the same thing with Arthur Young twenty-seven years ago. It was a sort of *pilgrimage :* but, as the distance was ten miles, we thought it best to perform it on horseback.—We passed through the parish of *Highclere*, where they have *enclosed commons*, worth, as tillage land, not one single farthing an acre, and never will and never can be. As a common it afforded a little picking for geese and asses, and, in the moory parts of it, a little fuel for the labourers. But now it really can afford nothing. It will all fall to common again by degrees. This madness, this blind eagerness to gain, is now, I hope, pretty nearly over. At *East Woody*, we passed the house of a Mr. Goddard, which is uninhabited, he residing at Bath.—At *West Woody* (Berks) is the estate of Mr. Sloper, a very pretty place. A beautiful sporting country. Large fields, small woods, dry soil. What has taken place here is an instance of the workings of the system. Here is a large gentleman's house. But the proprietor *lets it* (it is, just now, empty), and resides in a *farm house* and farms his own estate. Happy is the landlord, who has the good sense to do this in time. This is a fine farm, and here appears to be very judicious farming. Large tracts of turnips; clean land; stubbles ploughed up early; ploughing with oxen; and a very large and singularly fine flock of sheep. Everything that you see, land, stock, implements, fences, buildings; all do credit to the owner; bespeak his sound judgment, his industry and care. All that is wanted here is, the *radical husbandry;* because that would enable the owner to keep three times the quantity of stock. However, since I left home, I have seen but very few farms that I should prefer to that of Mr. Sloper, whom I have not the pleasure to know, and whom, indeed, I never heard of till I saw his farm. At a village (certainly named by some *author*) called *Inkpen*, we passed a neat little house and paddock, the residence of a Mr. Butler, a nephew of Dr. Butler, who died Bishop of Oxford, and whom I can remember hearing preach at Farnham in Surrey, when I was a very, very little boy. I have his features and his wig as clearly in my recollection as if I had seen them but yesterday; and, I dare say, I have not thought of Doctor Butler for forty years before to-day. The " loyal " (oh, the pious gang!) will say, that my memory is good as to the face and wig, but bad as to the doctor's *sermons.* Why I must confess that I have no recollection of them; but, then, do I not *make sermons myself?*—At about two miles from Inkpen we came to the end of our pilgrimage. The farm, which was Mr. *Tull's;* where he used the first drill that ever was used; where he practised his husbandry; where he wrote that book, which does so much honour to his memory, and to which the cultivators of England owe so much; this farm is on an open and somewhat bleak spot, in Berkshire, on the borders of Wiltshire, and within a very short distance of a part of Hampshire. The ground is a loam, mixed with flints, and has the chalk at no great distance beneath it. It is, therefore, free from *wet;* needs no water furrows; and is pretty good in its nature. The house, which has been improved by Mr. Blandy the present proprietor, is still but a plain farm-house. Mr. Blandy has lived here thirty years, and has brought up ten children to man's and woman's estate. Mr. Blandy was from home, but Mrs. Blandy received and entertained us in a very hospitable manner.—We returned, not along the low land, but along the top of the downs, and through Lord Caernarvon's park, and got home after a very pleasant day.

BURGHCLERE,
Wednesday, 21 *Nov.*

We intended to have a hunt; but the fox-hounds came across and rendered it impracticable. As an instance of the change which rural customs have undergone since the hellish paper-system has been so furiously at work, I need only mention the fact, that, forty years ago, there were *five* packs of *fox-hounds* and *ten* packs of *harriers* kept within *ten miles* of Newbury; and that now there is *one* of the former (kept, too, by *subscription*) and *none* of the latter, except the few couple of dogs kept by Mr. Budd! " So much the better," says the shallow fool, who cannot duly estimate the difference between a resident *native* gentry, attached to the soil, known to every farmer and labourer from their childhood, frequently mixing with them in those pursuits where all artificial distinctions are lost, practising hospitality without ceremony, from habit and not on calculation; and a gentry, only now-and-then residing at all, having no relish for country-delights, foreign in their manners, distant and haughty in their behaviour, looking to the soil only for its rents, viewing it as a mere object of speculation, unacquainted with its cultivators, despising them and their pursuits, and relying, for influence, not upon the good will of the vicinage, but upon the dread of their power. The war and paper-system has brought in nabobs, negro-drivers, generals, admirals, governors, commissaries, contractors, pensioners, sinecurists, commissioners, loan-jobbers, lottery-dealers, bankers, stock-jobbers; not to mention the long and *black list* in gowns and three-tailed wigs. You can see but few good houses not in possession of one or the other of these. These, with the parsons, are now the magistrates. Some of the *consequences* are before us; but they have not all yet arrived. A taxation that sucks up fifty millions a year *must* produce a new set of proprietors every twenty years or less; and the proprietors, while they last, can be little better than tax-collectors to the government, and scourgers of the people.—I must not quit *Burghclere* without noticing Mr. Budd's *radical* swedes and other things. His is but miniature farming; but it is very good, and very interesting. Some time in May, he drilled a piece of swedes on four feet ridges. The fly took them off. He had cabbage and mangel-wurzel plants to put in their stead. Unwilling to turn back the ridges, and thereby bring the dung to the top, he planted the cabbages and mangel-wurzel on the ridges where the swedes had been drilled. This was done in June. Late in July, his neighbour, a farmer Hulbert, had a field of swedes that he was hoeing. Mr. Budd now put some manure in the furrows between the ridges, and ploughed a furrow over it from each ridge. On this he planted swedes, taken from farmer Hulbert's field. Thus his plantation consisted of rows of plants *two feet apart*. The result is a prodigious crop. Of the mangel-wurzel (greens and all) he has not less than twenty tons to the acre. He can scarcely have less of the cabbages, some of which are *green savoys* as fine as I ever saw. And of the swedes, many of which weigh from five to nine pounds, he certainly has more than twenty tons to the acre. So that here is a crop of, at the very least, *forty tons to the acre*. This piece is not much more than half an acre; but, he will, perhaps, not find so much cattle food upon any four acres in the county. He is, and long has been, feeding four milch cows, large, fine, and in fine condition, upon cabbages sometimes, and sometimes on mangel-wurzel leaves. The butter is excellent. Not the smallest degree of bitterness or bad taste of any sort. Fine colour and fine taste. And here, upon not three-quarters of an acre of ground, he has, if he manage the thing well, enough food for these four cows to the month of May! Can any system of husbandry equal this? What would he do with these cows, if he had not this crop? He could not keep one of them, except on hay. And he owes all this crop to transplanting. He thinks that the transplanting, fetching the swede plants and all, might cost him ten or twelve shillings. It was done by women, who had never done such a thing before. —However, he must get in his crop before the hard weather comes; or my Lord Caernarvon's hares will help him. They have begun already; and, it is curious, that they have begun on the mangel-wurzel roots. So that hares, at any rate, have set the seal of merit upon this root.

WHITCHURCH,
Thursday (night), 22 Nov.

We have come round here, instead of going by Newbury, in consequence of a promise to Mr. Blount at Uphusband, that I would call on him on my return. We left Uphusband by lamplight, and, of course, we could see little on our way.

KENSINGTON,
Friday, 23 Nov.

Got home by the coach. At leaving Whitchurch we soon passed the mill where the Mother-Bank paper is made! Thank God, this mill is likely soon to want employment! Hard by is a pretty park and house, belonging to " *'Squire* " Portal, the *paper-maker*. The country people, who seldom want for sarcastic shrewdness, call it " *Rag Hall* "!—I perceive that they

are planting oaks on the "*wastes*," as the *Agriculturasses* call
them, about *Hartley Row;* which is very good; because the
herbage, after the first year, is rather increased than diminished
by the operation; while, in time, the oaks arrive at a timber
state, and add to the beauty and to the *real wealth* of the country,
and to the real and solid wealth of the descendants of the planter,
who, in every such case, merits unequivocal praise, because he
plants for his children's children.   The planter here is Lady
Mildmay, who is, it seems, Lady of the Manors about here.   It is
impossible to praise this act of hers too much, especially when
one considers her *age*.   I beg a thousand pardons!   I do not mean
to say that her ladyship is *old ;* but she has long had grandchildren.   If her ladyship had been a reader of old dread-death
and dread-devil Johnson, that teacher of moping and melancholy, she never would have planted an oak tree.   If the writings
of this time-serving, mean, dastardly old pensioner had got a
firm hold of the minds of the people at large, the people would
have been bereft of their very souls.   These writings, aided by
the charm of pompous sound, were fast making their way, till
light, reason, and the French revolution came to drive them
into oblivion; or, at least, to confine them to the shelves of
repentant, married old rakes, and those of old stock-jobbers
with young wives standing in need of something to keep down
the unruly ebullitions which are apt to take place while the
"dearies" are gone hobbling to 'Change. — "After *pleasure*
comes *pain*," says Solomon; and after the sight of Lady Mildmay's truly noble plantations, came that of the clouts of the
"gentlemen cadets" of the "*Royal Military College of Sand-
hurst !*"   Here, close by the road side, is the *drying-ground*.
Sheets, shirts, and all sorts of things were here spread upon lines,
covering, perhaps, an acre of ground!   We soon afterwards
came to "*York* Place" on "*Osnaburg* Hill."   And is there
never to be an *end* of these things?   Away to the left, we see
that immense building, which contains children *breeding up to
be military commanders !*   Has this plan cost so little as two
millions of pounds?   I never see this place (and I have seen it
forty times during the last twenty years) without asking myself
this question: Will this thing be suffered to go on; will this
thing, created by money *raised by loan ;* will this thing be upheld
by means of taxes, *while the interest of the debt is reduced*, on the
ground that the nation is *unable to pay the interest in full ?*—
Answer that question, Castlereagh, Sidmouth, Brougham, or
Scarlett.

KENTISH JOURNAL

FROM KENSINGTON TO DARTFORD, ROCHESTER, CHATHAM, AND FAVERSHAM

Tuesday, 4 December, 1821.
ELVERTON FARM, NEAR FAVERSHAM, KENT.

THIS is the first time, since I went to France, in 1792, that I have been on this side of *Shooters' Hill*. The land, generally speaking, from Deptford to Dartford is poor, and the surface ugly by nature, to which ugliness there has been made, just before we came to the latter place, a considerable addition by the inclosure of a common, and by the sticking up of some shabby-genteel houses, surrounded with dead fences and things called gardens, in all manner of ridiculous forms, making, all together, the bricks, hurdle-rods and earth say, as plainly as they can speak, "Here dwell *vanity* and *poverty*." This is a little excrescence that has grown out of the immense sums, which have been drawn from other parts of the kingdom to be expended on barracks, magazines, martello-towers, catamarans, and all the excuses for lavish expenditure, which the war for the Bourbons gave rise to. All things will return; these rubbishy flimsy things, on this common, will first be deserted, then crumble down, then be swept away, and the cattle, sheep, pigs and geese will once more graze upon the common, which will again furnish heath, furze and turf for the labourers on the neighbouring lands.—After you leave Dartford the land becomes excellent. You come to a bottom of chalk, many feet from the surface, and when that is the case the land is sure to be good; no *wet* at bottom, no deep ditches, no water furrows, necessary; sufficiently moist in dry weather, and no water lying about upon it in wet weather for any length of time. The chalk acts as a filtering-stone, not as a sieve, like gravel, and not as a dish, like clay. The chalk acts as the soft stone in Herefordshire does; but it is not so congenial to trees that have tap-roots.—Along through Gravesend towards Rochester the country presents a sort of gardening scene. Rochester (the bishop of which is, or lately was, *tax collector for London and Middlesex*), is a small but crowded place, lying on the south bank of the beautiful Medway, with a rising ground on the other side of the city.

Stroud, which you pass through before you come to the bridge, over which you go to enter Rochester; *Rochester* itself, and *Chatham*, form, in fact, one main street of about two miles and a half in length.—Here I was got into the scenes of my cap-and-feather days! Here, at between sixteen and seventeen, I enlisted for a soldier. Upon looking up towards the fortifications and the barracks, how many recollections crowded into my mind! The girls in these towns do not seem to be *so pretty* as they were thirty-eight years ago; or am I not so quick in discovering beauties as I was then? Have thirty-eight years corrected my taste, or made me a hypercritic in these matters? Is it that I now look at them with the solemnness of a " professional man," and not with the enthusiasm and eagerness of an " amateur? " I leave these questions for philosophers to solve. One thing I will say for the young women of these towns, and that is, that I always found those of them that I had the great happiness to be acquainted with, evince a sincere desire to do their best to smooth the inequalities of life, and to give us, " brave fellows," as often as they could, strong beer, when their churlish masters or fathers or husbands would have drenched us to death with small. This, at the out-set of life, gave me a high opinion of the judgment and justice of the female sex; an opinion which has been confirmed by the observations of my whole life.—This Chatham has had some monstrous *wens* stuck on to it by the lavish expenditure of the war. These will moulder away. It is curious enough that I should meet with a gentleman in an inn at Chatham to give me a picture of the house-distress in that enormous wen, which, during the war, was stuck on to Portsmouth. Not less than fifty thousand people had been drawn together there! These are now dispersing. The coagulated blood is diluting and flowing back through the veins. Whole streets are deserted, and the eyes of the houses knocked out by the boys that remain. The jack-daws, as much as to say, " Our turn to be inspired and to teach is come," are beginning to take possession of the Methodist chapels. The gentleman told me, that he had been down to Portsea to sell half a street of houses, left him by a relation; and that nobody would give him anything for them further than as very cheap fuel and rubbish! Good God! And is this " prosperity? " Is this the " prosperity of the war? " Have I not, for twenty long years, been regretting the existence of these unnatural embossments; these white-swellings, these odious wens, produced by *corruption* and engendering crime and misery and slavery?

We shall see the whole of these wens abandoned by the inhabitants, and, at last, the cannons on the fortifications may be of some use in battering down the buildings.—But what is to be the fate of the great wen of all? The monster, called, by the silly coxcombs of the press, " the metropolis of the empire? " What is to become of that multitude of towns that has been stuck up around it? The village of Kingston was smothered in the town of Portsea; and why? Because taxes, drained from other parts of the kingdom, were brought thither.

The dispersion of the wen is the only real difficulty that I see in settling the affairs of the nation and restoring it to a happy state. But dispersed it *must* be; and if there be half a million, or more, of people to suffer, the consolation is, that the suffering will be divided into half a million of parts. As if the swelling out of London, naturally produced by the funding system, were not sufficient; as if the evil were not sufficiently great from the inevitable tendency of the system of loans and funds, our pretty gentlemen must resort to positive institutions to augment the population of the Wen. They found that the increase of the Wen produced an increase of thieves and prostitutes, an increase of all sorts of diseases, an increase of miseries of all sorts; they saw that taxes drawn up to one point produced these effects; they must have a " *penitentiary*," for instance, to check the evil, and that they must needs have in the Wen! So that here were a million of pounds, drawn up in taxes, employed not only to keep the thieves and prostitutes still in the *Wen*, but to bring up to the Wen workmen to build the penitentiary, who and whose families, amounting, perhaps to thousands, make an addition to the cause of that crime and misery, to check which is the object of the penitentiary! People would follow, they must follow, the million of money. However, this is of a piece with all the rest of their goings on. They and their predecessors, ministers and *House*, have been collecting together all the materials for a dreadful explosion; and if the explosion be not dreadful, other heads must point out the means of prevention.

Wednesday, 5 Dec.

The land on quitting Chatham is chalk at bottom; but, before you reach Sittingbourne, there is a vein of gravel and sand under, but a great depth of loam above. Above Sittingbourne the chalk bottom comes again, and continues on to this place, where the land appears to me to be as good as it can possibly be.

Mr. *William Waller*, at whose house I am, has grown, this year, mangel-wurzel, the roots of which weigh, I think, on an average, twelve pounds, and in rows, too, at only about thirty inches distant from each other. In short, as far as *soil* goes, it is impossible to see a finer country than this. You frequently see a field of fifty acres, level as a die, clean as a garden and as rich. Mr. *Birkbeck* need not have crossed the Atlantic, and Alleghany into the bargain, to look for land *too rich to bear wheat ;* for here is a plenty of it. In short, this is a country of hop-gardens, cherry, apple, pear and filbert orchards, and quickset hedges. But, alas! what, in point of *beauty*, is a country without woods and lofty trees! And here there are very few indeed. I am now sitting in a room, from the window of which I look, *first*, over a large and level field of rich land, in which the drilled wheat is finely come up, and which is surrounded by clipped quickset hedges with a row of apple trees running by the sides of them; *next*, over a long succession of rich meadows, which are here called marshes, the shortest grass upon which will fatten sheep or oxen; *next*, over a little branch of the salt water which runs up to Faversham; *beyond that*, on the Isle of Shepry (or Shepway), which rises a little into a sort of ridge that runs along it; rich fields, pastures and orchards lie all around me; and yet, I declare, that I a million times to one prefer, as a spot to *live on*, the heaths, the miry coppices, the wild woods and the forests of Sussex and Hampshire.

Thursday, 6 Dec.

" Agricultural distress " is the great topic of general conversation. The *Webb Hallites* seem to prevail here. The fact is, farmers in general read nothing but the newspapers; these, in the Wen, are under the control of the corruption of one or the other of the factions; and in the country, nine times out of ten, under the control of the parsons and landlords, who are the magistrates, as they are pompously called, that is to say, Justices of the Peace. From such vehicles what are farmers to learn? They are, in general, thoughtful and sensible men; but their natural good sense is perverted by these publications, had it not been for which we never should have seen " *a sudden transition from war to peace* " lasting seven years, and more *sudden* in its destructive effects at last than at first. *Sir Edward Knatchbull* and *Mr. Honeywood* are the members of the " Collective Wisdom " for this county. The former was, till of late, a *tax-collector*. I hear that he is a great advocate for *corn-bills !* I suppose he does not wish to let people who have *leases* see the bottom of the evil. He may get his rents for this year; but it will be his last year, if the interest of the debt be not very greatly reduced. Some people here think, that corn is *smuggled in* even now! Perhaps it is, *upon the whole*, best that the delusion should continue for a year longer; as that would tend to make the destruction of the system more sure, or, at least, make the cure more radical.

Friday, 7 Dec.

I went through *Faversham*. A very pretty little town, and just ten minutes' walk from the market-place up to the Dover turnpike-road. Here are the *powder-affairs* that Mr. Hume so well exposed. An immensity of buildings and expensive things. Why are not these premises let or sold? However, this will never be done, until there be a *reformed parliament*. Pretty little *Van*, that beauty of all beauties; that orator of all orators; that saint of all saints; that financier of all financiers, said that, if Mr. Hume were to pare down the expenses of government to *his* wish, there would be others, " the Hunts, Cobbetts, and Carliles, who would still want the expense to be less." I do not know *how low* Mr. Hume would wish to go; but for myself I say, that if I ever have the power to do it, I will reduce the expenditure, and that in quick time too, down to what it was in the reign of Queen Anne; that is to say, to less than is now paid to tax-gatherers for their labour in collecting the taxes; and, monstrous as Van may think the idea, I do not regard it as impossible that I may have such power; which I would certainly not employ to do an act of *injustice* to any human being, and would, at the same time, maintain the throne in more real splendour than that in which it is now maintained. But I would have nothing to do with any Vans, except as door-keepers or porters.

Saturday, 8 Dec.

Came home very much pleased with my visit to Mr. Walker, in whose house I saw no drinking of wine, spirits, or even beer; where all, even to the little children, were up by candle-light in the morning, and where the most perfect sobriety was accompanied by constant cheerfulness. *Kent* is in a deplorable way. The farmers are skilful and intelligent, generally speaking. But there is infinite *corruption* in Kent, owing partly to the swarms of West Indians, nabobs, commissioners, and others of nearly the same description, that have selected it for the place of their residence; but owing still more to the immense sums of public money that have, during the last thirty years, been expended in it. And when one thinks of these, the conduct of the people of Dover, Canterbury, and other places, in the case of the ever-lamented queen, does them everlasting honour. The *fruit* in Kent is more *select* than in Herefordshire, where it is raised for *cyder*, while, in Kent, it is raised for sale in its fruit state, a great deal being sent to the *Wen*, and a great deal sent to the North of England and to Scotland. The orchards are beautiful indeed. Kept in the neatest order, and indeed, all belonging to them excels anything of the kind to be seen in Normandy; and, as to apples, I never saw any so good in France as those of Kent. This county, so blessed by Providence, has been cursed by the system in a peculiar degree. It has been the *receiver* of immense sums, raised on the other counties. This has puffed its *rents* to an unnatural height; and now that the drain of other counties is stopped, it feels like a pampered pony, turned out in winter to live upon a common. It is in an extremely " unsatisfactory state," and has certainly a greater mass of suffering to endure than any other part of the kingdom, the *Wens* only excepted. Sir Edward Knatchbull, who is a child of the system, does appear to see no more of the cause of these sufferings than if he were a baby. How should he? Not very bright by nature; never listening but to one side of the question; being a man who wants high rents to be paid him; not gifted with much light, and that little having to strive against prejudice, false shame, and self interest, what wonder is there that he should not see things in their true light?

NORFOLK AND SUFFOLK JOURNAL

BERGH APTON, NEAR NORWICH,
Monday, 10 *Dec*. 1821.

FROM the *Wen* to Norwich, from which I am now distant seven miles, there is nothing in Essex, Suffolk, or this county, that can be called a *hill*. Essex, when you get beyond the immediate influence of the gorgings and disgorgings of the Wen; that is to say, beyond the demand for crude vegetables and repayment in manure, is by no means a fertile county. There appears generally to be a bottom of *clay*; not *soft chalk*, which they persist in calling clay in Norfolk. I wish I had one of these Norfolk men in a coppice in Hampshire or Sussex, and I would show him what *clay* is. Clay is what pots and pans and jugs and tiles are made of; and not soft, whitish stuff that crumbles to pieces in the sun, instead of baking as hard as a stone, and which, in dry weather, is to be broken to pieces by nothing short of a sledge-hammer. The narrow ridges on which the wheat is sown; the water furrows; the water standing in the dips of the pastures; the rusty iron-like colour of the water coming out of some of the banks; the deep ditches; the rusty look of the pastures; all show that here is a bottom of clay. Yet there is gravel too; for the oaks do not grow well. It was not till I got nearly to Sudbury that I saw much change for the better. Here the bottom of chalk, the soft dirty-looking chalk that the Norfolk people call clay, begins to be the bottom, and this, with very little exception (as far as I have been), is the bottom of all the lands of these two fine counties of Suffolk and Norfolk.— Sudbury has some fine meadows near it on the sides of the river Stour. The land all along to Bury Saint Edmund's is very fine; but no trees worth looking at. *Bury*, formerly the seat of an abbot, the last of whom was, I think, hanged, or somehow put to death, by that matchless tyrant, Henry VIII., is a very pretty place; extremely clean and neat; no ragged or dirty people to be seen, and women (*young* ones I mean) very pretty and very neatly dressed.—On this side of Bury, a considerable distance lower, I saw a field of *rape*, transplanted very thick, for, I suppose, sheep feed in the spring. The farming all along to

Norwich is very good. The land clean, and everything done in a masterly manner.

Tuesday, 11 Dec.

Mr. Samuel Clarke, my host, has about 30 acres of *swedes* in rows. Some at 4 feet distances, some at 30 inches; and about 4 acres of the 4-feet swedes were transplanted. I have seen thousands of acres of swedes in these counties, and here are the largest crops that I have seen. The widest rows are decidedly the largest crops here. And the *transplanted*, though under disadvantageous circumstances, amongst the best of the best. The wide rows amount to at least 20 tons to the acre, exclusive of the greens taken off two months ago, which weighed 5 tons to the acre. Then there is the inter tillage, so beneficial to the land, and the small quantity of manure required in the broad rows, compared to what is required when the seed is drilled or sown upon the level. Mr. Nicholls, a neighbour of Mr. Clarke, has a part of a field transplanted on *seven turn ridges*, put in when in the other part of the field, drilled, the plants were a fortnight old. He has a much larger crop in the transplanted than in the drilled part. But if it had been a *fly-year*, he might have had *none* in the drilled part, while, in all probability, the crop in the transplanted part would have been better than it now is, seeing that a *wet* summer, though favourable to the hitting of the swedes, is by no means favourable to their attaining a great size of bulb. This is the case this year with all turnips. A great deal of leaf and neck, but not bulbs in proportion. The advantages of transplanting are, *first*, you make sure of a crop in spite of fly, and, *second*, you have six weeks or two months longer to prepare your ground. And the advantages of wide rows are, *first*, that you want only about half the quantity of manure; and, *second*, that you *plough* the ground two or three times during the summer.

GROVE, NEAR HOLT,

Thursday, 13 Dec.

Came to the Grove (Mr. Wither's), near Holt, along with Mr. Clarke. Through *Norwich* to *Aylsham* and then to *Holt*. On our road we passed the house of the late *Lord Suffield*, who married Castlereagh's wife's sister, who is a daughter of the late Earl of Buckinghamshire, who had for so many years that thumping sinecure of eleven thousand a year in Ireland, and who was the son of a man that, under the name of Mr. Hobart, cut such a figure in supporting Lord North and afterwards Pitt, and was made a peer under the auspices of the latter of these two heaven-born ministers. This house, which is a very ancient one, was, they say, the birthplace of Ann de Boleyne, the mother of Queen Elizabeth. Not much matter; for she married the king while his real wife was alive. I could have excused her, if there had been no marrying in the case; but, hypocrisy, always bad, becomes detestable when it resorts to religious ceremony as its mask. She, no more than Cranmer, seems, to her last moments, to have remembered her sins against her lawful queen. Foxe's *Book of Martyrs*, that ought to be called the *Book of Liars*, says that Cranmer, the recanter and re-recanter, held out his offending hand in the flames, and cried out " that hand, that hand! " If he had cried out *Catherine ! Catherine !* I should have thought better of him; but, it is clear, that the whole story is a lie, invented by the protestants, and particularly by the sectarians, to white-wash the character of this perfidious hypocrite and double apostate, who, if bigotry had something to do in bringing him to the stake, certainly deserved his fate, if any offences committed by man can deserve so horrible a punishment.—The present Lord Suffield is that Mr. Edward Harbord, whose father-in-law left him £500 to buy a seat in parliament, and who refused to carry an address to the late beloved and lamented queen, because Major Cartwright and myself were chosen to accompany him! Never mind, my lord; you will grow less fastidious! They say, however, that he is really good to his tenants, and has told them that he will take anything that they can give. There is some sense in this! He is a great Bible man; and it is strange that he cannot see that things are out of order, when *his* interference in this way can be at all *necessary*, while there is a Church that receives a tenth part of the produce of the earth.—There are some oak woods here, but very poor. Not like those, not near like the worst of those, in Hampshire and Herefordshire. All this eastern coast seems very unpropitious to trees of all sorts.— We passed through the estate of a Mr. Marsin, whose house is near the road, a very poor spot, and the first really poor ground I have seen in Norfolk. A nasty spewy black gravel on the top of a sour clay. It is worse than the heaths between Godalming and Liphook; for, while it is too poor to grow anything but heath, it is too cold to give you the chirping of the grasshopper in summer. However, Mr. Marsin has been too wise to enclose this wretched land, which is just like that which Lord Caernarvon has enclosed in the parishes of Highclere, and Burghclere, and which, for tillage, really is not worth a single farthing an acre.— Holt is a little, old-fashioned, substantially-built market-town. The land just about it, or, at least, towards the east, is poor, and has been lately enclosed.

Friday, 14 Dec.

Went to see the estate of Mr. Hardy at Leveringsett, a hamlet about two miles from Holt. This is the first time that I have seen a *valley* in this part of England. From Holt you look, to the distance of seven or eight miles, over a very fine valley, leaving a great deal of inferior hill and dell within its boundaries. At the bottom of this general valley, Mr. Hardy has a very beautiful estate of about four hundred acres. His house is at one end of it near the high road, where he has a malt-house and a brewery, the neat and ingenious manner of managing which I would detail if my total unacquaintance with machinery did not disqualify me for the task. His estate forms a valley of itself, somewhat longer than broad. The tops, and the sides of the tops of the hills round it, and also several little hillocks in the valley itself, are judiciously planted with trees of various sorts, leaving good wide roads, so that it is easy to ride round them in a carriage. The fields, the fences, the yards, the stacks, the buildings, the cattle, all showed the greatest judgment and industry. There was really nothing that the most critical observer could say was *out of order*. However, the forest trees do not grow well here. The oaks are mere scrubs, as they are about Brentwood in Essex, and in some parts of Cornwall; and, for some unaccountable reason, people seldom plant the *ash*, which no wind will *shave*, as it does the oak.

Saturday, 15 Dec.

Spent the evening amongst the farmers, at their market room at Holt; and very much pleased at them I was. We talked over the *cause of the low prices*, and I, as I have done everywhere, endeavoured to convince them that prices must fall a great deal lower yet; and that no man, who wishes not to be ruined, ought to keep or take a farm, unless on a calculation of best wheat at 4s. a bushel and a best South Down ewe at 15s. or even 12s. They heard me patiently, and, I believe, were well convinced of the truth of what I said. I told them of the correctness of the predictions of their great countrymen, Mr. Paine, and observed, how much better it would have been to take his advice, than to burn him in effigy. I endeavoured (but in such a care all human powers must fail!) to describe to them the sort and size of the talents of the Stern-path-of-duty man, of the great hole-digger, of the jester, of the Oxford-scholar, of the loan-jobber (who had just made an enormous grasp), of the Oracle, and so on. Here, as everywhere else, I hear every creature speak loudly in praise of *Mr. Coke*. It is well known to my readers, that I think nothing of him as a *public* man; that I think even his good qualities an injury to his country, because they serve the knaves whom he is duped by to dupe the people more effectually; but it would be base in me not to say, that I hear, from men of all parties, and sensible men too, expressions made use of towards him that affectionate children use towards the best of parents. I have not met with a single exception.

BERGH APTON,
Sunday, 16 *Dec.*

Came from Holt through Saxthorpe and Cawston. At the former village were on one end of a decent white house, these words, " *Queen Caroline ; for her Britons mourn,*" and a crown over all in black. I need not have looked to see: I might have been sure, that the owner of the house was a *shoe-maker*, a trade which numbers more men of sense and of public spirit than any other in the kingdom.—At Cawston we stopped at a public house, the keeper of which had taken and read the Register for years. I shall not attempt to describe the pleasure I felt at the hearty welcome given us by Mr. Pern and his wife and by a young miller of the village, who, having learnt at Holt that we were to return that way, had come to meet us, the house being on the side of the great road, from which the village is at some distance. This is the birthplace of the famous *Botley Parson*, all the history of whom we now learned, and if we could have gone to the village, they were prepared to *ring the bells*, and show us the old woman who nursed the *Botley Parson!* These Norfolk *baws* never do things by halves. We came away, very much pleased with our reception at Cawston, and with a promise, on my part, that, if I visited the county again, I would write a Register there; a promise which I shall certainly keep.

GREAT YARMOUTH,
Friday (morning), 21 *Dec.*

The day before yesterday I set out for Bergh Apton with Mr. Clarke, to come hither by the way of *Beccles* in Suffolk.

We stopped at Mr. Charles Clarke's at Beccles, where we saw some good and sensible men, who see clearly into all the parts of the works of the ' Thunderers," and whose anticipations, as to the " general working of events," are such as they ought to be. They gave us a humorous account of the " rabble " having recently crowned a Jack-ass, and of a struggle between them and the " Yeomanry Gavaltry." This *was* a place of most ardent and blazing *loyalty*, as the pretenders to it call it; but, it seems, it now blazes less furiously; it is milder, more measured in its effusions; and, with the help of low prices, will become bearable in time. This Beccles is a very pretty place, has watered meadows near it, and is situated amidst fine lands. What a *system* it must be to make people wretched in a country like this! Could he be *heaven-born* that invented such a system? Gaffer Gooch's father, a very old man, lives not far from here. We had a good deal of fun about the Gaffer, who will certainly never lose the name, unless he should be made a lord.—We slept at the house of a friend of Mr. Clarke on our way, and got to this very fine town of Great Yarmouth yesterday about noon. A party of friends met us and conducted us about the town, which is a very beautiful one indeed. What I liked best, however, was the hearty welcome that I met with, because it showed that the reign of calumny and delusion was passed. A company of gentlemen gave me a dinner in the evening, and in all my life I never saw a set of men more worthy of my respect and gratitude. Sensible, modest, understanding the whole of our case, and clearly foreseeing what is about to happen. One gentleman proposed, that, as it would be impossible for all to go to London, there should be a *Provincial Feast of the Gridiron*, a plan, which, I hope, will be adopted.—I leave Great Yarmouth with sentiments of the sincerest regard for all those whom I there saw and conversed with, and with my best wishes for the happiness of all its inhabitants; nay, even the *parsons* not excepted; for, if they did not come to welcome me, they collected in a group to *see* me, and that was one step towards doing justice to him whom their order have so much, so foully, and, if they knew their own interest, so foolishly slandered.

BERGH APTON,
22 *Dec.* (*night*).

After returning from Yarmouth yesterday, went to dine at Stoke-Holy-Cross, about six miles off; got home at midnight.

and came to Norwich this morning, this being market-day, and also the day fixed on for a Radical Reform Dinner at the Swan Inn, to which I was invited. Norwich is a very fine city, and the castle, which stands in the middle of it, on a hill, is truly majestic. The meat and poultry and vegetable market is beautiful. It is kept in a large open square in the middle, or nearly so, of the city. The ground is a pretty sharp slope, so that you see all at once. It resembles one of the French markets, only *there* the vendors are all standing and gabbling like parrots, and the meat is lean and bloody and nasty, and the people snuffy and grimy in hands and face, the contrary, precisely the contrary of all which is the case in this beautiful market at Norwich, where the women have a sort of uniform brown great coats, with white aprons and *bibs* (I think they call them) going from the apron up to the bosom. They equal in neatness (for nothing can surpass) the market women in Philadelphia.—The cattle-market is held on the hill by the castle, and many *fairs* are smaller in bulk of stock. The corn-market is held in a very magnificent place, called Saint Andrew's Hall, which will contain two or three thousand persons. They tell me that this used to be a most delightful scene; a most joyous one; and I think it was this scene that Mr. Curwen described in such glowing colours when he was talking of the Norfolk farmers, each worth so many thousands of pounds. Bear me witness, reader, that *I never was dazzled* by such sights; that the false glare never put my eyes out; and that, even then, twelve years ago, I warned Mr. Curwen of the *result!* Bear witness to this, my Disciples, and justify the doctrines of him, for whose sakes you have endured persecution. How different would Mr. Curwen find the scene *now!* What took place at the dinner has been already recorded in the Register; and I have only to add with regard to it, that my reception at Norfolk was such, that I have only to regret the total want of power to make those hearty Norfolk and Norwich friends any suitable return, whether by act or word.

KENSINGTON,
Monday, 24 Dec.

Went from Bergh Apton to Norwich in the morning, and from Norwich to London during the day, carrying with me great admiration of and respect for this county of *excellent farmers*, and hearty, open and spirited men. The Norfolk people are quick and smart in their motions and in their speaking. Very neat and *trim* in all their farming concerns, and very skilful. Their land is good, their roads are level, and the bottom of their soil is dry, to be sure; and these are great advantages; but they are diligent, and make the most of everything. Their management of all sorts of stock is most judicious; they are careful about manure; their teams move quickly; and, in short, it is a county of most excellent cultivators.—The churches in Norfolk are generally large and the towers lofty. They have all been well built at first. Many of them are of the Saxon architecture. They are, almost all (I do not remember an exception), placed on the *highest* spots to be found near where they stand; and it is curious enough, that the contrary practice should have prevailed in *hilly* countries, where they are generally found in valleys and in low, sheltered dells, even in those valleys! These churches prove that the people of Norfolk and Suffolk were always a superior people in point of wealth, while the size of them proves that the country parts were, at one time, a great deal more populous than they now are. The great drawbacks on the beauty of these counties are, their flatness and their want of fine woods; but to those who can dispense with these, Norfolk, under a wise and just government, can have nothing to ask more than Providence and the industry of man have given.

Landlord Distress Meetings

For, in fact, it is not the *farmer*, but the *landlord* and *parson*, who wants relief from the " *collective*." The tenant's remedy is, quitting his farm or bringing down his rent to what he can afford to give, wheat being 3 or 4 shillings a bushel. This is his remedy. What should *he* want high prices for? They can do *him* no good; and this I proved to the farmers last year. The fact is, the landlords and parsons are urging the farmers on to get *something done* to give them high rents and high tithes.

At *Hertford* there has been a meeting at which *some* sense was discovered, at any rate. The parties talked about the *fundholder*, the *debt*, the *taxes*, and so on, and seemed to be in a very warm temper. Pray, keep yourselves *cool*, gentlemen; for you have a great deal to endure yet. I deeply regret that I have not room to insert the resolutions of this meeting.

There is to be a meeting at *Battle* (East Sussex) on the 3rd instant, at which *I mean to be*. I want to *see* my friends on the *South-Downs*. To see how they *lock* now.

[At a public dinner given to Mr. Cobbett at Norwich, on the market-day above mentioned, the company drank the toast of *Mr. Cobbett and his "Trash,"* the name "two-penny trash," having been at one time applied by Lord Castlereagh to the *Register.* In acknowledging this toast Mr. Cobbett addressed the company in a speech, of which the following is a passage:]

My thanks to you for having drunk my health are great and sincere; but much greater pleasure do I feel at the approbation bestowed on that *trash*, which has, for so many years, been a mark for the finger of scorn to be pointed at by ignorant selfishness and arrogant and insolent power. To enumerate, barely to name, all, or a hundredth part of, the endeavours that have been made to stifle this *trash*, would require a much longer space of time than that which we have now before us. But, gentlemen, those endeavours must have *cost money ;* money must have been expended in the circulation of Anti-Cobbett, and the endless bale of papers and pamphlets put forth to check the progress of the *trash :* and when we take into view the immense sums expended in keeping down the spirit excited by the *trash*, who of us is to tell, whether these endeavours, taken altogether, may not have added *many millions* to that debt, of which (without any hint at a *concomitant measure*) some men have now the audacity, the unprincipled, the profligate assurance to talk of reducing the interest. The trash, gentlemen, is now triumphant; its triumph we are now met to celebrate; proofs of its triumph I myself witnessed not many hours ago, in that scene where the best possible evidence was to be found. In walking through St. Andrew's Hall, my mind was not so much engaged on the grandeur of the place, or on the gratifying reception I met with; those hearty shakes by the hand which I so much like, those smiles of approbation, which not to see with pride would argue an insensibility to honest fame: even these, I do sincerely assure you, engaged my mind much less than the melancholy reflection that, of the two thousand or fifteen hundred farmers then in my view, there were probably *three-fourths* who came to the hall with aching hearts, and who would leave it in a state of mental agony. What a thing to contemplate, gentlemen! What a scene is here! A set of men, occupiers of the land; producers of all that we eat, drink, wear, and of all that forms the buildings that shelter us; a set of men industrious and careful by habit; cool, thoughtful, and sensible from the instructions of nature; a set of men provident above all others, and engaged in pursuits in their nature stable as the very earth they till: to see a set of men like this plunged into anxiety, embarrassment, jeopardy, not to be described; and when the particular individuals before me were famed for their superior skill in this great and solid pursuit, and were blessed with soil and other circumstances to make them prosperous and happy: to behold this sight would have been more than sufficient to sink my heart within me, had I not been upheld by the reflection, that I had done all in my power to prevent these calamities, and that I still had in reserve that which, with the assistance of the sufferers themselves, would restore them and the nation to happiness.

SUSSEX JOURNAL

TO BATTLE, THROUGH BROMLEY, SEVENOAKS, AND TUNBRIDGE

Battle,
Wednesday, 2 Jan. 1822.

Came here to-day from Kensington, in order to see what goes on at the meeting to be held here to-morrow, of the " gentry, clergy, freeholders, and occupiers of land in the Rape of Hastings, to take into consideration the distressed state of the agricultural interest." I shall, of course, give an account of this meeting after it has taken place.—You come through part of *Kent* to get to *Battle* from the Great *Wen* on the Surrey side of the Thames, The first town is Bromley, the next Seven-Oaks, the next Tunbridge, and between Tunbridge and this place you cross the boundaries of the two counties.—From the Surrey Wen to Bromley the land is generally a deep loam on a gravel, and you see few trees except elm. A very ugly country. On quitting Bromley the land gets poorer; clay at bottom; the wheat sown on five, or seven, turn lands; the furrows shining with wet; rushes on the wastes on the sides of the road. Here there is a common, part of which has been inclosed and thrown out again, or, rather, the fences carried away.—There is a frost this morning, some, ice and the women look rosy-cheeked.—There is a very great variety of soil along this road; bottom of yellow clay; then of sand; then of sand-stone; then of solider stone; then (for about five miles) of chalk; then of red clay; then chalk again; here (before you come to Seven-Oaks) is a most beautiful and rich valley, extending from east to west, with rich corn-fields and fine trees; then comes sand-stone again; and the hop-gardens near Seven-Oaks, which is a pretty little town with beautiful environs, part of which consists of the park of *Knowle,* the seat of the Duchess of Dorset. It is a very fine place. And there is another park, on the other side of the town. So that this is a delightful place, and the land appears to be very good. The gardens and houses all look neat and nice. On quitting Seven-Oaks you come to a bottom of gravel for a short distance, and to a clay for many miles. When I say that I saw teams *carting* gravel from this spot to a distance of nearly *ten miles* along the road, the reader will be at no loss to know what sort of bottom the land has all along here. The bottom then becomes sand-stone again. This vein of land runs all along through the county of Sussex, and the clay runs into Hampshire, across the forests of Bere and Waltham, then across the parishes of Ousle-bury, Stoke, and passing between the sand hills of Southampton and chalk hills of Winchester, goes westward till stopped by the chalky downs between Romsey and Salisbury.—Tunbridge is a small but very nice town, and has some fine meadows and a navigable river.—The rest of the way to Battle presents, alternately, clay and sand-stone. Of course the coppices and oak woods are very frequent. There is now and then a hop-garden spot, and now and then an orchard of apples or cherries; but these are poor indeed compared with what you see about Canterbury and Maidstone. The agricultural state of the country or, rather, the quality of the land, from Bromley to Battle, may be judged of from the fact, that I did not see, as I came along, more than thirty acres of swedes during the fifty-six miles! In Norfolk I should, in the same distance, have seen five hundred acres! However, man was not the maker of the land; and, as to human happiness, I am of opinion that as much, and even more, falls to the lot of the leather-legged chaps that live in and rove about amongst those clays and woods as to the more regularly disciplined labourers of the rich and prime parts of England. As " God has made the back to the burthen," so the clay and coppice people make the dress to the stubs and bushes. Under the sole of the shoe is *iron ;* from the sole six inches upwards is a high-low; then comes a leather bam to the knee; then comes a pair of leather breeches; then comes a stout doublet; over this comes a smock-frock; and the wearer sets brush and stubs and thorns and mire at defiance. I have always observed that woodland and forest labourers are best off in the main. The coppices give them pleasant and profitable work in winter. If they have not so great a corn-harvest, they have a three weeks' harvest in April or May; that is to say, in the season of barking, which in Hampshire is called *stripping*, and in Sussex *flaying*, which employs women and children as well as men. And then in the great article of *fuel !* They *buy* none. It is miserable work where this is to be bought, and where, as at Salisbury, the poor take by turns the making of fires at their houses to boil four or five tea-kettles. What a winter-life must those lead, whose turn it is not to make the fire! At Launceston in Cornwall a man, a tradesman too, told me, that the people in general could not afford to have fire in ordinary, and that he himself paid 3d. for boiling a leg of mutton at another man's fire! The leather-legged-race know none of these miseries, at any rate. They literally get their fuel " by *hook* or by *crook*," whence, doubtless, comes that old and very expressive saying, which is applied to those cases where people *will have a thing* by one means or another.

BATTLE,
Thursday (night), 3 *Jan.* 1822.

To-day there has been a *meeting* here of the landlords and farmers in this part of Sussex, which is called the *Rape of Hastings*. The object was to agree on a petition to parliament praying for *relief !* Good God! Where is this to *end ?* We now see the effects of those *rags* which I have been railing against for the last twenty years. Here were collected together not less than 300 persons, principally landlords and farmers, brought from their homes by their distresses and by their alarms for the future! Never were such things heard in any country before; and it is useless to hope, for terrific must be the consequences, if an effectual remedy be not speedily applied. The town, which is small, was in a great bustle before noon; and the meeting (in a large room in the principal inn) took place about one o'clock. Lord Ashburnham was called to the chair, and there were present Mr. Curteis, one of the county members, Mr. Fuller, who formerly used to cut *such a figure* in the House of Commons, Mr. Lambe, and many other gentlemen of landed property within the rape, or district, for which the meeting was held. Mr. Curteis, after Lord Ashburnham had opened the business, addressed the meeting.

Mr. Fuller then tendered some resolutions, describing the fallen state of the landed interest, and proposing to pray, *generally*, for relief. Mr. Britton complained that it was not proposed to pray for some *specific measure*, and insisted, that the cause of the evil was the rise in the value of money without a corresponding r duction in the taxes.—A committee was appointed to draw up a petition, which was next produced. It merely described the distress, and prayed generally for relief. Mr. Holloway proposed an addition, containing an imputation of the distress to restricted currency and unabated taxation, and praying for a reduction of taxes. A discussion now arose upon two points: first, whether the addition were admissible at all! and, second, whether Mr. Holloway was qualified to offer it to the meeting. Both the points having been, at last, decided in the affirmative, the addition, or amendment, was put, and *lost ;* and then the original petition was adopted.

After the business of the day was ended, there was a dinner in the inn, in the same room where the meeting had been held. I was at this dinner; and Mr. Britton having proposed my health, and Mr. Curteis, who was in the chair, having given it, I thought it would have looked like mock-modesty, which is, in fact, only another term for hypocrisy, to refrain from expressing my opinions upon a point or two connected with the business of the day. I shall now insert a substantially correct sketch of what the company was indulgent enough to hear from me at the dinner; which I take from the report, contained in the *Morning Chronicle* of Saturday last. The report in the *Chronicle* has all the *pith* of what I advanced relative to *the inutility of Corn Bills*, and relative to *the cause of further declining prices ;* two points of the greatest importance in themselves, and which I was, and am, uncommonly anxious to press upon the attention of the public.

The following is a part of the speech so reported:—

I am decidedly of opinion, gentlemen, that a Corn Bill of no description, no matter what its principles or provisions, can do either tenant or landlord any good; and I am not less decidedly of opinion, that though prices are now low, they must, all the present train of public measures continuing, be yet lower, and continue lower upon an average of years and of seasons.—As to a Corn Bill; a law to prohibit or check the importation of human food is a perfect novelty in our history, and ought, therefore, independent of the reason, and the recent experience of the case, to be received and entertained with great suspicion. Heretofore, *premiums* have been given for the exportation, and at other times for the importation, of corn; but of laws to prevent the importation of human food our ancestors knew nothing. And what says recent experience? When the present Corn Bill was passed, I, then a farmer, unable to get my brother farmers to join me, *petitioned singly* against this Bill; and I stated to my brother farmers, that such a Bill could do us no good, while it would not fail to excite against us the ill-will of the other classes of the community; a thought by no means pleasant. Thus has it been. The distress of agriculture was considerable in magnitude then; but what is it now? And yet the Bill was passed; that Bill which was to remunerate and protect is still in force; the farmers got what they prayed to

have granted them; and their distress, with a short interval
of tardy pace, has proceeded rapidly increasing from that day
to this. What, in the way of Corn Bill, can you have, gentlemen, beyond absolute prohibition? And have you not, since
about April, 1819, had absolute prohibition? Since that time
no corn has been imported, and then only thirty millions of
bushels, which, supposing it all to have been wheat, was a
quantity much too insignificant to produce any sensible depression in the price of the immense quantity of corn raised in
this kingdom since the last bushel was imported. If your
produce had fallen in this manner, if your prices had come down
very low, immediately after the importation had taken place,
there might have been some colour of reason to impute the fall
to the importation; but it so happens, and as if for the express
purpose of contradicting the crude notions of Mr. Webb Hall,
that your produce has fallen in price at a greater rate, in proportion as time has removed you from the point of importation;
and as to the circumstance, so ostentatiously put forward by
Mr. Hall and others, that there is still some of the imported
corn *unsold*, what does it prove but the converse of what those
gentlemen aim at, that is to say, that the holders *cannot afford*
to sell it at present prices; for, if they could gain but ever so
little by the sale, would they keep it wasting and costing money
in warehouses? There appears with some persons to be a
notion, that the importation of corn is a *new thing*. They seem
to forget, that, during the last war, when agriculture was so
prosperous, the *ports were always open;* that prodigious quantities
of corn were imported during the war; that, so far from importation being prohibited, high *premiums* were given, paid out of the
taxes, partly raised upon English farmers, to induce men to
import corn. All this seems to be forgotten as much as if it had
never taken place; and now the distress of the English farmer
is imputed to a cause which was never before an object of his
attention, and a desire is expressed to put an end to a branch
of commerce which the nation has always freely carried on. I
think, gentlemen, that here are reasons quite sufficient to make
any man but Mr. Webb Hall slow to impute the present distress
to the importation of corn; but, at any rate, what can you have
beyond absolute efficient prohibition? No law, no duty, however high; nothing that the parliament can do can go beyond
this; and this you now have, in effect, as completely as if this
were the only country beneath the sky. For these reasons,
gentlemen (and to state more would be a waste of your time and

an affront to your understandings), I am convinced, that, in the way of Corn Bill, it is impossible for the parliament to afford you any, even the smallest, portion of relief. As to the other point, gentlemen, the tendency which the present measures and course of things have to carry prices *lower*, and considerably lower than they now are, and to keep them for a permanency at that low rate, this is a matter worthy of the serious attention of all connected with the land, and particularly of that of the renting farmer. During the *war* no importations distressed the farmer. It was not till peace came that the cry of distress was heard. But, during the war, there was a boundless issue of paper money. Those issues were instantly narrowed by the peace, the law being that the bank should pay in cash six months after the peace should take place. This was the cause of that distress which led to the present Corn Bill. The disease occasioned by the preparations for cash-payments has been brought to a crisis by Mr. Peel's Bill, which has, in effect, doubled, if not tripled, the real amount of the taxes, and violated all contracts for time; given triple gains to every lender, and placed every borrower in jeopardy.

KENSINGTON,
Friday, 4 Jan. 1822.

Got home from *Battle*. I had no time to see the town, having entered the inn on Wednesday in the dusk of the evening, having been engaged all day yesterday in the inn, and having come out of it only to get into the coach this morning. I had not time to go even to see *Battle Abbey*, the seat of the Webster family, now occupied by a man of the name of *Alexander !* Thus they *replace them !* It will take a much shorter time than most people imagine to put out all the ancient families. I should think, that six years will turn out all those who receive nothing out of taxes. The greatness of the estate is no protection to the owner; for, great or little, it will soon yield him *no* rents; and when the produce is nothing in either case, the small estate is as good as the large one. Mr. Curteis said, that the *land* was *immovable ;* yes; but the *rents are not.* And if freeholds cannot be seized for common contract debts, the carcass of the owner may. But, in fact, there will be no rents; and, without these, the ownership is an empty sound. Thus, at last, the burthen will, as I always said it would, fall upon the *landowner ;* and, as the fault of supporting the system has been wholly his, the burthen will fall upon the *right back.*

Whether he will now call in the people to help him to shake it off is more than I can say; but, if he do not, I am sure that he must sink under it. And then, will *revolution No. I.* have been accomplished; but far, and very far indeed, will that be from being the *close* of the drama!—I cannot quit Battle without observing that the country is very pretty all about it. All hill or valley. A great deal of woodland, in which the underwood is generally very fine, though the oaks are not very fine, and a good deal covered with *moss*. This shows that the clay ends before the *tap*-root of the oak gets as deep as it would go; for when the clay goes the full depth the oaks are always fine.— The woods are too large and too near each other for hare-hunting; and as to coursing it is out of the question here. But it is a fine country for shooting and for harbouring game of all sorts.—It was rainy as I came home; but the woodmen were at work. A great many *hop-poles* are cut here, which makes the coppices more valuable than in many other parts. The women work in the coppices, shaving the bark of the hop-poles, and, indeed, at various other parts of the business. These poles are shaved to prevent *maggots* from breeding in the bark and accelerating the destruction of the pole. It is curious that the bark of trees should generate maggots; but it has, as well as the wood, a *sugary* matter in it. The hickory wood in America sends out from the ends of the logs when these are burning great quantities of the finest syrup that can be imagined. Accordingly, that wood breeds maggots, or worms as they are usually called, surprisingly. Our *ash* breeds worms very much. When the tree or pole is cut, the moist matter between the outer bark and the wood, putrifies. Thence come the maggots, which soon begin to eat their way into the wood. For this reason the bark is shaved off the hop-poles, as it ought to be off all our timber trees, as soon as cut, especially the ash.—Little boys and girls shave hop-poles and assist in other coppice work very nicely. And it is pleasant work when the weather is dry over head. The woods, bedded with leaves as they are, are clean and dry underfoot. They are warm too, even in the coldest weather. When the ground is frozen several inches deep in the open fields, it is scarcely frozen at all in a coppice where the underwood is a good plant, and where it is nearly high enough to cut. So that the woodman's is really a pleasant life. We are apt to think that the birds have a hard time of it in winter. But we forget the warmth of the woods, which far exceeds any-thing to be found in farmyards. When Sidmouth started me from my farm, in 1817, I had just planted my farmyard round with a pretty coppice. But, never mind, Sidmouth, and I shall, I dare say, have plenty of time and occasion to talk about that coppice, and many other things, before we die. And, can I, when I think of these things now, *pity* those to whom Sidmouth *owed his power* of starting me!—But let me forget the subject for this time at any rate.—Woodland countries are interesting on many accounts. Not so much on account of their masses of green leaves, as on account of the variety of sights and sounds and incidents that they afford. Even in winter the coppices are beautiful to the eye, while they comfort the mind with the idea of shelter and warmth. In spring they change their hue from day to day during two whole months, which is about the time from the first appearance of the delicate leaves of the birch to the full expansion of those of the ash; and even before the leaves come at all to intercept the view, what in the vegetable creation is so delightful to behold as the bed of a coppice bespangled with primroses and bluebells? The opening of the birch leaves is the signal for the pheasant to begin to crow, for the blackbird to whistle, and the thrush to sing; and just when the oak-buds begin to look reddish, and not a day before, the whole tribe of finches burst forth in songs from every bough, while the lark, imitating them all, carries the joyous sounds to the sky. These are amongst the means which Providence has benignantly appointed to sweeten the toils by which food and raiment are produced; these the English Ploughman could once hear without the sorrowful reflection that he himself was *a pauper*, and that the bounties of nature had, for him, been scattered in vain! And shall he never see an end to this state of things! Shall he never have the due reward of his labour! Shall unsparing taxation never cease to make him a miserable dejected being, a creature famishing in the midst of abundance, fainting, expiring with hunger's feeble moans, surrounded by a carolling creation! O! accursed paper-money! Has hell a torment surpassing the wickedness of thy inventor!

SUSSEX JOURNAL

THROUGH CROYDON, GODSTONE, EAST-GRINSTEAD, AND UCKFIELD, TO LEWES, AND BRIGHTON; RETURNING BY CUCKFIELD, WORTH, AND RED-HILL

LEWES,
Tuesday, 8 Jan. 1822.

CAME here to-day, from home, to see what passes to-morrow at a meeting to be held here of the owners and occupiers of land in the rapes of Lewes and Pevensey.—In quitting the great Wen we go through Surrey more than half the way to Lewes. From *Saint George's Fields*, which now are covered with houses, we go, towards Croydon, between rows of houses, nearly half the way, and the whole way is nine miles. There are, erected within these four years, two entire miles of stock-jobbers' houses on this one road, and the work goes on with accelerated force! To be sure; for the taxes being, in fact, tripled by Peel's Bill, the fundlords increase in riches; and their accommodations increase of course. What an at once horrible and ridiculous thing this country would become, if this thing could go on only for a few years! And these rows of new houses, added to the Wen, are proofs of growing prosperity, are they? These make part of the increased capital of the country, do they? But how is this Wen to be *dispersed ?* I know not whether it be to be done by knife or by caustic; but dispersed it must be! And this is the only difficulty, which I do not see the *easy* means of getting over.—Aye! these are dreadful thoughts! I know they are; but they ought not to be banished from the mind; for they will *return*, and, at every return, they will be more frightful. The man who cannot coolly look at this matter is unfit for the times that are approaching. Let the interest of the debt be once well reduced (and that must be sooner or later) and then what is to become of *half a million* at least of the people congregated in this Wen? Oh! precious " Great Man now no more!" Oh! " Pilot that weathered the Storm!" Oh! " Heaven - born " pupil of Prettyman! Who but him who can number the sands of the sea, shall number the execrations with which thy memory will be loaded!— From London to

Croydon is as ugly a bit of country as any in England. A poor spewy gravel with some clay. Few trees but elms, and those generally stripped up and villainously ugly.—Croydon is a good market-town; but is, by the funds, swelled out into a *Wen.*—Upon quitting Croydon for Godstone, you come to the chalk hills, the juniper shrubs and the yew trees. This is an extension westward of the vein of chalk which I have before noticed (see page 57) between Bromley and Seven-Oaks. To the westward here lies Epsom Downs, which lead on to Merrow Downs and St. Margaret's Hill, then, skipping over Guildford, you come to the Hog's Back, which is still of chalk, and at the west end of which lies Farnham. With the Hog's Back this vein of chalk seems to end; for then the valleys become rich loam, and the hills sand and gravel till you approach the Winchester Downs by the way of Arlesford.—Godstone, which is in Surrey also, is a beautiful village, chiefly of one street with a fine large green before it and with a pond in the green. A little way to the right (going from London) lies the vile rotten Borough of *Blechingley;* but, happily for Godstone, out of sight. At and near Godstone the gardens are all very neat; and, at the inn, there is a nice garden well stocked with beautiful flowers in the season. I here saw, last summer, some double violets as large as small pinks, and the lady of the house was kind enough to give me some of the roots.—From Godstone you go up a long hill of clay and sand, and then descend into a level country of stiff loam at top, clay at bottom, corn-fields, pastures, broad hedge-rows, coppices, and oak woods, which country continues till you quit Surrey about two miles before you reach East-Grinstead. The woods and coppices are very fine here. It is the genuine *oak-soil;* a bottom of yellow clay to any depth, I dare say, that man can go. No moss on the oaks. No dead tops. Straight as larches. The bark of the young trees with dark spots in it; sure sign of free growth and great depth of clay beneath. The wheat is here sown on five-turn ridges, and the ploughing is amongst the best that I ever saw.—At East-Grinstead, which is a rotten borough and a very shabby place, you come to stiff loam at top with sand-stone beneath. To the south of the place the land is fine, and the vale on both sides a very beautiful intermixture of woodland and corn-fields and pastures.—At about three miles from Grinstead you come to a pretty village, called Forest-Row, and then, on the road to Uckfield, you cross Ashurst Forest, which is a heath, with here and there a few birch scrubs upon it, verily the most villainously ugly spot I ever saw in England. This lasts you for five miles, getting, if possible, uglier and uglier all the way, till, at last, as if barren soil, nasty spewy gravel, heath and even that stunted, were not enough, you see some rising spots, which instead of trees, present you with black, ragged, hideous rocks. There may be Englishmen who wish to see the coast of *Nova Scotia*. They need not go to sea; for here it is to the life. If I had been in a long trance (as our nobility seem to have been), and had been waked up here, I should have begun to look about for the Indians and the squaws, and to have heaved a sigh at the thought of being so far from England.—From the end of this forest without trees you come into a country of but poorish wettish land. Passing through the village of Uckfield, you find an enclosed country, with a soil of a clay cast all the way to within about three miles of Lewes, when you get to a chalk bottom, and rich land. I was at Lewes at the beginning of last harvest, and saw the fine farms of the Ellmans, very justly renowned for their improvement of the breed of *South-Down sheep*, and the younger Mr. John Ellman not less justly blamed for the part he had taken in propagating the errors of Webb Hall, and thereby, however unintentionally, assisting to lead thousands to cherish those false hopes that have been the cause of their ruin. Mr. Ellman may say, that he *thought* he was right; but if he had read my *New Year's Gift* to the farmers, published in the preceding January, he could not think that he was right. If he had not read it, he ought to have read it, before he appeared in print. At any rate, if no other person had a right to censure his publications, I *had* that right. I will here notice a calumny, to which the above visit to Lewes gave rise; namely, that I went into the neighbourhood of the Ellmans, to find out whether they illtreated their labourers! No man that knows me will believe this. The facts are these: the Ellmans, celebrated farmers, had made a great figure in the evidence taken before the committee. I was at Worth, about twenty miles from Lewes. The harvest was begun. Worth is a woodland country. I wished to know the state of the crops; for, I was, at that very time, as will be seen by referring to the date, beginning to write my First Letter to the Landlords. Without knowing anything of the matter myself, I asked my host, Mr. Brazier, what good corn country was nearest to us. He said Lewes. Off I went, and he with me, in a post-chaise. We had 20 miles to go and 20 back in the same chaise. A bad road, and rain all the day. We put up at the White Hart, took another chaise, went round and saw the farms, through the window of the chaise, having stopped at a little public-house to ask which were they, and having stopped now and then to get a sample out of the sheaves of wheat, came back to the White Hart, after being absent only about an hour and a half, got our dinner, and got back to Worth before it was dark; and never asked, and never intended to ask, one single question of any human being as to the conduct or character of the Ellmans. Indeed the evidence of the elder Mr. Ellman was so fair, so honest, and so useful, particularly as relating *to the labourers*, that I could not possibly suspect him of being a cruel or hard master. He told the committee that when he began business, forty-five years ago, every man in the parish brewed his own beer, and that now, not one man did it, unless he gave him the malt! Why, here was by far the most valuable part of the whole volume of evidence. Then, Mr. Ellman did not present a parcel of *estimates* and God knows what; but a plain and honest statement of facts, the rate of day wages, of job wages, for a long series of years, by which it clearly appeared how the labourer had been robbed and reduced to misery, and how the poor-rates had been increased. He did not, like Mr. George and other Bull-frogs, sink these interesting facts; but honestly told the truth. Therefore, whatever I might think of his endeavours to uphold the mischievous errors of Webb Hall, I could have no suspicion that he was a hard master.

LEWES,
Wednesday, 9 Jan. 1822.

The meeting and the dinner are now over. Mr. Davies Giddy was in the chair: the place the County Hall. A Mr. Partington, a pretty little oldish smart truss nice cockney-looking gentleman, with a yellow and red handkerchief round his neck, moved the petition, which was seconded by Lord Chichester, who lives in the neighbourhood. Much as I had read of that great doctor of *virtual representation* and *Royal Commissioner of Inimitable Bank Notes*, Mr. Davies Giddy, I had never seen him before. He called to my mind one of those venerable persons who administer spiritual comfort to the sinners of the " sister-kingdom; " and, whether I looked at the dress or the person, I could almost have sworn that it was the identical *Father Luke* that I saw about twenty-three years ago, at Philadelphia, in the farce of the Poor Soldier. Mr. Blackman (of Lewes I believe) disapproved of the petition, and in a speech of considerable

length, and also of considerable ability, stated to the meeting
that the evils complained of arose from the *currency*, and not
from the *importation of foreign corn*. A Mr. Donavon, an Irish
gentleman, who, it seems, is a magistrate in this "disturbed
county," disapproved of discussing anything at such a meeting,
and thought that the meeting should merely state its distresses,
and leave it to the wisdom of parliament to discover the remedy.
Upon which Mr. Chatfield observed; "So, sir, we are in a trap.
We cannot get ourselves out though we know the way. There
are others, who have got us in, and are able to get us out, but
they do not know how. And we are to tell them, it seems, that
we are in the trap; but are not to tell them the way to get us
out. I don't like long speeches, sir; but I like common sense."
This was neat and pithy. Fifty professed orators could not,
in a whole day, have thrown so much ridicule on the speech of
Mr. Donavon.—A Mr. Mabbott proposed an amendment to
include all classes of the community, and took a hit at Mr.
Curteis for his speech at Battle. Mr. Curteis defended himself,
and I thought very fairly. A Mr. Woodward, who said he was
a farmer, carried us back to the necessity of the war against
France; and told us of the horrors of plunder and murder and
rape that the war had prevented. This gentleman put an end
to my patience, which Donavon had put to an extremely severe
test; and so I withdrew.—After I went away Mr. Blackman
proposed some resolutions, which were carried by a great
majority by show of hands. But pieces of paper were then
handed about, for the voters to write their names on for and
against the petition. The greater part of the people were gone
away by this time; but, at any rate, there were more *signatures*
for the petition than for the resolutions. A farmer in Pennsylvania having a visitor, to whom he was willing to show how
well he treated his negroes as to food, bid the fellows (who were
at dinner) *to ask for a second or third cut of pork if they had not
enough.* Quite surprised at the novelty, but emboldened by a
repetition of the injunction, one of them did say, "Massa, I
wants another cut." He had it; but as soon as the visitor was
gone away, "D—n you," says the master, while he belaboured
him with the "cowskin." "I'll make you know *how to understand me* another time!"—The signers of this petition were in
the dark while the show of hands was going on; but when it
came to *signing* they knew well *what Massa meant!* This is a
petition to be sure; but, it is no more the petition of the farmers
in the rapes of Lewes and Pevensey than it is the petition of the

mermaids of Lapland.—There was a *dinner* after the meeting at the *Star Inn,* at which there occurred something rather curious regarding myself. When at Battle, I had no intention of going to Lewes, till on the evening of my arrival at Battle, a gentleman, who had heard of the before-mentioned calumny, observed to me that I would do well not to go to Lewes. That very observation made me resolve to go. I went, as a spectator, to the meeting; and I left no one ignorant of the place where I was to be found. I did not covet the noise of a dinner of from 200 to 300 persons; and I did not intend to go to it; but, being pressed to go, I finally went. After some previous commonplace occurrences, Mr. Kemp, formerly a member for Lewes, was called to the chair; and he having given as a toast, " *the speedy discovery of a remedy for our distresses,*" Mr. Ebenezer Johnstone, a gentleman of Lewes, whom I had never seen or heard of until that day, but who, I understand, is a very opulent and most respectable man, proposed *my health,* as that of a person likely to be able to point out the wished-for remedy.— This was the signal for the onset. Immediately upon the toast being given, a Mr. Hitchins, a farmer of Seaford, duly prepared for the purpose, got upon the table, and, with candle in one hand and *Register* in the other, read the following garbled passage from my *Letter to Lord Egremont.*—" But let us hear what the younger Ellman said: ' He had seen them employed in drawing beach gravel, as had been already described. One of them, the leader, worked with a bell about his neck.' Oh! the envy of surrounding nations and admiration of the world! Oh! what a ' glorious constitution!' Oh! what a happy country! Impudent Radicals, to want to reform a parliament, under which men enjoy such blessings! On such a subject it is impossible (under Six-Acts) to trust one's pen! However, this I will say; that here is much more than enough to make me rejoice in the ruin of the farmers; and I do, with all my heart, thank God for it; *seeing, that it appears absolutely necessary, that* the present race of them should be totally broken up, in Sussex at any rate, *in order to put an end to this cruelty and insolence towards the labourers, who are by far the greater number ; and who are men, and a little better men too, than such employers as these, who are, in fact, monsters in human shape !* "

I had not the *Register* by me, and could not detect the garbling. All the words that I have put in italics, this Hitchins left out in the reading. What sort of man he must be the public will easily judge.—No sooner had Hitchins done, than up started

Mr. Ingram, a farmer of Rottendean, who was the second person in the drama (for all had been duly prepared), and moved that I should be *put out of the room !* Some few of the Webb Hallites, joined by about six or eight of the dark, dirty-faced, half-whiskered, tax-eaters from Brighton (which is only eight miles off) joined in this cry. I rose, that they might see the man that they had to put out. Fortunately *for themselves*, not one of them attempted to approach me. They were like the mice that resolved that a bell should be put round the cat's neck!—However, a considerable hubbub took place. At last, however, the chairman, Mr. Kemp, whose conduct was fair and manly, having given my health, I proceeded to address the company in substance as stated here below; and, it is curious enough, that even those who, upon my health being given, had taken their hats and gone out of the room (and amongst whom Mr. Ellman the younger was one) came back, formed a crowd, and were just as silent and attentive as the rest of the company!

[NOTE, written at *Kensington*, 13 *Jan.*—I must here, before I insert the speech, which has appeared in the *Morning Chronicle*, the Brighton papers, and in most of the London papers, except the base sinking *Old Times* and the brimstone-smelling *Tramper*, or *Traveller*, which is, I well know, a mere tool in the hands of two snap-dragon Whig-lawyers, whose greediness and folly I have so often had to expose, and which paper is maintained by a contrivance which I will amply expose in my next; I must, before I insert this speech, remark, that Mr. Ellman the younger has, to a gentleman whom I know to be incapable of falsehood, disavowed the proceeding of Hitchins; on which I have to observe, that the disavowal, to have any weight, must be public, or be made to me.

As to the provocation that I have given the Ellmans, I am, upon reflection, ready to confess that I may have laid on the lash without a due regard to mercy. The fact is, that I have so long had the misfortune to be compelled to keep a parcel of badger-hided fellows, like Scarlett, in order, that I am, like a drummer that has been used to flog old offenders, become *heavy handed*. I ought to have considered the Ellmans as *recruits* and to have suited my tickler to the tenderness of their backs.—I hear that Mr. Ingram of Rottendean, who moved for my being turned out of the room, and who looked so foolish when he had to turn himself out, is an officer of Yeomanry "*Gavaltry.*" A ploughman spoiled! This man would, I dare say, have been a very good husbandman; but the unnatural working of the paper-system has sublimated him out of his senses. That greater doctor, Mr. Peel, will bring him down again.—Mr. Hitchins, I am told, after going away, came back, stood on the landing-place (the door being open), and, while I was speaking, exclaimed, "Oh! the fools! How they open their mouths! How they suck it all in."—Suck *what* in, Mr. Hitchins? Was it honey that dropped from my lips? Was it flattery? Amongst other things, I said that I liked the plain names of *farmer* and *husbandman* better than that of *agriculturist;* and the prospect I held out to them, was that of a description to catch their applause?—But this Hitchins seems to be a very silly person indeed.]

The following is a portion of the speech:—

The toast having been *opposed,* and that, too, in the extraordinary manner we have witnessed, I will, at any rate, with your permission, make a remark or two on that manner. If the person who has made the opposition had been actuated by a spirit of fairness and justice, he would not have confined himself to a detached sentence of the paper from which he has read; but would have taken the whole together; for, by taking a particular sentence, and leaving out all the rest, what writing is there that will not admit of a wicked interpretation? As to the particular part which has been read, I should not, perhaps, if I had seen it *in print,* and had had time to cool a little [it was in a *Register* sent from Norfolk], have sent it forth in terms so very general as to embrace all the farmers of this county; but as to those of them who put *the bell round the labourer's neck,* I beg leave to be now repeating, in its severest sense, every word of the passage that has been read.—Born in a farm-house, bred up at the plough tail, with a smock-frock on my back, taking great delight in all the pursuits of farmers, liking their society, and having amongst them my most esteemed friends, it is natural that I should feel, and I do feel, uncommonly anxious to prevent, as far as I am able, that total ruin which now menaces them. But the labourer, was I to have no feeling for him? Was not he my *countryman* too? And was I not to feel indignation against those farmers, who had had the hard-heartedness to put the bell round his neck, and thus wantonly insult and degrade the class to whose toils they owed their own ease? The statement of the fact was not mine; I read it in the newspaper as having come from Mr. Ellman the younger; he, in a very laudable manner, expressed his *horror* at it; and was not I to express *indignation* at what Mr. Ellman felt horror? That gentleman and Mr. Webb Hall may monopolise all the wisdom in matters of political economy; but are they, or rather is Mr. Ellman alone, to engross all the feeling too? [It was here denied that Mr. Ellman had said the bell had been put on by *farmers*.] Very well, then, the complained of passage has been productive of benefit to the farmers of this county; for, as the thing stood in the newspapers, the natural and unavoidable inference was, that that atrocious, that inhuman act, was an act of Sussex farmers.

BRIGHTON,
Thursday, 10 *Jan*. 1822.

Lewes is in a valley of the *South Downs*, this town is at eight miles distance, to the south-south-west or thereabouts. There is a great extent of rich meadows above and below Lewes. The town itself is a model of solidity and neatness. The buildings all substantial to the very outskirts; the pavements good and complete; the shops nice and clean; the people well-dressed; and, though last not least, the girls remarkably pretty, as, indeed, they are in most parts of Sussex; round faces, features small, little hands and wrists, plump arms, and bright eyes. The Sussex men, too, are remarkable for their good looks. A Mr. Baxter, a stationer at Lewes, showed me a *farmer's account book*, which is a very complete thing of the kind. The inns are good at Lewes, the people civil and not servile, and the charges really (considering the taxes) far below what one could reasonably expect.—From Lewes to Brighton the road winds along between the hills of the South Downs, which, in this mild weather, are mostly beautifully green even at this season, with flocks of sheep feeding on them.—Brighton itself lies in a valley cut across at one end by the sea, and its extension, or *Wen*, has swelled up the sides of the hills and has run some distance up the valley.—The first thing you see in approaching Brighton from Lewes, is a splendid *horse-barrack* on one side of the road, and a heap of low, shabby, nasty houses, irregularly built, on the other side. This is always the case where there is a barrack. How soon a reformed parliament would make both disappear! Brighton is a very pleasant place. For a *wen* remarkably so. The *Kremlin*, the very name of which has so long been a subject of laughter all over the country, lies in the gorge of the valley, and amongst the old houses of the town. The grounds, which cannot, I think, exceed a couple or three acres, are surrounded by a wall neither lofty nor good-looking. Above this rise some trees, bad in sorts, stunted in growth, and dirty with smoke. As to the " palace " as the Brighton newspapers call it, the apartments appear to be all upon the ground floor; and, when you see the thing from a distance, you think you see a parcel of *cradle-spits*, of various dimensions, sticking up out of the mouths of so many enormous squat decanters. Take a square box, the sides of which are three feet and a half, and the height a foot and a half. Take a large Norfolk-turnip, cut off the green of the leaves, leave the stalks 9 inches long, tie these round with a string three inches from the top, and put the turnip on the middle of the top of the box. Then take four turnips of half the size, treat them in the same way, and put them on the corners of the box. Then take a considerable number of bulbs of the crown-imperial, the narcissus, the hyacinth, the tulip, the crocus, and others; let the leaves of each have sprouted to about an inch, more or less according to the size of the bulb; put all these, pretty promiscuously, but pretty thickly, on the top of the box. Then stand off and look at your architecture. There! That's " *a Kremlin !* " Only you must cut some church-looking windows in the sides of the box. As to what you ought to put *into* the box, that is a subject far above my cut.—Brighton is naturally a place of resort for *expectants*, and a shifty ugly-looking swarm is, of course, assembled here. Some of the fellows, who had endeavoured to disturb our harmony at the dinner at Lewes, were parading, amongst this swarm, on the cliff. You may always know them by their lank jaws, the stiffeners round their necks, their hidden or *no* shirts, their stays, their false shoulders, hips and haunches, their half-whiskers, and by their skins, colour of veal kidney-suet, warmed a little, and then powdered with dirty dust.—These vermin excepted, the people at Brighton make a very fine figure. The trades-people are very nice in all their concerns. The houses are excellent, built chiefly with a blue or purple brick; and bow-windows appear to be the general taste. I can easily believe this to be a very healthy place: the open downs on the one side and the open sea on the other. No inlet, cove, or river; and, of course, no swamps.—I have spent this evening very pleasantly in a company of reformers, who, though plain tradesmen and mechanics, know I am quite satisfied more about the questions that agitate the country than any equal number of lords.

KENSINGTON,
Friday, 11 January, 1822.

Came home by the way of Cuckfield, Worth, and Red-Hill, instead of by Uckfield, Grinstead and Godstone, and got into the same road again at Croydon. The roads being nearly parallel lines and at no great distance from each other, the soil is nearly the same, with the exception of the fine oak country between Godstone and Grinstead, which does not go so far westward as my homeward bound road, where the land, opposite the spot just spoken of, becomes more of a moor than a clay, and though there are oaks, they are not nearly so fine as those on the other road. The tops are flatter; the side *shoots* are sometimes higher than the middle shoot; a certain proof that the *tap-root* has met with something that it does not like.—I see (Jan. 15) that Mr. Curteis has thought it necessary to state in the public papers, that *he* had *nothing to do* with my being at the dinner at Battle! Who the Devil thought he had? Why, was it not an ordinary; and had I not as much right there as he? He has said, too, that *he did not know* that I was to be at the dinner. How should he? Why was it necessary to apprise him of it any more than the porter of the inn? He has said, that he did not hear of any deputation to invite me to the dinner, and, "*upon inquiry*," cannot find that there was any. Have I said that there was any invitation at all? There was; but I have not said so. I went to the dinner for my half-crown like another man, without knowing, or caring, who would be at it. But, if Mr. Curteis thought it necessary to say so much, he might have said a little more. He might have said, that he twice addressed himself to me in a very peculiar manner, and that I never addressed myself to him except in answer; and, if he had thought "*inquiry*" necessary upon this subject also, he might have found that, though always the first to speak or hold out the hand to a hard-fisted artisan or labourer, I never did the same to a man of rank or riches in the whole course of my life. Mr. Curteis might have said, too, that unless I had gone to the dinner, the party would, according to appearances, have been very *select;* that I found him at the head of one of the tables, with less than thirty persons in the room; that the number swelled up to about one hundred and thirty; that no person was at the other table; that I took my seat at it; and that that table became almost immediately crowded from one end to the other. To these Mr. Curteis, when his hand was in, might have added, that he turned himself in his chair and listened to my speech with the greatest attention; that he bade me, by name, good-night, when he retired; that he took not a man away with him; and that the gentlemen who was called on to replace him in the chair (whose name I have forgotten) had got from his seat during the evening to come and shake me by the hand. All these things Mr. Curteis might have said; but the fact is, he has been bullied by the base newspapers, and he has not been able to muster up courage to act the manly part, and which, too, he would have found to be the *wise* part in the end. When he gave the toast " *more money and less taxes*," he turned himself towards me, and said, " That is a toast, that I am sure, *you* *approve* of, Mr. Cobbett." To which I answered, " It would be made good, sir, if *members of parliament would do their duty*."— I appeal to all the gentlemen present for the truth of what I say.—Perhaps Mr. Curteis, in his heart, did not like to give my health. If that was the case, he ought to have left the chair, and retired. *Straight forward* is the best course; and see what difficulties Mr. Curteis has involved himself in by not pursuing it! I have no doubt that he was agreeably surprised when he saw and heard me. Why not *say* then: " After all that has been said about Cobbett, he is a devilish pleasant, frank, and clever fellow, at any rate."—How much better this would have been, than to act the part that Mr. Curteis has acted.—The editors of the *Brighton Chronicle and Lewes Express* have, out of mere modesty, I dare say, fallen a little into Mr. Curteis's strain. In closing their account (in their paper of the 15th) of the Lewes meeting, they say, that I addressed the company at some length, as reported in their supplement published on Thursday the 10th. And then they think it necessary to add: " For ourselves, we can say, that we never saw Mr. Cobbett until the meeting at Battle." Now, had it not been for pure maiden-like bashfulness, they would, doubtless, have added, that when they did see me, they were profuse in expressions of their gratitude to me for having merely *named their paper* in my *Register*, a thing, which, as I told them, I myself had forgotten. When, too, they were speaking, in reference to a speech made in the hall, of " one of the finest specimens of oratory that has ever been given in any assembly," it was, without doubt,

out of pure compassion for the perverted taste of their Lewes
readers, that they suppressed the fact, that the agent of the
paper at Lewes sent them word, that it was useless for them
to send any account of the meeting, unless that account contained Mr. Cobbett's speech; that he, the agent, could have
sold a hundred papers that morning, if they had contained
Mr. Cobbett's speech; but could not sell one without it. I
myself, by mere accident, heard this message delivered to a
third person by their agent at Lewes. And, as I said before,
it must have been pure tenderness towards their readers that
made the editors suppress a fact so injurious to the reputation
of those readers in point of *taste !* However, at last, these editors
seem to have triumphed over all feelings of this sort; for, having
printed off a placard, advertising their supplement, in which
placard no menion was made of *me*, they, grown bold all of a
sudden, took a *painting brush*, and in large letters, put into
their placard, " *Mr. Cobbett's Speech at Lewes ;* " so that, at a
little distance, the placard seemed to relate to nothing else;
and there was " the finest specimen of oratory " left to find
its way into the world under the auspices of my rustic harangue.
Good God! What will this world come to! We shall, by and
by, have to laugh at the workings of envy in the very worms
that we breed in our bodies!— The fast-sinking *Old Times*
newspaper, its cat-and-dog opponent the *New Times*, the
Courier, and the Whig-lawyer *Tramper*, called the *Traveller ;*
the fellows who conduct these vehicles; these wretched fellows,
their very livers burning with envy, have hasted to inform their
readers, that " they have authority to state that Lord Ashburnham and Mr. Fuller were not present at the dinner at
Battle where Cobbett's health was drunk." These fellows have
now " authority " to state, that there were no two men who
dined at Battle, that I should not prefer as companions to Lord
Ashburnham and Mr. Fuller, commonly called " Jack Fuller,"
seeing that I am no admirer of *lofty reserve*, and that, of all things
on earth, I abhor a head like a drum, all noise and emptiness.
These scribes have also " authority " to state, that they amuse
me and the public too by declining rapidly in their sale from
their exclusion of my country lectures, which have only begun.
In addition to this the *Tramper* editor has " authority " to
state, that one of his papers of 5th Jan. has been sent to the
Register office by post, with these words written on it: " This
scoundrel paper has taken no notice of Mr. Cobbett's speech."

All these papers have " authority " to state beforehand, that they will insert no account of what shall take place, within these three or four weeks, at *Huntingdon*, at *Lynn*, at *Chichester*, and other places where I intend to be. And, lastly, the editors have full " authority " to state, that they may employ, without let or molestation of any sort, either private or public, the price of the last number that they shall sell in the purchase of hemp or ratsbane, as the sure means of a happy deliverance from their present state of torment.

HUNTINGDON JOURNAL

THROUGH WARE AND ROYSTON, TO HUNTINGDON

ROYSTON,
Monday morning, 21st Jan. 1822.

CAME from London, yesterday noon, to this town on my way to Huntingdon. My road was through Ware. Royston is just within the line (on the Cambridgeshire side), which divides Hertfordshire from Cambridgeshire. On this road, as on almost all the others going from it, the enormous *Wen* has swelled out to the distance of about six or seven miles.—The land till you come nearly to Ware which is in Hertfordshire, and which is twenty-three miles from the *Wen*, is chiefly a strong and deep loam, with the gravel a good distance from the surface. The land is good wheat-land; but I observed only three fields of swedish turnips in the 23 miles, and no wheat drilled. The wheat is sown on ridges of great width here and there; sometimes on ridges of ten, at others on ridges of seven, on those of five, four, three, and even two, feet wide. Yet the bottom is manifestly not very wet generally; and that there is not a bottom of clay is clear from the poor growth of the oak trees. All the trees are shabby in this country; and the eye is incessantly offended by the sight of *pollards*, which are seldom suffered to disgrace even the meanest lands in Hampshire or Sussex. As you approach Ware the bottom becomes chalk of a dirtyish colour, and, in some parts, far below the surface. After you quit Ware, which is a mere market town, the land grows by degrees poorer; the chalk lies nearer and nearer to the surface, till you come to the open common-fields within a few miles of Royston. Along here the land is poor enough. It is not the stiff red loam mixed with large blue-grey flints, lying upon the chalk, such as you see in the north of Hampshire; but a whitish sort of clay, with little yellow flattish stones amongst it; sure signs of a hungry soil. Yet this land bears wheat sometimes. —Royston is at the foot of this high poor land; or rather in a dell, the open side of which looks towards the North. It is a common market town. Not mean, but having nothing of beauty about it; and having on it, on three of the sides out of the four, those very ugly things, common-fields, which have all the nakedness, without any of the smoothness, of Downs.

HUNTINGDON,
Tuesday morning, 22 Jan. 1822.

Immediately upon quitting Royston, you come along, for a considerable distance, with enclosed fields on the left and open common-fields on the right. Here the land is excellent. A dark, rich loam, free from stones, on chalk beneath at a great distance. The land appears, for a mile or two, to resemble that at and near Faversham in Kent, which I have before noticed. The fields on the left seem to have been enclosed by act of parliament; and they certainly are the most beautiful tract of *fields* that I ever saw. Their extent may be from ten to thirty acres each. Divided by quick-set hedges, exceedingly well planted and raised. The whole tract is nearly a perfect level. The cultivation neat, and the stubble heaps, such as remain out, giving proof of great crops of straw, while, on land with a chalk bottom, there is seldom any want of a proportionate quantity of grain. Even here, however, I saw but few swedish turnips, and those not good. Nor did I see any wheat drilled; and observed, that, in many parts, the broad-cast sowing had been performed in a most careless manner, especially at about three miles from Royston, where some parts of the broad lands seemed to have had the seed flung along them with a shovel, while other parts contained only here and there a blade; or, at least, were so thinly supplied as to make it almost doubtful whether they had not been wholly missed. In some parts, the middles only of the ridges were sown thickly. This is shocking husbandry. A Norfolk or a Kentish farmer would have sowed a bushel and a half of seed to the acre here, and would have had a far better plant of wheat.—About four miles, I think it is, from Royston you come to the estate of Lord Hardwicke. You see the house at the end of an avenue about two miles long, which, however, wants the main thing, namely, fine and lofty trees. The soil here begins to be a very stiff loam at top; clay beneath for a considerable distance; and, in some places, beds of yellow gravel with very large stones mixed in it. The land is generally cold; a great deal of draining is wanted; and yet, the bottom is such as not to be favourable to the growth of the *oak*, of which sort I have not seen one *handsome* tree since I left London. A grove, such as I saw at Weston in Herefordshire,

would, here, be a thing to attract the attention of all ranks
and all ages. What, then, would they say, on beholding a
wood of oaks, hickories, chestnuts, walnuts, locusts, gum-trees,
and maples in America!—Lord Hardwicke's avenue appears to
be lined with elms chiefly. They are shabby. He might have
had *ash;* for the ash will grow *anywhere;* on sand, on gravel,
on clay, on chalk, or in swamps. It is surprising that those
who planted these rows of trees did not observe how well the
ash grows here! In the hedge-rows, in the plantations, everywhere the ash is fine. The ash is the *hardiest* of all our large
trees. Look at trees on any part of the sea coast. You will
see them all, even the firs, lean from the sea breeze, except the
ash. You will see the oak *shaved up* on the side of the breeze.
But the ash stands upright, as if in a warm woody dell. We
have no tree that attains a greater height than the ash; and
certainly none that equals it in beauty of leaf. It bears pruning
better than any other tree. Its timber is one of the most useful;
and as underwood and fire-wood it far exceeds all others of
English growth. From the trees of an avenue like that of Lord
Hardwicke a hundred pounds' worth of fuel might, if the trees
were ash, be cut every year in prunings necessary to preserve
the health and beauty of the trees. Yet, on this same land,
has his lordship planted many acres of larches and firs. These
appear to have been planted about twelve years. If instead of
these he had planted ash, four years from the seed bed and
once removed; had cut them down within an inch of the ground
the second year after planting; and had planted them at four
feet apart, he would now have had about six thousand ash-poles,
on an average twelve feet long, on each acre of land in his
plantation; which, at three-halfpence each, would have been
worth somewhere nearly forty pounds an acre. He might now
have cut the poles, leaving about 600 to stand upon an acre
to come to trees; and, while these were growing to timber, the
underwood would, for poles, hoops, broomsticks, spars, rods,
and faggots, have been worth twenty-five or thirty pounds an
acre every ten years. Can beggarly stuff, like larches and firs,
ever be profitable to this extent? Ash is timber, fit for the
wheelwright, at the age of twenty years, or less. What can you
do with a rotten fir thing at that age?—This estate of Lord
Hardwicke appears to be very large. There is a part which is,
apparently, in his own hands, as, indeed, the whole must soon
be, unless he give up all idea of rent, or unless he can *choack off*
the fundholder or get again afloat on the sea of paper-money.

In this part of his land there is a fine piece of *Lucerne* in rows at about eighteen inches distant from each other. They are now manuring it with *burnt-earth* mixed with some dung; and I see several heaps of burnt-earth hereabouts. The directions for doing this are contained in my *Year's Residence*, as taught me by Mr. William Gauntlet, of Winchester.—The land is, all along here, laid up in those wide and high ridges, which I saw in Gloucestershire, going from Gloucester to Oxford, as I have already mentioned. These ridges are ploughed *back* or *down ;* but they are ploughed up again for every sowing.—At an inn near Lord Hardwicke's I saw the finest parcel of dove-house pigeons I ever saw in my life.—Between this place and Hunting-don is the village of Caxton, which very much resembles almost a village of the same size in *Picardy*, where I saw the women dragging harrows to harrow in the corn. Certainly this village resembles nothing English, except some of the rascally rotten boroughs in Cornwall and Devonshire, on which a just Providence seems to have entailed its curse. The land just about here does seem to be really bad. The face of the country is naked. The few scrubbed trees that now and then meet the eye, and even the quick-sets, are covered with a yellow moss. All is bleak and comfortless; and, just on the most dreary part of this most dreary scene, stands almost opportunely, " *Caxton Gibbet*," tendering its friendly one arm to the passers-by. It has recently been fresh-painted, and written on in conspicuous characters, for the benefit, I suppose, of those who cannot exist under the thought of wheat at four shillings a bushel.—Not far from this is a new house, which, the coachman says, belongs to a Mr. Cheer, who, if report speaks truly, is not, however, not-withstanding his name, guilty of the sin of making people either drunkards or gluttons. Certainly the spot, on which he has built his house, is one of the most ugly that I ever saw. Few spots have everything that you could wish to find; but this, according to my judgment, has everything that every man of ordinary taste would wish to avoid.—The country changes but little till you get quite to Huntingdon. The land is generally quite open, or in large fields. Strong wheat-land, that wants a good deal of draining. Very few turnips of any sort are raised; and, of course, few sheep and cattle kept. Few trees, and those scrubbed. Few woods, and those small. Few hills, and those hardly worthy of the name. All which, when we see them, make us cease to wonder, that this country is so famous for *fox-hunting*. Such it has doubtless been, in all times, and to this circumstance Huntingdon, that is to say, Huntingdun, or Huntingdown, unquestionably owes its name; because *down* does not mean *unploughed* land, but open and *unsheltered* land, and the Saxon word is *dun*.—When you come down near to the town itself, the scene suddenly, totally, and most agreeably, changes. The *River Ouse* separates Godmanchester from Huntingdon, and there is, I think, no very great difference in the population of the two. Both together do not make up a population of more than about five thousand souls. Huntingdon is a slightly built town, compared with Lewes, for instance. The houses are not in general so high, nor made of such solid and costly materials. The shops are not so large and their contents not so costly. There is not a show of so much business and so much opulence. But Huntingdon is a very clean and nice place, contains many elegant houses, and the environs are beautiful. Above and below the bridge, under which the Ouse passes, are the most beautiful, and by far the most beautiful, meadows that I ever saw in my life. The meadows at Lewes, at Guildford, at Farnham, at Winchester, at Salisbury, at Exeter, at Gloucester, at Hereford, and even at Canterbury, are nothing, compared with those of Huntingdon in point of beauty. Here are no reeds, here is no sedge, no unevennesses of any sort. Here are *bowling-greens* of hundreds of acres in extent, with a river winding through them, full to the brink. *One* of these meadows is the *race-course;* and so pretty a spot, so level, so smooth, so green, and of such an extent I never saw, and never expected to see. From the bridge you look across the valleys, first to the west and then to the east; the valleys terminate at the foot of rising ground, well set with trees, from amongst which church spires raise their heads here and there. I think it would be very difficult to find a more delightful spot than this in the world. To my fancy (and every one to his taste) the prospect from this bridge far surpasses that from Richmond Hill.—All that I have yet seen of Huntingdon I like exceedingly. It is one of those pretty, clean, unstenched, unconfined places that tend to lengthen life and make it happy.

JOURNAL

HERTFORDSHIRE, AND BUCKINGHAMSHIRE: TO ST. ALBANS, THROUGH EDGWARE, STANMORE, AND WATFORD, RETURNING BY REDBOURN, HEMPSTEAD, AND CHESHAM

SAINT ALBANS,
19 *June*, 1822.

FROM Kensington to this place, through Edgware, Stanmore, and Watford, the crop is almost entirely hay, from fields of permanent grass, manured by dung and other matter brought from the *Wen*. Near the Wen, where they have had the *first haul* of the Irish and other perambulating labourers, the hay is all in rick. Some miles further down it is nearly all in. Towards Stanmore and Watford, a third, perhaps, of the grass remains to be cut. It is curious to see how the thing regulates itself. We saw, all the way down, squads of labourers, of different departments, migrating from tract to tract; leaving the cleared fields behind them and proceeding on towards the work to be yet performed; and then, as to the classes of labourers, the *mowers*, with their scythes on their shoulders, were in front, going on towards the standing crops, while the *hay-makers* were coming on behind towards the grass already cut or cutting. The weather is fair and warm; so that the pu'lic-houses on the road are pouring out their beer pretty fast, and are getting a good share of the wages of these thirsty souls. It is an exchange of beer for sweat; but the tax-eaters get, after all, the far greater part of the sweat; for, if it were not for the tax, the beer would sell for three-halfpence a pot, instead of fivepence. Of this threepence-halfpenny the Jews and jobbers get about twopence-halfpenny. It is curious to observe how the different labours are divided as to the *nations*. The mowers are all *English ;* the haymakers all *Irish*. Scotchmen toil hard enough in Scotland; but when they go from home it is not to *work*, if you please. They are found in gardens, and especially in gentlemen's gardens. Tying up flowers, picking dead leaves off exotics, peeping into melon-frames, publishing the banns of marriage between the " *male* " and " *female* " blossoms, tap-tap-tapping against a wall with a hammer that weighs half an ounce. They have backs as straight and shoulders as square as heroes of Waterloo; and who can blame them? The digging, the mowing, the carrying of loads; all the break-back and sweat-extracting work they leave to be performed by those who have less *prudence* than they have. The great purpose of human art, the great end of human study, is to obtain *ease*, to throw the burden of labour from our own shoulders, and fix it on those of others. The crop of hay is very large, and that part which is in, is in very good order. We shall have hardly any hay that is not fine and sweet; and we shall have it, carried to London, at less, I dare say, than £3 a load, that is 18 cwt. So that here the *evil* of "*over-production*" will be great indeed! Whether we shall have any projects for taking hay into *pawn* is more than any of us can say; for, after what we have seen, need we be surprised, if we were to hear it proposed to take butter and even milk into pawn? In after times, the mad projects of these days will become proverbial. The oracle and the over-production men will totally supplant the *March-hare*.—This is, all along here, and especially as far as Stanmore, a very dull and ugly country: flat, and all grass-fields and elms. Few *birds* of any kind, and few *constant* labourers being wanted; scarcely any cottages and gardens, which form one of the great beauties of a country. Stanmore is on a hill; but it looks over a country of little variety, though rich. What a difference between the view here and those which carry the eye over the coppices, the corn-fields, the hop-gardens and the orchards of Kent! It is miserable land from Stanmore to Watford, where we get into Hertfordshire. Hence to Saint Albans there is generally chalk at bottom with a red tenacious loam at top, with flints, grey on the outside and dark blue within. Wherever this is the soil, the wheat grows well. The crops, and especially that of the barley, are very fine and very forward. The wheat, in general, does not appear to be a heavy crop; but the ears seem as if they would be full from bottom to top; and we have had so much heat, that the grain is pretty sure to be plump, let the weather, for the rest of the summer, be what it may. The produce depends more on the weather, previous to the coming out of the ear, than on the subsequent weather. In the northern parts of America, where they have, some years, not heat enough to bring the Indian corn to perfection, I have observed, that, if they have about fifteen days with the thermometer at *ninety*, before the ear makes its appearance, the crop never fails, though the weather may be ever so unfavourable afterwards. This allies with the old remark of the country people in England, that "*May* makes or mars the wheat;" for it is in May that the ear and the grains are *formed*."

KENSINGTON,

24 June, 1822.

Set out at four this morning for Redbourn, and then turned off to the westward to go to High Wycombe, through Hempstead and Chesham. The *wheat* is good all the way. The barley and oats good enough till I came to Hempstead. But the land along here is very fine: a red tenacious flinty loam upon a bed of chalk at a yard or two beneath, which, in my opinion, is the very best *corn land* that we have in England. The fields here, like those in the rich parts of Devonshire, will bear perpetual grass. Any of them will become upland meadows. The land is, in short, excellent, and it is a real corn-country. The *trees* from Redbourn to Hempstead are very fine; oaks, ashes, and beeches. Some of the finest of each sort, and the very finest ashes I ever saw in my life. They are in great numbers, and make the fields look most beautiful. No villainous things of the *fir-tribe* offend the eye here. The custom is in this part of Hertfordshire (and I am told it continues into Bedfordshire) to leave a *border* round the ploughed part of the fields to bear grass and to make hay from, so that, the grass being now made into hay, every corn field has a closely mowed grass walk about ten feet wide all round it, between the corn and the hedge. This is most beautiful! The hedges are now full of the shepherd's rose, honeysuckles, and all sorts of wild flowers; so that you are upon a grass walk, with this most beautiful of all flower gardens and shrubberies on your one hand, and with the corn on the other. And thus you go from field to field (on foot or on horseback), the sort of corn, the sort of underwood and timber, the shape and size of the fields, the height of the hedge-rows, the height of the trees, all continually varying. Talk of *pleasure-grounds* indeed! What that man ever invented, under the name of pleasure-grounds, can equal these fields in Hertfordshire?—This is a profitable system too; for the ground under hedges bears little corn, and it bears very good grass. Something, however, depends on the nature of the soil: for it is not all land that will bear grass, fit for hay, perpetually; and, when the land will not do that, these headlands would only be a harbour for weeds and couch-grass, the seeds of which would fill the fields with their mischievous race.—Mr. Tull has observed upon the great use of headlands.—It is curious enough, that these headlands cease soon after you get into Buckinghamshire. At first you see now and then a field *without* a grass headland; then it comes to now and then a field *with* one; and, at the end of five or six miles, they wholly cease. Hempstead is a very pretty town, with beautiful environs, and there is a canal that comes near it, and that goes on to London. It lies at the foot of a hill. It is clean, substantially built, and a very pretty place altogether. Between Hempstead and Chesham the land is not so good. I came into Buckinghamshire before I got into the latter place. Passed over two commons. But still the land is not bad. It is drier; nearer the chalk, and not so red. The wheat continues good, though not heavy; but the barley, on the land that is not very good, is light, begins to look *blue*, and the backward oats are very short. On the still thinner lands the barley and oats must be a very short crop.—People do not sow *turnips*, the ground is so dry, and I should think that the *swede-crop* will be very short; for *swedes* ought to be *up* at least, by this time. If I had swedes to sow, I would sow them now, and upon ground very deeply and finely broken. I would sow directly after the plough, not being half an hour behind it, and would roll the ground as hard as possible. I am sure the plants would come up, even without rain. And the moment the rain came, they would grow famously.—Chesham is a nice little town, lying in a deep and narrow valley, with a stream of water running through it. All along the country that I have come, the labourers' dwellings are good. They are made of what they call *brick-nog ;* that is to say, a frame of wood, and a single brick thick, filling up the vacancies between the timber. They are generally covered with tile. Not *pretty* by any means; but they are good; and you see here, as in Kent, Sussex, Surrey and Hampshire, and, indeed, in almost every part of England, that most interesting of all objects, that which is such an honour to England, and that which distinguishes it from all the rest of the world, namely, those *neatly kept and productive little gardens round the labourers' houses*, which are seldom unornamented with more or less of flowers. We have only to look at these to know what sort of people English labourers are: these gardens are the answer to the *Malthuses* and the *Scarletts*. Shut your mouths, you Scotch economists; cease bawling, Mr. Brougham, and you Edinburgh Reviewers, till *you* can show us something, not *like*, but approaching towards a likeness of *this !*

The orchards all along this country are by no means bad.
Not like those of Herefordshire and the north of Kent; but a
great deal better than in many other parts of the kingdom.
The cherry-trees are pretty abundant and particularly good.
There are not many of the *merries*, as they call them in Kent
and Hampshire; that is to say, the little black cherry, the name
of which is a corruption from the French *merise*, in the singular,
and *merises* in the plural.   I saw the little boys, in many places,
set to keep the birds off the cherries, which reminded me of the
time when I followed the same occupation, and also of the toll
that I used to take in payment.   The children are all along
here, I mean the little children, locked out of the doors, while
the fathers and mothers are at work in the fields.   I saw many
little groups of this sort; and this is one advantage of having
plenty of room on the outside of a house.   I never saw the
country children better clad, or look cleaner and fatter than they
look here, and I have the very great pleasure to add, that I do
not think I saw three acres of *potatoes* in this whole tract
of fine country, from St. Albans to Redbourn, from Redbourn
to Hempstead, and from Hempstead to Chesham.   In all the
houses where I have been, they use the roasted rye instead of
coffee or tea, and I saw one gentleman who had sown a piece of
rye (a grain not common in this part of the country) for the
express purpose.   It costs about three farthings a pound,
roasted and ground into powder.—The pay of the labourers
varies from eight to twelve shillings a week.   Grass mowers get
two shillings-day, two quarts of what they call strong beer, and
as much small beer as they can drink.   After quitting Chesham,
I passed through a wood, resembling, as nearly as possible, the
woods in the more cultivated parts of Long Island, with these
exceptions, that there the woods consist of a great variety of
trees, and of more beautiful foliage.   Here there are only two
sorts of trees, beech and oak: but the wood at bottom was
precisely like an American wood: none of that stuff which we
generally call underwood: the trees standing very thick in some
places: the shade so complete as never to permit herbage below:
no bushes of any sort; and nothing to impede your steps but
little spindling trees here and there grown up from the seed.
The trees here are as lofty, too, as they generally are in the Long
Island woods, and as straight, except in cases where you find
clumps of the tulip-tree, which sometimes go much above a
hundred feet high as straight as a line.   The oaks seem here to
vie with the beeches in size as well as in loftiness and straightness.

I saw several oaks which I think were more than eighty feet high, and several with a clear stem of more than forty feet, being pretty nearly as far through at that distance from the ground as at bottom; and I think I saw more than one, with a clear stem of fifty feet, a foot and a half through at that distance from the ground. This is by far the finest *plank oak* that I ever saw in England. The road through the wood is winding and brings you out at the corner of a field, lying sloping to the south, three sides of it bordered by wood and the field planted as an orchard. This is precisely what you see in so many thousands of places in America. I had passed through Hempstead a little while before, which certainly gave its name to the township in which I lived in Long Island, and which I used to write *Hampstead*, contrary to the orthography of the place, never having heard of such a place as *Hempstead* in England. Passing through Hempstead I gave my mind a toss back to Long Island, and this beautiful wood and orchard really made me almost conceit that I was there, and gave rise to a thousand interesting and pleasant reflections. On quitting the wood I crossed the great road from London to Wendover, went across the park of Mr. Drake, and up a steep hill towards the great road leading to Wycombe. Mr. Drake's is a very beautiful place, and has a great deal of very fine timber upon it. I think I counted pretty nearly 200 oak trees, worth, on an average, five pounds apiece, growing within twenty yards of the road that I was going along. Mr. Drake has some thousands of these, I dare say, besides his beech; and, therefore, *he* will be able to stand a tug with the fundholders for some time. When I got to High Wycombe, I found everything a week earlier than in the rich part of Hertfordshire. High Wycombe, as if the name was ironical, lies along the bottom of a narrow and deep valley, the hills on each side being very steep indeed. The valley runs somewhere about from east to west, and the wheat on the hills facing the south will, if this weather continue, be fit to reap in ten days. I saw one field of oats that a bold farmer would cut next Monday. Wycombe is a very fine and very clean market town; the people all looking extremely well; the girls somewhat larger featured and larger boned than those in Sussex, and not so fresh-coloured and bright-eyed. More like the girls of America, and that is saying quite as much as any reasonable woman can expect or wish for. The hills on the south side of Wycombe form a park and estate now the property of Smith, who was a banker or stocking-maker at Nottingham, who was made a lord in the time of Pitt, and who purchased this estate of the late Marquis of Landsdowne, one of whose titles is Baron Wycombe. Wycombe is one of those famous things called boroughs, and 34 votes in this borough send Sir John Dashwood and Sir Thomas Baring to the " collective wisdom." The landlord where I put up " *remembered* " the name of Dashwood, but had " *forgotten* " who the " *other* " was! There would be no forgettings of this sort, if these thirty-four, together with *their* representatives, were called upon to pay the share of the national debt due from High Wycombe. Between High Wycombe and Beaconsfield, where the soil is much about that last described, the wheat continued to be equally early with that about Wycombe. As I approached Uxbridge I got off the chalk upon a gravelly bottom, and then from Uxbridge to Shepherd's Bush on a bottom of clay. Grass-fields and elm-trees, with here and there a wheat or a bean-field, form the features of this most ugly country, which would have been perfectly unbearable after quitting the neighbourhoods of Hempstead, Chesham and High Wycombe, had it not been for the diversion I derived from meeting, in all the various modes of conveyance, the cockneys going to *Ealing Fair*, which is one of those things which nature herself would almost seem to have provided for drawing off the matter and giving occasional relief to the overcharged *Wen*. I have traversed to-day what I think may be called an average of England as to corn-crops. Some of the best, certainly; and pretty nearly some of the worst. My observation as to the wheat is, that it will be a fair and average crop, and extremely early; because, though it is not a heavy crop, though the ears are not long they will be full; and the earliness seems to preclude the possibility of blight, and to ensure plump grain. The barley and oats must, upon an average, be a light crop. The peas a light crop; and as to beans, unless there have been rains where beans are mostly grown, they cannot be half a crop; for they will not endure heat. I tried masagan beans in Long Island, and could not get them to bear more than a pod or two upon a stem. Beans love cold land and shade. The earliness of the harvest (for early it must be) is always a clear advantage. This fine summer, though it may not lead to a good crop of turnips, has already put safe into store such a crop of hay as I believe England never saw before. Looking out of the window, I see the harness of the Wiltshire wagon-horses (at this moment going by) covered with the chalk-dust of that county; so that the fine weather continues in the west. The saintfoin hay has all been got in, in the chalk countries, without a drop of wet; and when that is the case, the farmers stand in no need of oats. The grass crops have been large everywhere, as well as got in in good order. The fallows must be in excellent order. It must be a sloven indeed that will sow his wheat in foul ground next autumn; and the sun, where the fallows have been well stirred, will have done more to enrich the land than all the dung-carts and all the other means employed by the hand of man. Such a summer is a great blessing; and the only drawback is, the dismal apprehension of not seeing such another for many years to come. It is favourable for poultry, for colts, for calves, for lambs, for young animals of all descriptions, not excepting the game. The partridges will be very early. They are now getting into the roads with their young ones, to roll in the dust. The first broods of partridges in England are very frequently killed by the wet and cold; and this is one reason why the game is not so plenty here as it is in countries more blest with sun. This will not be the case this year; and, in short, this is one of the finest years that I ever knew.

WM. COBBETT.

FROM KENSINGTON TO UPHUSBAND

INCLUDING A RUSTIC HARANGUE AT WINCHESTER,
AT A DINNER WITH THE FARMERS, ON THE
28TH SEPTEMBER—104 MILES

CHILWORTH, NEAR GUILDFORD, SURREY,
Wednesday, 25th Sept. 1822.

THIS morning I set off, in rather a drizzling rain, from Kensington, on horseback, accompanied by my son, with an intention of going to Uphusband, near Andover, which is situated in the north-west corner of Hampshire. It is very true that I could have gone to Uphusband by travelling only about 66 miles, and in the space of about eight hours. But my object was, not to see inns and turnpike-roads, but to see the *country ;* to see the farmers at home, and to see the labourers in the fields; and to do this you must go either on foot or on horseback. With a gig you cannot get about amongst byelanes and across fields, through bridle-ways and hunting-gates; and to *tramp it* is too slow, leaving the labour out of the question, and that is not a trifle.

We went through the turnpike-gate at Kensington, and immediately turned down the lane to our left, proceeded on to Fulham, crossed Putney-bridge into Surrey, went over Barnes Common, and then, going on the upper side of Richmond, got again into Middlesex, by crossing Richmond-bridge. All Middlesex is *ugly,* notwithstanding the millions upon millions which it is continually sucking up from the rest of the kingdom; and, though the Thames and its meadows now and then are seen from the road, the country is not less ugly from Richmond to Chertsey-bridge, through Twickenham, Hampton, Sunbury and Sheperton, than it is elsewhere. The soil is a gravel at bottom with a black loam at top near the Thames; further back it is a sort of spewy gravel; and the buildings consist generally of tax-eaters' showy, tea-garden-like boxes, and of shabby dwellings of labouring people who, in this part of the country, look to be about half *Saint Giles's :* dirty, and have every appearance of drinking gin.

At Chertsey, where we came into Surrey again, there was

a fair for horses, cattle and pigs. I did not see any sheep. Everything was exceedingly *dull*. Cart colts, two and three years old, were selling for *less than a third* of what they sold for in 1813. The cattle were of an inferior description to be sure; but the price was low almost beyond belief. Cows, which would have sold for £15 in 1813, did not get buyers at £3. I had no time to inquire much about the pigs, but a man told me that they were dirt-cheap. Near Chertsey is *Saint Anne's Hill* and some other pretty spots. Upon being shown this hill I was put in mind of Mr. Fox; and that brought into my head a grant that he obtained of *Crown lands* in this neighbourhood, in, I think, 1806. The Duke of York obtained, by Act of Parliament, a much larger grant of these lands, at Oatlands, in 1804, I think it was. But this was natural enough; this is what would surprise nobody. Mr. Fox's was another affair; and especially when taken into view with what I am now going to relate. In 1804 or 1805, Fordyce, the late Duchess of Gordon's brother, was collector-general (or had been) of taxes in Scotland, and owed a large arrear to the public. He was also surveyor of Crown lands. The then Opposition were for hauling him up. Pitt was again in power. Mr. Creevey was to bring forward the motion in the House of Commons, and Mr. Fox was to support it, and had actually spoken once or twice, in a preliminary way, on the subject. Notice of the motion was regularly given; it was put off from time to time, and, at last, *dropped*, Mr. Fox *declining* to support it. I have no books at hand; but the affair will be found recorded in the *Register*. It was not owing to Mr. Creevey that the thing did not come on. I remember well that it was owing to Mr. Fox. Other motives were stated; and those others might be the real motives; but, at any rate, the next year, or the year after, Mr. Fox got transferred to him a part of that estate which belongs to the *public*, and which was once so great, called the *Crown lands ;* and of these lands Fordyce long had been, and then was the surveyor. Such are the facts: let the reader reason upon them and draw the conclusion.

This county of Surrey presents to the eye of the traveller a greater contrast than any other county in England. It has some of the very best and some of the worst lands, not only in England, but in the world. We were here upon those of the latter description. For five miles on the road towards Guildford the land is a rascally common covered with poor heath, except where the gravel is so near the top as not to suffer even the heath to grow. Here we entered the enclosed lands, which have the gravel at bottom, but a nice light, black mould at top; in which the trees grow very well. Through bye-lanes and bridle-ways we came out into the London road, between Ripley and Guildford, and immediately crossing that road, came on towards a village called Merrow. We came out into the road just mentioned, at the lodge-gates of a Mr. Weston, whose mansion and estate have just passed (as to occupancy) into the hands of some new man. At Merrow, where we came into the Epsom road, we found that Mr. Webb Weston, whose mansion and park are a little further on towards London, had just walked out, and left it in possession of another new man. This gentleman told us, last year, at the *Epsom meeting*, that he was *losing his income*; and I told him *how it was* that he was losing it! He is said to be a very worthy man; very much respected; a very good landlord; but, I dare say, he is one of those who approved of yeomanry cavalry to keep down the " Jacobins and Levellers; " but who, in fact, as I always told men of this description, have *put down* themselves and their landlords; for without them this thing never could have been done. To ascribe the whole to *contrivance* would be to give to Pitt and his followers too much credit for profundity; but, if the knaves who assembled at the Crown and Anchor in the Strand, in 1793, to put down, by the means of prosecutions and spies, those whom they called " Republicans and Levellers; " if these knaves had said, " Let us go to work to induce the owners and occupiers of the land to convey their estates and their capital into our hands," and if the Government had corresponded with them in views, the effect could not have been more complete than it has, thus far, been. The yeomanry actually, as to the effect, drew their swords to keep the reformers at bay, while the tax-eaters were taking away the estates and the capital. It was the sheep surrendering up the dogs into the hands of the wolves.

Lord Onslow lives near Merrow. This is the man that was, for many years, so famous as a driver of four-in-hand. He used to be called *Tommy Onslow*. He has the character of being a very good landlord. I know he called me " a d——d *Jacobin* " several years ago, only, I presume, because I was labouring to preserve to him the means of still driving four-in-hand, while he, and others like him, and their yeomanry cavalry, were working as hard to defeat my wishes and endeavours. They say here, that, some little time back, his lordship, who has, at any rate, had the courage to retrench in all sorts of ways, was at Guildford in a gig with one horse, at the very moment when Spicer, the stockbroker, who was a chairman of the committee for prosecuting Lord Cochrane, and who lives at Esher, came rattling in with four horses and a couple of out-riders! They relate an observation made by his lordship, which may, or may not, be true, and which, therefore, I shall not repeat. But, my lord, there is another sort of courage; courage other than that of retrenching, that would become you in the present emergency: I mean *political* courage, and especially the courage of *acknowledging your errors ;* confessing that you were wrong, when you called the reformers jacobins and levellers; the courage of now joining them in their efforts to save their country, to regain their freedom, and to preserve to you your estate, which is to be preserved, you will observe, by no other means than that of a reform of the Parliament. It is now manifest, even to fools, that it has been by the instrumentality of a base and fraudulent paper-money, that loan-jobbers, stock-jobbers, and Jews have got the estates into their hands. With what eagerness, in 1797, did the nobility, gentry and clergy rush forward to give their sanction and their support to the system which then began, and which has finally produced what we now behold! They assembled in all the counties, and put forth declarations, that they would take the paper of the bank, and that they would support the system. Upon this occasion the county of Surrey was the very first county; and, on the list of signatures, the very *first* name was *Onslow !* There may be sales and conveyances; there may be recoveries, deeds, and other parchments; but this was the real transfer; this was the real signing away of the estates.

To come to Chilworth, which lies on the south side of St. Martha's Hill, most people would have gone along the level road to Guildford, and come round through Shawford under the hills; but we, having seen enough of streets and turnpikes, took across over Merrow Down, where the Guildford race-course is, and then mounted the " Surrey Hills," so famous for the prospects they afford. Here we looked back over Middlesex, and into Buckinghamshire and Berkshire, away towards the north-west, into Essex and Kent towards the east, over part of Sussex to the south, and over part of Hampshire to the west and south-west. We are here upon a bed of chalk, where the downs always afford good sheep food. We steered for St. Martha's Chapel, and went round at the foot of the lofty hill on which it stands. This brought us down the side of a steep hill, and along a bridle-way, into the narrow and exquisitely beautiful vale of Chilworth, where we were to stop for the night. This vale is skirted partly by woodlands and partly by sides of hills tilled as corn fields. The land is excellent, particularly towards the bottom. Even the arable fields are in some places, towards their tops, nearly as steep as the roof of a tiled house; and where the ground is covered with woods the ground is still more steep. Down the middle of the vale there is a series of ponds, or small *lakes*, which meet your eye, here and there, through the trees. Here are some very fine farms, a little strip of meadows, some hop-gardens, and the lakes have given rise to the establishment of powder-mills and paper-mills. The trees of all sorts grow well here; and coppices yield poles for the hop-gardens and wood to make charcoal for the powder-mills.

They are sowing wheat here, and the land, owing to the fine summer that we have had, is in a very fine state. The rain, too, which, yesterday, fell here in great abundance, has been just in time to make a really good wheat-sowing season. The turnips all the way that we have come, are good. Rather backward in some places; but in sufficient quantity upon the ground, and there is yet a good while for them to grow. All the fall fruit is excellent, and in great abundance. The grapes are as good as those raised under glass. The apples are much richer than in ordinary years. The crop of hops has been very fine here, as well as everywhere else. The crop not only large, but good in quality. They expect to get *six* pounds a hundred for them at Weyhill Fair. That is *one* more than I think they will get. The best Sussex hops were selling in the borough of Southwark at three pounds a hundred a few days before I left London. The Farnham hops *may* bring double that price; but that, I think, is as much as they will; and this is ruin to the hop-planter. The *tax*, with its attendant inconveniences, amount to a pound a hundred; the picking, drying, and bagging to 50s. The carrying to market not less than 5s. Here is the sum of £3 10s. of the money. Supposing the crop to be half a ton to the acre, the bare tillage will be 10s. The poles for an acre cannot cost less than £2 a year; that is another 4s. to each hundred of hops. This brings the outgoings to 82s. Then comes the manure, then come the poor-rates, and road-rates, and county-rates; and if these leave one single farthing for *rent* I think it is strange.

I hear that Mr. Birkbeck is expected home from America! It is said that he is coming to receive a large legacy; a thing not to be overlooked by a person who lives in a country where he can have *land for nothing!* The truth is, I believe, that there has lately died a gentleman, who has bequeathed a part of his property to pay the creditors of a relation of his who some years ago became a bankrupt, and one of whose creditors Mr. Birkbeck was. What the amount may be I know not; but I have heard that the bankrupt had a *partner* at the time of the bankruptcy; so that there must be a good deal of difficulty in settling the matter in an equitable manner. The *Chancery* would drawl it out (supposing the present system to continue) till, in all human probability, there would not be as much left for Mr. Birkbeck as would be required to pay his way back again to the Land of Promise. I hope he is coming here to remain here. He is a very clever man, though he has been very abusive and very unjust with regard to me.

LEA, NEAR GODALMING, SURREY,
Thursday, 26 Sept.

We started from Chilworth this morning, came down the vale, left the village of Shawford to our right, and that of Wonersh to our left, and crossing the river Wey, got into the turnpike-road between Guildford and Godalming, went on through Godalming, and got to Lea, which lies to the north-east snugly under Hind-Head, about 11 o'clock. This was coming only about eight miles, a sort of rest after the 32 miles of the day before. Coming along the road, a farmer overtook us, and as he had known me from seeing me at the meeting at Epsom last year, I had a part of my main business to perform, namely, to talk politics. He was going to *Haslemere* Fair. Upon the mention of that sink-hole of a borough, which sends, " *as clearly as the sun at noonday,*" the celebrated Charles Long, and the scarcely less celebrated Robert Ward, to the celebrated House of Commons, we began to talk, as it were, spontaneously about Lord Lonsdale and the Lowthers. The farmer wondered why the Lowthers, that were the owners of so many farms, should be for a system which was so manifestly taking away the estates of the landlords and the capital of the farmers, and giving them to Jews, loan-jobbers, stock-jobbers, placemen, pensioners, sinecure people, and people of the " dead weight." But his wonder ceased; his eyes were opened; and "his heart

seemed to burn within him as I talked to him on the way,"
when I explained to him the nature of *Crown lands* and "*Crown
tenants*," and when I described to him certain districts of
property in Westmoreland and other parts. I had not the
book in my pocket, but my memory furnished me with quite
a sufficiency of matter to make him perceive, that, in supporting
the present system, the Lowthers were by no means so foolish
as he appeared to think them. From the Lowthers I turned to
Mr. Poyntz, who lives at Midhurst in Sussex, and whose name
as a "*Crown tenant*" I find in a report lately laid before the
House of Commons, and the particulars of which I will state
another time for the information of the people of Sussex. I
used to wonder myself what made Mr. Poyntz call me a jacobin.
I used to think that Mr. Poyntz must be a fool to support the
present system. What I have seen in that report convinces
me that Mr. Poyntz is no fool, as far as relates to his own interest,
at any rate. There is a mine of wealth in these "*Crown lands.*"
Here are farms, and manors, and mines, and woods, and forests,
and houses, and streets, incalculable in value. What can
be so proper as to apply this public property towards the dis-
charge of a part, at least, of that public debt, which is hanging
round the neck of this nation like a mill-stone? Mr. Ricardo
proposes to seize upon a part of the private property of every
man, to be given to the stock-jobbing race. At an act of
injustice like this the mind revolts. The foolishness of it,
besides, is calculated to shock one. But in the *public property*
we see the suitable thing. And who can possibly object to this,
except those who, amongst them, now divide the possession or
benefit of this property? I have once before mentioned, but I
will repeat it, that *Marlborough House* in Pall Mall, for which
the Prince of Saxe Coburg pays a rent to the Duke of Marlborough of three thousand pounds a year, is rented of this
generous public by that most noble duke at the rate of less
than *forty pounds* a year. There are three houses in Pall Mall,
the whole of which pay a rent *to the public* of about fifteen
pounds a year, I think it is. I myself, twenty-two years ago,
paid three hundred pounds a year for one of them, to a man
that I thought was the owner of them; but I now find that
these houses belong to the public. The Duke of Buckingham's
house in Pall Mall, which is one of the grandest in all London,
and which is not worth less than seven or eight hundred pounds
a year, belongs to the public. The duke is the tenant; and I
think he pays for it much less than twenty pounds a year. I

speak from memory here all the way along; and therefore not positively; I will, another time, state the particulars from the books. The book that I am now referring to is also of a date of some years back; but I will mention all the particulars another time. Talk of *reducing rents*, indeed! Talk of *generous landlords !* It is the public that is the generous landlord. It is the public that lets its houses and manors and mines and farms at a cheap rate. It certainly would not be so good a landlord if it had a reformed Parliament to manage its affairs, nor would it suffer so many snug *corporations* to carry on their snugglings in the manner that they do, and therefore it is obviously the interest of the rich tenants of this poor public, as well as the interest of the snugglers in corporations, to prevent the poor public from having such a Parliament.

We got into free-quarter again at Lea; and there is nothing like free-quarter, as soldiers well know. Lea is situated on the edge of that immense heath which sweeps down from the summit of Hind-Head, across to the north over innumerable hills of minor altitude and of an infinite variety of shapes towards Farnham, to the north-east, towards the Hog's Back, leading from Farnham to Guildford, and to the east, or nearly so, towards Godalming. Nevertheless, the inclosed lands at Lea are very good and singularly beautiful. The timber of all sorts grows well; the land is light, and being free from stones, very pleasant to work. If you go southward from Lea about a mile you get down into what is called, in the old Acts of Parliament, the *Weald* of Surrey. Here the land is a stiff tenacious loam at top with blue and yellow clay beneath. This weald continues on eastward, and gets into Sussex near East Grinstead: thence it winds about under the hills, into Kent. Here the oak grows finer than in any part of England. The trees are more spiral in their form. They grow much faster than upon any other land. Yet the timber must be better; for, in some of the Acts of Queen Elizabeth's reign, it is provided that the oak for the royal navy shall come out of the Wealds of Surrey, Sussex, or Kent.

ODIHAM, HAMPSHIRE,
Friday, 27 Sept.

From Lea we set off this morning about six o'clock to get free-quarter again at a worthy old friend's at this nice little plain market-town. Our direct road was right over the heath through Tilford to Farnham; but we veered a little to the left after we came to Tilford, at which place on the green we stopped to look at an *oak tree*, which, when I was a little boy, was but a very little tree, comparatively, and which is now, take it altogether, by far the finest tree that I ever saw in my life. The stem or shaft is short; that is to say, it is short before you come to the first limbs; but it is full *thirty feet round*, at about eight or ten feet from the ground. Out of the stem there come not less than fifteen or sixteen limbs, many of which are from five to ten feet round, and each of which would, in fact, be considered a decent stick of timber. I am not judge enough of timber to say anything about the quantity in the whole tree, but my son stepped the ground, and as nearly as we could judge, the diameter of the extent of the branches was upwards of ninety feet, which would make a circumference of about three hundred feet. The tree is in full growth at this moment. There is a little hole in one of the limbs; but with that exception, there appears not the smallest sign of decay. The tree has made great shoots in all parts of it this last summer and spring; and there are no appearances of *white* upon the trunk, such as are regarded as the symptoms of full growth. There are many sorts of oak in England; two very distinct; one with a pale leaf, and one with a dark leaf: this is of the pale leaf. The tree stands upon Tilford-green, the soil of which is a light loam with a hard sand stone a good way beneath, and, probably, clay beneath that. The spot where the tree stands is about a hundred and twenty feet from the edge of a little river, and the ground on which it stands may be about ten feet higher than the bed of that river.

In quitting Tilford we came on to the land belonging to Waverly Abbey, and then, instead of going on to the town of Farnham, veered away to the left towards Wrecklesham, in order to cross the Farnham and Alton turnpike-road, and to come on by the side of Crondall to Odiham. We went a little out of the way to go to a place called the *Bourn*, which lies in the heath at about a mile from Farnham. It is a winding narrow valley, down which, during the wet season of the year, there runs a stream beginning at the *Holt Forest*, and emptying itself into the *Wey* just below Moor-Park, which was the seat of Sir William Temple when Swift was residing with him. We went to this bourn in order that I might show my son the spot where I received the rudiments of my education. There is a little hop-garden in which I used to work when from eight to ten years old; from which I have scores of times run to follow the hounds, leaving the hoe to do the best it could to destroy the weeds; but the most interesting thing was a *sand-hill*, which goes from a part of the heath down to the rivulet. As a due mixture of pleasure with toil, I, with two brothers, used occasionally to *desport* ourselves, as the lawyers call it, at this sand-hill. Our diversion was this: we used to go to the top of the hill, which was steeper than the roof of a house; one used to draw his arms out of the sleeves of his smock-frock, and lay himself down with his arms by his sides; and then the others, one at head and the other at feet, sent him rolling down the hill like a barrel or a log of wood. By the time he got to the bottom, his hair, eyes, ears, nose, and mouth were all full of this loose sand; then the others took their turn, and at every roll there was a monstrous spell of laughter. I had often told my sons of this while they were very little, and I now took one of them to see the spot. But that was not all. This was the spot where I was receiving my *education ;* and this was the sort of education; and I am perfectly satisfied that if I had not received such an education, or something very much like it; that, if I had been brought up a milksop, with a nursery-maid everlastingly at my heels, I should have been at this day as great a fool, as inefficient a mortal, as any of those frivolous idiots that are turned out from Winchester and Westminster School, or from any of those dens of dunces called colleges and universities. It is impossible to say how much I owe to that sand-hill; and I went to return it my thanks for the ability which it probably gave me to be one of the greatest terrors, to one of the greatest and most powerful bodies of knaves and fools that ever were permitted to afflict this or any other country.

From the Bourn we proceeded on to Wrecklesham, at the end of which we crossed what is called the river Wey. Here we found a parcel of labourers at parish-work. Amongst them was an old playmate of mine. The account they gave of their situation was very dismal. The harvest was over early. The hop-picking is now over; and now they are employed *by the parish ;* that is to say, not absolutely digging holes one day and filling them up the next; but at the expense of half-ruined farmers and tradesmen and landlords, to break stones into very small pieces to make nice smooth roads lest the jolting, in going along them, should create bile in the stomach of the over-fed tax-eaters. I call upon mankind to witness this scene; and to say, whether ever the like of this was heard of before. It is a state of things, where all is out of order; where self-preservation, that great law of nature, seems to be set at defiance; for here are farmers *unable* to pay men for working for them, and yet compelled to pay them for working in doing that which is really of no use to any human being. There lie the hop-poles unstripped. You see a hundred things in the neighbouring fields that want doing. The fences are not nearly what they ought to be. The very meadows, to our right and our left in crossing this little valley, would occupy these men advantageously until the setting in of the frost; and here are they, not, as I said before, actually digging holes one day and filling them up the next; but, to all intents and purposes, as uselessly employed. Is this Mr. Canning's " *Sun of Prosperity ?* " Is this the way to increase or preserve a nation's wealth? Is this a sign of wise legislation and of good government? Does this thing " work well," Mr. Canning? Does it prove that we want no change? True, you were born under a kingly government; and so was I as well as you; but I was not born under *Six-Acts ;* nor was I born under a state of things like this. I was not born under it, and I do not wish to live under it; and, with God's help, I will change it if I can.

We left these poor fellows, after having given them, not " religious tracts," which would, if they could, make the labourer content with half starvation, but something to get them some bread and cheese and beer, being firmly convinced that it is the body that wants filling and not the mind. However, in speaking of their low wages, I told them that the farmers and hop-planters were as much objects of compassion as themselves, which they acknowledged.

We immediately, after this, crossed the road, and went on towards Crondall upon a soil that soon became stiff loam and flint at top with a bed of chalk beneath. We did not go to Crondall; but kept along over Slade Heath, and through a very pretty place called Well. We arrived at Odiham about half after eleven, at the end of a beautiful ride of about seventeen miles, in a very fine and pleasant day.

WINCHESTER,
Saturday, 28th September.

Just after day-light we started for this place. By the turnpike we could have come through Basingstoke by turning off to the right, or through Alton and Alresford by turning off to the left. Being naturally disposed towards a middle course, we chose to wind down through Upton-Gray, Preston-Candover, Chilton-Candover, Brown-Candover, then down to Ovington, and into Winchester by the north entrance. From Wrecklesham to Winchester we have come over roads and lanes of flint and chalk. The weather being dry again, the ground under you, as solid as iron, makes a great rattling with the horses' feet. The country where the soil is stiff loam upon chalk, is never bad for corn. Not rich, but never poor. There is at no time anything deserving to be called dirt in the roads. The buildings last a long time, from the absence of fogs and also the absence of humidity in the ground. The absence of dirt makes the people habitually cleanly; and all along through this country the people appear in general to be very neat. It is a country for sheep, which are always sound and good upon this iron soil. The trees grow well, where there are trees. The woods and coppices are not numerous; but they are good, particularly the ash, which always grows well upon the chalk. The oaks, though they do not grow in the spiral form, as upon the clays, are by no means stunted; and some of them very fine trees; I take it, that they require a much greater number of years to bring them to perfection than in the *Wealds*. The wood, perhaps, may be harder; but I have heard that the oak, which grows upon these hard bottoms, is very frequently what the carpenters call *shaky*. The underwoods here consist, almost entirely, of hazel, which is very fine, and much tougher and more durable than that which grows on soils with a moist bottom. This hazel is a thing of great utility here. It furnishes rods wherewith to make fences; but its principal use is to make *wattles* for the folding of sheep in the fields. These things are made much more neatly here than in the south of Hampshire and in Sussex, or in any other part that I have seen. Chalk is the favourite soil of the *yew-tree ;* and at Preston-Candover there is an avenue of yew-trees, probably a mile long, each tree containing, as nearly as I can guess, from twelve to twenty feet of timber, which, as the reader knows, implies a tree of considerable size. They have probably been a century or two in growing; but, in any way that timber can be used, the timber of the yew will last, perhaps, ten times as long as the timber of any other tree that we grow in England.

Quitting the Candovers, we came along between the two estates of the two Barings. Sir Thomas, who has supplanted the Duke of Bedford, was to our right, while Alexander, who has supplanted Lord Northington, was on our left. The latter has enclosed, as a sort of outwork to his park, a pretty little down called Northington Down, in which he has planted, here and there, a clump of trees. But Mr. Baring, not reflecting that woods are not like funds, to be made at a heat, has planted his trees *too large ;* so that they are covered with moss, are dying at the top, and are literally growing downward instead of upward. In short, this enclosure and plantation have totally destroyed the beauty of this part of the estate. The down, which was before very beautiful, and formed a sort of *glacis* up to the park pales, is now a marred, ragged, ugly-looking thing. The dying trees, which have been planted long enough for you not to perceive that they have been planted, excite the idea of sterility in the soil. They do injustice to it; for, as a down, it was excellent. Everything that has been done here is to the injury of the estate, and discovers a most shocking want of taste in the projector. Sir Thomas's plantations, or, rather those of his father, have been managed more judiciously.

I do not like to be a sort of spy in a man's neighbourhood; but I will tell Sir Thomas Baring what I have heard; and if he be a man of sense I shall have his thanks, rather than his reproaches, for so doing. I may have been misinformed; but this is what I have heard, that he and also Lady Baring are very charitable; that they are very kind and compassionate to their poor neighbours; but that they tack a sort of condition to this charity; that they insist upon the objects of it adopting their notions with regard to religion; or, at least, that where the people are not what they deem *pious,* they are not objects of their benevolence. I do not say that they are not perfectly sincere themselves, and that their wishes are not the best that can possibly be; but of this I am very certain, that, by pursuing this principle of action, where they make one good man or woman, they will make one hundred hypocrites. It is not little books that can make a people good; that can make them moral; that can restrain them from committing crimes. I believe that books of any sort, never yet had that tendency. Sir Thomas does, I dare say, think me a very wicked man, since I aim at the destruction of the funding system, and what he would call a robbery of what he calls the public creditor; and yet, God help me, I have read books enough, and amongst the rest, a great part of the religious tracts. Amongst the labouring people, the first thing you have to look after is, *common honesty, speaking the truth,* and *refraining from thieving ;* and to secure these, the labourer must have *his belly-full* and be *free from fear;* and this belly-full must come to him from out of his *wages,* and not from benevolence of any description. Such being my opinion, I

think Sir Thomas Baring would do better, that he would discover more real benevolence, by using the influence which he
must naturally have in his neighbourhood, to prevent a diminution in the wages of labour.

WINCHESTER,
Sunday morning, 29 Sept.

Yesterday was market-day here. Everything cheap and falling
instead of rising. If it were *over-production* last year that
produced the *distress*, when are our miseries to have an end! They
will end when these men cease to have sway, and not before.

I had not been in Winchester long before I heard something
very interesting about the *manifesto* concerning the poor, which
was lately issued here, and upon which I remarked in my last
Register but one, in my letter to Sir Thomas Baring. Proceeding upon the true military principle, I looked out for free
quarter, which the reader will naturally think difficult for *me*
to find in a town containing a *cathedral*. Having done this,
I went to the Swan Inn to dine with the farmers. This is the
manner that I like best of doing the thing. *Six-Acts* do not,
to be sure, prevent us from *dining* together. They do not
authorise justices of the peace to kill us, because we meet to
dine without their permission. But I do not like dinner-
meetings on *my* account. I like much better to go and fall in
with the lads of the land, or with anybody else, at their own
places of resort; and I am going to place myself down at Uphusband, in excellent free-quarter, in the midst of all the great
fairs of the west, in order, before the winter campaign begins,
that I may see as many farmers as possible, and that they may
hear my opinions, and I theirs. I shall be at Weyhill Fair on
the 10th of October, and, perhaps, on some of the succeeding
days; and, on one or more of those days, I intend to dine at the
White Hart, at Andover. What other fairs or places I shall go
to I shall notify hereafter. And this I think the frankest and
fairest way. I wish to see many people, and to talk to them:
and there are a great many people who wish to see and to talk
to me. What better reason can be given for a man's going
about the country and dining at fairs and markets?

At the dinner at Winchester we had a good number of opulent
yeomen, and many gentlemen joined us after the dinner. The
state of the country was well talked over; and, during the
session (much more sensible than some other *sessions* that I have
had to remark on), I made the following

RUSTIC HARANGUE

GENTLEMEN,—Though many here are, I am sure, glad to *see me*, I am not vain enough to suppose that anything other than that of wishing to hear my opinions on the prospects before us can have induced many to choose to be here to dine with me to-day. I shall, before I sit down, propose to you a *toast*, which you will drink, or not, as you choose; but, I shall state one particular wish in that shape, that it may be the more distinctly understood, and the better remembered.

The wish to which I allude relates to the *tithes*. Under that word I mean to speak of all that mass of wealth which is vulgarly called *church property*; but which is, in fact, *public property*, and may, of course, be disposed of as the Parliament shall please. There appears at this moment an uncommon degree of anxiety on the part of the parsons to see the farmers enabled to pay *rents*. The business of the parsons being only with *tithes*, one naturally, at first sight, wonders why they should care so much about *rents*. The fact is this; they see clearly enough, that the landlords will never long go without rents, and suffer them to enjoy the tithes. They see, too, that there must be a struggle between the *land* and the *funds*: they see that there is such a struggle. They see, that it is the taxes that are taking away the rent of the landlord and the capital of the farmer. Yet the parsons are afraid to see the taxes reduced. Why? Because, if the taxes be reduced in any great degree (and nothing short of a great degree will give relief), they see that the interest of the debt cannot be paid; and they know well, that the interest of the debt can never be reduced, until their tithes have been reduced. Thus, then, they find themselves in a great difficulty. They wish the taxes to be kept up and rents to be paid too. Both cannot be, unless some means or other be found out of putting into, or keeping in, the farmer's pocket, money that is not now there.

The scheme that appears to have been fallen upon for this purpose is the strangest in the world, and it must, if attempted to be put into execution, produce something little short of open and general commotion; namely, that of reducing the wages of labour to a mark so low as to make the labourer a walking skeleton. Before I proceed further, it is right that I communicate to you an explanation, which, not an hour ago, I received from Mr. Poulter, relative to the *manifesto* lately issued in this town by a bench of magistrates of which that gentleman was chairman. I have not the honour to be personally acquainted with Mr. Poulter, but certainly, if I had misunderstood the manifesto, it was right that I should be, if possible, made to understand it. Mr. Poulter, in company with another gentleman, came to me in this inn, and said, that the bench did not mean that their resolutions should have the effect of *lowering the wages;* and that the sums, stated in the paper, were sums to be given in the way of *relief.* We had not the paper before us, and, as the paper contained a good deal about relief, I, in recollection, confounded the two, and said, that I had understood the paper agreeably to the explanation. But, upon looking at the paper again, I see that, as to the *words*, there was a clear recommendation to make the *wages* what is there stated. However, seeing that the chairman himself disavows this, we must conclude that the bench put forth words not expressing their meaning. To this I must add, as connected with the manifesto, that it is stated in that document, that such and such justices were present, and a large and respectable number of yeomen who had been invited to attend. Now, gentlemen, I was, I must confess, struck with this addition to the bench. These gentlemen have not been accustomed to treat farmers with so much attention. It seemed odd that they should want a set of farmers to be present, to give a sort of sanction to their acts. Since my arrival in Winchester, I have found, however, that having them present was not all; for that the names of some of these yeomen were actually inserted in the manuscript of the manifesto, and that those names were expunged *at the request of the parties named*. This is a very singular proceeding, then, altogether. It presents to us a strong picture of the diffidence, or modesty (call it which you please) of the justices; and it shows us, that the yeomen present did not like to have *their names* standing as giving sanction to the resolutions contained in the manifesto. Indeed, they knew well, that those resolutions never could be acted upon. They knew that they could not live in safety even in the same village with labourers, paid at the rate of 3, 4, and 5 shillings a week.

To return, now, gentlemen, to the scheme for squeezing rents out of the bones of the labourer, is it not, upon the face of it, most monstrously absurd, that this scheme should be resorted to, when the plain and easy and just way of insuring rents must present itself to every eye, and can be pursued by the Parliament whenever it choose? We hear loud outcries against the poor-rates; the *enormous* poor-rates; the *all-devouring* poor-rates; but what are the facts? Why, that, in Great Britain, *six millions* are paid in poor-rates; *seven millions* (or thereabouts) in *tithes*, and *sixty millions* to the fund-people, the army, place-men, and the rest. And yet, nothing of all this seems to be thought of but the *six* millions. Surely the other and so much larger sums ought to be thought of. Even the *six* millions are, for the far greater part, *wages* and not poor-rates. And yet all this outcry is made about these *six* millions, while not a word is said about the other *sixty-seven* millions.

Gentlemen, to enumerate all the ways in which the public money is spent would take me a week. I will mention two classes of persons who are receivers of taxes; and you will then see with what *reason* it is that this outcry is set up against the poor-rates and against the amount of wages. There is a thing called the *Dead Weight*. Incredible as it may seem that such a vulgar appellation should be used in such a way and by such persons, it is a fact that the ministers have laid before the Parliament an account, called the account of the *Dead Weight*. This account tells how five millions three hundred thousand pounds are distributed annually amongst half-pay officers, pensioners, retired commissaries, clerks, and so forth, employed during the last war. If there were nothing more entailed upon us by that war, this is pretty smart-money. Now unjust, unnecessary as that war was, detestable as it was in all its principles and objects, still, to every man, who really did *fight*, or who performed a soldier's duty abroad, I would give *some-thing :* he should not be left destitute. But, gentlemen, is it right for the nation to keep on paying for life crowds of young fellows such as make up the greater part of this *dead weight ?* This is not all, however, for, there are the widows and the children who have, and are to have, *pensions too.* You seem surprised, and well you may; but this is the fact. A young fellow who has a pension for life, aye, or an old fellow either, will easily get a wife to enjoy it with him, and he will, I'll warrant him, take care that *she* shall not be *old.* So that here is abso-lutely a premium for entering into the holy state of matrimony. The husband, you will perceive, cannot prevent the wife from having the pension after his death. She is *our widow*, in this respect, not his. She marries, in fact, with a jointure settled on her. The more children the husband leaves the better for the widow; for each child has a pension for a certain number of years. The man who, under such circumstances, does not marry, must be a woman-hater. An old man actually going into the grave may, by the mere ceremony of marriage, give any woman a pension for life. Even the widows and children of insane officers are not excluded. If an officer, now insane, but at large, were to marry, there is nothing as the thing now stands to prevent his widow and children from having pensions. Were such things as these ever before heard of in the world? Were such premiums ever before given for breeding gentlemen and ladies, and that, too, while all sorts of projects are on foot to check the breeding of the labouring classes? Can such a thing *go on?* I say it cannot; and, if it could, it must inevitably render this country the most contemptible upon the face of the earth. And yet, not a word of complaint is heard about these five millions and a quarter, expended in this way, while the country rings, fairly resounds, with the outcry about the six millions that are given to the labourers in the shape of poor-rates, but which, in fact, go, for the greater part, to pay what ought to be called *wages.* Unless, then, we speak out here; unless we call for redress here; unless we here seek relief, we shall not only be totally ruined, but we shall *deserve it.*

The other class of persons, to whom I have alluded, as having taxes bestowed on them, are the *poor clergy.* Not of the *church* as by *law* established, to be sure, you will say! Yes, gentlemen, even to the poor clergy of the Established Church. We know well how *rich* that church is; we know well how many millions it annually receives; we know how opulent are the bishops, how rich they die; how rich, in short, a body it is. And yet *fifteen hundred thousand pounds* have, within the same number of years, been given, out of the taxes, partly raised on the labourers, for the relief of the *poor* clergy of that Church, while it is notorious that the livings are given in numerous cases by twos and threes to the same person, and while a clamour, enough to make the sky ring, is made about what is given in the shape of *relief to the labouring classes!* Why, gentlemen, what do we want more than this one fact? Does not this one fact sufficiently characterise the system under which we live? Does not this prove that a change, a great change, is wanted? Would it not be more natural to propose to get this money back from the Church, than to squeeze so much out of the bones of the labourers? This the Parliament can do if it pleases; and this it will do, if you do your duty.

Passing over several other topics, let me, gentlemen, now

come to what, at the present moment, most nearly affects you; namely, the *prospect as to prices*. In the first place, this depends upon whether Peel's Bill will be repealed. As this depends a good deal upon the ministers, and as I am convinced that they know no more what to do in the present emergency than the little boys and girls that are running up and down the street before this house, it is impossible for me, or for any one, to say what will be done in this respect. But, my opinion is decided, that the Bill will *not* be repealed. The ministers see that, if they were *now* to go back to the paper, it would not be the paper of 1819; but a paper never to be redeemed by gold; that it would be *assignats* to all intents and purposes. That must of necessity cause the complete overthrow of the Government in a very short time. If, therefore, the ministers see the thing in this light, it is impossible that they should think of a repeal of Peel's Bill. There appeared, last winter, a strong disposition to repeal the Bill; and I verily believe that a repeal in effect, though not in name, was actually in contemplation. A Bill was brought in which was described beforehand as intended to prolong the issue of small notes, and also to prolong the time for making Bank of England notes a legal tender. This would have been a repealing of Peel's Bill in great part. The Bill, when brought in, and when passed, as it finally was, contained no clause relative to legal tender; and without that clause it was perfectly nugatory. Let me explain to you, gentlemen, what this Bill really is. In the seventeenth year of the late king's reign, an Act was passed for a time limited, to prevent the issue of notes payable to bearer on demand, for any sums less than five pounds. In the twenty-seventh year of the late king's reign, this Act was made *perpetual ;* and the preamble of the Act sets forth, that it is made perpetual, because the *preventing of small notes being made has been proved to be for the good of the nation.* Nevertheless, in just ten years afterwards; that is to say, in the year one thousand seven hundred and ninety-seven, when the bank stopped payment, this salutary Act was *suspended ;* indeed, it was absolutely necessary, for there was no gold to pay with. It continued suspended, until 1819, when Mr. Peel's Bill was passed, when a Bill was passed to suspend it still further, until the year 1825. You will observe, then, that last winter there were yet three years to come, during which the banks might make small notes if they would. Yet this new Bill was passed last winter to authorise them to make small notes until the year 1833. The measure was wholly uncalled for. It appeared to be altogether unnecessary; but, as I have just said, the intention was to introduce into this Bill a clause to continue the *legal tender* until 1833; and that would, indeed, have made a great alteration in the state of things; and, if extended to the Bank of England, would have been, in effect, a complete repeal of Peel's Bill.

It was fully expected by the country bankers, that the legal tender clause would have been inserted; but, before it came to the trial, the ministers gave way, and the clause was not inserted. The reason for their giving way, I do verily believe, had its principal foundation in their perceiving, that the public would clearly see that such a measure would make the paper-money merely assignats. The legal tender not having been enacted, the Small-note Bill can do nothing towards augmenting the quantity of circulating medium. As the law now stands, Bank of England notes are, in effect, a *legal tender*. If I owe a debt of twenty pounds, and tender Bank of England notes in payment, the law says that you shall not arrest me; that you may bring your action, if you like; that I may pay the notes into court; that you may go on with your action; that you shall pay all the costs, and I none. At last you gain your action; you obtain judgment and execution, or whatever else the everlasting law allows of. And what have you got then? Why the *notes ;* the same identical notes the sheriff will bring you. You will not take them. Go to law with the sheriff then. He pays the *notes* into court. More costs for you to pay. And thus you go on; but without ever touching or seeing gold!

Now, gentlemen, Peel's Bill puts an end to all this pretty work on the first day of next May. If you have a handful of a country banker's rags *now*, and go to him for payment, he will tender you Bank of England notes; and if you like the paying of costs you may go to law for gold. But when the first of next May comes, he must put gold into your hands in exchange for your notes, if you choose it; or you may clap a bailiff's hand upon his shoulder; and if he choose to pay into court, he must pay in gold, and pay your costs also as far as you have gone.

This makes a strange alteration in the thing! And everybody must see that the Bank of England and the country bankers—that all, in short, are preparing for the first of May. It is clear that there must be a farther diminution of the paper-money. It is hard to say the precise degree of effect that this will have upon prices; but that it must bring them down is clear; and, for my own part, I am fully persuaded, that they will come down to the standard of prices in France, be those prices what they may. This, indeed, was acknowledged by Mr. Huskisson in the Agricultural Report of 1821. That two countries so near together, both having gold as a currency or standard, should differ very widely from each other, in the prices of farm-produce, is next to impossible; and therefore, when our legal tender shall be completely done away, to the prices of France you must come; and those prices cannot, I think, in the present state of Europe, much exceed three or four shillings a bushel for good wheat.

You know, as well as I do, that it is impossible, with the present taxes and rates and tithes, to pay any rent at all with prices upon that scale. Let loan-jobbers, stock-jobbers, Jews, and the whole tribe of tax-eaters say what they will, you know that it is impossible, as you also know it would be cruelly unjust to wring from the labourer the means of paying rent, while those taxes and tithes remain. Something must be taken off. The labourers wages have already been reduced as low as possible. All public pay and salaries ought to be reduced; and the tithes also ought to be reduced, as they might be to a great amount without any injury to religion. The interest of the debt ought to be largely reduced; but, as none of the others can, with any show of justice, take place, without a reduction of the tithes, and as I am for confining myself to one object at present, I will give you as a toast, leaving you to drink it or not as you please, *A large Reduction of Tithes*.

Somebody proposed to drink this toast with *three times three*, which was accordingly done, and the sound might have been heard down to the close.—Upon some gentleman giving *my health*, I took occasion to remind the company, that, the last time I was at Winchester we had the memorable fight with Lockhart " the Brave " and his sable friends. I reminded them that it was in that same room that I told them, that it would not be long before Mr. Lockhart and those sable gentlemen would become enlightened; and I observed that, if we were to judge from a man's language, there was not a land-owner in England that more keenly felt than Mr. Lockhart the truth of those predictions which I had put forth at the castle on the day alluded to. I reminded the company that I sailed for America in a few days after that meeting; that they must be well aware that, on the day of the meeting, I knew that I was taking leave of the country, but, I observed, that I had not been in the least depressed by that circumstance; because I relied, with perfect confidence, on being in this same place again to enjoy, as I now did, a triumph over my adversaries.

After this, Mr. Hector gave a *Constitutional Reform in the Commons' House of Parliament*, which was drunk with great enthusiasm; and Mr. Hector's health having been given, he, in returning thanks, urged his brother yeomen and freeholders to do their duty by coming forward in county meeting and giving their support to those noblemen and gentlemen that were willing to stand forward for a reform and for a reduction of taxation. I held forth to them the example of the county of Kent, which had done itself so much honour by its conduct last spring. What these gentlemen in Hampshire will do, it is not for me to say. If nothing be done by them, they will certainly be ruined, and that ruin they will certainly deserve. It was to the farmers that the Government owed its strength to carry on the war. Having them with it, in consequence of a false and bloated prosperity, it cared not a straw for anybody else. If they, therefore, now do their duty; if they all, like the yeomen and farmers of Kent, come boldly forward, everything will be done necessary to preserve themselves and their country; and if they do not come forward, they will, as men of property, be swept from the face of the earth. The noblemen and gentlemen who are in Parliament, and who are disposed to adopt measures of effectual relief, cannot move with any hope of success unless backed by the yeomen and farmers, and the middling classes throughout the country generally. I do not mean to confine myself to yeomen and farmers, but to take in all tradesmen and men of property. With these at their back, or rather, at the back of these, there are men enough in both Houses of Parliament to propose and to urge measures suitable to the exigency of the case. But without the middling classes to *take the lead*, those noblemen and gentlemen can do nothing. Even the ministers themselves, if they were so disposed (and they must be so disposed at last) could make none of the reforms that are necessary, *without being actually urged on by the middle classes of the community.* This is a very important consideration. A new man, as minister, might indeed propose the reforms himself; but these men, opposition as well as ministry, are so *pledged* to the things that have brought all this ruin upon the country, that they absolutely stand in need of an overpowering call from the people to justify them in doing that which they themselves may think just, and which they may know to be necessary for the salvation of the country. They dare not take the lead in the necessary reforms. It is too much to be expected of any men upon the face of the earth, pledged and situated as these ministers are; and therefore, unless the people will do their duty, they will have themselves, and only themselves, to thank for their ruin, and for that load of disgrace, and for that insignificance worse than disgrace which seems, after so many years of renown, to be attaching themselves to the name of England.

UPHUSBAND,
Sunday Evening, 29 Sept. 1822.

We came along the turnpike-road, through Wherwell and Andover, and got to this place about 2 o'clock. This country, except at the village and town just mentioned, is very open, a thinnish soil upon a bed of chalk. Between Winchester and Wherwell we came by some hundreds of acres of ground that was formerly most beautiful down, which was broken up in dear-corn times, and which is now a district of thistles and other weeds. If I had such land as this I would soon make it down again. I would for once (that is to say if I had the money) get it quite clean, prepare it as for sowing turnips, get the turnips if possible, feed them off early, or plough the ground if I got no turnips; sow thick with saintfoin and meadow-grass seeds of all sorts, early in September; let the crop stand till the next July; feed it then slenderly with sheep, and dig up all thistles and rank weeds that might appear; keep feeding it, but not too close, during the summer and the fall; and ke p on feeding it for ever after as a down. The saintfoin itself would last for many years; and as it disappeared, its place would be supplied by the grass; that sort which was most congenial to the soil, would at last stifle all other sorts, and the land would become a valuable down as formerly.

I see that some plantations of ash and of hazel have been made along here; but, with great submission to the planters, I think they have gone the wrong way to work, as to the mode of preparing the ground. They have planted *small trees*, and that is right; they have *trenched* the ground, and that is also right; but they have brought the bottom soil to the top; and that is *wrong*, always; and especially where the bottom soil is gravel or chalk, or clay. I know that some people will say that this is a *puff;* and let it pass for that; but if any gentleman that is going to plant trees, will look into my *Book on Gardening*, and into the chapter on *Preparing the Soil*, he will, I think, see how conveniently ground may be trenched without bringing to the top that soil in which the young trees stand so long without making shoots.

This country, though so open, has its beauties. The home-steads in the sheltered bottoms with fine lofty trees about the houses and yards, form a beautiful contrast with the large open fields. The little villages, running straggling along the dells (always with lofty trees and rookeries) are very interesting objects, even in the winter. You feel a sort of satisfaction, when you are out upon the bleak hills yourself, at the thought of the shelter, which is experienced in the dwellings in the valleys.

Andover is a neat and solid market-town. It is supported entirely by the agriculture around it; and how the makers of *population returns* ever came to think of classing the inhabitants of such a town as this under any other head than that of " *persons employed in agriculture*," would appear astonishing to any man who did not know those population return makers as well as I do.

The village of Uphusband, the legal name of which is Hurst-bourn Tarrant, is, as the reader will recollect, a great favourite with me, not the less so certainly on account of the excellent free-quarter that it affords.

THROUGH HAMPSHIRE, BERKSHIRE, SURREY, AND SUSSEX, BETWEEN 7TH OCTOBER AND 1ST DECEMBER 1822—327 MILES

7 to 10 October, 1822.

AT Uphusband, a little village in a deep dale, about five miles to the north of Andover, and about three miles to the south of the hills at *Highclere*. The wheat is sown here, and up, and, as usual, at this time of the year, looks very beautiful. The wages of the labourers brought down to *six shillings a week !* a horrible thing to think of; but, I hear, it is still worse in Wiltshire.

11 October.

Went to Weyhill-fair, at which I was about 46 years ago, when I rode a little pony, and remember how proud I was on the occasion; but, I also remember, that my brothers, two out of three of whom were older than I, thought it unfair that my father selected me; and my own reflections upon the occasion have never been forgotten by me. The 11th of October is the Sheep-fair. About £300,000 used, some few years ago, to be carried home by the sheep-sellers. To-day, less, perhaps, than £70,000, and yet the *rents* of these sheep-sellers are, perhaps, as high, on an average, as they were then. The countenances of the farmers were descriptive of their ruinous state. I never, in all my life, beheld a more mournful scene. There is a horse-fair upon another part of the down; and there I saw horses keeping pace in depression with the sheep. A pretty numerous group of the tax-eaters, from Andover and the neighbourhood, were the only persons that had smiles on their faces. I was struck with a young farmer trotting a horse backward and forward to show him off to a couple of gentlemen, who were bargaining for the horse, and one of whom finally purchased him. These *gentlemen* were two of our " *dead-weight*," and the horse was that on which the farmer had pranced in the *Yeomanry Troop !* Here is a turn of things! Distress; pressing distress; dread of the bailiffs alone could have made the farmer sell his horse. If he had the firmness to keep the tears out of his eyes, his heart must have paid the penalty. What, then, must have been his feelings, if he reflected, as I did, that the purchase-money for the horse had first gone from his pocket into that of the *dead-weight!* And, further, that the horse had pranced about for years for the purpose of subduing all opposition to those very measures, which had finally dismounted the owner!

From this dismal scene, a scene formerly so joyous, we set off back to Uphusband pretty early, were overtaken by the rain, and got a pretty good soaking. The land along here is very good. This whole country has a chalk bottom; but, in the valley on the right of the hill over which you go from Andover to Weyhill, the chalk lies far from the top, and the soil has few flints in it. It is very much like the land about Malden and Maidstone. Met with a farmer who said he must be ruined, unless another " good war " should come! This is no un-common notion. They saw high prices *with* war, and they thought that the war was the *cause*.

12 *to* 16 *October.*

The fair was too dismal for me to go to it again. My sons went two of the days, and their account of the hop-fair was enough to make one gloomy for a month, particularly as my townsmen of Farnham were, in this case, amongst the sufferers. On the 12th I went to dine with and to harangue the farmers at Andover. Great attention was paid to what I had to say. The crowding to get into the room was a proof of nothing, perhaps, but *curiosity ;* but, there must have been a *cause* for the curiosity, and that cause would, under the present circum-stances, be matter for reflection with a wise government.

17 *October.*

Went to Newbury to dine with and to harangue the farmers. It was a fair-day. It rained so hard that I had to stop at Burghclere to dry my clothes, and to borrow a greatcoat to keep me dry for the rest of the way; so as not to have to sit in wet clothes. At Newbury the company was not less attentive or less numerous than at Andover. Some one of the tax-eating crew had, I understand, called me an " incendiary." The day is passed for those tricks. They deceive no longer. Here, at Newbury, I took occasion to notice the base accusation of *Dundas,* the member for the county. I stated it as something that I had heard of, and I was proceeding to charge him conditionally, when Mr. Tubb of Shillingford rose from his seat, and said, " I myself, sir, heard him say the words." I had heard of his vile conduct long before; but, I abstained from charging him with it, till an opportunity should offer for doing it in his own country. After the dinner was over I went back to Burghclere.

18 to 20 October.

At Burghclere, one half the time writing, and the other half hare-hunting.

21 October.

Went back to Uphusband.

22 October.

Went to dine with the farmers at Salisbury, and got back to Uphusband by ten o'clock at night, two hours later than I have been out of bed for a great many months.

In quitting Andover to go to Salisbury (17 miles from each other) you cross the beautiful valley that goes winding down amongst the hills to Stockbridge. You then rise into the open country that very soon becomes a part of that large tract of downs called Salisbury Plain. You are not in Wiltshire, however, till you are about half the way to Salisbury. You leave Tidworth away to your right. This is the seat of Asheton Smith; and the fine *coursing* that I once saw there I should have called to recollection with pleasure, if I could have forgotten the hanging of the men at Winchester last spring for resisting one of this Smith's gamekeepers! This Smith's son and a Sir John Pollen are the members for Andover. They are chosen by the corporation. One of the corporation, an attorney named Etwall, is a commissioner of the lottery, or something in that way. It would be a curious thing to ascertain how large a portion of the " public services " is performed by the voters in boroughs and their relations. These persons are singularly kind to the nation. They not only choose a large part of the " representatives of the people; " but they come in person, or by deputy, and perform a very considerable part of the " *public services.*" I should like to know how many of them are employed about the *Salt-Tax*, for instance. A list of these public-spirited persons might be produced to show the *benefit* of the boroughs.

Before you get to Salisbury, you cross the valley that brings down a little river from Amesbury. It is a very beautiful valley. There is a chain of farm-houses and little churches all the way up it. The farms consist of the land on the flats on each side of the river, running out to a greater or less extent, at different places, towards the hills and downs. Not far above Amesbury is a little village called Netherhaven, where I once saw an *acre of hares*. We were coursing at Everly, a few miles off; and one of the party happening to say that he had seen " an acre of hares " at Mr. Hicks Beech's at Netherhaven, we, who wanted to see the same, or to detect our informant, sent a messenger to beg a day's coursing, which being granted, we went over the next day. Mr. Beech received us very politely. He took us into a wheat stubble close by his paddock; his son took a gallop round, cracking his whip at the same time; the hares (which were very thickly in sight before) started all over the field, ran into a *flock* like sheep; and we all agreed that the flock did cover *an acre of ground*. Mr. Beech had an old greyhound, that I saw lying down in the shrubbery close by the house, while several hares were sitting and skipping about, with just as much confidence as cats sit by a dog in a kitchen or a parlour. Was this *instinct* in either dog or hares? Then, mind, this same greyhound went amongst the rest to course with us out upon the distant hills and lands; and then he ran as eagerly as the rest, and killed the hares with as little remorse. Philosophers will talk a long while before they will make men believe that this was *instinct alone*. I believe that this dog had much more reason than half of the Cossacks have; and I am sure he had a great deal more than many a negro that I have seen.

In crossing this valley to go to Salisbury, I thought of Mr. Beech's hares; but I really have neither thought of nor seen any *game* with pleasure, since the hanging of the two men at Winchester. If no other man will petition for the repeal of the law under which those poor fellows suffered, I will. But let us hope that there will be no need of petitioning. Let us hope that it will be repealed without any express application for it. It is curious enough that laws of this sort should *increase*, while *Sir James Mackintosh* is so resolutely bent on " *softening the criminal code !* "

The company at Salisbury was very numerous; not less than 500 farmers were present. They were very attentive to what I said, and, which rather surprised me, they received very docilely what I said against squeezing the labourers. A fire, in a farm-yard, had lately taken place near Salisbury; so that the subject was a ticklish one. But it was my very first duty to treat of it, and I was resolved, be the consequence what it might, not to neglect that duty.

23 to 26 October.

At Uphusband. At this village, which is a great thoroughfare for sheep and pigs, from Wiltshire and Dorsetshire to Berkshire, Oxfordshire, and away to the north and north-east, we see many farmers from different parts of the country; and, if I had had any doubts before as to the deplorableness of their state, those would now no longer exist. I did indeed, years ago, prove that if we returned to cash payments without a reduction of the debt, and without a rectifying of contracts, the present race of farmers must be ruined. But still, when the thing actually comes, it astounds one. It is like the death of a friend or relation. We talk of its approach without much emotion. We foretell the *when* without much seeming pain. We know it *must be*. But, when it comes, we forget our foretellings, and feel the calamity as acutely as if we had never expected it. The accounts we hear, daily, and almost hourly, of the families of farmers actually coming to the *parish-book*, are enough to make anybody but a boroughmonger feel. That species of monster is to be moved by nothing but his own pecuniary sufferings; and, thank God, the monster is now about to be *reached*. I hear, from all parts, that the parsons are in great alarm! Well they may, if their hearts be too much set upon the treasures of this world; for I can see no possible way of settling this matter justly, without resorting to their temporalities. They have long enough been calling upon all the industrious classes for " sacrifices for the good of the country." The time seems to be come for them to do something in this way themselves. In a short time there will be, because there can be, no rents. And we shall see whether the landlords will then suffer the parsons to continue to receive a tenth part of the produce of the land! In many places the farmers have had the sense and the spirit to *rate* the tithes to the *poor-rates*. This they *ought* to do in all cases, whether the tithes be taken up in kind or not. This, however, sweats the fire-shovel hat gentleman. It " bothers his wig." He does not know what to think of it. He does not know *who to blame* ; and, where a parson finds things not to his mind, the first thing he always does is, to look about for somebody to accuse of sedition and blasphemy. Lawyers always begin, in such cases, to hunt the books, to see if there be no *punishment* to apply. But, the devil of it is, neither of them have now anybody to lay on upon! I always told them that there would arise an enemy that would laugh at all their anathemas, informations, dungeons, halters, and bayonets. One positive good has, however, arisen out of the present calamities, and that is, the *parsons* are grown more *humble* than they were. Cheap corn and a good thumping debt have greatly conduced to the producing of the Christian virtue *humility*, necessary in us all, but doubly necessary in the priesthood. The parson is now one of the parties who is taking away the landlord's estate and the farmer's capital. When the farmer's capital is gone, there will be no rents; but, without a law upon the subject, the parson will still have his tithe, and a tithe upon the *taxes* too, which the land has to bear! Will the landlords stand this? No matter. If there be no reform of the Parliament, they must stand it. The two sets may, for aught I care, worry each other as long as they please. When the present race of farmers are gone (and that will soon be) the landlord and the parson may settle the matter between them. They will be the only parties interested; and which of them shall devour the other appears to be of little consequence to the rest of the community. They agreed most cordially in creating the debt. They went hand in hand in all the measures against the Reformers. They have made, actually made, the very thing that now frightens them, which now menaces them with *total extinction*. They cannot think it unjust, if their prayers be now treated as the prayers of the Reformers were.

27 to 29 October.

At Burghclere. Very nasty weather. On the 28th the fox hounds came to throw off at *Penwood*, in this parish. Having heard that *Dundas* would be out with the hounds, I rode to the place of meeting, in order to look him in the face, and to give him an opportunity to notice, on his own peculiar dunghill, what I had said of him at Newbury. He came. I rode up to him and about him; but he said not a word. The company entered the wood, and I rode back towards my quarters. They found a fox, and I quickly lost him. Then they came out of the wood and came back along the road, and met me, and passed me, they as well as I going at a foot pace. I had plenty of time to survey them all well, and to mark their looks. I watched Dundas's eyes, but the devil a bit could I get them to turn *my way*. He is *paid* for the present. We shall see whether he will go, or send an ambassador, or neither, when I shall be at Reading on the 9th of next month.

Set off for London. Went by Alderbridge, Crookham,
Brimton, Mortimer, Strathfield Say, Heckfield Heath, Eversley,
Blackwater, and slept at Oakingham. This is, with trifling
exceptions, a miserably poor country. Burghclere lies along
at the foot of a part of that chain of hills which, in this part,
divide Hampshire from Berkshire. The parish just named is,
indeed, in Hampshire, but it forms merely the foot of the Highclere and Kingsclere Hills. These hills, from which you can
see all across the country, even to the Isle of Wight, are of chalk,
and with them, towards the north, ends the chalk. The soil
over which I have come to-day is generally a stony sand upon
a bed of gravel. With the exception of the land just round
Crookham and the other villages, nothing can well be poorer or
more villainously ugly. It is all first cousin to Hounslow Heath,
of which it is, in fact, a continuation to the westward. There
is a clay at the bottom of the gravel; so that you have here
nasty stagnant pools without fertility of soil. The rushes grow
amongst the gravel; sure sign that there is clay beneath to
hold the water; for, unless there be water constantly at their
roots, rushes will not grow. Such land is, however, good for
oaks wherever there is soil enough on the top of the gravel for the
oak to get hold, and to send its tap-root down to the clay. The
oak is the thing to plant here; and, *therefore*, this whole country
contains not one single plantation of oaks! That is to say, as
far as I observed. Plenty of *fir*-trees and other rubbish have
been recently planted; but no oaks.

At *Strathfield Say* is that everlasting monument of English
Wisdom Collective, the *Heir Loom Estate* of the "*greatest
Captain of the Age!*" In his peerage it is said that it was
wholly out of the power of the nation to reward his services fully;
but that "she did what she could!" Well, poor devil! And
what could anybody ask for more? It was well, however,
that she gave what she did while she was drunk; for, if she had
held her hand till now, I am half disposed to think that her
gifts would have been very small. I can never forget that we
have to pay interest on £50,000 of the money merely owing to
the coxcombery of the late Mr. Whitbread, who actually moved
that *addition* to one of the grants proposed by the ministers!
Now, a great part of the grants is in the way of annuity or
pension. It is notorious that, when the grants were made,
the pensions would not purchase more than a third part of as

much wheat as they will now. The grants, therefore, have been augmented threefold. What right, then, has any one to say that the *labourer's wages* ought to fall, unless he say that these pensions ought to be reduced! The Hampshire magistrates, when they were putting forth their *manifesto* about the allowances to labourers, should have noticed these pensions of the lord-lieutenant of the county. However, real starvation cannot be inflicted to any very great extent. The present race of farmers must give way, and the attempts to squeeze rents out of the wages of labour must cease. And the matter will finally rest to be settled by the landlords, parsons, and tax-eaters. If the landlords choose to give the greatest captain three times as much as was granted to him, why, let him have it. According to all account, he is no *miser* at any rate; and the estates that pass through his hands may, perhaps, be full as well disposed of as they are at present. Considering the miserable soil I have passed over to-day, I am rather surprised to find Oakingham so decent a town. It has a very handsome market-place, and is by no means an ugly country-town.

31 October.

Set off at daylight and got to Kensington about noon. On leaving Oakingham for London, you get upon what is called *Windsor Forest;* that is to say, upon as bleak, as barren, and as villainous a heath as ever man set his eyes on. However, here are new enclosures without end. And here are houses too, here and there, over the whole of this execrable tract of country. "What!" Mr. Canning will say, "will you not allow that the owners of these new enclosures and these houses know their own interests? And are not these *improvements,* and are they not a proof of an addition to the national capital?" To the first I answer, *May be so ;* to the two last, *No.* These new enclosures and houses arise out of the beggaring of the parts of the country distant from the vortex of the funds. The farm-houses have long been growing fewer and fewer; the labourers' houses fewer and fewer; and it is manifest to every man who has eyes to see with, that the villages are regularly wasting away. This is the case all over the parts of the kingdom where the tax-eaters do not haunt. In all the really agricultural villages and parts of the kingdom, there is a *shocking decay ;* a great dilapidation and constant pulling down or falling down of houses. The farm-houses are not so many as they were forty years ago by three-fourths. That is to say, the infernal system of Pitt and his followers has annihilated three parts out of four of the farm-houses. The labourers' houses disappear also. And all the *useful* people become less numerous. While these spewy sands and gravel near London are enclosed and built on, good lands in other parts are neglected. These enclosures and buildings are a *waste ;* they are means *misapplied ;* they are a proof of national decline and not of prosperity. To cultivate and ornament these villainous spots the produce and the population are drawn away from the good lands. There all manner of schemes have been resorted to to get rid of the necessity of *hands;* and I am quite convinced that the population, upon the whole, has not increased, in England, one single soul since I was born; an opinion that I have often expressed, in support of which I have as often offered arguments, and those arguments have *never been answered.* As to this rascally heath, that which has ornamented it has brought misery on millions. The spot is not far distant from the stock-jobbing crew. The roads to it are level. They are smooth. The wretches can go to it from the 'Change without any danger to their worthless necks. And thus it is " *vastly improved, ma'am !*" A set of men who can look upon this as " improvement," who can regard this as a proof of the " increased capital of the country," are pretty fit, it must be allowed, to get the country out of its present difficulties ! At the end of this blackguard heath you come (on the road to Egham) to a little place called *Sunning Hill,* which is on the western side of Windsor Park. It is a spot all made into " grounds " and gardens by tax-eaters. The inhabitants of it have beggared twenty agricultural villages and hamlets.

From this place you go across a corner of Windsor Park, and come out at Virginia Water. To Egham is then about two miles. A much more ugly country than that between Egham and Kensington would with great difficulty be found in England. Flat as a pancake, and, until you come to Hammersmith, the soil is a nasty stony dirt upon a bed of gravel. Hounslow Heath, which is only a little worse than the general run, is a sample of all that is bad in soil and villainous in look. Yet this is now enclosed, and what they call " cultivated." Here is a fresh robbery of villages, hamlets, and farm and labourers' buildings and abodes ! But here is one of those " *vast improve-ments, ma'am,*" called *Barracks.* What an " improvement ! " What an " addition to the national capital ! " For, mind,

Monsieur de Snip, the Surrey Norman, actually said, that the new buildings ought to be reckoned an addition to the national capital! What, Snip! Do you pretend that the nation is *richer*, because the means of making this barrack have been drawn away from the people in taxes? Mind, Monsieur le Normand, the barrack did not drop down from the sky nor spring up out of the earth. It was not created by the unhanged knaves of paper-money. It came out of the people's labour; and when you hear Mr. Ellman tell the committee of 1821, that forty-five years ago every man in his parish brewed his own beer, and that now not one man in that same parish does it; when you hear this, Monsieur de Snip, you might, if you had brains in your skull, be able to estimate the effects of what has produced the barrack. Yet, barracks there must be, or *Gatton* and *Old Sarum* must fall; and the fall of these would break poor Mr. Canning's heart.

8 November.

From London to Egham in the evening.

9 November.

Started at day-break in a hazy frost, for Reading. The horses' manes and ears covered with the hoar before we got across Windsor Park, which appeared to be a blackguard soil, pretty much like Hounslow Heath, only not flat. A very large part of the park is covered with heath or rushes, sure sign of execrable soil. But the roads are such as might have been made by Solomon. "A greater than Solomon is here!" some one may exclaim. Of that I know nothing. I am but a traveller; and the roads in this park are beautiful indeed. My servant, whom I brought from amongst the hills and flints of Uphusband, must certainly have thought himself in Paradise as he was going through the park. If I had told him that the buildings and the labourers' clothes and meals, at Uphusband, were the *worse* for those pretty roads with edgings cut to the line, he would have wondered at me, I dare say. It would, nevertheless, have been perfectly true; and this is *feelosofee* of a much more useful sort than that which is taught by the Edinburgh Reviewers.

When you get through the park you come to Winkfield, and then (bound for Reading) you go through Binfield, which is ten miles from Egham and as many from Reading. At Binfield I stopped to breakfast, at a very nice country inn called the *Stag and Hounds*. Here you go along on the north border of that villainous tract of country that I passed over in going from Oakingham to Egham. Much of the land even here is but newly enclosed; and it was really not worth a straw before it was loaded with the fruit of the labour of the people living in the parts of the country distant from the *Fund-Wen*. What injustice! What unnatural changes! Such things cannot be, without producing convulsion in the end! A road as smooth as a die, a real stock-jobber's road, brought us to Reading by eleven o'clock. We dined at one; and very much pleased I was with the company. I have seldom seen a number of persons assembled together, whose approbation I valued more than that of the company of this day. Last year the prime minister said that his speech (the grand speech) was rendered necessary by the " pains that had been taken, in different parts of the country," to persuade the farmers that the distress had arisen out of the *measures of the government*, and *not from over-production!* To be sure I had taken some pains to remove that stupid notion about over-production from the minds of the farmers; but did the stern-path-man *succeed* in counter-acting the effect of my efforts? Not he, indeed. And, after his speech was made, and sent forth cheek by jowl with that of the sane Castlereagh, of hole-digging memory, the truths inculcated by me were only the more manifest. This has been a fine meeting at Reading! I feel very proud of it. The morn-ing was fine for me to ride in, and the rain began as soon as I was housed.

I came on horseback 40 miles, slept on the road, and finished my harangue at the end of *twenty-two hours* from leaving Ken-sington; and I cannot help saying that is pretty well for " *Old* Cobbett." I am delighted with the people that I have seen at Reading. Their kindness to me is nothing in my estimation compared with the sense and spirit which they appear to possess. It is curious to observe how things have *worked* with me. That combination, that sort of *instinctive* union, which has existed for so many years, amongst all the parties, to *keep me down* generally, and particularly, as the *County-Club* called it, to keep me out of Parliament " *at any rate*," this combination has led to the present *haranguing* system, which, in some sort, supplies the place of a seat in Parliament. It may be said, indeed, that I have not the honour to sit in the same room with those great Reformers, Lord John Russell, Sir Massey Lopez, and his guest, Sir Francis Burdett; but man's happiness here below is never perfect; and there may be, besides, people to believe that a man ought not to break his heart on account of being shut out of such company, especially when he can find such company as I have this day found at Reading.

10 October.

Went from Reading, through Aldermaston for Burghclere. The rain has been very heavy, and the water was a good deal out. Here, on my way, I got upon Crookham Common again, which is a sort of continuation of the wretched country about Oakingham. From Highclere I looked, one day, over the flat towards Marlborough; and I there saw some such rascally heaths. So that this villainous tract extends from east to west, with more or less of exceptions, from Hounslow to Hungerford. From north to south it extends from Binfield (which cannot be far from the borders of Buckinghamshire) to the South Downs of Hampshire, and terminates somewhere between Liphook and Petersfield, after stretching over Hindhead, which is certainly the most villainous spot that God ever made. Our ancestors do, indeed, seem to have ascribed its formation to another power; for the most celebrated part of it is called " *the Devil's Punch Bowl.*" In this tract of country there are certainly some very beautiful spots. But these are very few in number, except where the chalk-hills run into the tract. The neighbourhood of Godalming ought hardly to be considered as an exception; for there you are just on the outside of the tract, and begin to enter on the *Wealds ;* that is to say, clayey woodlands. All the part of Berkshire of which I have been recently passing over, if I except the tract from Reading to Crookham, is very bad land and a very ugly country.

11 November.

Uphusband *once more*, and, for the sixth time this year, over the North Hampshire Hills, which, notwithstanding their everlasting flints, I like very much. As you ride along, even in a *green lane*, the horses' feet make a noise like *hammering*. It seems as if you were riding on a mass of iron. Yet the soil is good, and bears some of the best wheat in England. All these high and, indeed, all chalky lands, are excellent for sheep. But on the top of some of these hills there are as fine meadows as I ever saw. Pasture richer, perhaps, than that about Swindon in the north of Wiltshire. And the singularity is, that this pasture is on the *very tops* of these lofty hills, from which you can see the Isle of Wight. There is a stiff loam, in some places twenty feet deep, on a bottom of chalk. Though the grass grows so finely, there is no apparent wetness in the land. The wells are more than three hundred feet deep. The main part of the water, for all uses, comes from the clouds; and, indeed, these are pretty constant companions of these chalk hills, which are very often enveloped in clouds and wet, when it is sunshine down at Burghclere or Uphusband. They manure the land here by digging *wells* in the fields, and bringing up the chalk, which they spread about on the land; and which, being free-chalk, is reduced to powder by the frosts. A considerable portion of the land is covered with wood; and as, in the clearing of the land, the clearers followed the good soil, without regard to shape of fields, the forms of the woods are of endless variety, which, added to the never-ceasing inequalities of the surface of the whole, makes this, like all the others of the same description, a very pleasant country.

17 November.

Set off from Uphusband for Hambledon. The first place I had to get to was Whitchurch. On my way, and at a short distance from Uphusband, down the valley, I went through a village called *Bourn*, which takes its name from the water that runs down this valley. A *bourn*, in the language of our forefathers, seems to be a river which is, part of the year, *without water*. There is one of these bourns down this pretty valley. It has, generally, no water till towards spring, and then it runs for several months. It is the same at the Candovers, as you go across the downs from Odiham to Winchester.

The little village of *Bourn*, therefore, takes its name from its situation. Then there are two *Hurstbourns*, one above and one below this village of Bourn. *Hurst* means, I believe, a forest. There were, doubtless, one of those on each side of Bourn; and when they became villages, the one above was called *Up*-hurstbourn, and the one below, *Down*-hurstbourn; which names have become *Uphusband* and *Downhusband*. The lawyers, therefore, who, to the immortal honour of high-blood and Norman descent, are making such a pretty story out for the lord chancellor, relative to a noble peer who voted for the bill against the queen, ought to leave off calling the seat of the noble person *Hursperne ;* for it is at Downhurstbourn where he lives, and where he was visited by Dr. Bankhead!

Whitchurch is a small town, but famous for being the place where the paper has been made for the *Borough-Bank !* I

passed by the *mill* on my way to get out upon the downs to go
to Alresford, where I intended to sleep. I hope the time will
come when a monument will be erected where that mill stands,
and when on that monument will be inscribed *the curse of
England*. This spot ought to be held accursed in all time hence-
forth and for evermore. It has been the spot from which have
sprung more and greater mischiefs than ever plagued mankind
before. However, the evils now appear to be fast recoiling on
the merciless authors of them; and, therefore, one beholds this
scene of paper-making with a less degree of rage than formerly.
My blood used to boil when I thought of the wretches who
carried on and supported the system. It does not boil now,
when I think of them. The curse, which they intended solely
for others, is now falling on themselves; and I smile at their
sufferings. Blasphemy! Atheism! Who can be an atheist,
that sees how *justly* these wretches are treated; with what exact
measure they are receiving the evils which they inflicted on
others for a time, and which they intended to inflict on them
for ever! If, indeed, the monsters had continued to prosper,
one might have been an atheist. The true history of the rise,
progress and fall of these monsters, of their *power*, their *crimes*
and their *punishment*, will do more than has been done before
to put an end to the doubts of those who have doubts upon this
subject.

Quitting Whitchurch, I went off to the left out of the Winchester road, got out upon the highlands, took an " observation," as the sailors call it, and off I rode, in a straight line, over
hedge and ditch, towards the rising ground between Stratton
Park and Micheldever Wood; but, before I reached this point,
I found some wet meadows and some running water in my way
in a little valley running up from the turnpike road to a little
place called *West Stratton*. I, therefore, turned to my left, went
down to the turnpike, went a little way along it, then turned
to my left, went along by Stratton Park pales down East
Stratton Street, and then on towards the Grange Park. Stratton
Park is the seat of Sir Thomas Baring, who has here several
thousands of acres of land; who has the living of Micheldever,
to which, I think, Northington and Swallowfield are joined.
Above all, he has Micheldever Wood, which, they say, contains
a thousand acres, and which is one of the finest oak-woods in
England. This large and very beautiful estate must have
belonged to the Church at the time of Henry the Eighth's " reformation." It was, I believe, given by him to the family of

Russell ; and it was, by them, sold to Sir Francis Baring about twenty years ago. Upon the whole, all things considered, the change is for the better. Sir Thomas Baring would not have moved, nay, he *did not* move, for the pardon of *Lopez,* while he left Joseph Swann in gaol for *four years and a half,* without so much as hinting at Swann's case! Yea, verily, I would rather see this estate in the hands of Sir Thomas Baring than in those of Lopez's friend. Besides, it seems to be acknowledged that any title is as good as those derived from the old wife-killer. Castlereagh, when the Whigs talked in a rather rude manner about the sinecure places and pensions, told them that the title of the sinecure man or woman was *as good as the titles of the Duke of Bedford !* this was *plagiarism,* to be sure; for *Burke* had begun it. He called the duke the *Leviathan of grants ;* and seemed to hint at the propriety of *overhauling* them a little. When the men of Kent petitioned for a "*just* reduction of the National Debt," Lord John Russell, with that wisdom for which he is renowned, reprobated the prayer; but, having done this in terms not sufficiently unqualified and strong, and having made use of a word of equivocal meaning, the man that cut his own throat at North Cray pitched on upon him and told him that the fundholder had as much right to his dividends as *the Duke of Bedford had to his estates.* Upon this the noble reformer and advocate for Lopez mended his expressions; and really said what the North Cray philosopher said he ought to say! Come, come: Micheldever Wood is in very proper hands! A little girl, of whom I asked my way down into East Stratton, and who was dressed in a camlet gown, white apron and plaid cloak (it was Sunday), and who had a book in her hand, told me that Lady Baring gave her the clothes, and had her taught to read and to sing hymns and spiritual songs.

As I came through the Strattons, I saw not less than a dozen girls clad in this same way. It is impossible not to believe that this is done with a good motive; but it is possible not to believe that it is productive of good. It must create hypocrites, and hypocrisy is the great sin of the age. Society is in a *queer* state when the rich think that they must *educate* the poor in order to insure their *own safety :* for this, at bottom, is the great motive now at work in pushing on the education scheme, though in this particular case, perhaps, there may be a little enthusiasm at work. When persons are glutted with riches; when they have their fill of them; when they are surfeited of all earthly pursuits, they are very apt to begin to think about the next world; and, the moment they begin to think of that, they begin to look over the *account* that they shall have to present. Hence the far greater part of what are called " charities." But it is the business of *governments* to take care that there shall be very little of this *glutting* with riches, and very little need of " charities."

From Stratton I went on to Northington Down; then round to the south of the Grange Park (Alex. Baring's), down to Abbotson, and over some pretty little green hills to Alresford, which is a nice little town of itself, but which presents a singularly beautiful view from the last little hill coming from Abbotson. I could not pass by the Grange Park without thinking of *Lord and Lady Henry Stuart,* whose lives and deaths surpassed what we read of in the most sentimental romances. Very few things that I have met with in my life ever filled me with sorrow equal to that which I felt at the death of this most virtuous and most amiable pair.

It began raining soon after I got to Alresford, and rained all the evening. I heard here, that a requisition for a county meeting was in the course of being signed in different parts of the county. They mean to petition for reform, I hope. At any rate, I intend to go to see what they do. I saw the *parsons* at the county meeting in 1817. I should like, of all things, to see them at another meeting *now.* These are the persons that I have most steadily in my eye. The war and the debt were for the *tithes* and the *boroughs.* These must stand or fall together now. I always told the parsons that they were the greatest fools in the world to put the tithes on board *the same boat* with the boroughs. I told them so in 1817; and, I fancy, they will soon see all about it.

18 *November.*

Came from Alresford to Hambledon, through Titchbourn, Cheriton, Beauworth, Kilmston, and Exton. This is all a high, hard, dry, fox-hunting country. Like that, indeed, over which I came yesterday. At Titchbourn there is a park, and " great house," as the country-people call it. The place belongs, I believe, to a Sir somebody *Titchbourne,* a family, very likely half as old as the name of the village, which, however, partly takes its name from the *bourn* that runs down the valley. I thought, as I was riding alongside of this park, that I had heard *good* of this family of Titchbourne, and I therefore saw the park *pales* with sorrow. There is not more than one pale in a yard, and those that remain, and the rails and posts and all, seem tumbling down. This park-paling is perfectly typical of those of the landlords who are *not tax-eaters*. They are wasting away very fast. The tax-eating landlords think to swim out the gale. They are deceived. They are "deluded" by their own greediness.

Kilmston was my next place after Titchbourn, but I wanted to go to Beauworth, so that I had to go through Cheriton; a little, hard, iron village, where all seems to be as old as the hills that surround it. In coming along you see Titchbourn church away to the right, on the side of the hill, a very pretty little view; and this, though such a hard country, is a pretty country.

At Cheriton I found a grand camp of *Gipsys*, just upon the move towards Alresford. I had met some of the scouts first, and afterwards the advanced guard, and here the main body was getting in motion. One of the scouts that I met was a young woman, who, I am sure, was six feet high. There were two or three more in the camp of about the same height; and some most strapping fellows of men. It is curious that this race should have preserved their dark skin and coal-black straight and coarse hair, very much like that of the American Indians. I mean the hair, for the skin has nothing of the copper-colour as that of the Indians has. It is not, either, of the Mulatto cast; that is to say, there is no yellow in it. It is a black mixed with our English colours of pale, or red, and the features are small, like those of the girls in Sussex, and often singularly pretty. The tall girl that I met at Titchbourn, who had a huckster basket on her arm, had most beautiful features. I pulled up my horse, and said, "Can you tell me my fortune, my dear?" She answered in the negative, giving me a look at the same time that seemed to say it was *too late ;* and that if I had been thirty years younger she might have seen a little what she could do with me. It is, all circumstances considered, truly surprising that this race should have preserved so perfectly all its distinctive marks.

I came on to Beauworth to inquire after the family of a worthy old farmer, whom I knew there some years ago, and of whose death I had heard at Alresford. A bridle road over some fields and through a coppice took me to Kilmston, formerly a large village, but now mouldered into two farms, and a few miserable tumble-down houses for the labourers. Here is a house that was formerly the residence of the landlord of the place, but is now occupied by one of the farmers. This is a fine country for fox-hunting, and Kilmston belonged to a Mr. Ridge who was a famous fox-hunter, and who is accused of having spent his fortune in that way. But what do people mean? He had a right to spend his *income*, as his fathers had done before him. It was the Pitt-system, and not the fox-hunting, that took away the principal. The place now belongs to a Mr. Long, whose origin I cannot find out.

From Kilmston I went right over the downs to the top of a hill called *Beacon Hill*, which is one of the loftiest hills in the country. Here you can see the Isle of Wight in detail, a fine sweep of the sea; also away into Sussex, and over the New Forest into Dorsetshire. Just below you, to the east, you look down upon the village of Exton; and you can see up this valley (which is called a *Bourn* too) as far as West-Meon, and down it as far as Soberton. Corhampton, Warnford, Meon-Stoke and Droxford come within these two points; so that here are six villages on this bourn within the space of about five miles. On the other side of the main valley down which the bourn runs, and opposite Beacon Hill, is another such a hill, which they call *Old Winchester Hill*. On the top of this hill there was once a camp, or rather fortress; and the ramparts are now pretty nearly as visible as ever. The same is to be seen on the Beacon Hill at Highclere. These ramparts had nothing of the principles of modern fortification in their formation. You see no signs of salient angles. It was a *ditch* and a *bank*, and that appears to have been all. I had, I think, a full mile to go down from the top of Beacon Hill to Exton. This is the village where that *Parson Baines* lives who, as described by me in 1817, bawled in Lord Cochrane's ear at Winchester in the month of March of that year. Parson *Poulter* lives at Meon-Stoke, which is not a mile further down. So that this valley has something in it besides picturesque views! I asked some countrymen how Poulter and Baines did; but their answer contained too much of *irreverence* for me to give it here.

At Exton I crossed the Gosport turnpike-road, came up the cross valley under the south side of Old Winchester Hill, over Stoke Down, then over West-End Down, and then to my friend's house at West-End in the parish of Hambledon.

Thus have I crossed nearly the whole of this country from the north-west to the south-east, without going five hundred yards on a turnpike-road, and, as nearly as I could do it, in a straight line.

The whole country that I have crossed is loam and flints, upon a bottom of chalk. At Alresford there are some

watered meadows, which are the beginning of a chain of
meadows that goes all the way down to Winchester, and
hence to Southampton; but even these meadows have, at
Alresford, chalk under them. The water that supplies them
comes out of *a pond*, called Alresford Pond, which is fed
from the high hills in the neighbourhood. These counties
are purely agricultural; and they have suffered most cruelly
from the accursed Pitt-system. Their hilliness, bleakness,
roughness of roads, render them unpleasant to the luxurious,
effeminate, tax-eating crew, who never come near them, and
who have pared them down to the very bone. The villages
are all in a state of *decay*. The farm-buildings dropping down,
bit by bit. The produce is, by a few great farmers, dragged to
a few spots, and all the rest is falling into decay. If this infernal
system could go on for forty years longer, it would make all the
labourers as much slaves as the negroes are, and subject to the
same sort of discipline and management.

19 to 23 November.

At West-End. Hambledon is a long, straggling village, lying
in a little valley formed by some very pretty but not lofty hills.
The environs are much prettier than the village itself, which is
not far from the north side of Portsdown Hill. This must have
once been a considerable place; for here is a church pretty
nearly as large as that at Farnham in Surrey, which is quite
sufficient for a large town. The means of living has been drawn
away from these villages, and the people follow the means.
Cheriton and Kilmston and Hambledon and the like have been
beggared for the purpose of giving tax-eaters the means of
making "*vast improvements, ma'am,*" on the villainous spewy
gravel of Windsor Forest! The thing, however, must go *back*.
Revolution here or revolution there: bawl, bellow, alarm, as
long as the tax-eaters like, *back* the thing must go. Back,
indeed, *it is going* in some quarters. Those scenes of glorious
loyalty, the sea-port places, are beginning to be deserted.
How many villages has that scene of all that is wicked and
odious, Portsmouth, Gosport, and Portsea; how many villages
has that hellish assemblage beggared! It is now being scattered
itself ! Houses which there let for forty or fifty pounds a year
each, now let for three or four shillings a week each; and thousands, perhaps, cannot be let at all to anybody capable of paying
rent. There is an absolute tumbling down taking place, where,
so lately, there were such "vast improvements, ma'am!"

Does Monsieur de Snip call those improvements, then? Does he insist that those houses form "an addition to the national capital?" Is it any wonder that a country should be miserable when such notions prevail? And when they can, even in the Parliament, be received with cheering?

24 Nov. Sunday.

Set off from Hambledon to go to Thursley in Surrey, about five miles from Godalming. Here I am at Thursley, after as interesting a day as I ever spent in all my life. They say that "*variety* is charming," and this day I have had of scenes and of soils a variety indeed!

To go to Thursley from Hambledon the plain way was up the downs to Petersfield, and then along the turnpike-road through Liphook, and over Hindhead, at the north-east foot of which Thursley lies. But I had been over that sweet Hindhead, and had seen too much of turnpike-road and of heath, to think of taking another so large a dose of them. The map of Hampshire (and we had none of Surrey) showed me the way to Headley, which lies on the west of Hindhead, down upon the flat. I knew it was but about five miles from Headley to Thursley; and I, therefore, resolved to go to Headley, in spite of all the remonstrances of friends, who represented to me the danger of breaking my neck at Hawkley and of getting buried in the bogs of Woolmer Forest. My route was through East-Meon, Froxfield, Hawkley, Greatham, and then over Woolmer Forest (a *heath* if you please), to Headley.

Off we set over the downs (crossing the bottom sweep of Old Winchester Hill) from West-End to East-Meon. We came down a long and steep hill that led us winding round into the village, which lies in a valley that runs in a direction nearly east and west, and that has a rivulet that comes out of the hills towards Petersfield. If I had not seen anything further to-day, I should have dwelt long on the beauties of this place. Here is a very fine valley, in nearly an elliptical form, sheltered by high hills sloping gradually from it; and not far from the middle of this valley there is a hill nearly in the form of a goblet-glass with the foot and stem broken off and turned upside down. And this is clapped down upon the level of the valley, just as you would put such goblet upon a table. The hill is lofty, partly covered with wood, and it gives an air of great singularity to the scene. I am sure that East-Meon has been a *large place*. The church has a *Saxon tower* pretty nearly equal, as far as I recollect, to that of the cathedral at Winchester. The rest of the church has been rebuilt, and, perhaps, several times; but the *tower* is complete; it has had *a steeple* put upon it; but it retains all its beauty, and it shows that the church (which is still large) must, at first, have been a very large building. Let those who talk so glibly of the increase of the population in England, go over the country from Highclere to Hambledon. Let them look at the size of the churches, and let them observe those numerous small inclosures on every side of every village, which had, to a certainty, *each its house* in former times. But let them go to East-Meon, and account for that church. Where did the hands come from to make it? Look, however, at the downs, the many square miles of downs near this village, all bearing the *marks of the plough*, and all out of tillage for many many years; yet not one single inch of them but what is vastly superior in quality to any of those great "improvements" on the miserable heaths of Hounslow, Bagshot, and Windsor Forest. It is the destructive, the murderous paper-system, that has transferred the fruit of the labour, and the people along with it, from the different parts of the country to the neighbourhood of the all-devouring *Wen*. I do not believe one word of what is said of the increase of the population. All observation and all reason is against the fact; and, as to the *parliamentary returns*, what need we more than this: that *they* assert that the population of Great Britain has increased from ten to fourteen millions in the last *twenty years !* That is enough! A man that can suck that in will believe, literally believe, that the moon is made of green cheese. Such a thing is too monstrous to be swallowed by anybody but Englishmen, and by any Englishman not brutified by a Pitt-system.

To Mr. Canning

WORTH (SUSSEX),
10 *December* 1822.

SIR,—The agreeable news from France, relative to the intended invasion of Spain, compelled me to break off, in my last letter, in the middle of my *Rural Ride* of Sunday, the 24th of November. Before I mount again, which I shall do in this letter, pray let me ask you what *sort of apology* is to be offered to the nation, if the French Bourbons be permitted to take quiet possession of

Cadiz and of the Spanish naval force? Perhaps you may be disposed to answer, when you have taken time to reflect; and, therefore, leaving you to *muse* on the matter, I will resume my ride.

24 November.

(Sunday.) From Hambledon to Thursley (continued).

From East-Meon, I did not go on to Froxfield church, but turned off to the left to a place (a couple of houses) called *Bower.* Near this I stopped at a friend's house, which is in about as lonely a situation as I ever saw. A very pleasant place however. The lands dry, a nice mixture of woods and fields, and a great variety of hill and dell.

Before I came to East-Meon, the soil of the hills was a shallow loam with flints, on a bottom of chalk; but, on this side of the valley of East-Meon; that is to say, on the north side, the soil on the hills is a deep, stiff loam, on a bed of a sort of gravel mixed with chalk; and the stones, instead of being grey on the outside and blue on the inside, are yellow on the outside and whitish on the inside. In coming on further to the north, I found that the bottom was sometimes gravel and sometimes chalk. Here, at the time when *whatever it was* that formed these hills and valleys, the stuff of which Hindhead is composed seems to have run down and mixed itself with the stuff of which *Old Winchester Hill* is composed. Free chalk (which is the sort found here) is excellent manure for stiff land, and it produces a complete change in the nature of *clays.* It is, therefore, dug here, on the north of East-Meon, about in the fields, where it happens to be found, and is laid out upon the surface, where it is crumbled to powder by the frost, and thus gets incorporated with the loam.

At Bower I got instructions to go to Hawkley, but accompanied with most earnest advice not to go that way, for that it was impossible to get along. The roads were represented as so bad; the floods so much out; the hills and bogs so dangerous; that, really, I began to *doubt;* and, if I had not been brought up amongst the clays of the Holt Forest and the bogs of the neighbouring heaths, I should certainly have turned off to my right, to go over Hindhead, great as was my objection to going that way. "Well, then," said my friend at Bower, "if you *will* go that way, by G—, you must go down *Hawkley Hanger;*" of which he then gave me *such* a description! But even this I found to fall short of the reality. I inquired simply,

whether *people were in the habit* of going down it; and the
answer being in the affirmative, on I went through green lanes
and bridle-ways till I came to the turnpike-road from Petersfield to Winchester, which I crossed, going into a narrow and
almost untrodden green lane, on the side of which I found a
cottage. Upon my asking the way to *Hawkley*, the woman at
the cottage said, "Right up the lane, sir: you'll come to a
hanger presently: you must take care, sir: you can't ride down:
will your horses *go alone?*"

On we trotted up this pretty green lane; and indeed, we had
been coming gently and generally uphill for a good while. The
lane was between highish banks and pretty high stuff growing
on the banks, so that we could see no distance from us, and
could receive not the smallest hint of what was so near at hand.
The lane had a little turn towards the end; so that, out we
came, all in a moment, at the very edge of the hanger! And
never, in all my life, was I so surprised and so delighted! I
pulled up my horse, and sat and looked; and it was like looking
from the top of a castle down into the sea, except that the
valley was land and not water. I looked at my servant, to see
what effect this unexpected sight had upon him. His surprise
was as great as mine, though he had been bred amongst the
North Hampshire hills. Those who had so strenuously dwelt
on the dirt and dangers of this route, had said not a word about
beauties, the matchless beauties of the scenery. These hangers
are woods on the sides of very steep hills. The trees and underwood *hang*, in some sort, to the ground, instead of *standing on*
it. Hence these places are called *Hangers*. From the summit
of that which I had now to descend, I looked down upon the
villages of Hawkley, Greatham, Selborne and some others.

From the south-east, round, southward, to the north-west,
the main valley has cross-valleys running out of it, the hills on
the sides of which are very steep, and, in many parts, covered
with wood. The hills that form these cross-valleys run out
into the main valley, like piers into the sea. Two of these
promontories, of great height, are on the west side of the main
valley, and were the first objects that struck my sight when
I came to the edge of the hanger, which was on the south. The
ends of these promontories are nearly perpendicular, and their
tops so high in the air, that you cannot look at the village below
without something like a feeling of apprehension. The leaves
are all off, the hop-poles are in stack, the fields have little verdure; but, while the spot is beautiful beyond description even

now, I must leave to imagination to suppose what it is when the trees and hangers and hedges are in leaf, the corn waving, the meadows bright, and the hops upon the poles!

From the south-west, round, eastward, to the north, lie the *heaths*, of which Woolmer Forest makes a part, and these go gradually rising up to Hindhead, the crown of which is to the north-west, leaving the rest of the circle (the part from north to north-west) to be occupied by a continuation of the valley towards Headley, Binstead, Frensham and the Holt Forest. So that even the *contrast* in the view from the top of the hanger is as great as can possibly be imagined. Men, however, are not to have such beautiful views as this without some trouble. We had had the view; but we had to go down the hanger. We had, indeed, some roads to get along, as we could, afterwards; but we had to get down the hanger first. The horses took the lead, and crept partly down upon their feet and partly upon their hocks. It was extremely slippery too; for the soil is a sort of marl, or, as they call it here, maume, or mame, which is, when wet, very much like *grey soap*. In such a case it was likely that I should keep in the rear, which I did, and I descended by taking hold of the branches of the underwood, and so letting myself down. When we got to the bottom, I bade my man, when he should go back to Uphusband, tell the people there that *Ashmansworth Lane* is not the *worst* piece of road in the world. Our worst, however, was not come yet, nor had we by any means seen the most novel sights.

After crossing a little field and going through a farmyard, we came into a lane, which was, at once, road and river. We found a hard bottom, however; and when we got out of the water, we got into a lane with high banks. The banks were quarries of white stone, like Portland-stone, and the bed of the road was of the same stone; and, the rains having been heavy for a day or two before, the whole was as clean and as white as the steps of a fundholder or dead-weight doorway in one of the squares of the *Wen*. Here were we, then, going along a stone road with stone banks, and yet the underwood and trees grew well upon the tops of the banks. In the solid stone beneath us, there were a horse-track and wheel-tracks, the former about three and the latter about six inches deep. How many many ages it must have taken the horses' feet, the wheels, and the water, to wear down this stone so as to form a hollow way! The horses seemed alarmed at their situation; they trod with fear; but they took us along very nicely, and, at last, got us safe into the indescribable dirt and mire of the road from Hawkley Green to Greatham. Here the bottom of all the land is this solid white stone, and the top is that *mame*, which I have before described. The hop-roots penetrate down into this stone. How deep the stone may go I know not; but, when I came to look up at the end of one of the piers, or promontories, mentioned above, I found that it was all of this same stone.

At Hawkley Green I asked a farmer the way to Thursley. He pointed to one of two roads going from the green; but, it appearing to me that that would lead me up to the London road and over Hindhead, I gave him to understand that I was resolved to get along, somehow or other, through the "low countries." He besought me not to think of it. However, finding me resolved, he got a man to go a little way to put me into the Greatham road. The man came, but the farmer could not let me go off without renewing his entreaties that I would go away to Liphook, in which entreaties the man joined, though he was to be paid very well for his trouble.

Off we went, however, to Greatham. I am thinking whether I ever did see *worse* roads. Upon the whole, I think, I have; though I am not sure that the roads of New Jersey, between Trenton and Elizabeth Town, at the breaking up of winter, be worse. Talk of *shows*, indeed! Take a piece of this road; just a cut across, and a rod long, and carry it up to London. That would be something like a *show !*

Upon leaving Greatham we came out upon Woolmer Forest. Just as we were coming out of Greatham, I asked a man the way to Thursley. "You *must* go to *Liphook*, sir," said he. "But," I said, "I *will not* go to Liphook." These people seemed to be posted at all these stages to turn me aside from my purpose, and to make me go over that *Hindhead*, which I had resolved to avoid. I went on a little further, and asked another man the way to Headley, which, as I have already observed, lies on the western foot of Hindhead, whence I knew there must be a road to Thursley (which lies at the north-east foot) without going over that miserable hill. The man told me that I must go across the *forest*. I asked him whether it was a *good* road: "It is a *sound* road," said he, laying a weighty emphasis upon the word *sound*. "Do people *go* it?" said I. "*Ye-es,*" said he. "Oh then," said I, to my man, "as it is a *sound* road, keep you close to my heels, and do not attempt to go aside, not even for a foot." Indeed, it was a *sound* road.

The rain of the night had made the fresh horse tracks visible. And we got to Headley in a short time, over a sand-road, which seemed so delightful after the flints and stone and dirt and sloughs that we had passed over and through since the morning! This road was not, if we had been benighted, without its dangers, the forest being full of quags and quicksands.   This is a tract of Crown-lands, or, properly speaking, *public-lands*, on some parts of which our land steward, Mr. Huskisson, is making some plantations of trees, partly fir, and partly other trees.   What he can plant the *fir* for, God only knows, seeing that the country is already over-stocked with that rubbish.   But this *public-land* concern is a very great concern.

If I were a member of Parliament, I *would* know what timber has been cut down, and what it has been sold for, since year 1790.   However, this matter must be *investigated*, first or last. It never can be omitted in the winding up of the concern; and that winding up must come out of wheat at four shillings a bushel.   It is said, hereabouts, that a man who lives near Liphook, and who is so mighty a hunter and game pursuer, that they call him *William Rufus ;* it is said that this man is *Lord of the Manor of Woolmer Forest.*   This he cannot be without *a grant* to that effect; and, if there be a grant, there must have been a *reason* for the grant.   This *reason* I should very much like to know; and this I would know if I were a member of Parliament.   That the people call him the *Lord of the Manor* is certain; but he can hardly make preserves of the plantations; for it is well known how marvellously *hares* and *young trees* agree together!   This is a matter of great public importance; and yet, how, in the present state of things, is an *investigation* to be obtained?   Is there a man in parliament that will call for it? Not one.   Would a dissolution of Parliament mend the matter? No: for the same men would be there still.   They are the same men that have been there for these thirty years; and the *same men* they will be, and they *must be*, until there be *a reform.* To be sure when one dies, or cuts his throat (as in the case of Castlereagh), another *one* comes; but it is the *same body.*   And, as long as it is that same body, things will always go on as they now go on.   However, as Mr. Canning says the body "*works well*," we must not say the contrary.

The soil of this tract is, generally, a black sand, which, in some places, becomes *peat*, which makes very tolerable fuel.   In some parts there is clay at bottom; and there the *oaks* would grow; but not while there are *hares* in any number on the forest.

If trees be to grow here, there ought to be no hares, and as little hunting as possible.

We got to Headley, the sign of the Holly Bush, just at dusk, and just as it began to rain. I had neither eaten nor drunk since eight o'clock in the morning; and as it was a nice little public-house, I at first intended to stay all night, an intention that I afterwards very indiscreetly gave up. I had *laid my plan*, which included the getting to Thursley that night. When, therefore, I had got some cold bacon and bread, and some milk, I began to feel ashamed of stopping short of my *plan*, especially after having so heroically persevered in the " stern path," and so disdainfully scorned to go over Hindhead. I knew that my road lay through a hamlet called *Churt*, where they grow such fine *bennet-grass* seed. There was a moon; but there was also a hazy rain. I had heaths to go over, and I might go into quags. Wishing to execute my plan, however, I at last brought myself to quit a very comfortable turf-fire, and to set off in the rain, having bargained to give a man three shillings to guide me out to the northern foot of Hindhead. I took care to ascertain that my guide knew the road perfectly well; that is to say, I took care to ascertain it as far as I could, which was, indeed, no further than his word would go. Off we set, the guide mounted on his own or master's horse, and with a white smock frock, which enabled us to see him clearly. We trotted on pretty fast for about half an hour; and I perceived, not without some surprise, that the rain, which I knew to be coming from the *south*, met me full in the face, when it ought, according to my reckoning, to have beat upon my right cheek. I called to the guide repeatedly to ask him if he was *sure that he was right*, to which he always answered, " Oh! yes, sir, I know the road." I did not like this, " *I know the road*." At last, after going about six miles in nearly a southern direction, the guide turned short to the left. That brought the rain upon my right cheek, and, though I could not very well account for the long stretch to the south, I thought that, at any rate, we were *now* in the right track; and, after going about a mile in this new direction, I began to ask the guide *how much further we had to go ;* for I had got a pretty good soaking, and was rather impatient to see the foot of Hindhead. Just at this time, in raising my head and looking forward as I spoke to the guide, what should I see but a long, high, and steep *hanger* arising before us, the trees along the top of which I could easily distinguish! The fact was, we were just getting to the outside of the heath, and were on the brow of a steep hill, which faced this hanging wood. The guide had begun to descend; and I had called to him to stop; for the hill was so steep, that, rain as it did and wet as my saddle must be, I got off my horse in order to walk down. But, now behold, the fellow discovered that he *had lost his way!*—Where we were I could not even guess. There was but one remedy, and that was to get back, if we could. I became guide now; and did as Mr. Western is advising the ministers to do, *retraced* my steps. We went back about half the way that we had come, when we saw two men, who showed us the way that we ought to go. At the end of about a mile, we fortunately found the turnpike-road; not, indeed, at the *foot*, but on the *tip-top* of that very Hindhead, on which I had so repeatedly *vowed* I would not go! We came out on the turnpike some hundred yards on the Liphook side of the buildings called *the Hut;* so that we had the whole of three miles of hill to come down at not much better than a foot pace, with a good pelting rain at our backs.

It is odd enough how differently one is affected by the same sight, under different circumstances. At the "*Holly Bush*" at Headley there was a room full of fellows in white smock frocks, drinking and smoking and talking, and I, who was then dry and warm, *moralised* within myself on their *folly* in spending their time in such a way. But when I got down from Hindhead to the public-house at Road Lane, with my skin soaking and my teeth chattering, I thought just such another group, whom I saw through the window sitting round a good fire with pipes in their mouths, the *wisest assembly* I had ever set my eyes on. A real *Collective Wisdom.* And I most solemnly declare, that I felt a greater veneration for them than I have ever felt even for the *Privy Council*, notwithstanding the Right Honourable Charles Wynn and the Right Honourable Sir John Sinclair belong to the latter.

It was now but a step to my friend's house, where a good fire and a change of clothes soon put all to rights, save and except the having come over Hindhead after all my resolutions. This mortifying circumstance; this having been *beaten*, lost the guide the *three shillings* that I had agreed to give him. "Either," said I, "you did not know the way well, or you did: if the former, it was dishonest in you to undertake to guide me: if the latter, you have wilfully led me miles out of my way." He grumbled; but off he went. He certainly deserved nothing; for he did not know the way, and he prevented some other man from earning and receiving the money. But had he not caused

me to *get upon Hindhead*, he would have had the three shillings.
I had, at one time, got my hand in my pocket; but the thought
of having been *beaten* pulled it out again.

Thus ended the most interesting day, as far as I know, that I
ever passed in all my life. Hawkley-hangers, promontories,
and stone-roads will always come into my mind when I see, or
hear of, picturesque views. I forgot to mention that, in going
from Hawkley to Greatham, the man who went to show me the
way, told me at a certain fork, " that road goes to *Selborne*."
This put me in mind of a book, which was once recommended
to me, but which I never saw, entitled *The History and Antiquities of Selborne* (or something of that sort), written, I
think, by a parson of the name of *White*, brother of Mr. *White*,
so long a bookseller in Fleet Street. This parson had, I think,
the living of the parish of Selborne. The book was mentioned
to me as a work of great curiosity and interest. But, at that
time, the THING was biting *so very sharply* that one had no attention to bestow on antiquarian researches. Wheat at 39s. a
quarter, and South-Down ewes at 12s. 6d. have so weakened the
THING's jaws and so filed down its teeth, that I shall now certainly
read this book if I can get it. By the bye, if *all the parsons* had,
for the last thirty years, employed their leisure time in writing
the histories of their several parishes, instead of living, as many
of them have, engaged in pursuits that I need not here name,
neither their situation nor that of their flocks would, perhaps,
have been the worse for it at this day.

25 Nov.
THURSLEY (SURREY).

In looking back into Hampshire, I see with pleasure the
farmers bestirring themselves to get a county meeting called.
There were, I was told, nearly five hundred names to a requisition, and those all of land-owners or occupiers.—Precisely what
they mean to petition for I do not know; but (and now I address
myself to you, Mr. Canning), if they do not petition *for a reform
of the Parliament*, they will do worse than nothing. You, sir,
have often told us that the House, however got together,
" works well." Now, as I said in 1817, just before I went to
America to get out of the reach of our friend, the *Old Doctor*,
and to use my *long arm ;* as I said then, in a letter addressed
to Lord Grosvenor, so I say now, show me the inexpediency of
reform, and I will hold my tongue. Show us, prove to us, that
the House " works well," and I, for my part, give the matter

up. It is not the construction or the motions of a machine that I ever look at: all I look after is *the effect*. When, indeed, I find that the effect is deficient or evil, I look to the construction. And as I now see, and have for many years seen, evil effect, I seek a remedy in an alteration in the machine. There is now nobody, no, not a single man, out of the regions of Whitehall, who will pretend that the country can, without the risk of some great and terrible convulsion, go on, even for twelve months longer, unless there be a great change of some sort in the mode of managing the public affairs.

Could you see and hear what I have seen and heard during this Rural Ride, you would no longer say that the House "works well." Mrs. Canning and your children are dear to you; but, sir, not more dear than are to them the wives and children of, perhaps, two hundred thousand men, who, by the Acts of this same House, see those wives and children doomed to beggary, and to beggary, too, never thought of, never regarded as more likely than a blowing up of the earth or a falling of the sun. It was reserved for this " working well " House to make the firesides of farmers scenes of gloom. These firesides, in which I have always so delighted, I now approach with pain. I was, not long ago, sitting round the fire with as worthy and as industrious a man as all England contains. There was his son, about 19 years of age; two daughters from 15 to 18; and a little boy sitting on the father's knee. I knew, but not from him, that there was *a mortgage* on his farm. I was anxious to induce him *to sell without delay*. With this view I, in an hypo-thetical and roundabout way, approached *his case*, and at last I came to final consequences. The deep and deeper gloom on a countenance once so cheerful told me what was passing in his breast, when turning away my looks in order to seem not to perceive the effect of my words, I saw the eyes of his wife full of tears. She had made the application; and there were her children before her! And am I to be *banished for life* if I express what I felt upon this occasion! And does this House, then, " work well? " How many men of the most industrious, the most upright, the most exemplary, upon the face of the earth, have been, by this one Act of this House, driven to despair, ending in madness or self-murder, or both! Nay, how many scores! And yet are we to be banished for life, if we endeavour to show that this House does not " work well? "—However, banish or banish not, these facts are notorious: *the House* made all the *Loans* which constitute the debt: *the House* contracted for the dead weight: *the House* put a stop to gold-payments in 1797: *the House* unanimously passed Peel's Bill. Here are *all* the causes of the ruin, the misery, the anguish, the despair, and the madness and self-murders. Here they are *all*. They have all been Acts of this House; and yet, we are to be banished if we sáy, in words suitable to the subject, that this House does not "*work well !* "

This one Act, I mean this *Banishment Act*, would be enough, with posterity, to characterise this House. When they read (and can believe what they read) that it actually passed a law to banish for life any one who should write, print, or publish anything having a *tendency* to bring it into *contempt ;* when posterity shall read this, and believe it, they will want nothing more to enable them to say what sort of an assembly it was! It was delightful, too, that they should pass this law just after they had passed *Peel's Bill !* Oh, God! thou art *just !* As to *reform*, it *must come.* Let what else will happen, it must come. Whether before, or after, all the estates be transferred, I cannot say. But this I know very well; that the later it come, the *deeper* will it go.

I shall, of course, go on remarking, as occasion offers, upon what is done by and said in this present House; but I know that it can do nothing efficient for the relief of the country. I have seen some men of late, who seem to think that even a reform, enacted or begun by this House, would be an evil; and that it would be better to let the whole thing go on, and produce its natural consequence. I am not of this opinion: I am for a reform as soon as possible, even though it be not, at first, precisely what I could wish; because, if the debt blow up before the reform take place, confusion and uproar there must be; and I do not want to see confusion and uproar. I am for a reform of *some sort*, and *soon ;* but when I say of *some sort*, I do not mean of Lord John Russell's sort; I do not mean a reform in the Lopez way. In short, what I want is to see the *men* changed. I want to see *other men* in the House; and as to *who* those other men should be, I really should not be very nice. I have seen the Tierneys, the Bankeses, the Wilberforces, the Michael Angelo Taylors, the Lambs, the Lowthers, the Davis Giddies, the Sir John Sebrights, the Sir Francis Burdetts, the Hobhouses, old or young, Whitbreads the same, the Lord Johns and the Lord Williams and the Lord Henries and the Lord Charleses, and, in short, all *the whole family ;* I have seen them all there, all the same faces and names, all my lifetime; I see that neither adjournment nor prorogation nor dissolution makes any change in *the men ;* and caprice let it be if you like, I want to see a change *in the men.* These have done enough in all conscience; or at least, they have done enough to satisfy me. I want to see some fresh faces, and to hear a change of some sort or other in the sounds. A " *hear, hear,*" coming everlastingly from the same mouths, is what I, for my part, am tired of.

I am aware that this is not what the " *great reformers* " in the House mean. They mean, on the contrary, no such thing as a change of men. They mean that *Lopez* should sit there for ever; or, at least, till succeeded by a legitimate heir. I believe that Sir Francis Burdett, for instance, has not the smallest idea of an Act of Parliament ever being made without his assistance, if he chooses to assist, which is not very frequently the case. I believe that he looks upon a seat in the House as being his property; and that the other seat is, and ought to be, held as a sort of leasehold or copyhold under him. My idea of reform, therefore, my change of faces and of names and of sounds will appear quite horrible to him. However, I think the nation begins to be very much of my way of thinking; and this I am very sure of, that we shall never see that change in the management of affairs which we most of us want to see, unless there be a pretty complete change of men.

Some people will blame me for speaking out so broadly upon this subject. But I think it the best way to disguise nothing; to do what is *right ;* to be sincere; and to let come what will.

GODALMING,
26 to 28 November.

I came here to meet my son, who was to return to London when we had done our business.—The turnips are pretty good all over the country, except upon the very thin soils on the chalk. At Thursley they are very good, and so they are upon all these nice light and good lands round about Godalming.

This is a very pretty country. You see few prettier spots than this. The chain of little hills that run along to the south and south-east of Godalming, and the soil, which is a good loam upon a sand-stone bottom, run down on the south side, into what is called the *Weald.* This Weald is a bed of clay, in which nothing grows well but oak trees. It is first the Weald of Surrey, and then the Weald of Sussex. It runs along on the south of Dorking, Reigate, Bletchingley, Godstone, and then winds away down into Kent. In no part of it, as far as I have observed, do the oaks grow finer than between the sand-hill on the south of Godstone and a place called Fellbridge, where the county of Surrey terminates on the road to East Grinstead.

At Godalming we heard some account of a lawsuit between Mr. Holme Sumner and his tenant, Mr. Nash; but the particulars I must reserve till I have them in black and white.

In all parts of the country, I hear of landlords that begin to *squeak*, which is a certain proof that they begin to feel the bottom of their tenants' pockets. No man can pay rent, I mean any rent at all, except out of capital; or except under some peculiar circumstances, such as having a farm near a spot where the fund-holders are building houses. When I was in Hampshire, I heard of terrible breakings up in the Isle of Wight. They say that the general rout is very near at hand there. I heard of one farmer, who held a farm at seven hundred pounds a year, who paid his rent annually, and punctually, who had, of course, seven hundred pounds to pay to his landlord last Michaelmas; but who, before Michaelmas came, thrashed out and sold (the harvest being so early) the whole of his corn; sold off his stock, bit by bit; got the very goods out of his house, leaving only a bed and some trifling things; sailed with a fair wind over to France with his family; put his mother-in-law into the house to keep possession of the house and farm, and to prevent the landlord from entering upon the land for a year or better, unless he would pay to the mother-in-law a certain sum of money! Doubtless the landlord had already sucked away about three or four times seven hundred pounds from this farmer. He would not be able to enter upon his farm without a process that would cost him some money, and without the farm being pretty well stocked with thistles and docks, and perhaps laid half to common. Farmers on the coast opposite France are not so firmly bounden as those in the interior. Some hundreds of these will have carried their allegiance, their capital (what they have left), and their skill, to go and grease the fat sow, our old friends the Bourbons. I hear of a sharp, greedy, hungry shark of a landlord, who says that " some law must be passed; " that " Parliament must do something to prevent this! " There is a pretty fool for you! There is a great jackass (I beg the real jackass's pardon), to imagine that the people at Westminster can do anything to prevent the French from suffering people to come with their money to settle in France! This fool does not know, perhaps, that there are members of Parliament that live in France more than they do in England. I have heard of one, who not only lives there, but carries on vineyards there, and is never absent from them, except when he comes over " to attend to his duties in Parliament." He perhaps sells his wine at the same time, and that being genuine, doubtless brings him a good price; so that the occupations harmonise together very well. The Isle of Wight must be rather peculiarly distressed; for it was the scene of monstrous expenditure. When the *pure* Whigs were in power, in 1806, it was proved to them and to the Parliament, that in several instances, *a barn* in the Isle of Wight was rented by the " envy of surrounding nations " for more money than the rest of the whole farm! These barns were wanted as *barracks ;* and, indeed, such things were carried on in that island as never could have been carried on under anything that was not absolutely " the admiration of the world." These sweet pickings caused, doubtless, a great rise in the rent of the farms; so that, in this island, there is not only the depression of price, and a greater depression than anywhere else, but also the loss of the pickings, and these together leave the tenants but this simple choice, beggary or flight; and as most of them have had a pretty deal of capital, and will be likely to have some left as yet, they will, as they perceive the danger, naturally flee for succour to the Bourbons. This is, indeed, something new in the history of English agriculture; and were not Mr. Canning so positive to the contrary, one would almost imagine that the thing which has produced it does not work so very well. However, that gentleman seems resolved to prevent us, by his *King of Bohemia* and his two *Red Lions*, from having any change in this thing; and therefore the landlords, in the Isle of Wight, as well as elsewhere, must make the best of the matter.

November 29.

Went on to Guildford, where I slept. Everybody that has been from Godalming to Guildford, knows that there is hardly another such a pretty four miles in all England. The road is good; the soil is good; the houses are neat; the people are neat: the hills, the woods, the meadows, all are beautiful. Nothing wild and bold, to be sure, but exceedingly pretty; and it is almost impossible to ride along these four miles without feelings of pleasure, though you have rain for your companion, as it happened to be with me.

I came over the high hill on the south of Guildford, and came down to Chilworth, and up the valley to Albury. I noticed, in my first Rural Ride, this beautiful valley, its hangers, its meadows, its hop-gardens, and its ponds. This valley of Chilworth has great variety, and is very pretty; but after seeing Hawkley, every other place loses in point of beauty and interest. This pretty valley of Chilworth has a run of water which comes out of the high hills, and which, occasionally, spreads into a pond; so that there is in fact a series of ponds connected by this run of water. This valley, which seems to have been created by a bountiful providence, as one of the choicest retreats of man; which seems formed for a scene of innocence and happiness, has been, by ungrateful man, so perverted as to make it instrumental in effecting two of the most damnable of purposes; in carrying into execution two of the most damnable inventions that ever sprang from the minds of men under the influence of the devil! namely, the making of *gunpowder* and of *bank-notes !* Here in this tranquil spot, where the nightingales are to be heard earlier and later in the year than in any other part of England; where the first bursting of the buds is seen in spring, where no rigour of seasons can ever be felt; where everything seems formed for precluding the very thought of wickedness; here has the devil fixed on as one of the seats of his grand manufactory; and perverse and ungrateful man not only lends him his aid, but lends it cheerfully! As to the gunpowder, indeed, we might get over that. In some cases that may be innocently, and, when it sends the lead at the hordes that support a tyrant, meritoriously employed. The alders and the willows, therefore, one can see, without so much regret, turned into powder by the waters of this valley; but, the *bank-notes !* To think that the springs which God has commanded to flow from the sides of these happy hills, for the comfort and the delight of man; to think that these springs should be perverted into means of spreading misery over a whole nation; and that, too, under the base and hypocritical pretence of promoting its *credit* and maintaining its *honour* and its *faith !* There was one circumstance, indeed, that served to mitigate the melancholy excited by these reflections; namely, that a part of these springs have, at times, assisted in turning rags into *Registers !* Somewhat cheered by the thought of this, but, still, in a more melancholy mood than I had been for a long while, I rode on with my friend towards *Albury*, up the valley, the sand-hills on one side of us and the chalk-hills on the other. Albury is a little village consisting of a few houses, with a large house or two near it. At the end of the village we came to a park, which is the residence of Mr. Drummond. — Having heard a great deal of this park, and of the gardens, I wished very much to see them. My way to Dorking lay through Shire, and it went along on the outside of the park. I *guessed*, as the Yankees say, that there must be a way through the park to Shire; and I fell upon the scheme of going into the park as far as Mr. Drummond's house, and then asking his leave to go out at the other end of it. This scheme, though pretty barefaced, succeeded very well. It is true that I was aware that I had not a *Norman* to deal with; or I should not have ventured upon the experiment. I sent in word that, having got into the park, I should be exceedingly obliged to Mr. Drummond if he would let me go out of it on the side next to Shire. He not only granted this request, but, in the most obliging manner, permitted us to ride all about the park, and to see his gardens, which, without any exception, are, to my fancy, the prettiest in England; that is to say, that I ever saw in England.

They say that these gardens were laid out for one of the Howards, in the reign of Charles the Second, by Mr. Evelyn, who wrote the *Sylva*. The mansion-house, which is by no means magnificent, stands on a little flat by the side of the parish church, having a steep, but not lofty, hill rising up on the south side of it. It looks right across the gardens, which lie on the slope of a hill which runs along at about a quarter of a mile distant from the front of the house. The gardens, of course, lie facing the south. At the back of them, under the hill, is a high wall; and there is also a wall at each end, running from north to south. Between the house and the gardens there is a very beautiful run of water, with a sort of little wild narrow sedgy meadow. The gardens are separated from this by a hedge, running along from east to west. From this hedge there go up the hill, at right angles, several other hedges, which divide the land here into distinct gardens, or orchards. Along at the top of these there goes a yew hedge, or, rather, a row of small yew trees, the trunks of which are bare for about eight or ten feet high, and the tops of which form one solid head of about ten feet high, while the bottom branches come out on each side of the row about eight feet horizontally. This hedge, or row, is *a quarter of a mile long*. There is a nice hard sand-road under this species of umbrella; and, summer and winter, here is a most delightful walk! Behind this row of yews there is a space, or garden (a quarter of a mile long you will observe), about thirty or forty feet wide, as nearly as I can recollect. At the back of this garden, and facing the yew-tree row, is a wall probably ten feet high, which forms the breastwork of a *terrace ;* and it is this terrace which is the most beautiful thing that I ever saw in the gardening way. It is a quarter of a mile long, and, I believe, between thirty and forty feet wide; of the finest green sward, and as level as a die.

The wall, along at the back of this terrace, stands close against the hill, which you see with the trees and underwood upon it rising above the wall. So that here is the finest spot for fruit trees that can possibly be imagined. At both ends of this garden the trees in the park are lofty, and there are a pretty many of them. The hills on the south side of the mansion-house are covered with lofty trees, chiefly beeches and chestnut: so that a warmer, a more sheltered, spot than this, it seems to be impossible to imagine. Observe, too, how judicious it was to plant the row of yew trees at the distance which I have described from the wall which forms the breastwork of the terrace: that wall, as well as the wall at the back of the terrace, are covered with fruit trees, and the yew-tree row is just high enough to defend the former from winds, without injuring it by its shade. In the middle of the wall, at the back of the terrace, there is a recess, about thirty feet in front and twenty feet deep, and here is a *basin*, into which rises a spring coming out of the hill. The overflowings of this basin go under the terrace and down across the garden into the rivulet below. So that here is water at the top, across the middle, and along at the bottom of this garden. Take it altogether, this, certainly, is the prettiest garden that I ever beheld. There was taste and sound judgment at every step in the laying out of this place. Everywhere utility and convenience is combined with beauty. The terrace is by far the finest thing of the sort that I ever saw, and the whole thing altogether is a great compliment to the taste of the times in which it was formed. I know there are some ill-natured persons who will say that I want a revolution that would turn Mr. Drummond out of this place and put me into it. Such persons will hardly believe me, but upon my word I do not. From everything that I hear, Mr. Drummond is very worthy of possessing it himself, seeing that he is famed for his justice and his kindness *towards the labouring classes,* who, God knows, have very few friends amongst the rich. If what I have heard be true, Mr. Drummond is singularly good in this way; for instead of hunting down an unfortunate creature who has exposed himself to the lash of the law; instead of regarding a crime committed as proof of an inherent disposition to commit crime; instead of rendering the poor creatures desperate by this species of *proscription*, and forcing them on to the *gallows*, merely because they have once merited the *Bridewell*; instead of this, which is the common practice throughout the country, he rather seeks for such unfortunate creatures to take them into his employ, and thus to reclaim them, and to make them repent of their former courses. If this be true, and I am credibly informed that it is, I know of no man in England so worthy of his estate. There may be others, to act in like manner; but I neither know nor have heard of any other. I had, indeed, heard of this, at Alresford in Hampshire; and, to say the truth, it was this circumstance, and this alone, which induced me to ask the favour of Mr. Drummond to go through his park. But, besides that Mr. Drummond is very worthy of his estate, what chance should I have of getting it if it came to a *scramble*? There are others who like pretty gardens, as well as I; and if the question were to be decided according to the law of the strongest, or, as the French call it, by the *droit du plus fort*, my chance would be but a very poor one. The truth is, that you hear nothing but *fool's* talk about revolutions *made for the purpose of getting possession of people's property*. They never have their spring in any such motives. They are *caused by governments themselves*; and though they do sometimes cause a new distribution of property to a certain extent, there never was, perhaps, one single man in this world that had anything to do, worth speaking of, in the causing of a revolution, that did it with any such view. But what a strange thing it is, that there should be men at this time to fear *the loss of estates* as the consequence of a convulsive revolution; at this time, when the estates are actually passing away from the owners before their eyes, and that, too, in consequence of measures which have been adopted for what has been called the *preservation of property*, against the designs of Jacobins and Radicals! Mr. Drummond has, I dare say, the means of preventing his estate from being actually taken away from him; but I am quite certain that that estate, except as a place to live at, is not worth to him, at this moment, one single farthing. What could a revolution do for him *more* than this? If one could suppose the power of doing what they like placed in the hands of the labouring classes; if one could suppose such a thing as this, which never was yet seen; if one could suppose anything so monstrous as that of a revolution that would leave no public authority anywhere; even in such a case, it is against nature to suppose that the people would come and turn him out of his house and leave him without food; and yet that they must do, to make him, as a landholder, worse off than he is; or, at least, worse off than he must be in a very short time. I saw, in the gardens at Albury Park, what I never saw before in all my life; that is, some plants of the *American Cranberry*. I never saw them in America; for there they grow in those swamps into which I never happened to go at the time of their bearing fruit. I may have seen the plant, but I do not know that I ever did. Here it not only grows, but bears; and there are still some cranberries on the plants now. I tasted them, and they appeared to me to have just the same taste as those in America. They grew in a long bed near the stream of water which I have spoken about, and therefore it is clear that they may be cultivated with great ease in this country. The road, through Shire along to Dorking, runs up the valley between the chalk-hills and the sand-hills; the chalk to our left and the sand to our right. This is called the Home Dale. It begins at Reigate and terminates at Shalford Common, down below Chilworth.

REIGATE,
December 1.

I set off this morning with an intention to go across the weald to Worth; but the red rising of the sun and the other appearances of the morning admonished me to keep upon *high ground;* so I crossed the mole, went along under Boxhill, through Betchworth and Buckland, and got to this place just at the beginning of a day of as heavy rain, and as boisterous wind, as I think I have ever known in England. *In* one rotten borough, one of the most rotten too, and with another still more rotten *up upon the hill*, in Reigate, and close by Gatton, how can I help reflecting, how can my mind be otherwise than filled with reflections on the marvellous deeds of the Collective Wisdom of the nation! At present, however (for I want to get to bed), I will notice only one of those deeds, and that one yet "*incohete*," a word which Mr. Canning seems to have coined for the *nonce* (which is not a coined word), when Lord Castle-reagh (who cut his throat the other day) was accused of making a *swap*, as the horse-jockeys call it, of a *writer-ship* against a *seat*. It is *barter, truck, change, dicker*, as the Yankees call it, but as our horse-jockeys call it, *swap*, or *chop*. The case was this: the chop had been *begun ;* it had been entered on; but had not been completed; just as two jockeys may have *agreed* on a chop and yet not actually *delivered* the horses to one another. Therefore, Mr. Canning said that the act was *incohete*, which means without cohesion, without consequence. Whereupon the House entered on its Journals a solemn resolution, that it was its duty to *watch over its purity with the greatest care ;* but that the said act being "*incohete*," the House did not think it necessary to proceed any farther in the matter! It unfortunately happened, however, that in a very few days afterwards, that is to say on the memorable eleventh of June 1809, Mr. Maddocks accused the very same Castlereagh of having actually sold and delivered a seat to Quintin Dick for three thousand pounds. The accuser said he was ready to bring to the bar proof of the fact; and he moved that he might be permitted so to do. Now then what did Mr. Canning say? Why, he said that the reformers were a low degraded crew, and he called upon the House to make a stand against democratical encroachment! And the House did not listen to him, surely? Yes, but it did! And it voted by a thundering majority, that it would not hear the evidence. And this vote was, by the leader of the Whigs, justified upon the ground that the deed complained of by Mr. Maddocks was according to a practice which was as notorious as *the sun at noonday*. So much for the word "*incohete*," which has led me into this long digression. The deed, or achievement, of which I am now about to speak, is not the Marriage Act; for that is *cohete* enough: that has had plenty of consequences. It is the New Turnpike Act, which though passed, is, as yet, "*incohete;*" and is not to be cohete for some time yet to come. I hope it will become *cohete* during the time that Parliament is sitting, for otherwise it will have *cohesion* pretty nearly equal to that of the Marriage Act. In the first place this Act makes *chalk* and *lime* everywhere liable to turnpike duty, which in many cases they were not before. This is a monstrous oppression upon the owners and occupiers of clay lands; and comes just at the time, too, when they are upon the point, many of them, of being driven out of cultivation, or thrown up to the parish, by other burdens. But it is the provision with regard to the *wheels* which will create the greatest injury, distress and confusion. The wheels which this law orders to be used on turnpike-roads, on pain of enormous toll, cannot be used on the *cross-roads* throughout more than nine-tenths of the kingdom. To make these roads and the *drove-lanes* (the private roads of farms) fit for the cylindrical wheels described in this Bill, would cost a pound an acre, upon an average, upon all the land in England, and especially in the counties where the land is poorest. It would, in those counties, cost a tenth part of the worth of the fee-simple of the land. And this is enacted, too, at a time when the wagons, the carts, and all the dead stock of a farm; when the whole is falling into a state of irrepair; when all is actually perishing for want of means in the farmer to keep it in repair! This is the time that the Lord Johns and the Lord Henries and the rest of that honourable body have thought proper to enact that the whole of the farmers in England shall have new wheels to their wagons and carts, or that they shall be punished by the payment of heavier tolls! It is useless, perhaps, to say anything about the matter; but I could not help noticing a thing which has created such a general alarm amongst the farmers in every part of the country where I have recently been.

WORTH (SUSSEX),
December 2.

I set off from Reigate this morning, and after a pleasant ride of ten miles, got here to breakfast.—Here, as everywhere else, the farmers appear to think that their last hour is approaching.—Mr. *Charles B——'s farms;* I believe it is *Sir* Charles B——; and I should be sorry to withhold from him his title, though, being said to be a very good sort of a man, he might, perhaps, be able to shift without it: this gentleman's farms are subject of conversation here. The matter is curious in itself, and very well worthy of attention, as illustrative of the present state of things. These farms were, last year, taken into hand by the owner. This was stated in the public papers about a twelvemonth ago. It was said that his tenants would not take the farms again at the rent which he wished to have, and that therefore he took the farms into hand. These farms lie somewhere down in the west of Sussex. In the month of August last I saw (and I think in one of the Brighton newspapers) a paragraph stating that Mr. B——, who had taken his farms into hand the Michaelmas before, had already got in his harvest, and that he had had excellent crops! This was a sort of bragging paragraph; and there was an observation added, which implied that the farmers were great fools for not having taken the farms! We now hear that Mr. B—— has let his farms. But, now, mark how he has let them. The custom in Sussex is this; when a tenant quits a farm, he receives payment, according to valuation, for what are called the dressings, the half-dressings, for seeds and lays, and for the growth of under-wood in coppices and hedgerows; for the dung in the yards; and, in short, for whatever he leaves behind him, which, if he had staid, would have been of value to him. The dressings and half-dressings include, not only the manure that has been recently put into the land, but also the summer ploughings; and, in short, everything which has been done to the land, and the benefit of which has not been taken out again by the farmer. This is a good custom; because it ensures good tillage to the land. It ensures, also, a fair start to the new tenant; but then, observe, it requires some money, which the new tenant must pay down before he can begin, and therefore this custom presumes a pretty deal of capital to be possessed by farmers. Bearing *these* general remarks in mind, we shall see, in a moment, the case of Mr. B——. If my information be correct, he has let his farms: he has found tenants for his farms; but not tenants to pay him anything for dressings, half-dressings, and the rest. He was obliged to pay the out-going tenants for these things. Mind that! He was obliged to pay them according to the custom of the country; but he has got nothing of this sort from his in-coming tenants! It must be a poor farm, indeed, where the valuation does not amount to some hundreds of pounds. So that here is a pretty sum sunk by Mr. B——; and yet even on conditions like these, he has, I dare say, been glad to get his farms off his hands. There can be very little security for the payment of rent where the tenant pays no in-coming; but even if he get no rent at all, Mr. B—— has done well to get his farms off his hands. Now, do I wish to insinuate that Mr. B—— asked too much for his farms last year, and that he wished to squeeze the last shilling out of his farmers? By no means. He bears the character of a mild, just, and very considerate man, by no means greedy, but the contrary. A man very much beloved by his tenants; or, at least, deserving it. But the truth is, he could not believe it possible that his farms were so much fallen in value. He could not believe it possible that his estate had been taken away from him by the leger-demain of the Pitt-system, which he had been supporting all his life: so that he thought, and very naturally thought, that his old tenants were endeavouring to impose upon him, and therefore resolved to take his farms into hand. Experience has shown him that farms yield no rent, in the hands of the landlord at least; and therefore he has put them into the hands of other people. Mr. B——, like Mr. Western, has not read the *Register*. If he had, he would have taken any trifle from his old tenants, rather than let them go. But he surely might have read the speech of his neighbour and friend Mr. Huskisson, made in the House of Commons in 1814, in which that gentleman said that, with wheat at less than double the price that it bore before the war, it would be impossible for any rent at all to be paid. Mr. B—— might have read this; and he might, having so many opportunities, have asked Mr. Huskisson for an explanation of it. This gentleman is now a great advocate for *national faith ;* but may not Mr. B—— ask him whether there be no faith to be kept with the landlord? However, if I am not deceived, Mr. B—— or Sir Charles B—— (for I really do not know which it is) is a member of the Collective! If this be the case he has had something to do with the thing himself; and he must muster up as much as he can of that " patience " which is so strongly recommended by our great new state doctor, Mr. Canning.

I cannot conclude my remarks on this Rural Ride without noticing the new sort of language that I hear everywhere made use of with regard to the parsons, but which language I do not care to repeat. These men may say that I keep company with none but those who utter " sedition and blasphemy; " and if they do say so, there is just as much veracity in their words as I believe there to be charity and sincerity in the hearts of the greater part of them. One thing is certain; indeed, two things: the first is, that almost the whole of the persons that I have conversed with are farmers; and the second is, that they are in this respect all of one mind! It was my intention, at one time, to go along the south of Hampshire to Portsmouth, Fareham, Botley, Southampton, and across the New Forest into Dorsetshire. My affairs made me turn from Hambledon this way; but I had an opportunity of hearing something about the neighbourhood of Botley. Take any one considerable circle where you know everybody, and the condition of that circle will teach you how to judge pretty correctly of the condition of every other part of the country. I asked about the farmers of my old neighbourhood, one by one; and the answers I received only tended to confirm me in the opinion, that the whole race will be destroyed; and that a new race will come, and enter upon farms without capital and without stock; be a sort of bailiffs to the landlord for a while, and then, if this system go on, bailiffs to the government as trustees for the fundholders. If the account which I have received of Mr. B——'s new mode of letting be true, here is one step further than has been before taken. In all probability the stock upon the farms belongs to him, to be paid for when the tenant can pay for it. Who does not see to what this tends? The man must be blind indeed who cannot see confiscation here; and can he be much less than blind, if he imagine that relief is to be obtained by the *patience* recommended by Mr. Canning?

Thus, sir, have I led you about the country. All sorts of things have I talked of, to be sure; but there are very few of these things which have not their interest of one sort or another. At the end of a hundred miles or two of travelling, stopping here and there; talking freely with everybody. Hearing what gentlemen, farmers, tradesmen, journeymen, labourers, women, girls, boys, and all have to say; reasoning with some, laughing with others, and observing all that passes; and especially if your manner be such as to remove every kind of reserve from every class; at the end of a tramp like this, you get impressed upon your mind a true picture, not only of the state of the country, but of the state of the people's minds throughout the country. And, sir, whether you believe me or not, I have to tell you, that it is my decided opinion that the people, high and low, with one unanimous voice, except where they live upon the taxes, *impute their calamities to the House of Commons*. Whether they be right or wrong is not so much the question, in this case. That such is the fact I am certain; and, having no power to make any change myself, I must leave the making or the refusing of the change to those who have the power. I repeat, and with perfect sincerity, that it would give me as much pain as it would give to any man in England, to see a change *in the form of the government*. With *King, Lords,* and *Commons,* this nation enjoyed many ages of happiness and of glory. *Without Commons,* my opinion is, it never can again see anything but misery and shame; and when I say Commons I *mean* Commons, and, by Commons, I mean men elected by the free voice of the untitled and unprivileged part of the people, who, in fact as well as in law, are the Commons of England.

I am, sir, you most obedient and most humble servant,

WM. COBBETT.

JOURNAL

RIDE FROM KENSINGTON TO WORTH, IN SUSSEX

Monday, May 5, 1823.

FROM London to Reigate, through Sutton, is about as villainous a tract as England contains. The soil is a mixture of gravel and clay, with big yellow stones in it, sure sign of really bad land. Before you descend the hill to go into Reigate, you pass *Gatton* ("Gatton and Old Sarum"), which is a very rascally spot of earth. The trees are here a week later than they are at Tooting. At Reigate they are (in order to save a few hundred yards length of road) cutting through a hill. They have lowered a little hill on the London side of Sutton. Thus is the money of the country actually thrown away: the produce of labour is taken from the industrious, and given to the idlers. Mark the process; the town of Brighton, in Sussex, 50 miles from the Wen, is on the seaside, and is thought by the stock-jobbers to afford a *salubrious air*. It is so situated that a coach, which leaves it not very early in the morning, reaches London by noon; and, starting to go back in two hours and a half afterwards, reaches Brighton not very late at night. Great parcels of stock-jobbers stay at Brighton with the women and children. They skip backward and forward on the coaches, and actually carry on stock-jobbing, in 'Change Alley, though they reside at Brighton. This place is, besides, a place of great resort with the *whiskered* gentry. There are not less than about twenty coaches that leave the Wen every day for this place; and there being three or four different roads, there is a great rivalship for the custom. This sets the people to work to shorten and to level the roads; and here you see hundreds of men and horses constantly at work to make pleasant and quick travelling for the jews and jobbers. The jews and jobbers pay the turnpikes, to be sure; but they get the money from the land and labourer. They drain these, from John-a-Groat's House to the Land's End, and they lay out some of the money on the Brighton roads! " Vast *improvements*, ma'am!" as Mrs. *Scrip* said to Mrs. *Omnium*, in speaking of the new enclosures on the villainous heaths of Bagshot and Windsor.—Now, some will say, "Well, it is only a change from hand to hand." Very true, and if Daddy Coke of Norfolk like the change, I know not why I should dislike it. More and more new houses are building as you leave the Wen to come on this road. *Whence come* the means of building these new houses and keeping the inhabitants? Do they come out of *trade* and *commerce?* Oh, no! they come from *the land;* but if Daddy Coke like this, what has any one else to do with it? Daddy Coke and Lord Milton like "national faith;" it would be a pity to disappoint their liking. The best of this is, it will bring *down to the very dirt;* it will bring down their faces to the very earth, and fill their mouths full of sand; it will thus pull down a set of the basest lick-spittles of power and the most intolerable tyrants towards their inferiors in wealth, that the sun ever shone on. It is time that these degenerate dogs were swept away at any rate. The blackthorns are in full bloom, and make a grand show. When you quit Reigate to go towards Crawley, you enter on what is called the *Weald of Surrey*. It is a level country, and the soil a very, very strong loam, with clay beneath to a great depth. The fields are small, and about a third of the land covered with oak-woods and coppice-woods. This is a country of wheat and beans; the latter of which are about three inches high, the former about seven, and both looking very well. I did not see a field of bad-looking wheat from Reigate Hill foot to Crawley, nor from Crawley across to this place, where, though the whole country is but poorish, the wheat looks very well; and if this weather hold about twelve days, we shall recover the lost time. They have been stripping trees (taking the bark off) about five or six days. The nightingales sing very much, which is a sign of warm weather. The house-martins and the swallows are come in abundance; and they seldom do come until the weather be set in for mild.

Wednesday, 7 May.

The weather is very fine and warm; the leaves of the *Oaks* are coming out very fast: some of the trees are nearly in half-leaf. The *Birches* are out in leaf. I do not think that I ever saw the wheat look, take it all together, so well as it does at this time. I see, in the stiff land, no signs of worm or slug. The winter, which destroyed so many turnips, must, at any rate, have destroyed these mischievous things. The oats look well. The barley is very young; but I do not see anything amiss with regard to it.—The land between this place and Reigate is stiff.

How the corn may be, in other places, I know not; but, in coming down, I met with a farmer of Bedfordshire, who said that the wheat looked very well in that county; which is not a county of clay, like the Weald of Surrey. I saw a Southdown farmer, who told me that the wheat is good there, and that is a fine corn-country. The bloom of the fruit trees is the finest I ever saw in England. The pear-bloom is, at a distance, like that of the *Gueldre Rose ;* so large and bold are the bunches. The plum is equally fine; and even the blackthorn (which is the hedge-plum) has a bloom finer than I ever saw it have before. It is rather *early* to offer any opinion as to the crop of corn; but if I were compelled to bet upon it, I would bet upon a good crop. Frosts frequently come after this time; and, if they come in May, they cause " things to come about " very fast. But if we have no more frosts: in short, if we have, after this, a good summer, we shall have a fine laugh at the Quakers' and the Jews' press. Fifteen days' sun will bring *things about* in reality. The wages of labour, in the country, have taken a rise, and the poor-rates an increase, since first of March. I am glad to hear that the *Straw Bonnet* affair has excited a good deal of attention. In answer to applications upon the subject, I have to observe, that all the information on the subject will be published in the first week of June. Specimens of the *straw* and *plat* will then be to be seen at No. 183, Fleet Street.

FROM THE [LONDON] WEN ACROSS SURREY, ACROSS THE WEST OF SUSSEX, AND INTO THE SOUTH-EAST OF HAMPSHIRE

REIGATE (SURREY),
Saturday, 26 July, 1823.

CAME from the Wen, through Croydon. It rained nearly all the way. The corn is good. A great deal of straw. The barley very fine; but all are backward; and, if this weather continue much longer, there must be that " heavenly blight " for which the wise friends of " social order " are so fervently praying. But if the wet now cease, or cease soon, what is to become of the " poor souls of farmers " God only knows! In one article the wishes of our wise government appear to have been gratified to the utmost; and that, too, without the aid of any express form of prayer. I allude to the hops, of which, it is said, that there will be, according to all appearance, none at all! Bravo! Courage, my Lord Liverpool! This article, at any rate, will not choak us, will not distress us, will not make us miserable by " over-production! "—The other day a gentleman (and a man of general good sense too) said to me: " What a deal of wet we have: what do you think of the weather *now ?* "—" More rain," said I. " D—n those farmers," said he, " what luck they have! They will be as rich as Jews! "—Incredible as this may seem, it is a fact. But, indeed, there is no folly, if it relate to these matters, which is, nowadays, incredible. The hop affair is a pretty good illustration of the doctrine of " relief " from " diminished production." Mr. Ricardo may now call upon any of the hop-planters for proof of the correctness of his notions. They are ruined, for the greater part, if their all be embarked in hops. How are they to pay rent? I saw a planter, the other day, who sold his hops (Kentish) last fall for sixty shillings a hundred. The same hops will now fetch the owner of them eight pounds, or a hundred and sixty shillings.

Thus the *Quaker* gets rich, and the poor devil of a farmer is squeezed into a gaol. The *Quakers* carry on the far greater part of this work. They are, as to the products of the earth, what the *Jews* are as to gold and silver. How they profit, or, rather, the degree in which they profit, at the expense of those who own and those who till the land, may be guessed at if we look at their immense worth, and if we, at the same time, reflect that they never work. Here is a sect of non-labourers. One would think that their religion bound them under a curse not to work. Some part of the people of all other sects work; sweat at work; do something that is useful to other people; but here is a sect of buyers and sellers. They make nothing; they cause nothing to come; they breed as well as other sects; but they make none of the raiment or houses, and cause none of the food to come. In order to justify some measure for paring the nails of this grasping sect, it is enough to say of them, which we may with perfect truth, that, if all the other sects were to act like them, *the community must perish.* This is quite enough to say of this sect, of the monstrous privileges of whom we shall, I hope, one of these days, see an end. If I had the dealing with them, I would soon teach them to use the *spade* and the *plough*, and the *musket* too when necessary.

The rye, along the roadside, is ripe enough; and some of it is reaped and in shock. At Mearstam there is a field of cabbages, which, I was told, belonged to Colonel Joliffe. They appear to be early Yorks, and look very well. The rows seem to be about eighteen inches apart. There may be from 15,000 to 20,000 plants to the acre; and I dare say that they will weigh three pounds each, or more. I know of no crop of cattle food equal to this. If they be early Yorks, they will be in perfection in October, just when the grass is almost gone. No five acres of common grass land will, during the year, yield cattle food equal, either in quantity or quality, to what one acre of land, in early Yorks, will produce during three months.

WORTH (SUSSEX),
Wednesday, 30 July.

Worth is ten miles from Reigate on the Brighton road, which goes through Horley. Reigate has the Surrey chalk hills close to it on the north, and sand hills along on its south, and nearly close to it also. As soon as you are over the sand hills, you come into a country of *deep* clay; and this is called the *Weald* of Surrey. This Weald winds away round, towards the west into Sussex, and towards the east into Kent. In this part of Surrey, it is about eight miles wide, from north to south, and ends just as you enter the parish of Worth, which is the first

parish (in this part) in the county of Sussex. All across the
Weald (the strong and stiff clays) the corn looks very well. I
found it looking well from the Wen to Reigate, on the villainous
spewy soil between the Wen and Croydon; on the chalk from
Croydon to near Reigate; on the loam, sand and chalk (for there
are all three) in the valley of Reigate; but not quite so well
on the sand. On the clay all the corn looks well. The wheat,
where it has begun to die, is dying of a good colour, not black,
nor in any way that indicates blight. It is, however, all backward. Some few fields of white wheat are changing colour;
but for the greater part it is quite green; and though a sudden
change of weather might make a great alteration in a short time,
it does appear that the harvest must be later than usual. When
I say this, however, I by no means wish to be understood as
saying, that it must be so late as to be injurious to the crop.
In 1816, I saw a barleyrick making in November. In 1821, I
saw wheat uncut, in Suffolk, in October. If we were now to
have good, bright, hot weather, for as long a time as we have had
wet, the whole of the corn, in these southern counties, would be
housed, and great part of it threshed out, by the 10th of September. So that all depends on the weather, which appears
to be clearing up in spite of Saint Swithin. This saint's birthday
is the 15th of July; and it is said that, if rain fall on his birthday, it will fall on *forty days* successively. But, I believe, that
you reckon retrospectively as well as prospectively; and if this
be the case, we may, this time, escape the extreme unction;
for it began to rain on the 26th of June; so that it rained 19
days before the 15th of July; and as it has rained 16 days
since, it has rained, in the whole, 35 days, and, of course, five
days more will satisfy this wet soul of a saint. Let him take
his five days; and there will be plenty of time for us to have
wheat at four shillings a bushel. But if the saint will give us
no credit for the 19 days, and will insist upon his forty daily
drenchings *after* the fifteenth of July; if he will have such a
soaking as this at the celebration of the anniversary of his birth,
let us hope that he is prepared with a miracle for feeding us, and
with a still more potent miracle for keeping the farmers from
riding over us, filled, as Lord Liverpool thinks their pockets
will be, by the annihilation of their crops!

The upland meadow grass is, a great deal of it, not cut yet,
along the Weald. So that, in these parts, there has not been
a great deal of hay spoiled. The clover hay was got in very
well: and only a small part of the meadow hay has been spoiled

in this part of the country. This is not the case, however, in other parts, where the grass was forwarder, and where it was cut before the rain came. Upon the whole, however, much hay does not appear to have been spoiled as yet. The farmers along here, have, most of them, begun to cut to-day. This has been a fine day; and it is clear that they expect it to continue. I saw but two pieces of swedish turnips between the Wen and Reigate, but one at Reigate, and but one between Reigate and Worth. During a like distance, in Norfolk or Suffolk, you would see two or three hundred fields of this sort of root. Those that I do see here, look well. The white turnips are just up, or just sown, though there are some which have rough leaves already. This Weald is, indeed, not much of land for turnips! but from what I see here, and from what I know of the weather, I think that the turnips must be generally good. The after-grass is surprisingly fine. The lands, which have had hay cut and carried from them, are, I think, more *beautiful* than I ever saw them before. It should, however, always be borne in mind, that this *beautiful* grass is by no means the *best*. An acre of this grass will not make a quarter part so much butter as an acre of rusty-looking pasture, made rusty by the rays of the sun. Sheep on the commons *die* of the *beautiful* grass produced by long-continued rains at this time of the year. Even geese, hardy as they are, die from the same cause. The rain will give quantity, but without sun the quality must be poor at the best. The woods have not shot much this year. The cold winds, the frosts, that we had up to midsummer, prevented the trees from growing much. They are beginning to shoot now; but the wood must be imperfectly ripened.

I met, at Worth, a beggar who told me, in consequence of my asking where he belonged, that he was born in South Carolina. I found, at last, that he was born in the English army, during the American rebel-war; that he became a soldier himself; and that it had been his fate to serve under the Duke of York, in Holland; under General Whitelock, at Buenos Ayres; under Sir John Moore, at Corunna; and under " the Greatest Captain," at Talavera! This poor fellow did not seem to be at all aware that, in the last case, he partook in *a victory!* He had never before heard of its being a victory. He, poor fool, thought that it was a *defeat.* "Why," said he, " we *ran away*, sir." Oh, yes! said I, and so you did afterwards, perhaps, in Portugal, when Massena was at your heels; but it is only in certain cases that running away is a mark of being defeated; or, rather, it is only with certain commanders. A matter of much more interest to us, however, is, that the wars for " social order," not forgetting Gatton and Old Sarum, have filled the country with beggars, who have been, or who pretend to have been, soldiers and sailors. For want of looking well into this matter, many good and just, and even sensible men are led to give to these army and navy beggars what they refuse to others. But if reason were consulted, she would ask what pretensions these have to a preference? She would see in them men who had become soliders or sailors because they wished to live without that labour by which other men are content to get their bread. She would ask the soldier beggar whether he did not voluntarily engage to perform services such as were performed at Manchester; and if she pressed him for *the motive* to this engagement, could he assign any motive other than that of wishing to live without work upon the fruit of the work of other men? And why should reason not be listened to? Why should she not be consulted in every such case? And, if she were consulted, which would she tell you was the most worthy of your compassion, the man, who, no matter from what cause, is become a beggar after forty years spent in the raising of food and raiment for others as well as for himself; or the man who, no matter again from what cause, is become a beggar after forty years living upon the labour of others, and, during the greater part of which time, he has been living in a barrack, there kept for purposes explained by Lord Palmerston, and always in readiness to answer those purposes? As to not giving to beggars, I think there is a law against giving! However, give to them people will, as long as they ask. Remove the *cause* of the beggary and we shall see no more beggars; but as long as there are *boroughmongers*, there will be beggars enough.

HORSHAM (SUSSEX),
Thursday, 31 *July*.

I left Worth this afternoon about 5 o'clock, and am got here to sleep, intending to set off for Petworth in the morning, with a view of crossing the South Downs and then going into Hampshire through Havant, and along at the southern foot of Portsdown Hill, where I shall see the earliest corn in England. From Worth you come to Crawley along some pretty good land; you then turn to the left and go two miles along the road from the Wen to Brighton; then you turn to the right, and go over six of the worst miles in England, which miles terminate but a few hundred yards before you enter Horsham. The first two of these miserable miles go through the estate of Lord Erskine. It was a bare heath with here and there, in the better parts of it, some scrubby birch. It has been, in part, planted with fir-trees, which are as ugly as the heath was: and, in short, it is a most villainous tract. After quitting it, you enter a forest; but a most miserable one; and this is followed by a large common, now enclosed, cut up, disfigured, spoiled, and the labourers all driven from its skirts. I have seldom travelled over eight miles so well calculated to fill the mind with painful reflections. The ride has, however, this in it: that the ground *is* pretty much elevated, and enables you to look about you. You see the Surrey hills away to the north; Hindhead and Blackdown to the north-west and west; and the South Downs from the west to the east. The sun was shining upon all these, though it was cloudy where I was. The soil is a poor, miserable, clayey-looking sand, with a sort of sandstone underneath. When you get down into this town, you are again in the Weald of Sussex. I believe that *Weald* meant *clay*, or low, wet, stiff land. This is a very nice, solid, country town. Very clean, as all the towns in Sussex are. The people very clean. The Sussex women are very nice in their dress and in their houses. The men and boys wear smock-frocks more than they do in some counties. When country people do not they always look dirty and comfortless. This has been a pretty good day; but there was a little rain in the afternoon; so that St. Swithin keeps on as yet, at any rate. The hay has been spoiled here, in cases where it has been cut; but a great deal of it is not yet cut. I speak of the meadows; for the clover-hay was all well got in. The grass, which is not cut, is receiving great injury. It is, in fact, in many cases, rotting upon the ground. As to corn, from Crawley to Horsham, there is none worth speaking of. What there is is very good, in general, considering the quality of the soil. It is about as backward as at Worth: the barley and oats green, and the wheat beginning to change colour.

BILLINGSHURST (SUSSEX),
Friday Morning, 1 *Aug.*

This village is 7 miles from Horsham, and I got here to break-fast about seven o'clock. A very pretty village, and a very nice breakfast, in a very neat little parlour of a very decent public-house. The landlady sent her son to get me some cream, and he was just such a chap as I was at his age, and dressed just in the same sort of way, his main garment being a blue smock-frock, faded from wear, and mended with pieces of *new* stuff, and, of course, not faded. The sight of this smock-frock brought to my recollection many things very dear to me. This boy will, I dare say, perform his part at Billingshurst, or at some place not far from it. If accident had not taken me from a similar scene, how many villains and fools, who have been well teased and tormented, would have slept in peace at night, and have fearlessly swaggered about by day! When I look at this little chap; at his smock-frock, his nailed shoes, and his clean, plain, and coarse shirt, I ask myself, will anything, I wonder, ever send this chap across the ocean to tackle the base, corrupt, perjured Republican judges of Pennsylvania? Will this little lively, but, at the same time, simple boy, ever become the terror of villains and hypocrites across the Atlantic? What a chain of strange circumstances there must be to lead this boy to thwart a miscreant tyrant like Mackeen, the chief justice and afterwards governor of Pennsylvania, and to expose the corruptions of the band of rascals, called a "Senate and a House of Representatives," at Harrisburgh, in that state!

I was afraid of rain, and got on as fast as I could: that is to say, as fast as my own diligence could help me on; for as to my horse, he is to go only *so fast*. However, I had no rain; and got to Petworth, nine miles further, by about ten o'clock.

PETWORTH (SUSSEX),
Friday Evening, 1 *Aug.*

No rain, until just at sunset, and then very little. I must now look back. From Horsham to within a few miles of Petworth is in the Weald of Sussex; stiff land, small fields, broad hedgerows, and, invariably, thickly planted with fine, growing oak trees. The corn here consists chiefly of wheat and oats. There are some bean-fields, and some few fields of peas; but very little barley along here. The corn is very good all along the Weald; backward; the wheat almost green; the oats quite green; but, late as it is, I see no blight; and the farmers tell me that there is no blight. There may be yet, however; and, therefore, our government, our "*paternal* government," so anxious to prevent "over production," need not *despair*, as yet, at any rate. The beans in the Weald are not very good. They got lousy before the wet came; and it came rather too late to make them recover what they had lost. What peas there are look well. Along here the wheat, in general, may be fit to cut in about 16 days' time; some sooner; but some later, for some is perfectly green. No swedish turnips all along this country. The white turnips are just up, coming up, or just sown. The farmers are laying out lime upon the wheat fallows, and this is the universal practice of the country. I see very few sheep. There are a good many orchards along in the Weald, and they have some apples this year; but, in general, not many. The apple trees are planted very thickly, and, of course, they are small; but they appear healthy in general; and, in some places, there is a good deal of fruit, even this year. As you approach Petworth, the ground rises and the soil grows lighter. There is a hill which I came over, about two miles from Petworth, whence I had a clear view of the Surrey chalk-hills, Leith Hill, Hindhead, Blackdown, and of the South Downs, towards one part of which I was advancing. The pigs along here are all black, thin-haired, and of precisely the same sort of those that I took from England to Long Island, and with which I pretty well stocked the American States. By the by, the trip which Old Sidmouth and crew gave me to America was attended with some interesting consequences; amongst which were the introducing of the Sussex pigs into the American farm-yards; the introduction of the swedish turnip into the American fields; the introduction of American apple-trees into England; and the introduction of the making, in England, of the straw plat, to supplant the Italian; for had my son not been in America, this last would not have taken place; and in America he would not have been, had it not been for Old Sidmouth and crew. One thing more, and that is of more importance than all the rest, Peel's Bill arose out of the " puff-out " Registers; these arose out of the trip to Long Island; and out of Peel's Bill has arisen the best bothering that the wigs of the boroughmongers ever received, which bothering will end in the destruction of the boroughmongering. It is curious, and very *useful*, thus to trace events to their causes.

Soon after quitting Billingshurst I crossed the river Arun, which has a canal running alongside of it. At this there are large timber and coal yards, and kilns for lime. This appears to be a grand receiving and distributing place. The river goes down to Arundale, and, together with the valley that it runs through, gives the town its name. This valley, which is very

pretty, and which winds about a good deal, is the dale of the
Arun: and the town is the town of the Arun-dale. To-day,
near a place called Westborough Green, I saw a woman bleaching
her home-spun and home-woven linen. I have not seen such
a thing before, since I left Long Island. There, and, indeed,
all over the American States, north of Maryland, and especially
in the New England States, almost the whole of both linen and
woollen, used in the country, and a large part of that used in
towns, is made in the farm-houses. There are thousands and
thousands of families who never use either, except of their own
making. All but the weaving is done by the family. There
is a loom in the house, and the weaver goes from house to house.
I once saw about three thousand farmers, or rather country
people, at a horse race in Long Island, and my opinion was,
that there were not five hundred who were not dressed in home-
spun coats. As to linen, no farmer's family thinks of buying
linen. The lords of the loom have taken from the land, in
England, this part of its due; and hence one cause of the
poverty, misery, and pauperism that are becoming so frightful
throughout the country. A national debt, and all the taxation
and gambling belonging to it, have a natural tendency to draw
wealth into great masses. These masses produce a power of
congregating manufactures, and of making the many work at
them, for the *gain of a few*. The taxing government finds great
convenience in these congregations. It can lay its hand easily
upon a part of the produce; as ours does with so much effect.
But the land suffers greatly from this, and the country must
finally feel the fatal effects of it. The country people lose part
of their natural employment. The women and children, who
ought to provide a great part of the raiment, have nothing to
do. The fields *must* have men and boys; but where there are
men and boys there will be *women* and *girls ;* and as the lords
of the loom have now a set of real slaves, by the means of whom
they take away a great part of the employment of the country-
women and girls, these must be kept by poor rates in whatever
degree they lose employment through the lords of the loom.
One would think that nothing can be much plainer than this;
and yet you hear the *jolterheads* congratulating one another
upon the increase of Manchester, and such places! My straw
affair will certainly restore to the land some of the employment
of its women and girls. It will be impossible for any of the
" rich ruffians; " any of the horse-power or steam-power or air-
power ruffians; any of these greedy, grinding ruffians, to draw

together bands of men, women and children, and to make them slaves, in the working of straw. The raw material comes of itself, and the hand, and the hand alone, can convert it to use. I thought well of this before I took one single step in the way of supplanting the Leghorn bonnets. If I had not been certain that no rich ruffian, no white slave holder, could ever arise out of it, assuredly one line upon the subject never would have been written by me. Better, a million times, that the money should go to Italy; better that it should go to enrich even the rivals and enemies of the country; than that it should enable these hard, these unfeeling men, to draw English people into crowds and make them slaves, and slaves too of the lowest and most degraded cast.

As I was coming into this town I saw a new-fashioned sort of stone-cracking. A man had a sledge-hammer, and was cracking the heads of the big stones that had been laid on the road a good while ago. This is a very good way; but this man told me that he was set at this, because the farmers had *no employment* for many of the men. " Well," said I, " but they pay you to do this!" " Yes," said he. " Well, then," said I, " is it not better for them to pay you for working *on their land ?* " " I can't tell, indeed, sir, how that is." But only think; here is half the haymaking to do: I saw, while I was talking to this man, fifty people in one hay-field of Lord Egremont, making and carrying hay; and yet, at a season like this, the farmers are so poor as to be unable to pay the labourers to work on the land! From this cause there will certainly be some falling off in production. This will, of course, have a tendency to keep prices from falling so low as they would do if there were no falling off. But can this *benefit* the farmer and landlord? The poverty of the farmers is seen in their diminished stock. The animals are sold *younger* than formerly. Last year was a year of great slaughtering. There will be less of everything produced; and the quality of each thing will be worse. It will be a lower and more mean concern altogether. Petworth is a nice market town, but solid and clean. The great abundance of *stone* in the land hereabouts has caused a corresponding liberality in paving and wall-building, so that everything of the building kind has an air of great strength, and produces the agreeable idea of durability. Lord Egremont's house is close to the town, and with its out-buildings, garden walls, and other erections, is, perhaps, nearly as big as the town; though the town is not a very small one. The park is very fine, and consists of a parcel of those hills and dells which

Nature formed here when she was in one of her most sportive modes. I have never seen the earth flung about in such a wild way as round about Hindhead and Blackdown; and this park forms a part of this ground. From an elevated part of it, and indeed, from each of many parts of it, you see all around the country to the distance of many miles. From the south-east to the north-west, the hills are so lofty and so near, that they cut the view rather short; but for the rest of the circle, you can see to a very great distance. It is, upon the whole, a most magnificent seat, and the Jews will not be able to get it from the *present* owner; though, if he live many years, they will give even him a *twist*. If I had time, I would make an actual survey of one whole county, and find out how many of the old gentry have lost their estates, and have been supplanted by the Jews, since Pitt began his reign. I am sure I should prove that, in number, they are one-half extinguished. But it is *now* that they go. The little ones are, indeed, gone; and the rest will follow in proportion as the present farmers are exhausted. These will keep on giving rents as long as they can beg or borrow the money to pay rents with. But a little more time will so completely exhaust them, that they will be unable to pay; and as that takes place, the landlords will lose their estates. Indeed many of them, and even a large portion of them, have, in fact, no estates now. They are *called* theirs; but the mortgagees and annuitants receive the rents. As the rents fall off, sales must take place, unless in cases of entails; and if this thing go on, we shall see acts passed to *cut off entails*, in order that the Jews may be put into full possession. Such, thus far, will be the result of our "glorious victories" over the French! Such will be, in part, the price of the deeds of Pitt, Addington, Perceval and their successors. For having applauded such deeds; for having boasted of the Wellesleys; for having bragged of battles won by *money* and by money *only*, the nation deserves that which it will receive; and as to the landlords, they, above all men living, deserve punishment. They put the power into the hands of Pitt and his crew to torment the people; to keep the people down; to raise soldiers and to build barracks for this purpose. These base landlords laughed when affairs like that of Manchester took place. They laughed at the *Blanketteers*. They laughed when Canning jested about Ogden's rupture. Let them, therefore, now take the full benefit of the measures of Pitt and his crew. They would fain have us believe that the calamities they endure do not arise from the acts of the government.

What do they arise from, then? The Jacobins did not contract the *Debt* of £800,000,000 sterling. The Jacobins did not create a *dead weight* of £150,000,000. The Jacobins did not cause a pauper-charge of £200,000,000 by means of "new inclosure bills," "vast improvements," paper-money, potatoes, and other "proofs of prosperity." The Jacobins did not do these things. And will the government pretend that "Providence" did it? That would be "blasphemy" indeed. — Poh! These things are the price of efforts to crush freedom in France, *lest the example of France should produce a reform in England*. These things are the price of that undertaking; which, however, has not yet been crowned with *success*; for the question is *not yet decided*. They boast of their victory over the French. The Pitt crew boast of their achievements in the war. They boast of the battle of Waterloo. Why! what fools could not get the same, or the like, if they had as much *money* to get it with? Shooting with *a silver gun* is a saying amongst game-eaters. That is to say, *purchasing* the game. A waddling, fat fellow that does not know how to prime and load, will, in this way, beat the best shot in the country. And this is the way that our crew "beat" the people of France. They laid out, in the first place, six hundred millions which they borrowed, and for which they mortgaged the revenues of the nation. Then they contracted for a "dead weight" to the amount of one hundred and fifty millions. Then they stripped the labouring classes of the commons, of their kettles, their bedding, their beer-barrels; and, in short, made them all paupers, and thus fixed on the nation a permanent annual charge of about 8 or 9 millions, or, a gross debt of £200,000,000. By these means, by these anticipations, our crew did what they thought would keep down the French nation for ages; and what they were sure would, for the present, enable them to keep up the *tithes* and other things of the same sort in England. But the crew did not reflect on the *consequences* of the anticipations! Or at least the landlords, who gave the crew their power, did not thus reflect. These consequences are now come, and are coming; and that must be a base man indeed, who does not see them with pleasure.

SINGLETON (SUSSEX),
Saturday, 2 Aug.

Ever since the middle of March, I have been trying remedies for the *hooping-cough*, and have, I believe, tried everything, except riding, wet to the skin, two or three hours amongst the clouds on the South Downs. This remedy is now under trial. As Lord Liverpool said, the other day, of the Irish Tithe Bill, it is "under experiment." I am treating my disorder (with better success I hope) in somewhat the same way that the pretty fellows at Whitehall treat the disorders of poor Ireland. There is one thing in favour of this remedy of mine, I shall *know* the effect of it, and that, too, in a short time. It rained a little last night. I got off from Petworth without baiting my horse, thinking that the weather looked suspicious, and that St. Swithin meant to treat me to a dose. I had no greatcoat, nor any means of changing my clothes. The hooping-cough made me anxious; but I had fixed on going along the South Downs from Donnington-hill down to Lavant, and then to go on the flat to the south foot of Portsdown-hill, and to reach Fareham to-night. Two men, whom I met soon after I set off, assured me that it would not rain. I came on to Donnington, which lies at the foot of that part of the South Downs which I had to go up. Before I came to this point, I crossed the Arun and its canal again; and here was another place of deposit for timber, lime, coals, and other things. White, in his history of Selborne, mentions a hill, which is one of the Hindhead group, from which two springs (one on each side of the hill) send water into the two *seas* : the *Atlantic* and the *German Ocean !* This is big talk; but it is a fact. One of the streams becomes the *Arun*, which falls into the Channel; and the other, after winding along amongst the hills and hillocks between Hindhead and Godalming, goes into the river *Wey*, which falls into the Thames at Weybridge. The soil upon leaving Petworth, and at Petworth, seems very good; a fine deep loam, a sort of mixture of sand and soft chalk. I then came to a sandy common; a piece of ground that seemed to have no business there; it looked as if it had been tossed from Hindhead or Blackdown. The common, however, during the rage for "improvements," has been *inclosed*. That impudent fellow, Old Rose, stated the number of Inclosure Bills as an indubitable proof of "national prosperity." There was some *rye* upon this common, the sight of which would have gladdened the heart of Lord Liverpool. It was, in parts, not more than eight inches high. It was ripe, and, of course, the straw dead; or I should have found out the owner, and have bought it to make *bonnets* of ! I defy the Italians to grow worse rye than this. The reader will recollect that I always said that we could grow *as poor* corn as any Italians that ever lived.

The village of Donton lies at the foot of one of these great chalk ridges, which are called the South Downs. The ridge, in this place, is, I think, about three-fourths of a mile high, by the high road, which is obliged to go twisting about, in order to get to the top of it. The hill sweeps round from about west-north-west to east-south-east; and, of course, it keeps off all the heavy winds, and especially the south-west winds, before which, in this part of England (and all the south and western part of it), even the oak trees seem as if they would gladly flee; from it shaves them up as completely as you see a quickset hedge shaved by hook or shears. Talking of hedges reminds me of having seen a box-hedge, just as I came out of Petworth, more than twelve feet broad, and about fifteen feet high. I dare say it is several centuries old. I think it is about forty yards long. It is a great curiosity.

The apple trees at Donnington show their gratitude to the hill for its shelter; for I have seldom seen apple trees in England so large, so fine, and, in general, so flourishing. I should like to have, or to see, an orchard of American apples under this hill. The hill, you will observe, does not shade the ground at Donnington. It slopes too much for that. But it affords complete shelter from the mischievous winds. It is very pretty to look down upon this little village as you come winding up the hill.

From this hill I ought to have had a most extensive view. I ought to have seen the Isle of Wight and the sea before me; and to have looked back to Chalk Hill at Reigate, at the foot of which I had left some bonnet-grass bleaching. But, alas! *Saint Swithin* had begun his works for the day, before I got to the top of the hill. Soon after the two turnip-hoers had assured me that there would be no rain, I saw, beginning to poke up over the South Downs (then right before me), several parcels of those white, curled clouds, that we call *Judges' Wigs*. And they are just like judges' wigs. Not the *parson-like* things which the judges wear when they have to listen to the dull wrangling and duller jests of the lawyers; but those *big* wigs which hang down about their shoulders, when they are about to tell you a little of *their intentions,* and when their very looks say, "*Stand clear!*" These clouds (if rising from the south-west) hold precisely the same language to the great-coatless traveller. Rain is *sure* to follow them. The sun was shining very beautifully when I first saw these judges' wigs rising over the hills. At the sight of them he soon began to hide his face!

and before I got to the top of the hill of Donton, the white clouds had become black, had spread themselves all around, and a pretty decent and sturdy rain began to fall. I had resolved to come to this place (Singleton) to breakfast. I quitted the turn-pike road (from Petworth to Chichester) at a village called Up-waltham, about a mile from Donnington Hill; and came down a lane, which led me first to a village called Eastdean; then to another called Westdean, I suppose; and then to this village of Singleton, and here I am on the turnpike road from Midhurst to Chichester. The lane goes along through some of the finest farms in the world. It is impossible for corn land and for agriculture to be finer than these. In cases like mine, you are pestered to death to find out the way to *set out* to get from place to place. The people you have to deal with are innkeepers, ostlers, and post-boys; and they think you mad if you express your wish to avoid turnpike roads; and a great deal more than half mad, if you talk of going, even from necessity, by any other road. They think you a strange fellow if you will not ride six miles on a turnpike road rather than two on any other road. This plague I experienced on this occasion. I wanted to go from Petworth to Havant. My way was through Single-ton and Funtington. I had no business at Chichester, which took me too far to the south. Nor at Midhurst, which took me too far to the west. But though I staid all day (after my arrival) at Petworth, and though I slept there, I could get no directions how to set out to come to Singleton, where I am now. I started, therefore, on the Chichester road, trusting to my inquiries of the country people as I came on. By these means I got hither, down a long valley, on the South Downs, which valley winds and twists about amongst hills, some higher and some lower, forming cross dells, inlets, and ground in such a variety of shapes that it is impossible to describe; and the whole of the ground, hill as well as dell, is fine, most beautiful, corn land, or is covered with trees or underwood. As to St. Swithin, I set him at defiance. The road was flinty, and very flinty. I rode a foot pace, and got here wet to the skin. I am very glad I came this road. The corn is all fine; all good; fine crops, and no appearance of blight. The barley extremely fine. The corn not forwarder than in the Weald. No beans here; few oats comparatively; chiefly wheat and barley; but great quantities of swedish turnips, and those very forward. More swedish turnips here upon one single farm than upon all the farms that I saw between the Wen and Petworth. These turnips are, in some places, a foot high, and nearly cover the ground. The farmers are, however, plagued by this St. Swithin, who keeps up a continual drip, which prevents the thriving of the turnips and the killing of the weeds. The *orchards* are good here in general. Fine walnut trees, and an abundant crop of walnuts. This is a series of villages all belonging to the Duke of Richmond, the outskirts of whose park and woods come up to these farming lands, all of which belong to him; and I suppose that every inch of land that I came through this morning belongs either to the Duke of Richmond or to Lord Egremont. No *harm* in that, mind, if those who till the land have *fair play ;* and I should act unjustly towards these noblemen, if I insinuated that the husbandmen have not fair play, as far as the landlords are concerned; for everybody speaks well of them. There is, besides, *no misery* to be seen here. I have seen no wretchedness in Sussex; nothing to be at all compared to that which I have seen in other parts; and as to these villages in the South Downs, they are beautiful to behold. Hume and other historians rail against the *feudal*-system; and we, " enlightened " and " free " creatures as we are, look back with scorn, or, at least, with surprise and pity, to the " vassalage " of our forefathers. But if the matter were well inquired into, not slurred over, but well and truly examined, we should find, that the people of these villages were *as free* in the days of William Rufus as are the people of the present day; and that vassalage, only under other names, exists now as completely as it existed then. Well; but out of this, if true, arises another question: namely, Whether the millions would derive any benefit from being transferred from these great lords who possess them by hundreds, to Jews and jobbers who would possess them by half-dozens, or by couples? One thing we may say with a certainty of being right: and that is, that the transfer would be bad for the lords themselves. There is an appearance of comfort about the dwellings of the labourers, all along here, that is very pleasant to behold. The gardens are neat, and full of vegetables of the best kinds. I see very few of " Ireland's lazy root; " and never, in this country, will the people be base enough to lie down and expire from starvation under the operation of the *extreme unction !* Nothing but a *potato-eater* will ever do that. As I came along between Upwaltham and Eastdean, I called to me a young man, who, along with other turnip-hoers, was sitting under the shelter of a hedge at breakfast. He came running to me with his victuals in his hand; and I was glad to see that his food consisted of a good lump of household bread and not a very small piece of *bacon*. I did not envy him his appetite, for I had at that moment a very good one of my own; but I wanted to know the distance I had to go before I should get to a good public-house. In parting with him, I said, " You do get some *bacon* then? " " Oh, yes! sir," said he, and with an emphasis and a swag of the head which seemed to say, " We *must* and *will* have *that.*" I saw, and with great delight, a pig at almost every labourer's house. The houses are good and warm; and the gardens some of the very best that I have seen in England. What a difference, good God! what a difference between this country and the neighbourhood of those corrupt places *Great Bedwin* and *Cricklade*. What sort of *breakfast* would this man have had in a mess of *cold potatoes ?* Could he have *worked*, and worked in the wet, too, with such food? Monstrous! No society ought to exist where the labourers live in a hog-like sort of way. The *Morning Chronicle* is everlastingly asserting the mischievous consequences of the want of *enlightening* these people " *i' th a sooth ;* " and telling us how well they are off in the north. Now, this I know, that in the north, the " enlightened " people eat *sowens, burgoo, porridge,* and *potatoes :* that is to say, *oatmeal and water*, or the root of *extreme unction*. If this be the effect of their *light*, give me the *darkness* " o' th a s⸗oth." This is according to what I have heard. If, when I go to the north, I find the labourers *eating more meat* than those of the " sooth," I shall then say that " enlightening " is a very good thing; but give me none of that " light," or of that " grace," which makes a man content with oatmeal and water, or that makes him patiently lie down and die of starvation amidst abundance of food. The *Morning Chronicle* hears the labourers crying out in Sussex. They are right to cry out in time. When they are actually brought down to the extreme unction, it is useless to cry out. And next to the extreme unction is the *porridge* of the " enlightened " slaves who toil in the factories for the lords of the loom. Talk of *vassals !* Talk of *villains !* Talk of *serfs !* Are there any of these, or did feudal times ever see any of them, so debased, so absolutely slaves, as the poor creatures who, in the " enlightened " north, are compelled to work fourteen hours in a day, in a heat of eighty-four degrees; and who are liable to punishment for looking out at a window of the factory!

This is really a soaking day, thus far. I got here at nine o'clock. I stripped off my coat, and put it by the kitchen fire. In a parlour just eight feet square I have another fire, and have dried my shirt on my back. We shall see what this does for a hooping cough. The clouds fly so low as to be seen passing by the sides of even little hills on these downs. The Devil is said to be busy in a *high* wind; but he really appears to be busy now in this south-west wind. The Quakers will, next market day, at Mark Lane, be as busy as he. They and the ministers and St. Swithin and Devil all seem to be of a mind.

I must not forget the *churches*. That of Donnington is very small, for a church. It is about twenty feet wide and thirty long. It is, however, sufficient for the population, the amount of which is two hundred and twenty-two, not one half of whom are, of course, ever at church at one time. There is, however, plenty of room for the whole: the " tower " of this church is about double the size of a *sentry-box*. The parson, whose name is Davidson, did not, when the return was laid before Parliament, in 1818, reside in the parish. Though the living is a large living, the parsonage house was let to " a lady and her three daughters." What impudence a man must have to put this into a return! The church at Upwaltham is about such another, and the " tower " still less than that at Donnington. Here the population is seventy-nine. The parish is a rectory, and, in the return before mentioned, the parson (whose name was Tripp), says, that the church will hold the population, but that the parsonage house will not hold him! And why? Because it is " a miserable cottage." I looked about for this " miserable cottage," and could not find it. What an impudent fellow this must have been! And, indeed, what a state of impudence have they not now arrived at! Did he, when he was ordained, talk anything about a fine house to live in? Did Jesus Christ and Saint Paul talk about fine houses? Did not this priest most solemnly vow to God, upon the altar, that he would be constant, in season and out of season, in watching over the souls of his flock? However, it is useless to remonstrate with this set of men. Nothing will have any effect upon them. They will keep grasping at the tithes as long as they can reach them. " A *miserable cottage !* " What impudence! What, Mr. Tripp, is it a fine house that you have been appointed and ordained to live in? Lord Egremont is the patron of Mr. Tripp; and he has a *duty* to perform too; for the living is *not his*: he is, in this case, only an hereditary *trustee* for the public; and he ought to see that this parson resides in the parish, which, according to his own return, yields him £125 a year. Eastdean is a vicarage, with a population of 353, a church which the parson says will hold 200, and which I say will hold 600 or 700, and a living worth £85 a year, in the gift of the Bishop of Chichester.

Westdean is united with Singleton, the living is in the gift of the church at Chichester and the Duke of Richmond alternately; it is a large living, it has a population of 613, and the two churches, says the parson, will hold 200 people! What careless, or what impudent fellows these must have been. These two churches will hold a thousand people, packed much less close than they are in meeting houses.

At Upwaltham there is a toll gate, and, when the woman opened the door of the house to come and let me through, I saw some *straw plat* lying in a chair. She showed it me; and I found that it was made by her husband, in the evenings, after he came home from work, in order to make him a hat for the harvest. I told her how to get better straw for the purpose; and when I told her that she must cut the grass, or the grain, *green*, she said, " Aye, I dare say it is so: and I wonder we never thought of that before; for we sometimes make hats out of rushes, cut green, and dried, and the hats are very durable." This woman ought to have my *Cottage Economy*. She keeps the toll-gate at Upwaltham, which is called Waltham, and which is on the turnpike road from Petworth to Chichester. Now, if any gentleman, who lives at Chichester, will call upon my son, at the office of the *Register* in Fleet Street, and ask for a copy of *Cottage Economy*, to be given to this woman, he will receive the copy, and my thanks, if he will have the goodness to give it to her, and to point to her the Essay on Straw Plat.

FAREHAM (HANTS),
Saturday, 2 August.

Here I am in spite of St. Swithin!—The truth is, that the saint is like most other oppressors; *rough* him! *rough* him! and he relaxes. After drying myself, and sitting the better part of four hours at Singleton, I started in the rain, boldly setting the saint at defiance, and expecting to have not one dry thread by the time I got to Havant, which is nine miles from Fareham, and four from Cosham. To my most agreeable surprise, the rain ceased before I got by Selsey, I suppose it is called, where Lord Selsey's house and beautiful and fine estate is. On I went, turning off to the right to go to Funtington and Westbourn, and getting to Havant to bait my horse, about four o'clock.

From Lavant (about two miles back from Funtington) the ground begins to be a sea-side flat. The soil is somewhat varied in quality and kind; but, with the exception of an enclosed common between Funtington and Westbourn, it is all good soil. The corn of all kinds good and earlier than further back. They have begun cutting peas here, and, near Lavant, I saw a field of wheat nearly ripe. The swedish turnips very fine, and still earlier than on the South Downs. Prodigicus crops of walnuts; but the apples bad along here. The south-west winds have cut them off; and, indeed, how should it be otherwise, if these winds happen to prevail in May, or early in June?

On the new enclosure near Funtington, the wheat and oats are both nearly ripe.

In a new enclosure, near Westbourn, I saw the only really blighted wheat that I have yet seen this year. "Oh!" exclaimed I, "that my Lord Liverpool; that my much respected stern-path-of-duty-man could but see that wheat, which God and the seedsman intended to be *white ;* but which the Devil (listening to the prayers of the Quakers) has made *black !* Oh! could but my lord see it, lying flat upon the ground, with the May-weed and the couch-grass pushing up through it, and with a whole flock of rooks pecking away at its ears! Then would my much valued lord say, indeed, that the 'difficulties' of agriculture are about to receive the 'greatest abatement!'"

But now I come to one of the great objects of my journey: that is to say, to see the state of the corn along at the south foot and on the south side of Portsdown Hill. It is impossible that there can be, anywhere, a better corn country than this. The hill is eight miles long, and about three-fourths of a mile high, beginning at the road that runs along at the foot of the hill. On the hill-side the corn land goes rather better than half way up; and, on the sea-side, the corn land is about the third (it may be half) a mile wide. Portsdown Hill is very much in the shape of an oblong tin cover to a dish. From Bedhampton, which lies at the eastern end of the hill, to Fareham, which is at the western end of it, you have brought under your eye not less than eight square miles of corn fields, with scarcely a hedge or ditch of any consequence, and being, on an average, from twenty to forty acres each in extent. The land is excellent. The situation good for manure. The spot the *earliest in the whole kingdom.* Here, if the corn were backward, then the harvest must be backward. We were talking at Reigate of the prospect of a backward harvest. I observed that it was a rule that if no *wheat were cut* under Portsdown Hill on the hill *fair-day*, 26th July, the harvest must be generally backward. When I made this observation, the fair-day was passed; but I determined in my mind to come and see how the matter stood. When, therefore, I got to the village of Bedhampton, I began to look out pretty sharply. I came on to Wimmering, which is just about the mid-way along the foot of the hill, and there I saw, at a good distance from me, five men reaping in a field of wheat of about 40 acres. I found, upon inquiry, that they began this morning, and that the wheat belongs to Mr. Boniface, of Wimmering. Here the first sheaf is cut that is cut in England: that the reader may depend upon. It was never known that the average even of Hampshire was less than ten days behind the average of Portsdown Hill. The corn under the hill is as good as I ever saw it, except in the year 1813. No beans here. No peas. Scarcely any oats. Wheat, barley, and turnips. The swedish turnips not so good as on the South Downs and near Funtington; but the wheat full as good, rather better; and the barley as good as it is possible to be. In looking at these crops, one wonders whence are to come the hands to clear them off.

A very pleasant ride to-day; and the pleasanter for my having set the wet saint at defiance. It is about thirty miles from Petworth to Fareham; and I got in in very good time. I have now come, if I include my *boltings*, for the purpose of looking at farms and woods, a round hundred miles from the Wen to this town of Fareham; and, in the whole of the hundred miles, I have not seen one single wheat rick, though I have come through as fine corn countries as any in England, and by the homesteads of the richest of farmers. Not one single wheat rick have I seen, and not one rick of any sort of corn. I never saw, nor heard of the like of this before; and if I had not witnessed the fact with my own eyes I could not have believed it. There are some farmers who have corn in their barns perhaps; but when there is no *rick* left, there is very little corn in the hands of farmers. Yet the markets, St. Swithin notwithstanding, do not rise. This harvest must be three weeks later than usual; and the last harvest was three weeks earlier than usual. The last crop was begun upon at once, on account of the badness of the wheat of the year before. So that the last crop will have had to give food for thirteen months and a half. And yet the markets do not rise! And yet there are men, farmers, mad enough to think, that they have " got past the bad place," and that things will come about, and are coming about! And Lethbridge, of the Collective, withdraws his motion because he has got what he wanted: namely, a return of good and "*remunerating* prices!" The *Morning Chronicle* of this day, which has met me at this place, has the following paragraph. "The weather is much improved, though it does not yet assume the character of being fine. At the Corn Exchange since Monday the arrivals consist of 7130 quarters of wheat, 450 quarters of barley, 8300 quarters of oats, and 9200 sacks of flour. The demand for wheat is next to zero, and for oats it is extremely dull. To effect sales, prices are not much attended to, for the demand cannot be increased at the present currency. The farmers should pay attention to oats, for the foreign new, under the king's lock, will be brought into consumption, unless a decline takes place immediately, and a weight will thereby be thrown over the markets, which under existing circumstances will be extremely detrimental to the agricultural interests. Its distress however does not deserve much sympathy, for as soon as there was a prospect of the payment of rents, the cause of the people was abandoned by the representatives of agriculture in the Collected Wisdom, and Mr. Brougham's most excellent measure for increasing the consumption of malt was neglected. Where there is no sympathy, none can be expected, and the land proprietors need not in future depend on the assistance of the mercantile and manufacturing interests, should their own distress again require a united effort to remedy the general grievances." As to the mercantile and manufacturing people, what is the land to expect from them? But I agree with the *Chronicle*, that the landlords deserve ruin. They abandoned the public cause the moment they thought that they saw a prospect of getting rents. That prospect will soon disappear, unless they pray hard to St. Swithin to insist upon forty days wet *after* his birthday. I do not see what the farmers can do about the price of oats. They have no power to do anything unless they come with their cavalry horses and storm the "king's lock." In short, it is all confusion in men's minds as well as in their pockets. There must be something completely out of joint, when the government are afraid of the effects of a good crop. I intend to set off to-morrow for Botley, and go thence to Easton; and then to Alton and Crondall and Farnham, to see how the *hops* are there. By the time that I get back to the Wen, I shall know nearly the real state of the case as to crops; and that, at this time, is a great matter.

THROUGH THE SOUTH-EAST OF HAMPSHIRE, BACK THROUGH THE SOUTH-WEST OF SURREY, ALONG THE WEALD OF SURREY, AND THEN OVER THE SURREY HILLS DOWN TO THE WEN

BOTLEY (HAMPSHIRE),
5 August, 1823.

I GOT to Fareham on Saturday night, after having got a soaking on the South Downs on the morning of that day. On the Sunday morning, intending to go and spend the day at Titchfield (about three miles and a half from Fareham), and perceiving, upon looking out of the window, about 5 o'clock in the morning, that it was likely to rain, I got up, struck a bustle, got up the ostler, set off and got to my destined point before 7 o'clock in the morning. And here I experienced the benefits of early rising; for I had scarcely got well and safely under cover, when St. Swithin began to pour down again, and he continued to pour during the whole of the day. From Fareham to Titchfield village a large part of the ground is a common enclosed some years ago. It is therefore amongst the worst of the land in the country. Yet, I did not see a bad field of corn along here, and the swedish turnips were, I think, full as fine as any that I saw upon the South Downs. But it is to be observed that this land is in the hands of dead-weight people, and is conveniently situated for the receiving of manure from Portsmouth. Before I got to my friend's house, I passed by a farm where I expected to find a wheat-rick standing. I did not, however; and this is the strongest possible proof that the stock of corn is gone out of the hands of the farmers. I set out from Titchfield at 7 o'clock in the evening, and had seven miles to go to reach Botley. It rained, but I got myself well furnished forth as a defence against the rain. I had not gone two hundred yards before the rain ceased; so that I was singularly fortunate as to rain this day; and I had now to congratulate myself on the success of the remedy for the hooping-cough which I used the day before on the South Downs; for really, though I had a spell or two of coughing on Saturday morning when I set out from Petworth, I have not had, up to this hour, any spell at all since I got wet upon the South Downs. I got to Botley about nine o'clock, having stopped two or three times to look about me as I went along; for I had, in the first place, to ride, for about three miles of my road, upon a turnpike road of which I was the projector, and, indeed, the maker. In the next place I had to ride, for something better than half a mile of my way, along between fields and coppices that were mine until they came into the hands of the mortgagee, and by the side of cottages of my own building. The only matter of much interest with me was the state of the inhabitants of those cottages. I stopped at two or three places, and made some little inquiries; I rode up to two or three houses in the village of Botley, which I had to pass through, and, just before it was dark, I got to a farm-house close by the church, and what was more, not a great many yards from the dwelling of that delectable creature, the Botley parson, whom, however, I have not seen during my stay at this place.

Botley lies in a valley, the soil of which is a deep and stiff clay. Oak trees grow well; and this year the wheat grows well, as it does upon all the clays that I have seen. I have never seen the wheat better in general, in this part of the country, than it is now. I have, I think, seen it heavier; but never clearer from blight. It is backward compared to the wheat in many other parts; some of it is quite green; but none of it has any appearance of blight. This is not much of a barley country. The oats are good. The beans that I have seen, very indifferent.

The best news that I have learnt here is, that the Botley parson is become quite a gentle creature, compared to what he used to be. The people in the village have told me some most ridiculous stories about his having been hoaxed in London! It seems that somebody danced him up from Botley to London, by telling him that a legacy had been left him, or some such story. Up went the parson on horseback, being in too great a hurry to run the risk of coach. The hoaxers, it appears, got him to some hotel, and there set upon him a whole tribe of applicants, wet-nurses, dry-nurses, lawyers with deeds of conveyance for borrowed money, curates in want of churches, coffin-makers, travelling companions, ladies' maids, dealers in Yorkshire hams, Newcastle coals, and dealers in dried night-soil at Islington. In short, if I am rightly informed, they kept the parson in town for several days, bothered him three parts out of his senses, compelled him to escape, as it were, from a fire; and then, when he got home, he found the village posted all over with handbills giving an account of his adventure, under the pretence of offering £500 reward for a discovery of the hoaxers! The good of it was the parson ascribed his disgrace *to me*, and they say that he perseveres to this hour in accusing me of it. Upon my word, I had nothing to do with the matter, and this affair only shows that I am not the only friend that the parson has in the world. Though this may have had a tendency to produce in the parson that amelioration of deportment which is said to become him so well, there is something else that has taken place, which has, in all probability, had a more powerful influence in this way; namely, a great reduction in the value of the parson's living, which was at one time little short of five hundred pounds a year, and which, I believe, is now not the half of that sum! This, to be sure, is not only a natural but a necessary consequence of the change in the value of money. The parsons are neither more nor less than another sort of landlords. They must fall, of course, in their demands, or their demands will not be paid. They may take in kind, but that will answer them no purpose at all. They will be less people than they have been, and will continue to grow less and less, until the day when the whole of the tithes and other church property, as it is called, shall be applied to public purposes.

EASTON (HAMPSHIRE),
Wednesday Evening, 6 August.

This village of Easton lies at a few miles towards the north-east from Winchester. It is distant from Botley by the way which I came about fifteen or sixteen miles. I came through Durley, where I went to the house of farmer Mears. I was very much pleased with what I saw at Durley, which is about two miles from Botley, and is certainly one of the most obscure villages in this whole kingdom. Mrs. Mears, the farmer's wife, had made, of the crested dog's tail grass, a bonnet which she wears herself. I there saw girls platting the straw. They had made plat of several degrees of fineness; and they sell it to some person or persons at Fareham, who, I suppose, makes it into bonnets. Mrs. Mears, who is a very intelligent and clever woman, has two girls at work, each of whom earns per week as much (within a shilling) as her father, who is a labouring man, earns per week. The father has at this time only 7s. per week. These two girls (and not very stout girls) earn six shillings a week each: thus the income of this family is, from seven shillings a week, raised to nineteen shillings a week. I shall suppose that this may in some measure be owing to the generosity of ladies in the neighbourhood, and to their desire to promote this domestic manufacture; but if I suppose that these girls receive double compared to what they will receive for the same quantity of labour when the manufacture becomes more general, is it not a great thing to make the income of the family thirteen shillings a week instead of seven? Very little, indeed, could these poor things have done in the field during the last forty days. And, besides, how clean; how healthful; how everything that one could wish, is this sort of employment! The farmer, who is also a very intelligent person, told me that he should endeavour to introduce the manufacture as a thing to assist the obtaining of employment, in order to lessen the amount of the poor-rates. I think it very likely that this will be done in the parish of Durley. A most important matter it is, *to put paupers in the way of ceasing to be paupers.* I could not help admiring the zeal as well as the intelligence of the farmer's wife, who expressed her readiness to teach the girls and women of the parish, in order to enable them to assist themselves. I shall hear, in all probability, of their proceedings at Durley, and if I do, I shall make a point of communicating to the public an account of those interesting proceedings. From the very first; from the first moment of my thinking about this straw affair, I regarded it as likely to assist in bettering the lot of the labouring people. If it has not this effect, I value it not. It is not worth the attention of any of us; but I am satisfied that this is the way in which it will work. I have the pleasure to know that there is one labouring family, at any rate, who are living well through my means. It is I, who, without knowing them, without ever having seen them, without even now knowing their names, have given the means of good living to a family who were before half-starved. This is indisputably my work; and when I reflect that there must necessarily be, now, some hundreds of families, and shortly, many thousands of families, in England, who are and will be, through my means, living well instead of being half-starved, I cannot but feel myself consoled; I cannot but feel that I have some compensation for the sentence passed upon me by Ellenborough, Grose, Le Blanc, and Bailey; and I verily believe, that, in the case of this one single family in the parish of Durley, I have done more good than Bailey ever did in the whole course of his life, notwithstanding his pious commentary on the Book of Common Prayer. I will allow nothing to be good, with regard to the labouring classes, unless it make an addition to their victuals, drink, or clothing. As to their *minds*, that is much too sublime matter for me to think about. I know that they are in rags, and that they have not a belly-full; and I know that the way to make them good, to make them honest, to make them dutiful, to make them kind to one another, is to enable them to live well; and I also know that none of these things will ever be accomplished by Methodist sermons, and by those stupid, at once stupid and malignant things, and roguish things, called Religious Tracts.

It seems that this farmer at Durley has always read the *Register*, since the first appearance of little *Two-penny Trash*. Had it not been for this reading, Mrs. Mears would not have thought about the grass; and had she not thought about the grass, none of the benefits above mentioned would have arisen to her neighbours. The difference between this affair and the spinning-jenny affairs is this; that the spinning-jenny affairs fill the pockets of "rich ruffians," such as those who would have murdered me at Coventry; and that this straw affair makes an addition to the food and raiment of the labouring classes, and gives not a penny to be pocketed by the rich ruffians.

From Durley I came on in company with farmer Mears through Upham. This Upham is the place where Young, who wrote that bombastical stuff, called *Night Thoughts*, was once the parson, and where, I believe, he was born. Away to the right of Upham lies the little town of Bishop's Waltham, whither I wished to go very much, but it was too late in the day. From Upham we came on upon the high land, called Black Down. This has nothing to do with that Black-down Hill, spoken of in my last ride. We are here getting up upon the chalk hills, which stretch away towards Winchester. The soil here is a poor blackish stuff, with little white stones in it, upon a bed of chalk. It was a down not many years ago. The madness and greediness of the days of paper-money led to the breaking of it up. The corn upon it is miserable, but as good as can be expected upon such land.

At the end of this tract, we come to a spot called Whiteflood, and here we cross the old turnpike-road which leads from Winchester to Gosport through Bishop's Waltham. Whiteflood is at the foot of the first of a series of hills over which you come to get to the top of that lofty ridge called Morning Hill. The farmer came to the top of the first hill along with me, and he was just about to turn back, when I, looking away to the left, down a valley which stretched across the other side of the down, observed a rather singular appearance, and said to the farmer, "What is that coming up that valley? is it smoke, or is it a cloud?" The day had been very fine hitherto; the sun was shining very bright where we were. The farmer answered, "Oh, it's smoke; it comes from Ouselberry, which is down in that bottom behind those trees." So saying, we bid each other good day; he went back, and I went on. Before I had got a hundred and fifty yards from him, the cloud which he had taken for the Ouselberry smoke, came upon the hill and wet me to the skin. He was not far from the house at Whiteflood; but I am sure that he could not entirely escape it. It is curious to observe how the clouds sail about in the hilly countries, and particularly, I think, amongst the chalk-hills. I have never observed the like amongst the sand-hills, or amongst rocks.

From Whiteflood you come over a series of hills, part of which form a rabbit-warren called Longwood warren, on the borders of which is the house and estate of Lord Northesk. These hills are amongst the most barren of the downs of England; yet a part of them was broken up during the rage for improvements; during the rage for what empty men think was an augmenting of the *capital* of the country. On about twenty acres of this land, sown with wheat, I should not suppose that there would be twice twenty bushels of grain! A man must be mad, or nearly mad, to sow wheat upon such a spot. However, a large part of what was enclosed has been thrown out again already, and the rest will be thrown out in a very few years. The down itself was poor; what then must it be as corn-land! Think of the destruction which has here taken place. The herbage was not good, but it was something: it was something for every year, and without trouble. Instead of grass it will now, for twenty years to come, bear nothing but that species of weeds which is hardy enough to grow where the grass will not grow. And this was "augmenting the capital of the nation." These new enclosure-bills were boasted of by George Rose and by Pitt as proofs of national prosperity! When men in power are ignorant to this extent, who is to expect anything but consequences such as we now behold.

From the top of this high land called *Morning Hill*, and the real name of which is *Magdalen Hill*, from a chapel which once stood there dedicated to Mary Magdalen; from the top of this land you have a view of a circle which is upon an average about seventy miles in diameter; and I believe in no one place so little as fifty miles in diameter. You see the Isle of Wight in one direction, and in the opposite direction you see the high lands in Berkshire. It is not a pleasant view, however. The fertile spots are all too far from you. Descending from this hill, you cross the turnpike-road (about two miles from Winchester), leading from Winchester to London through Alresford and Farnham. As soon as you cross the road, you enter the estate of the descendant of Rollo, Duke of Buckingham, which estate is in the parish of Avington. In this place the duke has a farm, not very good land. It is in his own hands. The corn is indifferent, except the barley, which is everywhere good. You come a full mile from the roadside down through this farm, to the duke's mansion-house at Avington, and to the little village of that name, both of them beautifully situated, amidst fine and lofty trees, fine meadows, and streams of clear water. On this farm of the duke I saw (in a little close by the farm-house) several hens in coops with broods of pheasants instead of chickens. It seems that a gamekeeper lives in the farm-house, and I dare say the duke thinks much more of the pheasants than of the corn. To be very solicitous to preserve what has been raised with so much care and at so much expense, is by no means unnatural; but then there is a measure to be observed here; and that measure was certainly outstretched in the case of Mr. Deller. I here saw, at this gamekeeping farm-house, what I had not seen since my departure from the Wen; namely, a wheat-rick! Hard, indeed, would it have been if a Plantagenet, turned farmer, had not a wheat-rick in his hands. This rick contains, I should think, what they call in Hampshire ten loads of wheat, that is to say, fifty quarters, or four hundred bushels. And this is the only rick, not only of wheat, but of any corn whatever that I have seen since I left London. The turnips, upon this farm, are by no means good; but I was in some measure compensated for the bad turnips by the sight of the duke's turnip-hoers, about a dozen females, amongst whom there were several very pretty girls, and they were as merry as larks. There had been a shower that had brought them into a sort of huddle on the roadside. When I came up to them, they all fixed their eyes upon me, and upon my smiling, they bursted out into laughter. I observed to them that the Duke of Buckingham was a very happy man to have such turnip-hoers, and really they seemed happier and better off than any work-people that I saw in the fields all the way from London to this spot. It is curious enough, but I have always observed that the women along this part of the country are usually tall. These girls were all tall, straight, fair, round-faced, excellent complexion, and uncommonly gay. They were well dressed, too, and I observed the same of all the men that I saw down at Avington. This could not be the case if the duke were a cruel or hard master; and this is an act of justice due from me to the descendant of Rollo. It is in the house of Mr. Deller that I make these notes, but as it is *injustice* that we dislike, I must do Rollo justice; and I must again say that the good looks and happy faces of his turnip-hoers spoke much more in his praise than could have been spoken by fifty lawyers, like that Storks who was employed, the other day, to plead against the editor of the *Bucks Chronicle*, for publishing an account of the selling-up of farmer Smith, of Ashendon, in that county. I came through the duke's park to come to Easton, which is the next village below Avington. A very pretty park. The house is quite in the bottom; it can be seen in no direction from a distance greater than that of four or five hundred yards. The river Itchen, which rises near Alresford, which runs down through Winchester to Southampton, goes down the middle of this valley, and waters all its immense quantity of meadows. The duke's house stands not far from the river itself. A stream of water is brought from the river to feed a pond before the house. There are several avenues of trees which are very beautiful, and some of which give complete shelter to the kitchen garden, which has, besides, extraordinarily high walls. Never was a greater contrast than that presented by this place and the place of Lord Egremont. The latter is all loftiness. Every-thing is high about it; it has extensive views in all directions. It sees and can be seen by all the country around. If I had the ousting of one of these noblemen, I certainly, however, would oust the duke, who, I dare say, will by no means be desirous of seeing arise the occasion of putting the sincerity of the compli-ment to the test. The village of Easton is, like that of Avington, close by the waterside. The meadows are the attraction; and, indeed, it is the meadows that have caused the villages to exist.

SELBORNE (HANTS),
Thursday, 7 August, Noon.

I took leave of Mr. Deller this morning, about 7 o'clock. Came back through Avington Park, through the village of Avington, and, crossing the Itchen river, came over to the village of Itchen Abas. *Abas* means *below*. It is a French word that came over with Duke Rollo's progenitors. There

needs no better proof of the high descent of the duke, and of
the antiquity of his family. This is that Itchen Abas where
that famous parson-justice, the Reverend Robert Wright, lives,
who refused to hear Mr. Deller's complaint against the duke's
servant at his own house, and who afterwards, along with Mr.
Poulter, bound Mr. Deller over to the quarter sessions for the
alleged assault. I have great pleasure in informing the public
that Mr. Deller has not had to bear the expenses in this case
himself; but that they have been borne by his neighbours, very
much to the credit of those neighbours. I hear of an affair
between the Duke of Buckingham and a Mr. Bird, who resides
in this neighbourhood. If I had had time I should have gone
to see Mr. Bird, of whose treatment I have heard a great deal,
and an account of which treatment ought to be brought before
the public. It is very natural for the Duke of Buckingham to
wish to preserve that game which he calls his hobby-horse. It
is very natural for him to delight in his hobby; but *hobbies,* my
lord duke, ought to be gentle, inoffensive, perfectly harmless
little creatures. They ought not to be suffered to kick and fling
about them: they ought not to be rough-shod, and, above all
things, they ought not to be great things like those which are
ridden by the Life Guards: and, like them, be suffered to dance,
and caper, and trample poor devils of farmers under foot.
Have your hobbies, my lords of the soil, but let them be gentle;
in short, let them be hobbies in character with the commons
and forests, and not the high-fed hobbies from the barracks at
Knightsbridge, such as put poor Mr. Sheriff Waithman's life in
jeopardy. That the game should be preserved, every one that
knows anything of the country will allow; but every man of any
sense must see that it cannot be preserved by sheer force. It
must be rather through love than through fear; rather through
good-will than through ill-will. If the thing be properly
managed, there will be plenty of game, without any severity
towards any good man. Mr. Deller's case was so plain: it was
so monstrous to think that a man was to be punished for being
on his own ground in pursuit of wild animals that he himself had
raised: this was so monstrous, that it was only necessary to
name it to excite the indignation of the country. And Mr.
Deller has, by his spirit and perseverance, by the coolness and
the good sense which he has shown throughout the whole of this
proceeding, merited the commendation of every man who is not
in his heart an oppressor. It occurs to me to ask here, who it
is that finally *pays* for those " counsels' opinions " which Poulter

and Wright said they took in the case of Mr. Deller; because, if these counsels' opinions are paid for by the county, and if a justice of the peace can take as many counsels' opinions as he chooses, I should like to know what fellow, who chooses to put on a bobtail wig and call himself a lawyer, may not have a good living given to him by any crony justice at the expense of the county. This never can be legal. It never can be binding on the county to pay for these counsels' opinions. However, leaving this to be inquired into another time, we have here, in Mr. Deller's case, an instance of the worth of counsels' opinions. Mr. Deller went to the two justices, showed them the Register with the Act of Parliament in it, called upon them to act agreeably to that Act of Parliament; but they chose to take counsels' opinion first. The two " counsel," the two " lawyers," the two " learned friends," told them that they were right in rejecting the application of Mr. Deller and in binding him over for the assault; and, after all, this grand jury threw out the bill, and in that throwing out showed that they thought the counsels' opinions not worth a straw.

Being upon the subject of matter connected with the conduct of these parson-justices, I will here mention what is now going on in Hampshire respecting the accounts of the *treasurer of the county*. At the last quarter sessions, or at a meeting of the magistrates previous to the opening of the sessions, there was a discussion relative to this matter. The substance of which appears to have been this; that the treasurer, Mr. George Hollis, whose accounts had been audited, approved of, and passed, every year by the magistrates, is in arrear to the county to the amount of about four thousand pounds. Sir Thomas Baring appears to have been the great stickler against Mr. Hollis, who was but feebly defended by his friends. The treasurer of a county is compelled to find securities. These securities have become *exempted*, in consequence of the annual passing of the accounts by the magistrates! Nothing can be more just than this exemption. I am security, suppose, for a treasurer. The magistrates do not pass his accounts on account of a deficiency. I make good the deficiency. But the magistrates are not to go on year after year passing his accounts, and then, at the end of several years, come and call upon me to make good the deficiencies. Thus say the securities of Mr. Hollis. The magistrates, in fact, are to blame. One of the magistrates, a Reverend Mr. Orde, said that the magistrates were more to blame than the treasurer; and really I think so too; for though Mr. Hollis has been a tool

for many, many years of Old George Rose and the rest of that
crew, it seems impossible to believe that he could have intended
anything dishonest, seeing that the detection arose out of an
account, published by himself in the newspaper, which account
he need not have published until three months later than the
time when he did publish it. This is, as he himself states, the
best possible proof that he was unconscious of any error or any
deficiency. The fact appears to be this; that Mr. Hollis, who
has for many years been under sheriff as well as treasurer of the
county, who holds several other offices, and who has, besides,
had large pecuniary transactions with his bankers, has for years
had his accounts so blended that he has not known how this
money belonging to the county stood. His own statement
shows that it was all a mass of confusion. The errors, he says,
have arisen, entirely from the negligence of his clerks, and from
causes which produced a confusion in his accounts. This is
the fact; but he has been in good fat offices too long not to have
made a great many persons think that his offices would be better
in *their* hands; and they appear resolved to oust him. I, for
my part, am glad of it; for I remember his coming up to me in
the grand jury chamber, just after the people of St. Stephen's
had passed Power-of-Imprisonment Bill in 1817; I remember
his coming up to me as the under-sheriff of Willis, the man that
we now call Flemming, who has *begun* to build a house at North
Stoneham; I remember his coming up to me, and with all the
base sauciness of a thorough-paced Pittite, *telling me to disperse
or he would take me into custody !* I remember this of Mr. Hollis,
and I am therefore glad that calamity has befallen him; but I
must say that after reading his own account of the matter;
after reading the debate of the magistrates; and after hearing the
observations and opinions of well-informed and impartial persons
in Hampshire who dislike Mr. Hollis as much as I do; I must say
that I think him perfectly clear of all intention to commit anything like fraud, or to make anything worthy of the name of
false account; and I am convinced that this affair, which will
now prove extremely calamitous to him, might have been laughed
at by him at the time when wheat was fifteen shillings a bushel.
This change in the affairs of the government; this penury now
experienced by the Pittites at Whitehall, reaches, in its influence,
to every part of the country. The Barings are now the great
men in Hampshire. They were not such in the days of George
Rose, while George was able to make the people believe that
it was necessary to give their money freely to preserve the

" blessed comforts of religion." George Rose would have thrown his shield over Mr. Hollis; his broad and brazen shield. In Hampshire the *bishop* too is changed. The present is, doubtless, as pious as the last, every bit, and has the same bishop-like views; but it is not the same family; it is not the Garniers and Poulters and Norths and De Grays and Haygarths; it is not precisely the same set who have the power in their hands. Things, therefore, take another turn. The Pittite jolterheads are all broken-backed; and the Barings come forward with their well-known weight of metal. It was exceedingly unfortunate for Mr. Hollis that Sir Thomas Baring happened to be against him. However, the thing will do good altogether. The county is placed in a pretty situation: its treasurer has had his accounts regularly passed by the magistrates; and these magistrates come at last and discover that they have for a long time been passing accounts that they ought not to pass. These magistrates have exempted the securities of Mr. Hollis, but not a word do they say about making good the deficiencies. What redress, then, have the people of the county? They have no redress, unless they can obtain it by petitioning the Parliament; and if they do not petition; if they do not state their case, and that boldly, too, they deserve everything that can befall them from similar causes. I am astonished at the boldness of the magistrates. I am astonished that they should think of calling Mr. Hollis to account without being prepared for rendering an account of their own conduct. However, we shall see what they will do in the end. And when we have seen that, we shall see whether the county will rest quietly under the loss which it is likely to sustain.

I must now go back to Itchen Abas, where, in the farm-yard of a farmer, Courtenay, I saw another wheat-rick. From Itchen Abas I came up the valley to Itchen Stoke. Soon after that I crossed the Itchen river, came out into the Alresford turnpike-road, and came on towards Alresford, having the valley now upon my left. If the hay be down all the way to Southampton in the same manner that it is along here, there are thousands of acres of hay rotting on the sides of this Itchen river. Most of the meadows are watered artificially. The crops of grass are heavy, and they appear to have been cut precisely in the right time to be spoiled. Coming on towards Alresford, I saw a gentleman (about a quarter of a mile beyond Alresford) coming out of his gate with his hat off, looking towards the south-west, as if to see what sort of weather it was likely to be. This was no other than Mr. Rolleston or Rawlinson, who, it appears, has a box and some land here. This gentleman was, when I lived in Hampshire, one of those worthy men who, in the several counties of England, executed " without any sort of remuneration," such a large portion of that justice which is the envy of surrounding nations and admiration of the world. We are often told, especially in Parliament, of the *disinterestedness* of these persons; of their worthiness, their piety, their loyalty, their excellent qualities of all sorts, but particularly of their *disinterestedness*, in taking upon them the office of justice of the peace; spending so much time, taking so much trouble, and all for nothing at all, but for the pure love of their king and country. And the worst of it is, that our ministers *impose* upon this disinterestedness and generosity; and, as in the case of Mr. Rawlinson, at the end of, perhaps, a dozen years of *services* voluntarily rendered to " king and country," they force him, sorely against his will, no doubt, to become a police magistrate in London! To be sure, there are five or six hundred pounds a year of public money attached to this; but what are these paltry pounds to a " country gentleman," who so disinterestedly rendered us services for so many years? Hampshire is fertile in persons of this disinterested stamp. There is a 'Squire Greme, who lives across the country, not many miles from the spot where I saw " Mr. Justice " Rawlinson. This 'squire also has served the country for nothing during a great many years; and, of late years, the 'squire junior, eager apparently to emulate his sire, has become a distributor of stamps for this famous county of Hants! What *sons* 'Squire Rawlinson may have is more than I know at present, though I will endeavour to know it, and to find out whether they also be *serving* us. A great deal has been said about the debt of gratitude due from the people to the justices of the peace. An account, containing the names and places of abode of the justices, and of the public money, or titles, received by them and by their relations; such an account would be a very useful thing. We should then know the real amount of this debt of gratitude. We shall see such an account by and by; and we should have seen it long ago, if there had been, in a certain place, only one single man disposed to do his duty.

I came through Alresford about eight o'clock, having loitered a good deal in coming up the valley. After quitting Alresford you come (on the road towards Alton) to the village of Bishop's Sutton; and then to a place called Ropley Dean, where there is a house or two. Just before you come to Ropley Dean, you see the beginning of the Valley of Itchen. The *Itchen* river falls into the salt water at Southampton. It rises, or rather has its first rise, just by the roadside at Ropley Dean, which is at the foot of that very high land which lies between Alresford and Alton. All along by the Itchen river, up to its very source, there are meadows; and this vale of meadows, which is about twenty-five miles in length, and is, in some places, a mile wide, is, at the point of which I am now speaking, only about twice as wide as my horse is long! This vale of Itchen is worthy of particular attention. There are few spots in England more fertile or more pleasant; and none, I believe, more healthy. Following the bed of the river, or rather, the middle of the vale, it is about five-and-twenty miles in length, from Ropley Dean to the village of South Stoneham, which is just above Southampton. The average width of the meadows is, I should think, a hundred rods at the least; and if I am right in this conjecture, the vale contains about five thousand acres of meadows, large part of which is regularly watered. The sides of the vale are, until you come down to within about six or eight miles of Southampton, hills or rising grounds of chalk, covered more or less thickly with loam. Where the hills rise up very steeply from the valley, the fertility of the corn-lands is not so great; but for a considerable part of the way, the corn-lands are excellent, and the farm-houses, to which those lands belong, are, for the far greater part, under covert of the hills on the edge of the valley. Soon after the rising of the stream, it forms itself into some capital ponds at Alresford. These, doubtless, were augmented by art, in order to supply Winchester with fish. The fertility of this vale, and of the surrounding country, is best proved by the fact that, besides the town of Alresford and that of Southampton, there are seventeen villages, each having its parish church, upon its borders. When we consider these things we are not surprised that a spot situated about half way down this vale should have been chosen for the building of a city, or that that city should have been for a great number of years a place of residence for the kings of England.

Winchester, which is at present a mere nothing to what it once was, stands across the vale at a place where the vale is made very narrow by the jutting forward of two immense hills. From the point where the river passes through the city, you go, whether eastward or westward, a full mile up a very steep hill all the way. The city is, of course, in one of the deepest holes that can be imagined. It never could have been thought of as a place to be defended since the discovery of gunpowder; and, indeed, one would think that very considerable annoyance might be given to the inhabitants even by the flinging of the flint-stones from the hills down into the city.

At Ropley Dean, before I mounted the hill to come on towards Rotherham Park, I baited my horse. Here the ground is precisely like that at Ashmansworth on the borders of Berkshire, which, indeed, I could see from the ground of which I am now speaking. In coming up the hill, I had the house and farm of Mr. Duthy to my right. Seeing some very fine swedish turnips, I naturally expected that they belonged to this gentleman who is secretary to the Agricultural Society of Hampshire; but I found that they belonged to a farmer Mayhew. The soil is, along upon this high land, a deep loam, bordering on a clay, red in colour, and pretty full of large, rough, yellow-looking stones, very much like some of the land in Huntingdonshire; but here is a bed of chalk under this. Everything is backward here. The wheat is perfectly green in most places; but it is every-where pretty good. I have observed, all the way along, that the wheat is good upon the stiff, strong land. It is so here; but it is very backward. The greater part of it is full three weeks behind the wheat under Portsdown Hill. But few farm-houses come within my sight along here; but in one of them there was a wheat-rick, which is the third I have seen since I quitted the Wen. In descending from this high ground, in order to reach the village of East Tisted, which lies on the turnpike-road from the Wen to Gosport through Alton, I had to cross Rotherham Park. On the right of the park, on a bank of land facing the north-east, I saw a very pretty farm-house, having everything in excellent order, with fine corn-fields about it, and with a wheat-rick standing in the yard. This farm, as I afterwards found, belongs to the owner of Rotherham Park, who is also the owner of East Tisted, who has recently built a new house in the park, who has quite metamorphosed the village of Tisted, within these eight years, who has, indeed, really and truly improved the whole country just round about here, whose name is Scot, well known as a brickmaker at North End, Fulham, and who has, in Hampshire, supplanted a Norman of the name of Powlet. The process by which this transfer has taken place is visible enough, to all eyes but the eyes of the jolterheads. Had there been no debt created to crush liberty in France and to keep down reformers in England, Mr. Scot would not have had bricks to burn to build houses for the Jews and jobbers and other eaters of taxes; and the Norman Powlet would not have had to pay in taxes, through his own hands and those of his tenants and labourers, the amount of the estate at Tisted, first to be given to the Jews, jobbers and tax-eaters, and then by them to be given to " 'Squire Scot " for his bricks. However, it is not 'Squire Scot who has assisted to pass laws to make people pay double toll on a Sunday. 'Squire Scot had nothing to do with passing the New Game-laws and Old Ellenborough's Act; 'Squire Scot never invented the New Trespass law, in virtue of which John Cockbain of Whitehaven in the county of Cumberland was, by two clergymen and three other magistrates of that county, sentenced to pay one half-penny for damages and seven shillings costs, for going upon a field, the property of William, Earl of Lonsdale. In the passing of this Act, which was one of the first passed in the present reign, 'Squire Scot, the brickmaker, had nothing to do. Go on, good 'squire, thrust out some more of the Normans: with the fruits of the augmentations which you make to the Wen, go, and take from them their mansions, parks, and villages!

At Tisted I crossed the turnpike-road before mentioned, and entered a lane which, at the end of about four miles, brought me to this village of Selborne. My readers will recollect that I mentioned this Selborne when I was giving an account of Hawkley Hanger, last fall. I was desirous of seeing this village, about which I have read in the book of Mr. White, and which a reader has been so good as to send me. From Tisted I came generally up hill till I got within half a mile of this village, when, all of a sudden, I came to the edge of a hill, looked down over all the larger vale of which the little vale of this village makes a part. Here Hindhead and Black Down Hill came full in my view. When I was crossing the forest in Sussex, going from Worth to Horsham, these two great hills lay to my west and north-west. To-day I am got just on the opposite side of them, and see them, of course, towards the east and the south-east, while Leith Hill lies away towards the north-east. This hill, from which you descend down into Selborne, is very lofty; but, indeed, we are here amongst some of the highest hills in the island, and amongst the sources of rivers. The hill over which I have come this morning sends the Itchen river forth from one side of it, and the river Wey, which rises near Alton, from the opposite side of it. Hindhead which lies before me, sends, as I observed upon a former occasion, the Arun forth towards the south and a stream forth towards the north, which meets the river Wey, somewhere above Godalming. I am told that the springs of these two streams rise in the Hill of Hindhead, or rather, on one side of the hill, at not many yards from each other. The village of Selborne is precisely what it is described by Mr. White. A straggling irregular street, bearing all the marks of great antiquity, and showing, from its lanes and its vicinage generally, that it was once a very considerable place. I went to look at the spot where Mr. White supposes the convent formerly stood. It is very beautiful. Nothing can surpass in beauty these dells and hillocks and hangers, which last are so steep that it is impossible to ascend them, except by means of a serpentine path. I found here deep hollow ways, with beds and sides of solid white stone; but not quite so white and so solid, I think, as the stone which I found in the roads at Hawkley. The churchyard of Selborne is most beautifully situated. The land is good, all about it. The trees are luxuriant and prone to be lofty and large. I measured the yew-tree in the churchyard, and found the trunk to be, according to my measurement, twenty-three feet, eight inches, in circumference. The trunk is very short, as is generally the case with yew-trees; but the head spreads to a very great extent, and the whole tree, though probably several centuries old, appears to be in perfect health. Here are several hop-plantations in and about this village; but, for this once, the prayers of the over-production men will be granted, and the devil of any hops there will be. The bines are scarcely got up the poles; the bines and the leaves are black, nearly, as soot; full as black as a sooty bag or dingy coal-sack, and covered with lice. It is a pity that these hop-planters could not have a parcel of Spaniards and Portuguese to louse their hops for them. Pretty devils to have liberty, when a favourite recreation of the Donna is to crack the lice in the head of the Don! I really shrug up my shoulders thinking of the beasts. Very different from such is my landlady here at Selborne, who, while I am writing my notes, is getting me a rasher of bacon, and has already covered the table with a nice clean cloth. I have never seen such quantities of grapes upon any vines as I see upon the vines in this village, badly pruned as all the vines have been. To be sure, this is a year for grapes, such, I believe, as has been seldom known in England, and the cause is, the perfect ripening of the wood by the last beautiful summer. I am afraid, however, that the grapes come in vain; for this summer has been so cold, and is now so wet, that we can hardly expect grapes, which are not under glass, to ripen. As I was coming into this village, I observed to a farmer who was standing at his gateway, that people ought to be happy here, for that God had done everything for them. His answer was, that he did not believe there was a more unhappy place in England: for that there were always quarrels of some sort or other going on. This made me call to mind the king's proclamation, relative to a reward for discovering the person who had recently *shot at the parson of this village.* This parson's name is Cobbold, and it really appears that there was a shot fired through his window. He has had law-suits with the people; and I imagine that it was these to which the farmer alluded. The hops are of considerable importance to the village, and their failure must necessarily be attended with consequences very inconvenient to the whole of a population so small as this. Upon inquiry, I find that the hops are equally bad at Alton, Froyle, Crondall, and even at Farnham. I saw them bad in Sussex; I hear that they are bad in Kent; so that hop-planters, at any rate, will be, for once, free from the dreadful evils of abundance. A correspondent asks me what is meant by the statements which he sees in the *Register,* relative to the *hop-duty ?* He sees it, he says, continually falling in amount; and he wonders what this means. The thing has not, indeed, been properly explained. It is *a gamble ;* and it is hardly right for me to state, in a publication like the *Register,* anything relative to a gamble. However, the case is this: a taxing system is necessarily a system of gambling; a system of betting; stock-jobbing is no more than a system of betting, and the wretched dogs that carry on the traffic are little more, except that they are more criminal, than the waiters at an *E O Table,* or the markers at billiards. The hop duty is so much per pound. The duty was imposed at two separate times. One part of it, therefore, is called the Old Duty, and the other part the New Duty. The old duty was a penny to the pound of hops. The amount of this duty, which can always be ascertained at the Treasury as soon as the hopping season is over, is the surest possible guide in ascertaining the total amount of the growth of hops for the year. If, for instance, the duty were to amount to no more than eight shillings and fourpence, you would be certain that only a hundred pounds of hops had been grown during the year. Hence a system of gambling precisely like the gambling in the funds. I bet you that the duty will not exceed so much. The duty has sometimes exceeded two hundred thousand pounds. This year, it is supposed, that it will not exceed twenty, thirty, or forty thousand. The gambling fellows are betting all this time; and it is, in fact, an account of the betting which is inserted in the *Register*.

This vile paper-money and funding-system; this system of Dutch descent, begotten by Bishop Burnet, and born in hell; this system has turned everything into a gamble. There are hundreds of men who live by being the agents to carry on gambling. They reside here in the Wen; many of the gamblers live in the country; they write up to their gambling agent, whom they call their stockbroker; he gambles according to their order; and they receive the profit or stand to the loss. Is it possible to conceive a viler calling than that of an agent for the carrying on of gambling? And yet the vagabonds call themselves gentlemen; or, at least, look upon themselves as the superiors of those who sweep the kennels. In like manner is the hop-gamble carried on. The gambling agents in the Wen make the bets for the gamblers in the country; and, perhaps, millions are betted during the year upon the amount of a duty which, at the most, scarcely exceeds a quarter of a million. In such a state of things how are you to expect young men to enter on a course of patient industry? How are you to expect that they will seek to acquire fortune and fame by study or by application of any kind?

Looking back over the road that I have come to-day, and perceiving the direction of the road going from this village in another direction, I perceive that this is a very direct road from Winchester to Farnham. The road, too, appears to have been, from ancient times, sufficiently wide; and when the Bishop of Winchester selected this beautiful spot whereon to erect a monastery, I dare say the roads along here were some of the best in the country.

THURSLEY (SURREY),
Thursday, 7 August.

I got a boy at Selborne to show me along the lanes out into Woolmer Forest on my way to Headley. The lanes were very deep; the wet *malme* just about the colour of rye-meal mixed up with water, and just about as clammy, came, in many places, very nearly up to my horse's belly. There was this comfort, however, that I was sure that there was a bottom, which is by no means the case when you are among clays or quick-sands. After going through these lanes, and along between some fir-plantations, I came out upon Woolmer Forest, and, to my great satisfaction, soon found myself on the side of those identical plantations, which have been made under the orders of the smooth Mr. Huskisson, and which I noticed last year in my ride from Hambledon to this place. These plantations are of fir, or, at least, I could see nothing else, and they never can be of any more use to the nation than the sprigs of heath which cover the rest of the forest. Is there nobody to inquire what becomes of the income of the crown lands? No, and there never will be, until the whole system be changed. I have seldom ridden on pleasanter ground than that which I found between Woolmer Forest and this beautiful village of Thursley. The day has been fine, too; notwithstanding I saw the judges' terrific wigs as I came up upon the turnpike-road from the village of Itchen. I had but one little scud during the day: just enough for St. Swithin to swear by; but when I was upon the hills, I saw some showers going about the country. From Selborne, I had first to come to Headley, about five miles. I came to the identical public-house where I took my blind guide last year, who took me such a dance to the southward, and led me up to the top of Hindhead at last. I had no business there. My route was through a sort of hamlet called Churt, which lies along on the side and towards the foot of the north of Hindhead, on which side, also, lies the village of Thursley. A line is hardly more straight than is the road from Headley to Thursley; and a prettier ride I never had in the course of my life. It was not the less interesting from the circumstance of its giving me all the way a full view of Crooksbury Hill, the grand scene of my exploits when I was a taker of the nests of crows and magpies.

At Churt I had, upon my left, three hills out upon the common, called the *Devil's Jumps*. The Unitarians will not believe in the Trinity, because they cannot account for it. Will they come here to Churt, go and look at these " Devil's Jumps," and account to me for the placing of these three hills, in the shape of three rather squat sugar-loaves, along in a line upon this heath, or the placing of a rock-stone upon the top of one of them as big as a church tower? For my part, I cannot account for this placing of these hills. That they should have been formed by mere chance is hardly to be believed. How could waters rolling about have formed such hills? How could such hills have bubbled up from beneath? But, in short, it is all wonderful alike: the stripes of loam running down through the chalk-hills; the circular parcels of loam in the midst of chalk-hills;

the lines of flint running parallel with each other horizontally along the chalk-hills; the flints placed in circles as true as a hair in the chalk-hills; the layers of stone at the bottom of hills of loam; the chalk first soft, then some miles further on becoming chalk-stone; then, after another distance, becoming burr-stone, as they call it; and at last, becoming hard white-stone, fit for any buildings; the sand-stone at Hindhead becoming harder and harder till it becomes very nearly iron in Hereford-shire, and quite iron in Wales; but, indeed, they once dug iron out of this very Hindhead. The clouds, coming and settling upon the hills, sinking down and creeping along, at last coming out again in springs, and those becoming rivers. Why, it is all equally wonderful, and as to not believing in this or that, because the thing cannot be proved by logical deduction, why is any man to believe in the existence of a God any more than he is to believe in the doctrine of the Trinity? For my part, I think the "Devil's Jumps," as the people here call them, full as wonderful and no more wonderful than hundreds and hundreds of other wonderful things. It is a strange taste which our ancestors had to ascribe no inconsiderable part of these wonders of nature to the Devil. Not far from the Devil's Jumps is that singular place which resembles a sugar-loaf inverted, hollowed out and an outside rim only left. This is called the "*Devil's Punch Bowl;*" and it is very well known in Wiltshire that the forming, or, perhaps, it is the breaking up of Stonehenge is ascribed to the Devil, and that the mark of one of his feet is now said to be seen in one of the stones.

I got to Thursley about sunset, and without experiencing any inconvenience from the wet. I have mentioned the state of the corn as far as Selborne. On this side of that village I find it much forwarder than I found it between Selborne and Ropley Dean. I am here got into some of the very best barley-land in the kingdom; a fine, buttery, stoneless loam, upon a bottom of sand or sand-stone. Finer barley and tu nip-land it is im-possible to see. All the corn is good here. The wheat not a heavy crop; but not a light one; and the barley all the way along from Headley to this place as fine, if not finer, than I ever saw it in my life. Indeed I have not seen a bad field of barley since I left the Wen. The corn is not so forward here as under Portsdown Hill; but some farmers intend to begin reap-ing wheat in a few days. It is monstrous to suppose that the price of corn will not come down. It must come down, good weather or bad weather. If the weather be bad, it will be so much the worse for the farmer, as well as for the nation at large, and can be of no benefit to any human being but the Quakers, who must now be pretty busy, measuring the crops all over the kingdom. It will be recollected that, in the Report of the Agricultural Committee of 1821, it appeared, from the evidence of one Hodgson, a partner of Cropper, Benson, and Co., Quakers, of Liverpool, that these Quakers sent a set of corn-gaugers into the several counties, just before every harvest; that these fellows stopped here and there, went into the fields, measured off square yards of wheat, clipped off the ears, and carried them off. These they afterwards packed up and sent off to Cropper and Co. at Liverpool. When the whole of the packets were got together, they were rubbed out, measured, weighed, and an estimate made of the amount of the coming crop. This, according to the confession of Hodgson himself, enabled these Quakers to speculate in corn, with the greater chance of gain. This has been done by these men for many years. Their disregard of worldly things; their desire to lay up treasures in heaven; their implicit yielding to the Spirit; these have induced them to send their corn-gaugers over the country regularly year after year; and I will engage that they are at it at this moment. The farmers will bear in mind that the New Trespass - law, though clearly not intended for any such purpose, enables them to go and seize by the throat any of these gaugers that they may catch in their fields. They could not do this formerly; to cut off standing corn was merely a trespass, for which satisfaction was to be attained by action of law. But now you can seize the caitiff who is come as a spy amongst your corn. Before, he could be off and leave you to find out his name as you could; but now you can lay hold of him, as Mr. Deller did of the duke's man, and bring him before a magistrate at once. I do hope that the farmers will look sharp out for these fellows, who are neither more nor less than so many spies. They hold a great deal of corn; they want blight, mildew, rain, hurricanes; but happy I am to see that they will get no blight, at any rate. The grain is formed; everywhere everybody tells me that there is no blight in any sort of corn, except in the beans.

I have not gone through much of a bean country. The beans that I have seen are some of them pretty good, more of them but middling, and still more of them very indifferent.

I am very happy to hear that that beautiful little bird, the American partridge, has been introduced with success to this neighbourhood, by Mr. Leech at Lea. I am told that they have been heard whistling this summer; that they have been frequently seen, and that there is no doubt that they have broods of young ones. I tried several times to import some of these birds; but I always lost them, by some means or other, before the time arrived for turning them out. They are a beautiful little partridge, and extremely interesting in all their manners. Some persons call them *quail*. If any one will take a quail and compare it with one of these birds, he will see that they cannot be of the same sort. In my *Year's Residence in America*, I have, I think, clearly proved that these birds are partridges, and not quails. In the United States, north of New Jersey, they are called quail: south and south-west of New Jersey they are called partridges. They have been called quail solely on account of their size; for they have none of the manners of quail belonging to them. Quails assemble in flocks like larks, starlings or rooks. Partridges keep in distinct coveys; that is to say, the brood lives distinct from all other broods until the ensuing spring, when it forms itself into pairs and separates. Nothing can be a distinction more clear than this. Our own partridges stick to the same spot from the time that they are hatched to the time that they pair off, and these American partridges do the same. Quails, like larks, get together in flocks at the approach of winter, and move about according to the season, to a greater or less distance from the place where they were bred. These, therefore, which have been brought to Thursley, are partridges; and if they be suffered to live quietly for a season or two, they will stock the whole of that part of the country, where the delightful intermixture of corn-fields, coppices, heaths, furze-fields, ponds and rivulets, is singularly favourable to their increase.

The turnips cannot fail to be good in such a season and in such land; yet the farmers are most dreadfully tormented with the weeds, and with the superabundant turnips. Here, my Lord Liverpool, is over production indeed! They have sown their fields broad-cast; they have no means of destroying the weeds by the plough; they have no intervals to bury them in; and they *hoe*, or *scratch*, as Mr. Tull calls it; and then comes St. Swithin and sets the weeds and the hoed-up turnips again. Then there is another hoeing or scratching; and then comes St. Swithin again: so that there is hoe, hoe, muddle, muddle, and such a fretting and stewing; such a looking up to Hindhead to see when it is going to be fine; when, if that beautiful field of twenty acres, which I have now before my eyes, and wherein

I see half a dozen men hoeing and poking and muddling, looking up to see how long it is before they must take to their heels to get under the trees to obtain shelter from the coming shower; when, I say, if that beautiful field had been sowed upon ridges at four feet apart, according to the plan in my *Year's Residence*, not a weed would have been to be seen in the field, the turnip-plants would have been three times the size that they now are, the expense would have not been a fourth part of that which has already taken place, and all the muddling and poking about of weeds, and all the fretting and all the stewing would have been spared; and as to the amount of the crop, I am now looking at the best land in England for swedish turnips, and I have no scruple to assert that, if it had been sown after my manner, it would have had a crop double the weight of that which it now will have. I think I know of a field of turnips, sown much later than the field now before me, and sown in rows at nearly four feet apart, which will have a crop double the weight of that which will be produced in yon beautiful field.

REIGATE (SURREY),
Friday, 8 *August*.

At the end of a long, twisting-about ride, but a most delightful ride, I got to this place about nine o'clock in the evening. From Thursley I came to Brook, and there crossed the turnpike-road from London to Chichester through Godalming and Midhurst. Thence I came on, turning upon the left upon the sandhills of Hambledon (in Surrey, mind). On one of these hills is one of those precious jobs, called "*Semaphores*." For what reason this pretty name is given to a sort of telegraph house, stuck up at public expense upon a high hill; for what reason this outlandish name is given to the thing, I must leave the reader to guess; but as to the thing itself, I know that it means this: a pretence for giving a good sum of the public money away every year to some one that the borough-system has condemned this labouring and toiling nation to provide for. The Dead Weight of nearly about six millions sterling a year; that is to say, this curse entailed upon the country on account of the late wars against the liberties of the French people, this Dead Weight is, however, falling, in part, at least, upon the landed jolterheads who were so eager to create it, and who thought that no part of it would fall upon themselves. Theirs has been a grand mistake. They saw the war carried on without any loss or any cost to themselves. By the means of paper-money and loans, the labouring classes were made to pay the whole of the expenses of the war. When the war was over, the jolterheads thought they would get gold back again to make all secure; and some of them really said, I am told, that it was high time to put an end to the gains of the paper-money people. The jolterheads quite overlooked the circumstance that, in returning to gold, they doubled and trebled what they had to pay on account of the debt, and that, at last, they were bringing the burden upon themselves. Grand, also, was the mistake of the jolterheads, when they approved of the squanderings upon the Dead Weight. They thought that the labouring classes were going to pay the whole of the expenses of the Knights of Waterloo, and of the other heroes of the war. The jolterheads thought that they should have none of this to pay. Some of them had relations belonging to the Dead Weight, and all of them were willing to make the labouring classes toil like asses for the support of those who had what was called " fought and bled " for Gatton and Old Sarum. The jolterheads have now found, however, that a pretty good share of the expense is to fall upon themselves. Their mortgagees are letting them know that *Semaphores* and such pretty things cost something, and that it is unreasonable for a loyal country gentleman, a friend of " social order " and of the " blessed comforts of religion " to expect to have semaphores and to keep his estate too.

This Dead Weight is, unquestionably, a thing such as the world never saw before. Here are not only a tribe of pensioned naval and military officers, commissaries, quarter-masters, pursers, and God knows what besides; not only these, but their wives and children are to be pensioned, after the death of the heroes themselves. Nor does it signify, it seems, whether the hero were married, before he became part of the Dead Weight, or since. Upon the death of the man, the pension is to begin with the wife, and a pension for each child; so that, if there be a large family of children, the family, in many cases, actually gains by the death of the father! Was such a thing as this ever before heard of in the world? Any man that is going to die has nothing to do but to marry a girl to give her a pension for life to be paid out of the sweat of the people; and it was distinctly stated, during the session of Parliament before the last, that the widows and children of insane officers were to have the same treatment as the rest! Here is the envy of surrounding nations and the admiration of the world! In addition, then, to twenty thousand parsons, more than twenty thousand stockbrokers and stockjobbers perhaps; forty or fifty thousand tax-gatherers; thousands upon thousands of military and naval officers in full pay; in addition to all these, here are the thousands upon thousands of pairs of this Dead Weight, all busily engaged in breeding gentlemen and ladies; and all while Malthus is wanting to put a check upon the breeding of the labouring classes; all receiving a *premium for breeding!* Where is Malthus? Where is this check-population parson! Where are his friends, the Edinburgh Reviewers? Faith, I believe they have given him up. They begin to be ashamed of giving countenance to a man who wants to check the breeding of those who labour, while he says not a word about those two hundred thousand breeding pairs, whose offspring are necessarily to be maintained at the public charge. Well may these fatteners upon the labour of others rail against the Radicals! Let them once take the fan to their hand, and they will, I warrant it, thoroughly purge the floor. However, it is a consolation to know that the jolter-heads who have been the promoters of the measures that have led to these heavy charges; it is a consolation to know that the jolterheads have now to bear part of the charges, and that they cannot any longer make them fall exclusively upon the shoulders of the labouring classes. The disgust that one feels at seeing the whiskers, and hearing the copper heels rattle, is in some measure compensated for by the reflection that the expense of them is now beginning to fall upon the malignant and tyrannical jolter-heads who are the principal cause of their being created.

Bidding the *Semaphore* good-bye, I came along by the church at Hambledon, and then crossed a little common and the turnpike-road, from London to Chichester through Godalming and Petworth; not Midhurst, as before. The turnpike-road here is one of the best that ever I saw. It is like the road upon Horley Common, near Worth, and like that between Godstone and East Grinstead; and the cause of this is, that it is made of precisely the same sort of stone, which, they tell me, is brought, in some cases, even from Blackdown Hill, which cannot be less, I should think, than twelve miles distant. This stone is brought in great lumps, and then cracked into little pieces. The next village I came to after Hambledon was Hascomb, famous for its *beech*, insomuch that it is called *Hascomb Beech*.

There are two lofty hills here, between which you go out of the sandy country down into the Weald. Here are hills of all heights and forms. Whether they came in consequence of a

boiling of the earth, I know not; but, in form, they very much
resemble the bubbles upon the top of the water of a pot which
is violently boiling. The soil is a beautiful loam upon a bed of
sand. Springs start here and there at the feet of the hills; and
little rivulets pour away in all directions. The roads are difficult merely on account of their extreme unevenness; the bottom
is everywhere sound, and everything that meets the eye is
beautiful; trees, coppices, cornfields, meadows; and then the
distant views in every direction. From one spot I saw this
morning Hindhead, Blackdown Hill, Lord Egremont's house
and park at Petworth, Donnington Hill, over which I went to
go on the South Downs, the South Downs near Lewes: the
forest at Worth, Turner's Hill, and then all the way round into
Kent and back to the Surrey Hills at Godstone. From Hascomb I began to descend into the low country. I had Leith
Hill before me; but my plan was, not to go over it or any part of
it, but to go along below it in the real Weald of Surrey. A little
way back from Hascomb, I had seen a *field of carrots ;* and now
I was descending into a country where, strictly speaking, only
three things will grow well—grass, wheat, and oak trees. At
Goose Green, I crossed a turnpike-road leading from Guildford
to Horsham and Arundel. I next come, after crossing a canal,
to a common called Smithwood Common. Leith Hill was full
in front of me, but I turned away to the right, and went through
the lanes to come to Ewhurst, leaving Crawley to my right.
Before I got to Ewhurst, I crossed another turnpike-road, leading
from Guildford to Horsham, and going on to Worthing or some
of those towns.

At Ewhurst, which is a very pretty village, and the church
of which is most delightfully situated, I treated my horse to
some oats, and myself to a rasher of bacon. I had now to come,
according to my project, round among the lanes at about a couple
of miles distance from the foot of Leith Hill, in order to get
first to Ockley, then to Holmwood, and then to Reigate. From
Ewhurst the first three miles was the deepest clay that I ever
saw, to the best of my recollection. I was warned of the difficulty of getting along; but I was not to be frightened at the
sound of clay. Wagons, too, had been dragged along the lanes
by some means or another; and where a wagon-horse could go,
my horse could go. It took me, however, a good hour and a
half to get along these three miles. Now, mind, this is the real
weald, where the clay is *bottomless ;* where there is no stone of
any sort underneath, as at Worth and all along from Crawley

to Billingshurst through Horsham. This clayey land is fed with water soaking from the sand-hills; and in this particular place from the immense hill of Leith. All along here the oak-woods are beautiful. I saw scores of acres by the roadside, where the young oaks stood as regularly as if they had been planted. The orchards are not bad along here, and, perhaps, they are a good deal indebted to the shelter they receive. The wheat very good, all through the weald, but backward.

At Ockley I passed the house of a Mr. Steer, who has a great quantity of hay-land, which is very pretty. Here I came along the turnpike-road that leads from Dorking to Horsham. When I got within about two or three miles of Dorking, I turned off to the right, came across the Holmwood, into the lanes leading down to Gadbrook Common, which has of late years been inclosed. It is all clay here; but, in the whole of my ride, I have not seen much finer fields of wheat than I saw here. Out of these lanes I turned up to " Betchworth " (I believe it is), and from Betchworth came along a chalk hill to my left and the sand hills to my right, till I got to this place.

WEN,
Sunday, 10 August.

I stayed at Reigate yesterday, and came to the Wen to-day, every step of the way in a rain; as good a soaking as any devotee of St. Swithin ever underwent for his sake. I promised that I would give an account of the effect which the soaking on the South Downs, on Saturday the 2nd instant, had upon the hooping-cough. I do not recommend the remedy to others; but this I will say, that I had a spell of the hooping-cough, the day before I got that soaking, and that I have not had a single spell since; though I have slept in several different beds, and got a second soaking in going from Botley to Easton. The truth is, I believe, that rain upon the South Downs, or at any place near the sea, is by no means the same thing with rain in the interior. No man ever catches cold from getting wet with sea water; and, indeed, I have never known an instance of a man catching cold at sea. The air upon the South Downs is saltish, I dare say; and the clouds may bring something a little partaking of the nature of sea water.

At Thursley I left the turnip-hoers poking and pulling and muddling about the weeds, and wholly incapable, after all, of putting the turnips in anything like the state in which they ought to be. The weeds that had been hoed up twice, were growing again, and it was the same with the turnips that had been hoed up. In leaving Reigate this morning, it was with great pleasure that I saw a field of swedish turnips, drilled upon ridges at about four feet distance, the whole field as clean as the cleanest of garden ground. The turnips standing at equal distances in the row, and having the appearance of being, in every respect, in a prosperous state. I should not be afraid to bet that these turnips, thus standing in rows at nearly four feet distance, will be a crop twice as large as any in the parish of Thursley, though there is, I imagine, some of the finest turnip-land in the kingdom. It seems strange, that men are not to be convinced of the advantage of the row-culture for turnips. They will insist upon believing that there is some *ground lost*. They will also insist upon believing that the row-culture is the most expensive. How can there be ground lost if the crop be larger? And as to the expense, take one year with another, the broadcast method must be twice as expensive as the other. Wet as it has been to-day, I took time to look well about me as I came along. The wheat, even in this raga-muffin part of the country, is good, with the exception of one piece, which lies on your left hand as you come down from Banstead Down. It is very good at Banstead itself, though that is a country sufficiently poor. Just on the other side of Sutton there is a little good land, and in a place or two I thought I saw the wheat a little blighted. A labouring man told me that it was where the heaps of dung had been laid. The barley here is most beautiful, as, indeed, it is all over the country.

Between Sutton and the Wen there is, in fact, little besides houses, gardens, grass plats and other matters to accommodate the Jews and jobbers, and the mistresses and bastards that are put out a-keeping. But, in a dell, which the turnpike-road crosses about a mile on this side of Sutton, there are two fields of as stiff land, I think, as I ever saw in my life. In summer time this land bakes so hard that they cannot plough it unless it be wet. When you have ploughed it, and the sun comes again, it bakes again. One of these fields had been thus ploughed and cross-ploughed in the month of June, and I saw the ground when it was lying in lumps of the size of portmanteaus, and not very small ones either. It would have been impossible to reduce this ground to small particles, except by the means of sledge hammers. The two fields, to which I alluded just now, are alongside of this ploughed field, and they are now in wheat. The heavy rain of to-day, aided by the south-west wind, made the wheat bend pretty nearly to lying down; but you shall rarely see two finer fields of wheat. It is red wheat; a coarseish kind, and the straw stout and strong; but the ears are long, broad and full; and I did not perceive anything approaching towards a speck in the straw. Such land as this, such very stiff land, seldom carries a very large crop; but I should think that these fields would exceed four quarters to an acre; and the wheat is by no means so backward as it is in some places. There is no corn, that I recollect, from the spot just spoken of, to almost the street of Kensington. I came up by Earl's Court, where there is, amongst the market gardens, a field of wheat. One would suppose that this must be the finest wheat in the world. By no means. It rained hard, to be sure, and I had not much time for being particular in my survey; but this field appears to me to have some blight in it; and as to crop, whether of corn or of straw, it is nothing to compare to the general run of the wheat in the wealds of Sussex or of Surrey; what, then, is it, if compared with the wheat on the South Downs, under Portsdown Hill, on the sea-flats at Havant and at Tichfield, and along on the banks of the Itchen!

Thus I have concluded this " rural ride," from the Wen and back again to the Wen, being, taking in all the turnings and windings, as near as can be, two hundred miles in length. My objects were to ascertain the state of the crops, both of hops and of corn. The hop-affair is soon settled, for there will be no hops. As to the corn, my remark is this: that on all the clays, on all the stiff lands upon the chalk; on all the rich lands, indeed, but more especially on all the stiff lands, the wheat is as good as I recollect ever to have seen it, and has as much straw. On all the light lands and poor lands, the wheat is thin, and, though not short, by no means good. The oats are pretty good almost everywhere; and I have not seen a bad field of barley during the whole of my ride; though there is no species of soil in England, except that of the fens, over which I have not passed. The state of the farmers is much worse than it was last year, notwithstanding the ridiculous falsehoods of the London newspapers, and the more ridiculous delusion of the jolterheads. In numerous instances the farmers, who continue in their farms, have ceased to farm for themselves, and merely hold the land for the landlords. The delusion caused by the rise of the price of corn has pretty nearly vanished already; and if St. Swithin would but get out of the way with his drippings for about a month, this delusion would disappear, never to return. In the

meanwhile, however, the London newspapers are doing what
they can to keep up the delusion; and in a paper called *Bell's
Weekly Messenger*, edited, I am told, by a place-hunting lawyer;
in that stupid paper of this day, I find the following passage:—
" So late as January last, the average price of wheat was 39*s.*
per quarter, and on the 29th ult. it was above 62*s.* As it has
been rising ever since, it may *now be quoted as little under* 65*s.*
So that in this article alone, there is a rise of more than *thirty-
five* per cent. Under these circumstances, it is not likely that
we shall hear anything of *agricultural distress.* A writer of
considerable talents, but no prophet, had *frightened* the kingdom
by a confident prediction that wheat, after the 1st of May,
would sink to 4*s.* per bushel, and that under the effects of Mr.
Peel's bill, and the payments in cash by the Bank of England,
it would *never again exceed that price !* Nay, so assured was
Mr. Cobbett of the mathematical certainty of his deductions on
the subject, that he did not hesitate to make use of the following language: ' And farther, if what I say do not come to pass,
I will give any one leave to broil me on a gridiron, and for that
purpose I will get one of the best gridirons I can possibly get
made, and it shall be hung out as near to my premises as possible,
in the Strand, so that it shall be seen by everybody as they pass
along.' The 1st of May has now passed, Mr. Peel's bill has not
been repealed, and the Bank of England has paid its notes in
cash, and yet wheat has risen nearly 40 per cent."
Here is a tissue of falsehoods! But only think of a country
being "*frightened* " by the prospect of a low price of provisions!
When such an idea can possibly find its way even into the
shallow brain of a cracked-skull lawyer; when such an idea
can possibly be put into print at any rate, there must be something totally wrong in the state of the country. Here is this
lawyer telling his readers that I had frightened the kingdom,
by saying that wheat would be sold at four shillings a bushel.
Again I say, that there must be something wrong, something
greatly out of place, some great disease at work in the community,
or such an idea as this could never have found its way *into print.*
Into the head of a cracked-skull lawyer, it might, perhaps, have
entered at any time; but for it to find its way into print, there
must be something in the state of society wholly out of joint.
As to the rest of this article, it is a tissue of down-right lies. The
writer says that the price of wheat is sixty-five shillings a quarter.
The fact is, that on the second instant, the price was fifty-nine
shillings and seven-pence: and it is now about two shillings less

than that. Then again, this writer must know, that I never said that wheat would not rise above four shillings a bushel; but that on the contrary I always expressly said that the price would be affected by the seasons, and that I thought that the price would vibrate between three shillings a bushel and seven shillings a bushel. Then again, Peel's bill has, in part, been repealed; if it had not, there could have been no small note in circulation at this day. So that this lawyer is "*All lie.*" In obedience to the wishes of a lady, I have been reading about the plans of Mr. Owen; and though I do not as yet see my way clear as to how we can arrange matters with regard to the young girls and the young fellows, I am quite clear that his institution would be most excellent for the disposal of the lawyers. One of his squares would be at a great distance from all other habitations; in the midst of *Lord Erskine's estate* for instance, mentioned by me in a former ride; and nothing could be so fitting, his lordship long having been called *the father of the Bar ;* in the midst of this estate, with no town or village within miles of them, we might have one of Mr. Owen's squares, and set the bob-tailed brotherhood most effectually at work. Pray, can any one pretend to say that a spade or shovel would not become the hands of this blunder-headed editor of *Bell's Messenger* better than a pen? However, these miserable falsehoods can cause the delusion to exist but for a very short space of time.

The quantity of the harvest will be great. If the quality be bad, owing to wet weather, the price will be still lower than it would have been in case of dry weather. The price, therefore, must come down; and if the newspapers were conducted by men who had any sense of honour or shame, those men must be covered with confusion.

RIDE THROUGH THE NORTH-EAST PART OF SUSSEX, AND ALL ACROSS KENT, FROM THE WEALD OF SUSSEX, TO DOVER

WORTH (SUSSEX),
Friday, 29 August, 1823.

I HAVE so often described the soil and other matters appertaining to the country between the Wen and this place, that my readers will rejoice at being spared the repetition here. As to the harvest, however, I find that they were deluged here on Tuesday last, though we got but little, comparatively, at Kensington. Between Mitcham and Sutton they were making wheat-ricks. The corn has not been injured here worth notice. Now and then an ear in the butts *grown ;* and grown wheat is a sad thing! You may almost as well be without wheat altogether. However, very little harm has been done here as yet.

At Walton Heath I saw a man who had suffered most terribly from the *game-laws.* He saw me going by, and came out to tell me his story; and a horrible story it is, as the public will find, when it shall come regularly and fully before them. Apropos of game-works: I asked who was *the judge* at the Somersetshire Assizes, the other day. A correspondent tells me that it was Judge Burrough. I am well aware that, as this correspondent observes, " gamekeepers ought not to be *shot at.*" This is not the point. It is not a *gamekeeper* in the usual sense of that word; it is a man seizing another without a warrant. That is what it is; and this, and Old Ellenborough's Act, are *new things* in England, and things of which the laws of England, " the birthright of Englishmen," knew nothing. Yet farmer Voke ought not to have shot at the gamekeeper, or seizer, without warrant: he ought not to have shot at him; and he would not had it not been for the law that put him in danger of being transported on the evidence of this man. So that it is, clearly, the terrible law that, in these cases, produces the violence. Yet, admire with me, reader, the singular turn of the mind of Sir James Mackintosh, whose whole soul appears to have been long bent on the " amelioration of the Penal Code," and who has never said one single word about this new and most terrible part of it! Sir James, after years of incessant toil, has, I believe, succeeded in getting a repeal of the laws for the punishment of " witchcraft," of the very existence of which laws the nation was unacquainted. But the devil a word has he said about the *game-laws*, which put into the gaols a full third part of the prisoners, and to hold which prisoners the gaols have actually been enlarged in all parts of the country! Singular turn of mind! Singular " humanity! " Ah! Sir James knows very well what he is at. He understands the state of his constituents at Knaresborough too well to meddle with game-laws. He has a " friend," I dare say, who knows more about game-laws than he does. However, the poor *witches* are safe: thank Sir James for that. Mr. Carlile's sister and Mrs. Wright are in gaol, and may be there for life! But the poor witches are safe. No hypocrite; no base pretender to religion; no atrocious, savage, *black*-hearted wretch, who would murder half mankind rather than not live on the labours of others; no monster of this kind can now persecute the poor witches, thanks to Sir James, who has obtained security for them in all their rides through the air, and in all their sailings upon the horseponds!

TONBRIDGE WELLS (KENT),
Saturday, 30 August.

I came from Worth about seven this morning, passed through East Grinstead, over Holthigh Common, through Ashurst, and thence to this place. The morning was very fine, and I left them at Worth making a wheat-rick. There was no show for rain till about one o'clock, as I was approaching Ashurst. The shattering that came at first I thought nothing of; but the clouds soon grew up all round, and the rain set in for the afternoon. The buildings at Ashurst (which is the first parish in Kent on quitting Sussex) are a mill, an alehouse, a church, and about six or seven other houses. I stopped at the alehouse to bait my horse; and, for want of bacon, was compelled to put up with bread and cheese for myself. I waited in vain for the rain to cease or to slacken, and the *want of bacon* made me fear as to a *bed*. So, about five o'clock, I, without greatcoat, got upon my horse, and came to this place, just as fast and no faster than if it had been fine weather. A very fine soaking! If the South Downs have left any little remnant of the hooping cough, *this* will take it away to be sure. I made not the least haste to get out of the rain, I stopped, here and there, as usual, and asked questions about the corn, the hops, and other things. But the moment I got in I got a good fire, and set about the work of drying in good earnest. It costing me nothing for drink, I can afford to have plenty of fire. I have not been in the house an hour; and all my clothes are now as dry as if they had never been wet. It is not getting wet that hurts you, if you keep moving while you are wet. It is the suffering of yourself to be *inactive*, while the wet clothes are on your back.

The country that I have come over to-day is a very pretty one. The soil is a pale yellow loam, looking like brick earth, but rather sandy; but the bottom is a softish stone. Now and then, where you go through hollow ways (as at East Grinstead) the sides are solid rock. And, indeed, the rocks sometimes (on the sides of hills) show themselves above ground, and, mixed amongst the woods, make very interesting objects. On the road from the Wen to Brighton, through Godstone and over Turner's Hill, and which road I crossed this morning in coming from Worth to East Grinstead; on that road, which goes through Lindfield, and which is by far the pleasantest coach-road from the Wen to Brighton; on the side of this road, on which coaches now go from the Wen to Brighton, there is a long chain of rocks, or, rather, rocky hills, with trees growing amongst the rocks, or apparently out of them, as they do in the woods near Ross in Herefordshire, and as they do in the Blue Mountains in America, where you can see no earth at all; where all seems rock, and yet where the trees grow most beautifully. At the place, of which I am now speaking, that is to say, by the side of this pleasant road to Brighton, and between Turner's Hill and Lindfield, there is a rock, which they call "*Big-upon-Little;*" that is to say, a rock upon another, having nothing else to rest upon, and the top one being longer and wider than the top of the one it lies on. This big rock is no trifling concern, being as big, perhaps, as a not very small house. How, then, *came* this big upon little? What lifted up the big? It balances itself naturally enough; but what tossed it up? I do not like to *pay* a parson for teaching me, while I have "*God's own word*" to teach me; but if any parson will tell me *how* big *came* upon little, I do not know that I shall grudge him a trifle. And if he cannot tell me this: if he say, All that we have to do is to *admire* and *adore ;* then I tell him, that I can admire and adore without his *aid*, and that I will keep my money in my pocket.

To return to the soil of this country, it is such a loam as I have described with this stone beneath; sometimes the top soil is lighter and sometimes heavier; sometimes the stone is harder and sometimes softer; but this is the general character of it all the way from Worth to Tonbridge Wells. This land is what may be called the *middle kind*. The wheat crop about 20 to 24 bushels to an acre, on an average of years. The grass fields not bad, and all the fields will grow grass; I mean make upland meadows. The woods good, though not of the finest. The land seems to be about thus divided: three-tenths *woods*, two-tenths *grass*, a tenth of a tenth *hops*, and the rest *corn-land*. These make very pretty surface, especially as it is a rarity to see a *pollard tree*, and as nobody is so beastly as to *trim trees up* like the elms near the Wen. The country has no *flat* spot in it; yet the hills are not high. My road was a gentle rise or a gentle descent all the way. Continual new views strike the eye; but there is little variety in them: all is pretty, but nothing strikingly beautiful. The labouring people look pretty well. They have pigs. They invariably do best in the *woodland* and *forest* and *wild* countries. Where the mighty grasper has *all under his eye*, they can get but little. These are cross-roads, mere parish roads; but they are very good. While I was at the alehouse at Ashurst, I heard some labouring men talking about the roads; and they having observed that the parish roads had become so wonderfully better within the last seven or eight years, I put in my word, and said: " It is odd enough, too, that the parish roads should become *better and better* as the farmers become *poorer and poorer !* " They looked at one another, and put on a sort of *expecting* look; for my observation seemed to *ask for information*. At last one of them said, " Why, it is because the farmers *have not the money to employ men*, and so they are put on the roads." " Yes," said I, " but they must pay them there." They said no more, and only *looked hard at one another*. They had, probably, never thought about this before. They seemed puzzled by it, and well they might, for it has bothered the wigs of boroughmongers, parsons and lawyers, and will bother them yet. Yes, this country now contains a body of occupiers of the land, who suffer the land to go to decay for want of means to pay a sufficiency of labourers; and, at the same time, are compelled to pay those labourers for doing that which is of no use to the occupiers! There, Collective Wisdom! Go: brag of that! Call that " the envy of surrounding nations and the admiration of the world."

This is a great *nut* year. I saw them hanging very thick on the way-side during a great part of this day's ride; and they put me in mind of the old saying, "That a great *nut* year is a great year for that class whom the lawyers, in their Latin phrase, call the 'sons and daughters of nobody.'" I once asked a farmer, who had often been overseer of the poor, whether he really thought that there was any ground for this old saying, or whether he thought it was mere banter? He said that he was sure that there were good grounds for it; and he even cited instances in proof, and mentioned one particular year, when there were four times as many of this class as ever had been born in a year in the parish before; an effect which he ascribed solely to the crop of nuts of the year before. Now, if this be the case, ought not Parson Malthus, Lawyer Scarlett, and the rest of that tribe, to turn their attention to the nut-trees? The *Vice Society* too, with that holy man Wilberforce at its head, ought to look out sharp after these mischievous nut-trees. A law to cause them all to be grubbed up, and thrown into the fire, would, certainly, be far less unreasonable than many things which we have seen and heard of.

The corn from Worth to this place is pretty good. The farmers say it is a small crop; other people, and especially the labourers, say that it is a good crop. I think it is not large and not small; about an average crop; perhaps rather less, for the land is rather light, and this is not a year for light lands. But there is no blight, no mildew, in spite of all the prayers of the "loyal." The wheat about a third cut, and none carried. No other corn begun upon. Hops very bad till I came within a few miles of this place, when I saw some, which I should suppose, would bear about six hundredweight to the acre. The orchards no great things along here. Some apples here and there; but small and stunted. I do not know that I have seen to-day any one *tree* well loaded with fine apples.

TENTERDEN (KENT),
Sunday, 31 *August.*

Here I am after a most delightful ride of twenty-four miles, through Frant, Lamberhurst, Goudhurst, Milkhouse Street, Benenden, and Rolvenden. By making a great stir in rousing waiters and "boots" and maids, and by leaving behind me the name of "a d—d noisy, troublesome fellow," I got clear of "*the Wells*," and out of the contagion of its Wen-engendered inhabitants, time enough to meet the first rays of the sun, on the hill that you come up in order to get to Frant, which is a most beautiful little village at about two miles from "*the*

Wells." Here the land belongs, I suppose, to Lord Abergavenny, who has a mansion and park here. A very pretty place, and kept, seemingly, in very nice order. I saw here what I never saw before: the bloom of the *common heath* we wholly overlook; but it is a very pretty thing; and here, when the plantations were made, and as they grew up, heath was *left to grow* on the sides of the roads in the plantations. The heath is not so much of a dwarf as we suppose. This is four feet high; and, being in full bloom, it makes the prettiest border that can be imagined. This place of Lord Abergavenny is, altogether, a very pretty place; and so far from grudging him the possession of it, I should feel pleasure at seeing it in his possession, and should pray God to preserve it to him, and from the unholy and ruthless touch of the Jews and jobbers; but I cannot forget this lord's *sinecure!* I cannot forget that he has, for doing nothing, received of the public money more than sufficient to buy such an estate as this. I cannot forget that this estate may, perhaps, have actually been bought with that money. Not being able to forget this, and with my mind filled with reflections of this sort, I got up to the church at Frant, and just by I saw a *School-house* with this motto on it: "*Train up a child as he should walk,*" etc. That is to say, try to breed up the boys and girls of this village in such a way that they may never know anything about Lord Abergavenny's sinecure; or, knowing about it, that they may think it *right* that he should roll in wealth coming to him in such a way. The projectors deceive nobody but themselves! They are working for the destruction of their own system. In looking back over "*the Wells*" I cannot but admire the operation of the gambling system. This little *toadstool* is a thing created entirely by the gamble; and the means have, hitherto, come out of the wages of labour. These means are *now* coming out of the farmer's capital and out of the landlord's estate; the labourers are stripped; they can give no more; the saddle is now fixing itself upon the right back.

In quitting Frant I descended into a country more woody than that behind me. I asked a man whose fine woods those were that I pointed to, and I fairly gave *a start* when he said, the Marquis Camden's. Milton talks of the *Leviathan* in a way to make one draw in one's shoulders with fear; and I appeal to any one, who has been at sea when a whale has come near the ship, whether he has not, at the first sight of the monster, made a sort of involuntary movement, as if to *get out of the way*. Such was the movement that I now made. However, soon coming to myself, on I walked my horse by the side of my pedestrian informant. It is Bayham Abbey that this great and awful sinecure placeman owns in this part of the county. Another great estate he owns near Sevenoaks. But here alone he spreads his length and breadth over more, they say, than ten or twelve thousand acres of land, great part of which consists of oak-woods. But, indeed, what estates might he not purchase? Not much less than thirty years he held a place, a sinecure place, that yielded him about thirty thousand pounds a-year! At any rate, he, according to Parliamentary accounts, has received, of public money, little short of a million of guineas. These, at 30 guineas an acre, would buy thirty thousand acres of land. And what did he have all this money *for?* Answer me that question, Wilberforce, you who called him a " bright star," when he gave up *a part* of his enormous sinecure. He gave up all but the *trifling* sum of nearly three thousand pounds a-year! What a bright star! And *when* did he give it up? When the *Radicals* had made the country ring with it. When his name was, by their means, getting into every mouth in the kingdom; when every radical speech and petition contained the name of Camden. Then it was, and not till then, that this " bright star," let fall part of its " brilliancy." So that Wilberforce ought to have thanked the *Radicals*, and not Camden. When he let go his grasp, he talked of the merits of his father. His father was a lawyer, who was exceedingly well paid for what he did without a million of money being given to his son. But there is something rather out of common-place to be observed about this father. This father was the contemporary of Yorke, who became Lord Hardwicke. Pratt and Yorke, and the merit of Pratt was, that he was constantly opposed to the principles of Yorke. Yorke was called a *Tory* and Pratt a *Whig;* but the devil of it was, both got to be lords; and, in one shape or another, the families of both have, from that day to this, been receiving great parcels of the public money! Beautiful system! The Tories were for *rewarding Yorke;* the Whigs were for *rewarding Pratt.* The ministers (all in good time!) humoured both parties; and the stupid people, divided into *tools of two factions,* actually applauded, now one part of them, and now the other part of them, the squandering away of their substance. They were like the man and his wife in the fable who, to spite one another, gave away to the cunning mumper the whole of their dinner bit by bit. *This species* of folly is over at any rate. The people are no longer fools enough to be *partisans.* They make no distinctions. The nonsense about " court party " and " country party " is at an end. Who thinks anything more of the name of *Erskine* than of that of *Scott?* As the people told the two factions at Maidstone, when they, with Camden at their head, met to congratulate the Regent on the marriage of his daughter, " they are all tarred with the same brush; " and tarred with the same brush they must be, until there be a real reform of the parliament. However, the people are no longer deceived. They are not duped. They *know* that the thing is that which it is. The people of the present day would laugh at disputes (carried on with so much gravity!) about the *principles* of Pratt and the *principles* of Yorke. " You are all tarred with the same brush," said the sensible people of Maidstone; and, in those words, they expressed the opinion of the whole country, boroughmongers and tax-eaters excepted.

The country from Frant to Lamberhurst is very woody. I should think five-tenths woods and three grass. The corn, what there is of it, is about the same as farther back. I saw a hop-garden just before I got to Lamberhurst, which will have about two or three hundredweight to the acre. This Lamberhurst is a very pretty place. It lies in a valley with beautiful hills round it. The pastures about here are very fine; and the roads are as smooth and as handsome as those in Windsor Park.

From the last-mentioned place I had three miles to come to Goudhurst, the tower of the church of which is pretty lofty of itself, and the church stands upon the very summit of one of the steepest and highest hills in this part of the country. The church-yard has a view of about twenty-five miles in diameter; and the whole is over a very fine country, though the character of the country differs little from that which I have before described.

Before I got to Goudhurst, I passed by the side of a village called Horsenden, and saw some very large hop-grounds away to my right. I should suppose there were fifty acres; and they appeared to me to look pretty well. I found that they belonged to a Mr. Springate, and people say that it will grow half as many hops as he grew last year, while people in general will not grow a tenth part so many. This hop growing and dealing have always been a *gamble;* and this puts me in mind of the horrible treatment which Mr. Waddington received on account of what was called his *forestalling* in hops! It is useless to talk: as long as that gentleman remains uncompensated for his sufferings, there can be no hope of better days. Ellenborough was his counsel; he afterwards became judge; but nothing was ever done to undo what Kenyon had done. However, Mr. Waddington will, I trust, yet live to obtain justice. He has, in the meanwhile, given the thing now and then a blow; and he has the satisfaction to see it reel about like a drunken man.

I got to Goudhurst to breakfast, and as I heard that the Dean of Rochester was to preach a sermon in behalf of the *National Schools*, I stopped to hear him. In waiting for his reverence I went to the Methodist Meeting-house, where I found the Sunday school boys and girls asembled, to the almost filling of the place, which was about thirty feet long and eighteen wide. The "minister" was not come, and the schoolmaster was reading to the children out of a *tract-book*, and shaking the brimstone bag at them most furiously. This schoolmaster was a *sleek*-looking young fellow: his skin perfectly tight: well fed, I'll warrant him: and he has discovered the way of living, without work, on the labour of those that do work. There were 36 little fellows in smock-frocks, and about as many girls listening to him; and I dare say he eats as much meat as any ten of them. By this time the *dean*, I thought, would be coming on; and, therefore, to the church I went; but to my great disappointment, I found that the parson was operating *preparatory* to the appearance of the dean, who was to come on in the afternoon, when I, agreeably to my plan, must be off. The sermon was from 2 Chronicles xxxi. 21., and the words of this text described King Hezekiah as a most *zealous man*, doing whatever he did *with all his heart*. I write from *memory*, mind, and, therefore, I do not pretend to quote exact words; and I may be a little in error, perhaps, as to chapter or verse. The object of the preacher was to hold up to his hearers the example of Hezekiah, and particularly in the case of the school affair. He called upon them to subscribe with all their hearts; but, alas! how little of *persuasive power* was there in what he said! No effort to make them see *the use of the schools*. No inducement *proved* to exist. No argument, in short, nor anything to move. No appeal either to the *reason*, or to the *feeling*. All was general, commonplace, cold observation; and that, too, in language which the far greater part of the hearers could not understand. This church is about 110 feet long and 70 feet wide in the clear. It would hold *three thousand people*, and it had in it 214, besides 53 Sunday School or National School boys; and these sat together, in a sort of lodge, up in a corner, 16 feet long and 10 feet wide. Now, will any Parson Malthus, or anybody else, have the impudence to tell me that this church was built for the use of a population not more numerous than the present? To be sure, when this church was built, there could be no idea of a Methodist meeting coming to *assist* the church, and as little, I dare say, was it expected that the preachers in the church would ever call upon the faithful to subscribe money to be sent up to one Joshua Watson (living in a Wen) to be by him laid out in " promoting Christian knowledge; " but, at any rate, the Methodists cannot take away above four or five hundred; and what, then, was this great church built *for*, if there were no more people, in those days, at Goudhurst, than there are now? It is very true that the *labouring* people have, in a great measure, ceased to go to church. There were scarcely any of that class at this great country church to-day. I do not believe there were *ten*. I can remember when they were so numerous that the parson could not attempt to begin till the rattling of their nailed shoes ceased. I have seen, I am sure, five hundred boys and men in smock-frocks coming out of church at one time. To-day has been a fine day: there would have been many at church to-day, if ever there are; and here I have another to add to the many things that convince me that the labouring classes have, in great part, ceased to go to church; that their way of thinking and feeling with regard to both church and clergy are totally changed; and that there is now very little *moral hold* which the latter possess. This preaching for money to support the schools is a most curious affair altogether. The king sends a *circular letter* to the bishops (as I understand it) to cause subscriptions for the schools; and the bishops (if I am rightly told) tell the parish clergy to send the money, when collected, to Joshua Watson, the treasurer of a society in the Wen, " for promoting Christian knowledge! " What! the church and all its clergy put into motion to get money from the people, to send up to one Joshua Watson, a wine-merchant, or late a wine-merchant, in Mincing Lane, Fenchurch Street, London, in order that the said wine-merchant may apply the money to the " promoting of Christian knowledge! " What! all the deacons, priests, curates perpetual, vicars, rectors, prebends, doctors, deans, archdeacons and fathers in God, right reverend and most reverend; all! yea all, engaged in getting money together to send to a wine-merchant that he may lay it out in the promoting of Christian knowledge *in their own flocks !* Oh, brave wine-merchant! What a prince of godliness must this wine-merchant be! I say wine-merchant, or late wine-merchant, of Mincing Lane, Fenchurch Street, London. And, for God's sake, some good parson, do send me up a copy of the king's circular, and also of the bishop's order to send the money to Joshua Watson; for some precious sport we will have with Joshua and his " society " before we have done with them!

After " service " I mounted my horse and jogged on through Milkhouse Street to Benenden, where I passed through the estate, and in sight of the house of Mr. Hodges. He keeps it very neat and has planted a good deal. His *ash* do very well; but the *chesnut* do not, as it seems to me. He ought to have the American chesnut, if he have any. If I could discover *an everlasting hop-pole*, and one, too, that would grow faster even than the ash, would not these Kentish hop-planters put me in the Kalendar along with their famous Saint Thomas of Canterbury? We shall see this, one of these days.

Coming through the village of Benenden, I heard a man at my right talking very loud about *houses! houses! houses!* It was a Methodist parson, in a house close by the road side. I pulled up, and stood still, in the middle of the road, but looking, in silent soberness, into the window (which was open) of the room in which the preacher was at work. I believe my stopping rather disconcerted him; for he got into shocking *repetition.* " Do you *know*," said he, laying great stress on the word *know :* " do you *know*, that you have ready for you houses, houses I say; I say do you know; do you know that you have houses in the heavens not made with hands? Do you know this from *experience ?* Has the blessed Jesus *told you so ?* " And on he went to say that, if Jesus had told them so, they would be saved, and that if he had not, and did not, they would be damned. Some girls whom I saw in the room, plump and rosy as could be, did not seem at all daunted by these menaces; and indeed, they appeared to me to be thinking much more about getting houses for themselves *in this world first ;* just to *see a little* before they entered, or endeavoured to enter, or even thought much about, those " *houses* " of which the parson was speaking: houses with pig-styes and little snug gardens attached to them, together with all the other domestic and conjugal circumstances, these girls seemed to me to be preparing themselves for. The truth is, these fellows have no power on the minds of any but the miserable.

Scarcely had I proceeded a hundred yards from the place where this fellow was bawling, when I came to the very situation which he ought to have occupied, I mean the *stocks*, which the people of Benenden have, with singular humanity, fitted up with a *bench*, so that the patient, while he is receiving the benefit of the remedy, is not exposed to the danger of catching cold by sitting, as in other places, upon the ground, always damp, and sometimes actually wet. But I would ask the people of Benenden what is the *use* of this humane precaution, and, indeed, what is the use of the stocks themselves, if, while a fellow is ranting and bawling in the manner just described, at the distance of a hundred yards from the stocks, the stocks (as is here actually the case) are almost hidden by grass and nettles? This, however, is the case all over the country; not nettles and grass indeed smothering the stocks, but I never see any feet peeping through the holes, anywhere, though I find Methodist parsons everywhere, and though *the law compels the parishes to keep up* all the pairs of stocks that exist in all parts of them; and, in some parishes, they have to keep up several pairs. I am aware that a good part of the use of the stocks is the *terror* they ought to produce. I am not supposing that they are of no use because not continually furnished with legs. But there is a wide difference between *always* and *never ;* and it is clear that a fellow, who has had the stocks under his eye all his lifetime, and has *never* seen a pair of feet peeping through them, will stand no more in awe of the stocks than rooks do of an old shoy-hoy, or than the ministers or their agents do of Hobhouse and Burdett. Stocks that never pinch a pair of ankles are like ministerial responsibility; a thing to talk about, but for no other use; a mere mockery; a thing laughed at by those whom it is intended to keep in check. It is time that the stocks were again *in use*, or that the expense of keeping them up were put an end to.

This mild, this gentle, this good-humoured sort of correction is *not enough* for our present rulers. But mark the consequence; gaols ten times as big as formerly; houses of correction; treadmills; the hulks; and the country filled with *spies* of one sort and another, *game-spies*, or other spies, and if a hare or pheasant come to an untimely death, *police-officers* from the Wen are not unfrequently called down to find out and secure the bloody offender! *Mark this*, Englishmen! Mark how we take to those things, which we formerly ridiculed in the French; and take them up too just as that brave and spirited people have shaken them off! I saw, not long ago, an account of a Wen police-officer being sent into the country, where he assumed *a disguise*, joined some poachers (as they are called), got into their secrets, went out in the night with them, and then (having laid his plans with the game-people) assisted to take them and convict them.

What! is this *England!* Is this the land of " manly hearts? " Is this the country that laughed at the French for their submissions? What! are police-officers kept for this? Does the law say so? However, thank God Almighty the estates are passing away into the hands of those who have had borrowed from them the money to uphold this monster of a system. The Debt! The blessed Debt will, at last, restore to us freedom.

Just after I quitted Benenden, I saw some bunches of *straw* lying upon the quickset hedge of a cottage garden. I found, upon inquiry, that they were bunches of the straw of grass. Seeing a face through the window of the cottage, I called out and asked what that straw was for. The person within said, it was to make *Leghorn-plat* with. I asked him (it was a young man) how he knew how to do it. He said he had got a little book that had been made by Mr. Cobbett. I told him that I was the man, and should like to see some of his work; and asked him to bring it out to me, I being afraid to tie my horse. He told me that he was a *cripple*, and that he could not come out. At last I went in, leaving my horse to be held by a little girl. I found a young man, who has been a cripple for fourteen years. Some ladies in the neighbourhood had got him the book, and his family had got him the grass. He had made some very nice plat, and he had knitted the greater part of the crown of a bonnet, and had done the whole very nicely, though, as to the knitting, he had proceeded in a way to make it very tedious. He was knitting upon a block. However, these little matters will soon be set to rights. There will soon be persons to teach knitting in all parts of the country. I left this unfortunate young man with the pleasing reflection that I had, in all likelihood, been the cause of his gaining a good living, by his labour, during the rest of his life. How long will it be before my calumniators, the false and infamous London press, will take the whole of it together, and leave out its evil, do as much good as my pen has done in this one instance! How long will it be ere the ruffians, the base hirelings, the infamous traders who own and who conduct that press; how long ere one of them, or all of them together, shall cause a cottage to smile; shall add one ounce to the meal of the labouring man!

Rolvenden was my next village, and thence I could see the lofty church of Tenterden on the top of a hill at three miles distance. This Rolvenden is a very beautiful village; and, indeed, such are all the places along here. These villages are not like those in the *iron* counties, as I call them; that is, the counties of flint and chalk. Here the houses have gardens in front of them as well as behind; and there is a good deal of show and finery about them and their gardens. The high roads are without a stone in them; and everything looks like *gentility*. At this place, I saw several *arbutuses* in one garden, and much finer than we see them in general; though, mind, this is no proof of a mild climate; for the arbutus is a native of one much colder than that of England, and indeed than that of Scotland.

Coming from Benenden to Rolvenden I saw some swedish turnips, and, strange as the reader will think it, the first I saw after leaving Worth! The reason I take to be this: the farms are all furnished with grass fields as in Devonshire about Honiton. These grass fields give hay for the sheep and cattle in winter, or, at any rate, they do all that is not done by the white turnips. It may be a question, whether it would be more *profitable* to break up, and sow swedes; but this is the reason of their not being cultivated along here. White turnips are more easily got than swedes; they may be sown later; and, with good hay, they will fat cattle and sheep; but the swedes will do this business without hay. In Norfolk and Suffolk the land is not generally of a nature to make hay-fields. Therefore the people there resort to swedes. This has been a sad time for these hay-farmers, however, all along here. They have but just finished haymaking; and I see, all along my way, from East Grinstead to this place, hay-ricks the colour of dirt and *smoking* like dung-heaps.

Just before I got to this place (Tenterden), I crossed a bit of marsh land, which I found, upon inquiry, is a sort of little branch or spray running out of that immense and famous tract of country called *Romney Marsh*, which, I find, I have to cross to-morrow, in order to get to Dover, along by the seaside, through Hythe and Folkestone.

This Tenterden is a market town, and a singularly bright spot. It consists of one street, which is, in some places, more, perhaps, than two hundred feet wide. On one side of the street the houses have gardens before them, from 20 to 70 feet deep. The town is upon a hill; the afternoon was very fine, and just as I rose the hill and entered the street, the people had come out of church and were moving along towards their houses. It was a very fine sight. *Shabbily-dressed people do not go to church.* I saw, in short, drawn out before me, the dress and beauty of the town; and a great many very, very pretty girls I saw; and saw them, too, in their best attire. I remember the girls in the

Pays de Caux, and, really, I think those of Tenterden resemble them. I do not know why they should not; for there is the *Pays de Caux*, only just over the water; just opposite this very place.

The hops about here are not so very bad. They say that one man, near this town, will have eight tons of hops upon ten acres of land! This is a great crop any year: a very great crop. This man may, perhaps, sell his hops for 1600 pounds! What a *gambling* concern it is! However, such hop-growing always was and always must be. It is a thing of perfect hazard.

The church at this place is a very large and fine old building. The tower stands upon a base thirty feet square. Like the church at Goudhurst, it will hold three thousand people. And, let it be observed, that, when these churches were built, people had not yet thought of cramming them with *pews*, as a stable is filled with stalls. Those who built these churches had no idea that worshipping God meant going to *sit* to hear a man talk out what he called preaching. By *worship*, they meant very different things; and, above all things, when they had made a fine and noble building, they did not dream of disfiguring the inside of it by filling its floor with large and deep boxes made of deal boards. In short, the floor was the place for the worshippers to stand or to kneel; and there was *no distinction;* no *high* place and no *low* place; all were upon a level *before God* at any rate. Some were not stuck into pews lined with green or red cloth, while others were crammed into corners to stand erect, or sit on the floor. These odious distinctions are of Protestant origin and growth. This lazy lolling in pews we owe to what is called the *Reformation*. A place filled with benches and boxes looks like an eating or a drinking place; but certainly not like a place of worship. A Frenchman, who had been driven from St. Domingo to Philadelphia by the Wilberforces of France, went to church along with me one Sunday. He had never been in a Protestant place of *worship* before. Upon looking round him, and seeing everybody comfortably seated, while a couple of good stoves were keeping the place as warm as a slack oven, he exclaimed: "*Pardi! On sert Dieu bien à son aise ici!*" That is: "Egad! they serve God very much at their ease here!" I always think of this, when I see a church full of pews; as, indeed, is now always the case with our churches. Those who built these churches had no idea of this: they made their calculations as to the people to be contained in them, not making any allowance for *deal boards*. I often wonder how it is that the present parsons are not ashamed to call the churches *theirs!* They must know the origin of them; and how they can look at them, and, at the same time, revile the Catholics, is astonishing to me.

This evening I have been to the Methodist Meeting-house. I was attracted, fairly drawn all down the street, by the *singing*. When I came to the place the parson was got into prayer. His hands were clenched together and held up, his face turned up and back so as to be nearly parallel with the ceiling, and he was bawling away with his "do thou," and "mayest thou," and "may we," enough to stun one. Noisy, however, as he was, he was unable to fix the attention of a parcel of girls in the gallery, whose eyes were all over the place, while his eyes were so devoutly shut up. After a deal of this rigmarole called prayer, came the *preachy*, as the negroes call it; and a *preachy* it really was. Such a mixture of whining cant and of foppish affectation I scarcely ever heard in my life. The text was (I speak from memory) one of Saint Peter's epistles (if he have more than one) the 18th chapter and 4th verse. The words were to this amount: that, *as the righteous would be saved with difficulty, what must become of the ungodly and the sinner!* After as neat a dish of nonsense and of impertinences as one could wish to have served up, came the distinction between the *ungodly* and the *sinner*. The sinner was one who did moral wrong; the ungodly, one who did no moral wrong, but who was not regenerated. *Both*, he positively told us, were to be damned. One was just as bad as the other. Moral rectitude was to do nothing in saving the man. He was to be damned, unless born again, and how was he to be born again, unless he came to the regeneration shop, and gave the fellows money? He distinctly told us that a man perfectly moral might be damned; and that "the vilest of the vile, and the basest of the base " (I quote his very words) "would be saved if they became regenerate; and that colliers, whose souls had been as black as their coals, had by regeneration become bright as the saints that sing before God and the Lamb." And will the *Edinburgh Reviewers* again find fault with me for cutting at this bawling, canting crew? Monstrous it is to think that the clergy of the church really encourage these roving fanatics. The church seems aware of its loss of credit and of power. It seems willing to lean even upon these men; who, be it observed, seem, on their part, to have taken the church under their protection. They always pray for the *Ministry*; I mean the ministry at *Whitehall*. They are most "loyal " souls. The THING *protects them;* and they lend their aid *in upholding the* THING. What silly, nay, what base creatures those must be, who really give their money, give their pennies, which ought to buy bread for their own children; who thus give their money to these lazy and impudent fellows, who call themselves ministers of God, who prowl about the country living easy and jovial lives upon the fruit of the labour of other people. However, it is, in some measure, these people's fault. If they did not give, the others could not receive. I wish to see every labouring man well fed and well clad; but, really, the man who gives any portion of his earnings to these fellows deserves to want: he deserves to be pinched with hunger: misery is the just reward of this worst species of prodigality.

The *singing* makes a great part of what passes in these meeting-houses. A number of women and girls singing together make very sweet sounds. Few men there are who have not felt *the power* of sounds of this sort. Men are sometimes pretty nearly bewitched without knowing how. *Eyes* do a good deal, but *tongues* do more. We may talk of sparkling eyes and snowy bosoms as long as we please; but what are these with a croaking, masculine voice? The parson seemed to be fully aware of the importance of this part of the " service." The subject of his hymn was something about *love :* Christian love; love of Jesus; but still it was about *love ;* and the parson read, or gave out, the verses, in a singularly *soft* and *sighing* voice, with his head on one side, and giving it rather a swing. I am satisfied that the singing forms great part of the *attraction.* Young girls like to sing; and young men like to hear them. Nay, old ones too; and, as I have just said, it was the singing that *drew* me three hundred yards down the street at Tenterden, to enter this meeting-house. By the by, I wrote some hymns myself, and published them in " *Twopenny Trash.*" I will give any Methodist parson leave to put them into his hymn book.

FOLKESTONE (KENT),
Monday (Noon), 1 *Sept.*

I have had a fine ride, and I suppose the Quakers have had a fine time of it at Mark Lane.

From Tenterden I set off at five o'clock, and got to Appledore after a most delightful ride, the high land upon my right, and the low land on my left. The fog was so thick and white along some of the low land that I should have taken it for water, if little hills and trees had not risen up through it here and there. Indeed, the view was very much like those which are presented in the deep valleys, near the great rivers in New Brunswick

(North America) at the time when the snows melt in the spring, and when, in sailing over those valleys, you look down from the side of your canoe, and see the lofty woods beneath you! I once went in a log canoe across a *sylvan sea* of this description, the canoe being paddled by two Yankees. We started in a stream; the stream became a wide water, and that water got deeper and deeper, as I could see by the trees (all was woods), till we got to sail amongst *the top branches of the trees*. By and by we got into a large open space; a piece of water a mile or two, or three or four wide, with *the woods under us !* A fog, with the tops of trees rising through it, is very much like this; and such was the fog that I saw this morning in my ride to Appledore. The church at Appledore is very large. Big enough to hold 3000 people; and the place does not seem to contain half a thousand old enough to go to church.

In coming along I saw a wheat-rick making, though I hardly think the wheat can be dry under the bands. The corn is all good here; and I am told they give twelve shillings an acre for reaping wheat.

In quitting this Appledore I crossed a canal and entered on Romney Marsh. This was grass-land on both sides of me to a great distance. The flocks and herds immense. The sheep are of a breed that takes its name from the marsh. They are called Romney Marsh sheep. Very pretty and large. The wethers, when fat, weigh about twelve stone, or one hundred pounds. The faces of these sheep are white; and, indeed, the whole sheep is as white as a piece of writing-paper. The wool does not look dirty and oily like that of other sheep. The cattle appear to be all of the *Sussex* breed. Red, loosed-limbed, and, they say, a great deal better than the Devonshire. How curious is the *natural economy* of a country! The *forests* of Sussex; those miserable tracts of heath and fern and bushes and sand called Ashdown Forest and Saint Leonard's Forest, to which latter Lord Erskine's estate belongs; these wretched tracts and the not much less wretched farms in their neighbourhood, *breed the cattle* which we see *fatting* in Romney Marsh! They are calved in the spring; they are weaned in a little bit of grass-land; they are then put into stubbles and about in the fallows for the first summer; they are brought into the yard to winter on rough hay, peas-haulm, or barley-straw; the next two summers they spend in the rough woods or in the forests; the two winters they live on straw; they then pass another summer on the forest or at *work ;* and then they come here or go elsewhere to be fatted. With cattle of this kind and with sheep such as I have spoken of before, this Marsh abounds in every part of it; and the sight is most beautiful.

At three miles from Appledore I came through Snargate, a village with five houses, and with a church capable of containing two thousand people! The vagabonds tell us, however, that we have a wonderful increase of population! These vagabonds will be hanged by and by, or else justice will have fled from the face of the earth.

At Brenzett (a mile further on) I with great difficulty got a rasher of bacon for breakfast. The few houses that there are, are miserable in the extreme. The church here (only a *mile* from the last) nearly as large; and nobody to go to it. What! will the *vagabonds* attempt to make us believe that these churches were *built for nothing!* "*Dark ages*" indeed those must have been, if these churches were erected without there being any more people than there are now. But *who* built them? Where did the *means*, where did the hands come from? This place presents another proof of the truth of my old observation: *rich land* and *poor labourers*. From the window of the house in which I could scarcely get a rasher of bacon, and not an egg, I saw numberless flocks and herds fatting, and the fields loaded with corn!

The next village, which was two miles further on, was Old Romney, and along here I had, for great part of the way, corn-fields on one side of me and grass-land on the other. I asked what the amount of the crop of wheat would be. They told me better than five quarters to the acre. I thought so myself. I have a sample of the red wheat and another of the white. They are both very fine. They reap the wheat here nearly two feet from the ground; and even then they cut it three feet long! I never saw corn like this before. It very far exceeds the corn under Portsdown Hill, that at Gosport and Tichfield. They have here about eight hundred large, very large, sheaves to an acre. I wonder how long it will be after the end of the world before Mr. Birkbeck will see the American "Prairies" half so good as this Marsh. In a garden here I saw some very fine onions, and a prodigious crop; sure sign of most excellent land. At this Old Romney there is a church (two miles only from the last mind!) fit to contain one thousand five hundred people, and there are for the people of the parish to live in twenty-two or twenty-three houses! And yet the *vagabonds* have the impudence to tell us, that the population of England has vastly increased! Curious system that depopulates Romney Marsh and peoples Bagshot Heath! It is an unnatural system. It is the *vagabond's* system. It is a system that must be destroyed, or that will destroy the country.

The rotten borough of New Romney came next in my way; and here, to my great surprise, I found myself upon the sea-beach; for I had not looked at a map of Kent for years, and perhaps, never. I had got a list of places from a friend in Sussex, whom I asked to give me a route to Dover, and to send me through those parts of Kent which he thought would be most interesting to me. Never was I so much surprised as when I saw *a sail*. This place, now that the *squanderings* of the THING are over, is, they say, become miserably poor.

From New Romney to Dimchurch is about four miles: all along I had the sea-beach on my right, and, on my left, sometimes grass-land and sometimes corn-land. They told me here, and also further back in the Marsh, that they were to have 15s. an acre for reaping wheat.

From Dimchurch to Hythe you go on the sea beach, and nearly the same from Hythe to Sandgate, from which last place you come over the hill to Folkestone. But let me look back. Here has been the squandering! Here has been the pauper-making work! Here we see some of these causes that are now sending some farmers to the workhouse and driving others to flee the country or to cut their throats!

I had baited my horse at New Romney, and was coming jogging along very soberly, now looking at the sea, then looking at the cattle, then the corn, when my eye, in swinging round, lighted upon a great round building, standing upon the beach. I had scarcely had time to think about what it could be, when twenty or thirty others, standing along the coast, caught my eye; and if any one had been behind me, he might have heard me exclaim, in a voice that made my horse bound, "The *Martello Towers* by——!" Oh, Lord! To think that I should be destined to behold these monuments of the wisdom of Pitt and Dundas and Perceval! Good God! Here they are, piles of bricks in a circular form about three hundred feet (*guess*) circumference at the base, about forty feet high, and about one hundred and fifty feet circumference at the top. There is a door-way, about midway up, in each, and each has two windows. Cannons were to be fired from the top of these things, in order to defend the country against the French Jacobins!

I think I have counted along here upwards of thirty of these ridiculous things, which I dare say cost five, perhaps ten, thousand pounds each; and one of which was, I am told, *sold* on the coast of Sussex, the other day, for two hundred pounds! There is, they say, a chain of these things all the way to Hastings! I dare say they cost millions. But far indeed are these from being all, or half, or a quarter of the squanderings along here. Hythe is half *barracks ;* the hills are covered with barracks; and barracks most expensive, most squandering, fill up the side of the hill. Here is a canal (I crossed it at Appledore) made for the length of thirty miles (from Hythe, in Kent, to Rye, in Sussex) to *keep out the French ;* for those armies who had so often crossed the Rhine and the Danube, were to be kept back by a canal, made by Pitt, thirty feet wide at the most! All along the coast there are works of some sort or other; incessant sinks of money; walls of immense dimensions; masses of stone brought and put into piles. Then you see some of the walls and buildings falling down; some that have never been finished. The whole thing, all taken together, looks as if a spell had been, all of a sudden, set upon the workmen; or, in the words of the Scripture, here is the " *desolation of abomination, standing in high places.*" However, all is right. These things were made with the hearty good will of those who are now coming to ruin in consequence of the debt, contracted for the purpose of making these things! This is all *just.* The load will come, at last, upon the right shoulders.

Between Hythe and Sandgate (a village at about two miles from Hythe) I first saw the French coast. The chalk cliffs at Calais are as plain to the view as possible, and also the land, which they tell me is near Boulogne.

Folkestone lies under a hill here, as Reigate does in Surrey, only here the sea is open to your right as you come along. The corn is very early here, and very fine. All cut, even the beans; and they will be ready to cart in a day or two. Folkestone is now a little place; probably a quarter part as big as it was formerly. Here is a church one hundred and twenty feet long and fifty feet wide. It is a sort of little cathedral. The churchyard has evidently been three times as large as it is now.

Before I got into Folkestone I saw no less than eighty-four men, women, and boys and girls gleaning or leasing in a field of about ten acres. The people all along here complain most bitterly of the *change of times.* The truth is that the squandered millions are gone! The nation has now to suffer for this squandering. The money served to silence some; to make others bawl; to cause the good to be oppressed; to cause the bad to be exalted; to "crush the Jacobins": and what is the *result?* What is the *end?* The *end* is not yet come; but as to the result thus far, go, ask the families of those farmers, who, after having, for so many years, threatened to shoot Jacobins, have, in instances not a few, shot themselves! Go, ask the ghosts of Pitt and of Castlereagh what has, thus far, been the *result!* Go, ask the Hampshire farmer, who, not many months since, actually blowed out his own brains with one of those very pistols which he had long carried in his yeomanry cavalry holsters, to be ready "to keep down the Jacobins and Radicals!" O God! inscrutable are thy ways; but thou art just, and of thy justice what a complete proof have we in the case of these very martello towers! They were erected to keep out the Jacobin French, lest they should come and assist the Jacobin English. The *loyal* people of this coast were fattened by the building of them. Pitt and his loyal *Cinque Ports* waged interminable war against Jacobins. These very towers are now used to keep these *loyal* Cinque Ports themselves in order. These towers are now used to lodge men, whose business it is to sally forth, not upon Jacobins, but upon *smugglers!* Thus, after having sucked up millions of the nation's money, these loyal Cinque Ports are squeezed again: kept in order, kept down, by the very towers which they rejoiced to see rise to keep down the Jacobins.

DOVER,
Monday, 1 Sept., Evening.

I got here this evening about six o'clock, having come to-day thirty-six miles; but I must defer my remarks on the country between Folkestone and this place; a most interesting spot, and well worthy of particular attention. What place I shall date from after Dover I am by no means certain; but be it from what place it may, the continuation of my journal shall be published, in due course. If the Atlantic Ocean could not cut off the communication between me and my readers, a mere strip of water, not much wider than an American river, will hardly do it. I am, in real truth, undecided, as yet, whether I shall go on to France, or back to the *Wen.* I think I shall, when I go out of this inn, toss the bridle upon my horse's neck, and let him decide for me. I am sure he is more fit to decide on such a point than our ministers are to decide on any point connected with the happiness, greatness, and honour of this kingdom.

FROM DOVER, THROUGH THE ISLE OF THANET, BY CANTERBURY AND FAVERSHAM, ACROSS TO MAIDSTONE, UP TO TONBRIDGE, THROUGH THE WEALD OF KENT AND OVER THE HILLS BY WESTERHAM AND HAYS, TO THE WEN

DOVER,
Wednesday, 3 Sept. 1823 *(Evening).*

ON Monday I was balancing in my own mind whether I should go to France or not. To-day I have decided the question in the negative, and shall set off this evening for the Isle of Thanet; that spot so famous for corn.

I broke off without giving an account of the country between Folkestone and Dover, which is a very interesting one in itself, and was peculiarly interesting to me on many accounts. I have often mentioned, in describing the parts of the country over which I have travelled; I have often mentioned the *chalk-ridge* and also the *sand-ridge*, which I had traced, running parallel with each other from about Farnham, in Surrey, to Sevenoaks, in Kent. The reader must remember how particular I have been to observe that, in going up from Chilworth and Albury, through Dorking, Reigate, Godstone, and so on, the two chains, or ridges, approach so near to each other, that, in many places, you actually have a chalk-bank to your right and a sand-bank to your left, at not more than forty yards from each other. In some places, these chains of hills run off from each other to a great distance, even to a distance of twenty miles. They then approach again towards each other, and so they go on. I was always desirous to ascertain whether these chains, or ridges, continued on thus *to the sea*. I have now found that they do. And if you go out into the channel, at Folkestone, there you see a sand cliff and a chalk cliff. Folkestone stands upon the sand, in a little dell about seven hundred or eight hundred yards from the very termination of the ridge. All the way along, the chalk ridge is the most lofty, until you come to Leith Hill and Hindhead; and here, at Folkestone, the sand-ridge tapers off in a sort of flat towards the sea. The land is like what it is at

Reigate, a very steep hill; a hill of full a mile high, and bending exactly in the same manner as the hill at Reigate does. The turnpike-road winds up it and goes over it in exactly the same manner as that at Reigate. The land to the south of the hill begins a poor, thin, white loam upon the chalk; soon gets to be a very fine rich loam upon the chalk; goes on till it mingles the chalky loam with the sandy loam; and thus it goes on down to the sea-beach, or to the edge of the cliff. It is a beautiful bed of earth here, resembling in extent that on the south side of Portsdown Hill rather than that of Reigate. The crops here are always good if they are good anywhere. A large part of this fine tract of land, as well as the little town of Sandgate (which is a beautiful little place upon the beach itself), and also great part of the town of Folkestone belong, they tell me, to Lord Radnor, who takes his title of viscount from Folkestone. Upon the hill begins, and continues on for some miles, that stiff red loam, approaching to a clay, which I have several times described as forming the soil at the top of this chalk-ridge. I spoke of it in the *Register* of the 16th of August last, page 409, and I then said that it was like the land on the top of this very ridge at Ashmansworth in the north of Hampshire. At Reigate you find precisely the same soil upon the top of the hill, a very red, clayey sort of loam, with big yellow flint stones in it. Everywhere, the soil is the same upon the top of the high part of this ridge. I have now found it to be the same, on the edge of the sea, that I found it on the north-east corner of Hampshire.

From the hill, you keep descending all the way to Dover, a distance of about six miles, and it is absolutely six miles of down hill. On your right, you have the lofty land which forms a series of chalk cliffs, from the top of which you look into the sea; on your left, you have ground that goes rising up from you in the same sort of way. The turnpike-road goes down the middle of a valley, each side of which, as far as you can see, may be about a mile and a half. It is six miles long, you will remember; and here, therefore, with very little interruption, very few chasms, there are *eighteen square miles of corn*. It is a patch such as you very seldom see, and especially of corn so good as it is here. I should think that the wheat all along here would average pretty nearly four quarters to the acre. A few oats are sown. A great deal of barley, and that a very fine crop.

The town of Dover is like other sea-port towns; but really much more clean, and with less blackguard people in it than I ever observed in any sea-port before. It is a most picturesque place, to be sure. On one side of it rises, upon the top of a very steep hill, the Old Castle, with all its fortifications. On the other side of it there is another chalk hill, the side of which is pretty nearly perpendicular, and rises up from sixty to a hundred feet higher than the tops of the houses, which stand pretty nearly close to the foot of the hill.

I got into Dover rather late. It was dusk when I was going down the street towards the quay. I happened to look up, and was quite astonished to perceive cows grazing upon a spot apparently fifty feet above the tops of the houses, and measuring horizontally not, perhaps, more than ten or twenty feet from a line which would have formed a continuation into the air. I went up to the same spot, the next day, myself; and you actually look down upon the houses, as you look out of a window upon people in the street. The valley that runs down from Folkestone is, when it gets to Dover, crossed by another valley that runs down from Canterbury, or, at least, from the Canterbury direction. It is in the gorge of this cross valley that Dover is built. The two chalk hills jut out into the sea, and the water that comes up between them forms a harbour for this ancient, most interesting, and beautiful place. On the hill to the north stands the castle of Dover, which is fortified in the ancient manner, except on the sea side, where it has the steep *Cliff* for a fortification. On the south side of the town the hill is, I believe, rather more lofty than that on the north side; and here is that cliff which is described by Shakespeare in the play of *King Lear*. It is fearfully steep, certainly. Very nearly perpendicular for a considerable distance. The grass grows well, to the very tip of the cliff; and you see cows and sheep grazing there with as much unconcern as if grazing in the bottom of a valley.

It was not, however, these natural curiosities that took me over *this* hill; I went to see, with my own eyes, something of the sorts of means that had been made use of to squander away countless millions of money. Here is a hill containing, probably, a couple of square miles or more, hollowed like a honeycomb. Here are line upon line, trench upon trench, cavern upon cavern, bomb-proof upon bomb-proof; in short the very sight of the thing convinces you that either madness the most humiliating, or profligacy the most scandalous must have been at work here for years. The question that every man of sense asks is: What reason had you to suppose that the *French would ever come to this hill* to attack it, while the rest of the country was so much more easy to assail? However, let any man of good plain understanding go and look at the works that have here been performed and that are now all tumbling into ruin. Let him ask what this cavern was for; what that ditch was for; what this tank was for; and why all these horrible holes and hiding-places at an expense of millions upon millions? Let this scene be brought and placed under the eyes of the people of England, and let them be told that Pitt and Dundas and Perceval had these things done to prevent the country from being conquered; with voice unanimous the nation would instantly exclaim: Let the French or let the devil take us, rather than let us resort to means of defence like these. This is, perhaps, the only set of fortifications in the world ever framed for mere *hiding*. There is no appearance of any intention to annoy an enemy. It is a parcel of holes made in a hill, to hide Englishmen from Frenchmen. Just as if the Frenchmen would come to this hill! Just as if they would not go (if they came at all) and land in Romney Marsh, or on Pevensey Level, or anywhere else, rather than come to this hill; rather than come to crawl up Shakespeare's Cliff. All the way along the coast, from this very hill to Portsmouth; or pretty nearly all the way, is a flat. What the devil should they come to this hill for, then? And when you ask this question, they tell you that it is to have an army here *behind* the French, after they had marched into the country! And for a purpose like this; for a purpose so stupid, so senseless, so mad as this, and withal, so scandalously disgraceful, more brick and stone have been buried in this hill than would go to build a neat new cottage for every labouring men in the counties of Kent and of Sussex!

Dreadful is the scourge of such ministers. However, those who supported them will now have to suffer. The money must have been squandered purposely, and for the worst ends. Fool as Pitt was; unfit as an old hack of a lawyer, like Dundas, was to judge of the means of defending the country, stupid as both these fellows were, and as their brother lawyer, Perceval, was too: unfit as these lawyers were to judge in any such case, they must have known that this was an useless expenditure of money. They must have known that; and, therefore, their general folly, their general ignorance, is no apology for their conduct. What they wanted was to prevent the landing, not of Frenchmen, but of French principles; that is to say, to prevent the example of the French from being alluring to the people of England. The devil a bit did they care for the Bourbons. They rejoiced at the killing of the king. They rejoiced at the atheistical decree. They rejoiced at everything calculated to alarm the timid and to excite horror in the people of England in general. They wanted to keep out of England those principles which had a natural tendency to destroy boroughmongering, and to put an end to peculation and plunder. No matter whether by the means of martello towers, making a great chalk hill a honeycomb, cutting a canal thirty feet wide to stop the march of the armies of the Danube and the Rhine: no matter how they squandered the money, so that it silenced some and made others bawl to answer their great purpose of preventing French example from having an influence in England. Simply their object was this: to make the French people miserable; to force back the Bourbons upon them as a *means* of making them miserable; to degrade France, to make the people wretched; and then to have to say to the people of England, Look there: *see what they have got by their attempts to obtain liberty!* This was their object. They did not want martello towers and honeycombed chalk hills and mad canals: they did not want these to keep out the French armies. The boroughmongers and the parsons cared nothing about the French armies. It was the French example that the lawyers, boroughmongers and parsons wished to keep out. And what have they done? It is impossible to be upon this honeycombed hill, upon this enormous mass of anti-jacobin expenditure, without seeing the chalk cliffs of Calais and the cornfields of France. At this season it is impossible to see those fields without knowing that the farmers are getting in their corn there as well as here; and it is impossible to think of that fact without reflecting, at the same time, on the example which the farmers of France hold out to the farmers of England. Looking down from this very anti-jacobin hill, this day, I saw the parsons' shocks of wheat and barley, left in the field after the farmer had taken his away. Turning my head, and looking across the Channel, "There," said I, pointing to France, "there the spirited and sensible people have ridded themselves of this burden, of which our farmers so bitterly complain." It is impossible not to recollect here, that, in numerous petitions, sent up, too, by the *loyal*, complaints have been made that the English farmer has to carry on a competition against the French farmer who has *no tithes to pay!* Well, *loyal gentlemen*, why do not you petition, then, to be relieved from tithes? What do you mean else? Do you mean to call upon our big gentlemen at Whitehall for them to compel the French to pay tithes? Oh, you loyal fools! Better hold your tongues about the French not paying tithes. Better do that, at any rate; for never will they pay tithes again.

Here is a large tract of *land* upon these hills at Dover, which is the property of the public, having been purchased at an enormous expense. This is now let out as pasture land to people of the town. I dare say that the letting of this land is a curious affair. If there were a member for Dover who would do what he ought to do, he would soon get before the public a list of the tenants, and of the rents paid by them. I should like very much to see such list. Butterworth, the bookseller in Fleet Street, he who is a sort of metropolitan of the Methodists, is one of the members for Dover. The other is, I believe, that Wilbraham or Bootle or Bootle Wilbraham, or some such name, that is a Lancashire magistrate. So that Dover is prettily set up. However, there is nothing of this sort that can, in the present state of things, be deemed to be of any real consequence. As long as the people at Whitehall can go on paying the interest of the debt in full, so long will there be no change worth the attention of any rational man. In the meanwhile, the French nation will be going on rising over us; and our ministers will be cringing and crawling to every nation upon earth who is known to possess a cannon or a barrel of powder.

This very day I have read Mr. Canning's speech at Liverpool, with a Yankee consul sitting on his right hand. Not a word now about the bits of bunting and the fir frigates; but now, America is the lovely daughter, who in a moment of excessive love has gone off with a lover (to wit, the French) and left the tender mother to mourn! What a fop! And this is the man that talked so big and so bold. This is the clever, the profound, the blustering, too, and above all things, " the high spirited " Mr. Canning. However, more of this hereafter. I must get from this Dover, as fast as I can.

SANDWICH,
Wednesday, 3 Sept., Night.

I got to this place about half an hour after the ringing of the eight o'clock bell, or curfew, which I heard at about two miles distance from the place. From the town of Dover you come up the Castle Hill, and have a most beautiful view from the top of it. You have the sea, the chalk cliffs of Calais, the high land at Boulogne, the town of Dover just under you, the valley towards Folkestone, and the much more beautiful valley towards Canterbury; and going on a little further, you have the Downs and the Essex or Suffolk coast in full view, with a most beautiful corn country to ride along through. The corn was chiefly cut between Dover and Walmer. The barley almost all cut and tied up in sheaf. Nothing but the beans seemed to remain standing along here. They are not quite so good as the rest of the corn; but they are by no means bad. When I came to the village of Walmer, I inquired for the castle; that famous place, where Pitt, Dundas, Perceval, and all the whole tribe of plotters against the French Revolution had carried on their plots. After coming through the village of Walmer, you see the entrance of the castle away to the right. It is situated pretty nearly on the water's edge, and at the bottom of a little dell, about a furlong or so from the turnpike-road. This is now the habitation of our great minister, Robert Bankes Jenkinson, son of Charles of that name. When I was told, by a girl who was leasing in a field by the road side, that that was Walmer Castle, I stopped short, pulled my horse round, looked steadfastly at the gateway, and could not help exclaiming: "Oh, thou who inhabitest that famous dwelling; thou, who hast always been in place, let who might be out of place! Oh, thou everlasting placeman! thou sage of 'over-production,' do but cast thine eyes upon this barley field, where, if I am not greatly deceived, there are from seven to eight quarters upon the acre! Oh, thou whose *Courier* newspaper has just informed its readers that wheat will be seventy shillings the quarter in the month of November: oh, thou wise man, I pray thee come forth from thy castle, and tell me what thou wilt do if wheat should happen to be, at the appointed time, thirty-five shillings, instead of seventy shillings, the quarter. Sage of over-production, farewell. If thou hast life, thou wilt be minister as long as thou canst pay the interest of the debt in full, but not one moment longer. The moment thou ceasest to be able to squeeze from the Normans a sufficiency to count down to the Jews their full tale, that moment, thou great stern-path-of-duty man, thou wilt begin to be taught the true meaning of the words *Ministerial Responsibility*."

Deal is a most villainous place. It is full of filthy-looking people. Great desolation of abomination has been going on here; tremendous barracks, partly pulled down and partly tumbling down, and partly occupied by soldiers. Everything seems upon the perish. I was glad to hurry along through it, and to leave its inns and public-houses to be occupied by the tarred, and trowsered, and blue - and - buff crew whose very vicinage I always detest. From Deal you come along to Upper Deal, which, it seems, was the original village; thence upon a beautiful road to Sandwich, which is a rotten borough. Rottenness, putridity is excellent for land, but bad for boroughs. This place, which is as villainous a hole as one would wish to see, is surrounded by some of the finest land in the world. Along on one side of it lies a marsh. On the other sides of it is land which they tell me bears *seven quarters* of wheat to an acre. It is certainly very fine; for I saw large pieces of radish-seed on the roadside; this seed is grown for the seedsmen in London; and it will grow on none but rich land. All the corn is carried here except some beans and some barley.

CANTERBURY,
Thursday Afternoon, 4 Sept.

In quitting Sandwich, you immediately cross a river up which vessels bring coals from the sea. This marsh is about a couple of miles wide. It begins at the sea-beach, opposite the Downs, to my right hand, coming from Sandwich, and it wheels round to my left and ends at the sea-beach, opposite Margate roads. This marsh was formerly covered with the sea, very likely; and hence the land within this sort of semicircle, the name of which is Thanet, was called an *Isle*. It is, in fact, an island now, for the same reason that Portsea is an island, and that New York is an island; for there certainly is the water in this river that goes round and connects one part of the sea with the other. I had to cross this river, and to cross the marsh, before I got into the famous Isle of Thanet, which it was my intention to cross. Soon after crossing the river, I passed by a place for making salt, and could not help recollecting that there are no excisemen in these salt-making places in France, that, before the Revolution, the French were most cruelly oppressed by the duties on salt, that they had to endure, on that account, the most horrid tyranny that ever was known, except, perhaps, that practised in an *Exchequer* that shall here be nameless; that thousands and thousands of men and women were every year sent to the galleys for what was called smuggling salt; that the fathers and even the mothers were imprisoned or whipped if the children were detected in smuggling salt: I could not help reflecting, with delight, as I looked at these salt-pans in the Isle of Thanet; I could not help reflecting, that in spite of Pitt, Dundas, Perceval, and the rest of the crew, in spite of the caverns of Dover and the martello towers in Romney Marsh: in spite of all the spies and all the bayonets, and the six hundred millions of debt and the hundred and fifty millions of dead-weight, and the two hundred millions of poor-rates that are now squeezing the borough-mongers, squeezing the farmers, puzzling the fellows at White-hall and making Mark Lane a scene of greater interest than the Chamber of the Privy Council; with delight as I jogged along under the first beams of the sun, I reflected that, in spite of all the malignant measures that had brought so much misery upon England, the gallant French people had ridded themselves of the tyranny which sent them to the galleys for endeavouring to use without tax the salt which God sent upon their shores. Can any man tell why we should still be paying five, or six, or seven shillings a bushel for salt, instead of one? We did pay fifteen shillings a bushel, tax. And why is two shillings a bushel kept on? Because, if they were taken off, the salt-tax-gathering crew must be discharged! This tax of two shillings a bushel causes the consumer to pay five, at the least, more than he would if there were no tax at all! When, great God! when shall we be allowed to enjoy God's gifts, in freedom, as the people of France enjoy them?

On the marsh I found the same sort of sheep as on Romney Marsh; but the cattle here are chiefly Welsh; black, and called runts. They are nice hardy cattle; and, I am told, that this is the description of cattle that they fat all the way up on this north side of Kent.—When I got upon the corn land in the Isle of Thanet, I got into a garden indeed. There is hardly any fallow; comparatively few turnips. It is a country of corn. Most of the harvest is in; but there are some fields of wheat and of barley not yet housed. A great many pieces of lucerne, and all of them very fine. I left Ramsgate to my right about three miles, and went right across the island to Margate; but that place is so thickly settled with stock-jobbing cuckolds, at this time of the year, that, having no fancy to get their horns stuck into me, I turned away to my left when I got within about half a mile of the town. I got to a little hamlet, where I breakfasted; but could get no corn for my horse, and no bacon for myself! All was corn around me. Barns, I should think, two hundred feet long; ricks of enormous size and most numerous; crops of wheat, five quarters to an acre, on the average; and a public-house without either bacon or corn! The labourers' houses, all along through this island, beggarly in the extreme. The people dirty, poor-looking; ragged, but particularly *dirty*. The men and boys with dirty faces, and dirty smock-frocks, and dirty shirts; and, good God! what a difference between the wife of a labouring man here, and the wife of a labouring man in the forests and woodlands of Hampshire and Sussex! Invariably have I observed that the richer the soil, and the more destitute of woods; that is to say, the more purely a corn country, the more miserable the labourers. The cause is this, the great, the big bull frog grasps all. In this beautiful island every inch of land is appropriated by the rich. No hedges, no ditches, no commons, no grassy lanes: a country divided into great farms; a few trees surround the great farm-house. All the rest is bare of trees; and the wretched labourer has not a stick of wood, and has no place for a pig or cow to graze, or even to lie down upon. The rabbit countries are the countries for labouring men. There the ground is not so valuable. There it is not so easily appropriated by the few. Here, in this island, the work is almost all done by the horses. The horses plough the ground; they sow the ground; they hoe the ground; they carry the corn home; they thresh it out; and they carry it to market: nay, in this island, they *rake* the ground; they rake up the straggling straws and ears; so that they do the whole, except the reaping and the mowing. It is impossible to have an idea of anything more miserable than the state of the labourers in this part of the country.

After coming by Margate, I passed a village called Monckton, and another called Sarr. At Sarr there is a bridge, over which you come out of the island, as you go into it over the bridge at Sandwich. At Monckton they had *seventeen men working on the roads*, though the harvest was not quite in, and though, of course, it had all to be threshed out; but, at Monckton, they had *four threshing machines;* and they have three threshing machines at Sarr, though there, also, they have several men upon the roads! This is a shocking state of things; and in spite of everything that the Jenkinsons and the Scots can do, this state of things must be changed.

At Sarr, or a little way further back, I saw a man who had just begun to reap a field of canary seed. The plants were too far advanced to be cut in order to be bleached for the making of plat; but I got the reaper to select me a few green stalks that grew near a bush that stood on the outside of the piece. These I have brought on with me, in order to give them a trial.

At Sarr I began to cross the marsh, and had, after this, to come through the village of Up-street, and another village called Steady, before I got to Canterbury. At Up-street I was struck with the words written upon a board which was fastened upon a pole, which pole was standing in a garden near a neat little box of a house. The words were these. "PARADISE PLACE. *Spring guns and steel traps are set here.*" A pretty idea it must give us of Paradise to know that spring guns and steel traps are set in it! This is doubtless some stock-jobber's place; for, in the first place, the name is likely to have been selected by one of that crew; and, in the next place, whenever any of them go to the country, they look upon it that they are to begin a sort of warfare against everything around them. They invariably look upon every labourer as a thief.

As you approach Canterbury, from the Isle of Thanet, you have another instance of the squanderings of the lawyer ministers. Nothing equals the ditches, the caverns, the holes, the tanks, and hiding-places of the hill at Dover; but, considerable as the city of Canterbury is, that city, within its gates, stands upon less ground than those horrible erections, the barracks of Pitt, Dundas, and Perceval. They are perfectly enormous; but thanks be unto God, they begin to crumble down. They have a sickly hue: all is lassitude about them: endless are their lawns, their gravel walks, and their ornaments; but their lawns are unshaven, their gravel walks grassy, and their ornaments putting on the garments of ugliness. You see the grass growing opposite the doorways. A hole in the window strikes you here and there. Lamp posts there are, but no lamps. Here are horse-barracks, foot-barracks, artillery-barracks, engineer-barracks: a whole country of barracks; but only here and there a soldier. The thing is actually perishing. It is typical of the state of the great Thing of things. It gave me inexpressible pleasure to perceive the gloom that seemed to hang over these barracks, which once swarmed with soldiers and their blithe companions, as a hive swarms with bees. These barracks now look like the environs of a hive in winter. Westminster Abbey Church is not the place for the monument of Pitt; the statue of the great snorting bawler ought to be stuck up here, just in the midst of this hundred or two of acres covered with barracks. These barracks, too, were erected in order to compel the French to return to the payment of tithes; in order to bring their necks again under the yoke of the lords and the clergy. That has not been accomplished. The French, as Mr. Hoggart assures us, have neither tithes, taxes, nor rates; and the people of Canterbury know that they have a *hop-duty* to pay, while Mr. Hoggart, of Broad Street, tells them that he has farms to let, in France, where there are hop-gardens and where there is no hop-duty. They have lately had races at Canterbury; and the mayor and aldermen, in order to get the Prince Leopold to attend them, presented him with the Freedom of the City; but it rained all the time and he did not come! The mayor and aldermen do not understand things half so well as this German gentleman, who has managed his matters as well, I think, as any one that I ever heard of.

This fine old town, or rather city, is remarkable for cleanliness and niceness, notwithstanding it has a cathedral in it. The country round it is very rich, and this year, while the hops are so bad in most other parts, they are not so very bad just about Canterbury.

ELVERTON FARM, NEAR FAVERSHAM,
Friday Morning, 5 Sept.

In going through Canterbury, yesterday, I gave a boy sixpence to hold my horse, while I went into the cathedral, just to thank St. Swithin for the trick that he had played my friends, the Quakers. Led along by the wet weather till after the harvest had actually begun, and then to find the weather turn fine, all of a sudden! This must have soused them pretty decently; and I hear of one, who, at Canterbury, has made a bargain by which he will certainly lose two thousand pounds. The land where I am now is equal to that of the Isle of Thanet. The harvest is nearly over, and all the crops have been prodigiously fine. In coming from Canterbury, you come to the top of a hill, called Baughton Hill, at four miles from Canterbury on the London Road; and you there look down into one of the finest flats in England. A piece of marsh comes up nearly to Faversham; and at the edge of that marsh lies the farm where I now am. The land here is a deep loam upon chalk; and this is also the nature of the land in the Isle of Thanet and all the way from that to Dover. The orchards grow well upon this soil. The trees grow finely, the fruit is large and of fine flavour.

In 1821 I gave Mr. William Waller, who lives here, some American apple-cuttings; and he has now some as fine Newtown Pippins as one would wish to see. They are very large of their sort; very free in their growth; and they promise to be very fine apples of the kind. Mr. Waller had cuttings from me of several sorts, in 1822. These were cut down last year; they have, of course, made shoots this summer; and great numbers of these shoots have fruit-spurs, which will have blossom, if not fruit, next year. This very rarely happens, I believe; and the state of Mr. Waller's trees clearly proves to me that the introduction of these American trees would be a great improvement.

My American apples, when I left Kensington, promised to be very fine; and the apples, which I have frequently mentioned as being upon cuttings imported last spring, promised to come to perfection; a thing which, I believe, we have not an instance of before.

MERRYWORTH,
Friday Evening, 5 *Sept.*

A friend at Tenterden told me that, if I had a mind to know Kent, I must go through Romney Marsh to Dover, from Dover to Sandwich, from Sandwich to Margate, from Margate to Canterbury, from Canterbury to Faversham, from Faversham to Maidstone, and from Maidstone to Tonbridge. I found from Mr. Waller, this morning, that the regular turnpike route, from his house to Maidstone, was through Sittingbourne. I had been along that road several times; and besides, to be covered with dust was what I could not think of, when I had it in my power to get to Maidstone without it. I took the road across the country, quitting the London road, or rather, crossing it, in the dell, between Ospringe and Green Street. I instantly began to go up hill, slowly, indeed; but up hill. I came through the villages of Newnham, Doddington, Ringlestone, and to that of Hollingbourne. I had come up hill for thirteen miles, from Mr. Waller's house. At last, I got to the top of this hill, and went along, for some distance, upon level ground. I found I was got upon just the same sort of land as that on the hill at Folkestone, at Reigate, at Ropley, and at Ashmansworth. The red clayey loam, mixed up with great yellow flint stones. I found fine meadows here, just such as are at Ashmansworth (that is to say, on the north Hampshire hills). This sort of ground is characterised by an astonishing depth that they have to go for the water. At Ashmansworth, they go to a depth of more than three hundred feet. As I was riding along upon the top of this hill in Kent, I saw the same beautiful sort of meadows that there are at Ashmansworth; I saw the corn backward; I was just thinking to go up to some house, to ask how far they had to go for water, when I saw a large well-bucket, and all the chains and wheels belonging to such a concern; but here was also the tackle for a *horse* to work in drawing up the water! I asked about the depth of the well; and the information I received must have been incorrect; because I was told it was three hundred yards. I asked this of a public-house keeper further on, not seeing anybody where the farm-house was. I make no doubt that the depth is, as near as possible, that of Ashmansworth. Upon the top of this hill, I saw the finest field of beans that I have seen this year, and, by very far, indeed, the *finest piece of hops*. A beautiful piece of hops, surrounded by beautiful plantations of young ash, producing poles for hop-gardens. My road here pointed towards the west. It soon wheeled round towards the south; and, all of a sudden, I found myself upon the edge of a hill, as lofty and as steep as that at Folkestone, at Reigate, or at Ashmansworth. It was the same famous chalk ridge that I was crossing again. When I got to the edge of the hill, and before I got off my horse to lead him down this more than mile of hill, I sat and surveyed the prospect before me, and to the right and to the left. This is what the people of Kent call the *Garden of Eden*. It is a district of meadows, corn fields, hop-gardens, and orchards of apples, pears, cherries and filberts, with very little if any land which cannot, with propriety, be called good. There are plantations of chestnut and of ash frequently occurring; and as these are cut when long enough to make poles for hops, they are at all times objects of great beauty.

At the foot of the hill of which I have been speaking is the village of Hollingbourne; thence you come on to Maidstone. From Maidstone to this place (Merryworth) is about seven miles, and these are the finest seven miles that I have ever seen in England or anywhere else. The Medway is to your left, with its meadows about a mile wide. You cross the Medway, in coming out of Maidstone, and it goes and finds its way down to Rochester, through a break in the chalk ridge. From Maidstone to Merryworth, I should think that there were hop-gardens on one half of the way on both sides of the road. Then looking across the Medway, you see hop-gardens and orchards two miles deep, on the side of a gently rising ground: and this continues with you all the way from Maidstone to Merryworth. The orchards form a great feature of the country; and the plantations of ashes and of chestnuts that I mentioned before, add greatly to the beauty. These gardens of hops are kept very clean, in general, though some of them have been neglected this year owing to the bad appearance of the crop. The culture is sometimes mixed: that is to say, apple-trees or cherry-trees or filbert-trees and hops, in the same ground. This is a good way, they say, of raising an orchard. I do not believe it; and I think that nothing is gained by any of these mixtures. They plant apple-trees or cherry-trees in rows here; they then plant a filbert-tree close to each of these large fruit-trees; and then they cultivate the middle of the ground by planting potatoes. This is being too greedy. It is impossible that they can gain by this. What they gain one way they lose the other way; and I verily believe that the most profitable way would be never to mix things at all. In coming from Maidstone I passed through a village called Teston, where Lord Basham has a seat.

TONBRIDGE,
Saturday Morning, 6 Sept.

I came off from Merryworth a little before five o'clock, passed the seat of Lord Torrington, the friend of Mr. Barretto. This Mr. Barretto ought not to be forgotten so soon. In 1820 he sued for articles of the peace against Lord Torrington, for having menaced him, in consequence of his having pressed his lordship about some money. It seems that Lord Torrington had known him in the East Indies; that they came home together, or soon after one another; that his lordship invited Mr. Barretto to his best parties in India; that he got him introduced at court in England by Sidmouth; that he got him made a *Fellow of the Royal Society ;* and that he tried to get him introduced into Parliament. His lordship, when Barretto rudely pressed him for his money, reminded him of all this, and of the many difficulties that he had had to overcome with regard to his *colour* and so forth. Nevertheless, the dingy skinned court visitant pressed in such a way that Lord Torrington was obliged to be pretty smart with him, whereupon the other sued for articles of the peace against his lordship; but these were not granted by the court. This Barretto issued a handbill at the last election as a candidate for St. Albans. I am truly sorry that he was not elected. Lord Camelford threatened to put in his black fellow; but he was a sad swaggering fellow; and had, at last, too much of the boroughmonger in him to do a thing so meritorious. Lord Torrington's is but an indifferent looking place.

I here began to see South Down sheep again, which I had not seen since the time I left Tenterden. All along here the villages are at not more than two miles distance from each other. They have all large churches, and scarcely anybody to go to them. At a village called Hadlow, there is a house belonging to a Mr. May, the most singular looking thing I ever saw. An immense house stuck all over with a parcel of chimneys, or things like chimneys; little brick columns, with a sort of caps on them, looking like carnation sticks, with caps at the top to catch the earwigs. The building is all of brick, and has the oddest appearance of anything I ever saw. This Tonbridge is but a common country town, though very clean, and the people looking very well. The climate must be pretty warm here, for in entering the town I saw a large Althea Frutex in bloom, a thing rare enough, any year, and particularly a year like this.

WESTERHAM,
Saturday, Noon, 6. Sept.

Instead of going on to the Wen along the turnpike-road through Sevenoaks, I turned to my left when I got about a mile out of Tonbridge, in order to come along that tract of country called the Weald of Kent; that is to say, the solid clays, which have no bottom, which are unmixed with chalk, sand, stone, or anything else; the country of dirty roads and of oak trees. I stopped at Tonbridge only a few minutes; but in the Weald I stopped to breakfast at a place called Leigh. From Leigh I came to Chittingstone causeway, leaving Tonbridge Wells six miles over the hills to my left. From Chittingstone I came to Bough-beach, thence to Four Elms, and thence to this little market-town of Westerham, which is just upon the border of Kent. Indeed, Kent, Surrey, and Sussex form a joining very near to this town. Westerham, exactly like Reigate and Godstone, and Sevenoaks, and Dorking, and Folkestone, lies between the sand-ridge and the chalk-ridge. The valley is here a little wider than at Reigate, and that is all the difference there is between the places. As soon as you get over the sand hill to the south of Reigate, you get into the Weald of Surrey; and here, as soon as you get over the sand hill to the south of Westerham, you get into the Weald of Kent.

I have now, in order to get to the Wen, to cross the chalk-ridge once more, and at a point where I never crossed it before. Coming through the Weald I found the corn very good; and low as the ground is, wet as it is, cold as it is, there will be very little of the wheat which will not be housed before Saturday night. All the corn is good, and the barley excellent. Not far from Bough-beach, I saw two oak trees, one of which was, they told me, more than thirty feet round, and the other more than twenty-seven; but they have been hollow for half a century. They are not much bigger than the oak upon Tilford Green, if any. I mean in the trunk; but they are hollow, while that tree is sound in all its parts, and growing still. I have had a most beautiful ride through the Weald. The day is very hot; but I have been in the shade; and my horse's feet very often in the rivulets and wet lanes. In one place I rode above a mile completely arched over by the boughs of the underwood, growing in the banks of the lane. What an odd taste that man must have who prefers a turnpike-road to a lane like this.

Very near to Westerham there are hops: and I have seen now and then a little bit of hop garden, even in the Weald. Hops will grow well where lucerne will grow well; and lucerne will grow well where there is a rich top and a dry bottom. When therefore you see hops in the Weald, it is on the side of some hill, where there is sand or stone at bottom, and not where there is real clay beneath. There appear to be hops, here and there, all along from nearly at Dover to Alton, in Hampshire. You find them all along Kent; you find them at Westerham; across at Worth, in Sussex; at Godstone, in Surrey; over to the north of Merrow Down, near Guildford; at Godalming; under the Hog's-back, at Farnham; and all along that way to Alton. But there, I think, they end. The whole face of the country seems to rise, when you get just beyond Alton, and to keep up. Whether you look to the north, the south, or west, the land seems to rise, and the hops cease, till you come again away to the north-west, in Herefordshire.

KENSINGTON,
Saturday Night, 6 Sept.

Here I close my day, at the end of forty-four miles. In coming up the chalk hill from Westerham, I prepared myself for the red stiff clay-like loam, the big yellow flints and the meadows; and I found them all. I have now gone over this chalk-ridge in the following places: at Coombe in the north-west of Hampshire; I mean the north-west corner, the very extremity of the county. I have gone over it at Ashmansworth, or High-clere, going from Newbury to Andover; at King's Clere, going from Newbury to Winchester; at Ropley, going from Alresford to Selborne; at Dippinghall going from Crondall to Thursly; at

Merrow, going from Chertsey to Chilworth; at Reigate; at Westerham, and then, between these, at Godstone; at Sevenoaks, going from London to Battle; at Hollingbourne, as mentioned above, and at Folkestone. In all these places I have crossed this chalk-ridge. Everywhere, upon the top of it, I have found a flat, and the soil of all these flats I have found to be a red stiff loam mingled up with big yellow flints. A soil difficult to work; but by no means bad, whether for wood, hops, grass, orchards or corn. I once before mentioned that I was assured that the pasture upon these bleak hills was as rich as that which is found in the north of Wiltshire, in the neighbourhood of Swindon, where they make some of the best cheese in the kingdom. Upon these hills I have never found the labouring people poor and miserable, as in the rich vales. All is not appropriated where there are coppices and wood, where the cultivation is not so easy and the produce so very large.

After getting up the hill from Westerham, I had a general descent to perform all the way to the Thames. When you get to Beckenham, which is the last parish in Kent, the country begins to assume a cockney-like appearance; all is artificial, and you no longer feel any interest in it. I was anxious to make this journey into Kent, in the midst of harvest, in order that I might *know* the real state of the crops. The result of my observations and my inquiries is, that the crop is a *full average* crop of everything except barley, and that the barley yields a great deal more than an average crop. I thought that the beans were very poor during my ride into Hampshire; but I then saw no real bean countries. I have seen such countries now; and I do not think that the beans present us with a bad crop. As to the quality, it is, in no case (except perhaps the barley), equal to that of last year. We had, last year, an Italian summer. When the wheat or other grain has to *ripen in wet weather*, it will not be *bright*, as it will when it has to ripen in fair weather. It will have a dingy or clouded appearance; and perhaps the flour may not be quite so good. The wheat, in fact, will not be so heavy. In order to enable others to judge, as well as myself, I took samples from the fields as I went along. I took them very fairly, and as often as I thought that there was any material change in the soil or other circumstances. During the ride I took sixteen samples. These are now at the office of the *Register*, in Fleet Street, where they may be seen by any gentleman who thinks the information likely to be useful to him. The samples are numbered, and there is a reference pointing out the place where each sample was taken. The opinions that I gather amount to this: that there is an average crop of everything, and a little more of barley.

Now then we shall see how all this tallies with the schemes, with the intentions and expectations of our matchless gentlemen at Whitehall. These wise men have put forth their views in the *Courier* of the 27th of August, and in words which ought never to be forgotten, and which, at any rate, shall be recorded here.

" GRAIN.—During the present unsettled state of the weather, it is impossible for the best informed persons to anticipate upon good grounds what will be the future price of agricultural produce. Should the season even yet prove favourable, for the operations of the harvest, there is every probability of the average price of grain continuing at that exact price, which will prove most conducive to the interests of the corn growers, and at the same time encouraging to the agriculture of our colonial possessions. We do not speak lightly on this subject, for we are aware that his majesty's ministers have been fully alive to the inquiries from all qualified quarters as to the effect likely to be produced on the markets from the addition of the present crops to the stock of wheat already on hand. The result of these inquiries is, that in the highest quarters there exists the full expectation that towards the month of November the price of wheat will nearly approach to seventy shillings, a price which, while it affords the extent of remuneration to the British farmer recognised by the corn laws, will at the same time admit of the sale of the Canadian bonded wheat; and the introduction of this foreign corn, grown by British colonists, will contribute to keeping down our markets, and exclude foreign grain from other quarters."

There's nice gentlemen of Whitehall! What pretty gentlemen they are! " *Envy of surrounding nations*," indeed, to be under command of pretty gentlemen who can make calculations so nice, and put forth predictions so positive upon such a subject! " *Admiration of the world* " indeed, to live under the command of men who can so control seasons and markets; or, at least, who can so dive into the secrets of trade, and find out the contents of the fields, barns, and ricks, as to be able to balance things so nicely as to cause the Canadian corn to find a market, without injuring the sale of that of the British farmer, and without admitting that of the French farmer and the other farmers of the continent! Happy, too happy, rogues that we are, to be under the guidance of such pretty gentlemen, and right just is it that we should be banished for life, if we utter a word *tending* to bring such pretty gentlemen into contempt.

Let it be observed that this paragraph *must* have come from Whitehall. This wretched paper is the demi-official organ of the government. As to the owners of the paper, Daniel Stewart, that notorious fellow, Street, and the rest of them, not excluding the brother of the great Oracle, which brother bought, the other day, a share of this vehicle of baseness and folly; as to these fellows, they have no control other than what relates to the expenditure and the receipts of the vehicle. They get their news from the offices of the Whitehall people, and their paper is the mouthpiece of those same people. Mark this, I I pray you, reader; and let the French people mark it, too, and then take their revenge for the Waterloo insolence. This being the case, then, this paragraph proceeding from the pretty gentlemen, what a light it throws on their expectations, their hopes, and their fears. They see that wheat at seventy shillings a quarter is *necessary* to them! Ah! pray mark that! They see that wheat at seventy shillings a quarter is necessary to them; and, therefore, they say that wheat will be at seventy shillings a quarter, the price, as they call it, necessary to re-munerate the British farmer. And how do the conjurors at Whitehall know this? Why, they have made full inquiries " in qualified quarters." And the qualified quarters have satisfied the " highest quarters," that, " towards the month of November, the price of wheat will nearly approach to seventy shillings the quarter! " I wonder what the words towards the " end of November " may mean. Devil's in't if middle of September is not " *towards* November; " and the wheat, instead of going on towards seventy shillings, is very fast coming down to forty. The beast who wrote this paragraph; the pretty beast; this " envy of surrounding nations " wrote it on the 27th of August, *a soaking wet Saturday !* The pretty beast was not aware that the next day was going to be fine, and that we were to have only the succeeding Tuesday and half the following Saturday of wet weather until the whole of the harvest should be in. The pretty beast wrote while the rain was spattering against the window; and he did " not speak lightly," but was fully aware that the highest quarters, having made inquiries of the qualified quarters, were sure that wheat would be at seventy shillings during the ensuing year. What will be the price of wheat it is impossible for any one of say. I know a gentleman, who is a very good judge of such matters, who is of opinion that the average price of wheat will be thirty-two shillings a quarter, or lower, before Christmas; this is not quite half what the *highest quarters* expect, in consequence of the inquiries which they have made of the *qualified quarters*. I do not say that the average of wheat will come down to thirty-two shillings; but this I know, that at Reading, last Saturday, about forty-five shillings was the price; and I hear that, in Norfolk, the price is forty-two. The *highest quarters*, and the infamous London press, will, at any rate, be prettily exposed before Christmas. Old Sir Thomas Lethbridge, too, and Gaffer Gooch, and his base tribe of Pittites at Ipswich; Coke and Suffield, and their crew; all these will be prettily laughed at; nor will that " tall soul," Lord Milton, escape being reminded of his profound and patriotic observation relative to " this self-renovating country." No sooner did he see the wheat get up to sixty or seventy shillings than he lost all his alarms; found that all things were right, turned his back on Yorkshire reformers, and went and toiled for Scarlett at Peter-borough: and discovered that there was nothing wrong, at last, and that the " self-renovating country " would triumph over all its difficulties!—So it will, " tall soul; " it will triumph over all its difficulties: it will renovate itself: it will purge itself of rotten boroughs, of vile boroughmongers, their tools and their stopgaps; it will purge itself of all the villainies which now corrode its heart; it will, in short, free itself from those curses which the expenditure of eight or nine hundred millions of English money took place in order to make perpetual; it will, in short, become as free from oppression, as easy and as happy as the gallant and sensible nation on the other side of the Channel. This is the sort of renovation, but not renovation by the means of wheat at seventy shillings a quarter. Renovation it will have: it will rouse and will shake from itself curses like the pension which is paid to Burke's executors. This is the sort of renovation, " tall soul; " and not wheat at seventy shillings a quarter, while it is at twenty-five shillings a quarter in France. Pray observe, reader, how the " tall soul " *catched* at the rise in the price of wheat: how he *snapped* at it: how quickly he ceased his attacks upon the Whitehall people and upon the system. He thought he had been deceived: he thought that things were coming about again; and so he drew in his horns, and began to talk about the self-renovating country. This was the tone of them *all*. This was the tone of all the boroughmongers; all the friends of the system; all those who, like Lethbridge, had begun to be staggered. They had deviated, for a moment, into our path! but they popped back again the moment they saw the price of wheat rise! All the enemies of reform, all the calumniators of reformers, all the friends of the system, most anxiously desired a rise in the price of wheat. Mark the curious fact that all the vile press of London; the whole of that infamous press; that newspapers, magazines, reviews: the whole of the base thing; and a baser surely this world never saw; that the whole of this base thing rejoiced, exulted, crowed over me, and told an impudent lie, in order to have the crowing; crowed, for what? *Because wheat and bread were become dear!* A newspaper hatched under a corrupt priest, a profligate priest, and recently espoused to the hell of Pall Mall; even this vile thing crowed because wheat and bread had become dear! Now, it is notorious that, heretofore, every periodical publication in this kingdom was in the constant habit of lamenting when bread became dear, and of rejoicing when it became cheap. This is notorious. Nay, it is equally notorious, that this infamous press was everlastingly assailing bakers, and millers, and butchers, for not selling bread, flour, and meat cheaper than they were selling them. In how many hundreds of instances has this infamous press caused attacks to be made by the mob upon tradesmen of this description! All these things are notorious. Moreover, notorious it is that, long previous to every harvest, this infamous, this execrable, this beastly press, was engaged in stunning the public with accounts of the *great crop* which was just coming forward! There was always, with this press, a prodigiously large crop. This was invariably the case. It was never known to be the contrary.

Now these things are perfectly well known to every man in England. How comes it, then, reader, that the profligate, the trading, the lying, the infamous press of London, has now totally changed its tone and bias. The base thing never now tells us that there is a great crop or even a good crop. It never now wants cheap bread and cheap wheat and cheap meat. It never now finds fault of bakers and butchers. It now always endeavours to make it appear that corn is dearer than it is. The base *Morning Herald*, about three weeks ago, not only suppressed the fact of the fall of wheat, but asserted that there had been a rise in the price. Now *why is all this?* That is a great question, reader. That is a very interesting question. Why has this infamous press, which always pursues that which it thinks its own interest; why has it taken this strange turn? This is the reason: stupid as the base thing is, it has arrived at a conviction that if the price of the produce of the land cannot be kept up to something approaching ten shillings a bushel for good wheat, the hellish system of funding must be blown up. The infamous press has arrived at a conviction that that cheating, that fraudulent system by which this press lives, must be destroyed unless the price of corn can be kept up. The infamous traders of the press are perfectly well satisfied that the interest of the debt must be reduced, unless wheat can be kept up to nearly ten shillings a bushel. Stupid as they are, and stupid as the fellows down at Westminster are, they know very well that the whole system, stock-jobbers, Jews, cant and all, go to the devil at once as soon as a deduction is made from the interest of the debt. Knowing this, they want wheat to sell high; because it has, at last, been hammered into their skulls that the interest cannot be paid in full if wheat sells low. Delightful is the dilemma in which they are. Dear bread does not suit their manufactories, and cheap bread does not suit their debt. "*Envy of surrounding nations*," how hard it is that Providence will not enable your farmers to sell dear and the consumers to buy cheap! These are the things that you want. Admiration of the world you are; but have these things you will not. There may be those, indeed, who question whether you yourself know what you want; but, at any rate, if you want these things, you will not have them.

Before I conclude, let me ask the reader to take a look at the *singularity* of the tone and tricks of this Six-Acts Government. Is it not a novelty in the world to see a government, and in ordinary seasons, too, having its whole soul absorbed in considerations relating to the price of corn? There are our neighbours, the French, who have got a government engaged in taking military possession of a great neighbouring kingdom to free which from these very French we have recently expended a *hundred and fifty millions of money*. Our neighbours have got a government that is thus engaged, and we have got a government that employs itself in making incessant "inquiries in all the qualified quarters" relative to the price of wheat! Curious employment for a government! Singular occupation for the ministers of the Great George! They seem to think nothing of Spain, with its eleven millions of people, being in fact added to France. Wholly insensible do they appear to concerns of this sort, while they sit thinking, day and night, upon the price of the bushel of wheat!

However, they are not, after all, such fools as they appear to be. Despicable, indeed, must be that nation whose safety or whose happiness does, in any degree, depend on so fluctuating a thing as the price of corn. This is a matter that we must take as it comes. The seasons will be what they will be; and all the calculations of statesmen must be made wholly independent of the changes and chances of seasons. This has always been the case, to be sure. What nation could ever carry on its affairs, if it had to take into consideration the price of corn? Nevertheless, such is the situation of *our government* that its very existence, in its present way, depends upon the price of corn. The pretty fellows at Whitehall, if you may say to them: Well, but look at Spain; look at the enormous strides of the French; think of the consequences in case of another war; look, too, at the growing marine of America. See, Mr. Jenkinson, see, Mr. Canning, see, Mr. Huskisson, see, Mr. Peel, and all ye tribe of Grenvilles, see, what tremendous dangers are gathering together about us! "*Us!*" Aye, about *you*; but pray think what tremendous dangers wheat at four shillings a bushel will bring about *us!* This is the gist. Here lies the whole of it. We laugh at a government employing itself in making calculations about the price of corn, and in employing its press to put forth market puffs. We laugh at these things; but we should not laugh, if we considered that it is on the price of wheat that the duration of the power and the profits of these men depends. They know what they want; and they wish to believe themselves, and to make others believe, that they shall have it. I have observed before, but it is necessary to observe again, that all those who are for the system, let them be Opposition or Opposition not, feel as Whitehall feels about the price of corn. I have given an instance in the " tall soul; " but it is the same with the whole of them, with the whole of those who do not wish to see this infernal system changed. I was informed, and I believe it to be true, that the Marquis of Lansdowne said, last April, when the great rise took place in the price of corn, that he had always thought that the cash-measures had but little effect on prices; but that he was now satisfied that those measures had no effect at all on prices! Now, what is our situation; what is the situation of this country, if we must have the present ministry, or a ministry of which the Marquis of Lansdowne is to be a member, if the Marquis of Lansdowne did utter these words? And again, I say, that I verily believe he did utter them.

Ours is a government that now seems to depend very much

upon the *weather*. The old type of a ship at sea will not do now, ours is a weather government; and to know the state of it, we must have recourse to those glasses that the Jews carry about. Weather depends upon the winds, in a great measure; and I have no scruple to say, that the situation of those two right honourable youths, that are now gone to the Lakes in the north; that their situation, next winter, will be rendered very irksome, not to say perilous, by the present easterly wind, if it should continue about fifteen days longer. Pitt, when he had just made a monstrous issue of paper, and had, thereby, actually put the match which blowed up the old She Devil in 1797—Pitt, at that time, congratulated the nation that the wisdom of parliament had established a solid system of finance. Anything but solid it assuredly was; but his system of finance was as worthy of being called solid, as that system of government which now manifestly depends upon the weather and the winds.

Since my return home (it is now Thursday, 11th September), I have received letters from the east, from the north, and from the west. All tell me that the harvest is very far advanced, and that the crops are free from blight. These letters are not particular as to the weight of the crop; except that they all say that the barley is excellent. The wind is now coming from the east. There is every appearance of the fine weather continuing. Before Christmas, we shall have the wheat down to what will be a fair average price in future. I always said that the late rise was a mere puff. It was, in part, a scarcity rise. The wheat of 1821 was grown and bad. That of 1822 had to be begun upon in July. The crop has had to last thirteen months and a half. The present crop will have to last only eleven months, or less. The crop of barley, last year, was so very bad; so very small; and the crop of the year before so very bad in quality that wheat was malted, last year, in great quantities, instead of barley. This year, the crop of barley is prodigious. All these things considered, wheat, if the cash-measures had had no effect, must have been a hundred and forty shillings a quarter, and barley eighty. Yet the first never got to seventy, and the latter never got to forty! And yet there was a man who calls himself a statesman to say that that mere puff of a rise satisfied him that the cash-measures had never had any effect! Ah! they are all *afraid* to believe in the effect of those cash-measures: they tremble like children at the sight of the rod, when you hold up before them the effect of those cash-measures. Their only hope is, that I am wrong in my opinions upon that subject; because, if I am right, their system is condemned to speedy destruction!

I thus conclude, for the present, my remarks relative to the harvest and the price of corn. It is the great subject of the day; and the comfort is that we are now speedily to see whether I be right or whether the Marquis of Lansdowne be right. As to the infamous London press, the moment the wheat comes down to forty shillings, that is to say, an average government return of forty shillings, I will spend ten pounds in placarding this infamous press, after the manner in which we used to placard the base and detestable enemies of the queen. This infamous press has been what is vulgarly called "running its rigs" for several months past. The *Quakers* have been urging it on, underhanded. They have, I understand, been bribing it pretty deeply, in order to calumniate me, and to favour their own monopoly, but, thank God, the cunning knaves have outwitted themselves. They won't play at cards; but they will play at *Stocks;* they will play at lottery tickets, and they will play at Mark Lane. They have played a silly game, this time. Saint Swithin, that good old Roman Catholic Saint, seemed to have set a trap for them: he went on, wet, wet, wet, even until the harvest began. Then, after two or three days' sunshine, shocking wet again. The ground soaking, the wheat growing, and the "*Friends*," the gentle Friends, seeking the Spirit, were as busy amongst the sacks at Mark Lane as the devil in a high wind. In short they bought away, with all the gain of Godliness, *and a little more*, before their eyes. All of a sudden, Saint Swithin took away his clouds; out came the sun; the wind got round to the east; just sun enough and just wind enough; and as the wheat ricks everywhere rose up, the long jaws of the Quakers dropped down; and their faces of slate became of a darker hue. That sect will certainly be punished this year; and let us hope that such a change will take place in their concerns as will compel a part of them to labour, at any rate; for, at present, their sect is a perfect monster in society; a whole sect, not one man of whom earns his living by the sweat of his brow. A sect a great deal worse than the Jews; for some of them do work. However, God send us the easterly wind for another fortnight, and we shall certainly see some of this sect at work.

FROM KENSINGTON, ACROSS SURREY, AND ALONG THAT COUNTY

HAVING some business at Hartswood, near Reigate, I intended to come off this morning on horseback, along with my son Richard, but it rained so furiously the last night that we gave up the horse project for to-day, being, by appointment, to be at Reigate by ten o'clock to-day: so that we came off this morning at five o'clock in a post-chaise, intending to return home and take our horses. Finding, however, that we cannot quit this place till Friday, we have now sent for our horses, though the weather is dreadfully wet. But we are under a farm-house roof, and the wind may whistle and the rain fall as much as they like.

Having done my business at Hartswood to-day about eleven o'clock, I went to a sale at a farm, which the farmer is quitting. Here I had a view of what has long been going on all over the country. The farm, which belongs to *Christ's Hospital,* has been held by a man of the name of Charington, in whose family the lease has been, I hear, a great number of years. The house is hidden by trees. It stands in the Weald of Surrey, close by the *River Mole,* which is here a mere rivulet, though just below this house the rivulet supplies the very prettiest flour-mill I ever saw in my life.

Everything about this farm-house was formerly the scene of *plain manners* and *plentiful living.* Oak clothes-chests, oak bedsteads, oak chests of drawers, and oak tables to eat on, long, strong, and well supplied with joint stools. Some of the things were many hundreds of years old. But all appeared to be in a state of decay and nearly of *disuse.* There appeared to have been hardly any *family* in that house, where formerly there were, in all probability, from ten to fifteen men, boys, and maids: and, which was the worst of all, there was a *parlour.* Aye, and a *carpet* and *bell-pull* too! One end of the front of this once plain and substantial house had been moulded into a " *parlour ;* " and there was the mahogany table, and the fine chairs, and the fine glass, and all as bare-faced upstart as any stock-jobber in the kingdom can boast of. And there were the decanters, the glasses, the " dinner-set " of crockery-ware, and all just in the true stock-jobber style. And I dare say it has been 'Squire Charington and the *Miss* Charington's; and not plain Master Charington, and his son Hodge, and his daughter Betty Charington, all of whom this accursed system has, in all likelihood, transmuted into a species of mock gentlefolks, while it has ground the labourers down into real slaves. Why do not farmers now *feed* and *lodge* their work-people, as they did formerly? Because they cannot keep them *upon so little* as they give them in wages. This is the real cause of the change. There needs no more to prove that the lot of the working classes has become worse than it formerly was. This fact alone is quite sufficient to settle this point. All the world knows that a number of people, boarded in the same house, and at the same table, can, with as good food, be boarded much cheaper than those persons divided into twos, threes, or fours, can be boarded. This is a well-known truth: therefore, if the farmer now shuts his pantry against his labourers, and pays them wholly in money, is it not clear that he does it because he thereby gives them a living *cheaper* to him; that is to say, a *worse* living than formerly? Mind, he has *a house* for them; a kitchen for them to sit in, bedrooms for them to sleep in, tables, and stools, and benches, of everlasting duration. All these he has: all these *cost him nothing ;* and yet so much does he gain by pinching them in wages that he lets all these things remain as of no use rather than feed labourers in the house. Judge, then, of the *change* that has taken place in the condition of these labourers! And be astonished, if you can, at the *pauperism* and the *crimes* that now disgrace this once happy and moral England.

The land produces, on an average, what it always produced, but there is a new distribution of the produce. This 'Squire Charington's father used, I dare say, to sit at the head of the oak-table along with his men, say grace to them, and cut up the meat and the pudding. He might take a cup of *strong beer* to himself, when they had none; but that was pretty nearly all the difference in their manner of living. So that *all* lived well. But the *'squire* had many *wine-decanters* and *wine-glasses* and " *a dinner set,*" and a " *breakfast set,*" and " *dessert knives ;* " and these evidently imply carryings on and a consumption that must of necessity have greatly robbed the long oak table if it had remained fully tenanted. That long table could not share in the work of the decanters and the dinner set. Therefore, it became almost untenanted; the labourers retreated to hovels, called cottages; and instead of board and lodging, they got money; so little of it as to enable the employer to drink wine; but, then, that he might not reduce them to *quite starvation*, they were enabled to come to him, in the *king's name*, and demand food *as paupers*. And now, mind, that which a man receives in the *king's name*, he knows well he has *by force;* and it is not in nature that he should *thank* anybody for it, and least of all the party *from whom it is forced.* Then, if this sort of force be insufficient to obtain him enough to eat and to keep him warm, is it surprising if he think it no great offence against God (who created no man to starve) to use another sort of force more within his own control? Is it, in short, surprising, if he resort to *theft* and *robbery?*

This is not only the *natural* progress, but it *has been* the progress in England. The blame is not justly imputed to 'Squire Charington and his like: the blame belongs to the infernal stock-jobbing system. There was no reason to expect that farmers would not endeavour to keep pace, in point of show and luxury, with fund-holders, and with all the tribes that *war* and *taxes* created. Farmers were not the authors of the mischief; and *now* they are compelled to shut the labourers out of their houses, and to pinch them in their wages, in order to be able to pay their own taxes; and, besides this, the manners and the principles of the working class are so changed that a sort of self-preservation bids the farmer (especially in some counties) to keep them from beneath his roof.

I could not quit this farm-house without reflecting on the thousands of scores of bacon and thousands of bushels of bread that had been eaten from the long oak-table which, I said to myself, is now perhaps going at last to the bottom of a bridge that some stock-jobber will stick up over an artificial river in his cockney garden. " By —— it shan't," said I, almost in a real passion: and so I requested a friend to buy it for me; and if he do so, I will take it to Kensington, or to Fleet Street, and keep it for the good it has done in the world.

When the old farm-houses are down (and down they must come in time) what a miserable thing the country will be! Those that are now erected are mere painted shells, with a mistress within, who is stuck up in a place she calls a *parlour*, with, if she have children, the " young ladies and gentlemen " about her: some showy chairs and a sofa (a *sofa* by all means): half a dozen prints in gilt frames hanging up: some swinging book-shelves with novels and tracts upon them: a dinner brought in by a girl that is perhaps better " educated " than she: two or three nick-nacks to eat instead of a piece of bacon and a pudding: the house too neat for a dirty-shoed carter to be allowed to come into; and everything proclaiming to every sensible beholder that there is here a constant anxiety to make a *show* not warranted by the reality. The children (which is the worst part of it) are all too clever to *work:* they are all to be *gentlefolks*. Go to plough! Good God! What, " young gentlemen " go to plough! They become *clerks*, or some skimmy-dish thing or other. They flee from the dirty *work* as cunning horses do from the bridle. What misery is all this! What a mass of materials for producing that general and *dreadful convulsion* that must, first or last, come and blow this funding and jobbing and enslaving and starving system to atoms!

I was going, to-day, by the side of a plat of ground, where there was a very fine flock of *turkeys*. I stopped to admire them, and observed to the owner how fine they were, when he answered, " We owe them entirely *to you*, sir, for we never raised one till we read your *Cottage Economy*." I then told him that we had, this year, raised two broods at Kensington, one black and one white, one of nine and one of eight; but that, about three weeks back, they appeared to become dull and pale about the head; and that, therefore, I sent them to a farm-house, where they recovered instantly, and the broods being such a contrast to each other in point of colour, they were now, when prowling over a grass field, amongst the most agreeable sights that I had ever seen. I intended, of course, to let them get their full growth at Kensington, where they were in a grass plat about fifteen yards square, and where I thought that the feeding of them, in great abundance, with lettuces and other greens from the garden, together with grain, would carry them on to perfection. But I found that I was wrong; and that though you may raise them to a certain size in a small place and with such management, they then, if so much confined, begin to be sickly. Several of mine began actually to droop: and the very day they were sent into the country, they became as gay as ever, and in three days all the colour about their heads came back to them.

This town of Reigate had, in former times, a priory, which

had considerable estates in the neighbourhood; and this is brought to my recollection by a circumstance which has recently taken place in this very town. We all know how long it has been the fashion for us to take it for *granted* that the monasteries were *bad things;* but of late I have made some hundreds of thousands of very good Protestants begin to suspect that monasteries were better than *poor-rates,* and that monks and nuns, who *fed the poor,* were better than sinecure and pension men and women, who *feed upon the poor.* But how came the monasteries! How came this that was at Reigate, for instance? Why it was, if I recollect correctly, *founded by a Surrey gentleman,* who gave this spot and other estates to it, and who, as was usual, provided that masses were to be said in it for his soul and those of others, and that it should, as usual, give aid to the poor and needy.

Now, upon the face of the transaction, what *harm* could this do the community? On the contrary, it must, one would think, do it *good;* for here was this estate given to a set of landlords who never could quit the spot; who could have no families; who could save no money; who could hold no private property; who could make no will; who must spend all their income at Reigate and near it; who, as was the custom, fed the poor, administered to the sick, and taught some, at least, of the people, *gratis.* This, upon the face of the thing, seems to be a very good way of disposing of a rich man's estate.

"Aye, but," it is said, "he left his estate away from his relations." That is not *sure,* by any means. The contrary is fairly to be presumed. Doubtless, it was the custom for Catholic priests, before they took their leave of a dying rich man, to advise him to think of the *Church and the Poor;* that is to say, to exhort him to bequeath something to them; and this has been made a monstrous charge against that Church. It is surprising how blind men are, when they have a mind to be blind; what despicable dolts they are, when they desire to be cheated. We of the Church of England must have a special deal of good sense and of modesty, to be sure, to rail against the Catholic Church on this account, when our own Common Prayer Book, copied from an act of parliament, *commands our parsons to do just the same thing!*

Ah! say the Dissenters, and particularly the Unitarians; that queer sect, who will have all the wisdom in the world to themselves; who will believe and won't believe; who will be Christians and who won't have *a Christ;* who will laugh at you, if

you believe in the Trinity, and who would (if they could) boil
you in oil if you do not believe in the Resurrection: " Oh! "
say the Dissenters, " we know very well that your *Church parsons*
are commanded to get, if they can, dying people to give their
money and estates to the Church and *the poor*, as they call the
concern, though the *poor*, we believe, come in for very little
which is got in this way. But what is *your Church?* We are
the real Christians; and we, upon our souls, never play such
tricks; never, no never, terrify old women out of their stockings
full of guineas." " And as to us," say the Unitarians, " we,
the most *liberal* creatures upon earth; we, whose virtue is
indignant at the tricks by which the monks and nuns got
legacies from dying people to the injury of heirs and other
relations; we, who are the really enlightened, the truly con-
sistent, the benevolent, the disinterested, the exclusive patentees
of the *salt of the earth*, which is sold only at, or by express permission from our old and original warehouse and manufactory,
Essex Street, in the Strand, first street on the left, going from
Temple Bar towards Charing Cross; we defy you to show that
Unitarian parsons. . . ."

Stop your protestations and hear my Reigate anecdote, which,
as I said above, brought the recollection of the Old Priory into
my head. The readers of the *Register* heard me, several times,
some years ago, mention Mr. Baron Maseres, who was, for a
great many years, what they call Cursitor Baron of the Exchequer. He lived partly in London and partly at Reigate,
for more, I believe, than half a century; and he died, about
two years ago, or less, leaving, I am told, *more than a quarter of
a million of money*. The Baron came to see me, in Pall Mall,
in 1800. He always came frequently to see me, wherever I was
in London; not by any means omitting to *come to see me in
Newgate*, where I was imprisoned for two years, with a thousand
pounds fine and seven years' heavy bail, for having expressed
my indignation at the flogging of Englishmen, in the heart of
England, under a guard of German bayonets; and to Newgate
he always came in *his wig and gown*, in order, as he said, to show
his abhorrence of the sentence. I several times passed a week,
or more, with the Baron at his house, at Reigate, and might
have passed many more, if my time and taste would have
permitted me to accept of his invitations. Therefore, I knew
the Baron well. He was a most conscientious man; he was
when I first knew him still a very clever man; he retained all
his faculties to a very great age; in 1815, I think it was, I got

a letter from him, written in a firm hand, correctly as to grammar and ably as to matter, and he must then have been little short of ninety. He never was a bright man; but had always been a very sensible, just and humane man, and a man too who always cared a great deal for the public good; and he was the only man that I ever heard of, who refused to have his salary augmented, when an augmentation was offered, and when all other such salaries were augmented. I had heard of this: I asked him about it when I saw him again; and he said: " There was no *work* to be added, and I saw no justice in adding to the salary. It must," added he, " be *paid by somebody*, and the more I take, the less that somebody must have."

He did not save money for money's sake. He saved it because his habits would not let him spend it. He kept a house in Rathbone Place, chambers in the Temple, and his very pretty place at Reigate. He was by no means stingy, but his scale and habits were cheap. Then, consider, too, a bachelor of nearly a hundred years old. His father left him a fortune, his brother (who also died a very old bachelor), left him another; and the money lay in the funds, and it went on doubling itself over and over again, till it became that immense mass which we have seen above, and which, when the Baron was making his will, he had neither Catholic priest nor Protestant parson to exhort him to leave to the Church and the poor, instead of his relations; though, as we shall presently see, he had somebody else to whom to leave his great heap of money.

The Baron was a most implacable enemy of the Catholics, as Catholics. There was rather a peculiar reason for this, his grandfather having been a *French Hugonot* and having fled with his children to England, at the time of the revocation of the Edict of Nantz. The Baron was a very humane man; his humanity made him assist to support the French emigrant priests; but, at the same time, he caused Sir Richard Musgrave's book against the Irish Catholics to be published at his own expense. He and I never agreed upon this subject; and this subject was, with him, a *vital* one. He had no asperity in his nature; he was naturally all gentleness and benevolence; and, therefore, he never *resented* what I said to him on this subject (and which nobody else ever, I believe, ventured to say to him): but he did not like it; and he liked it the less because I certainly beat him in the argument. However, this was long before he visited me in Newgate: and it never produced (though the dispute was frequently revived) any difference in his conduct towards me, which was uniformly friendly to the last time I saw him before his memory was gone.

There was great excuse for the Baron. From his very birth he had been taught to hate and abhor the Catholic religion. He had been told that his father and mother had been driven out of France by the Catholics: and there was *that mother* dinning this in his ears, and all manner of horrible stories along with it, during all the tender years of his life. In short, the prejudice made part of his very frame. In the year 1803, in August, I think it was, I had gone down to his house on a Friday, and was there on a Sunday. After dinner he and I and his brother walked to the Priory, as is still called the mansion house, in the dell at Reigate, which is now occupied by Lord Eastnor, and in which a Mr. Birket, I think, then lived. After coming away from the Priory, the Baron (whose native place was Betchworth, about two or three miles from Reigate), who knew the history of every house and everything else in this part of the country, began to tell me why the place was called *the Priory*. From this he came to the *superstition* and *dark ignorance* that induced people to found monasteries; and he dwelt particularly on the *injustice to heirs and relations ;* and he went on, in the usual Protestant strain, and with all the bitterness of which he was capable, against those *crafty priests*, who thus *plundered families* by means of the influence which they had over people in their dotage, or who were naturally weak-minded.

Alas! poor Baron! he does not seem to have at all foreseen what was to become of his own money! What would he have said to me, if I had answered his observations by predicting, that *he* would give his great mass of money to a little parson for that parson's own private use; leave only a mere pittance to his own relations; leave the little parson his house in which we were then sitting (along with all his other real property); that the little parson would come into the house and take possession; and that his own relations (two nieces) would walk out! Yet all this has actually taken place, and that, too, after the poor old Baron's four score years of jokes about the tricks of *Popish* priests, practised, in the *dark ages,* upon the *ignorant* and *superstitious* people of Reigate.

When I first knew the Baron he was a staunch *Church of England man.* He went to church every Sunday once, at least. He used to take me to Reigate church: and I observed that he was very well versed in his prayer book. But a decisive proof of his zeal as a Church of England man is, that he settled an annual sum on the incumbent of Reigate, in order to induce him to preach, or pray (I forget which), in the church, twice on a Sunday, instead of once; and in case this additional preaching, or praying, were not performed in Reigate church, the annuity was to go (and sometimes it does now go) to the poor of an adjoining parish, and not to those of Reigate, lest I suppose the parson, the overseers, and other ratepayers, might happen to think that the Baron's annuity would be better laid out in food for the bodies than for the souls of the poor; or, in other words, lest the money should be taken annually and added to the poor-rates to ease the purses of the farmers.

It did not, I dare say, occur to the poor Baron (when he was making this settlement), that he was now giving money to make a church parson put up additional prayers, though he had, all his lifetime, been laughing at those who, in the *dark* ages, gave money for this purpose to Catholic priests. Nor did it, I dare say, occur to the Baron that, in his contingent settlement of the annuity on the poor of an adjoining parish he as good as de-clared his opinion that he distrusted the piety of the parson, the overseers, the churchwardens, and, indeed, of all the people of Reigate: yes, at the very moment that he was providing additional prayers for them, he in the very same parchment put a provision which clearly showed that he was thoroughly convinced that they, overseers, churchwardens, people, parson and all, loved money better than prayers.

What was this, then? Was it hypocrisy; was it ostentation? No: mistake. The Baron thought that those who could not go to church in the morning ought to have an opportunity of going in the afternoon. He was aware of the power of money; but when he came to make his obligatory clause, he was com-pelled to do that which reflected great discredit on the very Church and religion which it was his object to honour and uphold.

However, the Baron *was* a staunch churchman as this fact clearly proves: several years he had become what they call an *Unitarian*. The first time (I think) that I perceived this was in 1812. He came to see me in Newgate, and he soon began to talk about *religion*, which had not been much his habit. He went on at a great rate, laughing about the Trinity; and I remember that he repeated the Unitarian distich, which makes *a joke* of the idea of there being a devil, and which they all repeat to you, and at the same time laugh and look as cunning and as priggish as jackdaws; just as if they were wiser than all the rest in the world! I hate to hear the conceited and disgusting prigs seeming to take it for granted that they only are wise because others *believe* in the incarnation without being able to reconcile it to *reason*. The prigs don't consider that there is no more *reason* for the *resurrection* than for the *incarnation ;* and yet having taken it into their heads to *come up again*, they would murder you, if they dared, if you were to deny the *resurrection*. I do most heartily despise this priggish set for their conceit and impudence; but seeing that they want *reason* for the incarnation; seeing that they will have *effects*, here, ascribed to none but *usual causes*, let me put a question or two to them.

1. *Whence* comes the *white clover*, that comes up and covers all the ground, in America, where hard-wood trees, after standing for thousands of years, have been burnt down?

2. *Whence* come (in similar cases as to self-woods) the hurtleberries in some places, and the raspberries in others?

3. *Whence* come fish in new made places where no fish have ever been put?

4. *What causes* horse-hair to become living things?

5. *What causes* frogs to come in drops of rain, or those drops of rain to turn to frogs, the moment they are on the earth?

6. *What causes* musquitoes to come in rain water caught in a glass, covered over immediately with oil paper, tied down and so kept till full of these winged torments?

7. *What causes* flounders, real little *flat fish*, brown on one side, white on the other, mouth side-ways, with tail, fins, and all, *leaping alive*, in the *inside* of a rotten sheep's, and of every rotten sheep's, *liver ?*

There, prigs; answer these questions. Fifty might be given you; but these are enough. Answer these. I suppose you will not deny the facts? They are all notoriously true. The *last*, which of itself would be quite enough for you, will be attested on oath, if you like it, by any farmer, ploughman, and shepherd in England. Answer this question 7, or hold your conceited gabble about the " *impossibility* " of that which I need not here name.

Men of sense do not attempt to discover that which it is *impossible* to discover. They leave things pretty much as they

find them; and take care, at least, not to make changes of any
sort without very evident necessity. The poor Baron, however,
appeared to be quite eaten up with his " *rational* Christianity."
He talked like a man who has made a *discovery* of his *own*. He
seemed as pleased as I, when I was a boy, used to be, when I had
just found a rabbit's stop, or a blackbird's nest full of young
ones. I do not recollect what I said upon this occasion. It is
most likely that I said nothing in contradiction to him. I saw
the Baron many times after this, but I never talked with him
about religion.

Before the summer of 1822, I had not seen him for a year or
two, perhaps. But in July of that year, on a very hot day, I
was going down Rathbone Place, and, happening to cast my eye
on the Baron's house, I knocked at the door to ask how he was.
His man-servant came to the door, and told me that his master
was at dinner. " Well," said I, " never mind; give my best
respects to him." But the servant (who had always been with
him since I knew him) begged me to come in, for that he was sure
his master would be glad to see me. I thought, as it was likely
that I might never see him again, I would go in. The servant
announced me, and the Baron said, " Beg him to walk in."
In I went, and there I found the Baron at dinner; but *not quite
alone ;* nor without *spiritual* as well as carnal and vegetable
nourishment before him: for there, on the opposite side of his
vis-à-vis dining table, sat that nice, neat, straight, prim piece of
mortality, commonly called the Reverend Robert Fellowes,
who was the chaplain to the unfortunate queen until Mr. Alderman Wood's son came to supply his place, and who was now,
I could clearly see, in a fair way enough. I had dined, and so
I let them dine on. The Baron was become quite a child, or
worse, as to mind, though he ate as heartily as I ever saw him,
and he was always a great eater. When his servant said, " Here
is Mr. Cobbett, sir; " he said, " How do you do, sir? I have
read much of your writings, sir; but *never had the pleasure to see
your person before*." After a time I made him recollect me; but
he, directly after, being about to relate something about America,
turned towards me and said, " *Were you ever in America,* sir ? "
But I must mention one proof of the state of his mind. Mr.
Fellowes asked me about the news from Ireland, where the
people were then in a state of starvation (1822), and I answering
that it was likely that many of them would actually be starved
to death, the Baron, quitting his green goose and green pease,
turned to me and said, " *Starved,* sir! Why don't they go to

the parish?" "Why," said I, "you know, sir, that there are no poor-rates in Ireland." Upon this he exclaimed, "What! no poor-rates in Ireland? Why not? I did not know that; I can't think how that can be." And then he rambled on in a childish sort of way.

At the end of about half an hour, or it might be more, I shook hands with the poor old Baron for the last time, well convinced that I should never see him again, and not less convinced that I had seen his *heir*. He died in about a year or so afterwards, left to his own family about £20,000, and to his ghostly guide, the Holy Robert Fellowes, all the rest of his immense fortune, which, as I have been told, amounts to more than a quarter of a million of money.

Now, the public will recollect that, while Mr. Fellowes was at the queen's, he was, in the public papers, charged with being an *Unitarian*, at the same time that he officiated *as her chaplain*. It is also well known that he never publicly contradicted this. It is, besides, the general belief at Reigate. However, this we know well, that he is a parson, of one sort or the other, and that he is not a Catholic priest. That is enough for me. I see this poor, foolish old man leaving a monstrous mass of money to this little Protestant parson, whom he had not even known more, I believe, than about three or four years. When the will was made I cannot say. I know nothing at all about that. I am supposing that all was perfectly fair; that the Baron had his senses when he made his will; that he clearly meant to do that which he did. But, then, I must insist that, if he had left the money to a *Catholic priest*, to be by him expended on the endowment of a convent, wherein to say masses and to feed and teach the poor, it would have been a more sensible and public-spirited part in the Baron, much more beneficial to the town and environs of Reigate, and beyond all measure more honourable to his own memory.

CHILWORTH,
Friday Evening, 21 Oct.

It has been very fine to-day. Yesterday morning there was *snow* on Reigate Hill, enough to look white from where we were in the valley. We set off about half-past one o'clock, and came all down the valley, through Buckland, Betchworth, Dorking, Sheer and Aldbury, to this place. Very few prettier rides in England, and the weather beautifully fine. There are more meeting-houses than churches in the vale, and I have heard of no less than five people, in this vale, who have gone crazy on account of religion.

To-morrow we intend to move on towards the west; to take a look, just a look, at the Hampshire parsons again. The turnips seem fine; but they cannot be large. All other things are very fine indeed. Everything seems to prognosticate a hard winter. All the country people say that it will be so.

FROM CHILWORTH, IN SURREY, TO WINCHESTER

WE set out from Chilworth to-day about noon. This is a little hamlet, lying under the south side of St. Martha's Hill; and on the other side of that hill, a little to the north-west, is the town of Guildford, which (taken with its environs) I, who have seen so many, many towns, think the prettiest, and, taken all together, the most agreeable and most happy-looking that I ever saw in my life. Here are hill and dell in endless variety. Here are the chalk and the sand, vieing with each other in making beautiful scenes. Here is a navigable river and fine meadows. Here are woods and downs. Here is something of everything but *fat marshes* and their skeleton-making *agues.* The vale, all the way down to Chilworth from Reigate, is very delightful.

We did not go to Guildford, nor did we cross the *River Wey,* to come through Godalming; but bore away to our left, and came through the village of Hambleton, going first to Hascomb to show Richard the South Downs from that high land, which looks southward over the *Wealds* of Surrey and Sussex, with all their fine and innumerable oak-trees. Those that travel on turnpike-roads know nothing of England.—From Hascomb to Thursley almost the whole way is across fields, or commons, or along narrow lands. Here we see the people without any disguise or affectation. Against a *great road* things are made for *show.* Here we see them *without any show.* And here we gain real knowledge as to their situation.—We crossed to-day three turnpike-roads, that from Guildford to Horsham, that from Godalming to Worthing, I believe, and that from Godalming to Chichester.

THURSLEY,
Wednesday, 26 Oct.

The weather has been beautiful ever since last Thursday morning; but there has been a white frost every morning, and the days have been coldish. *Here*, however, I am quite at home in a room where there is one of my *American fireplaces*, bought by my host of Mr. Judson of Kensington, who has made many a score of families comfortable, instead of sitting shivering in the cold. At the house of the gentleman whose house I am now in, there is a good deal of *fuel-wood;* and here I see in the parlours those fine and cheerful fires that make a great part of the happiness of the Americans. But these fires are to be had only in this sort of fireplace. Ten times the fuel; nay, no quantity, would effect the same object, in any other fireplace. It is equally good for coal as for wood; but, for *pleasure*, a wood-fire is the thing. There is round about almost every gentleman's or great farmer's house more wood suffered to rot every year, in one shape or another, than would make (with this fireplace) a couple of rooms constantly warm, from October to June. *Here*, peat, turf, saw-dust, and wood, are burnt in these fireplaces. My present host has three of the fireplaces.

Being out a-coursing to-day, I saw a queer-looking building upon one of the thousands of hills that nature has tossed up in endless variety of form round the skirts of the lofty Hindhead. This building is, it seems, called a *Semaphore*, or *Semiphare*, or something of that sort. What this word may have been hatched out of I cannot say; but it means a *job*, I am sure. To call it an *alarm-post* would not have been so convenient; for people not endued with Scotch *intellect* might have wondered why the devil we should have to pay for alarm-posts; and might have thought that, with all our " glorious victories," we had " brought our hogs to a fine market " if our dread of the enemy were such as to induce us to have alarm-posts all over the country! Such unintellectual people might have thought that we had " conquered France by the immortal Wellington " to little purpose, if we were still in such fear as to build alarm-posts; and they might, in addition, have observed that for many hundred of years England stood in need of neither signal-posts nor standing army of mercenaries; but relied safely on the courage and public spirit of the people themselves. By calling the thing by an outlandish name, these reflections amongst the unintellectual are obviated. *Alarm-post* would be a nasty name; and it would puzzle people exceedingly, when they saw one of these at a place like Ashe, a little village on the north side of the chalk-ridge (called the Hog's Back) going from Guildford to Farnham! What can this be *for?* Why are these expensive things put up all over the country? Respecting the movements of *whom* is wanted this *alarm-system?* Will no member ask this in parliament? Not one: not a man: and yet it is a thing to ask about. Ah! it is in vain, THING, that you thus are *making your preparations;* in vain that you are setting your trammels! The debt, the blessed debt, that best ally of the people, will break them all; will snap them, as the hornet does the cobweb; and even these very "Semaphores" contribute towards the force of that ever-blessed debt. Curious to see how things *work!* The "glorious revolution," which was made for the avowed purpose of maintaining the Protestant ascendency, and which was followed by such terrible persecution of the Catholics; that "glorious" affair, which set aside a race of kings, because they were Catholics, served as the *precedent* for the American revolution, also called "glorious," and this second revolution compelled the successors of the makers of the first to begin to cease their persecutions of the Catholics! Then again, the debt was made to raise and keep armies on foot to prevent reform of parliament, because, as it was feared by the aristocracy, reform would have humbled them; and this debt, created for this purpose, is fast sweeping the aristocracy out of their estates, as a clown, with his foot, kicks field-mice out of their nests. There was a hope that the debt could have been reduced by stealth, as it were; that the aristocracy could have been saved in this way. That hope now no longer exists. In all likelihood the funds will keep going down. What is to prevent this, if the interest of Exchequer Bills be raised, as the broadsheet tells us it is to be? What! the funds fall in time of peace; and the French funds not fall in time of peace! However, it will all happen just as it ought to happen. Even the next session of parliament will bring out matters of some interest. The thing is now working in the surest possible way.

The great business of life, in the country, appertains, in some way or other, to the *game,* and especially at this time of the year. If it were not for the game, a country life would be like an *everlasting honeymoon,* which would, in about half a century, put an end to the human race. In towns, or large villages, people make a shift to find the means of rubbing the rust off from each other by a vast variety of sources of contest. A couple of wives meeting in the street, and giving each other a wry look, or a look not quite civil enough, will, if the parties be hard pushed for a ground of contention, do pretty well. But in the country there is, alas! no such resource. Here are no walls for people to take of each other. Here they are so placed as to prevent the possibility of such lucky local contact. Here is more than room of every sort, elbow, leg, horse, or carriage, for them all. Even *at church* (most of the people being in the meeting-houses) the pews are surprisingly too large. Here, therefore, where all circumstances seem calculated to cause never-ceasing concord with its accompanying dullness, there would be no relief at all, were it not for the *game*. This, happily, supplies the place of all other sources of alternate dispute and reconciliation; it keeps all in life and motion, from the lord down to the hedger. When I see two men, whether in a market-room, by the way-side, in a parlour, in a church-yard, or even in the church itself, engaged in manifestly deep and most momentous discourse, I will, if it be any time between September and February, bet ten to one that it is, in some way or other, about *the game*. The wives and daughters hear so much of it that they inevitably get engaged in the disputes; and thus all are kept in a state of vivid animation. I should like very much to be able to take a spot, a circle of 12 miles in diameter, and take an exact account of all the *time* spent by each individual, above the age of ten (that is the age they begin at), in talking, during the game season of one year, about the game and about sporting exploits. I verily believe that it would amount, upon an average, to six times as much as all the other talk put together; and, as to the anger, the satisfaction, the scolding, the commendation, the chagrin, the exultation, the envy, the emulation, where are there any of these in the country uncon-nected with *the game* ?

There is, however, an important distinction to be made between *hunters* (including coursers) and *shooters*. The latter are, as far as relates to their exploits, a disagreeable class compared with the former; and the reason of this is, their doings are almost wholly their own; while, in the case of the others, the achievements are the property of the dogs. Nobody likes to hear another talk *much* in praise of his own acts, unless those acts have a manifest tendency to produce some good to the hearer; and shooters do talk *much* of their own exploits, and those exploits rather tend to *humiliate* the hearer. Then, a *greater shooter* will, nine times out of ten, go so far as almost to *lie a little ;* and though people do not tell him of it, they do not like him the better for it; and he but too frequently discovers that they do not believe him: whereas, hunters are mere followers of the dogs, as mere spectators; their praises, if any are called for, are bestowed on the greyhounds, the hounds, the fox, the hare, or the horses. There is a little rivalship in the riding, or in the behaviour of the horses; but this has so little to do with the personal merit of the sportsmen, that it never produces a want of good fellowship in the evening of the day. A shooter who has been *missing* all day, must have an uncommon share of good sense not to feel mortified while the slaughterers are relating the adventures of that day; and this is what cannot exist in the case of the hunters. Bring me into a room, with a dozen men in it, who have been sporting all day; or rather let me be in an adjoining room, where I can hear the sound of their voices, without being able to distinguish the words, and I will bet ten to one that I tell whether they be hunters or shooters.

I was once acquainted with a *famous shooter* whose name was William Ewing. He was a barrister of Philadelphia, but became far more renowned by his gun than by his law cases. We spent scores of days together a shooting, and were extremely well matched, I having excellent dogs and caring little about my reputation as a shot, his dogs being good for nothing, and he caring more about his reputation as a shot than as a lawyer. The fact which I am going to relate respecting this gentleman ought to be a warning to young men how they become enamoured of this species of vanity. We had gone about ten miles from our home, to shoot where partridges were said to be very plentiful. We found them so. In the course of a November day, he had, just before dark, shot, and sent to the farm-house, or kept in his bag, *ninety-nine* partridges. He made some few *double shots*, and he might have a *miss* or two, for he sometimes shot when out of my sight, on account of the woods. However, he said that he killed at every shot; and as he had counted the birds, when he went to dinner at the farm-house and when he cleaned his gun, he, just before sunset, knew that he had killed *ninety-nine* partridges, every one upon the wing, and a great part of them in woods very thickly set with largish trees. It was a grand achievement; but, unfortunately, he wanted to make it *a hundred*. The sun was setting, and, in that country, darkness comes almost at once; it is more like the going out of a candle than that of a fire; and I wanted to be off, as we had a very bad road to go, and as he, being under strict petticoat government, to which he most loyally and dutifully submitted, was compelled to get home that night, taking me with him, the vehicle (horse and gig) being mine. I, therefore, pressed him to come away,

and moved on myself towards the house (that of old John Brown,
in Bucks county, grandfather of that General Brown, who gave
some of our whiskered heroes such a rough handling last war,
which was waged for the purpose of " deposing James Madison "),
at which house I would have stayed all night, but from which I
was compelled to go by that watchful government, under which
he had the good fortune to live. Therefore I was in haste to be
off. No: he would kill the *hundredth* bird! In vain did I talk of
the bad road and its many dangers for want of moon. The poor
partridges, which we had scattered about, were *calling* all around
us; and, just at this moment, up got one under his feet, in a
field in which the wheat was three or four inches high. He shot
and *missed*. " That's it," said he, running as if to *pick up* the
bird. " What! " said I, " you don't think you *killed*, do you?
Why there is the bird now, not only alive, but *calling* in that
wood; " which was at about a hundred yards' distance. He,
in that *form of words* usually employed in such cases, asserted
that he shot the bird and saw it fall; and I, in much about the
same form of words, asserted that he had *missed*, and that I, with
my own eyes, saw the bird fly into the wood. This was too
much! To *miss* once out of a hundred times! To lose such a
chance of immortality! He was a good-humoured man; I
liked him very much; and I could not help feeling for him, when
he said, " Well, *sir*, I killed the bird; and if you choose to go
away and take your dog away, so as to prevent me from *finding*
it, you must do it; the dog is yours, to be sure." " The *dog*,"
said I, in a very mild tone, " why, Ewing, there is the spot; and
could we not see it, upon this smooth green surface, if it were
there? " However, he began to *look about ;* and I called the
dog, and affected to join him in the search. Pity for his weakness got the better of my dread of the bad road. After walking
backward and forward many times upon about twenty yards
square with our eyes to the ground, looking for what both of us
knew was not there, I had passed him (he going one way and I
the other), and I happened to be turning round just after I had
passed him, when I saw him, putting his hand behind him,
take a partridge out of his bag and let it fall upon the ground ! I
felt no temptation to detect him, but turned away my head, and
kept looking about. Presently he, having returned to the spot
where the bird was, called out to me, in a most triumphant tone,
" Here ! here ! Come here! " I went up to him, and he, pointing with his finger down to the bird, and looking hard in my face
at the same time, said, " There, Cobbett ; I hope that will be a

warning to you never to be obstinate again!" "Well," said I, "come along:" and away we went as merry as larks. When we got to Brown's, he told them the story, triumphed over me most clamorously; and though he often repeated the story to my face, I never had the heart to let him know that I knew of the imposition, which puerile vanity had induced so sensible and honourable a man to be mean enough to practise.

A *professed shot* is, almost always, a very disagreeable brother sportsman. He must, in the first place, have a head rather of the emptiest to *pride himself* upon so poor a talent. Then he is always out of temper, if the game fail, or if he miss it. He never participates in that great delight which all sensible men enjoy at beholding the beautiful action, the docility, the zeal, the wonderful sagacity of the pointer and the setter. He is always thinking about *himself :* always anxious to surpass his companions. I remember that, once, Ewing and I had lost our dog. We were in a wood, and the dog had gone out and found a covey in a wheat stubble joining the wood. We had been whistling and calling him for, perhaps, half an hour or more. When we came out of the wood we saw him pointing, with one foot up; and soon after, he, keeping his foot and body unmoved, gently turned round his head towards the spot where he heard us, as if to bid us come on, and when he saw that we saw him, turned his head back again. I was so delighted that I stopped to look with admiration. Ewing, astonished at my want of alacrity, pushed on, shot one of the partridges, and thought no more about the conduct of the dog than if the sagacious creature had had nothing at all to do with the matter. When I left America, in 1800, I gave this dog to Lord Henry Stuart, who was, when he came home a year or two afterwards, about to bring him to astonish the sportsmen even in England; but those of Pennsylvania were resolved not to part with him, and therefore they *stole* him the night before his lordship came away. Lord Henry had plenty of pointers after his return, and he *saw* hundreds; but always declared that he never saw anything approaching in excellence this American dog. For the information of sportsmen I ought to say that this was a small-headed and sharpnosed pointer, hair as fine as that of a greyhound, little and short ears, very light in the body, very long legged, and swift as a good lurcher. I had him a puppy, and he never had any *breaking*, but he pointed staunchly at once; and I am of opinion that this sort is, in all respects, better than the heavy breed. Mr. Thornton (I beg his pardon, I believe he is now a knight of some sort), who was, and perhaps still is, our envoy in Portugal, at the time here referred to was a sort of partner with Lord Henry in this famous dog; and gratitude (to the memory of *the dog* I mean) will, I am sure, or at least, I hope so, make him bear witness to the truth of my character of him; and if one could hear an ambassador *speak out*, I think that Mr. Thornton would acknowledge that his calling has brought him in pretty close contact with many a man who was possessed of most tremendous political power, without possessing half the sagacity, half the understanding, of this dog, and without being a thousandth part so faithful to his trust.

I am quite satisfied that there are as many *sorts* of men as there are of dogs. Swift was a man, and so is Walter the base. But is the *sort* the same? It cannot be *education* alone that makes the amazing difference that we see. Besides, we see men of the very same rank and riches and education differing as widely as the pointer does from the pug. The name, *man*, is common to all the sorts, and hence arises very great mischief. What confusion must there be in rural affairs, if there were no names whereby to distinguish hounds, greyhounds, pointers, spaniels, terriers, and sheep dogs, from each other! And what pretty work if, without regard to the *sorts* of dogs, men were to attempt to *employ them!* Yet this is done in the case of *men!* A man is always *a man;* and without the least regard as to the *sort*, they are promiscuously placed in all kinds of situations. Now, if Mr. Brougham, Doctors Birkbeck, Macculloch and Black, and that profound personage, Lord John Russell, will, in their forthcoming " London University," teach us how to divide men *into sorts*, instead of teaching us to " augment the capital of the nation " by making paper-money, they will render us a real service. That will be *feelosofy* worth attending to. What would be said of the 'squire who should take a fox-hound out to find partridges for him to shoot at? Yet would this be *more* absurd than to set a man to law-making who was manifestly formed for the express purpose of sweeping the streets or digging out sewers?

FARNHAM, SURREY,
Thursday, 27 Oct.

We came over the heath from Thursley, this morning, on our way to Winchester. Mr. Wyndham's fox-hounds are coming to Thursley on Saturday. More than three-fourths of all the interesting talk in that neighbourhood, for some days past, has been about this anxiously looked-for event. I have seen no man, or boy, who did not talk about it. There had been a false report about it; the hounds did *not come ;* and the anger of the disappointed people was very great. At last, however, the *authentic* intelligence came, and I left them all as happy as if all were young and all just going to be married. An abatement of my pleasure, however, on this joyous occasion was, that I brought away with me *one,* who was as eager as the best of them. Richard, though now only 11 years and 6 months old, had, it seems, one fox-hunt, in Herefordshire, last winter; and he actually has begun to talk rather *contemptuously* of hare hunting. To show me that he is in no *danger,* he has been leaping his horse over banks and ditches by the road side, all our way across the country from Reigate; and he joined with such glee in talking of the expected arrival of the fox-hounds that I felt some little pain at bringing him away. My engagement at Winchester is for Saturday; but if it had not been so, the deep and hidden ruts in the heath, in a wood in the midst of which the hounds are sure to find, and the immense concourse of horsemen that is sure to be assembled, would have made me bring him away. Upon the high, hard and open countries I should not be afraid for him, but here the danger would have been greater than it would have been right for me to suffer him to run.

We came hither by the way of Waverley Abbey and Moore Park. On the commons I showed Richard some of my old hunting scenes, when I was of his age, or younger, reminding him that I was obliged to hunt on foot. We got leave to go and see the grounds at Waverley where all the old monks' garden walls are totally gone, and where the spot is become a sort of lawn. I showed him the spot where the strawberry garden was, and where I, when sent to gather *hautboys,* used to eat every remarkably fine one, instead of letting it go to be eaten by Sir Robert Rich. I showed him a tree, close by the ruins of the Abbey, from a limb of which I once fell into the river, in an attempt to take the nest of a *crow,* which had artfully placed it upon a branch so far from the trunk as not to be able to bear the weight of a boy eight years old. I showed him an old elm-tree, which was hollow even then, into which I, when a very little boy, once saw a cat go, that was as big as a middle-sized spaniel dog, for relating which I got a great scolding, for standing to which I, at last, got a beating; but stand to which I still did. I have since many times repeated it; and I would take my oath of it to this day. When in New Brunswick I saw the great wild grey cat, which is there called a *Lucifee*; and it seemed to me to be just such a cat as I had seen at Waverley. I found the ruins not very greatly diminished; but it is strange how small the mansion, and ground, and everything but the trees, appeared to me. They were all great to my mind when I saw them last; and that early impression had remained, whenever I had talked or thought of the spot; so that, when I came to see them again, after seeing the sea and so many other immense things, it seemed as if they had all been made small. This was not the case with regard to the trees, which are nearly as big here as they are any where else; and the old cat-elm, for instance, which Richard measured with his whip, is about 16 or 17 feet round.

From Waverley we went to Moore Park, once the seat of Sir William Temple, and when I was a very little boy, the seat of a lady, or a Mrs. Temple. Here I showed Richard Mother Ludlum's Hole; but, alas! it is not the enchanting place that I knew it, nor that which Grose describes in his Antiquities! The semicircular paling is gone; the basins, to catch the never-ceasing little stream, are gone; the iron cups, fastened by chains, for people to drink out of, are gone; the pavement all broken to pieces; the seats for people to sit on, on both sides of the cave, torn up and gone; the stream that ran down a clean paved channel now making a dirty gutter; and the ground opposite, which was a grove, chiefly of laurels, intersected by closely mowed grass-walks, now become a poor, ragged-looking alder-coppice. Near the mansion, I showed Richard the hill upon which Dean Swift tells us he used to run for exercise, while he was pursuing his studies here; and I would have showed him the garden-seat, under which Sir William Temple's heart was buried, agreeably to his will; but the seat was gone, also the wall at the back of it; and the exquisitely beautiful little lawn in which the seat stood was turned into a parcel of divers-shaped cockney-clumps, planted according to the strictest rules of artificial and refined vulgarity.

At Waverley, Mr. Thompson, a merchant of some sort, has succeeded (after the monks) the Orby Hunters and Sir Robert Rich. At Moore Park, a Mr. Laing, a West India planter or merchant, has succeeded the Temples; and at the castle of Farnham, which you see from Moore Park, Bishop Prettyman Tomline has, at last, after perfectly regular and due gradations, succeeded William of Wykham! In coming up from Moore Park to Farnham town, I stopped opposite the door of a little old house, where there appeared to be a great parcel of children.

" There, Dick," said I, " when I was just such a little creature as that whom you see in the door-way, I lived in this very house with my grandmother Cobbett." He pulled up his horse, and looked *very hard at it*, but said nothing, and on we came.

WINCHESTER,
Sunday Noon, 30 *Oct.*

We came away from Farnham about noon on Friday, promising Bishop Prettyman to notice him and his way of living more fully on our return. At Alton we got some bread and cheese at a friend's, and then came to Alresford by Medstead, in order to have fine turf to ride on, and to see on this lofty land that which is, perhaps, the finest *beech-wood* in all England. These high down countries are not garden plats, like Kent; but they have, from my first seeing them, when I was about *ten*, always been my delight. Large sweeping downs, and deep dells here and there, with villages amongst lofty trees, are my great delight. When we got to Alresford it was nearly dark, and not being able to find a room to our liking, we resolved to go, though in the dark, to Easton, a village about six miles from Alresford down by the side of the Hichen River.

Coming from Easton yesterday, I learned that Sir Charles Ogle, the eldest son and successor of Sir Chaloner Ogle, had sold, to some *general*, his mansion and estate at Martyr's Worthy, a village on the north side of the Hichen, just opposite Easton. The Ogles had been here for *a couple of centuries* perhaps. They are *gone off now*, " for good and all," as the country people call it. Well, what I have to say to Sir Charles Ogle upon this occasion is this: " It was *you*, who moved at the county meeting, in 1817, that *Address to the Regent*, which you brought ready engrossed upon parchment, which Fleming, the sheriff, declared to have been carried, though a word of it never was heard by the meeting; which address *applauded the power of imprisonment bill, just then passed;* and the like of which address you will not in all human probability ever again move in Hampshire, and, I hope, nowhere else. So, you see, Sir Charles, there is one consolation, at any rate."

I learned, too, that Greame, a famously loyal 'squire and justice, whose son was, a few years ago, made a distributor of stamps in this county, was become so modest as to exchange his big and ancient mansion at Cheriton, or somewhere there, for a very moderate-sized house in the town of Alresford! I saw his household goods advertised in the Hampshire newspaper, a little while ago, to be sold by public auction. I rubbed my eyes, or, rather, my spectacles, and looked again and again; for I remembered the loyal 'squire; and I, with singular satisfaction, record this change in his scale of existence, which has, no doubt, proceeded solely from that prevalence of mind over matter which the Scotch *feelosofers* have taken such pains to inculcate, and which makes him flee from greatness as from that which diminishes the quantity of " *intellectual* enjoyment "; and so now he,

> " Wondering man can want the larger pile,
> Exults, and owns his cottage with a smile."

And they really tell me that his present house is not much bigger than that of my dear, good old grandmother Cobbett. But (and it may not be wholly useless for the 'squire to know it) she never burnt *candles ;* but *rushes* dipped in grease, as I have described them in my *Cottage Economy ;* and this was one of the means that she made use of in order to secure a bit of good bacon and good bread to eat, and that made her never give me *potatoes*, cold or hot. No bad hint for the 'squire, father of the distributor of stamps. Good bacon is a very nice thing, I can assure him; and if the quantity be small, it is all the sweeter; provided, however, it be not *too small*. This 'squire used to be a great friend of Old George Rose. But his patron's taste was different from his. George preferred a big house to a little one: and George *began* with a little one, and *ended* with a big one.

Just by Alresford, there was another old friend and supporter of Old George Rose, 'Squire Rawlinson, whom I remember a a very great 'squire in this county. He is now a *police-*'squire in London, and is one of those guardians of the Wen, respecting whose proceedings we read eternal columns in the broadsheet.

This being Sunday, I heard, about 7 o'clock in the morning, a sort of a jangling, made by a bell or two in the *cathedral*. We were getting ready to be off, to cross the country to Burghclere, which lies under the lofty hills at Highclere, about 22 miles from this city; but hearing the bells of the cathedral, I took Richard to show him that ancient and most magnificent pile, and particularly to show him the tomb of that famous bishop of Winchester, William of Wykham; who was the chancellor and the minister of the great and glorious king, Edward III.; who sprang from poor parents in the little village of Wykham, three miles from Botley; and who, amongst other great and most munificent deeds, founded the famous college, or school, of Winchester, and also one of the colleges of Oxford. I told Richard about this as we went from the inn down to the cathedral; and when I *showed him the tomb*, where the bishop lies on his back, in his Catholic robes, with his mitre on his head, his shepherd's crook by his side, with little children at his feet, their hands put together in a praying attitude, he looked with a degree of inquisitive earnestness that pleased me very much. I took him as far as I could about the cathedral. The " service " was now begun. There is a *dean*, and God knows how many *prebends* belonging to this immensely rich bishopric and chapter: and there were, at this " service," *two or three men* and *five or six boys* in white surplices, with a congregation of *fifteen women* and *four men !* Gracious God! If William of Wykham could, at that moment, have been raised from his tomb! If Saint Swithin, whose name the cathedral bears, or Alfred the Great, to whom St. Swithin was tutor: if either of these could have come, and had been told, that *that* was *now* what was carried on by men, who talked of the " *damnable* errors " of those who founded that very church! But it beggars one's feelings to attempt to find words whereby to express them upon such a subject and such an occasion. How, then, am I to describe what I felt when I yesterday saw in Hyde Meadow a *county bridewell* standing on the very spot where stood the abbey which was founded and endowed by Alfred, which contained the bones of that maker of the English name, and also those of the learned monk, St. Grimbald, whom Alfred brought to England *to begin the teaching at Oxford !*

After we came out of the cathedral, Richard said, " Why, papa, nobody can build such places *now*, can they? " " No, my dear," said I. " That building was made when there were no poor wretches in England called *paupers ;* when there were no *poor-rates ;* when every labouring man was clothed in good woollen cloth; and when all had a plenty of meat and bread and beer." This talk lasted us to the inn, where, just as we were going to set off, it most curiously happened that a parcel which had come from Kensington by the night coach was put into my hands by the landlord, containing, amongst other things, a pamphlet, sent to me from Rome, being an Italian translation of No. I. of the *Protestant Reformation.* I will here insert the title for the satisfaction of Doctor Black, who, some time ago expressed his utter astonishment that " *such* a work should be published in the *nineteenth* century." Why, Doctor? Did you want me to stop till the *twentieth* century? That would have been a little too long, Doctor.

Storia

Della

Riforma Protestante

In Inghilterra ed in Irlanda

La quale Dimostra

Come un tal' avvenimento ha impoverito

E degradato il grosso del popolo in que' paesi

in una serie di lettere indirizzate

A tutti i sensati e guisti inglesi

Da

Guglielmo Cobbett

E

Dall' inglese recate in italiano

Da

Dominico Gregorj.

Roma 1825.

Presso Francesco Bourlie.

Con Approvazione.

There, Doctor Black. Write *you* a book that shall be translated into *any* foreign language; and when you have done that, you may *again* call mine " pig's meat."

FROM WINCHESTER TO BURGHCLERE

WE had, or I had, resolved not to breakfast at Winchester yesterday: and yet we were detained till nearly noon. But at last off we came, *fasting*. The turnpike-road from Winchester to this place comes through a village called Sutton Scotney, and then through Whitchurch, which lies on the Andover and London road, through Basingstoke. We did not take the cross-turnpike till we came to Whitchurch. We went to King's Worthy; that is about two miles on the road from Winchester to London; and then, turning short to our left, came up upon the downs to the north of Winchester race-course. Here, looking back at the city and at the fine valley above and below it, and at the many smaller valleys that run down from the high ridges into that great and fertile valley, I could not help admiring the taste of the ancient kings, who made this city (which once covered all the hill round about, and which contained 92 churches and chapels) a chief place of their residence. There are not many finer spots in England; and if I were to take in a circle of eight or ten miles of semi-diameter, I should say that I believe there is not one so fine. Here are hill, dell, water, meadows, woods, corn-fields, downs: and all of them very fine and very beautifully disposed. This country does not present to us that sort of beauties which we see about Guildford and Godalming, and round the skirts of Hindhead and Black-down, where the ground lies in the form that the surface-water in a boiling copper would be in, if you could, by word of command, *make it be still*, the variously-shaped bubbles all sticking up; and really, to look at the face of the earth, who can help imagining that some such process has produced its present form? Leaving this matter to be solved by those who laugh at mysteries, I repeat, that the country round Winchester does not present to us beauties of *this sort ;* but of a sort which I like a great deal better. Arthur Young calls the vale between Farnham and Alton *the finest ten miles* in England. Here is a river with fine meadows on each side of it, and with rising grounds on each outside of the meadows, those grounds having some hop-gardens and some pretty woods. But, though I was born in this vale, I must confess that the ten miles between Maidstone and Tunbridge (which the Kentish folks call the *Garden of Eden*) is a great deal finer; for here, with a river three times as big, and a vale three times as broad, there are, on rising grounds six times as broad, not only hop-gardens and beautiful woods, but immense orchards of apples, pears, plums, cherries and filberts, and these, in many cases, with gooseberries and currants and raspberries beneath; and, all taken together, the vale is really worthy of the appellation which it bears. But even this spot, which I believe to be the very finest, as to fertility and diminutive beauty, in this whole world, I, for my part, do not like so well; nay, as a spot to *live on*, I thing nothing at all of it, compared with a country where high downs prevail, with here and there a large wood on the top or the side of a hill, and where you see, in the deep dells, here and there a farm-house, and here and there a village, the buildings sheltered by a group of lofty trees.

This is my taste, and here, in the north of Hampshire, it has its full gratification. I like to look at the winding side of a great down, with two or three numerous flocks of sheep on it, belonging to different farms; and to see, lower down, the folds, in the fields, ready to receive them for the night. We had, when we got upon the downs, after leaving Winchester, this sort of country all the way to Whitchurch. Our point of destination was this village of Burghclere, which lies close under the north side of the lofty hill at Highclere, which is called Beacon-hill, and on the top of which there are still the marks of a Roman encampment. We saw this hill as soon as we got on Winchester downs; and without any regard to *roads*, we *steered* for it, as sailors do for a land-mark. Of these 13 miles (from Winchester to Whitchurch) we rode about eight or nine upon the *green-sward*, or over fields equally smooth. And here is one great pleasure of living in countries of this sort: no sloughs, no ditches, no nasty dirty lanes, and the hedges, where there are any, are more for boundary marks than for fences. Fine for hunting and coursing: no impediments; no gates to open; nothing to impede the dogs, the horses, or the view. The water is not *seen running ;* but the great bed of chalk *holds it,* and the sun draws it up for the benefit of the grass and the corn; and whatever inconvenience is experienced from the necessity of deep wells, and of driving sheep and cattle far to water, is amply made up for by the goodness of the water, and by the complete absence of floods, of drains, of ditches and of water-furrows. As *things now are*, however, these countries have one great draw-back: the poor day-labourers suffer from the want of fuel, and they have nothing but their *bare pay*. For these reasons they are greatly worse off than those of the *woodland countries*; and it is really surprising what a difference there is between the faces that you see here, and the round, red faces that you see in the *wealds* and the *forests*, particularly in Sussex, where the labourers *will* have a *meat-pudding* of some sort or other; and where they *will* have *a fire* to sit by in the winter.

After steering for some time, we came down to a very fine farm-house, which we stopped a little to admire; and I asked Richard whether *that* was not a place to be happy in. The village, which we found to be Stoke-Charity, was about a mile lower down this little vale. Before we got to it, we overtook the owner of the farm, who knew me, though I did not know him; but when I found it was Mr. Hinton Bailey, of whom and whose farm I had heard so much, I was not at all surprised at the fineness of what I had just seen. I told him that the word *charity*, making, as it did, part of the name of this place, had nearly inspired me with boldness enough to go to the farm-house, in the ancient style, and ask for something to eat; for that we had not yet breakfasted. He asked us to go back; but at Burghclere we were *resolved to dine*. After, however, crossing the village, and beginning again to ascend the downs, we came to a labourer's (*once a farm-house*), where I asked the man whether he had any *bread and cheese*, and was not a little pleased to hear him say " *Yes*." Then I asked him to give us a bit, protesting that we had not yet broken our fast. He answered in the affirmative, at once, though I did not talk of payment. His wife brought out the cut loaf, and a piece of Wiltshire cheese, and I took them in hand, gave Richard a good hunch, and took another for myself. I verily believe that all the pleasure of eating enjoyed by all the feeders in London in a whole year does not equal that which we enjoyed in gnawing this bread and cheese, as we rode over this cold down, whip and bridle-reins in one hand, and the hunch in the other. Richard, who was purse bearer, gave the woman, by my direction, about enough to buy two quartern loaves: for she told me that they had to buy their bread *at the mill*, not being able to bake them-selves for *want of fuel;* and this, as I said before, is one of the draw-backs in this sort of country. I wish every one of these people had an *American fireplace*. Here they might then, even in these bare countries, have comfortable warmth. Rubbish of any sort would, by this means, give them warmth. I am now, at six o'clock in the morning, sitting in a room where one of these fireplaces, with very light *turf* in it, gives as good and steady a warmth as it is possible to feel, and which room has, too, been *cured of smoking* by this fireplace.

Before we got this supply of bread and cheese, we, though in ordinary times a couple of singularly jovial companions, and seldom going a hundred yards (except going very fast) without one or the other speaking, began to grow *dull*, or rather *glum*. The way seemed long; and, when I had to speak in answer to Richard, the speaking was as brief as might be. Unfortunately, just at this critical period, one of the loops that held the straps of Richard's little portmanteau broke; and it became necessary (just before we overtook Mr. Bailey) for me to fasten the port-manteau on before me, upon my saddle. This, which was not the work of more than five minutes, would, had I had *a breakfast*, have been nothing at all, and, indeed, matter of laughter. But, *now*, it was *something*. It was his "*fault*" for capering and jerking about "*so*." I jumped off, saying, "*Here!* I'll carry it *myself*." And then I began to take off the remaining strap, pulling with great violence and in great haste. Just at this time my eyes met his, in which I saw *great surprise ;* and, feeling the just rebuke, feeling heartily ashamed of myself, I instantly changed my tone and manner, cast the blame upon the saddler, and talked of the effectual means which we would take to prevent the like in future.

Now, if such was the effect produced upon me by the want of food for only two or three hours; me, who had dined well the day before and eaten toast and butter the over-night; if the missing of only one breakfast, and that, too, from my own whim, while I had money in my pocket, to get one at any public-house, and while I could get one only for asking for at any farm-house; if the not having breakfasted could, and under such circum-stances, make me what you may call "*cross*" to a child like this, whom I must necessarily love so much, and to whom I never speak but in the very kindest manner; if this mere absence of a breakfast could thus put me *out of temper*, how great are the allowances that we ought to make for the poor creatures who, in this once happy and now miserable country, are doomed to lead a life of constant labour and of half-starvation. I suppose that, as we rode away from the cottage, we gnawed up, between us, a pound of bread and a quarter of a pound of cheese. Here was about *five-pence* worth at present prices. Even this, which was only a mere *snap*, a mere *stay-stomach*, for us, would, for us two, come to 3*s.* a week all but a penny. How, then, gracious God! is a labouring man, his wife, and, perhaps, four or five small children, to exist upon 8*s.* or 9*s.* a week! Aye, and to find house-rent, clothing, bedding and fuel out of it? Richard and I ate here, at his snap, more, and much more, than the average of labourers, their wives and children, have to eat in a whole day, and that the labourer has to *work* on too!

When we got here to Burghclere, we were again as *hungry* as hunters. What, then, must be the life of these poor creatures? But is not the state of the country, is not the hellishness of the system, all depicted in this one disgraceful and damning fact, that the magistrates, who settle on what the *labouring poor* ought to have to live on, ALLOW THEM LESS THAN IS ALLOWED TO FELONS IN THE GAOLS, and allow them *nothing for clothing and fuel and house-rent !* And yet, while this is notoriously the case, while the main body of the working class in England are fed and clad and even lodged worse than felons, and are daily becoming even worse and worse off, the king is advised to tell the parliament, and the world, that we are in a state of *un-exampled prosperity*, and that this prosperity must be *permanent*, because *all the* GREAT *interests* are *prospering !* THE WORK-ING PEOPLE ARE NOT, THEN, " A *GREAT* INTEREST " ! THEY WILL BE FOUND TO BE ONE, BY AND BY. What is to be the *end* of this? What can be the *end* of it, but dreadful convulsion? What other can be produced by a system, which allows the *felon* better food, better clothing, and better lodging than the *honest labourer ?*

I see that there has been a grand *humanity-meeting* in Norfolk, to assure the parliament that these humanity-people will *back* it in any measures that it may adopt for freeing the NEGROES. Mr. Buxton figured here, also Lord Suffield, who appear to have been the two principal actors, or *showers-off*. This same Mr. Buxton opposed the bill intended to relieve the poor in England by breaking a little into the brewers' monopoly; and, as to Lord Suffield, if he really wish to *free slaves*, let him go to Wykham in this county, where he will see some drawing, like horses, gravel to repair the roads for the stock-jobbers and dead-weight and the seat-dealers to ride smoothly on. If he go down a little further, he will see CONVICTS AT PRECISELY THE SAME WORK, harnessed in JUST THE SAME WAY ; but the convicts he will find hale and ruddy-cheeked, in dresses sufficiently warm, and bawling and singing; while he will find the labourers thin, ragged, shivering, dejected mortals, such as never were seen in any other country upon earth. There is not a negro in the West Indies who has not more to eat in a day than the average of English labourers have to eat in a week, and of better food too. Colonel Wodehouse and a man of the name of Hoseason (whence came he?), who opposed this humanity-scheme, talked of the sums necessary to pay the owners of the slaves. They took special care not to tell the humanity-men *to look at home for slaves to free.* No, no! that would have applied to themselves, as well as to Lord Suffield and humanity Buxton. If it were worth while to *reason* with these people, one might ask them, whether they do not think that *another war* is likely to relieve them of all these cares, simply by making the colonies transfer their allegiance or assert their independence? But to reason with them is useless. If they can busy themselves with compassion for the negroes, while they uphold the system that makes the labourers of England more wretched, and beyond all measure more wretched than any negro slaves are, or ever were, or ever can be, they are unworthy of anything but our contempt.

But the " education " canters are the most curious fellows of all. They have seen " education " as they call it, and crimes, go on increasing together, till the gaols, though six times their former dimensions, will hardly suffice; and yet the canting creatures still cry that crimes arise from want of what they call " education! " They see the felon better fed and better clad than the honest labourer. They see this; and yet they continually cry that the crimes arise from a want of " education! " What can be the cause of this perverseness? It is not perverseness: it is *roguery, corruption,* and *tyranny.* The tyrant, the unfeeling tyrant, squeezes the labourers for gain's sake; and the corrupt politician and literary or tub rogue find an excuse for him by pretending that it is not want of food and clothing, but want of education, that makes the poor, starving wretches thieves and robbers. If the press, if only the press, were to do its duty, or but a tenth part of its duty, this hellish system could not go on. But it favours the system by ascribing the misery to wrong causes. The causes are these: the tax-gatherer presses the landlord; the landlord the farmer; and the farmer the labourer. Here it falls at last; and this class is made so miserable, that a *felon's* life is better than that of a *labourer.* Does there want any *other cause* to produce crimes? But on these causes, so clear to the eye of reason, so plain from experience, the press scarcely ever says a single word; while it keeps bothering our brains about education and morality; and about ignorance and immorality leading to *felonies*. To be sure immorality leads to felonies. Who does not know that? But who is to expect morality in a half-starved man, who is whipped if he do not work, though he has not, for his whole day's food, so much as I and my little boy snapped up in six or seven minutes upon Stoke-Charity down? Aye! but if the press were to ascribe the increase of crimes to the true causes, it must *go further back*. It must go to the *cause of the taxes*. It must go to the debt, the dead-weight, the thundering standing army, the enormous sine-cures, pensions, and grants; and this would suit but a very small part of *a press*, which lives and thrives principally by one or the other of these.

As with the press, so is it with Mr. Brougham, and all such politicians. They stop short, or, rather, they begin in the middle. They attempt to prevent the evils of the deadly ivy by cropping off, or, rather, bruising a little, a few of its leaves. They do not assail even its branches, while they appear to look upon the *trunk* as something *too sacred* even to be *looked at* with vulgar eyes. Is not the injury recently done to about *forty thousand poor families* in and near Plymouth, by the Small-note Bill, a thing that Mr. Brougham ought to think about before he thinks anything more about *educating* those poor families? Yet, will he, when he again meets the ministers, say a word about this monstrous evil? I am afraid that no member will say a word about it; I am rather more than afraid that *he* will not. And *why?* Because, if he reproach the ministers with this crying cruelty, they will ask him first, how this is to be prevented without a repeal of the Small-note Bill (by which Peel's Bill was partly repealed); then they will ask him how the prices are to be kept up without the small-notes; then they will say, " Does the honourable and learned gentleman *wish to see wheat at four shillings a bushel again?* "

B. No (looking at Mr. Western and Daddy Coke), no, no, no! Upon my honour, no!

MIN. Does the honourable and learned gentleman wish to see Cobbett again at county meetings, and to see petitions again coming from those meetings, calling for a reduction of the interest of the . . . ?

B. No, no, no, upon my soul, no!

MIN. Does the honourable and learned gentleman wish to see that "*equitable* adjustment," which Cobbett has a thousand times declared can never take place without an application, to new purposes, of that great mass of public property, commonly called Church property?

B. (Almost bursting with rage) How *dare* the honourable gentleman to suppose me capable of such a thought?

MIN. We suppose nothing. We only ask the question; and we ask it, because to put an end to the small notes would inevitably produce all these things; and it is impossible to have small notes to the extent necessary to *keep up prices*, without having, now and then, *breaking banks*. Banks cannot break without *producing misery*; you must have the *consequence*, if you will have the *cause*. The honourable and learned gentleman wants the feast without the reckoning. In short, is the honourable and learned gentleman for putting an end to "*public credit*"?

B. No, no, no, no!

MIN. Then would it not be better for the honourable and learned gentleman to *hold his tongue*?

All men of sense and sincerity will, at once, answer this last question in the affirmative. They will all say that this is not *opposition* to the ministers. The ministers do not *wish* to see 40,000 families, nor any families at all (who give them *no real annoyance*), reduced to misery; they do not *wish* to cripple their own tax-payers; very far from it. If they could carry on the debt and dead-weight and place and pension and barrack system, without reducing any *quiet* people to misery, they would like it exceedingly; But they *do* wish to carry on that system; and he does not *oppose* them who does not endeavour to put an end to the system.

This is done by nobody in parliament; and, therefore, there is, in fact, *no opposition ;* and this is felt by the whole nation; and this is the reason why *the people* now take so little interest in what is said and done in parliament, compared to that which they formerly took. This is the reason why there is no man, or men, whom the people seem to care at all about. A great portion of the people now clearly understand the nature and effects of the system; they are not now to be deceived by speeches and professions. If Pitt and Fox had *now to start*, there would be no "Pittites" and "Foxites." Those happy days of political humbug are gone for ever. The "gentlemen *opposite*" are opposite only as to mere *local position*. They sit on the opposite side of the house: that's all. In every other respect they are like parson and clerk; or, perhaps, rather more like the rooks and jackdaws: one *caw* and the other *chatter;* but both have the same object in view: both are in pursuit of the same sort of diet. One set is, to be sure, IN place, and the other OUT; but though the rooks keep the jackdaws on the inferior branches, these latter would be as clamorous as the rooks themselves against *felling the tree;* and just as clamorous would the "gentlemen opposite" be against any one who should propose to put down the system itself. And yet, unless you do *that*, things must go on in the present way, and *felons* must be *better fed* than *honest labourers;* and starvation and thieving and robbing and gaol-building and transporting and hanging and penal laws must go on increasing, as they have gone on from the day of the establishment of the debt to the present hour. Apropos of *penal laws*, Doctor Black (of the *Morning Chronicle*) is now filling whole columns with very just remarks on the new and terrible law, which makes the taking of an apple *felony;* but he says not a word about the *silence* of Sir Jammy (the humane *code-softener*) upon this subject! The "*humanity* and *liberality*" of the parliament have relieved men addicted to *fraud* and to *certain other crimes* from the disgrace of the pillory, and they have, since Castlereagh cut his own throat, relieved *self-slayers* from the disgrace of the cross-road burial; but the same parliament, amidst all the workings of this rare humanity and liberality, have made it *felony to take an apple off a tree*, which last year was a trivial trespass, and was formerly no offence at all! However, even this *is necessary*, as long as this bank note system continue in its present way; and all complaints about severity of laws, levelled at the poor, are useless and foolish; and these complaints are even base in those who do their best to uphold a system which has brought *the honest labourer to be fed worse than the felon*. What, short of such laws, can prevent *starving men* from coming to take away the dinners of those who have plenty? "*Education!*" Despicable cant and nonsense! What education, what moral precepts, can quiet the gnawings and ragings of hunger?

Looking, now, back again, for a minute to the little village of *Stoke Charity*, the name of which seems to indicate that its rents formerly belonged wholly to the poor and indigent part of the community: it is near to Winchester, that grand scene of ancient learning, piety and munificence. Be this as it may, the parish formerly contained ten farms, and it now contains but two, which are owned by Mr. Hinton Bailey and his nephew, and, therefore, which may probably become *one*. There used to be ten well-fed families in this parish, at any rate: these, taking five to a family, made fifty well-fed people. And now all are half-starved, except the curate and the two families. The *blame* is not the landowner's; it is nobody's; it is due to the infernal *funding* and *taxing* system, which *of necessity* drives property into large masses in order to *save itself ;* which crushes little proprietors down into labourers; and which presses them down in that state, there takes their wages from them and makes them *paupers*, their share of food and raiment being taken away to support debt and dead-weight and army and all the rest of the enormous expenses, which are required to sustain this intolerable system. Those, therefore, are fools or hypocrites who affect to wish to better the lot of the poor labourers and manufacturers, while they, at the same time, either actively or passively, uphold the system which is the manifest cause of it. Here is a system which, clearly as the nose upon your face, you see taking away the little gentleman's estate, the little farmer's farm, the poor labourer's meat-dinner and Sunday-coat; and while you see this so plainly, you, fool or hypocrite, as you are, cry out for supporting the system that causes it all! Go on, base wretch; but remember, that of such a progress dreadful must be the end. The day will come when millions of long-suffering creatures will be in a state that they and you now little dream of. All that we now behold of *combinations* and the like are mere *indications* of what the great body of the suffering people *feel*, and of the thoughts that are passing in their minds. The *coaxing* work of *schools* and *tracts* will only add to what would be quite enough without them. There is not a labourer in the whole country who does not see to the bottom of this *coaxing* work. They are *not deceived* in this respect. Hunger has opened their eyes. I'll engage that there is not, even in this obscure village of Stoke Charity, one single creature, however forlorn, who does not understand all about the *real motives* of the school and the tract and Bible affair as well as Butterworth, or Rivington, or as Joshua Watson himself.

Just after we had finished the bread and cheese, we crossed the turnpike-road that goes from Basingstoke to Stockbridge; and Mr. Bailey had told us that we were then to bear away to our right, and go to the end of a wood (which we saw one end of), and keep round with that wood, or coppice, as he called it, to our left; but we, seeing Beacon Hill more to the left, and resolving to go, as nearly as possible, in a straight line to it, steered directly over the fields; that is to say, pieces of ground from 30 to 100 acres in each. But a hill which we had to go over, had here hidden from our sight a part of this " coppice," which consists, perhaps, of 150 or 200 acres, and which we found sweeping round, in a crescent-like form so far, from towards our left, as to bring our land-mark over the coppice at about the mid-length of the latter. Upon this discovery we slackened sail; for this coppice might be a mile across; and though the bottom was sound enough, being a coverlet of flints upon a bed of chalk, the under-wood was too high and too thick for us to face, being, as we were, at so great a distance from the means of obtaining a fresh supply of clothes. Our leather leggings would have stood anything; but our coats were of the common kind; and before we saw the other side of the coppice we should, I dare say, have been as ragged as forest-ponies in the month of March.

In this dilemma I stopped, and looked at the coppice. Luckily two boys, who had been cutting sticks (to *sell*, I dare say, at least *I hope so*), made their appearance, at about half a mile off on the side for the coppice. Richard galloped off to the boys, from whom he found that, in one part of the coppice, there was a road cut across, the point of entrance into which road they explained to him. This was to us what the discovery of a canal across the isthmus of Darien would be to a ship in the Gulf of Mexico wanting to get into the Pacific without doubling Cape Horn. A beautiful road we found it. I should suppose the best part of a mile long, perfectly straight, the surface sound and smooth, about eight feet wide, the whole length seen at once, and, when you are at one end, the other end seeming to be hardly a yard wide. When we got about half way, we found a road that crossed this. These roads are, I suppose, cut for the hunters. They are very pretty, at any rate, and we found this one very convenient; for it cut our way short by a full half mile.

From this coppice to Whitchurch is not more than about four miles, and we soon reached it, because here you begin to descend into the *vale* in which this little town lies, and through which there runs that *stream* which turns the mill of 'Squire Portal, and which mill makes the Bank of England note-paper! Talk of the Thames and the Hudson with their forests of masts; talk of the Nile and the Delaware bearing the food of millions on their bosoms; talk of the Ganges and the Mississippi sending forth over the world their silks and their cottons; talk of the

Rio de la Plata and the other rivers, their beds pebbled with silver and gold and diamonds. What as to their effect on the condition of mankind, as to the virtues, the vices, the enjoyments and the sufferings of men; what are all these rivers put together compared with the *river of Whitchurch*, which a man of threescore may jump across dry-shod, which moistens a quarter of a mile wide of poor, rushy meadow, which washes the skirts of the park and game preserves of that bright patrician who wedded the daughter of Hanson, the attorney and late solicitor to the Stamp Office, and which is, to look at it, of far less importance than any gutter in the Wen! Yet this river, by merely turning a wheel, which wheel sets some rag-tearers and grinders and washers and re-compressers in motion, has produced a greater effect on the condition of men than has been produced on that condition by all the other rivers, all the seas, all the mines and all the continents in the world. The discovery of America, and the consequent discovery and use of vast quantities of silver and gold, did, indeed, produce great effects on the nations of Europe. They changed the value of money, and caused, as all such changes must, a *transfer of property*, raising up new families and pulling down old ones, a transfer very little favourable either to *morality*, or to real and *substantial liberty*. But this cause worked *slowly* ; its consequences came on by slow *degrees ;* it made a transfer of property, but it made that transfer in so small a degree, and it left the property quiet in the hands of the new possessor *for so long a time*, that the effect was not violent, and was not, at any rate, such as to uproot possessors by whole districts, as the hurricane uproots the forests.

Not so the product of the little sedgy rivulet of Whitchurch! It has, in the short space of a hundred and thirty-one years, and, indeed, in the space of the last *forty*, caused greater changes as to property than had been caused by all other things put together in the long course of seven centuries, though during that course there had been a sweeping, confiscating Protestant reformation. Let us look back to the place where I started on this present rural ride. Poor old Baron Maseres succeeded at Reigate by little Parson Fellowes, and at Betchworth (three miles on my road) by Kendrick, is no bad instance to begin with; for the Baron was nobly descended, though from French ancestors. At Albury, fifteen miles on my road, Mr. Drummond (a banker) is in the seat of one of the Howards, and, close by, he has bought the estate, just pulled down the house, and blotted out the memory of the Godschalls. At Chilworth, two miles further down the same vale, and close under St. Martha's Hill, Mr. Tinkler, a powder-maker (succeeding Hill, another powder-maker, who had been a breeches-maker at Hounslow) has got the old mansion and the estate of the old Duchess of Marlborough, who frequently resided in what was then a large quadrangular mansion, but the remains of which now serve as out farm-buildings and a farm-house, which I found inhabited by a poor labourer and his family, the farm being in the hands of the powder-maker, who does not find the once noble seat good enough for him. Coming on to Waverley Abbey, there is Mr. Thompson, a merchant, succeeding the Orby Hunters and Sir Robert Rich. Close adjoining, Mr. Laing, a West India dealer of some sort, has stepped into the place of the lineal descendants of Sir William Temple. At Farnham the park and palace remain in the hands of a Bishop of Winchester, as they have done for about eight hundred years: but why is this? Because they are public property; because they cannot, without express laws, be transferred. Therefore the product of the rivulet of Whitchurch has had no effect upon the ownership of these, which are still in the hands of a Bishop of Winchester; not of a William of Wykham, to be sure; but still in those of a bishop, at any rate. Coming on to old Alresford (twenty miles from Farnham) Sheriff, the son of a Sheriff, who was a commissary in the American war, has succeeded the Gages. Two miles further on, at Abbotston (down on the side of the Itchen) Alexander Baring has succeeded the heirs and successors of the Duke of Bolton, the remains of whose noble mansion I once saw here. Not above a mile higher up, the same Baring has, at the Grange, with its noble mansion, park and estate, succeeded the heirs of Lord Northington; and at only about two miles further, Sir Thomas Baring, at Stratton Park, has succeeded the Russells in the ownership of the estates of Stratton and Micheldover, which were once the property of Alfred the Great! Stepping back, and following my road, down by the side of the meadows of the beautiful river Itchen, and coming to Easton, I look across to Martyr's Worthy, and there see (as I observed before) the Ogles succeeded by a general or a colonel somebody; but who, or whence, I cannot learn.

This is all in less than four score miles, from Reigate even to this place where I now am. Oh! mighty rivulet of Whitchurch! All our properties, all our laws, all our manners, all our minds, you have changed! This, which I have noticed, has all taken place within forty, and, most of it, within *ten* years. The *small gentry*, to about the *third* rank upwards (considering there to be five ranks from the smallest gentry up to the greatest nobility), are *all gone*, nearly to a man, and the small farmers along with them. The Barings alone have, I should think, swallowed up thirty or forty of these small gentry without perceiving it. They, indeed, swallow up the biggest race of all; but innumerable small fry slip down unperceived, like caplins down the throats of the sharks, while these latter *feel* only the cod-fish. It frequently happens, too, that a big gentleman or nobleman, whose estate has been big enough to resist for a long while, and who has swilled up many caplin-gentry, goes down the throat of the loan-dealer with all the caplins in his belly.

Thus the Whitchurch rivulet goes on, shifting property from hand to hand. The big, in order to save themselves from being "*swallowed up quick*" (as we used to be taught to say, in our Church prayers against Buonaparte), make use of their *voices* to get, through place, pension, or sinecure, something back from the taxes. Others of them *fall in love* with the *daughters* and *widows* of paper-money people, big brewers, and the like; and sometimes their daughters *fall in love* with the paper-money people's sons, or the fathers of those sons; and whether they be *Jews*, or not, seems to be little matter with this all-subduing passion of love. But the *small gentry* have no resource. While *war* lasted, "*glorious* war," there was a resource; but *now*, alas! not only is there no war, but there is *no hope of war ;* and not a few of them will actually come to the *parish-book*. There is no place for them in the army, church, navy, customs, excise, pension-list, or anywhere else. All these are now wanted by "*their betters*." A stock-jobber's family will not look at such pennyless things. So that, while they have been the active, the zealous, the efficient instruments, in compelling the working classes to submit to half-starvation, they have at any rate been brought to the most abject ruin themselves; for which I most heartily thank God. The "harvest of war" is never to return without a total blowing up of the paper-system. Spain must belong to France, St. Domingo must pay her tribute. America must be paid for slaves taken away in war, she must have Florida, she must go on openly and avowedly making a navy for the purpose of humbling us; and all this, and ten times more, if France and America should choose; and yet we can have *no war* as long as the paper-system last; and if *that cease*, then *what is to come !*

BURGHCLERE,
Sunday Morning, 6 November.

It has been fine all the week, until to-day, when we intended
to set off for Hurstbourn-Tarrant, vulgarly called Uphusband,
but the rain seems as if it would stop us. From Whitchurch to
within two miles of this place, it is the same sort of country
as between Winchester and Whitchurch. High, chalk bottom,
open downs or large fields, with here and there a farm-house
in a dell, sheltered by lofty trees, which, to my taste, is the most
pleasant situation in the world.

This has been, with Richard, one whole week of hare-hunting,
and with me, three days and a half. The weather has been
amongst the finest that I ever saw, and Lord Caernarvon's
preserves fill the country with hares, while these hares invite
us to ride about and to see his park and estate, at this fine season
of the year, in every direction. We are now on the north side
of that Beacon Hill for which we steered last Sunday. This
makes part of a chain of lofty chalk-hills and downs, which
divides all the lower part of Hampshire from Berkshire, though
the ancient ruler, owner, of the former took a little strip all
along, on the flat, on this side of the chain, in order, I suppose,
to make the ownership of the hills themselves the more clear of
all dispute; just as the owner of a field-hedge and bank owns
also the ditch on his neighbour's side. From these hills you
look, at one view, over the whole of Berkshire, into Oxfordshire,
Gloucestershire and Wiltshire, and you can see the Isle of Wight
and the sea. On this north side the chalk soon ceases, the sand
and clay begin, and the oak-woods cover a great part of the
surface. Amongst these is the farm-house in which we are,
and from the warmth and good fare of which we do not mean
to stir until we can do it without the chance of a wet skin.

This rain has given me time to look at the newspapers of about
a week old. Oh, oh! The cotton lords are tearing! Thank
God for that! The lords of the anvil are snapping! Thank
God for that too! They have kept poor souls, then, in a heat
of 84 degrees to little purpose, after all. The " great interests "
mentioned in the king's speech do not, *then*, all continue to
flourish! The " prosperity " was not, then, " permanent "
though the king was advised to assert so positively that it
was! " Anglo-Mexican and Pasco-Peruvian " fall in price, and
the *Chronicle* assures me that " the respectable owners of the
Mexican mining shares mean to take measures to protect their

property." Indeed! Like *protecting* the Spanish bonds, I suppose? Will the *Chronicle* be so good as to tell us the names of these "*respectable* persons?" Doctor Black must know their names; or else he could not know them to be *respectable*. If the parties be those that I have heard, these mining works may possibly operate with them as an emetic, and make them throw up a part, at least, of what they have taken down.

There has, I see, at New York been that confusion which I, four months ago, said would and must take place; that breaking of merchants and all the ruin which, in such a case, spreads itself about, ruining families and producing fraud and despair. Here will be, between the two countries, an interchange of cause and effect, proceeding from the dealings in *cotton*, until, first and last, two or three hundred thousands of persons have, at one spell of paper-money work, been made to drink deep of misery. I pity none but the poor English creatures who are compelled to work on the wool of this accursed weed, which has done so much mischief to England. The slaves who cultivate and gather the cotton are well fed. They do not suffer. The sufferers are those who spin it and weave it and colour it, and the wretched beings who cover with it those bodies which, as in the time of old Fortescue, ought to be " clothed throughout in good woollens."

One newspaper says that Mr. Huskisson is gone to Paris, and thinks it *likely* that he will endeavour to " inculcate in the mind of the Bourbons wise principles of *free trade !*" What the devil next! Persuade them, I suppose, that it is for *their good* that English goods should be admitted into France and into St. Domingo with little or no duty? Persuade them to make a treaty of commerce with him; and, in short, persuade them to make *France help to pay the interest of our debt and dead-weight*, lest our system of paper should go to pieces, and lest that should be followed by *a radical reform*, which reform would be injurious to " the monarchical principle!" This newspaper politician does, however, *think* that the Bourbons will be " too dull " to comprehend these " *enlightened* and *liberal* " notions; and I think so too. I think the Bourbons, or, rather, those who will speak for them, will say: " No thank you. You contracted your debt without our participation; you made your *dead-weight* for your own purposes; the seizure of our museums and the loss of our frontier towns followed your victory of Waterloo, though we were ' your Allies ' at the time; you made us pay an enormous tribute after that battle, and kept possession of part of France till we had paid it; you *wished*, the other day, to keep us out of Spain, and you, Mr. Huskisson, in a speech at Liverpool, called our deliverance of the King of Spain an *unjust and unprincipled act of aggression*, while Mr. Canning *prayed to God* that we might not succeed. No thank you, Mr. Huskisson, no. No coaxing, sir: we saw, then, too clearly the *advantage we derived from your having a debt and a dead-weight*, to wish to assist in relieving you from either. 'Monarchical principle' here, or 'monarchical principle' there, we know that your mill-stone debt is our best security. We like to have your wishes, your prayers, and your abuse against us, rather than your *subsidies* and your *fleets*: and so, farewell, Mr. Huskisson: if you like, the English may drink French wine; but whether they do or not, the French shall not wear your rotten cottons. And, as a last word, how did you maintain the 'monarchical principle,' the 'paternal principle,' or as Castlereagh called it, the 'social system,' when you called that an unjust and unprincipled aggression which put an end to the bargain by which the convents and other church-property of Spain were to be transferred to the Jews and jobbers of London? Bon jour, Monsieur Huskisson, ci-devant membre et orateur du club de quatre vingt neuf!"

If they do not actually say this to him, this is what they will think; and that is, as to the effect, precisely the same thing. It is childishness to suppose that any nation will act from a desire of *serving all other nations, or any one other nation, as well as itself*. It will make, unless compelled, no compact by which it does not think itself *a gainer;* and amongst its gains, it must, and always does, reckon the injury to its rivals. It is a stupid idea that *all nations are to gain* by anything. Whatever is the gain of one, must, in some way or other, be a loss to another. So that this new project of "free trade" and "mutual gain" is as pure a humbug as that which the newspapers carried on, during the "glorious days" of loans, when they told us, at every loan, that the bargain was "equally advantageous to the contractors and to the public!" The fact is the "free trade" project is clearly the effect of a *consciousness of our weakness*. As long as we felt *strong*, we felt *bold*, we had no thought of *conciliating* the world; we upheld a system of *exclusion*, which long experience proved to be founded in *sound policy*. But we now find that our debts and our loads of various sorts cripple us. We feel our incapacity for the *carrying of trade sword in hand:* and so we have given up all our old maxims, and are endeavouring to persuade the world that we are anxious to enjoy no advantages that are not enjoyed also by our neighbours. Alas! the world sees very clearly the cause of all this; and the world *laughs at us* for our imaginary cunning. My old doggrel, that used to make me and my friends laugh in Long Island, is precisely pat to this case.

When his maw was stuffed with paper,
How John Bull did prance and caper!
How he foam'd and how he roar'd:
How his neighbours all he gored!
How he scrap'd the ground and hurl'd
Dirt and filth on all the world!
But John Bull of paper empty,
Though in midst of peace and plenty,
Is modest grown as worn-out sinner,
As Scottish laird that wants a dinner;
As Wilberforce, become content
A rotten burgh to represent;
As Blue and Buff, when, after hunting
On Yankee coasts their " *bits of bunting,*"
Came softly back across the seas,
And silent were as mice in cheese.

Yes, the whole world, and particularly the French and the Yankees, see very clearly the *course* of this fit of modesty and of liberality into which we have so recently fallen. They know well that a *war* would play the very devil with our national faith. They know, in short, that no ministers in their senses will think of supporting the paper system through another war. They know well that no ministers that now exist, or are likely to exist, will venture to endanger the paper-system; and therefore they know that (for England) they may now do just what they please. When the French were about to invade Spain, Mr. Canning said that his last despatch on the subject was to be understood as a *protest*, on the part of England, against permanent occupation of any part of Spain by France. There the French are, however; and at the end of two years and a half he says that he knows nothing about any intention that they have to quit Spain, or any part of it.

Why, Saint Domingo *was* independent. We had traded with it as an independent state. Is it not clear that if we had said the word (and had been known to be able to *arm*), France would not have attempted to treat that fine and rich country as a colony? Mark how wise this measure of France! How *just*, too; to obtain by means of a tribute from the St. Domingoians compensation for the *loyalists* of that country! Was this done with regard to the loyalists of *America*, in the reign of the good jubilee George III.? Oh, no! Those loyalists had to be paid, and many of them have even yet, at the end of more than half a century, to be paid out of taxes raised on *us*, for the losses occasioned by their disinterested loyalty! This was a master-stroke on the part of France; she gets about seven millions sterling in the way of tribute; she makes that rich island yield to her great commercial advantages; and she, at the same time, paves the way for effecting one of two objects; namely, getting the island back again, or throwing our islands into confusion, whenever it shall be her interest to do it.

This might have been prevented by *a word* from us, if we had been ready for *war*. But we are grown *modest ;* we are grown *liberal ;* we do not want to engross that which fairly belongs to our neighbours! We have undergone a change, somewhat like that which marriage produces on a blustering fellow, who, while single, can but just clear his teeth. This change is quite surprising, and especially by the time that the second child comes, the man is *loaded ;* he looks like a loaded man; his voice becomes so soft and gentle compared to what it used to be. Just such are the effects of *our load :* but the worst of it is, our neighbours are *not* thus loaded. However, far be it from me to *regret* this, or any part of it. The load is the people's best friend. If that could, *without reform ;* if that could be shaken off, leaving the seat-men and the parsons in their present state, I would not live in England another day! And I say this with as much seriousness as if I were upon my death-bed.

The wise men of the newspapers are for a repeal of the *Corn Laws*. With all my heart. I will join anybody in a petition for their repeal. But this will not be done. We shall stop short of this extent of " liberality," let what may be the consequence to the manufacturers. The cotton lords must all go, to the last man, rather than a repeal of these laws will take place: and of this the newspaper wise men may be assured. The farmers can but just rub along now, with all their high prices and low wages. What would be their state, and that of their landlords, if the wheat were to come down again to 4, 5, or even 6 shillings a bushel? Universal agricultural bankruptcy would be the almost instant consequence. Many of them are now deep in debt from the effects of 1820, 1821, and 1822. One more year like 1822 would have broken the whole mass up, and left the lands to be cultivated, under the overseers, for the benefit of the paupers. Society would have been nearly dissolved, and the state of nature would have returned. The Small-Note Bill, co-operating with the corn laws, have given a respite, and nothing more. This bill must remain *efficient*, paper-money must cover the country, and the corn laws must remain in force; or an " equitable adjustment " must take place; or to a state of nature this country must return. What, then, as *I want* a repeal of the corn laws, and also *want* to get rid of the paper-money, I must want to see this return to a state of nature? By no means. I want the " equitable adjustment," and I am quite sure that no adjustment can be *equitable* which does not apply *every penny's worth of public property* to the payment of the fund-holders and dead-weight and the like. Clearly just and reasonable as this is, however, the very mention of it makes the FIRE-SHOVELS, and some others, half mad. It makes them storm and rant and swear like Bedlamites. But it is curious to hear them talk of the impracticability of it; when they all know that, by only two or three acts of parliament, Henry VIII. did ten times as much as it would now I hope be necessary to do. If the duty were imposed *on me*, no statesman, legislator or lawyer, but a simple citizen, I think I could, in less than twenty-four hours, draw up an act, that would give satisfaction to, I will not say *every man;* but to, at least, ninety-nine out of every hundred; an act that would put all affairs of money and of religion to rights at once; but that would, I must confess, soon take from us that amiable *modesty*, of which I have spoken above, and which is so conspicuously shown in our works of free trade and liberality.

The weather is clearing up; our horses are saddled, and we are off.

FROM BURGHCLERE TO PETERSFIELD

HURSTBOURN TARRANT (OR UPHUSBAND),
Monday, 7 November, 1825.

WE came off from Burghclere yesterday afternoon, crossing Lord Caernarvon's park, going out of it on the west side of Beacon Hill, and sloping away to our right over the downs towards Woodcote. The afternoon was singularly beautiful. The downs (even the poorest of them) are perfectly green; the sheep on the downs look, this year, like fatting sheep: we came through a fine flock of ewes, and, looking round us, we saw, all at once, seven flocks, on different parts of the downs, each flock on an average containing at least 500 sheep.

It is about six miles from Burghclere to this place; and we made it about twelve; not in order to avoid the turnpike-road; but because we do not ride about to *see* turnpike-roads; and, moreover, because I had seen this most monstrously hilly turnpike-road before. We came through a village called Woodcote, and another called Binley. I never saw any inhabited places more recluse than these. Yet into these the all-searching eye of the taxing Thing reaches. Its exciseman can tell it what is doing even in the little odd corner of Binley; for even there I saw, over the door of a place not half so good as the place in which my fowls roost, " *Licensed to deal in tea and tobacco.*" Poor, half-starved wretches of Binley! The hand of taxation, the collection for the sinecures and pensions, must fix its nails even in them, who really appeared too miserable to be called by the name of *people.* Yet there was one whom the taxing Thing had licensed (good God! *licensed !*) to serve out cat-lap to these wretched creatures! And our impudent and ignorant newspaper scribes talk of the *degraded state of the people of Spain !* Impudent impostors! Can they show a group so wretched, so miserable, so truly enslaved as this, in all Spain? No: and those of them who are not sheer fools know it well. But there would have been misery equal to this in Spain if the Jews and jobbers could have carried the bond-scheme into effect. The people of Spain were, through the instrumentality of patriot-loan makers, within an inch of being made as " enlightened " as

the poor, starving things of Binley. They would soon have had
people " licensed " to make them pay the Jews for permission
to chew tobacco, or to have a light in their dreary abodes. The
people of Spain were preserved from this by the French army,
for which the Jews cursed the French army; and the same army
put an end to those " bonds," by means of which *pious* Protestants hoped to be able to get at the convents in Spain, and
thereby put down " idolatry " in that country. These bonds
seem now not to be worth a farthing; and so after all the Spanish
people will have no one " licensed " by the Jews to make them
pay for turning the fat of their sheep into candles and soap.
These poor creatures that I behold here *pass their lives amidst
flocks of sheep ;* but never does a morsel of mutton enter their
lips. A labouring man told me, at Binley, that he had not tasted
meat since harvest; and his looks vouched for the statement.
Let the Spaniards come and look at this poor shotten-herring
of a creature; and then let them estimate what is due to a set of
" enlightening " and loan-making " patriots." Old Fortescue
says that " the English are clothed in good woollens throughout,"
and that they have " plenty of flesh of all sorts to eat." Yes,
but at this time the nation was not mortgaged. The " enlightening " patriots would have made Spain what England now is.
The people must never more, after a few years, have tasted
mutton, though living surrounded with flocks of sheep.

EASTON, NEAR WINCHESTER,
Wednesday Evening, 9 Nov.

I intended to go from Uphusband to Stonehenge, thence to
Old Sarum, and thence through the New Forest, to Southampton and Botley, and thence across into Sussex, to see Up-
Park, and Cowdry House. But, then, there must be no loss of
time: I must adhere to a certain route as strictly as a regiment
on a march. I had written the route: and Laverstock, after
seeing Stonehenge and Old Sarum, was to be the resting-place of
yesterday (Tuesday); but when it came, it brought rain with it
after a white frost on Monday. It was likely to rain again to-day.
It became necessary to change the route, as I must get to London
by a certain day; and as the first day, on the new route, brought
us here.

I had been three times at Uphusband before, and had, as my
readers will, perhaps, recollect, described the bourn here, or the
brook. It has, in general, no water at all in it from August to

March. There is the bed of a little river; but no water. In March, or thereabouts, the water begins to boil up, in thousands upon thousands of places, in the little narrow meadows, just above the village; that is to say a little higher up the valley. When the chalk hills are full; when the chalk will hold no more water; then it comes out at the lowest spots near these immense hills and becomes a rivulet first, and then a river. But until this visit to Uphusband (or Hurstbourn Tarrant, as the map calls it), little did I imagine that this rivulet, dry half the year, was the head of the river Teste, which, after passing through Stock-bridge and Rumsey, falls into the sea near Southampton.

We had to follow the bed of this river to Bourne; but there the water begins to appear; and it runs all the year long about a mile lower down. Here it crosses Lord Portsmouth's out-park, and our road took us the same way to the village called Down Husband, the scene (as the broadsheet tells us) of so many of that noble lord's ringing and cart-driving exploits. Here we crossed the London and Andover road, and leaving Andover to our right and Whitchurch to our left, we came on to Long Parish, where, crossing the water, we came up again on that high country which continues all across to Winchester. After passing Bullington, Sutton, and Wonston, we veered away from Stoke Charity, and came across the fields to the high down, whence you see Winchester, or rather the cathedral; for, at this distance, you can distinguish nothing else clearly.

As we had to come to this place, which is three miles *up* the river Itchen from Winchester, we crossed the Winchester and Basingstoke road at King's Worthy. This brought us, before we crossed the river, along through Martyr's Worthy, so long the seat of the Ogles, and now, as I observed in my last *Register*, sold to a general or colonel. These Ogles had been deans, I believe; or prebends, or something of that sort: and the one that used to live here had been, and was when he died, an " admiral." However, this last one, " Sir Charles," the loyal address mover, is my man for the present. We saw, down by the water-side, opposite to " Sir Charles's " *late* family mansion, a beautiful strawberry garden, capable of being watered by a branch of the Itchen which comes close by it, and which is, I suppose, brought there on purpose. Just by, on the green-sward, under the shade of very fine trees, is an alcove, wherein to sit to eat the strawberries, coming from the little garden just mentioned, and met by bowls of cream coming from a little milk-house, shaded by another clump a little lower down the stream. What delight! What a terrestrial paradise! "Sir Charles" might be very frequently in this paradise, while that Sidmouth, whose bill he so applauded, had many men shut up in loathsome dungeons! Ah, well! "Sir Charles," those very men may, perhaps, at this moment, envy neither you nor Sidmouth; no, nor Sidmouth's son and heir, even though Clerk of the Pells. At any rate, it is not likely that "Sir Charles" will sit again in this paradise, contemplating another *loyal address*, to carry to a county meeting ready engrossed on parchment, to be presented by Fleming and supported by Lockhart and the "Hampshire parsons."

I think I saw, as I came along, the new owner of the estate. It seems that he bought it "stock and fluke" as the sailors call it; that is to say, that he bought movables and the whole. He appeared to me to be a keen man. I can't find out where he comes from, or what he, or his father, has been. I like to see the revolution going on; but I like to be able to trace the parties a little more *closely*. "Sir Charles," the loyal address gentleman, lives in London, I hear. I will, I think, call upon him (if I can find him out) when I get back, and ask how he does now? There is one Hollest, a George Hollest, who figured pretty bigly on that same loyal address day. This man is become quite an inoffensive harmless creature. If we were to have another county meeting, he would not, I think, threaten to put the sash down upon anybody's head! Oh! Peel, Peel, Peel! Thy bill, oh, Peel, did sicken them so! Let us, oh, thou offspring of the great Spinning Jenny promoter, who subscribed ten thousand pounds towards the late "glorious" war; who was, after that, made a baronet, and whose biographers (in the Baronetage) tell the world that he had a "presentiment that he should be the founder of a family." Oh, thou, thou great Peel, do thou let us have only two more years of thy bill! Or, oh, great Peel, minister of the interior, do thou let us have repeal of Corn Bill! Either will do, great Peel. We shall then see such *modest* 'squires, and parsons looking so queer! However, if thou wilt not listen to us, great Peel, we must, perhaps (and only perhaps), wait a little longer. It is sure to come *at last*, and to come, too, in the most efficient way.

The water in the Itchen is, they say, famed for its clearness. As I was crossing the river the other day, at Avington, I told Richard to look at it, and I asked him if he did not think it very clear. I now find that this has been remarked by very ancient writers. I see, in a newspaper just received, an account of dreadful fires in New Brunswick. It is curious that, in my *Register* of the 29th October (dated from Chilworth in Surrey), I should have put a question, relative to the white clover, the huckleberries, or the raspberries, which start up after the burning down of woods in America. These fires have been at two places which I saw when there were hardly any people in the whole country; and if there never had been any people there to this day, it would have been a good thing for England. Those colonies are a dead expense, without a possibility of their ever being of any use. There are, I see, a church and a barrack destroyed. And why a barrack? What! were there bayonets wanted already to keep the people in order? For as to an *enemy*, where was he to come from? And if there really be an enemy anywhere there about, would it not be a wise way to leave the worthless country to him, to use it after his own way? I was at that very Fredericton, where they say thirty houses and thirty-nine barns have now been burnt. I can remember when there was no more thought of there ever being a barn there than there is now thought of there being economy in our government. The English money used to be spent prettily in that country. What do *we* want with armies and barracks and chaplains in those woods? What does anybody want with them; but *we*, above all the rest of the world? There is nothing there, no house, no barrack, no wharf, nothing, but what is bought with taxes raised on the half-starving people of England. What do *we* want with these wildernesses? Ah! but they are wanted by creatures who will not work in England, and whom this fine system of ours sends out into those woods to live in idleness upon the fruit of English labour. The soldier, the commissary, the barrack-master, all the whole tribe, no matter under what *name;* what keeps them? They are paid " by government; " and I wish that we constantly bore in mind that the " government " pays *our* money. It is, to be sure, sorrowful to hear of such fires and such dreadful effects proceeding from them; but to me it is beyond all measure *more sorrowful* to see *the labourers of England worse fed than the convicts in the gaols;* and I know very well that these worthless and jobbing colonies have assisted to bring England into this horrible state. The honest labouring man is allowed (aye, by the magistrates) less food than the felon in the goal; and the felon is clothed and has fuel; and the labouring man has nothing allowed for these. These worthless colonies, which find places for people that the Thing provides for, have helped to produce this dreadful state in England.

Therefore, any *assistance* the sufferers should never have from me, while I could find an honest and industrious English labourer (unloaded with a family too) fed worse than a felon in the gaols; and this I can find in every part of the country.

We lost another day at Easton; the whole of yesterday it having rained the whole day; so that we could not have come an inch but in the wet. We started, therefore, this morning, coming through the Duke of Buckingham's park, at Avington, which is close by Easton, and on the same side of the Itchen. This is a very beautiful place. The house is close down at the edge of the meadow land; there is a lawn before it, and a pond supplied by the Itchen, at the end of the lawn, and bounded by the park on the other side. The high road, through the park, goes very near to this water; and we saw thousands of wild-ducks in the pond, or sitting round on the green edges of it, while, on one side of the pond, the hares and pheasants were moving about upon a gravel walk on the side of a very fine plantation. We looked down upon all this from a rising ground, and the water, like a looking-glass, showed us the trees, and even the animals. This is certainly one of the very prettiest spots in the world. The wild water-fowl seem to take particular delight in this place. There are a great many at Lord Caernarvon's; but there the water is much larger, and the ground and wood about it comparatively rude and coarse. Here, at Avington, everything is in such beautiful order; the lawn before the house is of the finest green, and most neatly kept; and the edge of the pond (which is of several acres) is as smooth as if it formed part of a bowling-green. To see so many *wild*-fowl, in a situation where everything is in the *parterre*-order, has a most pleasant effect on the mind; and Richard and I, like Pope's cock in the farm-yard, could not help *thanking* the duke and duchess for having generously made such ample provision for our pleasure, and that, too, merely to please us as we were passing along. Now this is the advantage of going about on *horseback*. On foot, the fatigue is too great, and you go too slowly. In any sort of carriage, you cannot get into the *real country places*. To travel in stage coaches is to be hurried along by force, in a box, with an air-hole in it, and constantly exposed to broken limbs, the *danger* being much greater than that of ship-board, and the *noise* much more disagreeable, while the *company* is frequently not a great deal more to one's liking.

From this beautiful spot we had to mount gradually the downs to the southward; but it is impossible to quit the vale of the Itchen without one more look back at it. To form a just estimate of its real value, and that of the lands near it, it is only necessary to know that, from its source, at Bishop's Sutton, this river has, on its two banks, in the distance of nine miles (before it reaches Winchester) thirteen parish churches. There must have been some *people* to erect these churches. It is not true, then, that Pitt and George III. *created the English nation*, notwithstanding all that the Scotch *feelosofers* are ready to swear about the matter. In short, there can be no doubt in the mind of any rational man that in the time of the Plantagenets England was more populous than it is now.

When we began to get up towards the downs we, to our great surprise, saw them covered with *snow*. "Sad times coming on for poor Sir Glory," said I to Richard. "Why?" said Dick. It was too cold to talk much; and, besides, a great sluggishness in his horse made us both rather serious. The horse had been too hard ridden at Burghclere, and had got cold. This made us change our route again, and instead of going over the downs towards Hambledon, in our way to see the park and the innumerable hares and pheasants of Sir Harry Featherstone, we pulled away more to the left, to go through Bramdean, and so on to Petersfield, contracting greatly our intended circuit. And besides, I had never seen Bramdean, the spot on which, it is said, Alfred fought his last great and glorious battle with the Danes. A fine country for a battle, sure enough!

A little to our right, as we came along, we left the village of Kimston, where Squire Græme once lived, as was before related. Here, too, lived a Squire Ridge, a famous fox-hunter, at a great mansion, now used as a farm-house; and it is curious enough that this squire's son-in-law, one Gunner, an attorney at Bishop's Waltham, is steward to the man who now owns the estate.

Before we got to Petersfield, we called at an old friend's and got some bread and cheese and small beer, which we preferred to strong. In approaching Petersfield we began to descend from the high chalk-country, which (with the exception of the valleys of the Itchen and the Teste) had lasted us from Uphusband (almost the north-west point of the county) to this place, which is not far from the south-east point of it. Here we quit flint and chalk and downs, and take to sand, clay, hedges, and coppices; and here, on the verge of Hampshire, we begin again to see those endless little bubble-formed hills that we before saw round the foot of Hindhead. We have got in in very good time, and got, at the Dolphin, good stabling for our horses. The waiters and people at inns *look so hard at us* to see us so liberal as to horse-feed, fire, candle, beds, and room, while we are so very very sparing in the article of *drink!* They seem to pity our taste. I hear people complain of the " exorbitant charges " at inns; but my wonder always is how the people can live with charging so little. Except in one single instance, I have uniformly, since I have been from home, thought the charges too low for people to live by.

This long evening has given me time to look at the *Star* newspaper of last night; and I see that, with all possible desire to disguise the fact, there is a great "*panic*" brewing. It is impossible that this thing can go on, in its present way, for any length of time. The talk about " speculations "; that is to say, " adventurous dealings or, rather, commercial gamblings;" the talk about *these* having been the cause of the breakings and the other symptoms of approaching convulsion, is the most miserable nonsense that ever was conceived in the heads of idiots. These are *effect;* not *cause.* The cause is the *Small-note Bill,* that last brilliant effort of the joint mind of Van and Castlereagh. That bill was, as I always called it, a *respite;* and it was, and could be, nothing more. It could only put off the evil hour; it could not prevent the final arrival of that hour. To have proceeded with Peel's bill was, indeed, to produce total convulsion. The land must have been surrendered to the overseers for the use of the poor. That is to say, without an " equitable adjustment." But that adjustment as prayed for by Kent, Norfolk, Hereford, and Surrey, might have taken place; it *ought* to have taken place: and it must, at last, take place, or convulsion must come. As to the *nature* of this " adjustment," is it not most distinctly described in the Norfolk petition? Is not that memorable petition now in the Journals of the House of Commons? What more is wanted than to act on the prayer of that very petition? Had I to draw up a petition again, I would not change a single word of that. It pleased Mr. Brougham's " best public instructor " to abuse that petition, and it pleased Daddy Coke and the Hickory Quaker, Gurney, and the wise barn-orator, to calumniate its author. They succeeded; but their success was but shame to them; and that author is yet destined to triumph over them. I have seen no London paper for ten days, until to-day; and I should not have seen this if the waiter had not forced it upon me. I know *very nearly* what will happen by *next May*, or thereabouts; and as to the manner in which things will work in the meanwhile, it is of far less consequence to the nation than it is what sort of weather I shall have to ride in to-morrow. One thing, however, I wish to observe, and that is, that if any attempt be made to repeal the *Corn Bill*, the main body of the farmers will be crushed into total ruin. I come into *contact* with few who are not gentlemen or very substantial farmers: but I know the state of the *whole ;* and I know that even with present prices, and with *honest labourers fed worse than felons*, it is *rub-and-go* with nineteen-twentieths of the farmers; and of this fact I beseech the ministers to be well aware. And with this fact staring them in the face! with that other horrid fact, that by the regulations of the *magistrates* (who cannot avoid it, mind), the honest labourer is fed worse than the convicted felon; with the breakings of merchants, so ruinous to confiding foreigners, so disgraceful to the name of England; with the thousands of industrious and care-taking creatures reduced to beggary by bank-paper; with panic upon panic, plunging thousands upon thousands into despair: with all this notorious as the sun at noon-day, will they again advise their royal master to tell the parliament and the world, that this country is "in a state of unequalled prosperity," and that this prosperity "must be permanent, because *all* the great interests are *flourishing ?* " Let them! That will not alter the *result.* I had been, for several weeks, saying, that the *seeming prosperity* was *fallacious ;* that the cause of it must lead to *ultimate* and shocking ruin; that it could not last, because it arose from causes so manifestly *fictitious ;* that, in short, it was the fair-looking, but poisonous, fruit of a miserable expedient. I had been saying this for several weeks, when out came the king's speech and gave me and my doctrines the *lie direct* as to every point. Well: now, then, we shall *soon see.*

FROM PETERSFIELD TO KENSINGTON

PETWORTH,
Saturday, 12 Nov. 1825.

I was at this town in the summer of 1823, when I crossed
Sussex from Worth to Huntington, in my way to Titchfield in
Hampshire. We came this morning from Petersfield, with an
intention to cross to Horsham, and go thence to Worth, and
then into Kent; but Richard's horse seemed not to be fit for
so strong a bout, and therefore we resolved to bend our course
homewards, and first of all to fall back upon our resources at
Thursley, which we intend to reach to-morrow, going through
North Chapel, Chiddingfold, and Brook.

At about four miles from Petersfield we passed through
a village called Rogate. Just before we came to it, I asked
a man who was hedging on the side of the road how much he
got a day. He said, 1s. 6d.: and he told me that the *allowed*
wages was 7d. a day for the man *and a gallon loaf a week for the
rest of his family;* that is to say, one pound and two and a
quarter ounces of bread for each of them; and nothing more!
And this, observe, is one-third short of the bread allowance of
gaols, to say nothing of the meat and clothing and lodging of
the inhabitants of gaols. If the man have full work; if he get
his eighteen-pence a day, the whole nine shillings does not
purchase a gallon loaf each for a wife and three children, and
two gallon loaves for himself. In the gaols, the convicted felons
have a pound and a half each of bread a day to begin with: they
have some meat generally, and it has been found absolutely
necessary to allow them meat when they work at the tread-mill.
It is impossible to make them work at the tread-mill without it.
However, let us take the bare allowance of bread allowed in the
gaols. This allowance is, for five people, fifty-two pounds and
a half in the week; whereas, the man's nine shillings will buy
but fifty-two pounds of bread; and this, observe, is a vast

deal better than the state of things in the north of Hampshire, where the day-labourer gets but eight shillings a week. I asked this man how much a day they gave to a young able man who had no family, and who was compelled to come to the parish-officers for work. Observe, that there are a great many young men in this situation, because the farmers will not employ single men *at full wages*, these full wages being wanted for the married man's family, just to keep them alive according to the calculation that we have just seen. About the borders of the north of Hampshire they give to these single men two gallon loaves a week, or, in money, two shillings and eightpence, and nothing more. Here, in this part of Sussex, they give the single man sevenpence a day, that is to say, enough to buy two pounds and a quarter of bread for six days in the week, and as he does not work on the Sunday, there is no sevenpence allowed for the Sunday, and of course nothing to eat: and this is the allowance, settled by the magistrates, for a young, hearty, labouring man; and that, too, in the part of England where, I believe, they live better than in any other part of it. The poor creature here has sevenpence a day for six days in the week to find him food, clothes, washing, and lodging! It is just sevenpence, less than one half of what the meanest foot soldier in the standing army receives; besides that the latter has clothing, candle, fire, and lodging into the bargain! Well may we call our happy state of things the "envy of surrounding nations, and the admiration of the world!" We hear of the efforts of Mrs. Fry, Mr. Buxton, and numerous other persons to improve the situation of felons in the gaols; but never, no never, do we catch them ejaculating one single pious sigh for these innumerable sufferers, who are doomed to become felons or to waste away their bodies by hunger.

When we came into the village of Rogate, I saw a little group of persons standing before a blacksmith's shop. The church-yard was on the other side of the road, surrounded by a low wall. The earth of the churchyard was about four feet and a half higher than the common level of the ground round about it; and you may see, by the nearness of the church windows to the ground, that this bed of earth has been made by the innumerable burials that have taken place in it. The group, consisting of the blacksmith, the wheelwright, perhaps, and three or four others, appeared to me to be in a deliberative mood. So I said, looking significantly at the churchyard, " It has taken a pretty many thousands of your forefathers to raise that ground up so high."

" Yes, sir," said one of them. " And," said I, " for about nine hundred years those who built that church thought about religion very differently from what we do." " Yes," said another. " And," said I, " do you think that all those who made that heap there are gone to the devil? " I got no answer to this. " At any rate," added I, " they never worked for a pound and a half of bread a day." They looked hard at me, and then looked hard at one other; and I, having trotted off, looked round at the first turning, and saw them looking after us still. I should suppose that the church was built about seven or eight hundred years ago, that is to say, the present church; for the first church built upon this spot was, I dare say, erected more than a thousand years ago. If I had had time, I should have told this group that, before the Protestant Reformation, the labourers of Rogate received fourpence a day from Michaelmas to Lady-day; five-pence a day from Lady-day to Michaelmas, except in harvest and grass-mowing time, when able labourers had sevenpence a day; and that, at this time, bacon was *not so much as a halfpenny a pound :* and, moreover, that the parson of the parish maintained out of the tithes all those persons in the parish that were reduced to indigence by means of old age or other cause of inability to labour. I should have told them this, and, in all probability, a great deal more, but I had not time; and, besides, they will have an opportunity of reading all about it in my little book called the *History of the Protestant Reformation*.

From Rogate we came on to Trotten, where a Mr. Twyford is the squire, and where there is a very fine and ancient church close by the squire's house. I saw the squire looking at some poor devils who were making " wauste improvements, ma'am," on the road which passes by the squire's door. He looked uncommonly hard at me. It was a scrutinising sort of look, mixed, as I thought, with a little surprise, if not of jealousy, as much as to say, " I wonder who the devil you can be? " My look at the squire was with the head a little on one side, and with the cheek drawn up from the left corner of the mouth, expressive of anything rather than a sense of inferiority to the squire, of whom, however, I had never heard speak before. Seeing the good and commodious and capacious church, I could not help reflecting on the intolerable baseness of this description of men, who have remained mute as fishes, while they have been taxed to build churches for the convenience of the cotton-lords and the stock-jobbers. First, their estates have been taxed to pay interest of debts contracted with these stock-jobbers, and to make wars for the sale of the goods of the cotton-lords. This drain upon their estates has collected the people into great masses, and now the same estates are taxed to build churches for them in these masses. And yet the tame fellows remain as silent as if they had been born deaf and dumb and blind. As towards the labourers, they are sharp and vigorous and brave as heart could wish; here they are bold as Hector. They pare down the wretched souls to what is below gaol allowance. But as towards the taxers they are gentle as doves. With regard, however, to this Squire Twyford, he is not, as I afterwards found, without some little consolation; for one of his sons, I understand, is like Squire Rawlinson of Hampshire, *a police justice in London!* I hear that Squire Twyford was always a distinguished champion of loyalty; what they call a staunch friend of government; and it is therefore natural that the government should be a staunch friend to him. By the taxing of his estate, and paying the stock-jobbers out of the proceeds, the people have been got together in great masses, and as there are justices wanted to keep them in order in those masses, it seems but reasonable that the squire should, in one way or another, enjoy some portion of the profits of keeping them in order. However, this cannot be the case with every loyal squire; and there are many of them who, for want of a share in the distribution, have been totally extinguished. I should suppose Squire Twyford to be in the second rank upwards (dividing the whole of the proprietors of land into five ranks). It appears to me that pretty nearly the whole of this second rank is gone; that the stock-jobbers have eaten them clean up, having less mercy than the cannibals, who usually leave the hands and the feet; so that this squire has had pretty good luck.

From Trotten we came to Midhurst, and, having baited our horses, went into Cowdry Park to see the ruins of that once noble mansion, from which the Countess of Salisbury (the last of the Plantagenets) was brought by the tyrant Henry VIII. to be cruelly murdered, in revenge for the integrity and the other great virtues of her son, Cardinal Pole, as we have seen in Number Four, paragraph 115, of the *History of the Protestant Reformation*. This noble estate, one of the finest in the whole kingdom, was seized on by the king, after the possessor had been murdered on his scaffold. She had committed no crime. No crime was proved against her. The miscreant Thomas Cromwell finding that no form of trial would answer his purpose, invented a new mode of bringing people to their death; namely, a bill brought into parliament, condemning her to death. The estate was then granted to a Sir Anthony Brown, who was physician to the king. By the descendants of this Brown, one of whom was afterwards created Lord Montague, the estate has been held to this day; and Mr. Poyntz, who married the sole remaining heiress of this family, a Miss Brown, is now the proprietor of the estate, comprising, I believe, *forty or fifty manors*, the greater part of which are in this neighbourhood, some of them, however, extending more than twenty miles from the mansion. We entered the park through a great iron gate-way, part of which being wanting, the gap was stopped up by a hurdle. We rode down to the house and all round about and in amongst the ruins, now in part covered with ivy, and inhabited by innumerable starlings and jackdaws. The last possessor was, I believe, that Lord Montague who was put an end to by the celebrated *nautical adventure* on the Rhine along with the brother of Sir Glory. These two sensible worthies took it into their heads to go down a place something resembling the waterfall of an overshot mill. They were drowned just as two young kittens or two young puppies would have been. And as an instance of the truth that it is an ill wind that blows nobody good, had it not been for this sensible enterprise, never would there have been a Westminster Rump to celebrate the talents and virtues of Westminster's Pride and England's Glory. It was this Lord Montague, I believe, who had this ancient and noble mansion completely repaired, and fitted up as a place of residence: and a few days, or a very few weeks, at any rate, after the work was completed, the house was set on fire (by accident, I suppose), and left nearly in the state in which it now stands, except that the ivy has grown up about it, and partly hidden the stones from our sight. You may see, however, the hour of the day or night at which the fire took place; for there still remains the brass of the face of the clock, and the hand pointing to the hour. Close by this mansion there runs a little river which runs winding away through the valleys, and at last falls into the Arron. After viewing the ruins, we had to return into the turnpike-road, and then enter another part of the park, which we crossed, in order to go to Petworth. When you are in a part of this road through the park, you look down and see the house in the middle of a very fine valley, the distant boundary of which, to the south and south-west, is the South Down Hills. Some of the trees here are very fine, particularly some most magnificent rows of the Spanish chestnut. I asked the people at Midhurst where

Mr. Poyntz himself lived; and they told me at the *lodge* in the park, which lodge was formerly the residence of the head keeper. The land is very good about here. It is fine rich loam at top, with clay further down. It is good for all sorts of trees, and they seem to grow here very fast.

We got to Petworth pretty early in the day. On entering it you see the house of Lord Egremont, which is close up against the park-wall, and which wall bounds this little vale on two sides. There is a sort of town-hall here, and on one side of it there is the bust of Charles II., I should have thought; but they tell me it is that of Sir William Wyndham, from whom Lord Egremont is descended. But there is *another building* much more capacious and magnificent than the town-hall; namely, the Bridewell, which, from the modernness of its structure, appears to be one of those " wauste improvements, ma'am," which distinguish this *enlightened* age. This structure vies, in point of magnitude, with the house of Lord Egremont itself, though that is one of the largest mansions in the whole kingdom. The Bridewell has a wall round it that I should suppose to be twenty feet high. This place was not wanted when the labourer got twice as much instead of half as much as the common standing soldier. Here you see the true cause why the young labouring man is " *content* " to exist upon 7*d*. a day, for six days in the week, and nothing for Sunday. Oh! we are a most free and enlightened people; our happy constitution in church and state has supplanted Popery and slavery; but we go to a Bridewell unless we quietly exist and work upon 7*d*. a day!

THURSLEY,
Sunday, 13 *Nov.*

To our great delight we found Richard's horse quite well this morning, and off we set for this place. The first part of our road, for about three miles and a half, was through Lord Egremont's park. The morning was very fine; the sun shining; a sharp frost after a foggy evening; the grass all white, the twigs of the trees white, the ponds frozen over; and everything looking exceedingly beautiful. The spot itself being one of the very finest in the world, not excepting, I dare say, that of the father of Saxe Cobourg itself, who has, doubtless, many such fine places.

In a very fine pond, not far from the house and close by the road, there are some little artificial islands, upon one of which I observed an arbutus loaded with its beautiful fruit (quite ripe) even more thickly than any one I ever saw even in America. There were, on the side of the pond, a most numerous and beautiful collection of water-fowl, foreign as well as domestic. I never saw so great a variety of water-fowl collected together in my life. They had been ejected from the water by the frost, and were sitting apparently in a state of great dejection: but this circumstance had brought them into a comparatively small compass; and we facing our horses about, sat and looked at them, at the pond, at the grass, at the house, till we were tired of admiring. Everything here is in the neatest and most beautiful state. Endless herds of deer, of all the varieties of colours; and what adds greatly to your pleasure in such a case, you see comfortable retreats prepared for them in different parts of the woods. When we came to what we thought the end of the park, the gate-keeper told us that we should find other walls to pass through. We now entered upon woods, we then came to another wall, and there we entered upon farms to our right and to our left. At last we came to a third wall, and the gate in that let us out into the turnpike-road. The gate-keeper here told us that the whole enclosure was *nine miles round ;* and this, after all, forms, probably, not a quarter part of what this nobleman possesses. And is it wrong that one man should possess so much? By no means; but in my opinion it is wrong that a system should exist which compels this man to have his estate taken away from him unless he throw the junior branches of his family for maintenance upon the public.

Lord Egremont bears an excellent character. Everything that I have ever heard of him makes me believe that he is worthy of this princely estate. But I cannot forget that his two brothers, who are now very old men, have had, from their infancy, enormous revenues in sinecure places in the West Indies, while the general property and labour of England is taxed to maintain those West Indies in their state of dependence upon England; and I cannot forget that the burden of these sinecures are amongst the grievances of which the West Indians justly complain. True, the taxing system has taken from the family of Wyndham, during the lives of these two gentlemen, as much, and even more, than what that family has gained by those sinecures; but then let it be recollected that it is not the helpless people of England who have been the cause of this system. It is not the fault of those who receive 7*d.* a day. It is the fault of the family of Wyndham and of such persons; and if they have chosen to suffer the Jews and jobbers to take away so large a part of their income, it is not fair for them to come to the people at large to make up for the loss.

Thus it has gone on. The great masses of property have, in general, been able to take care of themselves: but the little masses have melted away like butter before the sun. The little gentry have had not even any disposition to resist. They merit their fate most justly. They have vied with each other in endeavours to ingratiate themselves with power, and to obtain compensation for their losses. The big fishes have had no feeling for them, have seen them sink with a sneer rather than with compassion; but, at last, the cormorant threatens even themselves; and they are struggling with might and main for their own preservation. They everywhere "most liberally" take the stock-jobber or the Jew by the hand, though they hate him mortally at the same time for his power to outdo them on the sideboard, on the table, and in the equipage. They seem to think nothing of the extinguishment of the small fry; they hug themselves in the thought that they escape; and yet, at times, their minds misgive them, and they tremble for their own fate. The country people really gain by the change; for the small gentry have been rendered, by their miseries, so niggardly and so cruel, that it is quite a blessing, in a village, to see a rich Jew or jobber come to supplant them. They come, too, with far less cunning than the half-broken gentry. Cunning as the stock-jobber is in Change Alley, I defy him to be cunning enough for the country people, brought to their present state of duplicity by a series of cruelties which no pen can adequately describe. The stock-jobber goes from London with the *cant of humanity* upon his lips, at any rate; whereas the half-broken squire takes not the least pains to disguise the hardness of his heart.

It is impossible for any just man to regret the sweeping away of this base race of squires; but the sweeping of them away is produced by causes that have a wider extent. These causes reach the good as well as the bad: all are involved alike: like the pestilence, this horrible system is no respecter of persons: and decay and beggary mark the whole face of the *country*.

North Chapel is a little town in the Weald of Sussex where there were formerly post-chaises kept; but where there are none kept now. And here is another complete revolution. In almost every country town the post-chaise houses have been lessened in number, and those that remain have become comparatively solitary and mean. The guests at inns are not now gentlemen, but *bumpers*, who, from being called (at the inns) " riders," became

" travellers," and are now " commercial gentlemen," who go about in *gigs*, instead of on horseback, and who are in such numbers as to occupy a great part of the room in all the inns in every part of the country. There are, probably, twenty thousand of them always out, who may perhaps have, on an average throughout the year, three or four thousand " ladies " travelling with them. The expense of this can be little short of fifteen millions a year, all to be paid by the country-people who consume the goods, and a large part of it to be drawn up to the Wen.

From North Chapel we came to Chiddingfold, which is in the Weald of Surrey; that is to say, the country of oak-timber. Between these two places there are a couple of pieces of that famous commodity called " government property." It seems that these places, which have extensive buildings on them, were for the purpose of making gunpowder. Like most other of these enterprises, they have been given up, after a time, and so the ground and all the buildings, and the monstrous fences, erected at enormous expense, have been sold. They were sold, it seems, some time ago, in lots, with the intention of being pulled down and carried away, though they are now nearly new, and built in the most solid, substantial, and expensive manner; brick walls eighteen inches through, and the buildings covered with lead and slate. It appears that they have been purchased by a Mr. Stovell, a Sussex banker; but for some reason or other, though the purchase was made long ago, " government " still holds the possession; and, what is more, it keeps people there to take care of the premises. It would be curious to have a complete history of these pretty establishments at Chiddingfold; but this is a sort of history that we shall never be treated with until there be somebody in parliament to rummage things to the bottom. It would be very easy to call for a specific account of the cost of these establishments, and also of the quantity of powder made at them. I should not be at all surprised if the concern, all taken together, brought the powder to a hundred times the price at which similar powder could have been purchased.

When we came through Chiddingfold the people were just going to church; and we saw a carriage and pair conveying an old gentleman and some ladies to the churchyard steps. Upon inquiry, we found that this was Lord Winterton, whose name, they told us, was Turnour. I thought I had heard of all the lords, first or last; but if I had ever heard of this one before, I had forgotten him. He lives down in the Weald, between the gunpowder establishments and Horsham, and has the reputation of being a harmless, good sort of man, and that being the case I was sorry to see that he appeared to be greatly afflicted with the gout, being obliged to be helped up the steps by a stout man. However, it is as broad, perhaps, as it is long: a man is not to have all the enjoyments of making the gout, and the enjoyments of abstinence too: that would not be fair play; and I dare say that Lord Winterton is just enough to be content with the consequences of his enjoyments.

This Chiddingfold is a very pretty place. There is a very pretty and extensive green opposite the church; and we were at the proper time of the day to perceive that the modern system of education had by no means overlooked this little village. We saw *the schools* marching towards the church in military order. Two of them passed us on our road. The boys looked very hard at us, and I saluted them with " There's brave boys, you'll all be parsons or lawyers or doctors." Another school seemed to be in a less happy state. The scholars were too much in uniform to have had their clothes purchased by their parents; and they looked, besides, as if a little more victuals and a little less education would have done as well. There were about twenty of them without one single tinge of red in their whole twenty faces. In short I never saw more deplorable looking objects since I was born. And can it be of any use to expend money in this sort of way upon poor creatures that have not half a bellyfull of food? We had not breakfasted when we passed them. We felt, at that moment, what hunger was. We had some bits of bread and meat in our pockets, however; and these, which were merely intended as stay-stomachs, amounted, I dare say, to the allowance of any half dozen of these poor boys for the day. I could, with all my heart, have pulled the victuals out of my pocket and given it to them; but I did not like to do that which would have interrupted the march, and might have been construed into a sort of insult. To quiet my conscience, however, I gave a poor man that I met soon afterwards sixpence, under pretence of rewarding him for telling me the way to Thursley, which I knew as well as he, and which I had determined, in my own mind, not to follow.

We had now come on the turnpike - road from my Lord Egremont's park to Chiddingfold. I had made two or three attempts to get out of it, and to bear away to the north-west, to get through the oak-woods to Thursley; but I was constantly prevented by being told that the road which I wished to take would lead me to Haslemere. If you talk to ostlers, or landlords, or post-boys; or, indeed, to almost anybody else, they mean by a *road* a *turnpike-road;* and they positively will not talk to you about any other. Now, just after quitting Chidding-fold, Thursley lies over fine woods and coppices, in a north-west direction, or thereabouts; and the turnpike-road, which goes from Petworth to Godalming, goes in a north-north-east direction. I was resolved, be the consequences what they might, not to follow the turnpike-road one single inch further; for I had not above three miles or thereabouts to get to Thursley, through the woods; and I had, perhaps, six miles at least to get to it the other way; but the great thing was to see the interior of these woods; to see the stems of the trees, as well as the tops of them. I saw a lane opening in the right direction; I saw indeed that my horses must go up to their knees in clay; but I resolved to enter and go along that lane, and long before the end of my journey I found myself most amply compensated for the toil that I was about to encounter. But talk of toil! It was the horse that had the toil; and I had nothing to do but to sit upon his back, turn my head from side to side and admire the fine trees in every direction. Little bits of fields and meadows here and there, shaded all over, or nearly all over, by the surrounding trees. Here and there a labourer's house buried in the woods. We had drawn out our luncheons and eaten them while the horses took us through the clay; but I stopped at a little house and asked the woman, who looked very clean and nice, whether she would let us dine with her. She said " Yes," with all her heart, but that she had no place to put our horses in, and that her dinner would not be ready for an hour, when she expected her husband home from church. She said they had a bit of bacon and a pudding and some cabbage; but that she had not much bread in the house. She had only one child, and that was not very old, so we left her, quite convinced that my old observation is true, that people in the woodland countries are best off, and that it is absolutely impossible to reduce them to that state of starvation in which they are in the corn-growing part of the kingdom. Here is that great blessing, abundance of fuel at all times of the year, and particularly in the winter.

We came on for about a mile further in these clayey lanes, when we renewed our inquiries as to our course, as our road now seemed to point towards Godalming again. I asked a man how I should get to Thursley? He pointed to some fir-trees upon a hill, told me I must go by them, and that there was no other way. "Where then," said I, "is Thursley?" He pointed with his hand, and said, "Right over those woods; but there is no road there, and it is impossible for you to get through those woods." "Thank you," said I; "but through those woods we mean to go." Just at the border of the woods I saw a cottage. There must be some way to that cottage; and we soon found a gate that let us into a field, across which we went to this cottage. We there found an old man and a young one. Upon inquiry we found that it was *possible* to get through these woods. Richard gave the old man threepence to buy a pint of beer, and I gave the young one a shilling to pilot us through the woods. These were oak-woods with underwood beneath; and there was a little stream of water running down the middle of the woods, the annual and long overflowings of which has formed a meadow sometimes a rod wide, and sometimes twenty rods wide, while the bed of the stream itself was the most serpentine that can possibly be imagined, describing, in many places, nearly a complete circle, going round for many rods together, and coming within a rod or two of a point that it had passed before. I stopped the man several times to sit and admire this beautiful spot, shaded in great part by lofty and wide-spreading oak-trees. We had to cross this brook several times, over bridges that the owner had erected for the convenience of the fox-hunters. At last, we came into an ash-coppice, which had been planted in regular rows, at about four feet distances, which had been once cut, and which was now in the state of six years' growth. A road through it, made for the fox-hunters, was as straight as a line, and of so great a length that, on entering it, the further end appeared not to be a foot wide. Upon seeing this, I asked the man whom these coppices belonged to, and he told me to Squire Leech, at Lea. My surprise ceased, but my admiration did not.

A piece of ordinary coppice ground, close adjoining this, and with no timber in it, and upon just the same soil (if there had been such a piece), would, at ten years' growth, be worth, at present prices, from five to seven pounds the acre. This coppice, at ten years' growth, will be worth twenty pounds the acre; and, at the next cutting, when the stems will send out so many more shoots, it will be worth thirty pounds the acre. I did not ask the question when I afterwards saw Mr. Leech, but, I dare say, the ground was trenched before it was planted; but what is that expense when compared with the great, the permanent profit of such an undertaking! And, above all things, what a convenient species of property does a man here create. Here are no tenants' rack, no anxiety about crops and seasons; the rust and the mildew never come here; a man knows what he has got, and he knows that nothing short of an earthquake can take it from him, unless, indeed, by attempting to vie with the stock-jobber in the expense of living, he enable the stock-jobber to come and perform the office of the earthquake. Mr. Leech's father planted, I think it was, forty acres of such coppice in the same manner; and, at the same time, he *sowed the ground with acorns*. The acorns have become oak-trees, and have begun and made great progress in diminishing the value of the ash, which have now to contend against the shade and the roots of the oak. For present profit, and, indeed, for permanent profit, it would be judicious to grub up the oak; but the owner has determined otherwise. He cannot endure the idea of destroying an oak wood.

If such be the profit of planting ash, what would be the profit of planting locust, even for poles or stakes? The locust would outgrow the ash, as we have seen in the case of Mr. Gunter's plantation, more than three to one. I am satisfied that it will do this upon any soil, if you give the trees fifteen years to grow in; and, in short, that the locusts will be trees when the ash are merely poles, if both are left to grow up in single stems. If in coppice, the locust will make as good poles; I mean as large and as long poles in six years as the ash will in ten years: to say nothing of the superior durability of the locust. I have seen locusts, at Mr. Knowles's, at Thursley, sufficient for a hop-pole, for an ordinary hop-pole, with only five years' growth in them, and leaving the last year's growth to be cut off, leaving the top of the pole three quarters of an inch through. There is nothing that we have ever heard of, of the timber kind, equal to this in point of quickness of growth. In parts of the country where hop-poles are not wanted, espalier stakes, wood for small fencing, hedge stakes, hurdle stakes, fold-shores, as the people call them, are always wanted; and is it not better to have a thing that will last twenty years than a thing that will last only three? I know of no English underwood which gives a hedge stake to last even *two years*. I should think that a very profitable way of employing the locust would be this. Plant a coppice, the plants two feet apart. Thus planted, the trees will protect one another against the wind. Keep the side shoots pruned off. At the end of six years, the coppice, if well planted and managed, will be, at the very least, twenty feet high to the tips of the trees. Not if the grass and weeds are suffered to grow up to draw all the moisture up out of the ground, to keep the air from the young plants, and to intercept the gentle rains and the dews; but trenched ground, planted carefully, and kept clean; and always bearing in mind that hares and rabbits and young locust trees will never live together; for the hares and rabbits will not only bite them off; but will gnaw them down to the ground, and, when they have done that, will scratch away the ground to gnaw into the very root. A gentleman bought some locust trees of me last year, and brought me a dismal account in the summer of their being all dead; but I have since found that they were all eaten up by the hares. He saw some of my refuse; some of those which were too bad to send to him, which were a great deal higher than his head. His ground was as good as mine, according to his account; but I had no hares to fight against; or else mine would have been all dead too.

I say, then, that a locust plantation, in pretty good land, well managed, would be twenty feet high in six years; suppose it, however, to be only fifteen, there would be, at the bottom, wood to make two locust PINS for ship-building; two locust pins at the bottom of each tree. Two at the very least; and here would be twenty-two thousand locust pins to the acre, probably enough for the building of a seventy-four gun ship. These pins are about eighteen inches long, and, perhaps, an inch and half through; and there is this surprising quality in the wood of the locust, that it is just as hard and as durable at five or six years' growth as it is at fifty years' growth. Of which I can produce an abundance of instances. The *stake* which I brought home from America, and which is now at Fleet Street, had stood as a stake for about eight-and-twenty years, as certified to me by Judge Mitchell, of North Hampstead in Long Island, who gave me the stake, and who said to me at the time, " Now are you really going to take that crooked miserable stick to England! " Now it is pretty well known, at least I have been so informed, that our government have sent to America in consequence of my writings about the locust to endeavour to get locust pins for the navy. I have been informed that they have been told that the American government has bought them all up. Be this as it may, I know that a waggon load of these pins is, in America itself, equal in value to a waggon load of barrels of the finest flour. This being undeniable, and the fact being undeniable that we can grow locust pins here, that I can take a seed to-day, and say that it shall produce two pins in seven years' time, will it not become an article of heavy accusation against the government if they neglect even one day to set about tearing up their infernal Scotch firs and larches in Wolmer Forest and elsewhere, and putting locust trees in their stead, in order, first to provide this excellent material for ship-building; and next to have some fine plantations in the Holt Forest, Wolmer Forest, the New Forest, the Forest of Dean, and elsewhere, the only possible argument against doing which being, that I may possibly take a ride round amongst their plantations, and that it may be everlastingly recorded that it was I who was the cause of the government's adopting this wise and beneficial measure?

I am disposed to believe, however, that the government will not be brutish enough obstinately to reject the advice given to them on this head, it being observed, however, that I wish to have no hand in their proceedings, directly or indirectly. I can sell all the trees that I have for sale to other customers. Let them look out for themselves; and as to any reports that their creatures may make upon the subjects I shall be able to produce proofs enough that such reports, if unfavourable, are false. I wrote, in a *Register* from Long Island, that I could if I would tell insolent Castlereagh, who was for making Englishmen dig holes one day and fill them up the next, how he might *profitably put something into those holes*, but that I would not tell him as long as the boroughmongers should be in the state in which they then were. They are no longer in that state, I thank God. There has been no positive law to alter their state, but it is manifest that there must be such law before it be long. Events are working together to make the country worth living in, which, for the great body of the people, is at present hardly the case. Above all things in the world, it is the duty of every man, who has it in his power, to do what he can to promote the creation of materials for the building of ships in the best manner; and it is now a fact of perfect notoriety that, with regard to the building of ships, it cannot be done in the best manner without the assistance of this sort of wood.

I have seen a specimen of the locust wood used in the making of furniture. I saw it in the posts of a bedstead; and anything more handsome I never saw in my life. I had used it myself in the making of rules; but I never saw it in this shape before. It admits of a polish nearly as fine as that of box. It is a bright and beautiful yellow. And in bedsteads, for instance, it would last for ever, and would not become loose at the joints, like oak and other perishable wood; because, like the live oak and the red cedar, no worm or insect ever preys upon it. There is no fear of the quantity being too great. It would take a century to make as many plantations as are absolutely wanted in England. It would be a prodigious creation of real and solid wealth. Not such a creation as that of paper money, which only takes the dinner from one man and gives it to another, which only gives an unnatural swell to a city or a watering place by beggaring a thousand villages; but it would be a creation of money's worth things. Let any man go and look at a farm-house that was built a hundred years ago. He will find it, though very well built with stone or brick, actually falling to pieces, unless very frequently repaired, owing entirely to the rotten wood in the window-sills, the door-sills, the plates, the pins, the door-frames, the window frames, and all those parts of the beams, the joists, and the rafters, that come in contact with the rain or the moisture. The two parts of a park paling which give way first, are the parts of the post that meet the ground, and the pins which hold the rails to the post. Both these rot long before the paling rots. Now all this is avoided by the use of locust as sills, as joists, as posts, as frames, and as pins. Many a roof has come down merely from the rotting of the pins. The best of spine oak is generally chosen for these pins. But after a time, the air gets into the pin-hole. The pin rots from the moist air, it gives way, the wind shakes the roof, and down it comes, or it swags, the wet gets in, and the house is rotten. In ships, the pins are the first things that give way. Many a ship would last twenty years after it is broken up, if put together with locust pins. I am aware that some readers will become tired of this subject, and nothing but my conviction of its being of the very first importance to the whole kingdom could make me thus dwell upon it.

We got to Thursley after our beautiful ride through Mr. Leech's coppices, and the weather being pretty cold, we found ourselves most happily situated here by the side of an *American fireplace*, making extremely comfortable a room which was formerly amongst the most uncomfortable in the world. This is another of what the malignant parsons call Cobbett's Quackeries. But my real opinion is that the whole body of them, all put together, have never, since they were born, conferred so much benefit upon the country as I have conferred upon it by introducing this fireplace. Mr. Judson of Kensington, who is the manufacturer of them, tells me that he has a great demand, which gives me much pleasure; but really, coming to conscience, no man ought to sit by one of these fireplaces that does not go the full length with me both in politics and religion. It is not fair for them to enjoy the warmth without subscribing to the doctrines of the giver of the warmth. However, as I have nothing to do with Mr. Judson's affair, either as to the profit or the loss, he must sell the fireplaces to whomsoever he pleases.

KENSINGTON,
Sunday, 20 Nov.

Coming to Godalming on Friday, where business kept us that night, we had to experience at the inn the want of our American fireplace. A large and long room to sit in, with a miserable thing called a screen to keep the wind from our backs, with a smoke in the room half an hour after the fire was lighted, we, consuming a full bushel of coals in order to keep us warm, were not half so well off as we should have been in the same room, and without any screen, and with two gallons of coals, if we had our American fireplace. I gave the landlord my advice upon the subject, and he said he would go and look at the fireplace at Mr. Knowles's. That was precisely one of those rooms which stand in absolute need of such a fireplace. It is, I should think, five-and-thirty or forty feet long, and pretty nearly twenty feet wide. I could sooner dine with a labouring man upon his allowance of bread, such as I have mentioned above, than I would, in winter time, dine in that room upon turbot and surloin of beef. An American fireplace, with a good fire in it, would make every part of that room pleasant to dine in in the coldest day in winter. I saw a public-house drinking-room, where the owner has tortured his invention to get a little warmth for his guests, where he fetches his coals in a waggon from a distance of twenty miles or thereabouts, and where he consumes these coals by the bushel, to effect that which he cannot effect at all, and which he might effect completely with about a fourth part of the coals.

It looked like rain on Saturday morning, we therefore sent our horses on from Godalming to Ripley, and took a post-chaise to convey us after them. Being shut up in the post-chaise did not prevent me from taking a look at a little snug house stuck under the hill on the road side, just opposite the old chapel on St. Catherine's Hill, which house was not there when I was a boy. I found that this house is now occupied by the family Molyneux, for ages the owners of Losely Park, on the out-skirts of which estate this house stands. The house at Losely is of great antiquity, and had, or perhaps has, attached to it the great manors of Godalming and Chiddingfold. I believe that Sir Thomas More lived at Losely, or, at any rate, that the Molyneuxes are, in some degree, descended from him. The estate is, I fancy, theirs yet; but here they are, in this little house, while one Gunning (an East Indian, I believe) occupies the house of their ancestors. At Send, or Sutton, where Mr. Webb Weston inhabited, there is a baron somebody, with a De before his name. The name is German or Dutch, I believe. How the baron came there I know not; but as I have read his name amongst the *justices of the peace* for the county of Surrey, he must have been born in England, or the law has been violated in making him a justice of the peace, seeing that no person not born a subject of the king, and a subject in this country too, can lawfully hold a commission under the crown, either civil or military. Nor is it lawful for any man born abroad of Scotch or Irish parents to hold such commission under the crown, though such commissions have been held, and are held, by persons who are neither natural born subjects of the king, nor born of English parents abroad. It should also be known and borne in mind by the people that it is unlawful to grant any pension from the crown to any foreigner whatever. And no naturalisation act can take away this disability. Yet the Whigs, as they call themselves, granted such pensions during the short time that they were in power.

When we got to Ripley, we found the day very fine, and we got upon our horses and rode home to dinner, after an absence of just one month, agreeably to our original intention, having seen a great deal of the country, having had a great deal of sport, and having, I trust, laid in a stock of health for the winter, sufficient to enable us to withstand the suffocation of this smoking and stinking Wen.

But Richard and I have done something else besides ride, and hunt, and course, and stare about us, during this month. He was eleven years old last March, and it was now time for him to begin to know something about letters and figures. He has learned to work in the garden, and having been a good deal in the country, knows a great deal about farming affairs. He can ride anything of a horse, and over anything that a horse will go over. So expert at hunting, that his first teacher, Mr. Budd, gave the hounds up to his management in the field; but now he begins to talk about nothing but *fox-hunting!* That is a dangerous

thing. When he and I went from home, I had business at
Reigate. It was a very wet morning, and we went off long before
daylight in a post-chaise, intending to have our horses brought
after us. He began to talk in anticipation of the sport he was
going to have, and was very inquisitive as to the probability of
our meeting with fox-hounds, which gave me occasion to address
him thus: " Fox-hunting is a very fine thing, and very proper
for people to be engaged in, and it is very desirable to be able to
ride well and to be in at the death; but that is not ALL; that
is not everything. Any fool can ride a horse and draw a cover;
any groom or any stable-fellow, who is as ignorant as the horse,
can do these things; but all gentlemen that go a fox-hunting
[I hope God will forgive me for the lie] are scholars, Richard.
It is not the riding, nor the scarlet coats, that make them gentlemen; it is their scholarship." What he thought I do not know;
for he sat as mute as a fish, and I could not see his countenance.
" So," said I, " you must now begin to learn something, and you
must begin with arithmetic." He had learned from mere play
to read, being first set to work of his own accord to find out what
was said about Thurtell, when all the world was talking and
reading about Thurtell. That had induced us to give him
Robinson Crusoe; and that had made him a passable reader.
Then he had scrawled down letters and words upon paper, and
had written letters to me in the strangest way imaginable. His
knowledge of figures he had acquired from the necessity of knowing the several numbers upon the barrels of seeds brought from
America, and the numbers upon the doors of houses. So that
I had pretty nearly a blank sheet of paper to begin upon; and I
have always held it to be stupidity to the last degree to attempt
to put book-learning into children who are too young to reason
with.

I began with a pretty long lecture on the utility of arithmetic;
the absolute necessity of it, in order for us to make out our
accounts of the trees and seeds that we should have to sell in the
winter, and the utter impossibility of our getting paid for our
pains unless we were able to make out our accounts, which
accounts could not be made out unless we understood something
about arithmetic. Having thus made him understand the
utility of the thing, and given him a very strong instance in the
case of our nursery affairs, I proceeded to explain to him the
meaning of the word arithmetic, the power of figures, according
to the place they occupied. I then, for it was still dark, taught
him to add a few figures together, I naming the figures one after

another, while he, at the mention of each new figure said the amount, and if incorrectly, he was corrected by me. When we had got a sum of about 24, I said now there is another line of figures on the left of this, and therefore you are to put down the 4 and carry 2. "What is *carrying* ?" said he. I then explained to him the *why* and the *wherefore* of this, and he perfectly understood me at once. We then did several other little sums; and by the time we got to Sutton, it becoming daylight, I took a pencil and set him a little sum upon paper, which, after making a mistake or two, he did very well. By the time we got to Reigate he had done several more, and at last a pretty long one, with very few errors. We had business all day, and thought no more of our scholarship until we went to bed, and then we did, in our post-chaise fashion, a great many lines in arithmetic before we went to sleep. Thus we went on mixing our riding and hunting with our arithmetic, until we quitted Godalming, when he did a sum very nicely in *multiplication of money*, falling a little short of what I had laid out, which was to make him learn the four rules in whole numbers first, and then in money, before I got home.

Friends' houses are not so good as inns for executing a project like this; because you cannot very well be by yourself; and we slept but four nights at inns during our absence. So that we have actually stolen the time to accomplish this job, and Richard's journal records that he was more than fifteen days out of the thirty-one coursing or hunting. Nothing struck me more than the facility, the perfect readiness with which he at once performed addition of money. There is a *pence table* which boys usually learn, and during the learning of which they usually get no small number of thumps. This table I found it wholly unnecessary to set him. I had written it for him in one of the leaves of his journal book. But upon looking at it, he said, " I don't want this, because, you know, I have nothing to do but to *divide by twelve*." That is right, said I, you are a clever fellow, Dick; and I shut up the book.

Now when there is so much talk about education, let me ask how many pounds it generally costs parents to have a boy taught this much of arithmetic; how much time it costs also; and, which is a far more serious consideration, how much mortification, and very often how much loss of health, it costs the poor scolded broken-hearted child, who becomes dunder-headed and dull for all his life-time, merely because that has been imposed upon him as a task which he ought to regard as an object of pleasant pursuit. I never even once desired him to stay a

moment from any other thing that he had a mind to go at. I
just wrote the sums down upon paper, laid them upon the table,
and left him to tackle them when he pleased. In the case of the
multiplication-table, the learning of which is something of a
job, and which it is absolutely necessary to learn perfectly, I
advised him to go up into his bedroom and read it twenty
times over out loud every morning before he went a hunting,
and ten times over every night after he came back, till it all
came as pat upon his lips as the names of persons that he knew.
He did this, and at the end of about a week he was ready to set
on upon multiplication. It is the irksomeness of the thing
which is the great bar to learning of every sort. I took care
not to suffer irksomeness to seize his mind for a moment, and the
consequence was that which I have described. I wish clearly
to be understood as ascribing nothing to extraordinary *natural*
ability. There are, as I have often said, as many *sorts* of men
as there are of dogs; but I do not pretend to be of any peculiarly
excellent sort, and I have never discovered any indications of
it. There are, to be sure, sorts that are naturally stupid; but
the generality of men are not so; and I believe that every boy of
the same age, equally healthy, and brought up in the same
manner, would (unless of one of the stupid kinds) learn in just
the same sort of way; but not if begun to be thumped at five or
six years old, when the poor little things have no idea of the
utility of anything; who are hardly sensible beings, and have
but just understanding enough to know that it will hurt them if
they jump down a chalk pit. I am sure, from thousands of
instances that have come under my own eyes, that to begin to
teach children book-learning before they are capable of reasoning
is the sure and certain way to enfeeble their minds for life; and
if they have natural genius, to cramp, if not totally to destroy,
that genius.

I think I shall be tempted to mould into a little book these
lessons of arithmetic given to Richard. I think that a boy of
sense, and of age equal to that of my scholar, would derive great
profit from such a little book. It would not be equal to my
verbal explanations, especially accompanied with the other
parts of my conduct towards my scholar; but, at any rate, it
would be plain; it would be what a boy could understand; it
would encourage him by giving him a glimpse at the reasons for
what he was doing: it would contain principles; and the difference between principles and rules is this, that the former are
persuasions and the latter are commands. There is a great deal

of difference between carrying 2 for such and such a reason, and carrying 2 because you *must* carry 2. You see boys that can cover reams of paper with figures, and do it with perfect correctness too; and at the same time can give you not a single reason for any part of what they have done. Now this is really doing very little. The rule is soon forgotten, and then all is forgotten. It would be the same with a lawyer that understood none of the principles of law. As far as he could find and remember cases exactly similar in all their parts to the case which he might have to manage, he would be as profound a lawyer as any in the world; but if there was the slightest difference between his case and the cases he had found upon record, there would be an end of his law.

Some people will say, here is a monstrous deal of vanity and egotism, and if they will tell me how such a story is to be told without exposing a man to this imputation, I will adopt their mode another time. I get nothing by telling the story. I should get full as much by keeping it to myself; but it may be useful to others, and therefore I tell it. Nothing is so dangerous as supposing that you have eight wonders of the world. I have no pretensions to any such possession. I look upon my boy as being like other boys in general. Their fathers can teach arithmetic as well as I; and if they have not a mind to pursue my method, they must pursue their own. Let them apply to the outside of the head and to the back, if they like; let them bargain for thumps and the birch rod; it is their affair and not mine. I never yet saw in my house a child that was *afraid;* that was in any fear whatever; that was ever for a moment under any sort of apprehension, on account of the learning of anything; and I never in my life gave a command, an order, a request, or even advice, to look into any book; and I am quite satisfied that the way to make children dunces, to make them detest books, and justify that detestation, is to tease them and bother them upon the subject.

As to the *age* at which children ought to begin to be taught, it is very curious that, while I was at a friend's house during my ride, I looked into, by mere accident, a little child's abridgment of the History of England: a little thing about twice as big as a crown-piece. Even into this abridgment the historian had introduced the circumstance of Alfred's father, who, " through a *mistaken notion* of kindness to his son, had suffered him to live to the age of twelve years without any attempt being made to give him education." How came this writer to know that it was a *mistaken notion?* Ought he not rather, when he looked at the result, when he considered the astonishing knowledge and great deeds of Alfred—ought he not to have hesitated before he thus criticised the notions of the father? It appears from the result that the notions of the father were perfectly correct; and I am satisfied that if they had begun to thump the head of Alfred when he was a child, we should not at this day have heard talk of Alfred the Great.

Great apologies are due to the OLD LADY from me, on account of my apparent inattention towards her, during her recent, or rather, I may say, her present, fit of that tormenting disorder which, as I observed before, comes upon her by *spells*. Dr. M'Culloch may say what he pleases about her being "*wi'* bairn." I say its the wet gripes; and I saw a poor old mare down in Hampshire in just the same way; but God forbid the catas- trophe should be the same, for they shot poor old Ball for the hounds. This disorder comes by spells. It sometimes seems as if it were altogether going off; the pulse rises, and the appetite returns. By and by a fresh grumbling begins to take place in the bowels. These are followed by acute pains; the patient becomes tremulous; the pulse begins to fall, and the most gloomy apprehensions begin again to be entertained. At every spell the pulse does not cease falling till it becomes lower than it was brought to by the preceding spell; and thus, spell after spell, finally produces the natural result.

It is useless at present to say much about the equivocating and blundering of the newspapers relative to the cause of the fall. They are very shy, extremely cautious; become wonderfully *wary* with regard to this subject. They do not know what to make of it. They all remember that I told them that their prosperity was delusive; that it would soon come to an end, while they were telling me of the falsification of all my pre- dictions. I told them the Small-note Bill had only given a *respite*. I told them that the foreign loans, and the shares, and all the astonishing enterprises, arose purely out of the Small-note Bill; and that a short time would see the Small-note Bill driving the gold out of the country, and bring us back to another restriction, OR, to wheat at four shillings a bushel. They remember that I told them all this; and now some of them begin to *regard me as the principal cause of the present embarrassments.* This is pretty work indeed! What! I! The poor deluded creature, whose predictions were all falsified, who knew nothing at all about such matters, who was a perfect pedlar in political economy, who was

"a conceited and obstinate old dotard," as that polite and
enlightened paper, the *Morning Herald*, called me: is it possible
that such a poor miserable creature can have had the power to
produce effects so prodigious? Yet this really appears to be
the opinion of one, at least, of these Mr. Brougham's best
possible public instructors. The *Public Ledger*, of the 16th of
November, has the following passage.

"It is fully ascertained that the country banking establishments in England have latterly been compelled to limit their
paper circulation, for the writings of Mr. Cobbett are widely
circulated in the agricultural districts, and they have been so
successful as to induce the *boobies* to call for gold in place of
country paper, a circumstance which has *produced a greater effect
on the currency than any exportation of the precious metals* to
the Continent, either of Europe or America, could have done,
although it too must have contributed to render money for a
season scarce."

And, so, the "*boobies*" call for gold instead of country bank-
notes! Bless the "*boobies*"! I wish they would do it to a
greater extent, which they would, if they were not so dependent
as they are upon the ragmen. But does the *Public Ledger* think
that those unfortunate creatures who suffered the other day at
Plymouth would have been "*boobies*" if they had gone and got
sovereigns before the banks broke? This brother of the broadsheet should act justly and fairly as I do. He should ascribe
these demands for gold to Mr. Jones of Bristol and not to me.
Mr. Jones taught the "boobies" that they might have gold for
asking for, or send the ragmen to gaol. It is Mr. Jones, therefore, that they should blame, and not me. But, seriously
speaking, what a mess, what a pickle, what a horrible mess,
must the thing be in, if any man, or any thousand of men, or any
hundred thousand of men, can change the value of money, un-
hinge all contracts and all engagements, and plunge the pecuniary
affairs of a nation into confusion? I have been often accused of
wishing to be thought the cleverest man in the country; but
surely it is no vanity (for vanity means unjust pretension) for
me to think myself the cleverest man in the country, if I can of
my own head, and at my own pleasure, produce effects like
these. Truth, however, and fair dealing with my readers, call
upon me to disclaim so haughty a pretension. I have no such
power as this public instructor ascribes to me. Greater causes
are at work to produce such effects; causes wholly uncontrollable
by me, and, what is more, wholly uncontrollable in the long run

by the government itself, though heartily co-operating with the bank directors. These united can do nothing to arrest the progress of events. Peel's bill produced the horrible distresses of 1822; the part repeal of that bill produced a respite, that respite is now about to expire; and neither government nor bank, nor both joined together, can prevent the ultimate conse-quences. They may postpone them for a little; but mark, every postponement will render the catastrophe the more dreadful.

I see everlasting attempts by the " Instructor " to cast blame upon the bank. I can see no blame in the bank. The bank has issued no small notes, though it has liberty to do it. The bank pays in gold agreeably to the law. What more does any-body want with the bank. The bank lends money I suppose when it chooses; and is not it to be the judge when it shall lend and when it shall not? The bank is blamed for putting out paper and causing high prices; and blamed at the same time for not putting out paper to accommodate merchants and keep them from breaking. It cannot be to blame for both, and, indeed, it is blamable for neither. It is the fellows that put out the paper and then break that do the mischief. However, a breaking merchant, whom the bank will no longer prop up, will naturally blame the bank, just as every insolvent blames a solvent that will not lend him money.

When the foreign loans first began to go on, Peter Macculloch and all the Scotch were cock o' whoop. They said that there were prodigious advantages in lending money to South America, that the interest would come home to enrich us; that the amount of the loans would go out chiefly in English manufactures; that the commercial gains would be enormous; and that this country would thus be made rich, and powerful, and happy, by employing in this way its " surplus capital," and thereby contributing at the same time to the uprooting of despotism and superstition, and the establishing of freedom and liberality in their stead. Unhappy and purblind, I could not for the life of me see the matter in this light. My perverted optics could perceive no *surplus capital* in bundles of bank-notes. I could see no gain in sending out goods which somebody in England was to pay for, without, as it appeared to me, the smallest chance of ever being paid again. I could see no chance of gain in the purchase of a bond, nominally bearing interest at six per cent., and on which, as I thought, no interest at all would ever be paid. I despised the idea of paying bits of paper by bits of paper. I knew that a bond, though said to bear six per cent. interest, was not worth a farthing, unless some interest were paid upon it. I declared, when Spanish bonds were at seventy-five, that I would not give a crown for a hundred pounds in them, if I were compelled to keep them unsold for seven years; and I now declare, as to South American bonds, I think them of less value than the Spanish bonds now are, if the owner be compelled to keep them unsold for a year. It is very true that these opinions agree with my *wishes ;* but they have not been created by those wishes. They are founded on my knowledge of the state of things, and upon my firm conviction of the folly of expecting that the interest of these things will ever come from the respective countries to which they relate.

Mr. Canning's despatch, which I shall insert below, has doubtless had a tendency (whether expected or not) to prop up the credit of these sublime speculations. The propping up of the credit of them can, however, do no sort of good. The keeping up the price of them for the present may assist some of the actual speculators, but it can do nothing for the speculation in the end, and this speculation, which was wholly an effect of the Small-note Bill, will finally have a most ruinous effect. How is it to be otherwise? Have we ever received any evidence, or anything whereon to build a belief, that the interest of these bonds will be paid? Never; and the man must be mad; mad with avarice or a love of gambling, that could advance his money upon any such a thing as these bonds. The fact is, however, that it was not *money :* it was paper: it was borrowed, or created, for the purpose of being advanced. Observe too, that when the loans were made, money was at a lower value than it is now; therefore those who would have to pay the interest would have too much to pay if they were to fulfil their engagement. Mr. Canning's state paper clearly proves to me that the main object of it is to make the loans to South America finally be paid, because, if they be not paid, not only is the amount of them lost to the bond-holders, but there is an end, at once, to all that brilliant *commerce* with which that shining minister appears to be so much enchanted. All the silver and gold, all the Mexican and Peruvian dreams vanish in an instant, and leave behind the wretched cotton lords and wretched Jews and jobbers to go to the workhouse or to Botany Bay. The whole of the loans are said to amount to about twenty-one or twenty-two millions. It is supposed that twelve millions have actually been sent out in goods. These goods have perhaps been paid for here, but they have been paid for out of English money or by English promises. The money to pay with has come from those who gave money for the South American bonds, and these bond-holders are to be repaid, if repaid at all, *by the South Americans*. If not paid at all, then England will have sent away twelve millions worth of goods for nothing; and this would be the Scotch way of obtaining enormous advantages for the country by laying out its "*surplus capital*" in foreign loans. I shall conclude this subject by inserting a letter which I find in the *Morning Chronicle* of the 18th instant. I perfectly agree with the writer. The editor of the *Morning Chronicle* does not, as appears by the remark which he makes at the head of it; but I shall insert the whole, his remark and all, and add a remark or two of my own.—[See *Register*, vol. 56, p. 556.]

This is a pretty round sum—a sum, the very naming of which would make anybody but half-mad Englishmen stare. To make comparisons with *our own debt* would have little effect, that being so monstrous that every other sum shrinks into nothingness at the sight of it. But let us look at the United States, for they have *a debt*, and a debt is a debt; and this debt of the United States is often cited as an apology for ours, even the parsons having at last come to cite the United States as presenting us with a system of perfection. What, then, is this debt of the United States? Why, it was on the 1st of January 1824 this, 90,177,962; that is to say dollars; that is to say, at four shillings and sixpence the dollar, just *twenty millions sterling;* that is to say, £594,000 *less* than our "surplus capital" men have lent to the South Americans! But now let us see what is the net revenue of this same United States. Why, 20,500,755, that is to say, in sterling money, three millions, three hundred and thirty thousand, and some odd hundreds; that is to say, almost to a mere fraction, a *sixth part* of the whole gross amount of the debt. Observe this well, that the whole of the debt amounts to only six times as much as one single year's net revenue. Then, again, look at the exports of the United States. These exports, in one single year, amount to 74,699,030 dollars, and in pounds sterling £16,599,783. Now, what can the South American state show in this way? Have they any exports? Or, at least, have they any that any man can speak of with certainty? Have they any revenue, wherewith to pay the interest of a debt, when they are borrowing the very means of maintaining themselves now against the bare name of their king? We are often told that the Americans borrowed their money to carry on their revolutionary war with. *Money !* Aye;

a farthing is money, and a double sovereign is no more than money. But surely some regard is to be had to the *quantity ;* some regard is to be had to the amount of the money; and is there any man in his senses that will put the half million, which the Americans borrowed of the Dutch, in competition, that will name on the same day, this half million, with the twenty-one millions and a half borrowed by the South Americans as above stated? In short, it is almost to insult the understandings of my readers, to seem to institute any comparison between the two things; and nothing in the world, short of this gambling, this unprincipled, this maddening paper-money system, could have made men look with patience for one single moment at loans like these, tossed into the air with the hope and expectation of repayment. However, let the bond-owners keep their bonds. Let them feel the sweets of the Small-note Bill, and of the consequent puffing up of the English funds. The affair is theirs. They have rejected my advice; they have listened to the broadsheet; and let them take all the consequences. Let them, with all my heart, die with starvation, and as they expire, let them curse Mr. Brougham's best possible public instructor.

UPHUSBAND (HAMPSHIRE),
Thursday, 24 *Aug.* 1826.

We left Burghclere last evening in the rain; but as our distance was only about seven miles, the consequence was little. The crops of corn, except oats, have been very fine hereabouts; and there are never any pease, nor any beans, grown here. The sainfoin fields, though on these high lands, and though the dry weather has been of such long continuance, look as green as watered meadows, and a great deal more brilliant and beautiful. I have often described this beautiful village (which lies in a deep dell) and its very variously shaped environs, in my *Register* of November 1822. This is one of those countries of chalk and flint and dry-top soil and hard roads and high and bare hills and deep dells, with clumps of lofty trees here and there, which are so many rookeries: this is one of those countries, or rather, approaching towards those countries, of downs and flocks of sheep, which I like so much, which I always get to when I can, and which many people seem to flee from as naturally as men flee from pestilence. They call such countries *naked* and *barren*, though they are, in the summer months, actually covered with meat and with corn.

I saw, the other day, in the *Morning Herald*, London, " best public instructor," that all those had *deceived themselves* who had expected to see the price of agricultural produce brought down by the lessening of the quantity of paper-money. Now in the first place, corn is, on an average, a seventh lower in price than it was last year at this time; and what would it have been if the crop and the stock had now been equal to what they were last year? All in good time, therefore, good Mr. Thwaites. Let us have a little time. The " best public instructors " have, as yet, only fallen, in number sold, about a third, since this time last year. Give them a little time, good Mr. Thwaites, and you will see them come down to your heart's content. Only let us fairly see an end to small notes, and there will soon be not two daily " best public instructors " left in all the " entire " great " British Empire."

But as man is not to live on bread alone, so corn is not the *only* thing that the owners and occupiers of the land have to look to. There are timber, bark, underwood, wool, hides, pigs, sheep, and cattle. All these together make, in amount, four times the corn, at the very least. I know that *all* these have greatly fallen in price since last year; but I am in a sheep and wool country, and can speak positively as to them, which are two articles of very great importance. As to sheep; I am speaking of South Downs, which are the great stock of these counties; as to sheep they have fallen one-third in price since last August, lambs as well as ewes. And as to the wool, it sold, in 1824, at 40s. a tod; it sold last year at 35s. a tod; and it now sells at 19s. a tod! A tod is 28lb. avoirdupois weight; so that the price of South Down wool now is 8d. a pound and a fraction over; and this is, I believe, cheaper than it has ever been known within the memory of the oldest man living! The " best public instructor " may, perhaps, think that sheep and wool are a trifling affair. There are many thousands of farmers who keep each a flock of at least a thousand sheep. An ewe yields about 3lb. of wool, a wether 4lb., a ram 7lb. Calculate, good Mr. Thwaites, what a difference it is when this wool becomes 8d. a pound instead of 17d., and instead of 30d. as it was not many years ago! In short, every middling sheep farmer receives, this year, about £250 less, as the produce of sheep and wool, than he received last year; and, on an average, £250 is more than half his rent.

There is a great falling off in the price of horses, and of all cattle except fat cattle; and observe, when the prospect is good, it shows a rise in the price of lean cattle; not in that of the meat which is just ready to go into the mouth. Prices will go on gradually falling, as they did from 1819 to 1822 inclusive, unless upheld by untoward seasons, or by an issue of assignats; for, mind, it would be no joke, no sham, *this time;* it would be an issue of as real, as *bona fide* assignats as ever came from the mint of any set of rascals that ever robbed and enslaved a people in the names of " liberty and law."

EAST EVERLEY (WILTSHIRE),
Sunday Evening, 27 August.

We set off from Uphusband on Friday, about ten o'clock, the morning having been wet. My sons came round, in the chaise, by Andover and Weyhill, while I came right across the country towards Ludgarshall, which lies in the road from Andover to this place. I never knew the *flies* so troublesome in England as I found them in this ride. I was obliged to carry a great bough, and to keep it in constant motion, in order to make the horse peaceable enough to enable me to keep on his back. It is a country of fields, lanes, and high hedges; so that no *wind* could come to relieve my horse; and, in spite of all I could do, a great part of him was covered with foam from the sweat. In the midst of this, I got, at one time, a little out of my road in or near a place called Tangley. I rode up to the garden-wicket of a cottage, and asked the woman, who had two children, and who seemed to be about thirty years old, which was the way to Ludgarshall, which I knew could not be more than about *four miles* off. She did *not know!* A very neat, smart, and pretty woman; but she did not know the way to this rotten borough, which was, I was sure, only about four miles off! " Well, my dear good woman," said I, " but you *have been* at Ludgarshall? " — " No." — " Nor at Andover? " (six miles another way)—" No."—" Nor at Marlborough? " (nine miles another way)—" No."—" Pray, were you born in this house? " — " Yes." — " And how far have you ever been from this house? "—" Oh! I have been *up in the parish* and over *to Chute.*" That is to say, the utmost extent of her voyages had been about two and a half miles! Let no one laugh at her, and, above all others, let not me, who am convinced that the *facilities* which now exist of *moving human bodies from place to place* are amongst the *curses* of the country, the destroyers of industry, of morals, and, of course, of happiness. It is a great error to suppose that people are rendered stupid by remaining always in the same place. This was a very acute woman, and as well behaved as need to be. There was in July last (last month) a Preston man who had never been further from home than Chorley (about eight or ten miles), and who started off, *on foot*, and went, *alone*, to Rouen, in France, and back again to London, in the space of about ten days; and that, too, without being able to speak, or to understand, a word of French. N.B.—Those gentlemen who, at Green Street, in Kent, were so kind to this man, *upon finding that he had voted for me*, will be pleased to accept of my best thanks. Wilding (that is the man's name) was full of expressions of gratitude towards these gentlemen. He spoke of others who were good to him on his way; and even at Calais he found friends on my account; but he was particularly loud in his praises of the gentlemen in Kent, who had been so good and so kind to him, that he seemed quite in an ecstasy when he talked of their conduct.

Before I got to the rotten borough I came out upon a down, just on the border of the two counties Hampshire and Wiltshire. Here I came up with my sons, and we entered the rotten borough together. It contained some rashers of bacon and a very civil landlady; but it is one of the most mean and beggarly places that man ever set his eyes on. The curse attending corruption seems to be upon it. The look of the place would make one swear that there never was a clean shirt in it since the first stone of it was laid. It must have been a large place once, though it now contains only 479 persons, men, women, and children. The borough is, as to all practical purposes, as much private property as this pen is my private property. Aye, aye! Let the petitioners of Manchester bawl as long as they like against all other evils; but until they touch this *master-evil*, they do nothing at all.

Everley is but about three miles from Ludgarshall, so that we got here in the afternoon of Friday: and in the evening a very heavy storm came and drove away all flies, and made the air delightful. This is a real *down*-country. Here you see miles and miles square without a tree, or hedge, or bush. It is country of greensward. This is the most famous place in all England for *coursing*. I was here, at this very inn, with a party eighteen years ago; and the landlord, who is still the same, recognised me as soon as he saw me. There were forty brace of greyhounds taken out into the field on one of the days, and every brace had one course, and some of them two. The ground is the finest in the world; from two to three miles for the hare to run to cover, and not a stone nor a bush nor a hillock. It was here proved to me that the hare is, by far, the swiftest of all English animals; for I saw three hares, in one day, *run away* from the dogs. To give dog and hare a fair trial there should be but *one* dog. Then, if that dog got so close as to compel the hare *to turn*, that would be a proof that the dog ran fastest. When the dog, or dogs, never get near enough to the hare to induce her to *turn*, she is said, and very justly, to "*run away*" from them; and as I saw three hares do this in one day, I conclude that the hare is the swiftest animal of the two.

This inn is one of the nicest, and, in summer, one of the pleasantest, in England; for I think that my experience in this way will justify me in speaking thus positively. The house is large, the yard and the stables good, the landlord *a farmer* also, and, therefore, no cribbing your horses in hay or straw and yourself in eggs and cream. The garden, which adjoins the south side of the house, is large, of good shape, has a terrace on one side, lies on the slope, consists of well-disposed clumps of shrubs and flowers, and of short grass very neatly kept. In the lower part of the garden there are high trees, and, amongst these, the tulip-tree and the live-oak. Beyond the garden is a large clump of lofty sycamores, and in these a most populous rookery, in which, of all things in the world, I delight. The village, which contains 301 souls, lies to the north of the inn, but adjoining its premises. All the rest, in every direction, is bare down or open arable. I am now sitting at one of the southern windows of this inn, looking across the garden towards the rookery. It is nearly sun-setting; the rooks are skimming and curving over the tops of the trees; while under the branches I see a flock of several hundred sheep coming nibbling their way in from the down and going to their fold.

Now, what ill-natured devil could bring Old Nic Grimshaw into my head in company with these innocent sheep? Why, the truth is this: nothing is *so swift* as *thought*: it runs over a life-time in a moment; and while I was writing the last sentence of the foregoing paragraph, *thought* took me up at the time when I used to wear a smock-frock and to carry a wooden bottle like that shepherd's boy; and, in an instant, it hurried me along through my no very short life of adventure, of toil, of peril, of pleasure, of ardent friendship and not less ardent enmity; and after filling me with wonder that a heart and mind so wrapped up in everything belonging to the gardens, the fields, and the woods should have been condemned to waste themselves away amidst the stench, the noise, and the strife of cities, it brought me *to the present moment*, and sent my mind back to what I have yet to perform about Nicholas Grimshaw and his *ditches !*

My sons set off about three o'clock to-day on their way to Herefordshire, where I intend to join them when I have had a pretty good ride in this country. There is no pleasure in travelling except on horse-back or on foot. Carriages take your body from place to place, and if you merely want to be *conveyed* they are very good; but they enable you to see and to know nothing at all of the country.

EAST EVERLEY,
Monday Morning, 5 *o'clock,* 28 *Aug.* 1826.

A very fine morning; a man, *eighty-two years of age*, just beginning to mow the short-grass in the garden: I thought it, even when I was young, the *hardest work* that man had to do. To *look on*, this work seems nothing; but it tries every sinew in your frame if you go upright and do your work well. This old man never knew how to do it well, and he stoops, and he hangs his scythe wrong; but with all this, it must be a surprising man to mow short-grass as well as he does at *eighty*. *I wish I* may be able to mow short-grass at eighty! That's all I have to say of the matter. I am just setting off for the source of the Avon, which runs from near Marlborough to Salisbury, and thence to the sea; and I intend to pursue it as far as Salisbury. In the distance of thirty miles here are, I see by the books, more than thirty churches. I wish to see, with my own eyes, what evidence there is that those thirty churches were built without hands, without money, and without a congregation; and thus to find matter, if I can, to justify the mad wretches who, from committee-rooms and elsewhere, are bothering this half-distracted nation to death about a " surplus popalashon, mon."

My horse is ready; and the rooks are just gone off to the stubble-fields. These rooks rob the pigs; but they have a *right* to do it. I wonder (upon my soul I do) that there is no lawyer, Scotchman, or parson-justice, to propose a law to punish the rooks for *trespass.*

DOWN THE VALLEY OF THE AVON IN WILTSHIRE

"Thou shalt not muzzle the ox when he treadeth out the corn; and,
The labourer is worthy of his reward."—Deuteronomy, xxv. 4; 1 Cor.
ix. 9; 1 Tim. v. 9.

MILTON,
Monday, 28 August.

I CAME off this morning on the Marlborough road about two
miles, or three, and then turned off, over the downs, in a north-
westerly direction, in search of the source of the Avon river,
which goes down to Salisbury. I had once been at Netheravon,
a village in this valley; but I had often heard this valley described as one of the finest pieces of land in all England; I knew
that there were about thirty parish churches, standing in a
length of about thirty miles, and in an average width of hardly
a mile; and I was resolved to see a little into the *reasons* that
could have induced our fathers to build all these churches,
especially if, as the Scotch would have us believe, there were
but a mere handful of people in England *until of late years*.

The first part of my ride this morning was by the side of Sir
John Astley's park. This man is one of the members of the
county (gallon-loaf Bennet being the other). They say that
he is good to the labouring people; and he ought to be good for
something, being a member of parliament of the Lethbridge and
Dickenson stamp. However, he has got a thumping estate;
though be it borne in mind, the working-people and the fund-
holders and the dead-weight have each their separate mortgage
upon it; of which this baronet has, I dare say, too much justice
to complain, seeing that the amount of these mortgages was
absolutely necessary to carry on Pitt and Perceval and Castlereagh wars; to support Hanoverian soldiers in England; to
fight and beat the Americans on the Serpentine river; to give
Wellington a kingly estate; and to defray the expenses of
Manchester and other yeomanry cavalry; besides all the various
charges of Power-of-Imprisonment Bills and of Six-Acts. These
being the cause of the mortgages, the "worthy baronet" has,
I will engage, too much justice to complain of them.

In steering across the down, I came to a large farm, which

34

a shepherd told me was Milton Hill Farm. This was upon the high land, and before I came to the edge of this *Valley of Avon*, which was my land of promise; or at least, of great expectation; for I could not imagine that thirty churches had been built *for nothing* by the side of a brook (for it is no more during the greater part of the way) thirty miles long. The shepherd showed me the way towards Milton; and at the end of about a mile, from the top of a very high part of the down, with a steep slope towards the valley, I first saw this *Valley of Avon ;* and a most beautiful sight it was! Villages, hamlets, large farms, towers, steeples, fields, meadows, orchards, and very fine timber trees, scattered all over the valley. The shape of the thing is this: on each side *downs*, very lofty and steep in some places, and sloping miles back in other places; but each *out-side* of the valley are downs. From the edge of the downs begin capital *arable fields* generally of very great dimensions, and, in some places, running a mile or two back into little *cross-valleys*, formed by hills of downs. After the corn-fields come *meadows* on each side, down to the *brook* or *river*. The farm-houses, mansions, villages, and hamlets are generally situated in that part of the arable land which comes nearest the meadows.

Great as my expectations had been, they were more than fulfilled. I delight in this sort of country; and I had frequently seen the vale of the Itchen, that of the Bourn, and also that of the Teste in Hampshire; I had seen the vales amongst the South Downs; but I never before saw anything to please me like this valley of the Avon. I sat upon my horse and looked over Milton and Easton and Pewsey for half an hour, though I had not breakfasted. The hill was very steep. A road, going slanting down it, was still so steep, and washed so very deep by the rains of ages, that I did not attempt to *ride* down it, and I did not like to lead my horse, the path was so narrow. So seeing a boy with a drove of pigs going out to the stubbles, I beckoned him to come up to me; and he came and led my horse down for me. But now, before I begin to ride down this beautiful vale, let me give, as well as my means will enable me, a plan or map of it, which I have made in this way: a friend has lent me a very old map of Wiltshire describing the spots where all the churches stand, and also all the spots where manor-houses or mansion-houses stood. I laid a piece of very thin paper upon the map, and thus traced the river upon my paper, putting *figures* to represent the spots where churches stand, and putting *stars* to represent the spots where manor-houses or mansion-

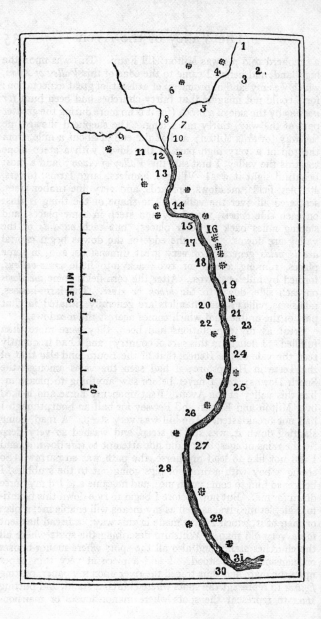

houses formerly stood. Endless is the variety in the shape of the high lands which form this valley. Sometimes the slope is very gentle, and the arable lands go back very far. At others, the downs come out into the valley almost like piers into the sea, being very steep in their sides, as well as their ends towards the valley. They have no slope at their other ends: indeed they have no *back ends,* but run into the main high land. There is also great variety in the width of the valley; great variety in the width of the meadows; but the land appears all to be of the very best; and it must be so, for the farmers confess it.

It seemed to me that one way, and that not, perhaps, the least striking, of exposing the folly, the stupidity, the inanity, the presumption, the insufferable emptiness and insolence and barbarity, of those numerous wretches who have now the audacity to propose to *transport* the people of England, upon the principle of the monster Malthus, who has furnished the unfeeling oligarchs and their toad-eaters with the pretence that *man has a natural propensity to breed faster than food can be raised for the increase;* it seemed to me that one way of exposing this mixture of madness and of blasphemy was to take a look, now that the harvest is in, at the produce, the mouths, the condition, and the changes that have taken place, in a spot like this, which God has favoured with every good that he has had to bestow upon man.

From the top of the hill I was not a little surprised to see, in every part of the valley that my eye could reach, a due, a large, portion of fields of swedish turnips, all looking extremely well. I had found the turnips of both sorts by no means bad from Salt Hill to Newbury; but from Newbury through Burghclere, Highclere, Uphusband, and Tangley, I had seen but few. At and about Ludgarshall and Everley I had seen hardly any. But when I came this morning to Milton Hill Farm, I saw a very large field of what appeared to me to be fine swedish turnips. In the valley, however, I found them much finer, and the fields were very beautiful objects, forming, as their colour did, so great a contrast with that of the fallows and the stubbles, which latter are, this year, singularly clean and bright.

Having gotten to the bottom of the hill, I proceeded on to the village of Milton, the church of which is, in the map, represented by the figure 3. I left Easton (2) away at my right, and I did not go up to Watton Rivers (1) where the river Avon rises, and which lies just close to the south-west corner of Marlborough Forest, and at about 5 or 6 miles from the town of Marlborough. Lower

down the river, as I thought, there lived a friend, who was a
great farmer, and whom I intended to call on. It being my way,
however, always to begin making inquiries soon enough, I asked
the pig-driver where this friend lived; and, to my surprise, I
found that he lived in the parish of Milton. After riding up to
the church, as being the centre of the village, I went on towards
the house of my friend, which lay on my road down the valley.
I have many, many times witnessed agreeable surprise; but I
do not know that I ever in the whole course of my life saw people
so much surprised and pleased as this farmer and his family
were at seeing me. People often *tell* you that they are *glad to
see* you; and in general they speak truth. I take pretty good
care not to approach any house, with the smallest appearance
of a design to eat or drink in it, unless I be *quite sure* of a cordial
reception; but my friend at Fifield (it is in Milton parish) and
all his family really seemed to be delighted beyond all expression.

When I set out this morning, I intended to go all the way
down to the city of Salisbury (31) *to-day;* but I soon found that
to refuse to sleep at Fifield would cost me a great deal more
trouble than a day was worth. So that I made my mind up to
stay in this farm-house, which has one of the nicest gardens, and
it contains some of the finest flowers, that I ever saw, and all is
disposed with as much good taste as I have ever witnessed.
Here I am, then, just going to bed after having spent as pleasant
a day as I ever spent in my life. I have heard to-day that
Birkbeck lost his life by attempting to cross a river on horseback; but if what I have heard besides be true, that life must
have been hardly worth preserving; for they say that he was
reduced to a very deplorable state; and I have heard, from what
I deem unquestionable authority, that his two beautiful and
accomplished daughters are married to two common labourers,
one a Yankee and the other an Irishman, neither of whom has,
probably, a second shirt to his back, or a single pair of shoes to
put his feet into! These poor girls owe their ruin and misery
(if my information be correct), and, at any rate, hundreds besides
Birkbeck himself, owe their utter ruin, the most scandalous
degradation, together with great bodily suffering, to the vanity,
the conceit, the presumption of Birkbeck, who, observe, richly
merited all that he suffered, not excepting his death; for he
sinned with his eyes open; he rejected all advice; he persevered
after he saw his error; he dragged thousands into ruin along with
him; and he most vilely calumniated the man who, after
having most disinterestedly, but in vain, endeavoured to pre-

serve him from ruin, endeavoured to preserve those who were in danger of being deluded by him. When, in 1817, before he set out for America, I was, in Catherine Street, Strand, London, so earnestly pressing him not to go to the back countries, he had one of these daughters with him. After talking to him for some time, and describing the risks and disadvantages of the back countries, I turned towards the daughter and, in a sort of joking way, said: " Miss Birkbeck, take my advice: don't let anybody get *you* more than twenty miles from Boston, New York, Philadelphia, or Baltimore." Upon which he gave me a most *dignified* look and observed: " Miss Birkbeck has a *father*, sir, whom she knows it to be her duty to obey." This snap was enough for me. I saw that this was a man so full of self-conceit that it was impossible to do anything with him. He seemed to me to be bent upon his own destruction. I thought it my duty to warn *others* of their danger: some took the warning; others did not; but he and his brother adventurer, Flower, never forgave me, and they resorted to all the means in their power to do me injury. They did me no injury, no thanks to them; and I have seen them most severely, but most justly, punished.

AMESBURY,
Tuesday, 29 August.

I set off from Fifield this morning, and got here (25 on the map) about one o'clock, with my clothes wet. While they are drying, and while a mutton chop is getting ready, I sit down to make some notes of what I have seen since I left Enford . . . but here comes my dinner: and I must put off my notes till I have dined.

SALISBURY,
Wednesday, 30 August.

My ride yesterday, from Milton to this city of Salisbury, was, without any exception, the most pleasant; it brought before me the greatest number of, to me, interesting objects, and it gave rise to more interesting reflections than I remember ever to have had brought before my eyes, or into my mind, in any one day of my life; and therefore, this ride was, without any exception, the most pleasant that I ever had in my life, as far as my recollection serves me. I got a little wet in the middle of the day; but I got dry again, and I arrived here in very good time, though I went over the Accursed Hill (Old Sarum), and went across to Laverstoke, before I came to Salisbury.

Let us now, then, look back over this part of Wiltshire, and see whether the inhabitants ought to be " transported " by order of the " Emigration Committee," of which we shall see and say more by and by. I have before described this valley generally; let me now speak of it a little more in detail. The farms are all large, and, generally speaking, they were always large, I dare say; bcause *sheep* is one of the great things here; and sheep, in a country like this, must be kept in *flocks*, to be of any profit. The sheep principally manure the land. This is to be done only by *folding ;* and to fold, you must have a *flock*. Every farm has its portion of down, arable, and meadow; and, in many places, the latter are watered meadows, which is a great resource where sheep are kept in flocks; because these meadows furnish grass for the suckling ewes early in the spring; and indeed, because they have always food in them for sheep and cattle of all sorts. These meadows have had no part of the suffering from the drought this year. They fed the ewes and lambs in the spring, and they are now yielding a heavy crop of hay; for I saw men mowing in them, in several places, particularly about Netheravon (18 in the map), though it was raining at the time.

The turnips look pretty well all the way down the valley; but I see very few, except swedish turnips. The early common turnips very nearly all failed, I believe. But the stubbles are beautifully bright; and the rick-yards tell us that the crops are good, especially of wheat. This is not a country of pease and beans, nor of oats, except for home consumption. The crops are wheat, barley, wool and lambs, and these latter not to be sold to butchers, but to be sold, at the great fairs, to those who are going to keep them for some time, whether to breed from or finally to fat for the butcher. It is the pulse and the oats that appear to have failed most this year; and, therefore, this valley has not suffered. I do not perceive that they have many *potatoes;* but what they have of this base root seem to look well enough. It was one of the greatest villains upon earth (Sir Walter Raleigh) who (they say) first brought this root into England. He was hanged at last! What a pity, since he was to be hanged, the hanging did not take place before he became such a mischievous devil as he was in the latter two-thirds of his life!

The stack-yards down this valley are beautiful to behold. They contain from five to fifteen banging wheat-ricks, besides barley-ricks and hay-ricks, and also besides the contents of the barns, many of which exceed a hundred, some two hundred, and I saw one at Pewsey (4 in map), and another at Fittleton (16 in map), each of which exceeded two hundred and fifty feet in length. At a farm which, in the old maps, is called Chissenbury Priory (14 in map), I think I counted twenty-seven ricks of one sort and another, and sixteen or eighteen of them wheat-ricks. I could not conveniently get to the yard without longer delay than I wished to make; but I could not be much out in my counting. A very fine sight this was, and it could not meet the eye without making one look round (and in vain) *to see the people who were to eat all this food ;* and without making one reflect on the horrible, the unnatural, the base and infamous state in which we must be, when projects are on foot, and are openly avowed, for *transporting* those who raise this food, because they want to eat enough of it to keep them alive; and when no project is on foot for transporting the idlers who live in luxury upon this same food; when no project is on foot for transporting pensioners, parsons, or dead-weight people!

A little while before I came to this farm-yard I saw, in one piece, about four hundred acres of wheat-stubble, and I saw a sheep-fold which, I thought, contained an acre of ground, and had in it about four thousand sheep and lambs. The fold was divided into three separate flocks; but the piece of ground was one and the same; and I thought it contained about an acre. At one farm, between Pewsey and Upavon, I counted more than 300 hogs in one stubble. This is certainly the most delightful farming in the world. No ditches, no water-furrows, no drains, hardly any hedges, no dirt and mire, even in the wettest seasons of the year: and though the downs are naked and cold, the valleys are snugness itself. They are, as to the downs, what *ah-ahs !* are in parks or lawns. When you are going over the downs, you look *over* the valleys, as in the case of the *ah-ah ;* and if you be not acquainted with the country, your surprise, when you come to the edge of the hill, is very great. The shelter in these valleys, and particularly where the downs are steep and lofty on the sides, is very complete. Then the trees are everywhere lofty. They are generally elms, with some ashes, which delight in the soil that they find here. There are, almost always, two or three large clumps of trees in every parish, and a rookery or two (not *rag*-rookery) to every parish. By the water's edge there are willows; and to almost every farm there is a fine orchard, the trees being, in general, very fine, and this year they are, in general, well loaded with fruit. So that, all taken together, it seems impossible to find a more beautiful and pleasant country than this, or to imagine any life more easy and happy than men might here lead if they were untormented by an accursed system that takes the food from those that raise it, and gives it to those that do nothing that is useful to man.

Here the farmer has always an abundance of straw. His farm-yard is never without it. Cattle and horses are bedded up to their eyes. The yards are put close under the shelter of a hill, or are protected by lofty and thick-set trees. Every animal seems comfortably situated; and in the dreariest days of winter these are, perhaps, the happiest scenes in the world; or, rather, they would be such, if those, whose labour makes it all, trees, corn, sheep and everything, had but *their fair share* of the produce of that labour. What share they really have of it one cannot exactly say; but I should suppose that every labouring *man* in this valley raises as much food as would suffice for fifty or a hundred persons, fed like himself!

At a farm at Milton there were, according to my calculation, 600 quarters of wheat and 1200 quarters of barley of the present year's crop. The farm keeps, on an average, 1400 sheep, it breeds and rears an usual proportion of pigs, fats the usual proportion of hogs, and, I suppose, rears and fats the usual proportion of poultry. Upon inquiry, I found that this farm was, in point of produce, about one-fifth of the parish. Therefore, the land of this parish produces annually about 3000 quarters of wheat, 6000 quarters of barley, the wool of 7000 sheep, together with the pigs and poultry. Now, then, leaving green, or moist, vegetables out of the question as being things that human creatures, and especially *labouring* human creatures, ought never to use *as sustenance*, and saying nothing at present about milk and butter; leaving these wholly out of the question, let us see how many people the produce of this parish would keep, supposing the people to live all alike, and to have plenty of food and clothing. In order to come at the fact here, let us see what would be the consumption of one family; let it be a family of five persons; a man, wife, and three children, one child big enough to work, one big enough to eat heartily, and one a baby; and this is a pretty fair average of the state of people in the country. Such a family would want 5lb. of bread a day; they would want a pound of mutton a day; they would want two pounds of bacon a day; they would want, on an average, winter and summer, a gallon and a half of beer a day; for I mean that they should live without the aid of the eastern or the western

slave-drivers. If *sweets* were absolutely necessary for the baby, there would be quite *honey* enough in the parish. Now, then, to begin with the bread, a pound of good wheat makes a pound of good bread; for though the offal be taken out, the water is put in; and, indeed, the fact is, that a pound of wheat will make a pound of bread, leaving the offal of the wheat to feed pigs, or other animals, and to produce other human food in this way. The family would, then, use 1825lb. of wheat in the year, which at 60lb. a bushel, would be (leaving out a fraction) 30 bushels, or three quarters and six bushels, *for the year*.

Next comes the mutton, 365lb. for the year. Next the bacon, 730lb. As to the quantity of mutton produced; the sheep are bred here, and not fatted in general; but we may fairly suppose that each of the sheep *kept* here, each of the *standing-stock*, makes, first or last, half a fat sheep; so that a farm that keeps, on an average, 100 sheep, produces annually 50 fat sheep. Suppose the mutton to be 15lb. a quarter, then the family will want, within a trifle of, seven sheep a year. Of bacon or pork, 36 score will be wanted. Hogs differ so much in their propensity to fat that it is difficult to calculate about them: but this is a very good rule: when you see a fat hog, and know how many *scores* he will weigh, set down to his account a sack (half a quarter) of barley for every score of his weight; for, let him have been *educated* (as the French call it) as he may, this will be about the real cost of him when he is fat. A sack of barley will make a score of bacon, and it will not make more. Therefore, the family would want 18 quarters of barley in the year for bacon.

As to the *beer*, 18 gallons to the bushel of malt is very good; but as we allow of no spirits, no wine, and none of the slave produce, we will suppose that a *sixth* part of the beer is *strong* stuff. This would require two bushels of malt to the 18 gallons. The whole would, therefore, take 35 bushels of malt; and a bushel of barley makes a bushel of malt, and by the *increase* pays the expense of malting. Here, then, the family would want, for beer, four quarters and three bushels of barley. The annual consumption of the family, in victuals and drink, would then be as follows:

				Qrs.	Bush.
Wheat	.	.	.	3	6
Barley	.	.	.	22	3
Sheep	.	.	.	7	

This being the case, the 3000 quarters of wheat, which the parish annually produces, would suffice for 800 families. The 6000 quarters of barley would suffice for 207 families. The 3500 fat sheep, being half the number kept, would suffice for 500 families. So that here is produced in the parish of Milton *bread* for 800, *mutton* for 500, and *bacon and beer* for 207 families. Besides victuals and drink, there are clothes, fuel, tools, and household goods wanting; but there are milk, butter, eggs, poultry, rabbits, hares, and partridges, which I have not noticed, and these are all eatables, and are all eaten too. And as to clothing, and, indeed, fuel and all other wants beyond eating and drinking, are there not 7000 fleeces of South Down wool, weighing, all together, 21,000lb., and capable of being made into 8400 yards of broad cloth, at two pounds and a half of wool to the yard? Setting, therefore, the wool, the milk, butter, eggs, poultry, and game against all the wants beyond the solid food and drink, we see that the parish of Milton, that we have under our eye, would give bread to 800 families, mutton to 580, and bacon and beer to 207. The reason why wheat and mutton are produced in a proportion so much greater than the materials for making bacon and beer is that the wheat and the mutton are more loudly demanded *from a distance,* and are much more cheaply conveyed away in proportion to their value. For instance, the wheat and mutton are wanted in the infernal Wen, and some barley is wanted there in the shape of malt; but hogs are not fatted in the Wen, and a larger proportion of the barley is used where it is grown.

Here is, then, bread for 800 families, mutton for 500, and bacon and beer for 207. Let us take the average of the three, and then we have 502 families, for the keeping of whom, and in this good manner too, the parish of Milton yields a sufficiency. In the wool, the milk, butter, eggs, poultry, and game, we have seen ample, and much more than ample, provision for all wants, other than those of mere food and drink. What I have allowed in food and drink is by no means excessive. It is but a pound of bread and a little more than half-a-pound of meat a day to each person on an average; and the beer is not a drop too much. There are no green and moist vegetables included in my account; but there would be some, and they would not do any harm; but no man can say, or, at least, none but a base usurer, who would grind money out of the bones of his own father; no other man can, or will, say that I have been *too liberal* to this family; and yet, good God! what extravagance is here, if the labourers of England be now treated justly!

Is there a family, even amongst those who live the hardest, in the Wen, that would not shudder at the thought of living upon what I have allowed to this family? Yet what do labourers' families get compared to this? The answer to that question ought to make us shudder indeed. The amount of my allowance, compared with the amount of the allowance that labourers now have, is necessary to be stated here, before I proceed further. The wheat 3 qrs. and 6 bushels, at present price (56s. the quarter), amounts to £10 10s. The barley (for bacon and beer) 22 qrs. 3 bushels, at present price (34s. the quarter), amounts to £37 16s. 8d. The seven sheep, at 40s. each, amount to £14. The total is £62 6s. 8d.; and this, observe, for *bare victuals and drink ;* just food and drink enough to keep people in working condition.

What then *do* the labourers get? To what fare has this wretched and most infamous system brought them! Why such a family as I have described is allowed to have, *at the utmost,* only about 9s. a week. The parish allowance is only about 7s. 6d. for the five people, including clothing, fuel, bedding and everything! Monstrous state of things! But let us suppose it to be *nine shillings.* Even that makes only £23 8s. a year, for food, drink, clothing, fuel and everything, whereas I allow £62 6s. 8d. a year for the bare eating and drinking; and that is little enough. Monstrous, barbarous, horrible as this appears, we do not, however, see it in half its horrors; our indignation and rage against this infernal system is not half roused, till we see the small number of labourers who raise all the food and the drink, and, of course, the mere trifling portion of it that they are suffered to retain for their own use.

The parish of Milton does, as we have seen, produce food, drink, clothing, and all other things, enough for 502 families, or 2510 persons upon my allowance, which is a great deal more than three times the present allowance, because the present allowance includes clothing, fuel, tools and everything. Now, then, according to the " Population Return," laid before parliament, this parish contains 500 persons, or, according to my division, one hundred families. So that here are about *one hundred* families to raise food and drink enough, and to raise wool and other things to pay for all other necessaries, for *five hundred* and *two* families! Aye, and five hundred and two families fed and lodged, too, on my liberal scale. Fed and lodged according to the present scale, this one hundred families raise enough to supply more, and many more, than fifteen hundred families; or seven thousand five hundred persons! And yet those who do the work are half starved! In the 100 families there are, we will suppose, 80 able working men, and as many boys, sometimes assisted by the women and stout girls. What a handful of people to raise such a quantity of food! What injustice, what a hellish system it must be, to make those who raise it skin and bone and nakedness, while the food and drink and wool are almost all carried away to be heaped on the fund-holders, pensioners, soldiers, dead-weight, and other swarms of tax-eaters! If such an operation do not need putting an end to, then the devil himself is a saint.

Thus it must be, or much about thus, all the way down this fine and beautiful and interesting valley. There are 29 agricultural parishes, the two last (30 and 31) being in town; being Fisherton and Salisbury. Now, according to the "Population Return," the whole of these 29 parishes contain 9116 persons; or according to my division 1823 families. There is no reason to believe that the proportion that we have seen in the case of Milton does not hold good all the way through; that is, there is no reason to suppose that the produce does not exceed the consumption in every other case in the same degree that it does in the case of Milton. And indeed, if I were to judge from the number of houses and the number of ricks of corn, I should suppose that the excess was still greater in several of the other parishes. But supposing it to be no greater; supposing the same proportion to continue all the way from Watton Rivers (1 in map) to Stratford Dean (29 in map), then here are 9116 persons raising food and raiment sufficient for 45,580 persons, fed and lodged according to my scale; and sufficient for 136,740 persons, according to the scale on which the unhappy labourers of this fine valley are now fed and lodged!

And yet there is an "*emigration committee*" sitting to devise the means of getting *rid*, not of the idlers, not of the pensioners, not of the dead-weight, not of the parsons (to "relieve" whom we have seen the poor labourers taxed to the tune of a million and a half of money), not of the soldiers; but to devise means of getting rid of *these working people*, who are grudged even the miserable morsel that they get! There is in the men calling themselves "English country gentlemen" something superlatively base. They are, I sincerely believe, the most cruel, the most unfeeling, the most brutally insolent: but I know, I can

prove, I can safely take my oath, that they are the most base of all the creatures that God ever suffered to disgrace the human shape. The base wretches know well that the *taxes* amount to more than *sixty millions* a year, and that the *poor-rates* amount to about *seven millions ;* yet, while the cowardly reptiles never utter a word against the taxes, they are incessantly railing against the poor-rates, though it is (and they know it) the taxes that make the paupers. The base wretches know well that the sum of money given, even to the fellows that gather the taxes, is greater in amount than the poor-rates; the base wretches know well that the money given to the dead-weight (who ought not to have a single farthing) amounts to more than the poor receive out of the rates; the base wretches know well that the common foot soldier now receives more pay per week (7s. 7d.) exclusive of clothing, firing, candle, and lodging; the base wretches know that the common foot soldier receives more to go down his own single throat than the overseers and magistrates allow to a working man, his wife and three children; the base wretches know all this well; and yet their railings are confined to the *poor* and the *poor-rates ;* and it is expected that they will, next session, urge the parliament to pass a law to enable overseers and vestries and magistrates *to transport paupers beyond the seas !* They are base enough for this, or for anything; but the whole system will go to the devil long before they will get such an act passed; long before they will see perfected this consummation of their infamous tyranny.

It is manifest enough that the *population* of this valley was, at one time, many times over what it is now; for, in the first place, what were the twenty-nine churches built *for ?* The population of the twenty-nine parishes is now but little more than one-half of that of the single parish of Kensington; and there are several of the churches bigger than the church at Kensington. What, then, should all these churches have been built *for ?* And besides, where did the hands come from? And where did the money come from? These twenty-nine churches would now not only hold all the inhabitants, men, women, and children, but all the household goods, and tools, and implements, of the whole of them, farmers and all, if you leave out the waggons and carts. In three instances, Fifield, Milston, and Roach Fen (17, 23, and 24), the *church-porches* will hold all the inhabitants, even down to the bed-ridden and the babies. What, then, will any man believe that these churches were built for such little knots of people? We are told about the *great* superstition of our fathers, and of their readiness to gratify the priests by building altars and other religious edifices. But we must think those priests to have been most devout creatures indeed if we believe that they chose to have the money laid out in *useless* churches, rather than have it put into their own pockets! At any rate, we all know that Protestant priests have no whims of *this sort;* and that they never lay out upon churches any money that they can, by any means, get hold of.

But suppose that we were to believe that the priests had, in old times, this unaccountable taste; and suppose we were to believe that a knot of people, who might be crammed into a church-porch, were seized, and very frequently too, with the the desire of having a big church to go to; we must, after all this, believe that this knot of people were more than *giants*, or that they had surprising *riches*, else we cannot believe that they had *the means* of gratifying the strange wishes of their priests and their own not less strange *piety* and *devotion*. Even if we could believe that they thought that they were paving their way to heaven by building churches which were a hundred times too large for the population, still we cannot believe that the building could have been effected without bodily force; and where was this force to come from, if the people were not more numerous than they now are? What, again, I ask, were these twenty-nine churches stuck up not a mile from each other; what were twenty-nine churches made *for,* if the population had been no greater than it is now?

But, in fact, you plainly see all the traces of a great ancient population. The churches are almost all large, and built in the best manner. Many of them are very fine edifices; very costly in the building; and in the cases where the body of the church has been altered in the repairing of it, so as to make it smaller, the *tower*, which everywhere defies the hostility of time, shows you what the church must formerly have been. This is the case in several instances; and there are two or three of these villages which must formerly have been *market-towns*, and particularly Pewsey and Upavon (4 and 13). There are now no less than nine of the parishes, out of the twenty-nine, that have either no parsonage-houses, or have such as are in such a state that a parson will not, or cannot, live in them. Three of them are without any parsonage-houses at all, and the rest are become poor, mean, falling-down places. This latter is the case at Upavon, which was formerly a very considerable place. Nothing can more clearly show, than this, that all, as far as buildings and population are concerned, has been long upon the decline and decay. Dilapidation after dilapidation have, at last, almost effaced even the parsonage-houses, and that too in *defiance of the law*, ecclesiastical as well as civil. The land remains; and the crops and the sheep come as abundantly as ever; but they are now sent almost wholly away, instead of remaining as formerly, to be, in great part, consumed in these twenty-nine parishes.

The *stars*, in my map, mark the spots where manor-houses, or gentlemen's mansions, formerly stood, and stood, too, only about sixty years ago. Every parish had its manor-house in the first place; and then there were, down this valley, twenty-one others; so that, in this distance of about thirty miles, there stood fifty mansion-houses. Where are they *now?* I believe there are but eight that are at all worthy of the name of mansion-houses; and even these are but poorly kept up, and, except in two or three instances, are of no benefit to the labouring people; they employ but few persons; and, in short, do not half supply the place of any eight of the old mansions. All these mansions, all these parsonages, aye, and their goods and furniture, together with the clocks, the brass kettles, the brewing-vessels, the good bedding and good clothes and good furniture, and the stock in pigs, or in money, of the inferior classes, in this series of once populous and gay villages and hamlets; all these have been by the accursed system of taxing and funding and paper-money, by the well-known exactions of the state, and by the not less real, though less generally understood, extortions of the *monopolies* arising out of paper-money; all these have been, by these accursed means, conveyed away, out of this valley, to the haunts of the tax-eaters and the monopolisers. There are many of the *mansion-houses* the ruins of which you yet behold. At Milton (3 in my map) there are two mansion-houses, the walls and the roofs of which yet remain, but which are falling gradually to pieces, and the garden walls are crumbling down. At Enford (15 in my map) Bennet, the member for the county, had a large mansion-house, the stables of which are yet standing. In several places I saw, still remaining, indubitable traces of an ancient manor-house, namely a dove-cote or pigeon-house. The poor pigeons have kept possession of their heritage, from generation to generation, and so have the rooks, in their several rookeries, while the paper-system has swept away, or rather swallowed-up, the owners of the dove-cotes and of the lofty trees, about forty families of which owners have been ousted in this one valley, and have become dead-weight creatures, tax-gatherers, barrack-fellows, thief-takers, or, perhaps, paupers or thieves.

Senator Snip congratulated, some years ago, that preciously honourable " Collective *Wisdom* " of which he is a most worthy member; Snip congratulated it on the success of the late war in creating capital! Snip is, you must know, a great *feelosofer*, and a not less great *feenanceer*. Snip cited, as a proof of the great and glorious effects of paper-money, the new and fine houses in London, the new streets and squares, the new roads, new canals and bridges. Snip was not, I dare say, aware that this same paper-money had destroyed forty mansion-houses in this Vale of Avon, and had taken away all the goods, all the substance, of the little gentry and of the labouring class. Snip was not, I dare say, aware that this same paper-money had, in this one vale of only thirty miles long, dilapidated and, in some cases, wholly demolished, nine out of twenty-nine even of the parsonage-houses. I told Snip at the time (1821) that paper-money could create no valuable thing. I begged Snip to bear this in mind. I besought all my readers, and particularly Mr. Mathias Atwood (one of the members for *Lowther*-town), not to believe that paper-money ever did, or ever could, *create* anything of any value. I besought him to look well into the matter, and assured him that he would find that though paper-money could *create* nothing of value, it was able to *transfer* everything of value; able to strip a little gentry; able to dilapidate even parsonage-houses; able to rob gentlemen of their estates, and labourers of their Sunday-coats and their barrels of beer; able to snatch the dinner from the board of the reaper or the mower, and to convey it to the barrack-table of the Hessian or Hanoverian grenadier; able to take away the wool that ought to give warmth to the bodies of those who rear the sheep, and put it on the backs of those who carry arms to keep the poor, half-famished shepherds in order!

I have never been able clearly to comprehend what the beastly Scotch *feelosofers* mean by their " national wealth;" but, as far as I can understand them, this is their meaning: that national wealth means that which is *left* of the products of the country over and above what is *consumed*, or *used*, by those whose labour causes the products to be. This being the notion, it follows, of course, that the *fewer* poor devils you can screw the products out of, the *richer* the nation is.

This is, too, the notion of Burdett as expressed in his silly and most nasty, musty aristocratic speech of last session. What, then, is to be done with this *over-produce*? Who is to have it? Is it to go to pensioners, placemen, tax-gatherers, dead-weight people, soldiers, gendarmerie, police-people, and, in short, to whole millions *who do no work at all*? Is this a cause of "national wealth?" Is a nation made *rich* by taking the food and clothing from those who create them, and giving them to those who do nothing of any use? Aye, but this over-produce may be given to *manufacturers*, and to those who supply the food-raisers with what they want besides food. Oh! but this is merely an *exchange* of one valuable thing for another valuable thing; it is an exchange of labour in Wiltshire for labour in Lancashire; and, upon the whole, here is no *over-production*. If the produce be exported, it is the same thing: it is an exchange of one sort of labour for another. But *our course* is that there is not an exchange; that those who labour, no matter in what way, have a large part of the fruit of their labour taken away, and receive nothing in exchange. If the over-produce of this Valley of Avon were given, by the farmers, to the weavers in Lancashire, to the iron and steel chaps of Warwickshire, and to other makers or sellers of useful things, there would come an abundance of all these useful things into this valley from Lancashire and other parts; but if, as is the case, the over-produce goes to the fund-holders, the dead-weight, the soldiers, the lord and lady and master and miss pensioners and sinecure people; if the over-produce go to them, as a very great part of it does, nothing, not even the parings of one's nails, can come back to the valley in exchange. And can this operation, then, add to the "national wealth?" It adds to the "wealth" of those who carry on the affairs of state; it fills their pockets, those of their relatives and dependents; it fattens all tax-eaters; but it can give no wealth to the "nation," which means the whole of the people. National wealth means the commonwealth or com-monweal; and these mean, the general good, or happiness, of the people, and the safety and honour of the state; and these are not to be secured by robbing those who labour in order to support a large part of the community in idleness. Devizes is the market-town to which the corn goes from the greater part of this valley. If, when a waggon-load of wheat goes off in the morning, the waggon came back at night loaded with cloth, salt, or something or other, equal in value to the wheat, except what might be necessary to leave with the shopkeeper as his profit; then, indeed, the people might see the waggon go off without tears in their eyes. But, now, they see it go to carry away, and to bring next to nothing in return.

What a *twist* a head must have before it can come to the conclusion that the nation gains in wealth by the government being able to cause the work to be done by those who have hardly any share in the fruit of the labour! What a *twist* such a head must have! The Scotch *feelosofers*, who seem all to have been, by nature, formed for negro-drivers, have an insuperable objection to all those establishments and customs which occasion *holidays*. They call them a great hindrance, a great bar to industry, a great drawback from "national wealth." I wish each of these unfeeling fellows had a spade put into his hand for ten days, only ten days, and that he were compelled to dig only just as much as one of the common labourers at Fulham. The metaphysical gentleman would, I believe, soon discover the *use of holidays!* But *why* should men, why should *any* men, work *hard?* Why, I ask, should they work incessantly, if working part of the days of the week be sufficient? Why should the people at Milton, for instance, work incessantly, when they now raise food and clothing and fuel and every necessary to maintain well five times their number? Why should they not have some holidays? And, pray, say, thou conceited Scotch feelosofer, how the "national wealth" can be increased by making these people work incessantly, that they may raise food and clothing, to go to feed and clothe people who do not work at all?

The state of this valley seems to illustrate the infamous and really diabolical assertion of Malthus, which is, that the human kind have a natural tendency *to increase beyond the means of sustenance for them.* Hence all the schemes of this and the other Scotch writers for what they call checking population. Now look at this Valley of Avon. Here the people raise nearly twenty times as much food and clothing as they consume. They raise five times as much even according to my scale of living. They have been doing this for many, many years. They have been doing it for several generations. Where, then, is their natural tendency to increase beyond the means of sustenance for them? Beyond, indeed, the means of that sustenance which a system like this will leave them. Say that, Sawneys, and I agree with you. Far beyond the means that the taxing and monopolising system will leave in their hands: that is very true; for it leaves them nothing but the scale of the poor-book: they must cease to breed at all, or they must exceed this mark; but the *earth*, give them their fair share of its products, will always give sustenance in sufficiency to those who apply to it by skilful and diligent labour.

The villages down this Valley of Avon, and, indeed, it was the same in almost every part of this county, and in the north and west of Hampshire also, used to have great employment for the women and children in the carding and spinning of wool for the making of broad-cloth. This was a very general employment for the women and girls; but it is now wholly gone; and this has made a vast change in the condition of the people, and in the state of property and of manners and of morals. In 1816, I wrote and published a *Letter to the Luddites*, the object of which was to combat their hostility to the use of machinery. The arguments I there made use of were general. I took the matter in the abstract. The *principles* were all correct enough; but their application cannot be universal; and we have a case here before us, at this moment, which, in my opinion, shows that the mechanic inventions, pushed to the extent that they have been, have been productive of great calamity to this country, and that they will be productive of still greater calamity; unless, indeed, it be their brilliant destiny to be the immediate cause of putting an end to the present system.

The greater part of manufactures consists of *clothing* and *bedding*. Now, if by using a machine, we can get our coat with less labour than we got it before, the machine is a desirable thing. But, then, mind, we must have the machine at home, and we ourselves must have the profit of it; for if the machine be elsewhere; if it be worked by other hands; if other persons have the profit of it; and if, in consequence of the existence of the machine, we have hands at home who have nothing to do, and whom we must keep, then the machine is an injury to us, however advantageous it may be to those who use it, and whatever traffic it may occasion with foreign states.

Such is the case with regard to this cloth-making. The machines are at Upton-Level, Warminster, Bradford, Westbury, and Trowbridge, and here are some of the hands in the Valley of Avon. This valley raises food and clothing; but in order to raise them it must have *labourers*. These are absolutely necessary; for without them this rich and beautiful valley becomes worth nothing except to wild animals and their pursuers. The labourers are *men* and *boys*. Women and girls occasionally; but the men and the boys are as necessary as the light of day, or as the air and the water. Now if beastly Malthus, or any of his nasty disciples, can discover a mode of having men and boys without having women and girls, then, certainly, the machine must be a good thing; but if this valley must absolutely have the women and the girls, then the machine, by leaving them with nothing to do, is a mischievous thing and a producer of most dreadful misery. What, with regard to the poor, is the great complaint now? Why, that the *single man* does not receive the same, or anything like the same, wages as the *married* man. Aye, it is the wife and girls that are the burden; and to be sure a burden they must be, under a system of taxation like the present, and with no work to do. Therefore, whatever may be saved in labour by the machine is no benefit, but an injury to the mass of the people. For, in fact, all that the women and children earned was so much clear addition to what the family earns now. The greatest part of the clothing in the United States of America is made by the farm women and girls. They do almost the whole of it; and all that they do is done at home. To be sure, they might buy cheap; but they must buy for less than nothing, if it would not answer their purpose to *make* the things.

The survey of this valley is, I think, the finest answer in the world to the "Emigration Committee" fellows, and to Jerry Curteis (one of the members for Sussex), who has been giving "evidence" before it. I shall find out, when I can get to see the *report*, what this "Emigration Committee" would be *after*. I remember that last winter a young woman complained to one of the police justices that the overseers of some parish were going to transport her orphan brother to Canada because he became chargeable to their parish! I remember also, that the justice said that the intention of the overseers was "premature," for that "the bill had not yet passed"! This was rather an ugly story; and I do think that we shall find that there have been, and are, some pretty propositions before this "Committee." We shall see all about the matter, however, by and by; and when we get the transporting project fairly before us, shall we not then loudly proclaim "the envy of surrounding nations and admiration of the world"!

But what ignorance, impudence, and insolence must those base wretches have, who propose to transport the labouring people, as being too numerous, while the produce which is obtained by their labour is more than sufficient for three, four, or five, or even ten times their numbers! Jerry Curteis, who has, it seems, been a famous witness on this occasion, says that

poor people, for all that." *They ?* " said I, " who is *they ?* "
He was silent. " Oh, no, no! my friend," said I, " it is not
they ; it is that Accursed Hill that has robbed you of the supper
that you ought to find smoking on the table when you get
home." I gave him the price of a pot of beer, and on I went,
leaving the poor dejected assemblage of skin and bone to wonder
at my words.

The hill is very steep, and I dismounted and led my horse up.
Being as near to the top as I could conveniently get, I stood a
little while reflecting, not so much on the changes which that
hill had seen, as on the changes, the terrible changes, which, in
all human probability, it had *yet to see,* and which it would have
greatly *helped to produce.* It was impossible to stand on this
accursed spot without swelling with indignation against the
base and plundering and murderous sons of corruption. I have
often wished, and I, speaking out loud, expressed the wish now;
" May that man perish for ever and ever, who, having the power,
neglects to bring to justice the perjured, the suborning, the
insolent and perfidious miscreants, who openly sell their country's
rights and their own souls."

From the Accursed Hill I went to Laverstoke where " Jemmy
Burrough " (as they call him here), the judge, lives. I have not
heard much about " Jemmy " since he tried and condemned the
two young men who had wounded the game-keepers of Ashton
Smith and Lord Palmerston. His lordship (Palmerston) is, I
see, making a tolerable figure in the newspapers as a *share-man !*
I got into Salisbury about half-past seven o'clock, less tired than
I recollect ever to have been after so long a ride; for, including
my several crossings of the river and my deviations to look at
churches and farm-yards and rick-yards, I think I must have
ridden nearly forty miles.

FROM SALISBURY TO WARMINSTER, FROM WAR-MINSTER TO FROME, FROM FROME TO DEVIZES, AND FROM DEVIZES TO HIGHWORTH

" Hear this, O ye that swallow up the needy, even to make the poor of the land to fail: saying, When will the new moon be gone that we may sell corn? And the Sabbath, that we may set forth wheat, making the ephah small and the shekel great, and falsifying the balances by deceit; that we may buy the poor for silver, and the needy for a pair of shoes; yea, and sell the refuse of the wheat? Shall not the land tremble for this; and every one mourn that dwelleth therein? I will turn your feasting into mourning, saith the Lord God, and your songs into lamentations."—Amos, viii. 4 to 10.

HEYTESBURY (WILTS),
Thursday, 31 August 1826.

THIS place, which is one of the rotten boroughs of Wiltshire, and which was formerly a considerable town, is now but a very miserable affair. Yesterday morning I went into the cathedral at Salisbury about 7 o'clock. When I got into the nave of the church, and was looking up and admiring the columns and the roof, I heard a sort of *humming*, in some place which appeared to be in the transept of the building. I wondered what it was, and made my way towards the place whence the noise appeared to issue. As I approached it, the noise seemed to grow louder. At last I thought I could distinguish the sounds of the human voice. This encouraged me to proceed; and still following the sound, I at last turned in at a doorway to my left, where I found a priest and his congregation assembled. It was a parson of some sort, with a white covering on him, and five women and four men: when I arrived there were five couple of us. I joined the congregation, until they came to the *litany ;* and then, being monstrously hungry, I did not think myself bound to stay any longer. I wonder what the founders would say if they could rise from the grave and see such a congregation as this in this most magnificent and beautiful cathedral? I wonder what they would say if they could know *to what purpose* the endowments of this cathedral are now applied; and above all things, I wonder what they would say if they could see the half-starved labourers that now minister to the luxuries of those who wallow in the wealth of those endowments. There is one thing, at any rate,

58

that might be abstained from, by those that revel in the riches of those endowments; namely, to abuse and blackguard those of our forefathers from whom the endowments came, and who erected the edifice, and carried so far towards the skies that beautiful and matchless spire, of which the present possessors have the impudence to boast, while they represent as ignorant and benighted creatures those who conceived the grand design, and who executed the scientific and costly work. These fellows, in big white wigs, of the size of half a bushel, have the audacity, even within the walls of the cathedrals themselves, to rail against those who founded them; and Rennell and Sturges, while they were actually, literally, fattening on the spoils of the monastery of St. Swithin, at Winchester, were publishing abusive pamphlets against that catholic religion which had given them their very bread. For my part, I could not look up at the spire and the whole of the church at Salisbury without feeling that I lived in degenerate times. Such a thing never could be made *now*. We *feel* that, as we look at the building. It really does appear that if our forefathers had not made these buildings we should have forgotten, before now, what the Christian religion was!

At Salisbury, or very near to it, four other rivers fall into the Avon. The Wyly river, the Nadder, the Born, and another little river that comes from Norrington. These all become one, at last, just below Salisbury, and then, under the name of the Avon, wind along down and fall into the sea at Christchurch. In coming from Salisbury, I came up the road which runs pretty nearly parallel with the river Wyly, which river rises at Warminster and in the neighbourhood. This river runs down a valley twenty-two miles long. It is not so pretty as the valley of the Avon; but it is very fine in its whole length from Salisbury to this place (Heytesbury). Here are watered meadows nearest to the river on both sides; then the gardens, the houses, and the corn-fields. After the corn-fields come the downs; but, generally speaking, the downs are not so bold here as they are on the sides of the Avon. The downs do not come out in promontories so often as they do on the sides of the Avon. The *Ah-ah!* if I may so express it, is not so deep, and the sides of it not so steep, as in the case of the Avon; but the villages are as frequent; there is more than one church in every mile, and there has been a due proportion of mansion-houses demolished and defaced. The farms are very fine up this vale, and the meadows, particularly at a place called Stapleford, are singularly fine. They had just been mow(d at Stapleford, and the hay carried off. At Stapleford there is a little cross valley, running up between two hills of the down. There is a little run of water about a yard wide at this time, coming down this little vale across the road into the river. The little vale runs up three miles. It does not appear to be half a mile wide; but in those three miles there are four churches; namely, Stapleford, Uppington, Berwick St. James, and Winterborne Stoke. The present population of these four villages is 769 souls, men, women, and children, the whole of whom could very conveniently be seated in the chancel of the church at Stapleford. Indeed, the church and parish of Uppington seem to have been united with one of the other parishes, like the parish in Kent which was united with North Cray, and not a single house of which now remains. What were these four churches *built for* within the distance of three miles? There are three parsonage-houses still remaining; but, and it is a very curious fact, neither of them good enough for the parson to live in! Here are seven hundred and sixty souls to be taken care of, but there is no parsonage-house for a soul-curer to stay in, or at least that he *will* stay in; and all the three parsonages are, in the return laid before parliament, represented to be no better than miserable labourers' cottages, though the parish of Winterborne Stoke has a church sufficient to contain two or three thousand people. The truth is, that the parsons have been receiving the revenues of the livings, and have been suffering the parsonage-houses to fall into decay. Here were two or three mansion-houses, which are also gone, even from the sides of this little run of water.

To-day has been exceedingly hot. Hotter, I think, for a short time, than I ever felt it in England before. In coming through a village called Wishford, and mounting a little hill, I thought the heat upon my back was as great as I had ever felt it in my life. There were thunderstorms about, and it had rained at Wishford a little before I came to it.

My next village was one that I had lived in for a short time, when I was only about ten or eleven years of age. I had been sent down with a horse from Farnham, and I remember that I went by *Stonehenge*, and rode up and looked at the stones. From Stonehenge I went to the village of Steeple Langford, where I remained from the month of June till the fall of the year. I remembered the beautiful villages up and down this valley. I also remembered, very well, that the women at Steeple Langford used to card and spin dyed wool. I was, therefore, some-

what filled with curiosity to see this Steeple Langford again;
and indeed, it was the recollection of this village that made me
take a ride into Wiltshire this summer. I have, I dare say,
a thousand times talked about this Steeple Langford and about
the beautiful farms and meadows along this valley. I have
talked of these to my children a great many times; and I formed
the design of letting two of them see this valley this year, and to
go through Warminster to Stroud, and so on to Gloucester and
Hereford. But when I got to Everley, I found that they would
never get along fast enough to get into Herefordshire in time
for what they intended; so that I parted from them in the
manner I have before described. I was resolved, however, to
see Steeple Langford myself, and I was impatient to get to it,
hoping to find a public-house, and a stable to put my horse in,
to protect him, for a while, against the flies, which tormented
him to such a degree that to ride him was work as hard as
threshing. When I got to Steeple Langford, I found no public-
house, and I found it a much more miserable place than I had
remembered it. The *Steeple*, to which it owed its distinctive
appellation, was gone; and the place altogether seemed to me
to be very much altered for the worse. A little further on,
however, I came to a very famous inn, called Deptford Inn,
which is in the parish of Wyly. I stayed at this inn till about
four o'clock in the afternoon. I remembered Wyly very well,
and thought it a gay place when I was a boy. I remembered
a very beautiful garden belonging to a rich farmer and miller.
I went to see it; but, alas! though the statues in the water and
on the grass-plat were still remaining, everything seemed to be
in a state of perfect carelessness and neglect. The living of this
parish of Wyly was lately owned by Dampier (a brother of the
judge), who lived at, and I believe had the living of, Meon Stoke
in Hampshire. This fellow, I believe, never saw the parish of
Wyly but once, though it must have yielded him a pretty good
fleece. It is a rectory, and the great tithes must be worth, I
should think, six or seven hundred pounds a year, at the least.

It is a part of our system to have certain *families*, who have
no particular merit, but who are to be maintained, without
why or wherefore, at the public expense, in some shape, or
under some name, or other, it matters not much what shape or
what name. If you look through the old list of pensioners,
sinecurists, parsons, and the like, you will find the same names
everlastingly recurring. They seem to be a sort of creatures
that have an *inheritance in the public carcass*, like the maggots

that some people have in their skins. This family of Dampier seems to be one of those. What, in God's name, should have made one of these a bishop and the other a judge! I never heard of the smallest particle of talent that either of them possessed. This rector of Wyly was another of them. There was no harm in them that I know of, beyond that of living upon the public; but where were their merits? They had none to distinguish them and to entitle them to the great sums they received; and under any other system than such a system as this they would, in all human probability, have been gentlemen's servants or little shopkeepers. I dare say there is some of the *breed* left; and, if there be, I would pledge my existence that they are, in some shape or other, feeding upon the public. However, thus it must be, until that change come which will put an end to men paying *fourpence* in tax upon a pot of beer.

This Deptford Inn was a famous place of meeting for the *yeomanry cavalry* in glorious anti-jacobin times, when wheat was twenty shillings a bushel, and when a man could be crammed into gaol for years for only *looking* awry. This inn was a glorious place in the days of Peg Nicholson and her knights. Strangely altered now. The shape of the garden shows you what revelry used to be carried on here. Peel's bill gave this inn, and all belonging to it, a terrible souse. The unfeeling brutes, who used to brandish their swords, and swagger about, at the news of what was called " a victory," have now to lower their scale in clothing, in drink, in eating, in dress, in horseflesh, and everything else. They are now a lower sort of men than they were. They look at their rusty sword and their old dusty helmet and their once gay regimental jacket. They do not hang these up now in the " parlour " for everybody to see them: they hang them up in their bedrooms, or in a cockloft; and when they meet their eye, they look at them as a cow does at a bastard calf, or as the bridegroom does at a girl that the over-seers are about to compel him to marry. If their children should happen to see these implements of war twenty or thirty years hence, they will certainly think that their fathers were the greatest fools that ever walked the face of the earth; and that will be a most filial and charitable way of thinking of them; for it is not from ignorance that they have sinned, but from excessive baseness; and when any of them now complain of those acts of the government which strip them (as the late Order in Council does) of a fifth part of their property in an hour, let them recollect their own base and malignant conduct towards those persecuted reformers, who, if they had not been suppressed by these very yeomen, would long ago have put an end to the cause of that ruin of which these yeomen now complain. When they complain of their ruin, let them remember the toasts which they drank in anti-jacobin times; let them remember their base and insulting exultations on the occasion of the 16th of August at Manchester; let them remember their cowardly abuse of men who were endeavouring to free their country from that horrible scourge which they themselves now feel.

Just close by this Deptford Inn is the farm-house of the farm where that Gourlay lived, who has long been making a noise in the Court of Chancery, and who is now, I believe, confined in some place or other for having assaulted Mr. Brougham. This fellow, who is confined, the newspapers tell us, on a charge of being insane, is certainly one of the most malignant devils that I ever knew anything of in my life. He went to Canada about the time that I went last to the United States. He got into a quarrel with the government there about something, I know not what. He came to see me, at my house in the neighbourhood of New York, just before I came home. He told me his Canada story. I showed him all the kindness in my power, and he went away, knowing that I was just then coming to England. I had hardly got home before the Scotch newspapers contained communications from a person, pretending to derive his information from Gourlay, relating to what Gourlay had described as having passed between him and me; and which description was a tissue of most abominable falsehoods, all having a direct tendency to do injury to me, who had never, either by word or deed, done anything that could possibly have a tendency to do injury to this Gourlay. What the vile Scotch newspapers had begun, the malignant reptile himself continued after his return to England, and, in an address to Lord Bathurst, endeavoured to make his court to the government by the most foul, false, and detestable slanders upon me, from whom, observe, he had never received any injury, or attempt at injury, in the whole course of his life; whom he had visited; to whose house he had gone, of his own accord, and that too, as he said, out of *respect* for me; endeavoured, I say, to make his court to the government by the most abominable slanders against me. He is now, even now, putting forth, under the form of letters to me, a revival of what he pretends was a *conversation* that passed between us at my house near New York. Even if what he says were true, none but caitiffs as base as those who conduct the English newspapers would give circulation to his letters, containing, as they must, the substance of a conversation purely private. But I never had any conversation with him: I never talked to him at all about the things that he is now bringing forward: I heard the fellow's stories about Canada: I thought he told me lies; and, besides, I did not care a straw whether his stories were true or not; I looked upon him as a sort of gambling adventurer; but I treated him, as is the fashion of the country in which I was, with great civility and hospitality. There are two fellows of the name of Jacob and Johnson at Winchester, and two fellows at Salisbury of the name of Brodie and Dowding. These reptiles publish, each couple of them, a newspaper; and in these newspapers they seem to take particular delight in calumniating me. The two Winchester fellows insert the letters of this half crazy, half cunning, Scotchman, Gourlay; the other fellows insert still viler slanders; and if I had seen one of their papers before I left Salisbury which I have seen since, I certainly would have given Mr. Brodie something to make him remember me. This fellow, who was a little coal-merchant but a short while ago, is now, it seems, a paper-money maker, as well as a news-paper maker. Stop, Master Brodie, till I go to Salisbury again, and see whether I do not give you a *check*, even such as you did not receive during the late run! Gourlay, amongst other whims, took it into his head to write against the poor laws, saying that they were a bad thing. He found, however, at last, that they were necessary to keep him from starving; for he came down to Wyly, three or four years ago, and threw himself upon the parish. The overseers, who recollected what a swaggering blade it was, when it came here to teach the moon-rakers " hoo to farm, mon," did not see the sense of keeping him like a gentleman; so they set him to crack stones upon the highway; and that set him off again, pretty quickly. The farm that he rented is a very fine farm, with a fine large farm-house to it. It is looked upon as one of the best farms in the country: the present occupier is a farmer born in the neighbourhood; a man such as ought to occupy it; and Gourlay, who came here with his Scotch impudence to teach others how to farm, is much about where and how he ought to be. Jacob and Johnson, of Winchester, know perfectly well that all the fellow says about me is lies: they know also that their parson readers know that it is a mass of lies: they further know that the parsons know that they know that it is a mass of lies; but they know that their paper will sell the better for that; they know that to circulate lies about me will get them money, and this is what they do it for, and such is the character of English newspapers, and of a great part of the readers of those newspapers. Therefore, when I hear of people " suffering; " when I hear of people being " ruined; " when I hear of " unfortunate families; " when I hear a talk of this kind, I stop before I either express or feel compassion, to ascertain *who* and *what* the sufferers are; and whether they have or have not participated in, or approved of, acts like those of Jacob and Johnson and Brodie and Dowding; for, if they have, if they have malignantly calumniated those who have been labouring to prevent their ruin and misery, then a crushed earwig, or spider, or eft, or toad, is as much entitled to the compassion of a just and sensible man. Let the reptiles perish: it would be injustice; it would be to fly in the face of morality and religion to express sorrow for their ruin. They themselves have felt for no man, and for the wife and children of no man, if that man's public virtues thwarted their own selfish views, or even excited their groundless fears. They have signed addresses applauding everything tyrannical and inhuman. They have seemed to glory in the shame of their country, to rejoice in its degradation, and even to exult in the shedding of innocent blood, if these things did but tend, as they thought, to give them permanent security in the enjoyment of their unjust gains. Such has been their conduct; they are numerous: they are to be found in all parts of the kingdom: therefore again I say, when I hear of " ruin " or " misery," I must know what the conduct of the sufferers has been before I bestow my compassion.

WARMINSTER (WILTS),
Friday, 1 Sept.

I set out from Heytesbury this morning about six o'clock. Last night, before I went to bed, I found that there were some men and boys in the house who had come all the way from Bradford, about twelve miles, in order to get *nuts*. These people were men and boys that had been employed in the *cloth factories* at Bradford and about Bradford. I had some talk with some of these nutters, and I am quite convinced, not that the cloth making is at *an end*, but that it *never will be again what it has been.* Before last Christmas these manufacturers had full work, at one shilling and threepence a yard at broad-cloth weaving. They have now a quarter work, at one shilling a yard! One and threepence **a** yard for this weaving has been given at all times within the memory of man! Nothing can show more clearly than this, and in a stronger light, the great change which has taken place in the *remuneration for labour*. There was a turn out last winter, when the price was reduced to a shilling a yard; but it was put an end to in the usual way; the constable's staff, the bayonet, the gaol. These poor nutters were extremely ragged. I saved my supper, and I fasted instead of breakfasting. That was three shillings which I had saved, and I added five to them, with a resolution to save them afterwards, in order to give these chaps a breakfast for once in their lives. There were eight of them, six men and two boys; and I gave them two quartern loaves, two pounds of cheese, and eight pints of strong beer. The fellows were very thankful, but the conduct of the landlord and landlady pleased me exceedingly. When I came to pay my bill, they had said nothing about my bed, which had been a very good one; and when I asked why they had not put the bed into the bill, they said they would not charge anything for the bed since I had been so good to the poor men. Yes, said I, but I must not throw the expense upon you. I had no supper, and I have had no breakfast; and, therefore, I am not called upon to pay for them: but *I have had* the bed. It ended by my paying for the bed, and coming off, leaving the nutters at their breakfast, and very much delighted with the landlord and his wife; and I must here observe, that I have pretty generally found a good deal of compassion for the poor people to prevail amongst publicans and their wives.

From Heytesbury to Warminster is a part of the country singularly bright and beautiful. From Salisbury up to very near Heytesbury you have the valley as before described by me. Meadows next the water; then arable land; then the downs; but when you come to Heytesbury, and indeed, a little before, in looking forward you see the vale stretch out, from about three miles wide to ten miles wide, from high land to high land. From a hill before you come down to Heytesbury you see through this wide opening into Somersetshire. You see a round hill rising in the middle of the opening; but all the rest a flat enclosed country, and apparently full of wood. In looking back down this vale one cannot help being struck with the innumerable proofs that there are of a decline in point of population. In the first place, there are twenty-four parishes, each of which takes a little strip across the valley, and runs up through the arable land into the down. There are twenty-four parish churches, and there ought to be as many *parsonage-houses*; but seven of these, out of the twenty-four, that is to say, nearly one-third of them, are, in the returns laid before parliament (and of which returns I shall speak more particularly by and by), stated to be such miserable dwellings as to be unfit for a parson to reside in. Two of them, however, are gone. There are no parsonage-houses in those two parishes: there are the sites; there are the glebes; but the houses have been suffered to fall down and to be totally carried away. The tithes remain, indeed, and the parson sacks the amount of them. A journeyman parson comes and works in three or four churches of a Sunday; but the master parson is not there. He generally carries away the produce to spend it in London, at Bath, or somewhere else, to show off his daughters; and the overseers, that is to say, the farmers, manage the poor in their own way, instead of having, according to the ancient law, a third-part of all the tithes to keep them with.

The falling down and the beggary of these parsonage-houses prove beyond all question the decayed state of the population. And, indeed, the mansion-houses are gone, except in a very few instances. There are but five left that I could perceive, all the way from Salisbury to Warminster, though the country is the most pleasant that can be imagined. Here is water, here are meadows; plenty of fresh-water fish; hares and partridges in abundance, and it is next to impossible to destroy them. Here are shooting, coursing, hunting; hills of every height, size, and form; valleys the same; lofty trees and rookeries in every mile; roads always solid and good; always pleasant for exercise; and the air must be of the best in the world. Yet it is manifest that four-fifths of the mansions have been swept away. There is a parliamentary return to prove that nearly a third of the parsonage-houses have become beggarly holes or have disappeared. I have now been in nearly three score villages, and in twenty or thirty or forty hamlets of Wiltshire; and I do not know that I have been in one, however small, in which I did not see a house or two, and sometimes more, either tumbled down or beginning to tumble down. It is impossible for the eyes of man to be fixed on a finer country than that between the village of Codford and the town of Warminster; and it is not very easy for the eyes of man to discover labouring people more miserable. There are two villages, one called Norton Bovant and the other Bishopstrow, which I think form together one of the prettiest spots that my eyes ever beheld. The former village belongs to Bennet, the member for the county, who has a mansion there, in which two of his sisters live, I am told. There is a farm at Bishopstrow, standing at the back of the arable land, up in a vale formed by two very lofty hills, upon each of which there was formerly a Roman camp, in consideration of which farm, if the owner would give it me, I would almost consent to let Ottiwell Wood remain quiet in his seat, and suffer the pretty gentlemen of Whitehall to go on without note or comment till they had fairly blowed up their concern. The farm-yard is surrounded by lofty and beautiful trees. In the rick-yard I counted twenty-two ricks of one sort and another. The hills shelter the house and the yard and the trees most completely from every wind but the south. The arable land goes down before the house, and spreads along the edge of the down, going with a gentle slope down to the meadows. So that, going along the turnpike-road, which runs between the lower fields of the arable land, you see the large and beautiful flocks of sheep upon the sides of the down, while the horn-cattle are up to their eyes in grass in the meadows. Just when I was coming along here, the sun was about half an hour high; it shined through the trees most brilliantly; and, to crown the whole, I met, just as I was entering the village, a very pretty girl, who was apparently going a gleaning in the fields. I asked her the name of the place, and when she told me it was Bishopstrow, she pointed to the situation of the church, which, she said, was on the other side of the river. She really put me in mind of the pretty girls at Preston who spat upon the " individual " of the Derby family, and I made her a bow accordingly.

The whole of the population of the twenty-four parishes down this vale amounts to only 11,195 souls, according to the official return to parliament; and, mind, I include the parish of Fisherton Anger (a suburb of the city of Salisbury), which contains 893 of the number. I include the town of Heytesbury, with its 1023 souls; and I further include this very good and large market town of Warminster, with its population of 5000! So that I leave, in the other twenty-one parishes, only 4170 souls, men, women, and children! That is to say, a hundred and ninety-eight souls to each parish; or, reckoning five to a family, thirty-nine families to each parish. Above one half of the population never could be expected to be in the church at one time; so that here are one-and-twenty churches built for the purpose of holding 2080 people! There are several of these churches, any one of which would conveniently contain the whole of these people, the 2080! The church of Bishopstrow would contain the whole of the 2080 very well indeed; and it is curious enough to observe that the churches of Fisherton Anger, Heytesbury, and Warminster, though quite sufficient to contain the people that go to church, are none of them nearly so big as several of the village churches. All these churches are built long and long before the reign of Richard II.; that is to say, they were founded long before that time, and if the first churches were gone, these others were built in their stead. There is hardly one of them that is not as old as the reign of Richard II.; and yet that impudent Scotchman, George Chalmers, would make us believe that, in the reign of Richard II., the population of the country was hardly anything at all! He has the impudence, or the gross ignorance, to state the population of England and Wales at *two millions*, which, as I have shown in the last number of the Protestant Reformation, would allow only twelve able men to every parish church throughout the kingdom. What, I ask, for about the thousandth time I ask it, what were these twenty churches built for? Some of them stand within a quarter of a mile of each other. They are pretty nearly as close to each other as the churches in London and Westminster are.

What a monstrous thing to suppose that they were built without there being people to go to them; and built, too, without money and without hands! The whole of the population in these twenty-one parishes could stand, and without much crowding too, in the bottoms of the towers of the several churches. Nay, in three or four of the parishes, the whole of the people could stand in the church porches. Then the *church-yards* show you how numerous the population must have been. You see, in some cases, only here and there the mark of a grave, where the church-yard contains from half an acre to an acre of land, and sometimes more. In short, everything shows that here was once a great and opulent population; that there was an abundance to eat, to wear, and to spare; that all the land that is now under cultivation, and a great deal that is not now under cultivation, was under cultivation in former times. The Scotch beggars would make us believe that *we* sprang from beggars. The impudent scribes would make us believe that England was formerly nothing at all till they come to enlighten it and fatten upon it. Let the beggars answer me this question; let the impudent, the brazen scribes, that impose upon the credulous and cowed-down English; let them tell me *why* these twenty-one churches were built; what they were built FOR; why the large churches of the two Codfords were stuck up within a few hundred yards of each other, if the whole of the population could then, as it can now, be crammed into the chancel of either of the two churches? Let them answer me this question, or shut up their mouths upon this subject, on which they have told so many lies.

As to the produce of this valley, it must be at least ten times as great as its consumption, even if we include the three towns that belong to it. I am sure I saw produce enough in five or six of the farm-yards, or rick-yards, to feed the whole of the population of the twenty-one parishes. But the infernal system causes it all to be carried away. Not a bit of good beef, or mutton, or veal, and scarcely a bit of bacon is left for those who raise all this food and wool. The labourers here *look* as if they were half-starved. They answer extremely well to the picture that Fortescue gave of the French in his day.

Talk of " liberty," indeed; " civil and religious liberty ": the inquisition, with a belly full, is far preferable to a state of things like this. For my own part, I really am ashamed to ride a fat horse, to have a full belly, and to have a clean shirt upon my back, while I look at these wretched countrymen of mine; while I actually see them reeling with weakness; when I see their poor faces present me nothing but skin and bone, while they are toiling to get the wheat and the meat ready to be carried away to be devoured by the tax-eaters. I am ashamed to look at these poor souls, and to reflect that they are my countrymen; and particularly to reflect that we are descended from those amongst whom "beef, pork, mutton, and veal, were the food of the poorer sort of people." What! and is the " Emigration Committee " sitting to invent the means of getting rid of some part of the thirty-nine families that are employed in raising the immense quantities of food in each of these twenty-one parishes? Are there *schemers* to go before this conjuration committee; Wiltshire *schemers*, to tell the committee how they can get rid of a part of these one hundred and ninety-eight persons to every parish? Are there schemers of this sort of work still, while no man, no man at all, not a single man, says a word about getting rid of the dead-weight, or the supernumerary parsons, both of whom have actually a premium given them for breeding, and are filling the country with idlers? We are reversing the maxim of the Scripture: our laws almost say that those that work shall not eat, and that those who do not work shall have the food. I repeat, that the baseness of the English land-owners surpasses that of any other men that ever lived in the world. The cowards know well that the labourers that give value to their land are skin and bone. They are not such brutes as not to know that this starvation is produced by taxation. They know well how unjust it is to treat their labourers in this way. They know well that there goes down the common foot soldier's single throat more food than is allowed by them to a labourer, his wife, and three children. They know well that the present standing army in time of peace consumes more food and raiment than a million of the labourers consume; aye, than two millions of them consume; if you include the women and the children; they well know these things; they know that their poor labourers are taxed to keep this army in fatness and in splendour. They know that the dead-weight, which, in the opinion of most men of sense, ought not to receive a single farthing of the public money, swallow more of good food than a third or a fourth part of the real labourers of England swallow. They know that a million and a half of pounds sterling was taken out of the taxes, partly raised upon the labourers, to enable the poor clergy of the Church of England to marry and to breed. They know that a regulation has been recently adopted by which an old dead-weight man is enabled to sell his dead-weight to a young man; and that thus this burden would, if the system were to be continued, be rendered perpetual. They know that a good slice of the dead-weight money goes to *Hanover*; and that even these Hanoverians can sell their dead-weight claim upon us. The "country gentlemen" fellows know all this: they know that the poor labourers, including all the poor manufacturers, pay one-half of their wages in taxes to support all these things; and yet not a word about these things is ever said, or even hinted, by these mean, these cruel, these cowardly, these carrion, these dastardly reptiles. Sir James Graham, of Netherby, who, I understand, is a young fellow instead of an old one, may invoke our pity upon these "ancient families," but he will invoke in vain. It was their duty to stand forward and prevent Power-of-Imprisonment Bills, Six-Acts, Ellenborough's Act, Poaching Transportation Act, New Trespass Act, Sunday Tolls, and the hundreds of other things that could be named. On the contrary, *they were the cause of them all*. They were the cause of all the taxes and all the debts; and now let them take the consequences!

Saturday, 2 September.

After I got to Warminster yesterday it began to rain, which stopped me in my way to Frome in Somersetshire, which lies about seven or eight miles from this place; but as I meant to be quite in the northern part of the county by to-morrow noon, or thereabouts, I took a post-chaise in the afternoon of yesterday and went to Frome, where I saw, upon my entrance into the town, between two and three hundred weavers, men and boys, cracking stones, moving earth, and doing other sorts of work, towards making a fine road into the town. I drove into the town, and through the principal streets, and then I put my chaise up a little at one of the inns.

This appears to be a sort of little Manchester. A very small Manchester, indeed; for it does not contain above ten to twelve thousand people, but it has all the *flash* of a Manchester, and the innkeepers and their people look and behave like the Manchester fellows. I was, I must confess, glad to find proofs of the irretrievable decay of the place. I remembered how ready the bluff manufacturers had been to *call in the troops* of various descriptions. " Let them," said I to myself, " call the troops in now, to make their trade revive. Let them now resort to their friends of the yeomanry and of the army; let them now threaten their poor workmen with the gaol, when they dare to ask for the means of preventing starvation in their families. Let them, who have, in fact, lived and thriven by the sword, now call upon the parson-magistrate to bring out the soldiers to compel me, for instance, to give thirty shillings a yard for the superfine black broad-cloth (made at Frome), which Mr. Roe, at Kensington, offered me at seven shillings and sixpence a yard just before I left home! Yes, these men have ground down into powder those who were earning them their fortunes: let the grinders themselves now be ground, and, according to the usual wise and just course of Providence, let them be crushed by the system which they have delighted in, because it made others crouch beneath them." Their poor work-people cannot be worse off than they long have been. The parish pay, which they now get upon the roads, is 2s. 6d. a week for a man, 2s. for his wife, 1s. 3d. for each child under eight years of age, 3d. a week, in addition, to each child above eight, who can go to work: and if the children above eight years old, whether girls or boys, do not go to work upon the road, they have *nothing !* Thus a family of five people have just as much, and eightpence over, as goes down the throat of one single foot soldier; but, observe, the standing soldier, that "truly English institution," has clothing, fuel, candle, soap, and house-rent, over and above what is allowed to this miserable family! And yet the base reptiles, who are called "country gentlemen," and whom Sir James Graham calls upon us to commit all sorts of acts of injustice in order to *preserve*, never utter a whisper about the expenses of keeping the soldiers, while they are everlastingly railing against the working people of every description, and representing them, and them only, as the cause of the loss of their estates!

These poor creatures at Frome have pawned all their things, or nearly all. All their best clothes, their blankets and sheets; their looms; any little piece of furniture that they had, and that was good for anything. Mothers have been compelled to pawn all the tolerably good clothes that their children had. In case of a man having two or three shirts, he is left with only one, and sometimes without any shirt; and though this is a sort of manufacture that cannot very well come to a complete end; still it has received a blow from which it cannot possibly recover. The population of this Frome has been augmented to the degree of one-third within the last six or seven years. There are here all the usual signs of accommodation bills and all false paper stuff, called money: new houses in abundance, half finished; new gingerbread "places of worship," as they are called; great swaggering inns; parcels of swaggering fellows going about, with vulgarity imprinted upon their countenances, but with good clothes upon their backs.

I found the working people at Frome very intelligent; very well informed as to the cause of their misery; not at all humbugged by the canters, whether about religion or loyalty. When I got to the inn, I sent my post-chaise boy back to the road to tell one or two of the weavers to come to me at the inn. The landlord did not at first like to let such ragged fellows upstairs. I insisted, however, upon their coming up, and I had a long talk with them. They were very intelligent men; had much clearer views of what is likely to happen than the pretty gentlemen of Whitehall seem to have; and it is curious enough that they, these common weavers, should tell me, that they thought that the trade never would come back again to what it was before; or, rather, to what it has been for some years past. This is the impression everywhere; that the *puffing is over ;* that we must come back again to something like reality. The first factories that I met with were at a village called Upton Lovell, just before

I came to Heytesbury. There they were a doing not more than a quarter work. There is only one factory, I believe, here at Warminster, and that has been suspended, during the harvest, at any rate. At Frome they are all upon about a quarter work. It is the same at Bradford and Trowbridge; and, as curious a thing as ever was heard of in the world is, that here are, through all these towns, and throughout this country, weavers from the north, singing about the towns ballads of distress! They had been doing it at Salisbury just before I was there. The landlord at Heytesbury told me that people that could afford it generally gave them something; and I was told that they did the same at Salisbury. The landlord at Heytesbury told me that every one of them had a *licence to beg*, given them he said "by the government." I suppose it was some *pass* from a magistrate; though I know of no law that allows of such passes; and a pretty thing it would be to grant such licences, or such passes, when the law so positively commands that the poor of every parish shall be maintained in and by every such parish.

However, all law of this sort, all salutary and humane law, really seems to be drawing towards an end in this now miserable country, where the thousands are caused to wallow in luxury, to be surfeited with food and drink, while the millions are continually on the point of famishing. In order to form an idea of the degradation of the people of this country, and of the abandonment of every English principle, what need we of more than this one disgraceful and truly horrible fact, namely, that *the common soldiers of the standing army in time of peace subscribe in order to furnish the meanest of diet to keep from starving the industrious people who are taxed to the amount of one-half of their wages, and out of which taxes the very pay of these soldiers comes!* Is not this one fact; this disgraceful, this damning fact; is not this enough to convince us that *there must be a change;* that there must be a complete and radical change; or that England must become a country of the basest slavery that ever disgraced the earth?

DEVIZES (WILTS),
Sunday Morning, 3 Sept.

I left Warminster yesterday at about one o'clock. It is contrary to my practice to set out at all unless I can do it early in the morning; but at Warminster I was at the south-west corner of this county, and I had made a sort of promise to be to-day at Highworth, which is at the north-east corner, and which parish, indeed, joins up to Berkshire. The distance, including my little intended deviations, was more than fifty miles; and not liking to attempt it in one day, I set off in the middle of the day, and got here in the evening, just before a pretty heavy rain came on.

Before I speak of my ride from Warminster to this place, I must once more observe that Warminster is a very nice town; everything belonging to it is *solid* and *good*. There are no villainous gingerbread houses running up, and no nasty, shabby-genteel people; no women trapesing about with showy gowns and dirty necks; no jew-looking fellows with dandy coats, dirty shirts and half-heels to their shoes. A really nice and good town. It is a great corn-market: one of the greatest in this part of England; and here things are still conducted in the good old honest fashion. The corn is brought and pitched in the market before it is sold; and, when sold, it is paid for on the nail; and all is over, and the farmers and millers gone home by daylight. Almost everywhere else the corn is sold by sample; it is sold by juggling in a corner; the parties meet and drink first; it is night work; there is no fair and open market; the mass of the people do not know what the prices are; and all this favours that *monopoly* which makes the corn change hands many times, perhaps, before it reaches the mouth, leaving a profit in each pair of hands, and which monopoly is, for the greater part, carried on by the villainous tribe of *Quakers, none of whom ever work*, and all of whom prey upon the rest of the community, as those infernal devils, the wasps, prey upon the bees. Talking of the Devil, puts one in mind of his imps; and talking of *Quakers*, puts one in mind of Jemmy Cropper of Liverpool. I should like to know precisely (I know pretty nearly) what effect " late panic " has had, and is having, on Jemmy! Perhaps the reader will recollect that Jemmy told the public, through the columns of base Bott Smith, that " Cobbett's prophecies were falsified as soon as spawned." Jemmy, canting Jemmy, has now had time to ruminate on that! But does the reader remember James's project for " making Ireland as happy as England? " It was simply by introducing cotton-factories, steam-engines, and power-looms! That was all; and there was Jemmy in Ireland, speech-making before such lords and such bishops and such 'squires as God never suffered to exist in the world before: there was Jemmy, showing, proving, demonstrating, that to make the Irish cotton-workers would infallibly make them *happy!* If it had been now, instead of being two years ago, he might have produced the reports of the starvation-committees of Manchester to confirm his opinions. One would think that this instance of the folly and impudence of this canting son of the monopolising sect would cure this public of its proneness to listen to cant; but nothing will cure it; the very existence of this sect, none of whom ever work, and the whole of whom live like fighting cocks upon the labour of the rest of the community; the very *existence* of such a sect shows that the nation is, almost in its nature, *a dupe.* There has been a great deal of railing against the King of Spain; not to becall the King of Spain is looked upon as a proof of want of " liberality," and what must it be, then, to *applaud* any of the acts of the King of Spain! This I am about to do, however, think Dr. Black of it what he may.

In the first place, the mass of the people of Spain are better off, better fed, better clothed, than the people of any other country in Europe, and much better than the people of England are. That is one thing; and that is almost enough of itself. In the next place, the King of Spain has refused to mortgage the land and labour of his people for the benefit of an infamous set of Jews and jobbers. Next, the King of Spain has most essentially thwarted the Six-Acts people, the Manchester 16th of August, the Parson Hay, the Sidmouth's Circular, the Dungeoning, the Ogden's rupture people; he has thwarted, and most cunningly annoyed, these people, who are also the poacher transporting people, and the new trespass law, and the apple-felony and the horse-police (or gendarmerie) and the Sunday-toll people: the King of Spain has thwarted all these, and he has materially assisted in blowing up the brutal big fellows of Manchester; and, therefore, I applaud the King of Spain.

I do not much like weasels; but I hate rats; and, therefore, I say, success to the weasels. But there is one act of the King of Spain which is worthy of the imitation of every king, aye, and of every republic too; his edict for taxing traffickers, which edict was published about eight months ago. It imposes a pretty heavy annual tax on every one who is a *mere buyer and seller,* and who neither produces, nor consumes, nor makes, nor changes the state of the article, or articles, that he buys and sells. Those who bring things into the kingdom are deemed producers, and those who send things out of the kingdom are deemed changers of the state of things. These two classes embrace all *legitimate merchants.* Thus, then, the farmer who produces corn and meat and wool and wood is not taxed; nor is the coach-master who buys the corn to give to his horses, nor the miller who buys it to change the state of it, nor the baker who buys the flour to change its state; nor is the manufacturer who buys the wool to change its state; and so on: but the Jew, or Quaker, the *mere dealer*, who buys the corn of the producer to sell it to the miller, and to deduct *a profit*, which must, at last, fall upon the consumer; this Jew, or Quaker, or self-styled Christian, who acts the part of Jew or Quaker, is taxed by the King of Spain; and for this I applaud the King of Spain.

If we had a law like this, the pestiferous sect of non-labouring, sleek and fat hypocrites could not exist in England. But ours is altogether *a system of monopolies*, created by taxation and paper-money, from which monopolies are inseparable. It is notorious that the brewer's monopoly is the master even of the government; it is well known to all who examine and reflect that a very large part of our bread comes to our mouths loaded with the profit of nine or ten, or more, different dealers; and I shall, as soon as I have leisure, prove as clearly as anything ever was proved, that the people pay two millions of pounds a year in consequence of the monopoly in tea! that is to say, they pay two millions a year more than they would pay were it not for the monopoly; and, mind, I do not mean the monopoly of the East India Company; but the monopoly of the Quaker and other tea dealers, who buy the tea of that company! The people of this country are eaten up by monopolies. These compel those who labour to maintain those who do not labour; and hence the success of the crafty crew of Quakers, the very *existence* of which sect is a disgrace to the country.

Besides the corn market at Warminster, I was delighted and greatly surprised to see the *meat*. Not only the very finest veal and lamb that I had ever seen in my life, but so exceedingly beautiful that I could hardly believe my eyes. I am a great connoisseur in joints of meat; a great judge, if five-and-thirty years of experience can give sound judgment. I verily believe that I have bought and have roasted more whole sirloins of beef than any man in England; I know all about the matter; a very great visitor of Newgate market; in short, though a little eater, I am a very great provider. It is a fancy, I like the subject, and therefore I understand it; and with all this knowledge of the matter I say I never saw veal and lamb half so fine as what I saw at Warminster. The town is famed for fine meat; and I knew it, and, therefore, I went out in the morning to look at the meat. It was, too, 2*d*. a pound cheaper than I left it at Kensington.

My road from Warminster to Devizes lay through Westbury,
a nasty odious rotten borough, a really rotten place. It has
cloth factories in it, and they seem to be ready to tumble down
as well as many of the houses. God's curse seems to be upon
most of these rotten boroughs. After coming through this
miserable hole, I came along on the north side of the famous hill
called Bratton Castle, so renowned in the annals of the Romans
and of Alfred the Great. Westbury is a place of great ancient
grandeur; and it is easy to perceive that it was once ten or
twenty times its present size. My road was now the line of
separation between what they call South Wilts and North Wilts,
the former consisting of high and broad downs and narrow
valleys with meadows and rivers running down them; the latter
consisting of a rather flat, enclosed country: the former having
a chalk bottom; the latter a bottom of marl, clay, or flat stone:
the former a country for lean sheep and corn; and the latter a
country for cattle, fat sheep, cheese, and bacon: the former,
by far, to my taste, the most beautiful; and I am by no means
sure that it is not, all things considered, the most rich. All my
way along, till I came very near to Devizes, I had the steep and
naked downs up to my right, and the flat and enclosed country
to my left.

Very near to Bratton Castle (which is only a hill with deep
ditches on it) is the village of Eddington, so famed for the battle
fought here by Alfred and the Danes. The church in this
village would contain several thousands of persons; and the
village is reduced to a few straggling houses. The land here is
very good; better than almost any I ever saw; as black and,
apparently, as rich as the land in the market-gardens at Fulham.
The turnips are very good all along here for several miles; but
this is, indeed, singularly fine and rich land. The orchards very
fine; finely sheltered, and the crops of apples and pears and
walnuts very abundant. Walnuts *ripe now*, a month earlier than
usual. After Eddington I came to a hamlet called Earl's Stoke,
the houses of which stand at a few yards from each other, on the
two sides of the road; every house is white; and the front of
every one is covered with some sort or other of clematis, or with
rose-trees, or jasmines. It was easy to guess that the whole
belonged to one owner; and that owner I found to be a Mr.
Watson Taylor, whose very pretty seat is close by the hamlet,
and in whose park-pond I saw what I never saw before, namely,
some *black swans*. They are not nearly so large as the white, nor
are they so stately in their movements. They are a meaner bird.

HIGHWORTH (WILTS),
Monday, 4 Sept.

I got here yesterday after a ride, including my deviations, of about thirty-four miles, and that, too, *without breaking my fast.* Before I got into the rotten borough of Calne I had two *tributes* to pay to the aristocracy; namely, two *Sunday tolls ;* and I was resolved that the country in which these tolls were extorted should have not a farthing of my money that I could, by any means, keep from it. Therefore I fasted until I got into the free-quarters in which I now am. I would have made my horse fast too if I could have done it without the risk of making him unable to carry me.

FROM HIGHWORTH TO CRICKLADE AND THENCE TO MALMSBURY

HIGHWORTH (WILTS),

Monday, 4 *Sept.* 1826.

WHEN I got to Devizes, on Saturday evening, and came to look out of the inn-window into the street, I perceived that I had seen that place before, and always having thought that I should like to *see* Devizes, of which I had heard so much talk as a famous corn-market, I was very much surprised to find that it was not new to me. Presently a stage-coach came up to the door with " Bath and London " upon its panels; and then I recollected that I had been at this place on my way to Bristol last year. Devizes is, as nearly as possible, in the centre of the county, and the *canal*, that passes close by it, is the great channel through which the produce of the country is carried away to be devoured by the idlers, the thieves, and the prostitutes, who are all tax-eaters, in the Wens of Bath and London. Pottern, which I passed through in my way from Warminster to Devizes, was once a place much larger than Devizes; and it is now a mere ragged village, with a church large, very ancient, and of most costly structure. The whole of the people here might, as in most other cases, be placed in the *belfry*, or the church-porches.

All the way along the mansion-houses are nearly all gone. There is now and then a great place, belonging to a borough-monger, or some one connected with boroughmongers; but all the *little gentlemen* are gone; and hence it is that parsons are now made justices of the peace! There are few other persons left who are at all capable of filling the office in a way to suit the system! The monopolising brewers and rag-rooks are, in some places, the " magistrates; " and thus is the whole thing *changed*, and England is no more what it was. Very near to the sides of my road from Warminster to Devizes there were formerly (within a hundred years), 22 mansion-houses of suffi-cient note to be marked as such in the county-map, then made. There are now only seven of them remaining. There were five parish-churches nearly close to my road; and in one parish out

80

of the five the parsonage-house is, in the parliamentary return, said to be "too small" for the parson to live in, though the church would contain two or three thousand people, and though the living is a rectory, and a rich one too! Thus has the church property, or rather that public property which is called church property, been dilapidated! The parsons have swallowed the *tithes* and the rent of the glebes; and have, successively, suffered the parsonage-houses to fall into decay. But these parsonage-houses were, indeed, not intended for large families. They were intended for a priest, a main part of whose business it was to distribute the tithes amongst the poor and the strangers! The parson, in this case, at Corsley, says, "too small for an incumbent with a family." Ah! there is the mischief. It was never intended to give men tithes as a premium for breeding! Malthus does not seem to see any harm in *this* sort of increase of population. It is the *working* population, those who raise the food and the clothing, that he and Scarlett want to put a stop to the breeding of!

I saw, on my way through the down-countries, hundreds of acres of ploughed land in *shelves*. What I mean is, the side of a steep hill, made into the shape of *a stairs*, only the rising parts more sloping than those of a stairs, and deeper in proportion. The side of the hill, in its original form, was too steep to be ploughed, or even to be worked with a spade. The earth as soon as moved would have rolled down the hill; and, besides, the rains would have soon washed down all the surface earth, and have left nothing for plants of any sort to grow in. Therefore the sides of hills, where the land was sufficiently good, and where it was wanted for the growing of corn, were thus made into a sort of steps or shelves, and the horizontal parts (representing the parts of the stairs that we put our feet upon) were ploughed and sowed, as they generally are, indeed, to this day. Now, no man, not even the hireling Chalmers, will have the impudence to say that these shelves, amounting to thousands and thousands of acres in Wiltshire alone, were not made by the hand of man. It would be as impudent to contend that the churches were formed by the flood, as to contend that these shelves were formed by that cause. Yet thus the Scotch scribes must contend; or they must give up all their assertions about the ancient beggary and want of population in England; for, as in the case of the churches, what were these shelves made *for*? And could they be made at all without a great abundance of hands? These shelves are everywhere to be seen throughout the down-countries of Sussex, Hampshire, Wiltshire, Dorset-shire, Devonshire and Cornwall; and, besides this, large tracts of land, amounting to millions of acres, perhaps, which are now downs, heaths, or woodlands, still, if you examine closely, bear the marks of the plough. The fact is, I dare say, that the country has never varied much in the gross amount of its popula-tion; but formerly the people were pretty evenly spread over the country, instead of being, as the greater part of them now are, collected together in great masses, where, for the greater part, the idlers live on the labour of the industrious.

In quitting Devizes yesterday morning, I saw just on the outside of the town a monstrous building, which I took for *a barrack;* but upon asking what it was I found it was one of those other marks of the JUBILEE REIGN; namely *a most magnificent gaol!* It seemed to me sufficient to hold one-half of the able-bodied men in the county! And it would do it too, and do it well! Such a system must come to an end, and the end must be dreadful. As I came on the road, for the first three or four miles, I saw great numbers of labourers either digging potatoes for their Sunday's dinner, or coming home with them, or going out to dig them. The land-owners, or occupiers, let small pieces of land to the labourers, and these they cultivate with the spade for their own use. They pay, in all cases, a high rent, and, in most cases, an enormous one. The practice pre-vails all the way from Warminster to Devizes, and from Devizes to nearly this place (Highworth). The rent is, in some places, a shilling a rod, which is, mind, 160s. or £8 an acre! Still the poor creatures like to have the land: they work in it at their spare hours; and on Sunday mornings early: and the overseers, sharp as they may be, cannot ascertain precisely how much they get out of their plat of ground. But, good God! what a life to live! What a life to see people live; to see this sight in our own country, and to have the base vanity to *boast* of that country, and to talk of our " constitution " and our " liberties," and to affect to *pity* the Spaniards, whose working people live like gentlemen, compared with our miserable creatures. Again I say, give me the inquisition and well-healed cheeks and ribs, rather than " civil and religious liberty " and skin and bone. But, the fact is, that where honest and laborious men can be compelled to starve quietly, whether all at once or by inches, with old wheat-ricks and fat cattle under their eye, it is a mockery to talk of their " liberty " of any sort; for the sum total of their state is this, they have " liberty " to choose between death by starvation (quick or slow) and death by the halter!

Between Warminster and Westbury I saw thirty or more men *digging* a great field of, I dare say, twelve acres. I thought, " surely, that ' humane,' half-mad fellow, Owen, is not got at work here; that Owen, who, the *feelosofers* tell us, went to the Continent to find out how to prevent the increase of the labourers' children." No: it was not Owen: it was the over-seer of the parish who had set these men to dig up this field, previously to its being sown with wheat. In short, it was a digging instead of a ploughing. The men, I found upon inquiry, got 9*d*. a day for their work. Plain digging, in the market gardens near London, is, I believe, 3*d*. or 4*d*. a rod. If these poor men, who were chiefly weavers or spinners from Westbury, or had come home to their parish from Bradford or Trowbridge; if they digged six rods each in a day, and *fairly* did it, they must work well. This would be 1½*d*. a rod, or 20*s*. an acre; and that is as cheap as ploughing, and four times as good. But how much better to give the men higher wages, and let them do more work? If married, how are their miserable families to live on 4*s*. 6*d*. a week? And if single, they must and will have more, either by poaching or by taking without leave. At any rate, this is better than the *road work :* I mean better for those who pay the rates; for here is something which they get for the money that they give to the poor; whereas, in the case of the road work, the money given in relief is generally wholly so much lost to the rate-payer. What a curious spectacle this is: the manufactories *throwing the people back again upon the land!* It is not above eighteen months ago that the Scotch FEELOSOFERS, and especi-ally Dr. Black, were calling upon *the farm labourers to become manufacturers!* I remonstrated with the doctor at the time; but he still insisted that such a transfer of hands was the only remedy for the distress in the farming districts. However (and I thank God for it) the *feelosofers* have enough to do at *home* now; for the poor are crying for food in dear, cleanly, warm, fruitful Scotland herself, in spite of a' the Hamiltons and a' the Wallaces and a' the Maxwells and a' the Hope John-stones and a' the Dundases and a' the Edinbro' Reviewers and a' the Broughams and Birkbecks. In spite of all these, the poor of Scotland are now helping themselves, or about to do it, for want of the means of purchasing food.

From Devizes I came to the vile rotten borough of Calne, leaving the park and house of Lord Lansdown to my left. This man's name is Petty, and, doubtless, his ancestors "came in with the Conqueror;" for *Petty* is, unquestionably, a corruption of the French word *Petit;* and, in this case, there appears to have been not the least degeneracy; a thing rather rare in these days. There is a man whose name was Grimstone (that is, to a certainty, *Grindstone*) who is now called Lord Verulam, and who, according to his pedigree in the Peerage, is descended from a "standard-bearer of the Conqueror!" Now, the devil a bit is there the word Grindstone, or Grimstone, in the Norman language. Well, let them have all that their French descent can give them, since they will insist upon it that they are not of this country. So help me God, I would, if I could, *give them Normandy* to live in, and, if the people would let them, to possess.

This Petty family began or, at least, made its first *grand push* in poor, unfortunate Ireland! The *history* of that push would amuse the people of Wiltshire! Talking of Normans and high blood, puts me in mind of Beckford and his "Abbey"! The public knows that the *tower* of this thing fell down some time ago. It was built of Scotch-fir and cased with stone! In it there was a place which the owner had named, "The Gallery of Edward III., the frieze of which," says the account, "contains the achievements of seventy-eight Knights of the Garter, from whom the owner is lineally descended"! Was there ever vanity and impudence equal to these! the negro-driver brag of his high blood! I dare say that the old powder man, Farquhar, had as good pretension; and I really should like to know whether he took out Beckford's name, and put in his own, as the lineal descendant of the seventy-eight Knights of the Garter.

I could not come through that villainous hole, Calne, without cursing Corruption at every step; and when I was coming by an ill-looking, broken-winded place, called the town-hall, I suppose, I poured out a double dose of execration upon it. "Out of the frying-pan into the fire;" for in about ten miles more I came to another rotten hole called Wotten-Basset! This also is a mean, vile place, though the country all round it is very fine. On this side of Wotton-Basset I went out of my way to see the church of Great Lyddiard, which, in the parliamentary return, is called Lyddiard *Tregose.* In my old map it is called *Tregose;* and, to a certainty, the word was *Tregrosse;* that is to say, *très grosse,* or, *very big.* Here is a good old mansion-house and large walled-in garden and a park, belonging, they told me, to Lord Bolingbroke. I went quite down to the house, close to which stands the large and fine church. It appears *to have been* a noble place; the land is some of the finest in the whole country; the trees show that the land is excellent; but all, except the church, is in a state of irrepair and apparent neglect, if not abandonment. The parish is large, the living is a rich one, it is a rectory; but though the incumbent has the great and small tithes, he, in his return, tells the parliament that the parsonage-house is "worn out and incapable of repair!" And, observe, that parliament lets him continue to sack the produce of the tithes and the glebe, while they know the parsonage-house to be crumbling down, and while he has the impudence to tell them that he does not reside in it, though the law says that he shall! And while this is suffered to be, a *poor* man may be transported for being in pursuit of a hare! What coals, how hot, how red, is this flagitious system preparing for the backs of its supporters!

In coming from Wotton-Basset to Highworth, I left Swindon a few miles away to my left, and came by the village of Blunsdon. All along here I saw great quantities of hops in the hedges, and very fine hops, and I saw at a village called Stratton, I think it was, the finest *campanula* that I ever saw in my life. The main stalk was more than four feet high, and there were four stalks, none of which were less than three feet high. All through the country, poor, as well as rich, are very neat in their gardens, and very careful to raise a great variety of flowers. At Blunsdon I saw a clump, or, rather, a sort of orchard, of as fine walnut-trees as I ever beheld, and loaded with walnuts. Indeed I have seen great crops of walnuts all the way from London. From Blunsdon to this place is but a short distance, and I got here about two or three o'clock. This is a *cheese country ;* some corn, but, generally speaking, it is a country of dairies. The sheep here are of the large kind; a sort of Leicester sheep, and the cattle chiefly for milking. The ground is a stiff loam at top, and a yellowish stone under. The houses are almost all built of stone. It is a tolerably rich, but by no means a gay and pretty country. Highworth has a situation corresponding with its name. On every side you go up-hill to it, and from it you see to a great distance all round and into many counties.

HIGHWORTH,
Wednesday, 6 Sept.

The great object of my visit to the northern border of Wiltshire will be mentioned when I get to Malmsbury, whither I intend to go to-morrow, or next day, and thence, through

Gloucestershire, in my way to Herefordshire. But an additional inducement was to have a good long political *gossip* with some excellent friends who detest the borough ruffians as cordially as I do, and who, I hope, wish as anxiously to see their fall effected, and no matter by what means. There was, however, arising incidentally, a third object, which, had I known of its existence, would of itself have brought me from the south-west to the north-east corner of this county. One of the parishes adjoining to Highworth is that of Coleshill, which is in Berkshire, and which is the property of Lord Radnor, or Lord Folkestone, and is the seat of the latter. I was at Coleshill twenty-two or three years ago, and twice at later periods. In 1824, Lord Folkestone bought some locust-trees of me; and he has several times told me that they were growing very finely; but I did not know that they had been planted at Coleshill; and, indeed, I always thought that they had been planted somewhere in the south of Wiltshire. I now found, however, that they were growing at Coleshill, and yesterday I went to see them, and was, for many reasons, more delighted with the sight than with any that I have beheld for a long while. These trees stand in clumps of 200 trees in each, and the trees being four feet apart each way. These clumps make part of a plantation of 30 or 40 acres, perhaps 50 acres. The rest of the ground—that is to say, the ground where the clumps of locusts do not stand—was, at the same time that the locust clumps were, planted with chestnuts, elms, ashes, oaks, beeches, and other trees. These trees were stouter and taller than the locust trees were when the plantation was made. Yet, if you were now to place yourself at a mile's distance from the plantation, you would not think that there was any plantation at all, except the clumps. The fact is, that the other trees have, as they generally do, made, as yet, but very little progress; are not, I should think, upon an average, more than 4½ feet, or 5 feet, high; while the clumps of locusts are from 12 to 20 feet high; and I think that I may safely say that the average height is 16 feet. They are the most beautiful clumps of trees that I ever saw in my life. They were, indeed, planted by a clever and most trusty servant, who to say all that can be said in his praise, is, that he is worthy of such a master as he has.

The trees are, indeed, in good land, and have been taken good care of; but the other trees are in the same land; and, while they have been taken the same care of since they were planted, they had not, I am sure, worse treatment before planting than

these locust-trees had. At the time when I sold them to my
Lord Folkestone, they were in a field at Worth, near Crawley,
in Sussex. The history of their transport is this. A Wiltshire
waggon came to Worth for the trees on the 14th of March 1824.
The waggon had been stopped on the way by the snow; and,
though the snow was gone off before the trees were put upon the
waggon, it was very cold, and there were sharp frosts and harsh
winds. I had the trees taken up, and tied up in hundreds by
withes, like so many fagots. They were then put in and upon
the waggon, we doing our best to keep the roots inwards in the
loading, so as to prevent them from being exposed but as little
as possible to the wind, sun, and frost. We put some fern on the
top, and, where we could, on the sides; and we tied on the load
with ropes, just as we should have done with a load of fagots.
In this way they were several days upon the road; and I do
not know how long it was before they got safe into the ground
again. All this shows how hardy these trees are, and it ought
to admonish gentlemen to make pretty strict inquiries, when
they have gardeners, or bailiffs, or stewards, under whose hands
locust-trees die, or do not thrive.

N.B.—Dry as the late summer was, I never had my locust-trees
so fine as they are this year. I have some, they write me, five
feet high, from seed sown just before I went to Preston the first
time, that is to say, on the 13th of May. I shall advertise my
trees in the next *Register*. I never had them so fine, though the
great drought has made the number comparatively small. Lord
Folkestone bought of me 13,600 trees. They are, at this moment,
worth the money they cost him, and in addition the cost of
planting, and in addition to that, they are worth the fee simple
of the ground (very good ground) on which they stand; and this I
am able to demonstrate to any man in his senses. What a
difference in the value of Wiltshire if all its elms were locusts!
As fuel, a foot of locust-wood is worth four or five of any English
wood. It will burn better green than almost any other wood
will dry. If men want woods, beautiful woods, and *in a hurry*,
let them go and see the clumps at Coleshill. Think of a wood
16 feet high, and I may say 20 feet high, in twenty-nine months
from the day of planting; and the plants, on an average, not
more than two feet high when planted! Think of that: and any
one may see it at Coleshill. See what efforts gentlemen make
to get a wood ! How they look at the poor slow-growing things
for years; when they might, if they would, have it at once:
really almost at a wish; and, with due attention, in almost any

soil; and the most valuable of woods into the bargain. Mr. Palmer, the bailiff, showed me, near the house at Coleshill, a locust tree which was planted about 35 years ago, or perhaps 40. He had measured it before. It is eight feet and an inch round at a foot from the ground. It goes off afterwards into two principal limbs; which two soon become six limbs, and each of these limbs is three feet round. So that here are six everlasting gate posts to begin with. This tree is worth £20 at the least farthing.

I saw also at Coleshill the most complete farm-yard that I ever saw, and that I believe there is in all England, many and complete as English farm-yards are. This was the contrivance of Mr. Palmer, Lord Folkestone's bailiff and steward. The master gives all the credit of plantation, and farm, to the servant; but the servant ascribes a good deal of it to the master. Between them, at any rate, here are some most admirable objects in rural affairs. And here, too, there is no misery amongst those who do the work; those without whom there could have been no locust-plantations and no farm-yard. Here all are comfortable; gaunt hunger here stares no man in the face. That same disposition which sent Lord Folkestone to visit John Knight in the dungeons at Reading, keeps pinching hunger away from Coleshill. It is a very pretty spot all taken together. It is chiefly grazing land; and though the making of cheese and bacon is, I dare say, the most profitable part of the farming here, Lord Folkestone fats oxen, and has a stall for it, which ought to be shown to foreigners, instead of the spinning jennies. A fat ox is a finer thing than a cheese, however good. There is a dairy here too, and beautifully kept. When this stall is full of oxen, and they all fat, how it would make a French farmer stare! It would make even a Yankee think that "Old England" was a respectable "mother," after all. If I had to show this village off to a Yankee, I would blindfold him all the way to, and after I got him out of, the village, lest he should see the scarecrows of paupers on the road.

For a week or ten days before I came to Highworth, I had, owing to the uncertainty as to where I should be, had no newspapers sent me from London; so that, really, I began to feel that I was in the "dark ages." Arrived here, however, the *light* came bursting in upon me, flash after flash, from the Wen, from Dublin, and from Modern Athens. I had, too, for several days, had nobody to enjoy the light with. I had no sharers in the "*anteelactual*" treat, and this sort of enjoyment, unlike that of some other sorts, is augmented by being divided. Oh!

how happy we were, and how proud we were, to find (from the "instructor") that we had a king, that we were the subjects of a sovereign, who had graciously sent twenty-five pounds to Sir Richard Birnie's poor-box, there to swell the amount of the munificence of fined delinquents! Aye, and this, too, while (as the "instructor" told us) this same sovereign had just bestowed, unasked for (oh! the dear good man!), an annuity of £500 a year on Mrs. Fox, who, observe, and whose daughters, had already a banging pension, paid out of the taxes, raised, in part, and in the greatest part, upon a people who are half-starved and half-naked. And our admiration at the poor-box affair was not at all lessened by the reflection that more money than sufficient to pay all the poor-rates of Wiltshire and Berkshire will, this very year, have been expended on new palaces, on pullings down and alterations of palaces before existing, and on ornaments and decorations in and about Hyde Park, where a bridge is building, which, I am told, must cost a hundred thousand pounds, though all the water that has to pass under it would go through a sugar-hogshead; and does, a little while before it comes to this bridge, go through an arch which I believe to be smaller than a sugar-hogshead! besides, there was a bridge here before, and a very good one too.

Now will Jerry Curteis, who complains so bitterly about the poor-rates, and who talks of the poor working people as if their poverty were the worst of crimes; will Jerry say anything about this bridge, or about the enormous expenses at Hyde Park Corner and in St. James's Park? Jerry knows, or he ought to know, that this bridge alone will cost more money than half the poor-rates of the county of Sussex. Jerry knows, or he ought to know, that this bridge must be paid for out of the taxes. He must know, or else he must be what I dare not suppose him, that it is the taxes that make the paupers; and yet I am afraid that Jerry will not open his lips on the subject of this bridge. What they are going at, at Hyde Park Corner, nobody that I talk with seems to know. The "great captain of the age," as that nasty palaverer, Brougham, called him, lives close to this spot, where also the "English ladies'" naked Achilles stands, having, on the base of it, the word WELLINGTON in great staring letters, while all the other letters are very, very small; so that base tax-eaters and fund-gamblers from the country, when they go to crouch before this image, think it is the image of the great captain himself! The reader will recollect that after the battle of Waterloo, when we beat Napoleon with nearly a million of foreign bayonets in our pay, pay that came out of that *borrowed money*, for which we have *now* to wince and howl; the reader will recollect that at that " glorious " time, when the insolent wretches of tax-eaters were ready to trample us under foot; that, at that time, when the Yankees were defeated on the Serpentine River, and before they had thrashed Blue and Bluff so unmercifully on the ocean and on the lakes; that, at that time, when the creatures called " English ladies " were flocking, from all parts of the country, to present rings to " Old Blucher; " that at that time of exultation with the corrupt, and of mourning with the virtuous, the Collective, in the hey-day, in the delirium, of its joy, resolved to expend three millions of money on triumphal arches, or columns, or monuments of some sort or other, to commemorate the glories of the war! Soon after this, however, low prices came, and they drove triumphal arches out of the heads of the ministers, until " prosperity, unparalleled prosperity " came! This set them to work upon palaces and streets; and I am told that the triumphal-arch project is now going on at Hyde Park Corner! Good God! If this should be true, how apt will everything be! Just about the time that the arch, or arches, will be completed; just about the time that the scaffolding will be knocked away, down will come the whole of the horrid boroughmongering system, for the upholding of which the vile tax-eating crew called for the war! All these palaces and other expensive projects were hatched two years ago; they were hatched in the days of " prosperity," the plans and contracts were made, I dare say, two or three years ago! However, they will be completed much about in the nick of time! They will help to exhibit the system in its true light.

The " best possible public instructor " tells us that Canning is going to Paris. For what, I wonder? His brother, Huskisson, was there last year; and he did nothing. It is supposed that the " revered and ruptured Ogden " orator is going to try the force of his oratory in order to induce France and her allies to let Portugal alone. He would do better to arm some ships of war! Oh! no: never will that be done again; or, at least, there never will again be war for three months as long as this borough and paper system shall last! This system has run itself out. It has lasted a good while, and has done tremendous mischief to the people of England; but it is over; it is done for; it will live for a while, but it will go about drooping its wings and half shutting its eyes, like a cock that has got the pip; it will never crow again; and for that I most humbly and fervently thank

God! It has crowed over us long enough: it has pecked us and spurred us and slapped us about quite long enough. The nasty, insolent creatures that it has sheltered under its wings have triumphed long enough: they are now going to the workhouse; and thither let them go.

I *know* nothing of the politics of the Bourbons; but though I can easily conceive that they would not like to see an end of the paper system and a consequent reform in England; though I can see very good reasons for believing this, I do not believe that Canning will induce them to sacrifice their own obvious and immediate interests for the sake of preserving our funding system. He will not get them out of Cadiz, and he will not induce them to desist from interfering in the affairs of Portugal, if they find it their interest to interfere. They know that we *cannot go to war*. They know this as well as we do; and every sane person in England seems to know it well. No war for us *without Reform !* We are come to this at last. No war with *this Debt ;* and this debt defies every power but that of *Reform*. Foreign nations were, as to our real state, a good deal enlightened by "late panic." They had hardly any notion of our state before that. That opened their eyes, and led them to conclusions that they never before dreamed of. It made them see that that which they had always taken for a mountain of solid gold, was only a great heap of rubbishy, rotten paper! And they now, of course, estimate us accordingly. But it signifies not what *they* think, or what *they* do; unless they will subscribe and pay off this *Debt* for the people at Whitehall. The foreign governments (not excepting the American) all hate the English reformers; those of Europe, because our example would be so dangerous to despots; and that of America, because we should not suffer it to build fleets and to add to its territories at pleasure. So that we have not only our own boroughmongers and tax-eaters against us, but also all foreign governments. Not a straw, however, do we care for them all, so long as we have for us the ever-living, ever-watchful, ever-efficient, and all-sub-duing *Debt !* Let our foes subscribe, I say, and pay off that *Debt ;* for until they do that we snap our fingers at them.

HIGHWORTH,
Friday, 8 Sept.

" The best public instructor " of yesterday (arrived to-day) informs us that " A number of official gentlemen connected

with finance have waited upon Lord Liverpool "! Connected
with finance! And "a number" of them too! Bless their
numerous and united noddles! Good God! what a state of
things it is altogether! There never was the like of it seen in
this world before. Certainly never; and the end must be what
the far greater part of the people anticipate. It was this very
Lord Liverpool that ascribed the *sufferings* of the country to a
surplus of food ; and that, too, at the very time when he was
advising the king to put forth a begging proclamation to raise
money to prevent, or, rather, put a stop to, starvation in Ireland;
and when, at the same time, public money was granted for the
causing of English people to emigrate to Africa! Ah! Good
God! who is to record or recount the endless blessings of a
jubilee-government! The "instructor" gives us a sad account
of the state of the working classes in Scotland. I am not glad
that these poor people suffer: I am very sorry for it; and if I
could relieve them, out of my own means, without doing good
to and removing danger from the insolent boroughmongers
and tax-eaters of Scotland, I would share my last shilling with
the poor fellows. But I must be glad that something has
happened to silence the impudent Scotch quacks, who have been,
for six years past, crying up the doctrine of Malthus, and railing
against the English poor laws. Let us now see what *they* will
do with their poor. Let us see whether they will have the
impudence to call upon *us* to maintain their poor! Well, amidst
all this suffering there is one good thing; the Scotch political
economy is blown to the devil, and the *Edinburgh Review* and
Adam Smith along with it.

MALMSBURY (WILTS),
Monday, 11 *Sept.*

I was detained at Highworth partly by the rain and partly
by company that I liked very much. I left it at six o'clock
yesterday morning, and got to this town about three or four
o'clock in the afternoon, after a ride, including my deviations,
of 34 miles; and as pleasant a ride as man ever had. I got
to a farm-house in the neighbourhood of Cricklade to breakfast,
at which house I was very near to the source of the river Isis,
which is, they say, the first branch of the Thames. They call it
the "Old Thames," and I rode through it here, it not being
above four or five yards wide, and not deeper than the knees
of my horse.

The land here, and all round Cricklade, is very fine. Here

are some of the very finest pastures in all England, and some of the finest dairies of cows, from 40 to 60 in a dairy, grazing in them. Was not this *always* so? Was it created by the union with Scotland; or was it begotten by Pitt and his crew? Aye, it was always so; and there were formerly two churches here, where there is now only one, and five, six, or ten times as many people. I saw in one single farm-yard here more food than enough for four times the inhabitants of the parish; and this yard did not contain a tenth, perhaps, of the produce of the parish; but while the poor creatures that raise the wheat and the barley and cheese and the mutton and the beef are living upon potatoes, an accursed *canal* comes kindly through the parish to convey away the wheat and all the good food to the tax-eaters and their attendants in the Wen! What, then, is this " an improvement? " Is a nation *richer* for the carrying away of the food from those who raise it, and giving it to bayonet men and others, who are assembled in great masses? I could broom-stick the fellow who would look me in the face and call this " an improvement." What! was it not better for the con- sumers of the food to live near to the places where it was grown? We have very nearly come to the system of Hindostan, where the farmer is allowed by the *Aumil*, or tax-contractor, only so much of the produce of his farm to eat in the year! The thing is not done in so undisguised a manner here: here are assessor, collector, exciseman, supervisor, informer, constable, justice, sheriff, jailer, judge, jury, jack-ketch, barrack-man. Here is a great deal of ceremony about it; all is done according to law; it is the *free-est* country in the world: but, somehow or other, the produce is, at last, *carried away ;* and it is eaten, for the main part, by those who do not work.

I observed, some pages back, that, when I got to Malmsbury, I should have to explain my main object in coming to the north of Wiltshire. In the year 1818, the parliament, by *an Act*, ordered the bishops to cause the beneficed clergy to give in an account of their livings, which account was to contain the following particulars relating to each parish:

1. Whether a rectory, vicarage, or what.
2. In what rural deanery.
3. Population.
4. Number of churches and chapels.
5. *Number of persons they* (the churches and chapels) *can contain.*

In looking into this account, as it was finally made up and printed by the parliamentary officers, I saw that it was impossible for it to be true. I have always asserted, and indeed I have clearly proved, that one of the two last population returns is false, barefacedly false; and I was sure that the account of which I am now speaking was equally false. The falsehood consisted, I saw principally, in the account of the capacity of the church to contain people; that is, under the head No. 5, as above stated. I saw that, in almost every instance, this account must of necessity be false, though coming from under the pen of a beneficed clergyman. I saw that there was a constant desire to make it appear that the church was now become too small! And thus to help along the opinion of a great recent increase of population, an opinion so sedulously inculcated by all the tax-eaters of every sort, and by the most brutal and best public instructor. In some cases the falsehood of this account was impudent almost beyond conception; and yet it required going to the spot to get unquestionable proof of the falsehood. In many of the parishes, in hundreds of them, the population is next to nothing, far fewer persons than the church porch would contain. Even in these cases the parsons have seldom said that the church would contain more than the population! In such cases they have generally said that the church can contain " the population! " So it can; but it can contain ten times the number! And thus it was that, in words of truth, a lie in meaning was told to the parliament, and not one word of notice was ever taken of it. Little Langford, or Landford, for instance, between Salisbury and Warminster, is returned as having a population under twenty, and a church that " can contain the population." This church, which I went and looked at, can contain, very conveniently, two hundred people! But there was one instance in which the parson had been singularly impudent; for he had stated the population at eight persons, and had stated that the church could contain eight persons! This was the account of the parish of Sharncut, in this county of Wilts. It lies on the very northernmost edge of the county, and its boundary, on one side, divides Wiltshire from Gloucestershire. To this Sharncut, therefore, I was resolved to go, and to try the fact with my own eyes. When, therefore, I got through Cricklade, I was compelled to quit the Malmsbury road, and go away to my right. I had to go through a village called Ashton Keines, with which place I was very much stricken. It is now a straggling village; but, to a certainty, it has been a large market town. There is a market-cross still standing in an open place in it; and there are such numerous lanes, crossing each other, and cutting the land up into such little bits, that it must, at one time, have been a large town. It is a very curious place, and I should have stopped in it for some time, but I was now within a few miles of the famous Sharncut, the church of which, according to the parson's account, *could* contain eight persons!

At the end of about three miles more of road, rather difficult to find, but very pleasant, I got to Sharncut, which I found to consist of a church, two farm-houses, and a parsonage-house, one part of the buildings of which had become a labourer's house. The church has no tower, but a sort of crowning-piece (very ancient) on the transept. The church is sixty feet long, and, on an average, twenty-eight feet wide; so that the area of it contains one thousand six hundred and eighty square feet; or one hundred and eighty-six square yards! I found in the church eleven pews that would contain, that were made to contain, eighty-two people; and these do not occupy a third part of the area of the church; and thus more than two hundred persons, at the least, might be accommodated, with perfect convenience, in this church, which the parson says "*can* contain *eight*"! Nay, the church porch, on its two benches, would hold twenty people, taking little and big promiscuously. I have been thus particular, in this instance, because I would leave no doubt as to the barefacedness of the lie. A strict inquiry would show that the far greater part of the account is a most impudent lie, or rather string of lies. For as to the subterfuge, that this account was true, because the church "*can* contain *eight*," it is an addition to the crime of lying. What the parliament meant was, what "is the greatest number of persons that the church can contain at worship;" and therefore to put the figure of 8 against the church of Sharncut was to tell the parliament a wilful lie. This parish is a rectory; it has great and small tithes; it has a glebe, and a good solid house, though the parson says it is unfit for him to live in! In short, he is not here; a curate that serves, perhaps, three or four other churches, comes here at five o'clock in the afternoon.

The *motive* for making out the returns in this way is clear enough. The parsons see that they are getting what they get in a declining and a mouldering country. The size of the church tells them, everything tells them, that the country is a mean and miserable thing compared with what it was in former times.

They feel the facts; but they wish to disguise them, because they know that they have been one great cause of the country being in its present impoverished and dilapidated state. They know that the people look at them with an accusing eye: and they wish to put as fair a face as they can upon the state of things. If you talk to them, they will never acknowledge that there is any misery in the country; because they well know how large a share they have had in the cause of it. They were always haughty and insolent, but the anti-jacobin times made them ten thousand times more so than ever. The cry of Atheism, as of the French, gave these fellows of ours a fine time of it: they became identified with loyalty and, what was more, with property; and, at one time, to say, or hint, a word against a parson, do what he would, was to be an enemy of God and of all property! Those were the glorious times for them. They urged on the war: they were the loudest of all the trumpeters. They saw their tithes in danger. If they did not get the Bourbons restored there was no chance of re-establishing tithes in France; and then the example might be fatal. But they forgot that to restore the Bourbons a debt must be contracted; and that, when the nation could not pay the interest of that debt, it would, as it now does, begin to look hard at the tithes! In short, they over-reached themselves; and those of them who have common sense now see it: each hopes that the thing will last out his time; but they have, unless they be half-idiots, a constant dread upon their minds: this makes them a great deal less brazen than they used to be; and, I dare say, that if the parliamentary return had to be made out again, the parson of Sharncut would not state that the church "*can* contain *eight persons.*"

From Sharncut I came through a very long and straggling village, called Somerford, another called Ocksey, and another called Crudwell. Between Somerford and Ocksey I saw, on the side of the road, more *goldfinches* than I had ever seen together; I think fifty times as many as I had ever seen at one time in my life. The favourite food of the goldfinch is the seed of the *thistle*. This seed is just now dead ripe. The thistles are all cut and carried away from the fields by the harvest; but they grow alongside the roads; and, in this place, in great quantities. So that the goldfinches were got here in flocks, and, as they continued to fly along before me, for nearly half a mile, and still sticking to the road and the banks, I do believe I had, at last, a flock of ten thousand flying before me. *Birds* of every kind, including partridges and pheasants and all sorts of poultry, are most abundant this year. The fine, long summer has been singularly favourable to them; and you see the effect of it in the great broods of chickens and ducks and geese and turkeys in and about every farm-yard.

The churches of the last-mentioned villages are all large, particularly the latter, which is capable of containing, very conveniently, 3000 or 4000 people. It is a very large church; it has a triple roof, and is nearly 100 feet long; and master parson says, in his return, that it "*can* contain *three hundred* people"! At Ocksey the people were in church as I came by. I heard the singers singing; and, as the church-yard was close by the road-side, I got off my horse and went in, giving my horse to a boy to hold. The fellow says that his church "*can* contain *two hundred* people." I counted pews for about 450; the singing gallery would hold 40 or 50; two-thirds of the area of the church have no pews in them. On benches these two-thirds would hold 2000 persons, taking one with another! But this is nothing rare; the same sort of statement has been made, the same kind of falsehoods, relative to the whole of the parishes, throughout the country, with here and there an exception. Everywhere you see the indubitable marks of *decay* in mansions, in parsonage-houses and in people. Nothing can so strongly depict the great decay of the villages as the state of the parsonage-houses, which are so many parcels of public property, and to prevent the dilapidation of which there are laws so strict. Since I left Devizes, I have passed close by, or very near to, thirty-two parish churches; and in fifteen out of these thirty-two parishes the parsonage-houses are stated, in the parliamentary return, either as being unfit for a parson to live in or as being wholly tumbled down and gone! What then, are there Scotch vagabonds; are there Chalmerses and Colquhounds, to swear, "mon," that Pitt and Jubilee George *begat* all us Englishmen; and that there were only a few stragglers of us in the world before! And that our dark and ignorant fathers, who built Winchester and Salisbury Cathedrals, had neither hands nor money!

When I got in here yesterday, I went, at first, to an inn; but I very soon changed my quarters for the house of a friend, who and whose family, though I had never seen them before, and had never heard of them until I was at Highworth, gave me a hearty reception, and precisely in *the style* that I like. This town, though it has nothing particularly engaging in itself, stands upon one of the prettiest spots that can be imagined. Besides the river Avon, which I went down in the south-east part of the country, here is another river Avon, which runs down to Bath, and two branches, or sources, of which meet here. There is a pretty ridge of ground, the base of which is a mile or a mile and a half wide. On each side of this ridge a branch of the river runs down, through a flat of very fine meadows. The town and the beautiful remains of the famous old abbey stand on the rounded spot which terminates this ridge; and, just below, nearly close to the town, the two branches of the river meet; and then they begin to be called *the Avon*. The land round about is excellent, and of a great variety of forms. The trees are lofty and fine: so that what with the water, the meadows, the fine cattle and sheep, and, as I hear, the absence of *hard*-pinching poverty, this is a very pleasant place. There remains more of the abbey than, I believe, of any of our monastic buildings, except that of Westminster, and those that have become cathedrals. The church service is performed in the part of the abbey that is left standing. The parish church has fallen down and is gone; but the tower remains, which is made use of for the bells; but the abbey is used as the church, though the church-tower is at a considerable distance from it. It was once a most magnificent building; and there is now a *doorway* which is the most beautiful thing I ever saw, and which was, nevertheless, built in Saxon times, in "the *dark* ages," and was built by men who were not begotten by Pitt nor by Jubilee George.—What *fools*, as well as ungrateful creatures, we have been and are! There is a broken arch, standing off from the sound part of the building, at which one cannot look up without feeling shame at the thought of ever having abused the men who made it. No one need *tell* any man of sense; he *feels* our inferiority to our fathers upon merely beholding the remains of their efforts to ornament their country and elevate the minds of the people. We talk of our skill and learning, indeed! How do we know how skilful, how learned *they* were? If, in all that they have left us, we see that they surpassed us, why are we to conclude that they did not surpass us in all other things worthy of admiration?

This famous abbey was founded, in about the year 600, by Maidulf, a Scotch monk, who upon the suppression of a nunnery here at that time selected the spot for this great establishment. For the great magnificence, however, to which it was soon after brought, it was indebted to Aldhelm, a monk educated within its first walls, by the founder himself; and to St. Aldhelm, who by his great virtues became very famous, the church was dedicated in the time of King Edgar. This monastery continued flourishing during those *dark* ages, until it was sacked by the great enlightener, at which time it was found to be endowed to the amount of £16,077 11s. 8d. of the money of the present day! Amongst other, many other, great men produced by this Abbey of Malmsbury, was that famous scholar and historian, William de Malmsbury.

There is a *market-cross* in this town, the sight of which is worth a journey of hundreds of miles. Time, with his scythe, and "enlightened Protestant piety," with its pick-axes and crow-bars; these united have done much to efface the beauties of this monument of ancient skill and taste, and proof of ancient wealth; but in spite of all their destructive efforts this cross still remains a most beautiful thing, though possibly, and even probably, nearly, or quite, a thousand years old. There is a *market-cross* lately erected at Devizes, and intended to imitate the ancient ones. Compare that with this, and then you have, pretty fairly, a view of the difference between us and our fore-fathers of the "dark ages."

To-morrow I start for Bollitree, near Ross, Herefordshire, my road being across the county, and through the city of Gloucester.

FROM MALMSBURY, IN WILTSHIRE, THROUGH GLOUCESTERSHIRE, HEREFORDSHIRE, AND WORCESTERSHIRE

I SET off from Malmsbury this morning at 6 o'clock, in as sweet and bright a morning as ever came out of the heavens, and leaving behind me as pleasant a house and as kind hosts as I ever met with in the whole course of my life, either in England or America; and that is saying a great deal indeed. This circumstance was the more pleasant, as I had never before either seen or heard of these kind, unaffected, sensible, *sans-façons*, and most agreeable friends. From Malmsbury I first came, at the end of five miles, to Tutbury, which is in Gloucestershire, there being here a sort of dell, or ravine, which, in this place, is the boundary line of the two counties, and over which you go on a bridge, one-half of which belongs to each county. And now, before I take my leave of Wiltshire, I must observe that, in the whole course of my life (days of *courtship* excepted, of course), I never passed seventeen pleasanter days than those which I have just spent in Wiltshire. It is, especially in the southern half, just the sort of country that I like; the weather has been pleasant; I have been in good houses and amongst good and beautiful gardens; and, in *every* case, I have not only been most kindly entertained, but my entertainers have been of just the stamp that I like.

I saw again, this morning, large flocks of *goldfinches* feeding on the thistle-seed on the roadside. The French call this bird by a name derived from the thistle, so notorious has it always been that they live upon this seed. *Thistle* is, in French, *chardon;* and the French call this beautiful little bird *chardonaret.* I never could have supposed that such flocks of these birds would ever be seen in England. But it is a great year for all the feathered race, whether wild or tame: naturally so, indeed; for every one knows that it is the *wet*, and not the *cold*, that is injurious to the breeding of birds of all sorts, whether land-birds or water-birds. They say that there are, this year, double the usual quantity of ducks and geese: and, really, they do seem to swarm in the farm-yards, wherever I go. It is a

in universal abhorrence: people would hate him; and, in short, if rich as Ricardo or Baring, he might live by himself; for no man would look upon him as a neighbour.

Tutbury is a very pretty town, and has a beautiful ancient church. The country is high along here for a mile or two towards Avening, which begins a long and deep and narrow valley, that comes all the way down to Stroud. When I got to the end of the high country, and the lower country opened to my view, I was at about three miles from Tutbury, on the road to Avening, leaving the Minchinghampton road to my right. Here I was upon the edge of the high land, looking right down upon the village of Avening, and seeing, just close to it, a large and fine mansion-house, a beautiful park, and, making part of the park, one of the finest, most magnificent woods (of 200 acres, I dare say), lying facing me, going from a valley up a gently-rising hill. While I was sitting on my horse, admiring this spot, a man came along with some tools in his hand, as if going somewhere to work as plumber. "Whose beautiful place is that?" said I. "One 'Squire Ricardo, I think they call him, but . . . " — You might have "knocked me down with a feather," as the old women say . . . "but" (continued the plumber) "the Old Gentleman's dead, and . . . " "God —— the old gentleman and the young gentleman too!" said I; and, giving my horse a blow, instead of a word, on I went down the hill. Before I got to the bottom, my reflections on the present state of the "market" and on the probable results of "watching the turn of it," had made me better humoured; and as one of the first objects that struck my eye in the village was the sign of the CROSS, and of the Red, or Bloody, Cross too, I asked the landlord some questions, which began a series of joking and bantering that I had with the people, from one end of the village to the other. I set them all a laughing; and though they could not know my name, they will remember me for a long while.— This estate of Gatcomb belonged, I am told, to a Mr. Shepperd, and to his fathers before him. I asked where this Shepperd was NOW? A tradesman-looking man told me that he did not know where he was; but that he had heard that he was living somewhere near to Bath! Thus they go! Thus they are squeezed out of existence. The little ones are gone; and the big ones have nothing left for it but to resort to the bands of holy matrimony with the turn of the market watchers and their breed. This the big ones are now doing apace; and there is this comfort at any rate; namely, that the connection cannot make them baser than they are, a boroughmonger being, of all God's creatures, the very basest.

From Avening I came on through Nailsworth, Woodchester, and Rodborough to this place. These villages lie on the sides of a narrow and deep valley, with a narrow stream of water running down the middle of it, and this stream turns the wheels of a great many mills and sets of machinery for the making of *woollen-cloth*. The factories begin at Avening, and are scattered all the way down the valley. There are steam-engines as well as water powers. The work and the trade is so flat that in, I should think, much more than a hundred acres of ground, which I have seen to-day, covered with rails or racks, for the drying of cloth, I do not think that I have seen one single acre where the racks had cloth upon them. The workmen do not get half wages; great numbers are thrown on the parish; but overseers and magistrates in this part of England do not presume that they are to leave anybody to starve to death; there is law here; this is in England, and not in " the north," where those who ought to see that the poor do not suffer, talk of their dying with hunger as Irish 'squires do; aye, and applaud them for their patient resignation!

The Gloucestershire people have no notion of dying with hunger; and it is with great pleasure that I remark that I have seen no woe-worn creature this day. The sub-soil here is a yellowish ugly stone. The houses are all built with this; and it being ugly, the stone is made *white* by a wash of some sort or other. The land on both sides of the valley, and all down the bottom of it, has plenty of trees on it; it is chiefly pasture land, so that the green and the white colours, and the form and great variety of the ground, and the water, and altogether make this a very pretty ride. Here are a series of spots, every one of which a lover of landscapes would like to have painted. Even the buildings of the factories are not ugly. The people seem to have been constantly well off. A pig in almost every cottage sty; that is the infallible mark of a happy people. At present this valley suffers; and though cloth will always be wanted, there will yet be much suffering even here, while at Uly and other places they say the suffering is great indeed.

HUNTLEY,
Between Gloucester and Ross.

From Stroud I came up to Pitchcomb, leaving Painswick on my right. From the lofty hill at Pitchcomb I looked down into that great flat and almost circular vale, of which the city of Gloucester is in the centre. To the left I saw the Severn, become a sort of arm of the sea; and before me I saw the hills that divide this county from Herefordshire and Worcestershire. The hill is a mile down. When down, you are amongst dairy-farms and orchards all the way to Gloucester, and, this year, the orchards, particularly those of pears, are greatly productive. I intended to sleep at Gloucester, as I had, when there, already come twenty-five miles, and as the fourteen, which remained for me to go, in order to reach Bollitree, in Herefordshire, would make about nine more than either I or my horse had a taste for. But when I came to Gloucester, I found that I should run a risk of having no bed if I did not bow very low and pay very high; for what should there be here, but one of those scandalous and beastly fruits of the system, called a "music-meeting!" Those who founded the cathedrals never dreamed, I dare say, that they would have been put to such uses as this! They are, upon these occasions, made use of as *Opera-Houses*; and, I am told, that the money which is collected goes, in some shape or another, to the clergy of the church, or their widows, or children, or something. These assemblages of player-folks, half-rogues and half-fools, began with the small paper-money; and with it they will go. They are amongst the profligate pranks which idleness plays when fed by the sweat of a starving people. From this scene of prostitution and of pocket-picking I moved off with all convenient speed, but not before the ostler made me pay 9*d.* for merely letting my horse *stand* about ten minutes, and not before he had *begun* to abuse me for declining, though in a very polite manner, to make him a present in addition to the 9*d.* How he ended I do not know; for I soon set the noise of the shoes of my horse to answer him. I got to this village, about eight miles from Gloucester, by five o'clock: it is now half-past seven, and I am going to bed with an intention of getting to Bollitree (six miles only) early enough in the morning to catch my sons in bed if they play the sluggard.

BOLLITREE,
Wednesday, 13 Sept.

This morning was most beautiful. There has been rain here now, and the grass begins (but only begins) to grow. When I got within two hundred yards of Mr. Palmer's, I had the happiness to meet my son Richard, who said that he had been up an hour. As I came along I saw one of the prettiest sights in the *flower* way that I ever saw in my life. It was a little orchard; the grass in it had just taken a start, and was beautifully fresh; and very thickly growing amongst the grass was the purple flowered *Colchicum*, in full bloom. They say that the leaves of this plant which come out in the spring and die away in the summer, are poisonous to cattle if they eat much of them in the spring. The flower, if standing by itself, would be no great beauty; but contrasted thus with the fresh grass, which was a little shorter than itself, it was very beautiful.

BOLLITREE,
Saturday, 23 Sept.

Upon my arrival here, which, as the reader has seen, was ten days ago, I had a parcel of *letters* to open, amongst which were a large lot from correspondents, who had been good enough to set me right with regard to that conceited and impudent plagiarist, or literary thief, " Sir James Graham, Baronet of Netherby." One correspondent says that I have reversed the rule of the Decalogue by visiting the sins of the son upon the father. Another tells me anecdotes about the " Magnus Apollo." I hereby do the father justice by saying that, from what I have now heard of him, I am induced to believe that he would have been ashamed to commit flagrant acts of plagiarism, which the son has been guilty of. The whole of this plagiarist's pamphlet is bad enough. Every part of it is contemptible; but the passage in which he says that there was " no man, of any authority, who did not under-rate the distress that would arise out of Peel's bill; " this passage merits a broom-stick at the hands of any Englishman that chooses to lay it on, and particularly from me.

As to *crops* in Herefordshire and Gloucestershire, they have been very bad. Even the wheat here has been only a two-third part crop. The barley and oats really next to nothing. *Fed off* by cattle and sheep in many places, partly for want of grass and partly from their worthlessness. The cattle have been nearly starved in many places; and we hear the same from Worcestershire. In some places one of these beautiful calves (last spring calves) will be given for the wintering of another. Hay at Stroud was £6 a ton: last year it was £3 a ton: and yet meat and cheese are lower in price than they were last year. Mutton (I mean alive) was last year at this time 7½d.; it is now 6d. There has been in North Wilts and in Gloucestershire half the quantity of cheese made this year, and yet the price is lower than it was last year. Wool is half the last year's price. There has, within these three weeks, or a month, been a prodigious increase in the quantity of cattle food; the grass looks like the grass late in May; and the late and stubble-turnips (of which immense quantities have been sown) have grown very much, and promise large crops generally; yet lean sheep have, at the recent fairs, fallen in price; they have been lessening in price while the facility of keeping them has been augmenting! Aye; but the paper-money has not been augmenting, notwithstanding the branch-bank at Gloucester! This bank is quite ready, they say, to take deposits; that is to say, to keep people's spare money for them; but to lend them none, without such security as would get money even from the claws of a miser. This trick is, then, what the French call a *coup-manqué*, or a missing of the mark. In spite of everything as to the season calculated to cause lean sheep to rise in price, they fell, I hear, at Wilton fair (near Salisbury) on the 12th instant from 2s. to 3s. a head. And yesterday, 22nd Sept., at Newent fair, there was a fall since the last fair in this neighbourhood. Mr. Palmer sold, at this fair, sheep for 23s. a head, rather better than some which he sold at the same fair last year for 34s. a head: so that here is a falling off of a third! Think of the dreadful ruin, then, which must fall upon the renting farmers, whether they rent the land or rent the money which enables them to call the land their own! The recent order in council *has* ruined many. I was, a few days after that order reached us, in Wiltshire, in a rick-yard, looking at the ricks, amongst which were two of beans. I asked the farmer how much the order would take out of his pocket; and he said it had already taken out more than a hundred pounds! This is a pretty state of things for a man to live in! The winds are less uncertain than this calling of a farmer is now become, though it is a calling the affairs of which have always been deemed as little liable to accident as anything human.

The "best public instructor" tells us that the ministers are about to give the *militia-clothing* to the poor manufacturers! Coats, waistcoats, trousers, shoes and stockings! Oh, what a kind as well as wise "envy of surrounding nations" this is! Dear good souls! But what are the *women* to do? No *smocks*, pretty gentlemen! No royal commission to be appointed to distribute smocks to the suffering "females" of the "*disturbed* districts!" How fine our "manufacturing population" will look all dressed in *red !* Then indeed will the farming fellows have to repent that they did not follow the advice of Dr. Black and fly to the "*happy* manufacturing districts" where employment, as the doctor affirmed, was so abundant and so permanent, and where wages were so high! Out of evil comes good; and this state of things has blown the Scotch *poleeteecal ecoonoomy* to the devil, at any rate. In spite of all their plausibility and persevering brass, the Scotch writers are now generally looked upon as so many tricky humbugs. Mr. Sedgwick's affair is enough, one would think, to open men's eyes to the character of this greedy band of *invaders ;* for invaders they are, and of the very worst sort: they come only to live on the labour of others; never to work themselves; and while they do this, they are everlastingly publishing essays, the object of which is to keep the Irish out of England! Dr. Black has, within these four years, published more than a hundred articles, in which he has represented the invasion of the Irish as being ruinous to England! What monstrous impudence! The Irish come to help do the work; the Scotch to help eat the taxes; or to tramp "*aboot mon*" with a pack and licence; or, in other words, to cheat upon a small scale, as their superiors do upon a large one. This tricky and greedy set have, however, at last over-reached themselves, after having so long over-reached all the rest of mankind that have had the misfortune to come in contact with them. They are now smarting under the scourge, the torments of which they have long made others feel. They have been the principal inventors and executors of all that has been damnable to England. They are *now* bothered; and I thank God for it. It may, and it must, finally deliver us from their baleful influence.

To return to the kind and pretty gentlemen of Whitehall, and their *militia-clothing :* if they refuse to supply the women with smocks, perhaps they would have no objection to hand them over some petticoats; or, at any rate, to give their husbands a *musket* apiece, and a little powder and ball; just to amuse themselves with, instead of the employment of "digging holes one day and filling them up the next," as suggested by "that great statesman, now no more," who was one of that "noble, honourable, and venerable body" the Privy Council (to which Sturges Bourne belongs), and who cut his own throat at North Cray, in Kent, just about three years after he had brought in the bill which compelled me to make the *Register* contain two sheets and a quarter, and to compel printers to give, before they began to print, bail to pay any fines that might be inflicted on them for anything that they might print. Let me see: where was I? Oh! the muskets and powder and ball ought, certainly, to go with the red clothes; but how strange it is that the *real relief* never seems to occur, even for one single moment, to the minds of these pretty gentlemen; namely, *taking off the taxes*. What a thing it is to behold poor people receiving rates, or alms, to prevent them from starving; and to behold one half, at least, of what they receive taken from them in taxes! What a sight to behold soldiers, horse and foot, employed to prevent a distressed people from committing acts of violence, when the *cost* of the horse and foot would, probably, if applied in the way of relief to the sufferers, prevent the existence of the distress! A cavalry horse has, I think, ten pounds of oats a day and twenty pounds of hay. These at present prices cost 16s. a week. Then there is stable room, barracks, straw, saddle and all the trappings. Then there is the wear of the horse. Then the pay of them. So that one single horseman, with his horse, do not cost so little as 36s. a week; and that is more than the parish allowance to five labourers' or manufacturers' families, at five to a family; so that one horseman and his horse cost what would feed twenty-five of the distressed creatures. If there be ten thousand of these horsemen, they cost as much as would keep, at the parish rate, two hundred and fifty thousand of the distressed persons. Aye; it is even so, Parson Hay, stare at it as long as you like. But suppose it to be only half as much: then it would maintain a hundred and twenty-five thousand persons. However, to get rid of all dispute, and to state one staring and undeniable fact, let me first observe, that it is notorious that the poor-rates are looked upon as enormous; that they are deemed an insupportable burden; that Scarlett and Nolan have asserted that they threaten to swallow up the land; that it is equally notorious that a large part of the poor-rates ought to be called *wages ;* all this is undeniable, and now comes the damning fact; namely, that the whole amount of these poor-rates falls far short of the cost of the standing army in time of peace! So that, take away this army, which is to keep the distressed people from committing acts of violence, and you have at once ample means of removing all the distress and all the danger of acts of violence! *When* will this be done? Do not say, " *Never*," reader: if you do, you are not only a slave, but you ought to be one.

I cannot dismiss this *militia-clothing* affair without remarking that I do not agree with those who *blame* the ministers for having let in the foreign corn *out of fear*. Why not do it from that motive? " The fear of the Lord is the beginning of wisdom."

And what is meant by " fear of the Lord " but the fear of doing wrong, or of persevering in doing wrong? And whence is this fear to arise? From thinking of the *consequences*, to be sure: and therefore, if the ministers did let in the foreign corn for fear of popular commotion, they acted rightly, and their motive was as good and reasonable as the act was wise and just. It would have been lucky for them if the same sort of motive had prevailed when the Corn Bill was passed; but that *game-cock* statesman, who at last sent a spur into his own throat, was then in high feather, and he, while soldiers were drawn up round the Honourable, Honourable, Honourable House, said that he did not, for his part, care much about the bill; but since the mob had clamoured against *it*, he was resolved to support it! Alas! that such a *cock* statesman should have come to such an end! All the towns and cities in England petitioned against that odious bill. Their petitions were rejected, and that rejection is *amongst* the causes of the present embarrassments. Therefore I am not for blaming the ministers for acting from *fear*. They did the same in the case of the poor queen. Fear taught them wisely, then, also. What! would you never have people act from *fear* ? What but fear of the law restrains many men from committing crimes? What but fear of exposure prevents thousands upon thousands of offences, moral as well as legal? Nonsense about " acting from fear." I always hear with great suspicion your eulogists of " *vigorous* " government; I do not like vigorous governments; your game-cock governments. We saw enough of these, and *felt* enough of them, too, under Pitt, Dundas, Perceval, Gibbs, Ellenborough, Sidmouth and Castlereagh. I prefer governments like those of Edward I. of England and St. Louis of France; *cocks* as towards their enemies and rivals, and *chickens* as towards their own people: precisely the reverse of our modern " country gentlemen," as they call themselves; very lions as towards their poor, robbed, famishing labourers, but more than lambs as towards tax-eaters, and especially as towards the fierce and whiskered *dead-weight*, in the presence of any of whom they dare not say that their souls are their own. This base race of men, called " country gentlemen," must be speedily changed by almost a miracle; or they, big as well as little, must be swept away; and if it should be desirable for posterity to have a just idea of them, let posterity take this one fact; that the tithes are now, in part, received by men who are rectors and vicars, and who at the same time receive half-pay as naval or military officers; and that not one English " country gentleman " has had the courage even to complain of this, though many gallant half-pay officers have been dismissed and beggared upon the ground that the half-pay is not a reward for past services, but a retaining fee for future services; so that, put the two together, they amount to this: that the half-pay is given to church parsons, that they may be, when war comes, ready to serve as officers in the army or navy! Let the world match that if it can! And yet there are scoundrels to say that we do not want a *radical reform!* Why, there must be such a reform in order to prevent us from becoming a mass of wretches too corrupt and profligate and base even to carry on the common transactions of life.

RYALL, NEAR UPTON-ON-SEVERN (WORCESTERSHIRE),
Monday, 25 Sept.

I set off from Mr. Palmer's yesterday, after breakfast, having his son (about 13 years old) as my travelling companion. We came across the country, a distance of about 22 miles, and having crossed the Severn at Upton, arrived here, at Mr. John Price's, about two o'clock. On our road we passed by the estate and park of *another Ricardo!* This is Osmond; the other is David. This one has ousted two families of Normans, the Honeywood Yateses and the Scudamores. They suppose him to have ten thousand pounds a year in rent here! Famous " watching the turn of the market "! The Barings are at work down in this country too. They are everywhere, indeed, depositing their eggs about, like cunning old guinea-hens, in sly places, besides the great, open showy nests that they have. The " instructor " tells us that the Ricardos have received sixty-four thousand pounds commission on the " Greek loans," or rather " loans to the Greeks." Oh, brave Greeks, to have such patriots to aid you with their financial skill; such patriots as Mr. Galloway to make engines of war for you, while his son is making them for the Turks; and such patriots as Burdett and Hobhouse to talk of your political relations! Happy Greeks! Happy Mexicans, too, it seems; for the " best instructor " tells us that the Barings, whose progenitors came from Dutchland about the same time as, and perhaps in company with, the Ricardos; happy Mexicans too; for the " instructor " as good as swears that the Barings will see that the dividends on your loans are paid in future! Now, therefore, the riches, the loads, the shiploads of silver and gold are now to pour in upon us!

Never was there a nation so foolish as this! But, and this ought to be well understood, it is not *mere* foolishness; not mere harmless folly; it is foolishness, the offspring of *greediness* and of a *gambling*, which is little short of a *roguish* disposition; and this disposition prevails to an enormous extent in the country, as I am told, more than in the monstrous Wen itself. Most delightfully, however, have the greedy, mercenary, selfish, unfeeling wretches been bit by the *loans* and *shares!* The King of Spain gave the wretches a sharp bite, for which I always most cordially thank his majesty. I dare say that his sponging off of the roguish bonds has reduced to beggary, or caused to cut their throats, many thousands of the greedy, fund-loving, stockjobbing devils, who, if they regard it likely to raise their "securities" one per cent., would applaud the murder of half the human race. These vermin all, without a single exception, approved of and rejoiced at Sidmouth's *Power-of-Imprisonment Bill*, and they applauded his *Letter of Thanks to the Manchester Yeomanry Cavalry*. No matter what it is that puts an end to a system which engenders and breeds up vermin like these.

Mr. Hanford, of this county, and Mr. Canning of Gloucestershire, having dined at Mr. Price's yesterday, I went, to-day, with Mr. Price to see Mr. Hanford at his house and estate at Bredon Hill, which is, I believe, one of the highest in England. The ridge, or, rather, the edge of it, divides, in this part, Worcestershire from Gloucestershire. At the very highest part of it there are the remains of an encampment, or rather, I should think, citadel. In many instances in Wiltshire these marks of fortifications are called castles still; and doubtless there were once castles on these spots. From Bredon Hill you see into nine or ten counties; and those curious bubblings-up, the Malvern Hills, are right before you, and only at about ten miles' distance, in a straight line. As this hill looks over the counties of Worcester, Gloucester, Hereford and part of Warwick and the rich part of Stafford; and as it looks over the vales of Esham, Worcester, and Gloucester, having the Avon and the Severn winding down them, you certainly see from this Bredon Hill one of the very richest spots of England, and I am fully convinced a richer spot than is to be seen in any other country in the world; I mean *Scotland excepted*, of course, for fear Sawney should cut my throat, or, which is much the same thing, squeeze me by the hand, from which last I pray thee to deliver me, O Lord!

The Avon (this is the *third* Avon that I have crossed in this

great mistake to suppose that ducks and geese *need* water, except
to drink.   There is, perhaps, no spot in the world, in proportion
to its size and population, where so many of these birds are
reared and fatted as in Long Island; and it is not in one case
out of ten that they have any ponds to go to, or that they ever
see any water other than water that is drawn up out of a well.

A little way before I got to Tutbury I saw a woman digging
some potatoes in a strip of ground making part of a field nearly
an oblong square, and which field appeared to be laid out in
strips.   She told me that the field was part of a farm (to the
homestead of which she pointed); that it was, by the farmer,
let out in strips to labouring people; that each strip contained
a rood (or quarter of a statute acre); that each married labourer
rented one strip; and that the annual rent was *a pound* for
the strip.   Now the taxes being all paid by the farmer; the
fences being kept in repair by him; and, as appeared to me, the
land being exceedingly good: all these things considered, the
rent does not appear to be too high.—This fashion is certainly a
growing one; it is a little step towards a coming back to the
ancient small life and leaseholds and common-fields!   This field
of strips was, in fact, a sort of common-field; and the " agriculturists," as the conceited asses of landlords call themselves, at
their clubs and meetings, might, and they would if their skulls
could admit any thoughts except such as relate to high prices
and low wages; they might, and they would, begin to suspect
that the " dark age " people were not so very foolish when they
had so many common-fields, and when almost every man that
had a family had also a bit of land, either large or small.   It is
a very curious thing that the enclosing of commons, that the
shutting out of the labourers *from all share* in the land; that
the prohibiting of them to look at a wild animal, almost at a
lark or a frog; it is curious that this hard-hearted system should
have gone on until at last it has produced effects so injurious
and so dangerous to the grinders themselves that they have, of
their own accord and for their own safety, begun to make a step
towards the ancient system, and have, in the manner I have
observed, made the labourers sharers, in some degree, in the
uses, at any rate, of the soil.   The far greater part of these strips
of land have potatoes growing in them; but in some cases they
have borne wheat, and in others barley, this year; and these have
now turnips; very young most of them, but in some places very
fine, and in every instance nicely hoed out.   The land that will
bear 400 bushels of potatoes to the acre will bear 40 bushels of

wheat; and the ten bushels of wheat to the quarter of an acre would be a crop far more valuable than a hundred bushels of potatoes, as I have proved many times in the *Register*.

Just before I got into Tutbury I was met by a good many people, in twos, threes, or fives, some running, and some walking fast, one of the first of whom asked me if I had met an " old man " some distance back. I asked what *sort* of a man: " A *poor* man." " I don't recollect, indeed; but what are you all pursuing him for? " " He has been *stealing*." " What has he been stealing? " " Cabbages." " Where? " " Out of Mr. Glover, the hatter's, garden." " What! do you call that *stealing;* and would you punish a man, a poor man, and there-fore, in all likelihood, a hungry man too, and moreover an old man; do you set up a hue-and-cry after, and would you punish, such a man for taking a few cabbages, when that Holy Bible, which, I dare say, you profess to believe in, and perhaps assist to circulate, teaches you that the hungry man may, without committing any offence at all, go into his neighbour's vineyard and eat his fill of grapes, one bunch of which is worth a sack-full of cabbages? " " Yes; but he is a very bad character." " Why, my friend, very poor and almost starved people are apt to be ' bad characters; ' but the Bible, in both Testaments, commands us to be merciful to the poor, to feed the hungry, to have compassion on the aged; and it makes no exception as to the ' character ' of the parties." Another group or two of the pursuers had come up by this time; and I, bearing in mind the fate of Don Quixote when he interfered in somewhat similar cases, gave my horse the hint, and soon got away; but though doubtless I made no converts, I, upon looking back, perceived that I had slackened the pursuit! The pursuers went more slowly; I could see that they got to talking; it was now the step of deliberation rather than that of decision; and though I did not like to call upon Mr. Glover, I hope he was merciful. It is impossible for me to witness scenes like this; to hear a man called *a thief* for such a cause; to see him thus eagerly and vindictively pursued for having taken some cabbages in a garden: it is impossible for me to behold such a scene, without calling to mind the practice in the United States of America, where, if a man were even to talk of prosecuting another (especially if that other were poor or old) for taking from the land, or from the trees, any part of a growing crop, for his own personal and immediate use; if any man were even to talk of prosecuting another for such an act, such talker would be held *reform,* in 1817, my Lord Somers wrote and published a pamphlet under his own name, condemning our conduct and our principles, and insisting that we, if let alone, should produce " *a revolution, and endanger all property !* " The Barings are adding field to field and tract to tract in Herefordshire; and as to the Ricardos, they seem to be animated with the same laudable spirit. This Osmond Ricardo has a park at one of his estates called Broomsborough, and that park has a new porter's lodge, upon which there is a span new cross as large as life! Aye, big enough and long enough to crucify a man upon! I had never seen such an one before; and I know not what sort of thought it was that seized me at the moment; but, though my horse is but a clumsy goer, I verily believe I got away from it at the rate of ten or twelve miles an hour. My companion, who is always upon the look-out for cross-ditches, or pieces of timber on the road-side, to fill up the time of which my jog-trot gives him so wearisome a surplus, seemed delighted at this my new pace; and I dare say he has wondered ever since what should have given me wings just for that once and that once only.

WORCESTER,
Tuesday, 26 *Sept.*

Mr. Price rode with us to this city, which is one of the cleanest, neatest, and handsomest towns I ever saw: indeed, I do not recollect to have seen any one equal to it. The *cathedral* is, indeed, a poor thing, compared with any of the others, except that of Hereford; and I have seen them all but those of Carlisle, Durham, York, Lincoln, Chester, and Peterborough; but the *town* is, I think, the very best I ever saw; and which is, indeed, the greatest of all recommendations, the *people* are, upon the whole, the most suitably dressed and most decent looking people. The town is precisely in character with the beautiful and rich country, in the midst of which it lies. Everything you see gives you the idea of real, solid wealth; aye! and thus it was, too, before, long before Pitt, and even long before " good Queen Bess " and her military law and her Protestant racks, were ever heard or dreamed of.

At Worcester, as everywhere else, I find a group of cordial and sensible friends, at the house of one of whom, Mr. George Brooke, I have just spent a most pleasant evening, in company with several gentlemen whom he had had the goodness to invite to meet me. I here learned a fact which I must put upon record before it escape my memory. Some few years ago (about seven, perhaps), at the public sale by auction of the goods of a then recently deceased attorney of the name of Hyde in this city, there were, amongst the goods to be sold, the portraits of *Pitt*, *Burdett*, and *Paine*, all framed and glazed. Pitt, with hard driving and very lofty praises, fetched fifteen shillings; Burdett fetched twenty-seven shillings. Paine was, in great haste, knocked down at five pounds; and my informant was convinced that the lucky purchaser might have had fifteen pounds for it. I hear Colonel Davies spoken of here with great approbation: he will soon have an opportunity of showing us whether he deserve it.

The hop-picking and bagging is over here. The crop, as in the other hop-countries, has been very great, and the quality as good as ever was known. The average price appears to be about 75s. the hundredweight. The reader (if he do not belong to a hop-country) should be told that hop-planters, and even all their neighbours, are, as hop-ward, *mad*, though the most sane and reasonable people as to all other matters. They are ten times more jealous upon this score than men ever are of their wives; aye, and than they are of their mistresses, which is going a great deal farther. I, who am a *Farnham* man, was well aware of this foible; and therefore, when a gentleman told me that he would not brew with Farnham hops, if he could have them as a gift, I took special care not to ask him how it came to pass that the Farnham hops always sold at about double the price of the Worcester; but if he had said the same thing to any other Farnham man that I ever saw, I should have preferred being absent from the spot: the hops are bitter, but nothing is their bitterness compared to the language that my townsman would have put forth.

This city, or this neighbourhood at least, being the birthplace of what I have called the " Little-Shilling project," and Messrs. Atwood and Spooner being the originators of the project, and the project having been adopted by Mr. Western, and having been by him now again recently urged upon the ministers, in a letter to Lord Liverpool, and it being possible that some worthy persons may be misled, and even ruined, by the confident assertions and the pertinacity of the projectors; this being the case, and I having half an hour to spare, will here endeavour to show, in as few words as I can, that this project, if put into execution, would produce injustice the most crying that the world ever heard of, and would, in the present state of things, infallibly lead to a violent revolution. The project is to " lower the standard," as they call it; that is to say, to make a *sovereign pass for more than* 20*s*. In what *degree* they would reduce the standard they do not say; but a vile pamphlet writer, whose name is Crutwell, and who is a beneficed parson, and who has most foully abused me, because I laugh at the project, says that he would reduce it one half; that is to say, that he would make a sovereign pass for two pounds. Well, then, let us for plainness' sake suppose that the present sovereign is, all at once, to pass for two pounds. What will the consequences be? Why, here is a parson who receives his tithes in kind, and whose tithes are, we will suppose, a thousand bushels of wheat in a year, on an average; and he owes a thousand pounds to somebody. He will pay his debt with 500 sovereigns, and he will still receive his thousand bushels of wheat a year! I let a farm for £100 a year, by the year; and I have a mortgage of £2000 upon it, the interest just taking away the rent. Pass the project, and then I, of course, raise my rent to £200 a year, and I still pay the mortgagee £100 a year! What can be plainer than this? But the banker's is the fine case. I deposit with a banker a thousand whole sovereigns to-day. Pass the project to-morrow, and the banker pays me my deposit with a thousand half sovereigns! If, indeed, you could double the quantity of corn and meat and all goods by the same act of parliament, then all would be right; but that quantity will remain what it was before you passed the project; and, of course, the money being doubled in nominal amount, the price of the goods would be doubled. There needs not another word upon the subject; and whatever may be the national inference respecting the intellects of Messrs. Atwood and Spooner, I must say that I do most sincerely believe that there is not one of my readers who will not feel astonishment that any men, having the reputation of men of sound mind, should not clearly see that such a project must almost instantly produce a revolution of the most dreadful character.

STANFORD PARK,
Wednesday Morning, 27 Sept.

In a letter which I received from Sir Thomas Winnington (one of the members for this county) last year, he was good enough to request that I would call upon him if I ever came into Worcestershire, which I told him I would do; and accordingly here we are in his house, situated, certainly, in one of the finest spots in all England. We left Worcester yesterday about ten o'clock, crossed the Severn, which runs close by the town, and came on to this place, which lies in a north-western direction from Worcester, at 14 miles distance from that city, and at about six from the borders of Shropshire. About four miles back we passed by the park and through the estate of Lord Foley, to whom is due the praise of being a most indefatigable and successful *planter of trees*. He seems to have taken uncommon pains in the execution of this work; and he has the merit of disinterestedness, the trees being chiefly oaks, which he is *sure* he can never see grow to timber. We crossed the Teme river just before we got here. Sir Thomas was out shooting; but he soon came home, and gave us a very polite reception. I had time, yesterday, to see the place, to look at trees, and the like, and I wished to get away early this morning; but being prevailed on to stay to breakfast, here I am, at six o'clock in the morning, in one of the best and best-stocked private libraries that I ever saw; and, what is more, the owner, from what passed yesterday, when he brought me hither, convinced me that he was acquainted with the *insides* of the books. I asked, and shall ask, no questions about who got these books together; but the collection is such as, I am sure, I never saw before in a private house.

The house and stables and courts are such as they ought to be for the great estate that surrounds them; and the park is everything that is beautiful. On one side of the house, looking over a fine piece of water, you see a distant valley, opening between lofty hills: on another side the ground descends a little at first, then goes gently rising for a while, and then rapidly, to the distance of a mile perhaps, where it is crowned with trees in irregular patches, or groups, single and most magnificent trees being scattered all over the whole of the park; on another side, there rise up beautiful little hills, some in the form of barrows on the downs, only forty or a hundred times as large, one or two with no trees on them, and others topped with trees; but on one of these little hills, and some yards higher than the lofty trees which are on this little hill, you see rising up the tower of the parish church, which hill is, I think, taken all together, amongst the most delightful objects that I ever beheld.

"Well, then," says the devil of laziness, "and could you not be contented to live here all the rest of your life; and never again pester yourself with the cursed politics?" "Why, I think I have laboured enough. Let others work now. And such a pretty place for coursing and for hare-hunting and woodcock shooting, I dare say; and then those pretty wild ducks in the water, and the flowers and the grass and the trees and all the birds in spring and the fresh air, and never, never again to be stifled with the smoke that from the infernal Wen ascendeth for ever more and that every easterly wind brings to choke me at Kensington!" The *last word* of this soliloquy carried me back, slap, to my own study (very much unlike that which I am in), and bade me think of the GRIDIRON; bade me think of the complete triumph that I have yet to enjoy: promised me the pleasure of seeing a million of trees of my own, and sown by my own hands this very year. Ah! but the hares and the pheasants and the wild ducks! Yes, but the delight of seeing Prosperity Robinson hang his head for shame: the delight of beholding the tormenting embarrassments of those who have so long retained crowds of base miscreants to revile me; the delight of ousting spitten-upon Stanley and bound-over Wood! Yes, but, then, the flowers and the birds and the sweet air! What, then, shall Canning never again hear of the " revered and ruptured Ogden!" Shall he go into his grave without being again reminded of " driving at the whole herd, in order to get at the *ignoble animal!*" Shall he never again be told of Six-Acts and of his wish " to extinguish that *accursed torch of discord for ever!*" Oh! God forbid! farewell hares and dogs and birds! what, shall Sidmouth, then, never again hear of his *Power of Imprisonment Bill*, of his *Circular*, of his *Letter of Thanks to the Manchester Yeomanry!* I really jumped up when this thought came athwart my mind, and, without thinking of the breakfast, said to George who was sitting by me, " Go, George, and tell them to saddle the horses; " for it seemed to me that I had been meditating some crime. Upon George asking me whether I would not stop to breakfast? I bade him not order the horses out yet; and here we are, waiting for breakfast.

RYALL,
Wednesday Night, 27 Sept.

After breakfast we took our leave of Sir Thomas Winnington, and of Stanford, very much pleased with our visit. We wished to reach Ryall as early as possible in the day, and we did not, therefore, stop at Worcester. We got here about three o'clock, and we intend to set off, in another direction, early in the morning.

FROM RYALL, IN WORCESTERSHIRE, TO BURGH-CLERE, IN HAMPSHIRE

> "Alas, the country! How shall tongue or pen
> Bewail her now, *un*country gentlemen!
> The last to bid the cry of warfare cease,
> The first to make a malady of peace!
> For what were all these country patriots born?
> To hunt, and vote, and raise the price of corn.
> But corn, like ev'ry mortal thing, must fall:
> Kings, conquerors, and *markets most of all*."
>
> LORD BYRON.

RYALL,
Friday Morning, 29 September 1826.

I HAVE observed in this country, and especially near Worcester, that the working people seem to be better off than in many other parts, one cause of which is, I dare say, that *glove manufacturing*, which cannot be carried on by fire or by wind or by water, and which is, therefore, carried on by the *hands* of human beings. It gives work to women and children as well as to men; and that work is, by a great part of the women and children, done in their cottages, and amidst the fields and hop-gardens, where the husbands and sons must live, in order to raise the food and the drink and the wool. This is a great thing for the land. If this glove-making were to cease, many of these women and children, now not upon the parish, must instantly be upon the parish. The glove-trade is, like all others, slack from this last change in the value of money; but there is no horrible misery here, as at Manchester, Leeds, Glasgow, Paisley, and other Hell-Holes of 84 degrees of heat. There misery walks abroad in skin, bone and nakedness. There are no subscriptions wanted for Worcester; no militia-clothing. The working people suffer, trades-people suffer, and who is to escape, except the monopolisers, the Jews, and the tax-eaters, when the government chooses to raise the value of money and lower the price of goods? The whole of the industrious part of the country must suffer in such a case; but where manufacturing is mixed with agriculture, where the wife and daughters are at the needle, or the wheel, while the men and the boys are at plough, and where the manufacturing, of which one or two towns are the centres, is spread over the whole country round about, and particularly where it is, in very great part, performed by females at their *own homes*, and where the earnings come *in aid of the man's wages* ; in such case the misery cannot be so great; and accordingly, while there is an absolute destruction of life going on in the hell-holes, there is no *visible* misery at, or near, Worcester; and I cannot take my leave of this county without observing, that I do not recollect to have seen one miserable object in it. The working people all seem to have good large gardens, and pigs in their styes; and this last, say the *feelosofers* what they will about her " antallectual enjoyments," is the *only* security for happiness in a labourer's family.

Then this glove-manufacturing is not like that of cottons, a mere gambling concern, making baronets to-day and bankrupts to-morrow, and making those who do the work slaves. Here are no masses of people called together by a *bell*, and " kept *to it* " by a driver; here are no " patriots " who, while they keep Englishmen to it by fines, and almost by the scourge, in a heat of 84 degrees, are petitioning the parliament to " give freedom " to the South Americans, who, as these " patriots " have been informed, use a great quantity of *cottons !*

The dilapidation of parsonage-houses and the depopulation of villages appears not to have been so great just round about Worcester as in some other parts; but they have made great progress even here. No man appears to fat an ox, or hardly a sheep, except with a view of sending it to London, or to some other infernal resort of monopolisers and tax-eaters. Here, as in Wiltshire and Gloucestershire and Herefordshire, you find plenty of large churches without scarcely any people. I dare say that, even in this county, more than one half of the parishes have either no parsonage-houses at all, or have not one that a parson thinks fit for him to live in; and I venture to assert that one or the other of these is the case in four parishes out of every five in Herefordshire! Is not this a monstrous shame? Is this " a church? " Is this " law? " The parsons get the tithes and the rent of the glebe-lands, and the parsonage-houses are left to tumble down, and nettles and brambles to hide the spot where they stood. But the fact is, the Jew-system has swept all the little gentry, the small farmers, and the domestic manufacturers away. The land is now used to raise food and drink for the monopolisers and the tax-eaters and their purveyors and lackeys and harlots; and they get together in Wens.

Of all the mean, all the cowardly reptiles, that ever crawled

on the face of the earth, the *English land-owners* are the most
mean and the most cowardly: for while they support the
churches in their several parishes, while they see the population
drawn away from their parishes to the Wens, while they are
taxed to keep the people in the Wens, and while they see their
own parsons pocket the tithes and the glebe-rents, and suffer
the parsonage-houses to fall down; while they see all this, they,
without uttering a word in the way of complaint, suffer themselves and their neighbours to be taxed, to build new churches
for the monopolisers and tax-eaters in those Wens! Never was
there in this world a set of reptiles so base as this. Stupid as
many of them are, they must clearly see the flagrant injustice of
making the depopulated parishes pay for the aggrandisement of
those who have caused the depopulation, aye, actually pay taxes
to add to the Wens, and, of course, to cause a further depopulation of the taxed villages; stupid beasts as many of them are,
they must see the flagrant injustice of this, and mean and
cowardly as many of them are, some of them would remonstrate
against it; but, alas! the far greater part of them are, themselves, getting, or expecting, *loaves and fishes*, either in their own
persons or in those of their family. They smouch, or want to
smouch, some of the taxes; and, therefore, they must not complain. And thus the thing goes on. These land-owners see,
too, the churches falling down and the parsonage-houses either
tumbled down or dilapidated. But then, mind, they have
amongst them the giving away of the benefices! Of course, all
they want is the income, and the less the parsonage-house
costs the larger the spending income. But, in the meanwhile,
here is a destruction of public property; and also, from a
diversion of the income of the livings, a great injury, great
injustice, to the middle and the working classes.

Is this, then, is this " church " a thing to remain untouched?
Shall the widow and the orphan, whose money has been
borrowed *by the land-owners* (including the parsons) to purchase
" victories " with; shall they be stripped of their interest, of
their very bread, and shall the parsons who have let half the
parsonage-houses fall down or become unfit to live in still keep
all the tithes and the glebe-lands and the immense landed estates
called Church Lands? Oh, no! Sir James Graham " of
Netherby," though you are a descendant of the Earls of
Monteith, of John of the bright sword, and of the seventh Earl
of Galloway, K.T. (taking care, for God's sake, not to omit the
K.T.); though you may be the *Magnus Apollo ;* and, in short,

be you what you may, you shall never execute your project of sponging the fund-holders and of leaving messieurs the parsons untouched! In many parishes, where the livings are good too, there is neither parsonage-house nor church! This is the case at Draycot Foliot, in Wiltshire. The living is a rectory; the parson has, of course, both great and small tithes; these tithes and the glebe-lands are worth, I am told, more than three hundred pounds a year; and yet there is neither church nor parsonage-house; both have been suffered to fall down and disappear; and when a new parson comes to take possession of the living there is, I am told, a temporary tent, or booth, erected upon the spot where the church ought to be, for the performance of the *ceremony of induction !* What, then!—Ought not this church to be repealed? An act of parliament made this church; an act of parliament can unmake it; and is there any but a monster who would suffer this parson to retain this income, while that of the widow and the orphan was taken away? Oh, no? Sir James Graham of Netherby, who, with the *gridiron before you*, says, that there was "no man, of any authority, who foresaw the effects of Peel's bill;" oh, no! thou stupid, thou empty-headed, thou insolent aristocratic pamphleteer, the widow and the orphan *shall not* be robbed of their bread, while this parson of Draycot Foliot keeps the income of his living!

On my return from Worcester to this place, yesterday, I noticed, at a village called Severn Stoke, a very curiously-constructed grape house; that is to say a hot-house for the raising of grapes. Upon inquiry, I found that it belonged to a parson of the name of St. John, whose parsonage-house is very near to it, and who, being *sure* of having the benefice when the then rector should die, bought a piece of land, and erected his grapery on it, just facing, and only about 50 yards from, the windows, out of which the *old parson* had to look until the day of his death, with a view, doubtless, of piously furnishing his aged brother with a *memento mori* (remember death), quite as significant as a death's head and cross-bones, and yet done in a manner expressive of that fellow-feeling, that delicacy, that abstinence from self-gratification, which are well known to be characteristics almost peculiar to "the cloth!" To those, if there be such, who may be disposed to suspect that the grapery arose, upon the spot where it stands, merely from the desire to have the vines in bearing state, against the time that the old parson should die, or, as I heard the Botley Parson once call it, "kick the bucket;" to such persons I would just put this one question; did they ever either from Scripture or tradition learn that any of the apostles or their disciples erected graperies from motives such as this? They may, indeed, say that they never heard of the apostles erecting any graperies at all, much less of their having erected them from such a motive. Nor, to say the truth, did I ever hear of any such erections on the part of those apostles and those whom they commissioned to preach the word of God; and Sir William Scott (now a *lord* of some sort) never convinced me, by his parson-praising speech of 1802, that to give the church-clergy a due degree of influence over the minds of the people, to make the people revere them, it was necessary that the parsons and their wives should shine at *balls* and in *pump-rooms*. On the contrary, these and the like have taken away almost the whole of their spiritual influence. They never had much; but lately, and especially since 1793, they have had hardly any at all; and, wherever I go, I find them much better known as *Justices of the Peace* than as clergymen. What they would come to if this system could go on for only a few years longer I know not: but go on, as it is now going, it cannot much longer; there must be *a settlement of some sort :* and that settlement never can leave that mass, that immense mass, of public property, called " church property," to be used as it now is.

I have seen in this county, and in Herefordshire, several pieces of mangel wurzel; and I hear that it has nowhere failed, as the turnips have. Even the lucerne has, in some places, failed to a certain extent; but Mr. Walter Palmer, at Pencoyd, in Herefordshire, has cut a piece of lucerne four times this last summer, and when I saw it on the 17th Sept. (12 days ago) it was got a foot high towards another cut. But, with one exception (too trifling to mention), Mr. Walter Palmer's lucerne is on the Tullian plan; that is, it is in rows at four feet distance from each other; so that you plough between as often as you please, and thus, together with a little hand weeding between the plants, keep the ground, at all times, clear of weeds and grass. Mr. Palmer says that his acre (he has no more) has kept two horses all the summer; and he seems to complain that it has done no more. Indeed! A stout horse will eat much more than a fatting ox. This grass will fat any ox or sheep; and would not Mr. Palmer like to have ten acres of land that would fat a score of oxen? They would do this if they were managed well. But is it *nothing* to keep a team of four horses, for five months in the year, on the produce of two acres of land? If a man say that, he must, of course, be eagerly looking forward to another world; for nothing will satisfy him in this. A good crop of early cabbages may be had between the rows of lucerne.

Cabbages have, generally, wholly failed. Those that I see are almost all too backward to make much of heads; though it is surprising how fast they will grow and come to perfection as soon as there is *twelve hours of night*. I am here, however, speaking of the large sorts of cabbage; for the smaller sorts will loave in summer. Mr. Walter Palmer has now a piece of these, of which I think there are from 17 to 20 *tons* to the acre; and this too, observe, after a season which on the same farm has not suffered a turnip of any sort to come. If he had had 20 acres of these, he might have almost laughed at the failure of his turnips, and at the short crop of hay. And this is a crop of which a man may always be *sure*, if he take proper pains. These cabbages (Early Yorks or some such sort) should, if you want them in June or July, be sown early in the previous August. If you want them in winter, sown in April, and treated as pointed out in my *Cottage Economy*. These small sorts stand the winter better than the large; they are more nutritious; and they occupy the ground little more than half the time. *Dwarf savoys* are the finest and richest and most nutritious of cabbages. Sown early in April, and planted out early in July, they will, at 18 inches apart each way, yield a crop of 30 to 40 tons by Christmas. But all this supposes land very good, or very well manured, and plants of a good sort, and well raised and planted, and the ground well tilled after planting; and a crop of 30 tons is worth all these and all the care and all the pains that a man can possibly take.

I am here amongst the finest of cattle, and the finest sheep of the Leicester kind, that I ever saw. My host, Mr. Price, is famed as a breeder of cattle and sheep. The cattle are of the Hereford kind, and the sheep surpassing any animals of the kind that I ever saw. The animals seem to be made for the soil, and the soil for them.

In taking leave of this county I repeat, with great satisfaction, what I before said about the apparent comparatively happy state of the labouring people; and I have been very much pleased with the tone and manner in which they are spoken to and spoken of by their superiors. I hear of no *hard* treatment of them here, such as I have but too often heard of in some counties, and too often witnessed in others; and I quit Worcestershire, and particularly the house in which I am, with all those feelings which are naturally produced by the kindest of receptions from frank and sensible people.

FAIRFORD (GLOUCESTERSHIRE),
Saturday Morning, 30 Sept.

Though we came about 45 miles yesterday, we are up by daylight, and just about to set off to sleep at Hayden, near Swindon, in Wiltshire.

HAYDEN,
Saturday Night, 30 Sept.

From Ryall, in Worcestershire, we came yesterday (Friday) morning first to Tewksbury in Gloucestershire. This is a good, substantial town which, for many years, sent to parliament that sensible and honest and constant hater of Pitt and his infernal politics, James Martin, and which now sends to the same place his son, Mr. John Martin, who, when the memorable *Kentish Petition* was presented, in June 1822, proposed that it should not be received, or that, if it were received, " the House should not separate until it had resolved that the interest of the debt should never be reduced!" Castlereagh abused the petition; but was for *receiving* it, in *order to fix on it a mark of the House's reprobation.* I said, in the next Register, that this fellow was *mad ;* and in six or seven weeks from that day he cut his own throat, and was declared to have been mad at the time when this petition was presented! The mess that " *the House* " will be in will be bad enough as it is; but what would have been its mess if it had, in its strong fit of " good faith," been furious enough to adopt Mr. Martin's " resolution!"

The Warwickshire Avon falls into the Severn here, and on the sides of both, for many miles back, there are the finest meadows that ever were seen. In looking over them, and beholding the endless flocks and herds, one wonders what can become of all the meat! By riding on about eight or nine miles farther, however, this wonder is a little diminished; for here we come to one of the devouring Wens; namely, Cheltenham, which is what they call a " watering place "; that is to say, a place to which East India plunderers, West India floggers, English tax-gorgers, together with gluttons, drunkards, and debauchees of all descriptions, female as well as male, resort, at the suggestion of silently laughing quacks, in the hope of getting rid of the bodily consequences of their manifold sins and iniquities. When

I enter a place like this, I always feel disposed to squeeze up my nose with my fingers. It is nonsense, to be sure; but I conceit that every two-legged creature that I see coming near me is about to cover me with the poisonous proceeds of its impurities. To places like this come all that is knavish and all that is foolish and all that is base; gamesters, pickpockets, and harlots; young wife-hunters in search of rich and ugly and old women, and young husband-hunters in search of rich and wrinkled or half-rotten men, the former resolutely bent, be the means what they may, to give the latter heirs to their lands and tenements. These things are notorious; and Sir William Scott, in his speech of 1802, in favour of the non-residence of the clergy, expressly said that they and their families ought to appear at watering places, and that this was amongst the means of making them respected by their flocks! Memorandum: he was a member for Oxford when he said this!

Before we got into Cheltenham, I learned from a coal-carter which way we had to go in order to see " *The New Buildings*," which are now nearly at a stand. We rode up the main street of the town for some distance, and then turned off to the left, which soon brought us to the " desolation of abomination." I have seldom seen anything with more heartfelt satisfaction. " Oh! " said I to myself, " the accursed THING has certainly got *a blow*, then, in every part of its corrupt and corrupting carcass! " The whole town (and it was now ten o'clock) looked delightfully dull. I did not see more than four or five carriages and, perhaps, twenty people on horseback; and these seemed, by their hook-noses and round eyes, and by the long and sooty necks of the women, to be, for the greater part, *Jews and Jewesses*. The place really appears to be sinking very fast; and I have been told, and believe the fact, that houses, in Cheltenham, will now sell for only just about one-third as much as the same would have sold for only in last October. It is curious to see the names which the vermin owners have put upon the houses here. There is a new row of most gaudy and fantastical dwelling places, called " Colombia Place," given it, doubtless, by some dealer in *bonds*. There is what a boy told us was the " *New Spa;* " there is "*Waterloo House!*" Oh! how I rejoice at the ruin of the base creatures! There is "*Liverpool Cottage,*" " *Canning Cottage,*" " *Peel Cottage;* " and the good of it is, that the ridiculous beasts have put this word *cottage* upon scores of houses, and some very mean and shabby houses, standing along, and making part of an unbroken street! What a figure this place will cut in another year or two! I should not wonder to see it nearly wholly deserted. It is situated in a nasty, flat, stupid spot, without anything pleasant near it. A putting down of the one-pound notes will soon take away its *spa*-people. Those of the notes that have already been cut off have, it seems, lessened the quantity of ailments very considerably; another brush will cure all the complaints!

They have had some rains in the summer not far from this place; for we saw in the streets very fine turnips for sale as vegetables, and broccoli with heads six or eight inches over! But as to the meat it was nothing to be compared with that of Warminster, in Wiltshire; that is to say, the veal and lamb. I have paid particular attention to this matter, at Worcester and Tewksbury as well as at Cheltenham; and I have seen no veal and no lamb to be compared with those of Warminster. I have been thinking, but cannot imagine how it is, that the Wen-Devils, either at Bath or London, do not get this meat away from Warminster. I hope that my observations on it will not set them to work: for, if it do, the people of Warminster will never have a bit of good meat again.

After Cheltenham we had to reach this pretty little town of Fairford, the regular turnpike-road to which lay through Cirencester; but I had from a fine map, at Sir Thomas Winnington's, traced out a line for us along through a chain of villages, leaving Cirencester away to our right, and never coming nearer than seven or eight miles to it. We came through Dodeswell, Withington, Chedworth, Winston, and the two Colnes. At Dodeswell we came up a long and steep hill, which brought us out of the great vale of Gloucester and up upon the Cotswold Hills, which name is tautological, I believe; for I think that *wold* meant *high lands of great extent*. Such is the Cotswold, at any rate, for it is a tract of country stretching across, in a south-easterly direction, from Dodeswell to near Fairford, and in a north-easterly direction from Pitchcomb Hill, in Gloucester-shire (which, remember, I descended on the 12th September), to near Witney in Oxfordshire. Here we were, then, when we got fairly up upon the wold, with the vale of Gloucester at our back, Oxford and its vale to our left, the vale of Wiltshire to our right, and the vale of Berkshire in our front: and from one particular point I could see a part of each of them. This wold is, in itself, an ugly country. The soil is what is called a *stone brash* below, with a reddish earth mixed with little bits of this brash at top, and, for the greater part of the wold, even this soil is very shallow; and as fields are divided by walls made of this brash, and as there are for a mile or two together, no trees to be seen, and as the surface is not smooth and green like the downs, this is a sort of country having less to please the eye than any other that I have ever seen, always save and except the *heaths* like those of Bagshot and Hindhead. Yet even this wold has many fertile dells in it, and sends out, from its highest parts, several streams, each of which has its pretty valley and its meadows. And here has come down to us, from a distance of many centuries, a particular race of sheep, called the *Cotswold* breed, which are, of course, the best suited to the country. They are short and stocky, and appear to me to be about half way, in point of size, between the Rylands and the South Downs. When crossed with the Leicester, as they are pretty generally in the north of Wiltshire, they make very beautiful and even large sheep; quite large enough, and, people say, very profitable.

A *route*, when it lies through *villages*, is one thing on a *map*, and quite another thing on the ground. Our line of villages from Cheltenham to Fairford was very nearly straight upon the map; but upon the ground it took us round about a great many miles, besides now and then a little going back, to get into the right road; and, which was a great inconvenience, not a public-house was there on our road until we got within eight miles of Fairford. Resolved that not one single farthing of my money should be spent in the Wen of Cheltenham, we came through that place, expecting to find a public-house in the first or second of the villages; but not one was there over the whole of the wold; and though I had, by pocketing some slices of meat and bread at Ryall, provided against this contingency, as far as related to ourselves, I could make no such provision for our horses, and they went a great deal too far without baiting. Plenty of farm-houses, and, if they had been in America, we need have looked for no other. Very likely (I hope it at any rate) almost any farmer on the Cotswold would have given us what we wanted, if we had asked for it; but the fashion, the good old fashion, was, by the hellish system of funding and taxing and monopolising, driven across the Atlantic. And is England *never* to see it return! Is the hellish system to last *for ever!*

Doctor Black, in remarking upon my Ride down the vale of the Salisbury Avon, says that there has doubtless been a falling off in the population of the villages "lying amongst the chalk-hills;" aye, and lying everywhere else too; or how comes it that four-fifths of the parishes of Herefordshire, abounding in rich land, in meadows, orchards, and pastures, have either no parsonage-houses at all, or have none that a parson thinks fit for him to live in? I vouch for the fact; I will, whether in parliament or not, prove the fact to the parliament: and, if the fact be such, the conclusion is inevitable. But how melancholy is the sight of these decayed and still decaying villages in the dells of the Cotswold, where the building materials being stone, the ruins do not totally disappear for ages! The village of Withington (mentioned above) has a church like a small cathedral, and the whole of the population is now only 603 persons, men, women, and children! So that, according to the Scotch fellows, this immense and fine church, which is as sound as it was 700 or 800 years ago, was built by and for a population containing, at most, only about 120 grown-up and able-bodied men! But here, in this once populous village, or I think town, you see *all* the indubitable marks of most melancholy decay. There are several lanes, crossing each other, which *must* have been *streets* formerly. There is a large open space where the principal streets meet. There are, against this open place, two large, old, roomy houses, with gateways into back parts of them, and with large stone *upping-blocks* against the walls of them in the street. These were manifestly considerable *inns*, and in this open place markets or fairs, or both, used to be held. I asked two men, who were threshing in a barn, how long it was since their public-house was put down or dropped. They told me about sixteen years. One of these men, who was about fifty years of age, could remember *three* public-houses, one of which was what was called an *inn* ! The place stands by the side of a little brook, which here rises, or rather issues, from a high hill, and which, when it has winded down for some miles, and through several villages, begins to be called the River Colne, and continues on, under this name, through Fairford and along, I suppose, till it falls into the Thames. Withington is very prettily situated; it was, and not very long ago, a gay and happy place; but it now presents a picture of dilapidation and shabbiness scarcely to be equalled. Here are the yet visible remains of two gentlemen's houses. Great farmers have supplied their place as to inhabiting; and I dare say that some tax-eater, or some blaspheming Jew, or some still more base and wicked loan-mongering robber is now the owner of the land; aye, and all these people are his *slaves* as completely, and more to their wrong, than the blacks are the slaves of the planters in Jamaica, the farmers here acting, in fact, in a capacity corresponding with that of the negro-drivers there.

A part, and perhaps a considerable part, of the decay and misery of this place is owing to the use of *machinery*, and to the *monopolising*, in the manufacture of blankets, of which fabric the town of Witney (above mentioned) was the centre, and from which town the wool used to be sent round to, and the yarn, or warp, come back from, all these Cotswold villages, and quite into a part of Wiltshire. This work is all now gone, and so the women and the girls are a " surplus *popalashon, mon,*" and are, of course, to be dealt with by the " Emigration Committee " of the " Collective Wisdom "! There were, only a few years ago, above thirty blanket-manufacturers at Witney: twenty-five of these have been swallowed up by the five that now have all the manufacture in their hands! And all this has been done by that system of gambling and of fictitious money, which has conveyed property from the hands of the many into the hands of the few. But wise Burdett *likes* this! He wants the land to be cultivated by a few hands, and he wants machinery and all those things which draw money into *large masses ;* that make a nation consist of a few of very rich and of millions of very poor! Burdett must look sharp or this system will play him a trick before it come to an end.

The crops on the Cotswold have been pretty good; and I was very much surprised to see a scattering of early turnips, and, in some places, decent crops. Upon this wold I saw more early turnips in a mile or two than I saw in all Herefordshire and Worcestershire and in all the rich and low part of Gloucestershire. The high lands always, during the year, and especially during the summer, receive much more of rain than the low lands. The clouds hang about the hills, and the dews, when they rise, go, most frequently, and cap the hills.

Wheat-sowing is yet going on on the wold; but the greater part of it is sown, and not only sown, but up, and in some places high enough to " hide a hare." What a difference! In some parts of England no man thinks of sowing wheat till November, and it is often done in March. If the latter were done on this wold there would not be a bushel on an acre. The ploughing and other work, on the wold, is done in great part by oxen, and here are some of the finest ox-teams that I ever saw.

All the villages down to Fairford are pretty much in the same dismal condition as that of Withington. Fairford, which is quite on the border of Gloucestershire, is a very pretty little market-town, and has one of the prettiest churches in the kingdom. It was, they say, built in the reign of Henry VII.; and one is naturally surprised to see that its windows of beautiful stained glass had the luck to escape, not only the fangs of the ferocious " good Queen Bess "; not only the unsparing plundering minions of James I.; but even the devastating ruffians of Cromwell.

We got in here about four o'clock, and at the house of Mr. Iles, where we slept, passed, amongst several friends, a very pleasant evening. This morning, Mr. Iles was so good as to ride with us as far as the house of another friend at Kempsford, which is the last Gloucestershire parish in our route. At this friend's, Mr. Arkall, we saw a fine dairy of about 60 or 80 cows, and a cheese loft with, perhaps, more than two thousand cheeses in it; at least there were many hundreds. This village contains what are said to be the remnants and ruins of a mansion of John of Gaunt. The church is very ancient and very capacious. What tales these churches do tell upon us! What fools, what lazy dogs, what presumptuous asses, what lying braggarts, they make us appear! No people here, " *mon, teel the Scots cam to seevelise* " us! Impudent, lying beggars! Their stinking " *kelts* " ought to be taken up, and the brazen and insolent vagabonds whipped back to their heaths and their rocks. Let them go and thrive by their " cash-credits," and let their paper-money poet, Walter Scott, immortalise their deeds. That conceited, dunderheaded fellow, George Chalmers, *estimated* the whole of the population of England and Wales at a few persons more than *two millions*, when England was just at the highest point of her power and glory, and when all these churches had long been built and were resounding with the voice of priests, who resided in their parishes, and who relieved all the poor out of their tithes! But this same Chalmers signed his *solemn conviction* that Vortigern and the other Ireland-manuscripts, which were written by a lad of sixteen, were written by Shakespeare.

In coming to Kempsford we got wet, and nearly to the skin. But our friends gave us coats to put on while ours were dried and while we ate our breakfast. In our way to this house, where we now are, Mr. Tucky's at Heydon, we called at Mr. James Crowdy's, at Highworth, where I was from the 4th to the 9th of September inclusive; but it looked rainy, and therefore we did not alight. We got wet again before we reached this place; but our journey being short, we soon got our clothes dry again.

BURGHCLERE (HAMPSHIRE),
Monday, 2 October.

Yesterday was a really *unfortunate day*. The morning promised fair; but its promises were like those of Burdett! There was a little snivelling, wet, treacherous frost. We had to come through Swindon, and Mr. Tucky had the kindness to come with us, until we got three or four miles on this side (the Hungerford side) of that very neat and plain and solid and respectable market town. Swindon is in Wiltshire, and is in the real fat of the land, all being wheat, beans, cheese, or fat meat. In our way to Swindon, Mr. Tucky's farm exhibited to me what I never saw before, four score oxen, all grazing upon one farm, and all nearly fat! They were some Devonshire and some Herefordshire. They were fatting on the grass only, and I should suppose that they are worth, or shortly will be, thirty pounds each. But the great pleasure with which the contemplation of this fine sight was naturally calculated to inspire me was more than counterbalanced by the thought that these fine oxen, this primest of human food, was, aye, every mouthful of it, destined to be devoured in the Wen, and that too, for the far greater part, by the Jews, loan-jobbers, tax-eaters, and their base and prostituted followers, dependants, purveyors, parasites and pimps, literary as well as other wretches, who, if suffered to live at all, ought to partake of nothing but the offal, and ought to come but one cut before the dogs and cats!

Mind you, there is in my opinion no land in England that surpasses this. There is, I suppose, as good in the three last counties that I have come through; but *better* than this is, I should think, impossible. There is a pasture-field, of about a hundred acres, close to Swindon, belonging to a Mr. Goddard, which, with its cattle and sheep, was a most beautiful sight. But everything is full of riches; and as fast as skill and care and industry can extract these riches from the land, the unseen grasp of taxation, loan-jobbing and monopolising takes them away, leaving the labourers not half a belly-full, compelling the farmer to pinch them or to be ruined himself, and making even the landowner little better than a steward, or bailiff, for the tax-eaters, Jews and jobbers!

Just before we got to Swindon, we crossed a canal at a place where there is a wharf and a coal-yard, and close by these a gentleman's house, with coach-house, stables, walled-in-garden, paddock *orné*, and the rest of those things, which, all together, make up *a villa*, surpassing the second and approaching towards the first class. Seeing a man in the coal-yard, I asked him to what gentleman the house belonged: " to the *head un* o' the canal," said he. And when, upon further inquiry of him, I found that it was the villa of the chief manager, I could not help congratulating the proprietors of this aquatic concern; for though I did not ask the name of the canal, I could readily suppose that the profits must be prodigious, when the residence of the manager would imply no disparagement of dignity if occupied by a Secretary of State for the Home, or even for the Foreign, department. I mean an *English* Secretary of State; for as to an *American* one, his salary would be wholly inadequate to a residence in a mansion like this.

From Swindon we came up into the *down country ;* and these downs rise higher even than the Cotswold. We left Marlborough away to our right, and came along the turnpike-road towards Hungerford, but with a view of leaving that town to our left, further on, and going away, through Ramsbury, towards the northernmost Hampshire hills, under which Burghclere (where we now are) lies. We passed some fine farms upon these downs, the houses and homesteads of which were near the road. My companion, though he had been to London and even to France, had never seen *downs* before; and it was amusing to me to witness his surprise at seeing the immense flocks of sheep which were now (ten o'clock) just going out from their several folds to the downs for the day, each having its shepherd, and each shepherd his dog. We passed the homestead of a farmer Woodman, with *sixteen* banging wheat-ricks in the rick-yard, two of which were old ones; and rick-yard, farm-yard, waste-yard, horse-paddock, and all round about, seemed to be swarming with fowls, ducks, and turkeys, and on the whole of them not one feather but what was white! Turning our eyes from this sight, we saw, just going out from the folds of this same farm, three separate and numerous flocks of sheep, one of which (the *lamb*-flock) we passed close by the side of. The shepherd told us that his flock consisted of thirteen score and five; but, apparently, he could not, if it had been to save his soul, tell us how many hundreds he had: and, if you reflect a little, you will find that his way of counting is much the easiest and best. This was a most beautiful flock of lambs; short legged and, in every respect, what they ought to be. George, though born and bred amongst sheep-farms, had never before seen sheep with dark-coloured faces and legs; but his surprise, at this

sight, was not nearly so great as the surprise of both of us at
seeing numerous and very large pieces (sometimes 50 acres
together) of very good early turnips, swedish as well as white!
All the three counties of Worcester, Hereford and Gloucester
(except on the Cotswold) do not, I am convinced, contain as
great a weight of turnip bulbs as we here saw in one single
piece ; for here there are, for miles and miles, no hedges and no
fences of any sort.

Doubtless they must have had *rain* here in the months of
June and July; but as I once before observed (though I forget
when) a chalk bottom does not suffer the surface to burn, however shallow the top soil may be.   It seems to me to absorb and
to *retain* the water, and to keep it ready to be drawn up by the
heat of the sun.   At any rate the fact is that the surface above
it does not burn; for there never yet was a summer, not even
this last, when the downs did not *retain their greenness to a
certain degree*, while the rich pastures, and even the meadows
(except actually *watered*), were burnt so as to be as brown as the
bare earth.

This is a most pleasing circumstance attending the down-
countries; and there are no *downs* without a chalk bottom.

Along here the country is rather *too bare :* here, until you
come to Auborne, or Aldbourne, there are *no meadows* in the
valleys, and no trees, even round the homesteads.   This, therefore, is too naked to please me; but I love *the downs* so much
that, if I had to choose, I would live even here, and especially
I would *farm* here, rather than on the banks of the Wye in Herefordshire, in the vale of Gloucester, of Worcester, or of Evesham,
or even in what the Kentish men call their " garden of Eden."
I have now seen (for I have, years back, seen the vales of Taunton,
Glastonbury, Honiton, Dorchester and Sherburne) what are
deemed the richest and most beautiful parts of England; and
if called upon to name the spot which I deem the brightest and
most beautiful and, of its extent, *best* of all, I should say the
villages of *North Bovant and Bishopstrow,* between Heytesbury
and Warminster in Wiltshire; for there is, as appertaining to
rural objects, *everything* that I delight in.   Smooth and verdant
downs in hills and valleys of endless variety as to height and
depth and shape; rich corn - land, unencumbered by fences;
meadows in due proportion, and those watered at pleasure;
and, lastly, the homesteads, and villages, sheltered in winter
and shaded in summer by lofty and beautiful trees; to which
may be added roads never dirty and a stream never dry.

When we came to Auborne, we got amongst trees again. This is a *town* and was, manifestly, once a large town. Its church is as big as three of that of Kensington. It has a market now, I believe; but I suppose it is, like many others, become merely nominal, the produce being nearly all carried to Hungerford, in order to be forwarded to the Jew-devils and the tax-eaters and monopolisers in the Wen, and in small Wens on the way. It is a *decaying place;* and I dare say that it would be nearly depopulated in twenty years' time if this hellish jobbing system were to last so long.

A little after we came through Auborne, we turned off to our right to go through Ramsbury to Shallburn, where Tull, the father of the drill-husbandry, began and practised that husbandry at a farm called "Prosperous." Our object was to reach this place (Burghclere) to sleep, and to stay for a day or two; and as I knew Mr. Blandy of Prosperous, I determined upon this route, which, besides, took us out of the turnpike-road. We stopped at Ramsbury, to bait our horses. It is a large and, apparently, miserable village, or "town" as the people call it. It was in remote times a *bishop's see*. Its church is very large and very ancient. Parts of it were evidently built long and long before the Norman Conquest. Burdett owns a great many of the houses in the village (which contains nearly two thousand people), and will, if he live many years, own nearly the whole; for as his eulogist, William Friend, the actuary, told the public, in a pamphlet in 1817, he has resolved that his numerous *life-holds shall run out*, and that those who were life-holders under his aunt, from whom he got the estate, shall become *rack-renters to him*, or quit the occupations. Besides this, he is continually purchasing lands and houses round about and in this place. He has now let his house to a Mr. Acres; and, as the *Morning Herald* says, is safe landed at Bordeaux, with his family, for the winter! When here, he did not occupy a square inch of his land! He let it all, park and all; and only reserved "a right of road" from the highway to his door. "He had and has *a right* to do all this." A *right?* Who denies that? But is this giving us a specimen of that "liberality and generosity and hospitality" of those "English country gentlemen" whose praises he so loudly sang last winter? His name is Francis Burdett *Jones*, which last name he was obliged to take by his aunt's will; and he actually used it for some time after the estate came to him! "Jones" was too common a name for him, I suppose! Sounded too much of the *vulgar!*

However, what I have principally to do with is his *absence from the country* at a time like this, and, if the newspapers be correct, his intended absence during the whole of next winter; and such a winter, too, as it is likely to be! He for many years complained, and justly, of the *sinecure placemen;* and are we to suffer him to be thus a sinecure member of parliament! This is, in my opinion, a great deal worse than a sinecure placeman; for this is shutting an active member out. It is a dog-in-manger offence; and to the people of a place such as Westminster, it is not only an injury, but a most outrageous insult. If it be true that he intends to stay away during the coming session of parliament, I trust, not only that he will never be elected again, but that the people of Westminster will call upon him to resign; and this I am sure they will do too. The next session of parliament *must* be a most important one, and that he knows well. Every member will be put to the test in the next session of parliament. On the question of Corn Bills every man must declare for or against the people. He would declare against if he dared; and, therefore, he gets out of the way! Or this is what we shall have a clear right to presume if he be absent from the next session of parliament. He knows that there must be something like a struggle between the land-owners and the fund-holders. His interest lies with the former; he wishes to support the law-church and the army and all sources of aristocratical profit; but he knows that the people of Westminster would be on the other side. It is better, therefore, to hear at Bordeaux about this struggle than to be engaged in it! He must know of the great embarrassment, distress, and of the great bodily suffering now experienced by a large part of the people; and has he *a right*, after having got himself returned as member for such a place as Westminster, to go out of the country at such a time and leave his seat vacant? He must know that during the ensuing winter there *must* be great distress in Westminster itself; for there will be a greater mass of the working people out of employ than there ever was in any winter before; and this calamity will, too, be owing to that infernal system which he has been supporting, to those paper-money rooks, with whom he is closely connected, and the existence of whose destructive rags he expressed his wish to prolong: he knows all this very well: he knows that in every quarter the distress and danger are great; and is it not, then, his duty to be here? Is he, who, at his own request, has been entrusted with the representing of a great city, to get out of the way at a time like this, and under circumstances like these? If this be so, then is this great, and *once* public-spirited city, become more contemptible, and infinitely more mischievous, than the " accursed hill " of Wiltshire: but this is *not so : the people* of Westminster are what they always were, full of good sense and public spirit: they have been cheated by a set of bribed intriguers; and *how* this has been done I will explain to them when I *punish* Sir Francis Burdett Jones for the sins *committed for him* by a hired Scotch writer. I shall dismiss him, for the present, with observing that, if I had in me a millionth part of that malignity and vindictiveness which he so basely showed towards me, I have learned anecdotes sufficient to enable me to take ample vengeance on him for the stabs which he, in 1817, knew that he was sending to the hearts of the defenceless part of my family!

While our horses were baiting at Ramsbury it began to rain, and by the time that they had done it rained pretty hard, with every appearance of continuing to rain for the day; and it was now about eleven o'clock, we having 18 or 19 miles to go before we got to the intended end of our journey. Having, however, for several reasons, a very great desire to get to Burghclere that night, we set off in the rain; and as we carry no greatcoats, we were wet to the skin pretty soon. Immediately upon quitting Ramsbury, we crossed the river Kennet, and, mounting a highish hill, we looked back over friend Sir Glory's park, the sight of which brought into my mind the visit of Thimble and Cowhide, as described in the " intense comedy," and when I thought of the " baker's being starved to death," and of the " heavy fall of snow," I could not help bursting out a laughing, though it poured of rain and though I already felt the water on my skin.—MEM. To ask, when I get to London, what is become of the intense " Counsellor Bric "; and whether he have yet had the justice to put the K to the end of his name. I saw a lovely female shoy-hoy, engaged in keeping the rooks from a newly-sown wheat field on the Cotswold Hills, that would be a very *suitable match* for him; and as his manners appear to be mended; as he now praises to the skies those 40s. freeholders whom, in my hearing, he asserted to be " *beneath brute beasts ;* " as he does, in short, appear to be rather less offensive than he was, I should have no objection to promote the union; and, I am sure, *the farmer* would like it of all things; for if Miss *Stuffed-o'-straw* can, when *single*, keep the devourers at a distance, say, you who know him, whether the sight of the *husband's head* would leave a rook in the country!

Turning from viewing the scene of Thimble and Cowhide's cruel disappointment, we pushed through coppices and across fields to a little village called Froxfield, which we found to be on the great Bath road. Here, crossing the road and also a run of water, we, under the guidance of a man who was good enough to go about a mile with us, and to whom we gave a shilling and the price of a pot of beer, mounted another hill, from which, after twisting about for awhile, I saw and recognised the out-buildings of Prosperous Farm, towards which we pushed on as fast as we could, in order to keep ourselves in motion so as to prevent our catching cold; for it rained, and incessantly, every step of the way. I had been at Prosperous before, so that I knew Mr. Blandy, the owner, and his family, who received us with great hospitality. They took care of our horses, gave us what we wanted in the eating and drinking way, and clothed us, shirts and all, while they dried all our clothes; for not only the things on our bodies were soaked, but those also which we carried in little thin leather rolls, fastened on upon the saddles before us. Notwithstanding all that could be done in the way of despatch, it took more than three hours to get our clothes dry. At last, about three quarters of an hour before sunset, we got on our clothes again and set off: for, as an instance of real bad luck, it ceased to rain the moment we got to Mr. Blandy's. Including the numerous angles and windings, we had nine or ten miles yet to go; but I was so anxious to get to Burghclere, that, contrary to my practice as well as my principle, I determined to encounter the darkness for once, though in cross-country roads, presenting us, at every mile, with ways crossing each other; or forming a Y; or kindly giving us the choice of three, forming the upper part of a Y and a half. Add to this that we were in an enclosed country, the lanes very narrow, deep-worn, and banks and hedges high. There was no moon; but it was starlight, and as I could see the Hampshire hills all along to my right, and knew that I must not get above a mile or so from them, I had a guide that could not deceive me; for as to *asking* the road, in a case like this it is of little use, unless you meet some one at every half mile: for the answer is, *keep right on;* aye, but in ten minutes, perhaps, you come to a Y, or to a T, or to a +.

A fellow told me once, in my way from Chertsey to Guildford, "keep *right on*, you can't miss your way." I was in the perpendicular part of the T, and the top part was only a few yards from me. "*Right on*," said I, "what, over *that bank* into the

wheat?" "No, no," said he, "I mean *that road*, to be sure,"
pointing to the road that went off to the *left*. In *down countries*
the direction of shepherds and pig and bird boys is always in
precisely the same words; namely, "*right* over the down,"
laying great stress upon the word *right*. "But," said I to a boy
at the edge of the down at King's Worthy (near Winchester),
who gave me this direction to Stoke Charity; "but what do
you mean by *right* over the down?" "Why," said he, "*right*
on to Stoke, to be sure, zur." "Aye," said I, "but how am I,
who was never here before, to know *what is* right, my boy?"
That posed him. It set him to thinking: and after a bit he
proceeded to tell me that when I got up the hill I should see
some trees ; that I should go along by them; that I should then
see *a barn* right before me; that I should go down to that barn;
and that I should then see a *waggon track* that would lead me all
down to Stoke. "Aye!" said I, "*now* indeed you are a real
clever fellow." And I gave him a shilling, being part of my
savings of the morning. Whoever tries it will find that the *less
they eat and drink*, when travelling, the better they will be. I
act accordingly. Many days I have no breakfast and no dinner.
I went from Devizes to Highworth without breaking my fast,
a distance, including my deviations, of more than *thirty miles*.
I sometimes take, from a friend's house, a little bit of meat
between two bits of bread, which I eat as I ride along; but
whatever I save from this fasting work, I think I have a clear
right to give away; and, accordingly, I generally put the amount,
in copper, into my waistcoat pocket, and dispose of it during
the day. I know well *that I am the better* for not stuffing and
blowing myself out, and with the savings I make many and
many a happy boy; and now and then I give a whole family a
good meal with the cost of a breakfast, or a dinner, that would
have done me mischief. I do not do this because I grudge
innkeepers what they charge; for my surprise is how they can
live without charging *more* than they do in general.

It was dark by the time that we got to a village called East
Woodhay. Sunday evening is the time *for courting* in the
country. It is not convenient to carry this on before faces, and
at farm-houses and cottages there are no spare apartments; so
that the pairs turn out and pitch up, to carry on their negotiations, by the side of stile or a gate. The evening was auspicious;
it was *pretty dark*, the *weather mild*, and *Old Michaelmas* (when
yearly services end) was fast approaching; and, accordingly, I
do not recollect ever having before seen so many negotiations

going on within so short a distance. At West Woodhay my horse *cast a shoe*, and as the road was abominably flinty, we were compelled to go at a snail's pace: and I should have gone crazy with impatience had it not been for these ambassadors and ambassadresses of Cupid, to every pair of whom I said something or other. I began by asking the fellow *my road;* and from the tone and manner of his answer I could tell pretty nearly what prospect he had of success, and knew what to say to draw something from him. I had some famous sport with them, saying to them more than I should have said by daylight, and a great deal less than I should have said if my horse had been in a condition to carry me away as swiftly as he did from Osmond Ricardo's terrific cross! "There!" exclaims Mrs. Scrip, the stock-jobber's young wife to her old hobbling wittol of a spouse, "You see, my love, that this mischievous man could not let even these poor *peasants* alone." "*Peasants!* you dirty-necked devil, and where got you that word! You who, but a few years ago, came perhaps up from the country in a waggon; who *made* the bed you now *sleep* in; and who got the husband by helping him to get his wife out of the world, as some young parti-coloured blade is to get you and the old rogue's money by a similar process!"

We got to Burghclere about eight o'clock, after a very disagreeable day; but we found ample compensation in the house, and all within it, that we were now arrived at.

BURGHCLERE,
Sunday, 8 Sept.

It rained steadily this morning, or else, at the end of these six days of hunting for George, and two for me, we should have set off. The rain gives me time to give an account of Mr. Budd's crop of Tullian wheat. It was sown in rows and on ridges, with very wide intervals, ploughed all summer. If he reckon that ground only which the wheat grew upon, he had one hundred and thirty bushels to the acre; and even if he reckoned the whole of the ground, he had 28 bushels all but two gallons to the acre! But the best wheat he grew this year was dibbled in between rows of swedish turnips, in November, four rows upon a ridge, with an eighteen inch interval between each two rows, and a five feet interval between the outside rows on each ridge. It is the white cone that Mr. Budd sows. He had ears with 130 grains in each. This would be the farming for labourers in their little plots. They might grow thirty bushels of wheat to the acre, and have crops of cabbages, in the intervals, at the same time; or of potatoes, if they liked them better.

Before my arrival here, Mr. Budd had seen my description of the state of the labourers in Wiltshire, and had, in consequence, written to my son James (not knowing where I was) as follows: "In order to see how the labourers are now *screwed down*, look at the following facts: Arthur Young, in 1771 (55 years ago), allowed for a man, his wife and three children 13s. 1d. a week, according to present money-prices. By the Berkshire magistrates' table, made in 1795, the allowance was, for such family, according to the present money-prices, 11s. 4d. Now it is, according to the same standard, 8s. According to your father's proposal, the sum would be (supposing there to be no malt tax) 18s. a week; and little enough too." Is not that enough to convince any one of the hellishness of this system! Yet Sir Glory applauds it. Is it not horrible to contemplate millions in this half-starving state; and is it not the duty of "England's Glory," who has said that his estate is *"a retaining fee* for defending the rights of the people;" is it not his duty to stay in England and endeavour to restore the people, the millions, to what their fathers were instead of going abroad; selling off his carriage horses, and going abroad there to spend some part at least of the fruits of English labour? I do not say that he has *no right*, generally speaking, to go and spend his money abroad; but I do say that, having got himself elected for such a city as Westminster, he had no right, at a time like this, to be absent from parliament. However what cares he! His "retaining fee" indeed! He takes special care to augment that fee; but I challenge all his shoe-lickers, all the base worshippers of twenty thousand acres, to show me one single thing that he has ever done, or, within the last twelve years, attempted to do, for his *clients*. In short, this is a man that must now be brought to book: he must not be suffered to insult Westminster any longer: he must turn to or turn out: he is a sore to Westminster; a set-fast on its back; a cholic in its belly; a cramp in its limbs; a gag in its mouth: he is a nuisance, a monstrous nuisance, in Westminster, and he must be abated.

FROM BURGHCLERE TO LYNDHURST, IN THE NEW FOREST

" The reformers have yet many and powerful foes; we have to contend against a host, such as never existed before in the world. Nine-tenths of the press; all the channels of speedy communication of sentiment; all the pulpits; all the associations of rich people; all the taxing-people; all the military and naval establishments; all the yeomanry cavalry tribes. Your allies are endless in number and mighty in influence. But we have *one ally* worth the whole of them put together, namely, the DEBT! This is an ally whom no honours or rewards can seduce from us. She is a steady, unrelaxing, persevering, incorruptible ally. An ally that is proof against all blandishments, all intrigues, all temptations, and all open attacks. She sets at defiance all ' *military*,' all ' *yeomanry cavalry*.' They may as well fire at a ghost. She cares no more for the sabres of the yeomanry or the Life Guards than Milton's angels did for the swords of Satan's myrmidons. This ally cares not a straw about *spies* and *informers*. She laughs at the employment of *secret-service money*. She is always erect, day and night, and is always firmly moving on in our cause, in spite of all the terrors of gaols, dungeons, halters and axes. Therefore, Mr. Jabet, be not so pert. The combat is not so unequal as you seem to imagine; and, confident and insolent as you now are, the day of your humiliation may not be far distant."—LETTER TO MR. JABET, of Birmingham, *Register*, v. 31, p. 477 (Nov. 1816).

HURSTBOURN TARRANT
(COMMONLY CALLED UPHUSBAND),
Wednesday, 11 October 1826.

WHEN quarters are good you are apt to *lurk* in them; but really it was so wet that we could not get away from Burghclere till Monday evening. Being here, there were many reasons for our going to the great fair at Weyhill, which began yesterday, and, indeed, the day before at Appleshaw. These two days are allotted for the selling of sheep only, though the horse-fair begins on the 10th. To Appleshaw they bring nothing but those fine curled-horned and long-tailed ewes, which bring the house-lambs and the early Easter-lambs; and these, which, to my taste, are the finest and most beautiful animals of the sheep kind, come exclusively out of Dorsetshire and out of the part of Somersetshire bordering on that county.

To Weyhill, which is a village of half a dozen houses on a down just above Appleshaw, they bring from the down-farms in Wiltshire and Hampshire, where they are bred, the South Down sheep; ewes to go away into the pasture and turnip countries to have lambs, wethers to be fatted and killed, and lambs (nine months old) to be kept to be sheep. At both fairs there is supposed to be about two hundred thousand sheep. It was of some consequence to ascertain how the *price* of these had been affected by "*late* panic," which ended the "respite" of 1822; or by the "plethora of money" as loan-man Baring called it. I can assure this political doctor, that there was no such "plethora" at Weyhill yesterday, where, while I viewed the long faces of the farmers, while I saw consciousness of ruin painted on their countenances, I could not help saying to myself, "the loan-mongers think they are *cunning;* but, by ——, they will never escape the ultimate consequences of this horrible ruin!" The prices, take them on a fair average, were, at both fairs, just about one-half what they were last year. So that my friend Mr. Thwaites of the *Herald*, who had a lying Irish reporter at Preston, was rather hasty, about three months ago, when he told his *well-informed* readers that, "those politicians were deceived who had supposed that prices of farm produce would fall in consequence of '*late* panic' and the subsequent measures!" There were Dorsetshire ewes that sold last year for 50s. a head. We could hear of none this year that exceeded 25s. And only think of 25s. for one of these fine, large ewes, nearly fit to kill, and having two lambs in her, ready to be brought forth in, on an average, six weeks' time! The average is *three lambs* to *two of these ewes*. In 1812 these ewes were from 55s. to 72s. each, at this same Appleshaw fair; and in that year I bought South Down ewes at 45s. each, just such as were, yesterday, sold for 18s. Yet the sheep and grass and all things are the same in *real value*. What a false, what a deceptious, what an infamous thing, this paper-money system is!

However, it is a pleasure, it is real, it is great delight, it is boundless joy to me, to contemplate this infernal system in its hour of *wreck*: swag here: crack there: scroop this way: souse that way: and such a rattling and such a squalling: and the parsons and their wives looking so frightened, beginning, apparently, to think that the day of *judgment* is at hand! I wonder what master parson of Sharncut, whose church *can* contain *eight persons*, and master parson of Draycot Foliot, who is, for want of a church, inducted under a *tent*, or temporary *booth;* I wonder what they think of South Down lambs (9 months old) selling for 6 or 7 shillings each! I wonder what the Barings and the Ricardos think of it. I wonder what those master parsons think of it who are half-pay naval or military

officers, as well as master parsons of the church made by *law*.
I wonder what the Gaffer Gooches, with their parsonships and
military offices, think of it. I wonder what Daddy Coke and
Suffield think of it; and when, I wonder, do they mean to get
into their holes and barns again to cry aloud against the
" roguery of reducing the interest of the debt; " when, I wonder,
do these manly, these modest, these fair, these candid, these
open, and, above all things, these *sensible* fellows intend to
assemble again, and to call all " the house of Quidenham " and
the " house of Kilmainham," or *Kinsaleham*, or whatever it is
(for I really have forgotten); to call, I say, all these about them,
in the holes and the barns, and then and there again make a
formal and solemn protest against Cobbett and against his
roguish proposition for reducing the interest of the debt!
Now, I have these fellows on the hip; and brave sport will I
have with them before I have done.

Mr. Blount, at whose house (7 miles from Weyhill) I am,
went with me to the fair; and we took particular pains to
ascertain the prices. We saw, and spoke to, Mr. John Herbert
of Stoke (near Uphusband) who was *asking* 20s., and who did
not expect to *get* it, for South Down ewes, just such as he *sold*
last year (at this fair), for 36s. Mr. Jolliff, of Crux-Easton, was
asking 16s. for just such ewes as he sold last year (at this fair)
for 32s. Farmer Holdway had sold " for less than half " his
last year's price. A farmer that I did not know told us that
he had sold to a great sheep-dealer of the name of Smallpiece at
the latter's own price! I asked him what that " own price "
was; and he said that he was ashamed to say. The horse-fair
appeared to have no business at all going on: for, indeed, how
were people to purchase horses who had got only half-price for
their sheep?

The sales of sheep, at this one fair (including Appleshaw),
must have amounted, this year, to a hundred and twenty or
thirty thousand pounds less than last year! Stick a pin there,
master " Prosperity Robinson," and turn back to it again anon!
Then came the horses; not equal in amount to the sheep, but
of great amount. Then comes the cheese, a very great article;
and it will have a falling off, if you take quantity into view, in a
still greater proportion. The hops being a monstrous crop
their *price* is nothing to judge by. But all is fallen. Even
corn, though, in many parts, all but the wheat and rye have
totally failed, is, taking a quarter of each of the *six sorts* (wheat,
rye, barley, oats, pease and beans), 11s. 9d. cheaper upon the

whole; that is to say, 11s. 9d. upon 258s. And if the "*late panic*" had not come, it must and it would have been, and according to the small bulk of the crop it ought to have been, 150s. *dearer*, instead of 11s. 9d. cheaper. Yet, it is too dear, and far too dear, for the working people to eat! The masses, the assembled masses, must starve, if the price of bread be not reduced; that is to say, in Scotland and Ireland; for *in England* I hope that the people will "*demand and insist*" (to use the language of the Bill of Rights) on a just and suitable provision, agreeably to the law; and if they do not get it, I trust that law and justice will in due course be done, and strictly done, upon those who refuse to make such provision. Though in time the price of corn will come down without any repeal of the Corn Bill; and though it would have come down now if we had had a good crop, or an average crop; still the Corn Bill ought now to be repealed, because people must not be *starved* in waiting for the next crop; and the "landowners' monopoly," as the son of "John with the bright sword" calls it, ought to be swept away; and the sooner it is done the better for the country. I know very well that the landowners must lose their estates if such prices continue, and if the present taxes continue; I know this very well; and I like it well; for the landowners *may cause the taxes to be taken off if they will.* "Ah! wicked dog!" say they, "What, then, you would have us lose the half-pay and the pensions and sinecures which our children and other relations, or that we ourselves, are pocketing out of the taxes, which are squeezed, in great part, out of the labourer's skin and bone!" Yes, upon my word, I would; but if you prefer losing your estates, I have no great objection; for it is hard that, "in a free country," people should not have their choice of the different roads to the poor-house. Here is the *rub :* the vote-owners, the seat-owners, the big boroughmongers, have, directly and indirectly, so large a share of the loaves and fishes, that the share is, in point of clear income, equal to, and in some cases greater than, that from their estates; and though this is not the case with the small fry of jolterheads, they are so linked in with, and overawed by, the big ones, that they have all the same feeling; and that is, that to cut off half-pay, pensions, sinecures, commissionerships (such as that of Hobhouse's father), army, and the rest of the "good things," would be nearly as bad as to take away the estates, which, besides, are in fact, in many instances, nearly gone (at least from the present holder) already, by the means of mortgage, annuity, rent-charge, settlement, jointure, or something or other. Then there are the parsons, who with their keen noses have smelled out long enough ago that if any serious settlement should take place *they go* to a certainty. In short, they know well how the whole nation (the interested excepted) feel towards them. They know well that, were it not for their allies, it would soon be queer times with them.

Here, then, is the *rub*. Here are the reasons why the taxes are not taken off! Some of these jolterheaded beasts were ready to cry, and I know one that did actually cry to a farmer (his tenant) in 1822. The tenant told him that " Mr. Cobbett had been *right* about this matter." " What! " exclaimed he, " I hope you do not read Cobbett! He will ruin you, and he would ruin us all. He would introduce anarchy, confusion, and destruction of property! " Oh, no, Jolterhead! There is no *destruction* of property. Matter, the philosophers say, is *indestructible*. But it is all easily *transferable*, as is well-known to the base jolterheads and the blaspheming Jews. The former of these will, however, soon have the faint sweat upon them again. Their tenants will be ruined *first :* and here what a foul robbery these landowners have committed or, at least, enjoyed and pocketed the gain of! They have given their silent assent to the one-pound note abolition bill. They knew well that this must reduce the price of farm produce *one-half*, or thereabouts; and yet they were prepared to take and to insist on, and they do take and insist on, as high rents as if that bill had never been passed! What dreadful ruin will ensue! How many, many farmers' families are now just preparing the way for their entrance into the poor-house! How many; certainly many a score farmers did I see at Weyhill, yesterday, who came there as it were *to know their fate ;* and who are gone home thoroughly convinced that they shall, as farmers, never see Weyhill fair again!

When such a man, his mind impressed with such conviction, returns home and there beholds a family of children, half bred up, and in the notion that they were *not* to be mere working people, what must be his *feelings ?* Why, if he have been a bawler against Jacobins and Radicals; if he have approved of the Power-of-Imprisonment Bill and of Six-Acts; aye, if he did not rejoice at Castlereagh's cutting his own throat; if he have been a cruel screwer down of the labourers, reducing them to skeletons; if he have been an officious detector of what are called " poachers," and have assisted in, or approved of, the hard punishments inflicted on them; then, in either of these cases,

I say, that his feelings, though they put the suicidal knife into his own hand, are short of what he deserves! I say this, and this I repeat with all the seriousness and solemnity with which a man can make a declaration; for had it not been for these base and selfish and unfeeling wretches, the deeds of 1817 and 1819 and 1820 would never have been attempted. These hard and dastardly dogs, armed up to the teeth, were always ready to come forth to destroy, not only to revile, to decry, to belie, to calumniate in all sorts of ways, but, if necessary, absolutely to cut the throats of, those who had no object, and who could have no object, other than that of preventing a continuance in that course of measures which have finally produced the ruin, and threaten to produce the absolute destruction, of these base, selfish, hard and dastardly dogs themselves. *Pity* them! Let them go for pity to those whom they have applauded and abetted.

The farmers, I mean the renters, will not now, as they did in 1819, stand a good long emptying out. They had, in 1822, lost nearly all. The present stock of the farms is not, in one half of the cases, the property of the farmer. It is borrowed stock; and the sweeping out will be very rapid. The notion that the ministers will " do something " is clung on to by all those who are deeply in debt, and all who have leases, or other engagements for time. These *believe* (because they anxiously *wish*) that the paper-money, by means of some sort or other, will be put out again; while the ministers *believe* (because they anxiously *wish*) that the thing can go on, that they can continue to pay the interest of the debt, and meet all the rest of their spendings, without one-pound notes and without bank-restriction. Both parties will be deceived, and in the midst of the strife that the dissipation of the delusion will infallibly lead to, the whole THING is very likely to go to pieces; and that, too, *mind*, tumbling into the hands and placed at the mercy of a people the millions of whom have been fed upon less, to four persons, than what goes down the throat of one single common soldier! Please to *mind* that, messieurs the admirers of select vestries! You have *not done it*, Messieurs Sturges Bourne and the Hampshire Parsons! You *thought* you had! You meant well; but it was a *coup-manqué*, a missing of the mark, and that, too, as is frequently the case, by over-shooting it. The attempt will, however, produce its just consequences in the end, and those consequences will be of vast importance.

From Weyhill I was shown, yesterday, the wood in which took place the battle in which was concerned poor Turner, one of the young men who was hanged at Winchester in the year 1822. There was another young man, named Smith, who was, on account of another game-battle, hanged on the same gallows! And this for the preservation of the *game*, you will observe! This for the preservation of the *sports* of that aristocracy for whose sake, and solely for whose sake, " Sir James Graham, of Netherby, descendant of the Earls of Monteith and of the seventh Earl of Galloway, K.T." (being sure not to omit the K.T.); this hanging of us is for the preservation of the sports of that aristocracy, for the sake of whom this Graham, this barefaced plagiarist, this bungling and yet impudent pamphleteer, would *sacrifice*, would reduce to beggary, according to his pamphlet, *three hundred thousand families* (making, doubtless, *two millions* of persons), in the middle rank of life! It is for the preservation, for upholding what he insolently calls the " dignity " of this sporting aristocracy, that he proposes to rob all mortgagees, all who have claims upon land! The feudal lords in France had, as Mr. Young tells us, a right, when they came in, fatigued, from hunting or shooting, to cause the belly of one of their vassals to be ripped up, in order for the lord to soak his feet in the bowels! Sir James Graham of the bright sword does not propose to carry us back so far as this; he is willing to stop at taking away the money and the victuals of a very large part of the community; and, monstrous as it may seem, I will venture to say that there are scores of the Lord-Charles tribe who think him moderate to a fault!

But to return to the above-mentioned hanging at Winchester (a thing never to be forgotten by me), James Turner, aged 28 years, was accused of assisting to kill Robert Baker, gamekeeper to Thomas Asheton Smith, Esq., in the parish of South Tidworth; and Charles Smith, aged 27 years, was accused of shooting at (not killing) Robert Snellgrove, assistant gamekeeper to Lord Palmerston (Secretary at War), at Broadlands, in the parish of Romsey. Poor Charles Smith had better have been hunting after *shares* than after *hares!* *Mines*, however *deep*, he would have found less perilous than the pleasure grounds of Lord Palmerston! I deem this hanging at Winchester worthy of general attention, and particularly at this time, when the aristocracy near Andover, and one, at least, of the members for that town, of whom this very Thomas Asheton Smith was, until lately, one, was, if the report in the *Morning Chronicle* (copied into the *Register* of the 7th instant) be correct, endeavouring, at the late meeting at Andover, to persuade people that they (these aristocrats) wished to keep up the price of corn for the sake of the labourers, whom Sir John Pollen (Thomas Asheton Smith's son's present colleague as member for Andover) called "poor devils," and who, he said, had "hardly a rag to cover them!" Oh! wished to keep up the price of corn for the good of the "poor devils of labourers who have hardly a rag to cover them!" Amiable feeling, tender-hearted souls! Cared not a straw about *rents!* Did not; oh, no! did not care even about the farmers! It was only for the sake of the poor naked devils of labourers that the colleague of young Thomas Asheton Smith cared; it was only for those who were in the same rank of life as James Turner and Charles Smith were that these kind Andover aristocrats cared! This was the only reason in the world for their wanting corn to sell at a high price? We often say, "*that* beats everything;" but really, I think, that these professions of the Andover aristocrats do "*beat everything.*" Ah! but, Sir John Pollen, these professions come *too late* in the day: the people are no longer to be deceived by such stupid attempts at disguising hypocrisy. However, the attempt shall do this: it shall make me repeat here that which I published on the Winchester hanging in the *Regist.r* of the 6th of April, 1822. It made part of a "Letter to Landlords." Many boys have, since this article was published, grown up to the age of thought. Let them now read it, and I hope that they will *remember it well.*

I, last fall, addressed ten letters to you on the subject of the *Agricultural Report.* My object was to convince you that you would be ruined; and when I think of your general conduct towards the rest of the nation, and especially towards the labourers, I must say that I have great pleasure in seeing that my opinions are in a fair way of being verified to the full extent. I dislike the *Jews;* but the Jews are not so inimical to the industrious classes of the country as you are. We should do a great deal better with the 'squires from 'Change Alley who, at any rate, have nothing of the ferocious and bloody in their characters. Engrafted upon your native want of feeling is the sort of military spirit of command that you have acquired during the late war. You appeared, at the close of that war, to think that you had made a *conquest* of the rest of the nation for ever; and if it had not been for the burdens which the war left behind it, there would have been no such thing as air in England for any one but a slave to breathe. The Bey of Tunis never talked to his subjects in language more insolent than you talked to the people of England. The DEBT, the blessed Debt, stood our friend, made you soften your tone, and will finally place you where you ought to be placed.

This is the last Letter that I shall ever take the trouble to address to you. In a short time, you will become much too insignificant to merit any particular notice; but just in the way of *farewell*, and that there may be something on record to show what care has been taken of the partridges, pheasants, and hares, while the estates themselves have been suffered to slide away, I have resolved to address this one more Letter to you, which resolution has been occasioned by the recent *putting to death*, at Winchester, of two men denominated *Poachers*. This is a thing which, whatever you may think of it, has not been passed over, and is not to be passed over, without full notice and ample record. The account of the matter, as it appeared in the public prints, was very short; but the fact is such as never ought to be forgotten. And while you are complaining of your " distress " I will endeavour to lay before the public that which will show that the *law* has not been unmindful of even your *sports*. The time is approaching when the people will have an opportunity of exercising their judgment as to what are called " game laws; " when they will look back a little at what has been done for the sake of insuring sport to landlords. In short, landlords as well as labourers will *pass under review*. But I must proceed to my subject, reserving reflections for a subsequent part of my letter.

The account to which I have alluded is this:

" HAMPSHIRE. The Lent Assizes for this county concluded on Saturday morning. The Criminal Calendar contained 58 prisoners for trial, 16 of whom have been sentenced to suffer death, but two only of that number (*poachers*) were left by the judges for execution, viz.: James Turner, aged 28, for aiding and assisting in killing Robert Baker, gamekeeper to Thomas Asheton Smith, Esq., in the parish of South Tidworth, and Charles Smith, aged 27, for having wilfully and maliciously shot at Robert Snellgrove, assistant gamekeeper to Lord Palmerston, at Broadlands, in the parish of Romsey, with intent to do him grievous bodily harm. The judge (Burrough) observed, it became *necessary* to *these cases* that the *extreme sentence of the law should be inflicted* to *deter others, as resistance to gamekeepers was now arrived at an alarming height,* and many lives had been lost."

The first thing to observe here is, that there were *sixteen* persons sentenced to suffer death; and that the only persons actually put to death were those who had been endeavouring to get at the hares, pheasants or partridges of Thomas Asheton Smith and of our Secretary at War, Lord Palmerston. Whether the Judge Burrough (who was long chairman of the quarter sessions in Hampshire) uttered the words ascribed to him or not, I cannot say; but the words have gone forth in print, and the impression they are calculated to make is this: that it was necessary to put these two *men to death* in order to deter others from resisting gamekeepers. The putting of these men to death has excited a very deep feeling throughout the county of Hants; a feeling very honourable to the people of that county, and very natural to the breast of every human being.

In this case there appears to have been a killing, in which Turner *assisted ;* and Turner might, by possibility, have given the fatal blow; but in the case of Smith, there was no killing at all. There was a mere *shooting at*, with intention to do him bodily harm. This latter offence was not a crime for which men were put to death, even when there was no assault, or attempt at assault, on the part of the person shot at; this was not a crime punished with death until that terrible act, brought in by the late Lord Ellenborough, was passed, and formed a part of our matchless code, that code which there is such a talk about *softening ;* but which softening does not appear to have in view this act, or any portion of the game laws.

In order to form a just opinion with regard to the offence of these two men that have been hanged at Winchester, we must first consider the motives by which they were actuated in committing the acts of violence laid to their charge. For it is the intention, and not the mere act, that constitutes the crime. To make an act murder there must be *malice aforethought*. The question, therefore, is, did these men attack, or were they the attacked? It seems to be clear that they were the attacked parties: for they are executed, according to this publication, to deter others from *resisting* gamekeepers!

I know very well that there is law for this; but what I shall endeavour to show is, that the law ought to be altered; that the people of Hampshire ought to petition for such alteration; and that if you, the landlords, were wise, you would petition also for an alteration, if not a total annihilation of that terrible code, called the game laws, which has been growing harder and harder all the time that it ought to have been wearing away. It should never be forgotten that, in order to make punishments efficient in the way of example, they must be thought just by the community at large; and they will never be thought just if they aim at the protection of things belonging to one particular class of the community, and especially if those very things be grudged to this class by the community in general. When punishments of this sort take place, they are looked upon as unnecessary, the sufferers are objects of pity, the common feeling of the community is in their favour instead of being against them; and it is those who cause the punishment, and not those who suffer it, who become objects of abhorrence.

Upon seeing two of our countrymen hanging upon a gallows, we naturally and instantly run back to the cause. First we find the fighting with gamekeepers; next we find that the men would have been transported if caught in or near a cover with guns after dark; next we find that these trespassers are exposed to transportation because they are in pursuit, or supposed to be in pursuit, of partridges, pheasants or hares; and then, we ask, where is the foundation of a law to punish a man with transportation for being in pursuit of these animals? And where, indeed, is the foundation of the law to take from any man, be he who he may, the right of catching and using these animals? We know very well, we are instructed by mere feeling, that we have a right to live, to see and to move. Common sense tells us that there are some things which no man can reasonably call his property; and though poachers (as they are called) do not read *Blackstone's Commentaries*, they know that such animals as are of a wild and untameable disposition any man may seize upon and keep for his own use and pleasure. "All these things, so long as they remain in possession, every man has a right to enjoy without disturbance; but if once they escape from his custody, or he voluntarily abandons the use of them, they return to the common stock, and any man else has an equal right to seize and enjoy them afterwards." (Book 2, chapter 1.)

In the second book and twenty-sixth chapter of *Blackstone*, the poacher might read as follows: "With regard likewise to wild animals, all mankind had by the original grant of the Creator a right to pursue and take away any fowl or insect of the air, any fish or inhabitant of the waters, and any beast or reptile of the field: and this natural right still continues in every individual, unless where it is restrained by the civil laws of the country. And when a man has once so seized them, they become, while living, his qualified property, or, if dead, are absolutely his own: so that to steal them or otherwise invade this property is, according to the respective values, sometimes a criminal offence, sometimes only a civil injury."

Poachers do not read this; but that reason which is common to all mankind tells them that this is true, and tells them, also, *what to think* of any positive law that is made to restrain them from this right granted by the Creator. Before I proceed further in commenting upon the case immediately before me, let me once more quote this English judge, who wrote fifty years ago, when the game code was mild indeed compared to the one of the present day. "Another violent alteration," says he, "of the English Constitution consisted in the depopulation of whole countries, for the purposes of the king's royal diversion; and subjecting both them, and all the ancient forests of the kingdom, to the unreasonable severities of forest laws imported from the continent, whereby the slaughter of a beast was made almost as penal as the death of a man. In the Saxon times, though no man was allowed to kill or chase the king's deer, yet he might start any game, pursue and kill it upon his own estate. But the rigour of these new constitutions vested the sole property of all the game in England in the king alone; and no man was entitled to disturb any fowl of the air, or any beast of the field, of such kinds as were specially reserved for the royal amusement of the sovereign, without express licence from the king, by a grant of a chase or free warren: and those franchises were granted as much with a view to preserve the breed of animals, as to indulge the subject. From a similar principle to which, though the forest laws are now mitigated, and by degrees grown entirely obsolete, yet from this root has sprung up a bastard slip, known by the name of the game law, now arrived to and wantoning in its highest vigour: both founded upon the same unreasonable notions of permanent property in wild creatures; and both productive of the same tyranny to the commons: but with this difference; that the forest laws established only one mighty hunter throughout the land, the game laws have raised a little Nimrod in every manor." (Book 4, chapter 33.)

When this was written nothing was known of the present severity of the law. Judge Blackstone says that the game law was then wantoning in its *highest vigour;* what, then, would he have said if any one had proposed to make it *felony* to resist a gamekeeper? He calls it tyranny to the commons, as it existed in his time; what would he have said of the present code, which, so far from being thought a thing to be *softened,* is never so much as mentioned by those humane and gentle creatures, who are absolutely supporting a sort of reputation, and aiming at distinction in society, in consequence of their incessant talk about softening the criminal code?

The law may say what it will, but the feelings of mankind will never be in favour of this code; and whenever it produces putting to death, it will necessarily excite horror. It is impossible to make men believe that any particular set of individuals should have a permanent property in wild creatures. That the owner of land should have a quiet possession of it is reasonable and right and necessary; it is also necessary that he should have the power of inflicting pecuniary punishment, in a moderate degree, upon such as trespass on his lands; but his right can go no further according to reason. If the law give him ample compensation for every damage that he sustains, in consequence of a trespass on his lands, what right has he to complain?

The law authorises the king, in case of invasion or apprehended invasion, to call upon all his people to take up arms in defence of the country. The militia law compels every man, in his turn, to become a soldier. And upon what ground is this? There must be some reason for it, or else the law would be tyranny. The reason is, that every man has *rights* in the country to which he belongs; and that, therefore, it is his duty to defend the country. Some rights, too, beyond that of merely living, merely that of breathing the air. And then, I should be glad to know what rights an Englishman has, if the pursuit of even wild animals is to be the ground of transporting him from his country? There is a sufficient punishment provided by the law of trespass; quite sufficient means to keep men off your land altogether! how can it be necessary, then, to have a law to transport them for coming upon your land? No, it is not for coming upon the land, it is for coming after the wild animals, which nature and reason tells them are as much theirs as they are yours.

It is impossible for the people not to contrast the treatment of these two men at Winchester with the treatment of some gamekeepers that have killed or maimed the persons they call poachers; and it is equally impossible for the people, when they see these two men hanging on a gallows, after being recommended to mercy, not to remember the almost instant pardon given to the exciseman, who was not recommended to mercy, and who was found guilty of wilful murder in the county of Sussex!

It is said, and I believe truly, that there are more persons imprisoned in England for offences against the game laws than there are persons imprisoned in France (with more than twice the population) for all sorts of offences put together. When there was a loud outcry against the cruelties committed on the priests and the seigneurs by the people of France, Arthur Young bade them remember the cruelties committed on the people by the game laws, and to bear in mind how many had been made galley-slaves for having killed, or tried to kill, partridges, pheasants, and hares!

However, I am aware that it is quite useless to address observations of this sort to you. I am quite aware of that; and yet there are circumstances in your present situation which, one would think, ought to make you *not very gay* upon the hanging of the two men at Winchester. It delights me, I assure you, to see the situation that you are in; and I shall, therefore, now, once more, and for the last time, address you upon that subject. We all remember how haughty, how insolent, you have been. We all bear in mind your conduct for the last thirty-five years; and the feeling of pleasure at your present state is as general as it is just. In my *ten Letters* to you, I told you that you would lose your estates. Those of you who have any capacity, except that which is necessary to enable you to kill wild animals, see this now, as clearly as I do; and yet you evince no intention to change your courses. You hang on with unrelenting grasp; and cry " pauper " and " poacher " and " radical " and " lower orders " with as much insolence as ever! It is always thus; men like you may be convinced of error, but they never change their conduct. They never become just because they are convinced that they have been unjust: they must have a great deal more than that conviction to make them just.

Such was what I *then* addressed to the landlords. How well it fits the *present* time! They are just in the same sort of *mess* now that they were in 1822. But there is this most important difference, that the paper-money cannot *now* be put out, in a quantity sufficient to save them, without producing not only a " *late* panic," worse than the last, but, in all probability, a total blowing up of the whole system, game laws, new trespass laws, treadmill, Sunday tolls, six‑acts, sunset and sunrise laws, apple-felony laws, select-vestry laws, and all the whole THING, root and trunk and branch! Aye, not sparing, perhaps, even the tent or booth of induction at Draycot Foliot! Good Lord! How should we be able to live without game laws! And tread-mills, then? And Sunday tolls? How should we get on without pensions, sinecures, tithes and the other " glorious institutions " of this " mighty *empire?*" Let us turn, how-ever, from the thought; but bearing this in mind, if you please, messieurs the game-people; that if, no matter in what shape and under what pretence; if, I tell you, paper be put out again, sufficient to raise the price of a South Down ewe to the last year's mark, the whole system goes to atoms. I tell you that; mind it; and look sharp about you, O ye fat parsons; for tithes and half-pay will, be you assured, never from that day again go in company into parson's pocket.

In this north of Hampshire, as everywhere else, the churches and all other things exhibit indubitable marks of decay. There are along under the north side of that chain of hills which divide Hampshire from Berkshire, in this part, taking into Hampshire about two or three miles wide of the low ground along under the chain, eleven churches along in a string in about fifteen miles, the chancels of which would contain a great many more than all the inhabitants, men, women, and children, sitting at their ease with plenty of room. How should this be otherwise when, in the parish of Burghclere, one single farmer holds by lease, under Lord Carnarvon, as one farm, the lands that men now living can remember to have formed fourteen farms, bring-ing up, in a respectable way, fourteen families. In some instances these small farm-houses and homesteads are com-pletely gone; in others the buildings remain, but in a tumble-down state; in others the house is gone, leaving the barn for use as a barn or as a cattle-shed; in others the out-buildings are gone, and the house, with rotten thatch, broken windows, rotten door-sills, and all threatening to fall, remains as the dwelling of a half-starved and ragged family of labourers, the grandchildren, perhaps, of the decent family of small farmers that formerly lived happily in this very house.

This, with few exceptions, is the case all over England; and if we duly consider the nature and tendency of the hellish system of taxing, of funding, and of paper-money, it must be so. Then, in this very parish of Burghclere, there was, until a few months ago, a famous cock-parson, the " Honourable and Reverend " George Herbert, who had grafted the *parson* upon the *soldier* and the *justice* upon the parson; for he died a little while ago, a half-pay officer in the army, rector of two parishes, and chair-

man of the quarter sessions of the county of Hants!! Mr. Hone
gave us, in his memorable " *House that Jack built*," a portrait of
the " Clerical Magistrate." Could not he, or somebody else,
give us a portrait of the *military* and of the *naval parson ?* For
such are to be found all over the kingdom. Wherever I go I
hear of them. And yet there sits Burdett, and even Sir Bobby
of the Borough, and say not a word upon the subject! This is
the case: the king dismissed Sir Bobby from the half-pay list,
scratched his name out, turned him off, stopped his pay. Sir
Bobby complained, alleging that the half-pay was a reward for
past services. No, no, said the ministers: it is *a retaining fee*
for *future* services. Now, the law is, and the parliament
declared, in the case of parson Horne Tooke, that once a parson
always a parson, and that a parson cannot, of course, again serve
as an officer under the crown. Yet these military and naval
parsons have " a retaining fee for future military and naval
services! " Never was so barefaced a thing before heard of in
the world. And yet there sits Sir Bobby, stripped of his " retaining fee," and says not a word about the matter; and there
sit the *big Whigs*, who gave Sir Bobby the subscription, having
sons, brothers, and other relations, military and naval parsons,
and the *big Whigs*, of course, bid Sir Bobby (albeit given enough
to twattle) hold his tongue upon the subject; and there sit Mr.
Wetherspoon (I think it is), and the rest of Sir Bobby's Rump,"
toasting " *the independence* of the Borough and its member! "

" That's our case," as the lawyers say: match it if you can,
devil, in all your roamings up and down throughout the earth!
I have often been thinking, and, indeed, expecting, to see Sir
Bobby turn parson himself, as the likeliest way to get back his
half-pay. If he should have " a call," I do hope we shall have
him for parson at Kensington; and, as an inducement, I promise
him that I will give him a good thumping Easter-offering.

In former Rides, and especially in 1821 and 1822, I described
very fully this part of Hampshire. The land is a chalk bottom,
with a bed of reddish, stiff loam, full of flints at top. In those
parts where the bed of loam and flints is deep the land is arable
or woods: where the bed of loam and flints is so shallow as to
let the plough down to the chalk, the surface is downs. In the
deep and long valleys, where there is constantly or occasionally
a stream of water, the top soil is blackish and the surface
meadows. This has been the distribution from all antiquity,
except that, in ancient times, part of that which is now downs
and woods was *corn-land*, as we know from the *marks of the plough*.

And yet the Scotch fellows would persuade us that there were scarcely any inhabitants in England before it had the unspeakable happiness to be united to that fertile, warm, and hospitable country where the people are so well off that they are *above* having poor-rates!

The tops of the hills here are as good corn-land as any other part; and it is all excellent corn-land, and the fields and woods singularly beautiful. Never was there what may be called a more *hilly* country, and *all in use*. Coming from Burghclere you come up nearly a mile of steep hill, from the top of which you can see all over the country, even to the Isle of Wight; to your right a great part of Wiltshire; into Surrey on your left; and turning round, you see lying below you the whole of Berkshire, great part of Oxfordshire, and part of Gloucestershire. This chain of lofty hills was a great favourite with kings and rulers in ancient times. At Highclere, at Combe, and at other places there are remains of great encampments or fortifications; and Kingsclere was a residence of the Saxon kings, and continued to be a royal residence long after the Norman kings came. King John, when residing at Kingsclere, founded one of the charities which still exists in the town of Newbury, which is but a few miles from Kingsclere.

From the top of this lofty chain you come to Uphusband (or the Upper Hurstbourn) over two miles or more of ground, descending in the way that the body of a snake descends (when he is going fast) from the high part, near the head, down to the tail; that is to say, over a series of hill and dell, but the dell part going constantly on increasing upon the hilly part, till you come down to this village; and then you, continuing on (southward) towards Andover, go up, directly, half a mile of hill so steep as to make it very difficult for an ordinary team with a load to take that load up it. So this *Up*-hurstbourn (called so because *higher up the valley* than the other Hurstbourns), the flat part of the road to which, from the north, comes in between two side-hills, is in as narrow and deep a dell as any place that I ever saw.

The houses of the village are in great part scattered about, and are amongst very lofty and fine trees; and from many, many points round about, from the hilly fields, now covered with the young wheat, or with scarcely less beautiful sainfoin, the village is a sight worth going many miles to see. The lands, too, are pretty beyond description. These chains of hills make, below them, an endless number of lower hills, of varying shapes and sizes and aspects and of relative state as to each other; while the surface presents, in the size and form of the fields, in the woods, the hedgerows, the sainfoin, the young wheat, the turnips, the tares, the fallows, the sheep-folds and the flocks, and at every turn of your head a fresh and different set of these; this surface all together presents that which I, at any rate, could look at with pleasure for ever. Not a sort of country that I like so well as when there are *downs* and a *broader valley* and *more of meadow;* but a sort of country that I like next to that; for here, as there, there are no ditches, no water-furrows, no dirt, and never any drought to cause inconvenience. The chalk is at bottom, and it takes care of all. The crops of wheat have been very good here this year, and those of barley not very bad. The sainfoin has given a fine crop of the finest sort of hay in the world, and this year without a drop of wet.

I wish that, in speaking of this pretty village (which I always return to with additional pleasure), I could give *a good account* of the state of *those without whose labour there would be neither corn nor sainfoin nor sheep.* I regret to say that my account of this matter, if I gave it truly, must be a dismal account indeed! For I have, in no part of England, seen the labouring people so badly off as they are here. This has made so much impression on me that I shall enter fully into the matter with names, dates, and all the particulars in the fourth number of the *Poor Man's Friend.* This is one of the great purposes for which I take these "rides." I am persuaded that before the day shall come when my labours must cease *I shall have mended the meals of millions.* I may over-rate the effects of my endeavours; but this being my persuasion, I should be guilty of a great neglect of duty were I not to use those endeavours.

ANDOVER,
Sunday, 15 *October.*

I went to Weyhill yesterday, to see the close of the hop and of the cheese fair; for, after the sheep, these are the principal articles. The crop of hops has been, in parts where they are grown, unusually large and of super-excellent quality. The average price of the Farnham *hops* has been, as nearly as I can ascertain, seven pounds for a hundredweight; that of Kentish hops, five pounds, and that of the Hampshire and Surrey hops (other than those of Farnham), about five pounds also. The prices are, considering the great weight of the crop, very good; but if it had not been for the effects of "*late* panic" (proceeding, as Baring said, from a " plethora of money "), these prices would have been a full third, if not nearly one-half, higher; for though the crop has been so large and so good, there was hardly any stock on hand; the country was almost wholly without hops.

As to cheese, the price, considering the quantity, has been not one half so high as it was last year. The fall in the positive price has been about 20 per cent., and the quantity made in 1826 has not been above two-thirds as great as that made in 1825. So that here is a fall of *one-half* in real relative price; that is to say, the farmer, while he has the same rent to pay that he paid last year, has only half as much money to receive for cheese as he received for cheese last year; and observe, on some farms cheese is almost the only saleable produce.

After the fair was over yesterday, I came down from the Hill (3 miles) to this town of Andover; which has, within the last 20 days, been more talked of, in other parts of the kingdom, than it ever was before from the creation of the world to the beginning of those 20 days. The Thomas Asheton Smiths and the Sir John Pollens, famous as they have been under the banners of the Old Navy Purser, George Rose, and his successors, have never, even since the death of poor Turner, been half so famous, they and this corporation whom they represent, as they have been since the meeting which they held here, which ended in their defeat and confusion, pointing them out as worthy of that appellation of " poor devils," which Pollen thought proper to give to those labourers, without whose toil his estate would not be worth a single farthing.

Having laid my plan to sleep at Andover last night, I went with two Farnham friends, Messrs. Knowles and West, to dine at the ordinary at the George Inn, which is kept by one Sutton, a rich old fellow, who wore a round-skirted sleeved fustian waistcoat, with a dirty white apron tied round his middle, and with no coat on; having a look the *eagerest* and the *sharpest* that I ever saw in any set of features in my whole life-time; having an air of authority and of mastership which, to a stranger as I was, seemed quite incompatible with the meanness of his dress and the vulgarity of his manners: and there being, visible to every beholder, constantly going on in him a pretty even contest between the servility of avarice and the insolence of wealth. A great part of the farmers and other fair-people having gone off home, we found preparations made for dining only about ten people. But after we sat down, and it was seen that we designed to dine, guests came in apace, the preparations were augmented, and as many as could dine came and dined with us.

After the dinner was over the room became fuller and fuller; guests came in from the other inns, where they had been dining, till at last the room became as full as possible in every part, the door being opened, the door-way blocked up, and the stairs leading to the room crammed from bottom to top. In this state of things Mr. Knowles, who was our chairman, gave *my health*, which, of course, was followed by a *speech ;* and, as the reader will readily suppose, to have an opportunity of making a speech was the main motive for my going to dine at *an inn*, at any hour, and especially at *seven o'clock* at night. In this speech I, after descanting on the present devastating ruin, and on those successive acts of the ministers and the parliament by which such ruin had been produced; after remarking on the shuffling, the tricks, the contrivances from 1797 up to last March, I proceeded to offer to the company *my reasons* for believing that no attempt would be made to relieve the farmers and others by putting out the paper-money again, as in 1822, or by a bank restriction. Just as I was stating these my reasons on a prospective matter of such deep interest to my hearers, amongst whom were land-owners, land-renters, cattle and sheep dealers, hop and cheese producers and merchants, and even one, two, or more country bankers; just as I was engaged in stating *my reasons* for my opinion on a matter of such vital importance to the parties present, who were all listening to me with the greatest attention; just at this time a noise was heard, and a sort of row was taking place in the passage, the cause of which was, upon inquiry, found to be no less a personage than our landlord, our host Sutton, who, it appeared, finding that my speech-making had cut off or at least suspended all intercourse between the dining, now become a drinking, room and the *bar ;* who finding that I had been the cause of a great " restriction in the exchange " of our money for his " neat " " genuine " commodities downstairs, and being, apparently, an ardent admirer of the " liberal " system of " free trade "; who finding, in short, or rather supposing, that if my tongue were not stopped from running his taps would be, had, though an old man, fought, or at least forced, his way up the thronged stairs and through the passage and door-way into the room, and was (with what breath the struggle had left him) beginning to bawl out to me, when some one called to him, and told him that he was causing an interruption, to which he answered that that was what he had come to do! And then he went on to say, in so many words, that my speech injured his sale of liquor!

The disgust and abhorrence which such conduct could not fail to excite, produced at first a desire to quit the room and the house, and even a proposition to that effect. But after a minute or so to reflect, the company resolved not to quit the room, but to turn him out of it who had caused the interruption; and the old fellow, finding himself *tackled*, saved the labour of shoving or kicking him out of the room, by retreating out of the door-way with all the activity of which he was master. After this I proceeded with my speech-making; and this being ended, the great business of the evening, namely, drinking, smoking, and singing, was about to be proceeded in by a company who had just closed an arduous and anxious week, who had before them a Sunday morning to sleep in, and whose wives were, for the far greater part, at a convenient distance. An assemblage of circumstances more auspicious to " free-trade " in the " neat " and " genuine " has seldom occurred! But now behold, the old fustian-jacketed fellow, whose head was, I think, *powdered*, took it into that head not only to lay " restrictions " upon trade, but to impose an absolute embargo; cut off entirely all supplies whatever from his bar to the room, *as long as I remained in that room.* A message to this effect from the old fustian man having been, through the waiter, communicated to Mr. Knowles, and he having communicated it to the company, I addressed the company in nearly these words: " Gentlemen, born and bred, as you know I was, on the borders of this county, and fond as I am of bacon, *Hampshire hogs* have with me always been objects of admiration rather than of contempt; but that which has just happened here induces me to observe that this feeling of mine has been confined to hogs of *four legs.* For my part, I like your company too well to quit it. I have paid this fellow *six shillings* for the wing of a fowl, a bit of bread, and a pint of small beer. I have a right to sit here; I want no drink, and those who do, being refused it here, have a right to send to other houses for it, and to drink it here."

However, Mammon soon got the upper hand downstairs, all the fondness for " free trade " returned, and up came the old fustian-jacketed fellow, bringing pipes, tobacco, wine, grog, sling, and seeming to be as pleased as if he had just sprung a mine of gold! Nay, he soon after this came into the room with two gentlemen, who had come to him to ask where I was. He actually came up to me, making me a bow, and telling me that those gentlemen wished to be introduced to me, he, with a fawning look, laid his hand upon my knee! "Take away your *paw*," said I, and shaking the gentlemen by the hand, I said, "I am happy to see you, gentlemen, even though introduced by this fellow." Things now proceeded without interruption; songs, toasts, and speeches filled up the time, until half-past two o'clock this morning, though in the house of a landlord who receives the sacrament, but who, from his manifestly ardent attachment to the "liberal principles" of "free-trade," would, I have no doubt, have suffered us, if we could have found money and throats and stomachs, to sit and sing and talk and drink until two o'clock of a Sunday afternoon instead of two o'clock of a Sunday morning. It was not politics; it was not *personal* dislike to me; for the fellow knew nothing of me. It was, as I told the company, just this: he looked upon their bodies as so many gutters to drain off the contents of his taps, and upon their purses as so many small heaps from which to take the means of augmenting his great one; and finding that I had been, no matter how, the cause of suspending this work of "reciprocity," he wanted, and no matter how, to restore the reciprocal system to motion. All that I have to add is this: that the next time this old sharp-looking fellow gets *six shillings* from me for a dinner, he shall, if he choose, *cook me*, in any manner that he likes, and season me with hand so unsparing as to produce in the feeders thirst unquenchable.

To-morrow morning we set off for the New Forest; and, indeed, we have lounged about here long enough. But, as some apology, I have to state that while I have been in a sort of waiting upon this great fair, where one hears, sees and learns so much, I have been writing No. IV. of the *Poor Man's Friend*, which, price twopence, is published once a month.

I see in the London newspapers accounts of *despatches from Canning!* I thought that he went solely "on a party of pleasure!" So the "despatches" come to tell the king how the pleasure party gets on! No: what he is gone to Paris for is to endeavour to prevent the "*holy* allies" from doing anything which shall sink the English government in the eyes of the world, and *thereby favour the radicals*, who are enemies of *all* "regular government," and whose success in England would *revive republicanism* in France. This is my opinion. The subject, if I be right in my opinion, was too ticklish to be committed to paper: Granville Levison Gower (for that is the man that is now Lord Granville) was, perhaps, not thought quite a match for the French as *a talker;* and therefore the Captain of Eton, who, in 1817, said that the " ever living luminary of British prosperity was only hidden behind a cloud; " and who, in 1819, said that " Peel's bill had set the currency question at rest for ever; " therefore the profound captain is gone over to see what *he* can do.

But, captain, a word in your ear: we do not care for the Bourbons any more than we do for you! My real opinion is, that there is nothing that can put England to rights that will not shake the Bourbon government. This is my opinion; but I defy the Bourbons to save, or to assist in saving, the present system in England, unless they and their friends will subscribe and pay off your debt for you, captain of toad-eating and nonsensical and shoe-licking Eton! Let them pay off your debt for you, captain; let the Bourbons and their allies do that; or they cannot save you; no, nor can they help you, even in the smallest degree.

RUMSEY (HAMPSHIRE),
Monday Noon, 16 *Oct.*

Like a very great fool, I, out of senseless complaisance, waited this morning to breakfast with the friends at whose house we slept last night at Andover. We thus lost two hours of dry weather, and have been justly punished by about an hour's ride in the rain. I settled on Lyndhurst as the place to lodge at to-night; so we are here, feeding out horses, drying our clothes, and writing the account of our journey. We came, as much as possible, all the way through the villages, and almost all the way avoided the turnpike-roads. From Andover to Stockbridge (about seven or eight miles) is, for the greatest part, an open corn and sheep country, a considerable portion of the land being downs. The wheat and rye and vetch and sainfoin fields look beautiful here; and during the whole of the way from Andover to Rumsey the early turnips of both kinds are not bad, and the stubble turnips very promising. The downs are green as meadows usually are in April. The grass is most abundant in all situations where grass grows. From Stockbridge to Rumsey we came nearly by the river side, and had to cross the river several times. This, the river Teste, which, as I described in my Ride of last November, begins at Uphusband by springs, bubbling up in March out of the bed of that deep valley. It is at first a bourn, that is to say, a stream that runs only a part of the year, and is the rest of the year as dry as a road. About five miles from this periodical source it becomes a stream all the year round. After winding about between the chalk hills for many miles, first in a general direction towards the south-east and then in a similar direction towards the south-west and south, it is joined by the little stream that rises just above and that passes through the town of Andover. It is, after this, joined by several other little streams with names; and here, at Rumsey, it is a large and very fine river, famous all the way down for trout and eels, and both of the finest quality.

LYNDHURST (NEW FOREST),
Monday Evening, 16 October.

I have just time, before I go to bed, to observe that we arrived here about 4 o'clock, over about 10 or 11 miles of the best road in the world, having a choice too, for the great part of the way, between these smooth roads and green sward. Just as we came out of Rumsey (or Romsey), and crossed our river Teste once more, we saw to our left the sort of park called *Broadlands*, where poor Charles Smith (as mentioned above) was hanged for *shooting at* (*not killing*) one Snellgrove, an assistant gamekeeper of Lord Palmerston, who was then our Secretary at War, and who is in that office, I believe, now, though he is now better known as a director of the grand Mining Joint-Stock Company, which shows the great *industry* of this noble and "right honourable person," and also the great scope and the various nature and tendency of his talents. What would our old fathers of the "dark ages" have said if they had been told that their descendants would at last become so enlightened as to enable Jews and loan-jobbers to take away noblemen's estates by mere "watching the turn of the market," and to cause members, or at least one member, of that "most honourable, noble, and reverend assembly," the king's privy council, in which he himself sits: so *enlightened*, I say, as to cause one of this "most honourable and reverend body" to become a director in a mining speculation! How one *pities* our poor, "dark-age, bigoted" ancestors, who would, I dare say, have been as ready to *hang* a man for proposing such a "liberal" system as this, as they would have been to hang him for *shooting at* (not killing) an assistant gamekeeper! Poor old fellows! How much they lost by not living in our enlightened times! I am here close by the old purser's son George Rose's!

FROM LYNDHURST (NEW FOREST) TO BEAULIEU ABBEY; THENCE TO SOUTHAMPTON AND WESTON; THENCE TO BOTLEY, ALLINGTON, WEST END, NEAR HAMBLEDON; AND THENCE TO PETERSFIELD, THURSLEY, GODALMING

> ' But where is now the goodly audit ale?
> The purse-proud tenant, never known to fail?
> The farm which never yet was left on hand?
> The marsh reclaim'd to most improving land?
> The impatient hope of the expiring lease?
> The doubling rental? What an evil's peace!
> In vain the prize excites the ploughman's skill,
> In vain the Commons pass their patriot Bill;
> The *Landed Interest*—(you may understand
> The phrase much better leaving out the *Land*)—
> The land self-interest groans from shore to shore,
> For fear that plenty should attain the poor.
> Up, up again, ye rents! exalt your notes,
> Or else the ministry will lose their votes,
> And patriotism, so delicately nice,
> Her loaves will lower to the market price."
>
> LORD BYRON, *Age of Bronze.*

WESTON GROVE,
Wednesday, 18 *Oct.* 1826.

YESTERDAY, from Lyndhurst to this place was a ride, including our round-abouts, of more than forty miles; but the roads the best in the world, one half of the way green turf; and the day as fine an one as ever came out of the heavens. We took in a breakfast, calculated for a long day's work, and for no more eating till night. We had slept in a room, the access to which was only through another sleeping room, which was also occupied; and as I had got up about *two o'clock* at Andover, we went to bed, at Lyndhurst, about *half-past seven* o'clock. I was, of course, awake by three or four; I had eaten little over night; so that here lay I, not liking (even after daylight began to glimmer) to go through a chamber, where, by possibility, there might be " a lady " actually *in bed ;* here lay I, my bones aching with lying in bed, my stomach growling for victuals, imprisoned by my *modesty*. But at last I grew impatient; for, modesty here or modesty there, I was not to be penned up and starved: so after having shaved and dressed and got ready to go down,

I thrusted George out a little before me into the other room; and through we pushed, previously resolving, of course, not to look towards *the bed* that was there. But as the devil would have it, just as I was about the middle of the room, I, like Lot's wife, turned my head! All that I shall say is, first, that the consequences that befell her did not befall me, and, second, that I advise those who are likely to be hungry in the morning not to sleep in *inner rooms;* or, if they do, to take some bread and cheese in their pockets. Having got safe down stairs, I lost no time in inquiry after the means of obtaining a breakfast to make up for the bad fare of the previous day; and finding my land-lady rather tardy in the work, and not, seemingly, having a proper notion of the affair, I went myself, and having found a butcher's shop, bought a loin of small, fat, wether mutton, which I saw cut out of the sheep and cut into chops. These were brought to the inn; George and I ate about 2lb. out of the 5lb. and while I was writing a letter, and making up my packet, to be ready to send from Southampton, George went out and found a poor woman to come and take away the rest of the loin of mutton; for our *fastings* of the day before enabled us to do this; and though we had about forty miles to go to get to this place (through the route that we intended to take), I had resolved that we would go without any more *purchase* of victuals and drink this day also. I beg leave to suggest to my *well-fed* readers; I mean, those who have at their command more victuals and drink than they can possibly swallow; I beg to suggest to such, whether this would not be a good way for them all to find the means of bestowing charity? Some poet has said, that that which is given in *charity* gives a blessing on both sides; to the giver as well as the receiver. But I really think that if *in general* the food and drink given came out of food and drink *deducted* from the usual quantity swallowed by the giver, the *blessing* would be still greater, and much more certain. I can speak for myself, at any rate. I hardly ever eat more than *twice* a day; when at home, never; and I never, if I can well avoid it, eat any meat later than about one or two o'clock in the day. I drink a little tea or milk and water at the usual tea-time (about 7 o'clock); I go to bed at eight, if I can; I write or read from about four to about eight, and then hungry as a hunter I go to breakfast, eating *as small a parcel* of cold meat and bread as I can prevail upon my teeth to be satisfied with. I do just the same at dinner time. I very rarely taste *garden-stuff* of any sort. If any man can show me that he has done, or can do, *more work*, bodily and mentally united; I say nothing about good health, for of that the public can know nothing; but I refer to *the work* : the public know, they see what I can do, and what I actually have done, and what I do; and when any one has shown the public that he has done, or can do, more, then I will advise my readers attend to him on the subject of diet and not to me. As to *drink*, the less the better; and mine is milk and water, or *not-sour* small beer, if I can get the latter; for the former I always can. I like the milk and water best; but I do not like much water; if I drink much milk it loads and stupefies and makes me fat.

Having made all preparations for a day's ride, we set off, as our first point, for a station in the Forest called New Park, there to see something about *plantations* and other matters connected with the affairs of our prime cocks, the surveyors of woods and forests and crown lands and estates. But before I go forward any further, I must just step back again to Rumsey, which we passed rather too hastily through on the 16th, as noticed in the Ride that was published last week. This town was, in ancient times, a very grand place, though it is now nothing more than a decent market-town, without anything to entitle it to particular notice, except its church, which was the church of an abbey nunnery (founded more, I think, than a thousand years ago), and which church was the burial place of several of the Saxon kings, and of "Lady Palmerstone," who a few years ago "died in child-birth!" What a mixture! But there was another personage buried here, and who was, it would seem, a native of the place; namely, Sir William Petty, the ancestor of the present Marquis of Lansdown. He was the son of *a cloth-weaver*, and was, doubtless, himself a weaver when young. He became a surgeon, was first in the service of Charles I., then went into that of Cromwell, whom he served as physician-general to his army in Ireland (alas! poor Ireland), and in this capacity he resided at Dublin till Charles II. came, when he came over to London (having become very rich), was knighted by that profligate and ungrateful king, and he died in 1687 leaving a fortune of £15,000 a year! This is what his biographers say. He must have made pretty good use of his time while physician-general to Cromwell's army in poor Ireland! *Petty* by nature as well as by name, he got from Cromwell a "patent for *double - writing*, invented by him;" and he invented a "*double-bottomed ship to sail against wind and tide*, a model of which is still preserved in the library of the Royal Society," of which he was a most worthy member. His great art was, however, the amassing of money, and the getting of *grants of lands in poor Ireland*, in which he was one of the most successful of the English adventurers. I had, the other day, occasion to observe that the word *Petty* manifestly is the French word *Petit*, which means little; and that it is, in these days of degeneracy, pleasing to reflect that there is *one family*, at any rate, that " Old England " still boasts one family, which retains the character designated by its pristine name; a reflection that rushed with great force into my mind when, in the year 1822, I heard the present noble head of the family say, in the House of Lords, that he thought that a currency of paper, convertible into gold, was the best and most solid and safe, especially since *Platina* had been discovered! " Oh, God! " exclaimed I to myself, as I stood listening and admiring " below the bar; " " Oh, great God! there it is, there it is, still running in the blood, that genius which discovered the art of double writing, and of making ships with double-bottoms to sail against wind and tide! " This noble and profound descendant of Cromwell's army-physician has now seen that " paper, convertible into gold," is not quite so " solid and safe " as he thought it was! He has now seen what a " late panic " is! And he might, if he were not so very well worthy of his family name, openly confess that he was deceived when, in 1819, he as one of the committee who reported in favour of Peel's bill said that the country could pay the interest of the debt in gold! Talk of a *change of ministry*, indeed! What is to be *gained* by putting this man in the place of any of those who are in power now?

To come back now to Lyndhurst, we had to go about three miles to New Park, which is a *farm* in the New Forest, and nearly in the centre of it. We got to this place about nine o'clock. There is a good and large mansion-house here, in which the " commissioners " of woods and forests reside when they come into the forest. There is a garden, a farm-yard, a farm, and a nursery. The place looks like a considerable gentleman's seat; the house stands in a sort of *park*, and you can see that a great deal of expense has been incurred in levelling the ground and making it pleasing to the eye of my lords " the commissioners." My business here was to see whether anything had been done towards the making of *locust plantations*. I went first to Lyndhurst to make inquiries; but I was there told that New Park was the place, and the only place, at which to get information on the subject; and I was

told, further, that the commissioners were now at New Park;
that is to say those experienced tree-planters, Messrs. Arbuthnot,
Dawkins, and Company. Gad! thought I, I am here coming in
close contact with a branch, or at least a twig, of the great
THING itself! When I heard this, I was at breakfast, and of
course dressed for the day. I could not, out of my extremely
limited wardrobe, afford a clean shirt for the occasion; and so
off we set, just as we were, hoping that their worships, the
nation's tree-planters, would, if they met with us, excuse our
dress, when they considered the nature of our circumstances.
When we came to the house, we were stopped by a little fence and
fastened gate. I got off my horse, gave him to George to hold,
went up to the door, and rang the bell. Having told my business to a person, who appeared to be a foreman or bailiff, he,
with great civility, took me into a nursery which is at the back
of the house; and I soon drew from him the disappointing
fact that my lords, the tree-planters, had departed the day
before! I found, as to *locusts*, that a patch were sowed last
spring, which I saw, which are from one foot to four feet high,
and very fine and strong, and are, in number, about enough to
plant two acres of ground, the plants at four feet apart each way.
I found that last fall some few locusts had been put out into
plantations of other trees already made; but that they had *not
thriven*, and had been *barked* by the hares! But a little bunch
of these trees (same age), which were planted in the nursery,
ought to convince my lords, the tree-planters, that if they were
to do what they ought to do the public would very soon be
owners of fine plantations of locusts for the use of the navy.
And what are the *hares* kept *for* here? *Who* eats them? What
right have these commissioners to keep hares here to eat up the
trees? Lord Folkestone killed his hares before he made his
plantation of locusts; and why not kill the hares in the *people's*
forest; for the *people's* it is, and that these commissioners ought
always to remember. And then again, why this farm? What is
it *for*? Why, the pretence for it is this: that it is necessary to
give the deer *hay*, in winter, because the lopping down of limbs
of trees for them to *browse* (as used to be the practice) is injurious
to the growth of timber. That will be a very good reason for
having a *hay-farm* when my lords shall have proved two things;
first, that hay, in quantity equal to what is raised here, could
not be bought for a twentieth part of the money that this farm
and all its trappings cost; and, second, that there ought to be
any deer kept! What are these deer *for*? Who are to *eat*

them? Are they for the royal family? Why, there are more
deer bred in Richmond Park alone to say nothing of Bushy
Park, Hyde Park, and Windsor Park; there are more deer bred
in Richmond Park alone than would feed all the branches of
the royal family and all their households all the year round,
if every soul of them ate as hearty as ploughmen, and if they
never touched a morsel of any kind of meat but venison! For
what, and *for whom*, then, are deer kept in the New Forest;
and why an expense of hay-farm, of sheds, of racks, of keepers,
of lodges, and other things attending the deer and the game;
an expense amounting to more money annually than would
have given relief to all the starving manufacturers in the north!
And, again I say, *who* is all this venison and game *for*? There
is more game even in Kew Gardens than the royal family can
want! And, in short, do they ever taste, or even hear of, any
game, or any venison, from the New Forest.

What a pretty thing here is, then! Here is another deep bite
into us by the long and sharp-fanged aristocracy, who so love
Old Sarum! Is there a man who will say that this is right?
And that the game should be kept, too, to eat up trees, to destroy
plantations, to destroy what is first paid for the planting of!
And that the public should pay keepers to preserve this game!
And that the *people* should be *transported* if they go out by night
to catch the game that they pay for feeding! Blessed state of
an aristocracy! It is pity that it has not a nasty, ugly, obstinate
DEBT to deal with! It might possibly go on for ages, deer and all,
were it not for this DEBT. This New Forest is a piece of property
as much belonging *to the public* as the Custom House at London
is. There is no man, however poor, who has not a right in it.
Every man is owner of a part of the deer, the game, and of the
money that goes to the keepers; and yet any man may be *transported* if he go out by night to catch any part of this game!
We are compelled to pay keepers for preserving game to eat up
the trees that we are compelled to pay people to plant! Still
however there is comfort; we *might* be worse off; for the Turks
made the Tartars pay a tax called *tooth-money*; that is to say,
they eat up the victuals of the Tartars, and then made them pay
for the *use of their teeth*. No man can say that we are come
quite to that yet: and, besides, the poor Tartars had no DEBT,
no blessed debt to hold out hope to them.

The same person (a very civil and intelligent man) that showed
me the nursery, took me, in my way back, through some plantations of *oaks*, which have been made amongst fir-trees. It was,

indeed, a plantation of Scotch firs, about twelve years old, in rows, at six feet apart. Every third row of firs was left, and oaks were (about six years ago) planted instead of the firs that were grubbed up; and the winter shelter that the oaks have received from the remaining firs has made them grow very finely, though the land is poor. Other oaks planted in the *open, twenty years* ago, and in land deemed better, are not nearly so good. However, these oaks, between the firs, will take fifty or sixty good years to make them timber, and until they be *timber*, they are of very little use; whereas the same ground planted with locusts (and the *hares* of " my lords " kept down) would, at this moment, have been worth fifty pounds an acre. What do " my lords " care about this? *For them*, for " my lords," the New Forest would be no better than it is now; no, nor *so good* as it is now; for there would be no hares for them.

From New Park, I was bound to Beaulieu Abbey, and I ought to have gone in a south-easterly direction, instead of going back to Lyndhurst, which lay in precisely the opposite direction. My guide through the plantations was not apprised of my intended route, and, therefore, did not instruct me. Just before we parted, he asked me *my name :* I thought it lucky that he had not asked it before! When we got nearly back to Lyndhurst, we found that we had come three miles out of our way; indeed, it made six miles altogether; for we were, when we got to Lyndhurst, three miles further from Beaulieu Abbey than we were when we were at New Park. We wanted, very much, to go to the site of this ancient and famous abbey, of which the people of the New Forest seemed to know very little. They call the place *Bewley*, and even in the maps it is called *Bauley*. *Ley*, in the Saxon language, means *place*, or rather *open place :* so that they put *ley* in place of *lieu*, thus beating the Normans out of some part of the name at any rate. I wished, besides, to see a good deal of this New Forest. I had been, before, from Southampton to Lyndhurst, from Lyndhurst to Lymington, from Lymington to Sway. I had now come in on the north of Minstead from Romsey, so that I had seen the north of the forest and all the west side of it down to the sea. I had now been to New Park and had got back to Lyndhurst; so that, if I rode across the forest down to Beaulieu I went right across the middle of it, from north-west to south-east. Then, if I turned towards Southampton, and went to Dipten and on to Ealing, I should see, in fact, the whole of this forest, or nearly the whole of it.

We therefore started, or rather turned away from Lyndhurst, as soon as we got back to it, and went about six miles over a heath, even worse than Bagshot Heath; as barren as it is possible for land to be. A little before we came to the village of Beaulieu (which, observe, the people call *Beuley*), we went through a wood, chiefly of beech, and that beech seemingly destined to grow food for pigs, of which we saw, during this day, many, many thousands. I should think that we saw at least a hundred hogs to one deer. I stopped, at one time, and counted the hogs and pigs just round about me, and they amounted to 140, all within 50 or 60 yards of my horse. After a very pleasant ride on land without a stone in it, we came down to the Beaulieu river, the highest branch of which rises at the foot of a hill about a mile and a half to the north-east of Lyndhurst. For a great part of the way down to Beaulieu it is a very insignificant stream. At last, however, augmented by springs from the different sand-hills, it becomes a little river, and has, on the sides of it, lands which were, formerly, very beautiful meadows. When it comes to the village of Beaulieu, it forms a large pond of a great many acres; and on the east side of this pond is the spot where this famous abbey formerly stood, and where the external walls of which, or a large part of them, are now actually standing. We went down on the western side of the river. The abbey stood, and the ruins stand, on the eastern side.

Happening to meet a man before I got into the village I, pointing with my whip across towards the abbey, said to the man, " I suppose there is a bridge down here to get across to the abbey." "That's not the abbey, sir," says he: " the abbey is about four miles further on." I was astonished to hear this; but he was very positive; said that some people called it the abbey; but that the abbey was further on; and was at a farm occupied by farmer John Biel. Having chapter and verse for it, as the saying is, I believed the man; and pushed on towards farmer John Biel's, which I found, as he had told me, at the end of about four miles. When I got there (not having, observe, gone over the water to ascertain that the other was the spot where the abbey stood), I really thought, at first, that this must have been the site of the Abbey of Beaulieu; because, the name meaning *fine place*, this was a thousand times finer place than that where the abbey, as I afterwards found, really stood. After looking about it for some time, I was satisfied that it had not been an abbey; but the place is one of the finest that ever was seen in this world. It stands at about half a mile's distance from the water's edge at high-water mark, and at about the middle of the space along the coast from Calshot Castle to Lymington haven. It stands, of course, upon a rising ground; it has a gentle slope down to the water. To the right, you see Hurst Castle, and that narrow passage called the Needles, I believe; and, to the left, you see Spithead, and all the ships that are sailing or lie anywhere opposite Portsmouth. The Isle of Wight is right before you, and you have in view, at one and the same time, the towns of Yarmouth, Newton, Cowes, and Newport, with all the beautiful fields of the island, lying upon the side of a great bank before, and going up the ridge of hills in the middle of the island. Here are two little streams, nearly close to the ruin, which filled ponds for fresh-water fish; while there was the Beaulieu river at about half a mile or three quarters of a mile to the left, to bring up the salt-water fish. The ruins consist of part of the walls of a building about 200 feet long and about 40 feet wide. It has been turned into a barn, in part, and the rest into cattle-sheds, cow-pens, and inclosures and walls to inclose a small yard. But there is another ruin which was a church or chapel, and which stands now very near to the farm-house of Mr. John Biel, who rents the farm of the Duchess of Buccleugh, who is now the owner of the abbey-lands and of the lands belonging to this place. The little church or chapel, of which I have just been speaking, appears to have been a very beautiful building. A part only of its walls are standing; but you see, by what remains of the arches, that it was finished in a manner the most elegant and expensive of the day in which it was built. Part of the outside of the building is now surrounded by the farmer's garden; the interior is partly a pig-stye and partly a goose-pen. Under that arch which had once seen so many rich men bow their heads, we entered into the goose-pen, which is by no means one of the *nicest* concerns in the world. Beyond the goose-pen was the pig-stye, and in it a hog which, when fat, will weigh about 30 score, actually rubbing his shoulders against a little sort of column which had supported the font and its holy water. The farmer told us that there was a hole, which, indeed, we saw, going down into the wall, or rather into the column where the font had stood. And he told us that many attempts had been made to bring water to fill that hole, but that it never had been done.

Mr. Biel was very civil to us. As far as related to us, he performed the office of hospitality, which was the main business of those who formerly inhabited the spot. He asked us to dine with him, which we declined, for want of time; but being exceedingly hungry, we had some bread and cheese and some very good beer. The farmer told me that a great number of gentlemen had come there to look at that place; but that he never could find out what the place had been, or what the place at Beuley had been. I told him that I would, when I got to London, give him an account of it; that I would write the account down, and send it down to him. He seemed surprised that I should make such a promise, and expressed his wish not to give me so much trouble. I told him not to say a word about the matter, for that his bread and cheese and beer were so good that they deserved a full history to be written of the place where they had been eaten and drunk. " God bless me, sir, no, no!" I said I will, upon my soul, farmer. I now left him, very grateful on our part for his hospitable reception, and he, I dare say, hardly being able to believe his own ears at the generous promise that I had made him, which promise, however, I am now about to fulfil. I told the farmer a little, upon the spot, to begin with. I told him that the name was all wrong: that it was not *Beuley* but *Beaulieu ;* and that Beaulieu meant *fine place ;* and I proved this to him in this manner. You know, said I, farmer, that when a girl has a sweetheart, people call him her *beau ?* Yes, said he, so they do. Very well. You know also that we say, sometimes, you shall have this in *lieu* of that; and that when we say *lieu*, we mean in *place* of that. Now the *beau* means *fine*, as applied to the young man, and the *lieu* means *place ;* and thus it is, that the name of this place is *Beaulieu*, as it is so fine as you see it is. He seemed to be wonderfully pleased with the discovery; and we parted, I believe, with hearty good wishes on his part, and I am sure with very sincere thanks on my part.

The Abbey of Beaulieu was founded in the year 1204, by King John, for thirty monks of the reformed Benedictine Order. It was dedicated to the blessed Virgin Mary; it flourished until the year 1540, when it was suppressed, and the lands confiscated, in the reign of Henry VIII. Its revenues were, at that time, *four hundred and twenty-eight pounds, six shillings and eight-pence a year,* making in money of the present day upwards of *eight thousand five hundred pounds* a year. The lands and the abbey, and all belonging to it, were granted by the king to one Thomas Wriothesley, who was a court-pander of that day. From him it passed by sale, by will, by marriage or by something or another, till at last it has got, after passing through various hands, into the hands of the Duchess of Buccleugh.

So much for the abbey; and now as for the ruins on the farm of Mr. John Biel: they were the dwelling-place of Knights' Templars, or Knights of St. John of Jerusalem. The building they inhabited was called an hospital, and their business was to relieve travellers, strangers, and persons in distress; and, if called upon, to accompany the king in his wars to uphold Christianity. Their estate was also confiscated by Henry VIII. It was worth at the time of being confiscated upwards of *two thousand pounds a year*, money of the present day. This establishment was founded a little before the Abbey of Beaulieu was founded; and it was this foundation and not the other that gave the name of Beaulieu to both establishments. The abbey is not situated in a very fine place. The situation is low; the lands above it rather a swamp than otherwise; pretty enough, altogether; but by no means a fine place. The Templars had all the reason in the world to give the name of Beaulieu to their place. And it is by no means surprising that the monks were willing to apply it to their abbey.

Now, farmer John Biel, I dare say, that you are a very good Protestant; and I am a monstrous good Protestant too. We cannot bear the pope, nor " they there priests that makes men confess their sins and go down upon their marrow-bones before them." But, master Biel, let us give the devil his due; and let us not act worse by those Roman Catholics (who, by the by, were our forefathers) than we are willing to act by the devil himself. Now then, here were a set of monks, and also a set of Knights' Templars. Neither of them could marry; of course, neither of them could have wives and families. They could possess no private property; they could bequeath nothing; they could own nothing, but that which they owned in common with the rest of their body. They could hoard no money; they could save nothing. Whatever they received, as rent for their lands, they must necessarily spend upon the spot, for they never could quit that spot. They did spend it all upon the spot: they kept all the poor; Beuley, and all round about Beuley, saw no misery, and had never heard the damned name of pauper pronounced, as long as those monks and Templars continued! You and I are excellent Protestants, farmer John Biel; you and I have often assisted on the 5th of November to burn Guy Fawkes, the pope and the devil. But you and I, farmer John Biel, would much rather be life holders under monks and Templars, than rack-renters under duchesses. The monks and the knights were the *lords* of their manors; but the farmers under them were not rack-renters; the farmers under them held by lease of lives, continued in the same farms from father to son for hundreds of years; they were real yeomen, and not miserable rack-renters, such as now till the land of this once happy country, and who are little better than the drivers of the labourers for the profit of the landlords. Farmer John Biel, what the Duchess of Buccleugh does you know, and I do not. She may, for anything that I know to the contrary, leave her farms on lease of lives, with rent so very moderate and easy as for the farm to be half as good as the farmer's own, at any rate. The duchess may, for anything that I know to the contrary, feed all the hungry, clothe all the naked, comfort all the sick, and prevent the hated name of *pauper* from being pronounced in the district of Beuley; her grace may, for anything that I know to the contrary, make poor-rates to be wholly unnecessary and unknown in your country; she may receive, lodge, and feed the stranger; she may, in short, employ the rents of this fine estate of Beuley to make the whole district happy; she may not carry a farthing of the rents away from the spot; and she may consume, by herself, and her own family and servants, only just as much as is necessary to the preservation of their life and health. Her grace may do all this; I do not say or insinuate that she does not do it all; but, Protestant here or Protestant there, farmer John Biel, this I do say, that unless her grace do all this, the monks and the Templars were better for Beuley than her grace.

From the former station of the Templars, from real Beaulieu of the New Forest, we came back to the village of Beaulieu, and there crossed the water to come on towards Southampton. Here we passed close along under the old abbey walls, a great part of which are still standing. There is a mill here which appears to be turned by the fresh water, but the fresh water falls, here, into the salt water, as at the village of Botley. We did not stop to go about the ruins of the abbey; for you seldom make much out by minute inquiry. It is the political history of these places, or, at least, their connection with political events, that is interesting. Just about the banks of this little river there are some woods and coppices and some corn-land; but at the distance of half a mile from the water-side we came out again upon the intolerable heath, and went on for seven or eight miles over that heath, from the village of Beaulieu to that of Marchwood, having a list of trees and enclosed lands away to our right all the way along, which list of trees from the south-west side of that arm of the sea which goes from Calshot Castle to Redbridge, passing by Southampton, which lies on the north-east side. Never was a more barren tract of land than these seven or eight miles. We had come seven miles across the forest in another direction in the morning; so that a poorer spot than this New Forest there is not in all England; nor, I believe, in the whole world. It is more barren and miserable than Bagshot Heath. There are less fertile spots in it in proportion to the extent of each. Still it is so large, it is of such great extent, being, if moulded into a circle, not so little, I believe, as 60 or 70 miles in circumference, that it must contain some good spots of land, and if properly and honestly managed those spots must produce a prodigious quantity of timber. It is a pretty curious thing that while the admirers of the paper-system are boasting of our "*waust improvements, ma'am,*" there should have been such a visible and such an enormous dilapidation in all the solid things of the country. I have, in former parts of this ride, stated that in some counties, while the parsons have been pocketing the amount of the tithes and of the glebe, they have suffered the parsonage-houses either to fall down and to be lost, brick by brick and stone by stone, or to become such miserable places as to be unfit for anything bearing the name of a gentlemen to live in; I have stated, and I am at any time ready to prove, that in some counties this is the case in more than one half of the parishes!

And now, amidst all these "waust improvements," let us see how the account of timber stands in the New Forest! In the year 1608, a survey of the timber in the New Forest was made, when there were loads of oak timber fit for the navy, 315,477. Mark that, reader. Another survey was taken in the year 1783; that is to say, in the glorious jubilee reign. And when there were, in this same New Forest, loads of oak timber fit for the navy, 20,830. "Waust improvement, ma'am," under "the pilot that weathered the storm," and in the reign of jubilee! What the devil, some one would say, could have become of all this timber? Does the reader observe, that there were 315,477 *loads ?* and does he observe that a load is *fifty-two cubic feet ?* Does the reader know what is the price of this load of timber? I suppose it is now, taking in lop, top and bark, and bought upon the spot (timber fit for the navy, mind!), ten pounds a load at the least. But let us suppose that it has been, upon an average, since the year 1608, just the time that the Stuarts were mounting the throne; let us suppose that it has been, on an average, four pounds a load. Here is a pretty tough sum of money. This must have gone into the pockets of somebody. At any rate, if we had the same quantity of timber now that we had when the Protestant Reformation took place, or even when old Betsy turned up her toes, we should be now three millions of money richer than we are; not in *bills ;* not in notes payable to bearer on demand; not in Scotch " cash credits; " not, in short, in lies, falseness, impudence, downright blackguard cheatery and mining shares and " Greek cause " and the devil knows what.

I shall have occasion to return to this New Forest, which is, in reality, though, in general, a very barren district, a much more interesting object to Englishmen than are the services of my Lord Palmerston, and the warlike undertakings of Burdett, Galloway and Company; but I cannot quit this spot, even for the present, without asking the Scotch population-mongers and Malthus and his crew, and especially George Chalmers, if he should yet be creeping about upon the face of the earth, what becomes of all their notions of the scantiness of the ancient population of England; what becomes of all these notions, of all their bundles of ridiculous lies about the fewness of the people in former times; what becomes of them all, if historians have told us one word of truth with regard to the formation of the New Forest by William the Conqueror. All the historians say, every one of them says, that this king destroyed several populous towns and villages in order to make this New Forest.

FROM WESTON, NEAR SOUTHAMPTON, TO KENSINGTON

WESTERN GROVE,
18 *Oct.* 1826.

I BROKE off abruptly, under this same date, in my last Register, when speaking of William the Conqueror's demolishing of towns and villages to make the New Forest; and I was about to show that all the historians have told us lies the most abominable about this affair of the New Forest; or that the Scotch writers on population, and particularly Chalmers, have been the greatest of fools or the most impudent of impostors. I therefore now resume this matter, it being, in my opinion, a matter of great interest, at a time when, in order to account for the present notoriously *bad living* of the people of England, it is asserted that they are become greatly more numerous than they formerly were. This would be no defence of the government, even if the fact were so; but, as I have over and over again proved, the fact is false; and to this I challenge denial, that either churches and great mansions and castles were formerly made without hands; or England was, seven hundred years ago, much more populous than it is now. But what has the formation of the New Forest to do with this? A great deal; for the historians tell us that, in order to make this forest, William the Conqueror destroyed "many populous towns and villages, and thirty-six parish churches!" The devil he did! How *populous* then, good God, must England have been at that time, which was about the year 1090; that is to say, 736 years ago! For the Scotch will hardly contend that the *nature of the soil* has been changed for the worse since that time, especially as it has not been cultivated. No, no; *brassey* as they are, they will not do that. Come, then, let us see how this matter stands.

This forest has been crawled upon by favourites, and is now much smaller than it used to be. A time may, and *will* come, for inquiring *how* George Rose, and others, became *owners* of some of the very best parts of this once public property; a time for such inquiry *must* come, before the people of England will ever give their consent to *a reduction of the interest of the debt!* But this we know, that the New Forest formerly extended, westward, from the Southampton Water and the river Oux to the river Avon, and northward from Lymington Haven to the borders of Wiltshire. We know that this was its utmost extent; and we know also that the towns of Christchurch, Lymington, Ringwood, and Fordingbridge, and the villages of Bolder, Fawley, Lyndhurst, Dipden, Eling, Minsted, and all the other villages that now have churches; we know, I say (and pray mark it), that all these towns and villages existed before the Norman Conquest: because the *Roman names* of several of them (all the towns) are in print, and because an account of them all is to be found in *Doomsday Book*, which was made by this very William the Conqueror. Well then, now, Scotch population-liars, and you Malthusian blasphemers, who contend that God has implanted in man a *principle* that *leads him to starvation ;* come, now, and face this history of the New Forest. Cooke, in his *Geography of Hampshire*, says that the Conqueror destroyed here " many populous towns and villages, and thirty-six parish churches." The same writer says, that in the time of Edward the Confessor (*just* before the Conqueror came), " two-thirds of the forest was inhabited and cultivated." Guthrie says nearly the same thing. But let us hear the two historians who are now pitted against each other, Hume and Lingard. The former (vol. ii. p. 217) says: " There was one pleasure to which William, as well as all the Normans and ancient Saxons, was extremely addicted, and that was hunting; but this pleasure he indulged more at the expense of his unhappy subjects, whose interests he always disregarded, than to the loss or diminution of his own revenue. Not content with those large forests which former kings possessed in all parts of England, he resolved to make a new forest, near Winchester, the usual place of his residence: and for that purpose he *laid waste* the county of Hampshire, *for an extent of thirty miles, expelled the inhabitants* from their houses, seized their property, even *demolished churches and convents*, and made the sufferers no compensation for the injury." Pretty well for a pensioned Scotchman: and now let us hear Dr. Lingard, to prevent his society from *presenting whose work to me*, the sincere and pious Samuel Butler was ready to go down upon his *marrow bones ;* let us hear the good doctor upon this subject. He says (vol. i. pp. 452 and 453), " Though the king possessed sixty-eight forests, besides parks and chases, in different parts of England, he was not yet satisfied, but for the occasional accommodation of his court afforested an *extensive tract of country* lying between the city of Winchester and the sea coast. The *inhabitants were expelled :* the cottages and the *churches were burnt :* and more than *thirty square miles* of a *rich and populous* district were *withdrawn from cultivation,* and converted into a *wilderness,* to afford sufficient range for the deer and ample space for the royal diversion. The memory of this act of despotism has been perpetuated in the name of the New Forest, which it retains at the present day, after the lapse of seven hundred and fifty years."

" *Historians* " should be careful how they make statements relative to *places* which are within the scope of the reader's *inspection.* It is next to impossible not to believe that the Doctor has, in this case (a very interesting one), merely *copied* from Hume. Hume says that the king " *expelled* the inhabitants;" and Lingard says " the inhabitants *were expelled :* " Hume says that the king " *demolished* the churches;" and Lingard says that " the churches were *burnt ;* " but Hume says churches " and *convents,*" and Lingard *knew* that to be a lie. The Doctor was too learned upon the subject of " *convents* " to follow the Scotchman here. Hume says that the king " laid *waste* the country for an *extent of thirty miles.*" The Doctor says that a district of *thirty square miles* was withdrawn from cultivation and converted into a *wilderness.*" Now what Hume meant by the loose phrase, " an *extent* of *thirty miles,*" I cannot say; but this I know, that Dr. Lingard's " thirty square miles " is a piece of ground only five and a half miles each way! So that the Doctor has got here a curious " *district,*" and a not less curious " *wilderness ;* " and what number of *churches* could William find to *burn* in a space five miles and a half each way? If the Doctor meant thirty *miles square,* instead of *square miles,* the falsehood is so monstrous as to destroy his credit for ever; for here we have Nine Hundred Square Miles, containing *five hundred and seventy-six thousand acres of land ;* that is to say, 56,960 acres more than are contained in the whole of the county of Surrey, and 99,840 acres more than are contained in the whole of the county of Berks! This is " *history,*" is it! And these are " *historians.*"

The true statement is this: the New Forest, according to its ancient state, was bounded thus: by the line going from the river Oux to the river Avon, and which line there separates Wiltshire from Hampshire; by the river Avon; by the sea from Christchurch to Calshot Castle; by the Southampton Water; and by the river Oux. These are the boundaries; and (as any one may, by scale and compass, ascertain) there are, within these boundaries, about 224 square miles, containing 143,360 acres of land. Within these limits there are now remaining eleven parish churches, all of which were in existence before the time of William the Conqueror; so that if he destroyed thirty-six parish churches, what a populous country this must have been! There must have been forty-seven parish churches; so that there was, over this whole district, one parish church to every four and three quarters square miles! Thus, then, the churches must have stood, on an average, at within one mile and about two hundred yards of each other! And observe, the parishes could, on an average, contain no more, each, than 2966 acres of land! Not a very large farm; so that here was a parish church to every large farm, unless these historians are all fools and liars.

I defy any one to say that I make hazardous assertions: I have plainly described the ancient boundaries: there are *the maps :* any one can, with scale and compass, measure the area as well as I can. I have taken the statements of historians, as they call themselves: I have shown that their histories, as they call them, are fabulous; OR (and mind this *or*) that England was, at one time, and that too, eight hundred years ago, *beyond all measure more populous than it is now.* For observe, notwithstanding what Dr. Lingard asserts; notwithstanding that he describes this district as " *rich*," it is the very poorest in the whole kingdom. Dr. Lingard was, I believe, born and bred at Winchester, and how, then, could he be so careless, or, indeed, so regardless of truth (and I do not see why I am to mince the matter with him), as to describe this as a *rich district.* Innumerable persons have seen *Bagshot Heath ;* great numbers have seen the barren heaths between London and Brighton; great numbers also have seen that wide sweep of barrenness which exhibits itself between the Golden Farmer Hill and Blackwater. Nine-tenths of each of these are less barren than four-fifths of the land in the New Forest. Supposing it to be credible that a man so prudent and so wise as William the Conqueror; supposing that such a man should have pitched upon a *rich* and *populous* district wherewith to make a chase; supposing, in short, these historians to have spoken the truth, and supposing this barren land to have been all inhabited and cultivated, and the people so numerous and so rich as to be able to build and endow a parish church upon every four and three quarters square miles upon this extensive district; supposing them to have been so rich in the produce of the soil as to want

a priest to be stationed at every mile and 200 yards in order to
help them to eat it; supposing, in a word, these historians not
to be the most farcical liars that ever put pen upon paper, this
country must, at the time of the Norman Conquest, have
literally *swarmed* with people; for *there is the land now*, and all
the land too: neither Hume nor Dr. Lingard can change the
nature of that. There it is, an acre of it not having, upon an
average, so much of productive capacity in it as one single
square rod, taking the average, of Worcestershire; and if I were
to say one single *square yard* I should be right; there is the
land; and if that land were, as these historians say it was,
covered with people and with churches, what the devil must
Worcestershire have been! To this, then, we come at last:
having made out what I undertook to show; namely, that the
historians, as they call themselves, are either the greatest fools
or the greatest liars that ever existed, or that England was
beyond all measure more populous eight hundred years ago than
it is now.

Poor, however, as this district is, and culled about as it has
been for the best spots of land by those favourites who have got
grants of land or leases or something or other, still there are
some spots here and there which would grow trees; but never
will it grow trees, or anything else, *to the profit of this nation*,
until it become *private property*. Public property must, in some
cases, be in the hands of public officers; but this is not an affair
of that nature. This is too loose a concern; too little con-
trollable by superiors. It is a thing calculated for jobbing
above all others; calculated to promote the success of favouritism.
Who can imagine that the persons employed about plantations
and farms for the public are employed because *they are fit* for
the employment? Supposing the commissioners to hold in
abhorrence the idea of paying for services to themselves under
the name of paying for services to the public; supposing them
never to have heard of such a thing in their lives, can they
imagine that nothing of this sort takes place while they are in
London eleven months out of twelve in the year? I never feel
disposed to cast much censure upon any of the persons engaged
in such concerns. The temptation is too great to be resisted.
The public must pay for everything *à pois d'or*. Therefore, no
such thing should be in the hands of the public, or rather of the
government; and I hope to live to see this thing completely
taken out of the hands of this government.

It was night-fall when we arrived at Eling, that is to say, at the head of the Southampton Water. Our horses were very hungry. We stopped to bait them, and set off just about dusk to come to this place (Weston Grove), stopping at Southampton on our way, and leaving a letter to come to London. Between Southampton and this place we cross a bridge over the Itchen river, and coming up a hill into a common, which is called Town-hill Common, we passed, lying on our right, a little park and house, occupied by the Irish Bible-man, Lord Ashdown, I think they call him, whose real name is French, and whose family are so very *well known* in the most unfortunate sister-kingdom. Just at the back of his house, in another sort of paddock-place, lives a man, whose name I forget, who was, I believe, a coachmaker in the East Indies, and whose father, or uncle, kept a turnpike gate at Chelsea a few years ago. See the effects of " *industry* and *enterprise* " ! But even these would be nothing were it not for this wondrous system by which money can be snatched away from the labourer in this very parish, for instance, sent off to the East Indies, there help to make a mass to put into the hands of an adventurer, and then the mass may be brought back in the pockets of the adventurer and cause him to be called a 'squire by the labourer whose earnings were so snatched away! Wondrous system! Pity it cannot last for ever! Pity that it has got a debt of a thousand millions to pay! Pity that it cannot turn paper into gold! Pity that it will make such fools of Prosperity Robinson and his colleagues!

The moon shone very bright by the time that we mounted the hill; and now, skirting the enclosures upon the edge of the common, we passed several of those cottages which I so well recollected, and in which I had the satisfaction to believe that the inhabitants were sitting comfortably with bellies full by a good fire. It was eight o'clock before we arrived at Mr. Chamberlayne's, whom I had not seen since, I think, the year 1816; for in the fall of that year I came to London and I never returned to Botley (which is only about three miles and a half from Weston) to stay there for any length of time. To those who like water-scenes (as nineteen-twentieths of people do) it is the prettiest spot, I believe, in all England. Mr. Chamberlayne built the house about twenty years ago. He has been bringing the place to greater and greater perfection from that time to this. All round about the house is in the neatest possible order. I should think that, altogether, there cannot be so little as *ten acres of short grass ;* and, when I say *that,* those who know anything about gardens will form a pretty correct general notion as to the *scale* on which the thing is carried on. Until of late, Mr. Chamberlayne was owner of only a small part, comparatively, of the lands hereabouts. He is now the owner, I believe, of the whole of the lands that come down to the water's edge and that lie between the ferry over the Itchen at Southampton and the river which goes out from the Southampton Water at Hamble. And now let me describe, as well as I can, what this land and its situation are.

The Southampton Water begins at Portsmouth, and goes up by Southampton to Redbridge, being, upon an average, about two miles wide, having on the one side the New Forest and on the other side, for a great part of the way, this fine and beautiful estate of Mr. Chamberlayne. Both sides of this water have rising lands divided into hill and dale, and very beautifully clothed with trees, the woods and lawns and fields being most advantageously intermixed. It is very curious that, at the *back* of each of these tracts of land, there are extensive heaths, on this side as well as on the New Forest side. To stand here and look across the water at the New Forest, you would imagine that it was really *a country of woods*; for you can see nothing of the heaths from here; those heaths over which we rode, and from which we could see a windmill down among the trees, which windmill is now to be seen just opposite this place. So that the views from this place are the most beautiful that can be imagined. You see up the water and down the water, to Redbridge one way and out to Spithead the other way. Through the trees, to the right, you see the spires of Southampton, and you have only to walk a mile, over a beautiful lawn and through a not less beautiful wood, to find, in a little dell, surrounded with lofty woods, the venerable ruins of *Netley Abbey*, which make part of Mr. Chamberlayne's estate.

The woods here are chiefly of oak; the ground consists of a series of hill and dale, as you go long-wise from one end of the estate to the other, *about six miles in length*. Down almost every little valley that divides these hills or hillocks there is more or less of water, making the underwood, in those parts, very thick and dark to go through; and these form the most delightful contrast with the fields and lawns. There are innumerable vessels of various sizes continually upon the water; and to those that delight in water-scenes, this is certainly the very prettiest place that I ever saw in my life. I had seen it many years ago; and as I intended to come here on my way home, I told George, before we set out, that I would show him *another Weston* before we got to London. The parish in which his father's house is, is also called Weston, and a very beautiful spot it certainly is; but I told him I questioned whether I could not show him a still prettier Weston than that. We let him alone for the first day. He sat in the house, and saw great multitudes of pheasants and partridges upon the lawn before the window: he went down to the water-side by himself, and put his foot upon the ground to see the tide rise. He seemed very much delighted. The second morning at breakfast we put it to him which he would rather have; this Weston or the Weston he had left in Herefordshire; but though I introduced the question in a way almost to extort a decision in favour of the Hampshire Weston, he decided instantly and plumped for the other, in a manner very much to the delight of Mr. Chamberlayne and his sister. So true it is, that when people are uncorrupted, they always *like home best*, be it in itself what it may.

Everything that nature can do has been done here; and money most judiciously employed has come to her assistance. Here are a thousand things to give pleasure to any rational mind; but there is one thing which, in my estimation, surpasses, in pleasure to contemplate, all the lawns and all the groves and all the gardens and all the game and everything else; and that is the real, unaffected goodness of the owner of this estate. He is a member for Southampton; he has other fine estates; he has great talents; he is much admired by all who know him; but he has done more by his justice, by his just way of thinking with regard to the labouring people, than in all other ways put together. This was nothing new to me; for I was well informed of it several years ago, though I had never heard him speak of it in my life. When he came to this place the common wages of day-labouring men were *thirteen shillings a week*, and the wages of carpenters, bricklayers, and other tradesmen were in proportion. Those wages he *has given, from that time to this*, without any abatement whatever. With these wages a man can live, having, at the same time, other advantages attending the working for such a man as Mr. Chamberlayne. He has got less money in his bags than he would have had if he had ground men down in their wages; but if his sleep be not sounder than that of the hard-fisted wretch that can walk over grass and gravel, kept in order by a poor creature that is half-starved; if his sleep be not sounder than the sleep of such a wretch, then all that we have been taught is false, and there is no difference between the man who feeds and the man who starves the poor: all the Scripture is a bundle of lies, and instead of being propagated it ought to be flung into the fire.

It is curious enough that those who are the least disposed to give good wages to the labouring people should be the most disposed to discover for them *schemes for saving their money!* I have lately seen, I saw it at Uphusband, a prospectus, or scheme, for establishing what they call a *County Friendly Society.* This is a scheme for getting from the poor a part of the wages that they receive. Just as if a poor fellow could *put anything by* out of eight shillings a week! If, indeed, the schemers were to pay the labourers twelve or thirteen shillings a week, then these might have something to lay by at some times of the year; but then, indeed, there would be *no poor-rates wanted;* and it is to *get rid of the poor-rates* that these schemers have invented their society. What wretched drivellers they must be: to think that they should be able to make the pauper keep the pauper; to think that they shall be able to make the man that is half-starved lay by part of his loaf! I know of no county where the poor are worse treated than in many parts of this county of Hants. It is happy to know of one instance in which they are well treated; and I deem it a real honour to be under the roof of him who has uniformly set so laudable an example in this most important concern. What are all his riches to me? They form no title to my respect. 'Tis not for me to set myself up in judgment as to his taste, his learning, his various qualities and endowments; but of these his un-equivocal works I am a competent judge. I know how much good he must do; and there is a great satisfaction in reflecting on the great happiness that he must feel when, in laying his head upon his pillow of a cold and dreary winter night, he reflects that there are scores, aye scores upon scores, of his country-people, of his poor neighbours, of those whom the Scripture denominates his brethren, who have been enabled, through him, to retire to a warm bed after spending a cheerful evening and taking a full meal by the side of their own fire. People may talk what they will about *happiness;* but I can figure to myself no happiness surpassing that of the man who falls to sleep with reflections like these in his mind.

Now observe it is a duty, on my part, to relate what I have here related as to the conduct of Mr. Chamberlayne; not a duty towards *him;* for I can do him no good by it, and I do most sincerely believe that both he and his equally benevolent sister would rather that their goodness remained unproclaimed; but it is a duty towards my country, and particularly towards my readers. Here is a striking and a most valuable practical example. Here is a whole neighbourhood of labourers living as they ought to live; enjoying that happiness which is the just reward of their toil. And shall I suppress facts so honourable to those who are the cause of this happiness, facts so interesting in themselves, and so likely to be useful in the way of example; shall I do this, aye, and besides this, *tacitly* give a *false account* of Weston Grove, and this, too, from the stupid and cowardly fear of being accused of flattering a rich man?

Netley Abbey ought, it seems, to be called Letley Abbey, the Latin name being Lætus Locus, or Pleasant Place. *Letley* was made up of an abbreviation of the *Lætus* and of the Saxon word *ley*, which meant *place, field,* or *piece of ground*. This abbey was founded by Henry III. in 1239, for twelve monks of the Benedictine order; and when suppressed, by the wife-killer, its revenues amounted to £3200 a year of our present money. The possessions of these monks were by the wife-killing founder of the Church of England given away (though they belonged to the public) to one of his court sycophants, Sir William Paulet, a man the most famous in the whole world for sycophancy, time-serving, and for all those qualities which usually distinguish the favourites of kings like the wife-killer. This Paulet changed from the popish to Henry VIII.'s religion, and was a great actor in punishing the papists: when Edward VI. came to the throne, this Paulet turned Protestant, and was a great actor in punishing those who adhered to Henry VIII.'s religion: when Queen Mary came to the throne, this Paulet turned back to papist, and was one of the great actors in sending Protestants to be burnt in Smithfield: when Old Bess came to the throne, this Paulet turned back to Protestant again, and was, until the day of his death, one of the great actors in persecuting, in fining, in mulcting, and in putting to death those who still had the virtue and the courage to adhere to the religion in which they and he had been born and bred. The *head* of this family got, at last, to be Earl of Wiltshire, Marquis of Winchester, and Duke of Bolton. This last title is now *gone;* or, rather, it is changed to that of "Lord Bolton," which is now borne by a man of the name of Orde, who is the son of a man of that name, who died some years ago, and who married a daughter (I think it was) of the last "Duke of Bolton."

Pretty curious, and not a little interesting, to look back at the *origin* of this Dukedom of Bolton, and then to look at the person now bearing the title of *Bolton ;* and then to go to Abbotston, near Winchester, and survey the ruins of the proud palace once inhabited by the Duke of Bolton, which ruins, and the estate on which they stand, are now the property of the loanmaker, Alexander Baring! Curious turn of things! Henry the wife-killer and his confiscating successors *granted* the estates of Netley, and of many other monasteries, to the head of these Paulets: to maintain these and other similar grants, a thing called a " Reformation " was made: to maintain the " Reformation " a " Glorious Revolution " was made: to maintain the " Glorious Revolution " a *Debt* was made: to maintain the debt, a large part of the rents must go to the debt-dealers, or loan-makers: and thus, at last, the Barings only in this one neighbourhood have become the successors of the Wriothesleys, the Paulets, and the Russells, who, throughout all the reigns of confiscation, were constantly *in the way* when a distribution of good things was taking place! Curious enough all this; but the thing will not *stop here.* The loan-makers think that they shall outwit the old grantee-fellows; and so they might, and the people too, and the devil himself; but they cannot outwit *events.* Those events *will have a thorough rummaging ;* and of this fact the " turn - of - the - market " gentlemen may be assured. Can it be *law* (I put the question to *lawyers*), can it be *law* (I leave reason and justice out of the inquiry), can it be *law* that if I, to-day, see dressed in good clothes, and with a full purse, a man who was notoriously pennyless yesterday; can it be law that I (being a justice of the peace) have a right to demand of that man *how he came by his clothes and his purse ?* And can it be *law* that I, seeing with an estate a man who was notoriously not worth a crown piece a few years ago, and who is notoriously related to nothing more than one degree above beggary; can it be *law* that I, a magistrate, seeing this have not a right to demand of this man how he came by his estate? No matter, however; for if both these be law now, they will not, I trust, be law in a few years from this time.

Mr. Chamberlayne has caused the ancient *fish-ponds*, at Netley Abbey, to be " reclaimed," as they call it. What a loss, what a national loss, there has been in this way, and in the article of water fowl! I am quite satisfied that, in these two articles and in that of *rabbits*, the nation has lost, has had annihilated (within the last 250 years) food sufficient for two days in the week, on an average, taking the year throughout. These are things, too, which cost so little labour! You can see the marks of old fish-ponds in thousands and thousands of places. I have noticed, I dare say, five hundred, since I left home. A trifling expense would, in most cases, restore them; but, now-a-days, all is looked for at shops: all is to be had by trafficking: scarcely any one thinks of providing for his own wants out of his own land and other his own domestic means. To buy the thing, *ready made*, is the taste of the day; thousands, who are housekeepers, buy their dinners ready cooked: nothing is so common as to rent breasts for children to suck: a man actually advertised, in the London papers, about two months ago, to supply childless husbands with heirs! In this case, the articles were, of course, to be *ready made ;* for to make them " to order " would be the devil of a business; though, in desperate cases, even this is, I believe, sometimes resorted to.

HAMBLEDON,
Sunday, 22 Oct. 1826.

We left Weston Grove on Friday morning, and came across to Botley, where we remained during the rest of the day, and until after breakfast yesterday. I had not seen " the Botley Parson " for several years, and I wished to have a look at him now, but could not get a sight of him, though we rode close before his house, at much about his breakfast time, and though we gave him the strongest invitation that could be expressed by hallooing and by cracking of whips! The fox was too cunning for us, and do all we could, we could not provoke him to put even his nose out of kennel. From Mr. James Warner's at Botley we went to Mr. Hallett's, at Allington, and had the very great pleasure of seeing him in excellent health. We intended to go back to Botley, and then to go to Titchfield, and in our way to this place over Portsdown Hill, whence I intended to show George the harbour and the fleet, and (of still more importance) the spot on which we signed the " Hampshire Petition," in 1817; that petition which foretold that which the " Norfolk Petition " confirmed; that petition which will be finally acted upon, or . . . ! That petition was the very *last thing that I wrote at Botley.* I came to London in November 1816; the Power-of-Imprisonment Bill was passed in February 1817; just before it was passed, the meeting took place on Portsdown Hill; and I, in my way to the hill from London, stopped at Botley and wrote the petition. We had one meeting afterwards at Winchester, when I heard parsons swear like troopers, and saw one of them hawk up his spittle, and spit it into Lord Cochrane's poll! Ah! my bucks, we have you *now!* You are got nearly to the end of your tether; and, what is more, *you know it.* Pay off the debt, parsons! It is useless to swear and spit, and to present addresses applauding Power-of-Imprisonment Bills, unless you can pay off the debt! Pay off the debt, parsons! They say you can *lay* the devil. Lay *this* devil, then; or confess that he is too many for you; aye, and for Sturges Bourne, or Bourne Sturges (I forget which), at your backs!

From Allington we, fearing that it would rain before we could get round by Titchfield, came across the country over Waltham Chase and Soberton Down. The chase was very green and fine; but the down was the very greenest thing that I have seen in the whole country. It is not a large down; perhaps not more than five or six hundred acres; but the land is good, the chalk is at a foot from the surface, or more; the mould is a hazel mould; and when I was upon the opposite hill I could, though I knew the spot very well, hardly believe that it was a down. The green was darker than that of any pasture or even any sainfoin or clover that I had seen throughout the whole of my ride; and I should suppose that there could not have been many less than a thousand sheep in the three flocks that were feeding upon the down when I came across it. I do not speak with anything like positiveness as to the measurement of this down; but I do not believe that it exceeds six hundred and fifty acres. They must have had more rain in this part of the country than in most other parts of it. Indeed, no part of Hampshire seems to have suffered very much from the drought. I found the turnips pretty good, of both sorts, all the way from Andover to Rumsey. Through the New Forest you may as well expect to find loaves of bread growing in fields as turnips, where there are any fields for them to grow in. From Redbridge to Weston we had not light enough to see much about us; but when we came down to Botley, we there found the turnips as good as I had ever seen them in my life, as far as I could judge from the time I had to look at them. Mr. Warner has as fine turnip fields as I ever saw him have, swedish turnips and white also; and pretty nearly the same may be said of the whole of that neighbourhood for many miles round.

After quitting Soberton Down, we came up a hill leading to

*G 639

Hambledon, and turned off to our left to bring us down to Mr. Goldsmith's at West End, where we now are, at about a mile from the village of Hambledon. A village is *now* is; but it was formerly a considerable market-town, and it had three fairs in the year. There is now not even the name of market left, I believe; and the fairs amount to little more than a couple or three gingerbread-stalls, with dolls and whistles for children. If you go through the place, you see that it has been a considerable town. The church tells the same story; it is now a tumble-down rubbishy place; it is partaking in the fate of all those places which were formerly a sort of rendezvous for persons who had things to buy and things to sell. *Wens* have devoured market-towns and villages; and *shops* have devoured *markets and fairs*; and this, too, to the infinite injury of the most numerous classes of the people. Shop-keeping, merely as shop-keeping, is injurious to any community. What are the shop and the shop-keeper for? To receive and distribute the produce of the land. There are other articles, certainly; but the main part is the produce of the land. The shop must be paid for; the shop-keeper must be kept; and the one must be paid for and the other must be kept by the consumer of the produce; or, perhaps, partly by the consumer and partly by the producer.

When fairs were very frequent shops were not needed. A manufacturer of shoes, of stockings, of hats; of almost anything that man wants, could manufacture at home in an obscure hamlet, with cheap house-rent, good air, and plenty of room. He need pay no heavy rent for shop; and no disadvantages from confined situation; and then, by attending three or four or five or six fairs in a year, he sold the work of his hands, unloaded with a heavy expense attending the keeping of a shop. He would get more for ten shillings in a booth at a fair or market than he would get in a shop for ten or twenty pounds. Of course he could afford to sell the work of his hands for less; and thus a greater portion of their earnings remained with those who raised the food and the clothing from the land. I had an instance of this in what occurred to myself at Weyhill Fair. When I was at Salisbury, in September, I wanted to buy a whip. It was a common hunting-whip, with a hook to it to pull open gates with, and I could not get it for less than seven shillings and sixpence This was more than I had made up my mind to give, and I went on with my switch. When we got to Weyhill Fair, George had made shift to lose his whip some time

before, and I had made him go without one by way of punishment. But now, having come to the fair, and seeing plenty of
whips, I bought him one, just such a one as had been offered me
at Salisbury for seven and sixpence, for four and sixpence; and
seeing the man with his whips afterwards, I thought I would
have one myself; and he let me have it for three shillings. So
that here were two whips, precisely of the same kind and quality
as the whip at Salisbury, bought for the money which the man
at Salisbury asked me for one whip. And yet, far be it from me
to accuse the man at Salisbury of an attempt at extortion: he
had an expensive shop and a family in a town to support, while
my Weyhill fellow had been making his whips in some house in
the country, which he rented, probably, for five or six pounds a
year, with a good garden to it. Does not every one see, in a
minute, how this exchanging of fairs and markets for shops
creates *idlers and traffickers ;* creates those locusts called middle-
men who create nothing, who add to the value of nothing, who
improve nothing, but who live in idleness, and who live well,
too, out of the labour of the producer and the consumer. The
fair and the market, those wise institutions of our forefathers,
and with regard to the management of which they were so
scrupulously careful; the fair and the market bring the producer
and the consumer in contact with each other. Whatever is
gained is, at any rate, gained by one or the other of these. The
fair and the market bring them together, and enable them to
act for their mutual interest and convenience. The shop and
the trafficker keeps them apart; the shop hides from both
producer and consumer the real state of matters. The fair and
the market lay everything open: going to either, you see the
state of things at once; and the transactions are fair and just,
not disfigured, too, by falsehood, and by those attempts at
deception which disgrace traffickings in general.

Very wise, too, and very just, were the laws against *forestalling*
and *regrating*. They were laws to prevent the producer and the
consumer from being cheated by the trafficker. There are
whole bodies of men, indeed, a very large part of the community,
who live in idleness in this country in consequence of the whole
current of the laws now running in favour of the trafficking
monopoly. It has been a great object with all wise governments,
in all ages, from the days of Moses to the present day, to confine
trafficking, mere trafficking, to as few hands as possible. It
seems to be the main object of this government to give all possible
encouragement to traffickers of every description, and to make

them swarm like the lice of Egypt. There is that numerous sect the Quakers. This sect arose in England: they were engendered by the Jewish system of usury. Till *excises* and *loan-mongering* began, these vermin were never heard of in England. They seem to have been hatched by that fraudulent system, as maggots are bred by putrid meat, or as the flounders come in the livers of rotten sheep. The base vermin do not pretend to work: all they talk about is dealing; and the government, in place of making laws that would put them in the stocks, or cause them to be whipped at the cart's tail, really seem anxious to encourage them and to increase their numbers; nay, it is not long since Mr. Brougham had the effrontery to move for leave to bring in a bill to make men liable to be hanged upon the bare word of these vagabonds. This is, with me, something never to be forgotten. But everything tends the same way: all the regulations, all the laws that have been adopted of late years, have a tendency to give encouragement to the trickster and the trafficker, and to take from the labouring classes all the honour and a great part of the food that fairly belonged to them.

In coming along yesterday from Waltham Chase to Soberton Down, we passed by a big white house upon a hill that was, when I lived at Botley, occupied by one Goodlad, who was a cock justice of the peace, and who had been a chap of some sort or other in *India*. There was a man of the name of Singleton who lived in Waltham Chase, and who was deemed to be a great poacher. This man, having been forcibly ousted by the order of this Goodlad and some others from an encroachment that he had made in the forest, threatened revenge. Soon after this, a horse (I forget to whom it belonged) was stabbed or shot in the night-time in a field. Singleton was taken up, tried at Winchester, convicted and *transported*. I cannot relate exactly what took place. I remember that there were some curious circumstances attending the conviction of this man. The people in that neighbourhood were deeply impressed with these circumstances. Singleton was transported; but Goodlad and his wife were both dead and buried in less, I believe, than three months after the departure of poor Singleton. I do not know that any injustice really was done; but I do know that a great impression was produced, and a very sorrowful impression, too, on the minds of the people in that neighbourhood.

I cannot quit Waltham Chase without observing that I heard, last year, that a bill was about to be petitioned for to enclose that chase! Never was so monstrous a proposition in this world. The Bishop of Winchester is lord of the manor over this chase. If the chase be enclosed the timber must be cut down, young and old; and here are a couple of hundred acres of land, worth ten thousand acres of land in the New Forest. This is as fine timber land as any in the wealds of Surrey, Sussex or Kent. There are two enclosures of about 40 acres each, perhaps, that were simply surrounded by a bank being thrown up about twenty years ago, only twenty years ago, and on the poorest part of the chase, too; and these are now as beautiful plantations of young oak-trees as man ever set his eyes on; many of them as big or bigger round than my thigh! Therefore, besides the sweeping away of two or three hundred cottages; besides plunging into ruin and misery all these numerous families, here is one of the finest pieces of timber land in the whole kingdom, going to be cut up into miserable clay fields, for no earthly purpose but that of gratifying the stupid greediness of those who think that they must gain, if they add to the breadth of their private fields. But if a thing like this be permitted, we must be prettily furnished with commissioners of woods and forests! I do not believe that they will sit in parliament and see a bill like this passed and hold their tongues; but if they were to do it, there is no measure of reproach which they would not merit. Let them go and look at the two plantations of oaks, of which I have just spoken; and then let them give their consent to such a bill if they can.

THURSLEY,
Monday Evening, 23 October.

When I left Weston, my intention was to go from Hambledon to Up Park, thence to Arundel, thence to Brighton, thence to Eastbourne, thence to Wittersham in Kent, and then by Cranbrook, Tunbridge, Godstone and Reigate to London; but when I got to Botley, and particularly when I got to Hambledon, I found my horse's back so much hurt by the saddle that I was afraid to take so long a stretch, and therefore resolved to come away straight to this place, to go hence to Reigate, and so to London. Our way, therefore, this morning, was over Butser Hill to Petersfield, in the first place; then to Lyphook and then to this place, in all about twenty-four miles. Butser Hill belongs to the back chain of the South Downs; and, indeed, it terminates that chain to the westward. It is the highest hill in the whole country. Some think that Hindhead, which is the famous sand-hill over which the Portsmouth road goes at sixteen miles to the north of this great chalk-hill; some think that Hindhead is the highest hill of the two. Be this as it may, Butser Hill, which is the right-hand hill of the two between which you go at three miles from Petersfield going towards Portsmouth; this Butser Hill is, I say, quite high enough; and was more than high enough for us, for it took us up amongst clouds that wet us very nearly to the skin. In going from Mr. Goldsmith's to the hill, it is all up hill for five miles. Now and then a little stoop; not much; but regularly, with these little exceptions, uphill for these five miles. The hill appears, at a distance, to be a sharp ridge on its top. It is, however, not so. It is, in some parts, half a mile wide or more. The road lies right along the middle of it from west to east, and just when you are at the highest part of the hill, it is very narrow from north to south; not more, I think, than about a hundred or a hundred and thirty yards.

This is as interesting a spot, I think, as the foot of man ever was placed upon. Here are two valleys, one to your right and the other to your left, very little less than half a mile down to the bottom of them, and much steeper than a tiled roof of a house. These valleys may be, where they join the hill, three or four hundred yards broad. They get wider as they get farther from the hill. Of a clear day you see all the north of Hampshire; nay, the whole county, together with a great part of Surrey and of Sussex. You see the whole of the South Downs to the eastward as far as your eye can carry you; and, lastly, you see over Portsdown Hill, which lies before you to the south; and there are spread open to your view the isle of Portsea, Porchester, Wimmering, Fareham, Gosport, Portsmouth, the harbour, Spithead, the Isle of Wight and the ocean.

But something still more interesting occurred to me here in the year 1808, when I was coming on horseback over the same hill from Botley to London. It was a very beautiful day and in summer. Before I got upon the hill (on which I had never been before), a shepherd told me to keep on in the road in which I was till I came to the London turnpike-road. When I got to within a quarter of a mile of this particular point of the hill, I saw at this point what I thought was a cloud of dust; and speaking to my servant about it, I found that he thought so too; but this cloud of dust disappeared all at once. Soon after there appeared to arise another cloud of dust at the same place, and then that disappeared, and the spot was clear again. As we were trotting along a pretty smart pace, we soon came to this narrow place, having one valley to our right and the other valley to our left, and there, to my great astonishment, I saw the clouds come one after another, each appearing to be about as big as two or three acres of land, skimming along in the valley on the north side, a great deal below the tops of the hills; and successively, as they arrived at our end of the valley, rising up, crossing the narrow pass, and then descending down into the other valley and going off to the south; so that we who sate there upon our horses, were alternately in clouds and in sunshine. It is a universal rule that if there be a fog in the morning, and that fog go from the valleys to the tops of the hills, there will be rain that day; and if it disappear by sinking in the valley, there will be no rain that day. The truth is, that fogs are clouds, and clouds are fogs. They are more or less full of water; but they are all water; sometimes a sort of steam, and sometimes water that falls in drops. Yesterday morning the fogs had ascended to the tops of the hills; and it was raining on all the hills round about us before it began to rain in the valleys. We, as I observed before, got pretty nearly wet to the skin upon the top of Butser Hill; but we had the pluck to come on and let the clothes dry upon our backs.

I must here relate something that appears very interesting to me, and something which, though it must have been seen by every man that has lived in the country, or, at least, in any hilly country, has never been particularly mentioned by anybody as far as I can recollect. We frequently talk of clouds coming from *dews ;* and we actually see the heavy fogs become clouds. We see them go up to the tops of hills, and taking a swim round, actually come and drop down upon us and wet us through. But I am now going to speak of clouds coming out of the sides of hills in exactly the same manner that you see smoke come out of a tobacco pipe, and rising up, with a wider and wider head, like the smoke from a tobacco-pipe, go to the top of the hill or over the hill, or very much above it, and then come over the valleys in rain. At about a mile's distance from Mr. Palmer's house at Bollitree, in Herefordshire, there is a large, long beautiful wood, covering the side of a lofty hill, winding round in the form of a crescent, the bend of the crescent being towards Mr. Palmer's house. It was here that I first observed this mode of forming clouds. The first time I noticed it, I pointed it out to Mr. Palmer. We stood and observed cloud after cloud come out from different parts of the side of the hill, and tower up and go over the hill out of sight. He told me that that was a certain sign that it would rain that day, for that these clouds would come back again, and would fall in rain. It rained sure enough; and I found that the country people all round about had this mode of the forming of the clouds as a sign of rain. The hill is called Penyard, and this forming of the clouds they called Old Penyard's *smoking his pipe ;* and it is a rule that it is sure to rain during the day if Old Penyard smokes his pipe in the morning. These appearances take place especially in warm and sultry weather. It was very warm yesterday morning: it had thundered violently the evening before: we felt it hot even while the rain fell upon us at Butser Hill. Petersfield lies in a pretty broad and very beautiful valley. On three sides of it are very lofty hills, partly downs and partly covered with trees: and as we proceeded on our way from the bottom of Butser Hill to Petersfield, we saw thousands upon thousands of clouds continually coming puffing out from different parts of these hills and towering up to the top of them. I stopped George several times to make him look at them; to see them come puffing out of the chalk downs as well as out of the woodland hills; and bade him remember to tell his father of it when he should get home, to convince him that the hills of Hampshire could smoke their pipes as well as those of Herefordshire. This is a really curious matter. I have never read, in any book, anything to lead me to suppose that the observation has ever found its way into print before. Sometimes you will see only one or two clouds during a whole morning come out of the side of a hill; but we saw thousands upon thousands, bursting out, one after another, in all parts of these immense hills. The first time that I have leisure, when I am in the high countries again, I will have a conversation with some old shepherd about this matter: if he cannot enlighten me upon the subject I am sure that no philosopher can.

We came through Petersfield without stopping, and baited our horses at Lyphook, where we stayed about half an hour. In coming from Lyphook to this place, we overtook a man who asked for relief. He told me he was a weaver, and as his accent was northern, I was about to give him the balance that I had in hand arising from our savings in the fasting way, amounting to about three shillings and sixpence; but, unfortunately for him, I asked him what place he had lived at as a weaver; and he told me that he was a Spitalfields weaver. I instantly put on my glove and returned my purse into my pocket, saying, go, then, to Sidmouth and Peel and the rest of them " and get relief; for I have this minute, while I was stopping at Lyphook, read in the *Evening Mail* newspaper, an address to the king from the Spitalfields weavers, for which address they ought to suffer death from starvation. In that address those base wretches tell the king that they were loyal men: that they detested the designing men who were guilty of seditious practices in 1817; they, in short, express their approbation of the Power-of-Imprisonment Bill, of all the deeds committed against the reformers in 1817 and 1819; they, by fair inference, express their approbation of the thanks given to the Manchester yeomanry. You are one of them; my name is William Cobbett, and I would sooner relieve a dog than relieve you." Just as I was closing my harangue, we overtook a country-man and woman that were going the same way. The weaver attempted explanations. He said that they only said it in order to get relief; but that they did not mean it in their hearts. "Oh, base dogs!" said I: "it is precisely by such men that ruin is brought upon nations; it is precisely by such baseness and insincerity, such scandalous cowardice, that ruin has been brought upon them. I had two or three shillings to give you; I had them in my hand: I have put them back into my purse: I trust I shall find somebody more worthy of them: rather than give them to you, I would fling them into that sand-pit and bury them for ever."

How curiously things happen. It was by mere accident that I took up a newspaper to read: it was merely because I was compelled to stay a quarter of an hour in the room without doing anything, and above all things it was miraculous that I should take up the *Evening Mail*, into which, I believe, I never before looked in my whole life. I saw the royal arms at the top of the paper, took it for the *Old Times*, and, in a sort of lounging mood, said to George, "Give me hold of that paper, and let us see what that foolish devil Anna Brodie says." Seeing the words "*Spitalfields*," I read on till I got to the base and scoundrelly part of the address. I then turned over, and looked at the title of the paper and the date of it, resolving, in my mind, to have satisfaction, of some sort or other, upon these base vagabonds. Little did I think that an opportunity would so soon occur of showing my resentment against them, and that, too, in so striking, so appropriate and so efficient a manner. I dare say that it was some tax-eating scoundrel who drew up this address (which I will insert in the *Register*, as soon as I can find it); but that is nothing to me and my fellow sufferers of 1817 and 1819. This infamous libel upon us is published under

the name of the Spitalfields weavers; and if I am asked what
the poor creatures were to do, being without bread as they were,
I answer by asking whether they could find no knives to cut
their throats with; seeing that they ought to have cut their
throats ten thousand times over, if they could have done it,
rather than sanction the publication of so infamous a paper
as this.

It is not thus that the weavers in the north have acted.
Some scoundrel wanted to inveigle them into an applauding
of the ministers; but they, though nothing so infamous as this
address was proposed to them, rejected the proposition, though
they were ten times more in want than the weavers of Spitalfields have ever been. They were only called upon to applaud
the ministers for the recent orders in council; but they justly
said that the ministers had a great deal more to do before they
would merit their applause. What would these brave and
sensible men have said to a tax-eating scoundrel who should
have called upon them to present an address to the king, and
in that address to applaud the terrible deeds committed against
the people in 1817 and 1819! I have great happiness in reflecting that this baseness of the Spitalfields weavers will not bring
them one single mouthful of bread. This will be their lot; this
will be the fruit of their baseness: and the nation, the working
classes of the nation, will learn, from this, that the way to get
redress of their grievances, the way to get food and raiment in
exchange for their labour, the way to ensure good treatment
from the government, is not to crawl to that government, to
lick its hands, and seem to deem it an honour to be its slaves.

Before we got to Thursley, I saw three poor fellows getting
in turf for their winter fuel, and I gave them a shilling apiece.
To a boy at the bottom of Hindhead I gave the other sixpence
towards buying him a pair of gloves; and thus I disposed of the
money which was, at one time, actually out of my purse, and
going into the hand of the loyal Spitalfields weaver.

We got to this place (Mr. Knowles's of Thursley) about 5
o'clock in the evening, very much delighted with our ride.

KENSINGTON,
Thursday, 26 Oct.

We left Mr. Knowles's on Thursday morning, came through
Godalming, stopped at Mr. Rowland's at Chilworth, and then
came on through Dorking to Colley Farm, near Reigate, where

we slept. I have so often described the country from Hindhead to the foot of Reigate Hill, and from the top of Reigate Hill to the Thames, that I shall not attempt to do it again here. When we got to the river Wey, we crossed it from Godalming Pismarsh to come up to Chilworth. I desired George to look round the country, and asked him if he did not think it was very pretty. I put the same question to him when we got into the beautiful neighbourhood of Dorking, and when we got to Reigate, and especially when we got to the tip-top of Reigate Hill, from which there is one of the finest views in the whole world; but ever after our quitting Mr. Knowles's, George insisted that that was the prettiest country that we had seen in the course of our whole ride, and that he liked Mr. Knowles's place better than any other place that he had seen. I reminded him of Weston Grove; and I reminded him of the beautiful ponds and grass and plantations at Mr. Leach's; but he still persisted in his judgment in favour of Mr. Knowles's place, in which decision, however, the greyhounds and the beagles had manifestly a great deal to do.

From Thursley to Reigate inclusive, on the chalk-side as well as on the sand-side, the crops of turnips, of both kinds, were pretty nearly as good as I ever saw them in my life. On a farm of Mr. Drummond's at Aldbury, rented by a farmer Peto, I saw a piece of cabbages, of the large kind, which will produce, I should think, not much short of five-and-twenty tons to the acre; and here I must mention (I do not know *why* I must, by the bye) an instance of my own skill in measuring land by the eye. The cabbages stand upon half a field and on the part of it furthest from the road where we were. We took the liberty to open the gate and ride into the field, in order to get closer to the cabbages to look at them. I intended to notice this piece of cabbages, and I asked George how much ground he thought there was in the piece. He said *two acres ;* and asked me how much I thought. I said that there were *above four acres*, and that I should not wonder if there were *four acres and a half*. Thus divided in judgment, we turned away from the cabbages to go out of the field at another gate, which pointed towards our road. Near this gate we found a man turning a heap of manure. This man, as it happened, had hoed the cabbages by the acre, or had had a hand in it. We asked him how much ground there was in that piece of cabbages, and he told us, *four acres and a half !* I suppose it will not be difficult to convince the reader that George looked upon me as a sort of conjuror. At Mr. Pym's, at Colley Farm, we found one of the very finest pieces of mangel wurzel that I had ever seen in my life. We calculated that there would be little short of *forty tons to the acre;* and there being three acres to the piece, Mr. Pym calculates that this mangel wurzel, the produce of these three acres of land, will carry his ten or twelve milch-cows nearly, if not wholly, through the winter. There did not appear to be a spurious plant, and there was not one plant that had gone to seed, in the whole piece. I have never seen a more beautiful mass of vegetation, and I had the satisfaction to learn, after having admired the crop, that the seed came from my own shop, and that it had been saved by myself.

Talking of the shop, I came to it in a very few hours after looking at this mangel wurzel; and I soon found that it was high time for me to get home again; for here had been pretty devils' works going on. Here I found the "Greek cause," and all its appendages, figuring away in grand style. But I must make this matter of separate observation.

I have put an end to my ride of August, September, and October, 1826, during which I have travelled five hundred and sixty-eight miles, and have slept in thirty different beds, having written three monthly pamphlets, called the *Poor Man's Friend*, and have also written (including the present one) eleven *Registers*. I have been in three cities, in about twenty market towns, in perhaps five hundred villages; and I have seen the people no where so well off as in the neighbourhood of Weston Grove, and nowhere so badly off as in the dominions of the Select Vestry of Hurstbourn Tarrant, commonly called Uphusband. During the whole of this ride, I have very rarely been a-bed after daylight; I have drunk neither wine nor spirits. I have eaten no vege-tables, and only a very moderate quantity of meat; and it may be useful to my readers to know that the riding of twenty miles was not so fatiguing to me at the end of my tour as the riding of ten miles was at the beginning of it. Some ill-natured fools will call this "*egotism.*" Why is it egotism? Getting upon a good strong horse, and riding about the country has no merit in it; there is no conjuration in it; it requires neither talents nor virtues of any sort; but *health* is a very valuable thing; and when a man has had the experience which I have had in this instance, it is his duty to state to the world, and to his own countrymen and neighbours in particular, the happy effects of early rising, sobriety, abstinence and a resolution to be active. It is his duty to do this; and it becomes imperatively his duty when he has seen, in the course of his life, so many men, so many men of excellent hearts and of good talents, rendered permaturely old, cut off ten or twenty years before their time, by a want of that early rising, sobriety, abstinence and activity from which he himself has derived so much benefit and such inexpressible pleasure. During this ride I have been several times wet to the skin. At some times of my life, after having indulged for a long while in coddling myself up in the house, these soakings would have frightened me half out of my senses; but I care very little about them: I avoid getting wet if I can; but it is very seldom that rain, come when it would, has prevented me from performing the day's journey that I had laid out beforehand. And this is a very good rule: to stick to your intention whether it be attended with inconveniences or not; to look upon yourself as *bound* to do it. In the whole of this ride, I have met with no one untoward circumstance, properly so called, except the wounding of the back of my horse, which grieved me much more on his account than on my own. I have a friend who, when he is disappointed in accomplishing anything that he has laid out, says that he has been *beaten*, which is a very good expression for the thing. I was beaten in my intention to go through Sussex and Kent; but I will retrieve the affair in a very few months' time, or perhaps few weeks. The COLLECTIVE will be here now in a few days; and as soon as I have got the Preston Petition fairly before them, and find (as I dare say I shall) that the petition will not be *tried* until February, I shall take my horse and set off again to that very spot, in the London turnpike-road, at the foot of Butser Hill, whence I turned off to go to Petersfield, instead of turning the other way to go to Up Park: I shall take my horse and go to this spot, and, with a resolution not to be beaten next time, go along through the whole length of Sussex, and sweep round through Kent and Surrey till I come to Reigate again, and then home to Kensington; for I do not like to be beaten by horse's sore back, or by anything else; and, besides that, there are several things in Sussex and Kent that I want to see and give an account of. For the present, however, farewell to the country, and now for the Wen and its villainous corruptions.

TO TRING IN HERTFORDSHIRE

BARN-ELM FARM,
23 *Sept.* 1829.

As if to prove the truth of all that has been said in *The Woodlands* about the impolicy of cheap planting, as it is called, Mr. Elliman has planted another and larger field with a mixture of ash, locusts, and larches; not upon *trenched* ground, but upon ground moved with the plough. The larches made great haste to *depart this life,* bequeathing to Mr. Elliman a very salutary lesson. The ash appeared to be alive, and that is all: the locusts, though they had to share in all the disadvantages of their neighbours, appeared, it seems, to be doing pretty well, and had made decent shoots, when a neighbour's sheep invaded the plantation and, being fond of the locust leaves and shoots, as all cattle are, reduced them to mere stumps, as it were to put them upon a level with the ash. In *The Woodlands*, I have strongly pressed the necessity of effectual fences: without these, you plant and sow in vain: you plant and sow the plants and seeds of disappointment and mortification; and the earth, being always grateful, is sure to reward you with a plentiful crop. One half acre of Mr. Elliman's plantation of locusts before-mentioned, time will tell him, is worth more than the whole of the six or seven acres of this *cheaply* planted field.

Besides the 25,000 trees which Mr. Elliman had from me, he had some (and a part of them fine plants) which he himself had raised from seed, in the manner described in *The Woodlands* under the head "Locust." This seed he bought from me; and, as I shall sell but a very few more locust plants, I recommend gentlemen to sow the seed for themselves according to the directions given in *The Woodlands*, in paragraphs 383 to 386 inclusive. In that part of *The Woodlands* will be found the most minute directions for the sowing of this seed, and particularly in the preparing of it for sowing; for unless the proper precautions are taken here, one seed out of one hundred will not come up; and with the proper precautions one seed in one hundred will not fail to come up. I beg the reader who intends to sow locusts to read with great care the latter part of paragraph 368 of *The Woodlands*.

At this town of Tring, which is a very pretty and respectable place, I saw what reminded me of another of my endeavours to introduce useful things into this country. At the door of a shop I saw a large *case* with the lid taken off, containing *bundles of straw for platting*. It was straw of spring wheat tied up in small bundles with the ear on; just such as I myself have grown in England many times, and bleached for platting according to the instructions so elaborately given in the last edition of my *Cottage Economy ;* and which instructions I was enabled to give from the information collected by my son in America. I asked the shopkeeper where he got this straw: he said that it came from Tuscany; and that it was manufactured there at Tring and other places for, as I understood, some single individual master-manufacturer. I told the shopkeeper that I wondered that they should send to Tuscany for the straw, seeing that it might be grown, harvested, and equally well bleached at Tring; that it was now, at this time, grown, bleached, and manufactured into bonnets in Kent; and I showed to several persons at Tring a bonnet made in Kent from the straw of wheat grown in Kent, and presented by that most public-spirited and excellent man Mr. John Wood, of Wettersham, who died, to the great sorrow of the whole country round about him, three or four years ago. He had taken infinite pains with this matter, had brought a young woman from Suffolk at his own expense to teach the children at Wettersham the whole of this manufacture from beginning to end; and, before he died, he saw as handsome bonnets made as ever came from Tuscany. At Benenden, the parish in which Mr. Hodges resides, there is now a manufactory of the same sort begun in the first place, under the benevolent auspices of that gentleman's daughters, who began by teaching a poor fellow who had been a cripple from his infancy, who was living with a poor widowed mother, and who is now the master of a school of this description, in the beautiful villages of Benenden and Rolvenden in Kent. My wife, wishing to have her bonnet cleaned some time ago, applied to a person who performs such work at Brighton, and got into a conversation with her about the *English Leghorn* bonnets. The woman told her that they looked very well at first, but that they would not retain their colour, and added, " They will not clean, ma'am, like this bonnet that you have." She was left with a request to clean that; and the result being the same as with all Leghorn bonnets, she was surprised upon being told that that was an " English Leghorn." In short, there is no difference at all in the two; and if these people at Tring choose to grow the straw instead of importing it from Leghorn; and if they choose to make plat, and to make bonnets just as beautiful and as lasting as those which come from Leghorn, they have nothing to do but to read my *Cottage Economy*, paragraph 224 to paragraph 234, inclusive, where they will find, as plain as words can make it, the whole mass of directions for taking the seed of the wheat, and converting the produce into bonnets. There they will find directions, first, as to the sort of wheat; second, as to the proper land for growing the wheat; third, season for sowing; fourth, quantity of seed to the acre and manner of sowing; fifth, season for cutting the wheat; sixth, manner of cutting it; seventh, manner of bleaching; eighth, manner of housing the straw; ninth, platting; tenth, manner of knitting; eleventh, manner of pressing.

I request my correspondents to inform me, if any one can, where I can get some spring wheat. The botanical name of it is *Triticum Æstivum*. It is sown in the spring, at the same time that barley is; these Latin words mean *summer wheat*. It is a small-grained, bearded wheat. I know from experience that the little brown-grained winter wheat is just as good for the purpose: but that must be sown earlier; and there is danger of its being thinned on the ground by worms and other enemies. I should like to sow some this next spring, in order to convince the people of Tring, and other places, that they need not go to Tuscany for the straw.

Of " *Cobbett's corn* " there is no considerable piece in the neighbourhood of Tring; but I saw some plants, even upon the high hill where the locusts are growing, and which is very backward land, which appeared to be about as forward as my own is at this time. If Mr. Elliman were to have a patch of good corn by the side of his locust-trees, and a piece of spring wheat by the side of the corn, people might then go and see specimens of the three great undertakings, or rather great additions to the wealth of the nation, introduced under the name of *Cobbett*.

I am the more desirous of introducing this manufacture at Tring on account of the very marked civility which I met with at that place. A very excellent friend of mine, who is professionally connected with that town, was some time ago apprised of my intention of going thither to see Mr. Elliman's plantation. He had mentioned this intention to some gentlemen of that town and neighbourhood; and I, to my great surprise, found that a *dinner had been organised*, to which I was to be invited. I never like to disappoint anybody; and, therefore, to this dinner I went. The company consisted of about forty-five gentlemen of the town and neighbourhood; and certainly, though I have been at dinners in several parts of England, I never found, even in Sussex, where I have frequently been so delighted, a more sensible, hearty, entertaining, and hospitable company than this. From me something in the way of speech was expected, as a matter of course; and though I was from a cold so hoarse as not to be capable of making myself heard in a large place, I was so pleased with the company and with my reception, that, first and last, I dare say I addressed the company for an hour and a half. We dined at two and separated at nine; and, as I declared at parting, for many, many years I had not spent a happier day. There was present the editor, or some other gentleman, from the newspaper called *The Bucks Gazette and General Advertiser*, who has published in his paper the following account of what passed at the dinner. As far as the report goes it is substantially correct; and though this gentleman went away at a very early hour, that which he has given of my speech (which he has given very judiciously) contains matter which can hardly fail to be useful to great numbers of his readers.

MR. COBBETT AT TRING

" Mr. Elliman, a draper of Tring, has lately formed a considerable plantation of the locust-tree, which Mr. Cobbett claims the merit of having introduced into this country. The number he has planted is about 30,000, on five acres and a half of very indifferent land, and they have thrived so uncommonly well that not more than 500 of the whole number have failed. The success of the plantation being made known to Mr. Cobbett, induced him to pay a visit to Tring to inspect it, and during his sojourn it was determined upon by his friends to give him a dinner at the Rose and Crown Inn. Thursday was fixed for the purpose; when about forty persons, agriculturists and tradesmen of Tring and the neighbouring towns, assembled, and sat down to a dinner served up in very excellent style by Mr. Northwood, the landlord: Mr. Faithful, solicitor, of Tring, in the chair.

" The usual routine toasts having been given,

" The chairman said he was sure the company would drink the toast with which he should conclude what he was about to say with every mark of respect. In addressing the company he rose under feelings of no ordinary kind, for he was about to give the health of a gentleman who had the talent of communicating to his writings an energy and perspicuity which he had never met with elsewhere; who conveyed knowledge in a way so clear that all who read could understand. He (the chairman) had read the *Political Register*, from the first of them to the last, with pleasure and benefit to himself, and he would defy any man to put his finger upon a single line which was not direct in support of a kingly government. He advocated the rights of the people, but he always expressed himself favourable to our ancient form of government; he certainly had strongly, but not too strongly, attacked the corruption of the government; but had never attacked its form or its just powers. As a public writer he considered him the most impartial that he knew. He well recollected—he knew not if Mr. Cobbett himself recollected it—a remarkable passage in his writings: he was speaking of the pleasure of passing from censure to praise, and thus expressed himself. ' It is turning from the frowns of a surly winter, to welcome a smiling spring come dancing over the daisied lawn, crowned with garlands, and surrounded with melody.' Nature had been bountiful to him; it had blessed him with a constitution capable of enduring the greatest fatigues; and a mind of superior order. Brilliancy, it was said, was a mere meteor; it was so: it was the solidity and depth of understanding such as he possessed that were really valuable. He had visited this place in consequence of a gentleman having been wise and bold enough to listen to his advice, and to plant a large number of locust-trees; and he trusted he would enjoy prosperity and happiness in duration equal to that of the never-decaying wood of those trees. He concluded by giving Mr. Cobbett's health.

" Mr. Cobbett returned thanks for the manner in which his health had been drunk, and was certain that the trees which had been the occasion of their meeting would be a benefit to the children of the planter. Though it might appear like presumption to suppose that those who were assembled that day came solely in compliment to him, yet it would be affectation not to believe that it was expected he should say something on the subject of politics. Every one who heard him was convinced that there was something wrong, and that a change of some sort must take place, or ruin to the country would ensue. Though there was a diversity of opinions as to the cause of the distress— and as to the means by which a change might be effected, and though some were not so deeply affected by it as others, all now felt that a change must take place before long, whether they were manufacturers, brewers, butchers, bakers, or of any other description of persons, they had all arrived at the conviction that there must be a change. It would be presumptuous to suppose that many of those assembled did not understand the cause of the present distress, yet there were many who did not; and those gentlemen who did he begged to have the goodness to excuse him if he repeated what they already knew. Politics was a science which they ought not to have the trouble of studying; they had sufficient to do in their respective avocations without troubling themselves with such matters. For what were the ministers, and a whole tribe of persons under them, paid large sums of money from the country but for the purpose of governing its political affairs. Their fitness for their stations was another thing. He had been told that Mr. Huskisson was so ignorant of the cause of the distress that he had openly said he should be glad if any practical man would tell him what it all meant. If any man present were to profess his ignorance of the cause of the distress it would be no disgrace to him; he might be a very good butcher, a very good farmer, or a very good baker: he might well understand the business by which he gained his living; and if any one should say to him, because he did not understand politics, ' You are a very stupid fellow!' he might fairly reply, ' What is that to you?' But it was another thing in those who were so well paid to manage the affairs of the country to plead ignorance of the cause of the prevailing distress.

. . . .

" Mr. Goulburn, with a string of figures as long as his arm, had endeavoured to prove in the House of Commons that the withdrawal of the one-pound notes, being altogether so small an amount, little more than two millions, would be of no injury to the country, and that its only effect would be to make bankers more liberal in discounting with their fives. He would appeal to the company if they had found this to be the case. Mr. Goulburn had forgotten that the one-pound notes were the legs upon which the fives walked. He had heard the Duke of Wellington use the same language in the other House. Taught, as they now were, by experience, it would scarcely be believed fifty years hence that a set of men could have been found with so little foresight as to have devised measures so fraught with injury.

" He felt convinced that if he looked to the present company, or any other accidentally assembled, that he would find thirteen gentlemen more fit to manage the affairs of the kingdom than were those who now presided at the head of government; not that he imputed to them any desire to do wrong, or that they were more corrupt than others; it was clear that with the eyes of the public upon them they must wish to do right; it was owing to their sheer ignorance, their entire unfitness to carry on the government, that they did no better. Ignorance and unfitness were, however, pleas which they had no business to make. It was nothing to him if a man was ignorant and stupid under ordinary circumstances; but if he entrusted a man with his money, thinking that he was intelligent, and was deceived, then it was something; he had a right to say, ' You are not what I took you for, you are an ignorant fellow; you have deceived me, you are an impostor.' Such was the language proper to all under such circumstances: never mind their titles!

" A friend had that morning taken him to view the beautiful vale of Aylesbury, which he had never before seen; and the first thought that struck him on seeing the rich pasture, was this, ' Good God! is a country like this to be ruined by the folly of those who govern it?' When he was a naughty boy he used to say that if he wanted to select members for our Houses of Parliament he would put a string across any road leading *into* London, and that the first 1000 men that ran against his string he would choose for members, and he would bet a wager that they would be better qualified than those who now filled those Houses. That was when he was a naughty boy; but since that time a bill had been passed which made it banishment for life to use language that brought the Houses of Parliament into contempt, and therefore he did not say so now. The government, it should be recollected, had passed all these acts with the hearty concurrence of both Houses of Parliament; they were thus backed by these Houses, and they were backed by ninety-nine out of one hundred of the papers, which affected to see all their acts in rose-colour, for no one who was in the habit of reading the papers could have anticipated, from what they there saw, the ruin which had fallen on the country. Thus we had an ignorant government, an ignorant parliament, and something worse than an ignorant press; the latter being employed (some of them with considerable talent) to assail and turn into ridicule those who had the boldness and honesty to declare their dissent from the opinion of the wisdom of the measures of government. It was no easy task to stand unmoved their ridicule and sarcasms, and many were thus deterred from expressing any sentiments of their minds. In this country we had all the elements of prosperity; an industrious people, such as were nowhere else to be found; a country, too, which was once called the finest and greatest on the earth (for whatever might be said of the country in comparison with others, the turnips of England were worth more, this year, than all the vines of France). It was a glorious and a great country until the government had made it otherwise; and it ought still to be what it once was, and to be capable of driving the Russians back from the country of our old and best ally—the Turks. During the time of war we were told that it was necessary to make great sacrifices to save us from disgrace. The people made those sacrifices; they gave up their all. But had the government done its part; had it saved us from disgrace? No: we were now the laughing-stock of all other countries. The French and all other nations derided us; and by and by it would be seen that they would make a partition of Turkey with the Russians, and make a fresh subject for laughter. Never since the time of Charles had such disgrace been brought upon the country; and why was this? When were we again to see the labourer receiving his wages from the farmer instead of being sent on the road to break stones? Some people, under this state of things, consoled themselves by saying things would come about again; they had come about before, and would come about again. They deceived themselves, things did not come about; the seasons came about, it was true; but something must be *done* to bring things about. Instead of the *neuter* verb (to speak as a grammarian) they should use the *active ;* they should not say things will *come* about, but things must be *put* about. He thought that the distress would shortly become so great, perhaps about Christmas, that the parliamentary gentlemen, finding they received but a small part of their rents, without which they could not do, any more than the farmer without his crops, would endeavour to bring them about; and the measures they would propose for that purpose, as far as he could judge, would be bank restriction and the re-issue of one-pound notes, and what the effect of that would be they would soon see. One of those persons who were so profoundly ignorant would come down to the House prepared to propose a return to bank restriction and the issue of small notes, and a bill to that effect would be passed. If such a bill did pass, he would advise all persons to be cautious in their dealings; it would be perilous to make bargains under such a state of things. Money was the measure of value; but if this measure was liable to be three times as large at one time as at another, who could know what to do? how was any one to know how to purchase wheat, if the bushel was to be altered at the pleasure of the government to three times its present size? The remedy for the evils of the country was not to be found in palliatives; it was not to be found in strong measures. The first step must be taken in the House of Commons, but that was almost hopeless; for although many persons possessed the right of voting, it was of little use to them whilst a few great men could render their votes of no avail. If we had possessed a House of Commons that represented the feelings and wishes of the people, they would not have submitted to much of what had taken place; and until we had a reform we should never, he believed, see measures emanating from that House which would conduce to the glory and safety of the country. He feared that there would be no improvement until a dreadful convulsion took place, and that was an event which he prayed God to avert from the country.

" The chairman proposed ' *Prosperity to Agriculture,*' when—

" Mr. Cobbett again rose, and said the chairman had told him he was entitled to give a sentiment. He would give prosperity to the towns of Aylesbury and Tring; but he would again advise those who calculated upon the return of prosperity to be careful. Until there was an equitable adjustment, or government took off part of the taxes, which was the same thing, there could be no return of prosperity."

After the reporter went away, we had a great number of toasts, most of which were followed by more or less of speech; and before we separated I think that the seeds of common sense, on the subject of our distresses, were pretty well planted in the lower part of Hertfordshire and in Buckinghamshire.

The gentlemen present were men of information, well able to communicate to others that which they themselves had heard; and I endeavoured to leave no doubt in the mind of any man that heard me that the cause of the distress was the work of the government and House of Commons, and that it was nonsense to hope for a cure until the people had a real voice in the choosing of that House. I think that these truths were well implanted; and I further think that if I could go to the capital of every county in the kingdom, I should leave no doubt in the minds of any part of the people. I must not omit to mention, in conclusion, that though I am no eater or drinker, and though I tasted nothing but the breast of a little chicken, and drank nothing but water, the dinner was the best that ever I saw called a *public dinner*, and certainly unreasonably cheap. There were excellent joints of meat of the finest description, fowls and geese in abundance; and, finally, a very fine haunch of venison, with a bottle of wine for each person; and all for *seven shillings and sixpence per head*. Good waiting upon; civil landlord and landlady; and, in short, everything at this very pretty town pleased me exceedingly. Yet what is Tring but a fair specimen of English towns and English people? And is it right, and is it to be suffered, that such a people should be plunged into misery by the acts of those whom they pay so generously, and whom they so loyally and cheerfully obey?

As far as I had an opportunity of ascertaining the facts, the farmers feel all the pinchings of distress, and the still harsher pinchings of anxiety for the future; and the labouring people are suffering in a degree not to be described. The shutting of the male paupers up in pounds is common through Bedfordshire and Buckinghamshire. Left at large during the day, they roam about and maraud. What are the farmers to do with them? God knows how long the peace is to be kept if this state of things be not put a stop to. The natural course of things is that an attempt to impound the paupers in cold weather will produce resistance in some place; that those of one parish will be joined by those of another; that a formidable band will soon be assembled; then will ensue the rummaging of pantries and cellars; that this will spread from parish to parish; and that, finally, mobs of immense magnitude will set the law at open defiance. Gaols are next to useless in such a case: their want of room must leave the greater part of the offenders at large; the agonising distress of the farmers will make them comparatively indifferent with regard to these violences; and, at last, general confusion will come. This is by no means an unlikely progress, or an unlikely result. It therefore becomes those who have much at stake to join heartily in their applications to government for a timely remedy for these astounding evils.

NORTHERN TOUR

SHEFFIELD,
31 *January* 1830.

ON the 26th instant I gave my third lecture at Leeds. I should in vain endeavour to give an adequate description of the pleasure which I felt at my reception, and at the effect which I produced in that fine and opulent capital of this great county of York; for the *capital* it is in fact, though not in name. On the first evening, the playhouse, which is pretty spacious, was not completely filled in all its parts; but on the second and the third it was filled brim full, boxes, pit and gallery; besides a dozen or two of gentlemen who were accommodated with seats on the stage. Owing to a cold which I took at Huddersfield, and which I spoke of before, I was, as the players call it, not in very good *voice;* but the audience made allowance for that, and very wisely preferred sense to sound. I never was more delighted than with my audience at Leeds; and what I set the highest value on is, that I find I produced a prodigious effect in that important town.

There had been a meeting at Doncaster a few days before I went to Leeds from Ripley, where one of the speakers, a Mr. Becket Denison, had said, speaking of the taxes, that there must be an application of the *pruning hook* or of the *sponge.* This gentleman is a banker, I believe: he is one of the Beckets connected with the Lowthers; and he is a brother, or very near relation, of that Sir John Becket who is the judge advocate general. So that, at last, others can talk of the pruning hook and the sponge as well as I.

From Leeds I proceeded on to this place, not being able to stop at either Wakefield or Barnsley, except merely to change horses. The people in those towns were apprised of the time that I should pass through them; and, at each place, great numbers assembled to see me, to shake me by the hand, and to request me to stop. I was so hoarse as not to be able to make the post-boy hear me when I called to him; and, therefore, it would have been useless to stop; yet I promised to go back if my time and my voice would allow me. They do not; and I have written to the gentlemen of those places to inform them that when I go to Scotland in the spring I will not fail to stop in those towns, in order to express my gratitude to them. All the way along from Leeds to Sheffield it is coal and iron, and iron and coal. It was dark before we reached Sheffield; so that we saw the iron furnaces in all the horrible splendour of their everlasting blaze. Nothing can be conceived more grand or more terrific than the yellow waves of fire that incessantly issue from the top of these furnaces, some of which are close by the way-side. Nature has placed the beds of iron and the beds of coal alongside of each other, and art has taught man to make one to operate upon the other, as to turn the iron-stone into liquid matter, which is drained off from the bottom of the furnace, and afterwards moulded into blocks and bars, and all sorts of things. The combustibles are put into the top of the furnace, which stands thirty, forty, or fifty feet up in the air, and the ever-blazing mouth of which is kept supplied with coal and coke and iron-stone from little iron waggons forced up by steam, and brought down again to be refilled. It is a surprising thing to behold; and it is impossible to behold it without being convinced that, whatever other nations may do with cotton and with wool, they will never equal England with regard to things made of iron and steel. This Sheffield, and the land all about it, is one bed of iron and coal. They call it black Sheffield, and black enough it is; but from this one town and its environs go nine-tenths of the knives that are used in the whole world; there being, I understand, no knives made at Birmingham; the manufacture of which place consists of the larger sort of implements, of locks of all sorts, and guns and swords, and of all the endless articles of hardware which go to the furnishing of a house. As to the land, viewed in the way of agriculture, it really does appear to be very little worth. I have not seen, except at Harewood and Ripley, a stack of wheat since I came into Yorkshire; and even there, the whole I saw; and all that I have seen since I came into Yorkshire; and all that I saw during a ride of six miles that I took into Derbyshire the day before yesterday; all put together would not make the one-half of what I have many times seen in one single rick-yard of the vales of Wiltshire. But this is all very proper: these coal-diggers, and iron-melters, and knife-makers, compel us to send the food to them, which, indeed, we do very cheerfully, in exchange for the produce of their rocks, and the wondrous works of their hands.

The trade of Sheffield has fallen off less in proportion than that of the other manufacturing districts. North America, and particularly the United States, where the people have so much victuals to cut, form a great branch of the custom of this town. If the people of Sheffield could only receive a tenth part of what their knives sell for by retail in America, Sheffield might pave its streets with silver. A *gross* of knives and forks is sold to the Americans for less than three knives and forks can be bought at retail in a country store in America. No fear of rivalship in this trade. The Americans may lay on their tariff, and double it, and triple it; but as long as they continue to *cut* their victuals from Sheffield they must have the things to cut it with.

The ragged hills all round about this town are bespangled with groups of houses inhabited by the working cutlers. They have not suffered like the working weavers; for to make knives there must be the hand of man. Therefore, machinery cannot come to destroy the wages of the labourer. The home demand has been very much diminished; but still the depression has here not been what it has been, and what it is where the machinery can be brought into play. We are here just upon the borders of Derbyshire, a nook of which runs up and separates Yorkshire from Nottinghamshire. I went to a village, the day before yesterday, called *Mosborough*, the whole of the people of which are employed in the making of *sickles* and *scythes*; and where, as I was told, they are very well off even in these times. A prodigious quantity of these things go to the United States of America. In short, there are about twelve millions of people there continually consuming these things; and the hardware merchants here have their agents and their stores in the great towns of America; which country, as far as relates to this branch of business, is still a part of old England.

Upon my arriving here on Wednesday night, the 27th instant, I by no means intended to lecture until I should be a little recovered from my cold; but, to my great mortification, I found that the lecture had been advertised, and that great numbers of persons had actually assembled. To send them out again, and give back the money, was a thing not to be attempted. I, therefore, went to the music hall, the place which had been taken for the purpose, gave them a specimen of the state of my voice, asked them whether I should proceed, and they answering in the affirmative, on I went. I then rested until yesterday, and shall conclude my labours here to-morrow, and then proceed to "*fair Nottingham,*" as we used to sing when I was a boy, in celebrating the glorious exploits of "Robin Hood and Little John." By the by, as we went from Huddersfield to Dewsbury, we passed by a hill which is celebrated as being the burial-place of the famed Robin Hood, of whom the people in this country talk to this day.

At Nottingham they have advertised for my lecturing at the playhouse for the 3rd, 4th, and 5th of February, and for a public breakfast to be given to me on the first of those days, I having declined a dinner agreeably to my original notification, and my friends insisting upon something or other in that sort of way. It is very curious that I have always had a very great desire to see Nottingham. This desire certainly originated in the great interest that I used to take, and that all country boys took, in the history of Robin Hood, in the record of whose achievements, which were so well calculated to excite admiration in the country boys, this Nottingham, with the word "*fair*" always before it, was so often mentioned. The word *fair*, as used by our forefathers, meant fine; for we frequently read in old descriptions of parts of the country of such a district or such a parish containing a *fair* mansion, and the like; so that this town appears to have been celebrated as a very fine place, even in ancient times; but within the last thirty years Nottingham has stood high in my estimation from the conduct of its people; from their public spirit; from their excellent sense as to public matters; from the noble struggle which they have made from the beginning of the French war to the present hour; if only forty towns in England equal in size to Nottingham had followed its bright example, there would have been no French war against liberty; the debt would have been now nearly paid off, and we should have known nothing of those manifold miseries which now afflict, and those greater miseries which now menace, the country. The French would not have been in Cadiz; the Russians would not have been at Constantinople; the Americans would not have been in the Floridas; we should not have had to dread the combined fleets of America, France and Russia; and, which is the worst of all, we should not have seen the gaols four times as big as they were; and should not have seen Englishmen reduced to such a state of misery as for the honest labouring man to be fed worse than the felons in the gaols.

EASTERN TOUR

" You permit the Jews openly to preach in their synagogues and call
Jesus Christ an impostor; and you send women to gaol (to be brought to
bed there, too) for declaring their unbelief in Christianity."—*King of
Bohemia's Letter to Canning, published in the Register, 4th of January* 1823.

HARGHAM
22 March 1830.

I SET off from London on the 8th of March, got to Bury St.
Edmund's that evening; and to my great mortification saw the
county-election and the assizes both going on at Chelmsford,
where, of course, a great part of the people of Essex were met.
If I had been aware of that I should certainly have stopped at
Chelmsford in order to address a few words of *sense* to the unfortunate constituents of Mr. Western. At Bury St. Edmund's
I gave a lecture on the 9th and another on the 10th of March,
in the playhouse, to very crowded audiences. I went to
Norwich on the 12th, and gave a lecture there on that evening,
and on the evening of the 13th. The audience here was more
numerous than at Bury St. Edmund's, but not so numerous in
proportion to the size of the place; and, contrary to what has
happened in most other places, it consisted more of town's
people than of country people.

During the 14th and 15th I was at a friend's house at Yelver-
ton, half way between Norwich and Bungay, which last is in
Suffolk, and at which place I lectured on the 16th to an audience
consisting chiefly of farmers, and was entertained there in a
most hospitable and kind manner at the house of a friend.

The next day, being the 17th, I went to Eye, and there
lectured in the evening in the neat little playhouse of the place,
which was crowded in every part, stage and all. The audience
consisted almost entirely of farmers, who had come in from Diss,
from Harleston, and from all the villages round about, in this
fertile and thickly-settled neighbourhood. I stayed at Eye all
the day of the 18th, having appointed to be at Ipswich on the
19th. Eye is a beautiful little place, though an exceedingly
rotten borough.

All was harmony and good humour: everybody appeared to
be of one mind; and as these friends observed to me, so I

thought, that more effect had been produced by this one lecture
in that neighbourhood than could have been produced in a whole
year if the *Register* had been put into the hands of every one of
the hearers during that space of time; for though I never attempt
to put forth that sort of stuff which the " intense " people on
the other side of St. George's Chaennl call " *eloquence*," I bring
out strings of very interesting facts; I use pretty powerful arguments; and I hammer them down so closely upon the mind that
they seldom fail to produce a lasting impression.

On the 19th I proceeded to Ipswich, not imagining it to be
the fine, populous and beautiful place that I found it to be.
On that night, and on the night of the 20th, I lectured to boxes
and pit crowded principally with opulent farmers, and to a
gallery filled, apparently, with journeymen tradesmen and their
wives. On the Sunday before I came away I heard from all
quarters that my audiences had retired deeply impressed with
the truths which I had endeavoured to inculcate. One thing,
however, occurred towards the close of the lecture of Saturday,
the 20th, that I deem worthy of particular attention. In
general it would be useless for me to attempt to give anything
like *a report* of these speeches of mine, consisting as they do of
words uttered pretty nearly as fast as I can utter them during
a space of never less than two, and sometimes of nearly three
hours. But there occurred here something that I must notice.
I was speaking of *the degrees* by which the established church
had been losing its *legal influence* since the peace. First, the
Unitarian Bill, removing the penal act which forbade an im-
pugning of the doctrine of the Trinity; second, the repeal of the
Test Act, which declared, in effect, that the religion of any of
the Dissenters was as good as that of the Church of England;
third, the repeal of the penal and excluding laws with regard to
the *Catholics ;* and this last act, said I, does in effect declare
that the thing called " the *Reformation* " was *unnecessary.*
" No," said one gentleman, in a very loud voice, and he was
followed by four or five more, who said " No, no." " Then,"
said I, " we will, if you like, put it *to the vote.* Understand,
gentlemen, that *I do not say*, whatever I may think, that the
Reformation was unnecessary; but I say that *this act amounts
to a declaration* that it was unnecessary; and without losing our
good humour, we will, if that gentleman choose, put this question
to the vote." I paused a little while, receiving no answer, and
perceiving that the company were with me, I proceeded with
my speech, concluding with the complete demolishing blow

which the church would receive by the bill for giving civil and political power for training to the bar, and seating on the bench, for placing in the commons and amongst the peers, and for placing in the council, along with the king himself, *those who deny that there ever existed a Redeemer ;* who give the name of *impostor* to him whom *we worship as God,* and who boast of having hanged him upon the cross. " Judge you, gentlemen," said I, " of the figure which England will make when its laws will seat on the bench, from which people have been sentenced to suffer most severely for denying the truth of Christianity; from which bench it has been held that *Christianity is part and parcel of the law of the land ;* judge you of the figure which England will make amongst Christian nations when a Jew, a blasphemer of Christ, a professor of the doctrines of those who murdered him, shall be sitting upon that bench; and judge, gentlemen, what we must think of *the clergy* of this church of ours *if they remain silent* while such a law shall be passed."

We were entertained at Ipswich by a very kind and excellent friend, whom, as is generally the case, I had never seen or heard of before. The morning of the day of the last lecture I walked about five miles, then went to his house to breakfast, and stayed with him and dined. On the Sunday morning, before I came away, I walked about six miles, and repeated the good cheer at breakfast at the same place. Here I heard the first singing of the birds this year; and I here observed an instance of that *petticoat government* which, apparently, pervades the whole of animated nature. A lark, very near to me in a ploughed field, rose from the ground, and was saluting the sun with his delightful song. He was got about as high as the dome of St. Paul's, having me for a motionless and admiring auditor, when the hen started up from nearly the same spot whence the cock had risen, flew up and passed close by him. I could not hear what she said; but supposed that she must have given him a pretty smart reprimand; for down she came upon the ground, and he, ceasing to sing, took a twirl in the air and came down after her. Others have, I dare say, seen this a thousand times over; but I never observed it before.

About twelve o'clock, my son and I set off for this place (Hargham), coming through Needham Market, Stowmarket, Bury St. Enmund's, and Thetford, at which latter place I intended to have lectured to-day and to-morrow, where the theatre was to have been the scene, but the mayor of the town thought it best not to give his permission until the assizes (which commence to-day the 22nd) should be over, lest the judge should take offence, seeing that it is the custom, while his lordship is in the town, to give up the civil jurisdiction to him. Bless his worship! what in all the world should he think would take me to Thetford *except it being a time for holding the assizes!* At no *other* time should I have dreamed of finding an audience in so small a place, and in a country so thinly inhabited. I was attracted, too, by the desire of meeting some of my " *learned friends* " from the Wen; for I deal in arguments founded on the *law of the land,* and on *Acts of Parliament.* The deuce take this mayor for disappointing me; and now I am afraid that I shall not fall in with this learned body during the whole of my spring tour.

Finding Thetford to be forbidden ground, I came hither to Sir Thomas Beevor's, where I had left my two daughters, having, since the 12th inclusive, travelled 120 miles, and delivered six lectures. These 120 miles have been through a fine *farming country,* and without my seeing, until I came to Thetford, but one spot of waste or common land, and that not exceeding, I should think, from fifty to eighty acres. From this place to Norwich, and through Attleborough and Wymondham, the land is all good and the farming excellent. It is pretty nearly the same from Norwich to Bungay, where we enter Suffolk. Bungay is a large and fine town, with three churches, lying on the side of some very fine meadows. Harleston, on the road to Eye, is a very pretty market-town: of Eye I have spoken before. From Eye to Ipswich we pass through a series of villages, and at Ipswich, to my great surprise, we found a most beautiful town, with a population of about twelve thousand persons; and here our profound Prime Minister might have seen most abundant evidence of prosperity; for the *new houses* are, indeed, very numerous. But if our famed and profound Prime Minister, having Mr. Wilmot Horton by the arm, and standing upon one of the hills that surround this town, and which, each hill seeming to surpass the other hill in beauty, command a complete view of every house, or, at least, of the top of every house, in this opulent town; if he, thus standing, and thus accompanied, were to hold up his hands, clap them together, and bless God for the proofs of prosperity contained in the new and red bricks, and were to cast his eye southward of the town, and see the numerous little vessels upon the little arm of the sea which comes up from Harwich, and which here finds its termination; and were, in those vessels, to discover an additional proof of prosperity; if he were to be thus situated, and to be thus feeling, would not some doubts be awakened in his mind if I, standing behind him, were to whisper in his ear, " Do you not think that the greater part of these new houses have been created by taxes, which went to pay the about 20,000 *troops* that were stationed here for pretty nearly 20 years during the war, and some of which are stationed here still? Look at that immense building, my lord duke: it is fresh and *new* and fine and splendid, and contains indubitable marks of opulence; but it is a BARRACK; aye, and the money to build that barrack, and to maintain the 20,000 troops, has assisted to beggar, to dilapidate, to plunge into ruin and decay hundreds upon hundreds of villages and hamlets in Wiltshire, in Dorsetshire, in Somersetshire, and in other counties who shared not in the ruthless squanderings of the war. But," leaning my arm upon the duke's shoulder, and giving Wilmot a poke in the poll to make him listen and look, and pointing with my fore-finger to the twelve large, lofty, and magnificent churches, each of them at least 700 years old, and saying, " Do you think Ipswich was not larger and far more populous 700 years ago than it is at this hour? " Putting this question to him, would it not check his exultation, and would it not make even Wilmot begin to reflect?

Even at this hour, with all the unnatural swellings of the war, there are not two thousand people, *including the bed-ridden and the babies*, to each of the magnificent churches. Of adults, there cannot be more than about 1400 to a church; and there is one of the churches which, being well filled, as in ancient times, would contain from four to seven thousand persons, for the nave of it appears to me to be larger than St. Andrew's Hall at Norwich, which hall was formerly the church of the Benedictine Priory. And, perhaps, the great church here might have belonged to some monastery; for here were three Augustine priories, one of them founded in the reign of William the Conquerer, another founded in the reign of Henry II., another in the reign of King John, with an Augustine friary, a Carmelite friary, an hospital founded in the reign of King John; and here, too, was the college founded by Cardinal Wolsey, the gate-way of which, though built in brick, is still preserved, being the same sort of architecture as that of Hampton Court and St. James's Palace.

There is no doubt but that this was a much greater place than it is now. It is the great outlet for the immense quantities of corn grown in this most productive country, and by farmers the most clever that ever lived. I am told that wheat is worth six shillings a quarter more, at some times, at Ipswich than at Norwich, the navigation to London being so much more speedy and safe. Immense quantities of flour are sent from this town. The windmills on the hills in the vicinage are so numerous that I counted, whilst standing in one place, no less than seventeen. They are all painted or washed white; the sails are black; it was a fine morning, the wind was brisk, and their twirling altogether added greatly to the beauty of the scene, which, having the broad and beautiful arm of the sea on the one hand, and the fields and meadows, studded with farm-houses, on the other, appeared to me the most beautiful sight of the kind that I had ever beheld. The town and its churches were down in the dell before me, and the only object that came to disfigure the scene was THE BARRACK, and made me utter involuntarily the words of Blackstone: " The laws of England recognise no distinction between the citizen and the soldier; they know of no standing soldier; no inland fortresses; no barracks." " Ah!" said I myself, but loud enough for any one to have heard me a hundred yards, " such *were* the laws of England when mass was said in those magnificent churches, and such they continued until a *septennial* parliament came and deprived the people of England of their rights."

I know of no town to be compared with Ipswich, except it be Nottingham; and there is this difference in the two; that Nottingham stands high and, on one side, looks over a very fine country; whereas Ipswich is in a dell, meadows running up above it, and a beautiful arm of the sea below it. The town itself is substantially built, well paved, everything good and solid, and no wretched dwellings to be seen on its outskirts. From the town itself you can see nothing; but you can, in no direction, go from it a quarter of a mile without finding views that a painter might crave, and then the country round about it so well cultivated; the land in such a beautiful state, the farm-houses all white, and all so much alike; the barns, and everything about the homesteads so snug; the stocks of turnips so abundant everywhere; the sheep and cattle in such fine order; the wheat all drilled; the ploughman so expert; the furrows, if a quarter of a mile long, as straight as a line, and laid as truly as if with a level: in short, here is everything to delight the eye, and to make the people proud of their country; and this is the case throughout the whole of this county. I have always found Suffolk farmers great boasters of their superiority over others; and I must say that it is not without reason.

*H 639

But observe this has been a very *highly-favoured county* : it has had poured into it millions upon millions of money, drawn from Wiltshire and other inland counties. I should suppose that Wiltshire alone has, within the last forty years, had two or three millions of money drawn from it, *to be given to Essex and Suffolk.* At one time there were not less than sixty thousand men kept on foot in these counties. The increase of London, too, the swelling of the immortal Wen, have assisted to heap wealth upon these counties; but, in spite of all this, the distress pervades all ranks and degrees, except those who live on the taxes. At Eye, butter used to sell for eighteenpence a pound: it now sells for ninepence halfpenny, though the grass has not yet begun to spring; and eggs were sold at thirty for a shilling. Fine times for me whose principal food is eggs and whose sole drink is milk, but very bad times for those who sell me the food and the drink.

Coming from Ipswich to Bury St. Edmund's, you pass through Needham Market and Stowmarket, two very pretty market towns; and, like all the other towns in Suffolk, free from the drawback of shabby and beggarly houses on the outskirts. I remarked that I did not see in the whole county one single instance of paper or rags supplying the place of glass in any window, and did not see one miserable hovel in which a labourer resided. The county, however, is *flat :* with the exception of the environs of Ipswich, there is none of that beautiful variety of hill and dale and hanging woods that you see at every town in Hampshire, Sussex, and Kent. It is curious, too, that though the people, I mean the poorer classes of people, are extremely neat in their houses, and though I found all their gardens dug up and prepared for cropping, you do not see about their cottages (and it is just the same in Norfolk) that *ornamental gardening ;* the walks, and the flower borders, and the honeysuckles and roses trained over the doors or over arched sticks, that you see in Hampshire, Sussex, and Kent, that I have many a time sitten upon my horse to look at so long and so often, as greatly to retard me on my journey. Nor is this done for show or ostentation. If you find a cottage in those counties, by the side of a *by lane,* or in the midst of a forest, you find just the same care about the garden and the flowers. In those counties, too, there is great taste with regard *to trees* of every description, from the hazel to the oak. In Suffolk it appears to be just the contrary: here is the great dissight of all these three eastern counties. Almost every bank of every field is studded with *pollards*, that is to say, trees that have been *beheaded*, at from six to twelve feet from the ground, than which nothing in nature can be more ugly. They send out shoots from the head, which are lopped off once in ten or a dozen years for fuel, or other purposes. To add to the deformity, the ivy is suffered to grow on them which, at the same time, checks the growth of the shoots. These pollards become hollow very soon and, as timber, are fit for nothing but gateposts, even before they be hollow. Upon a farm of a hundred acres these pollards, by root and shade, spoil at least six acres of the ground, besides being most destructive to the fences. Why not plant six acres of the ground with timber and underwood? Half an acre a year would most amply supply the farm with poles and brush, and with everything wanted in the way of fuel; and why not plant hedges to be unbroken by these pollards? I have scarcely seen a single farm of a hundred acres without pollards sufficient to find the farm-house in fuel, without any assistance from coals, for several years.

However, the great number of farm-houses in Suffolk, the neatness of those houses, the moderation in point of extent which you generally see, and the great store of the food in the turnips, and the admirable management of the whole, form a pretty good compensation for the want of beauties. The land is generally as clean as a garden ought to be; and though it varies a good deal as to lightness and stiffness, they make it all bear prodigious quantities of swedish turnips; and on them pigs, sheep, and cattle all equally thrive. I did not observe a single poor miserable animal in the whole county.

To conclude an account of Suffolk and not to sing the praises of Bury St. Edmund's would offend every creature of Suffolk birth; even at Ipswich, when I was praising *that place*, the very people of that town asked me if I did not think Bury St. Edmund's the nicest town in the world. Meet them wherever you will, they have all the same boast; and indeed, as a town *in itself*, it is the neatest place that ever was seen. It is airy, it has several fine open places in it, and it has the remains of the famous abbey walls and the abbey gate entire; and it is so clean and so neat that nothing can equal it in that respect. It was a favourite spot in ancient times; greatly endowed with monasteries and hospitals. Besides the famous Benedictine Abbey, there was once a college and a friary; and as to the abbey itself, it was one of the greatest in the kingdom; and was so ancient as to have been founded only about forty years after the landing of Saint Austin in Kent. The land all round about it is good; and the soil is of that nature as not to produce much dirt at any time of the year; but the country about it is *flat*, and not of that beautiful variety that we find at Ipswich.

After all, what is the reflection now called for? It is that this fine county, for which nature has done all that she can do, soil, climate, sea-ports, people; everything that can be done, and an internal government, civil and ecclesiastical, the most complete in the world, wanting nothing but to *be let alone*, to make every soul in it as happy as people can be upon earth; the peace provided for by the county rates; property protected by the law of the land; the poor provided for by the poor-rates; religion provided for by the tithes and the church-rates; easy and safe conveyance provided for by the highway-rates; extraordinary danger provided against by the militia-rates; a complete government in itself; *but having to pay a portion of sixty millions a year in taxes over and above all this ; and that, too, on account of wars carried on, not for the defence of England ;* not for the upholding of *English liberty and happiness*, but for the purpose of crushing liberty and happiness in other countries; and all this because, and only because, a septennial parliament has deprived the people of their rights.

That which we *admire* most is not always that which would be *our choice*. One might imagine that after all that I have said about this fine county, I should certainly prefer it as a place of residence. I should not, however: my choice has been always very much divided between the woods of Sussex and the downs of Wiltshire. I should not like to be compelled to decide: but if I were compelled, I do believe that I should fix on some vale in Wiltshire. Water meadows at the bottom, corn-land going up towards the hills, those hills being *down land*, and a farmhouse, in a clump of trees, in some little cross vale between the hills, sheltered on every side but the south. In short, if Mr. Bennet would give me a farm, the house of which lies on the right-hand side of the road going from Salisbury to Warminster, in the parish of Norton Bovant, just before you enter that village; if he would but be so good as to do that, I would freely give up all the rest of the world to the possession of whoever may get hold of it. I have hinted this to him once or twice before, but I am sorry to say that he turns a deaf ear to my hinting.

CAMBRIDGE,
28 *March* 1830.

I went from Hargham to Lynn on Tuesday, the 23rd; but owing to the disappointment at Thetford, everything was deranged. It was market-day at Lynn, but no preparations of any sort had been made, and no notification given. I there fore resolved, after staying at Lynn on Wednesday, to make a short tour, and to come back to it again. This tour was to take in Ely, Cambridge, St. Ives, Stamford, Peterborough, Wisbeach, and was to bring me back to Lynn, after a very busy ten days. I was particularly desirous to have a little political preaching at *Ely*, the place where the flogging of the English local militia under a guard of German bayonets cost me so dear.

I got there about noon on Thursday the 25th, being market-day; but I had been apprised even before I left Lynn that no place had been provided for my accommodation. A gentleman at Lynn gave me the name of one at Ely who, as he thought, would be glad of an opportunity of pointing out a proper place, and of speaking about it; but just before I set off from Lynn, I received a notification from this gentleman that he could do nothing in the matter. I knew that Ely was a small place, but I was determined to go and see the spot where the militia-men were flogged, and also determined to find some opportunity or other of relating that story as publicly as I could at Ely, and of describing the *tail* of the story; of which I will speak presently. Arrived at Ely, I first walked round the beautiful cathedral, that honour to our Catholic forefathers, and that standing disgrace to our Protestant selves. It is impossible to look at that magnificent pile without *feeling* that we are a fallen race of men. The cathedral would, leaving out the palace of the bishop and the houses of the dean, canons, and prebendaries, weigh more, if it were put into a scale, than all the houses in the town, and all the houses for a mile round the neighbourhood if you exclude the remains of the ancient monasteries. You have only to open your eyes to be convinced that England must have been a far greater and more wealthy country in those days than it is in these days. The hundreds of thousands of loads of stone, of which this cathedral and the monasteries in the neighbourhood were built, must all have been brought by sea from distant parts of the kingdom. These foundations were laid more than a thousand years ago; and yet there are vagabonds who have the impudence to say that it is the Protestant religion that has made England a great country.

Ely is what one may call a miserable little town: very prettily situated, but poor and mean. Everything seems to be on the decline, as, indeed, is the case everywhere, where the clergy are the masters. They say that this bishop has an income of £18,000 a year. He and the dean and chapter are the owners of all the land and tithes for a great distance round about in this beautiful and most productive part of the country; and yet this famous building, the cathedral, is in a state of disgraceful irrepair and disfigurement. The great and magnificent windows to the east have been shortened at the bottom, and the space plastered up with brick and mortar, in a very slovenly manner, for the purpose of saving the expense of keeping the glass in repair. Great numbers of the windows in the upper part of the building have been partly closed up in the same manner, and others quite closed up. One door-way, which apparently had stood in need of repair, has been rebuilt in modern style, because it was cheaper; and the churchyard contained a flock of sheep acting as vergers for those who live upon the immense income, not a penny of which ought to be expended upon themselves while any part of this beautiful building is in a state of irrepair. This cathedral was erected " to the honour of God and the Holy Church." My daughters went to the service in the afternoon, in the choir of which they saw God honoured by the presence of *two old men*, forming the whole of the congregation. I dare say that in Catholic times five thousand people at a time have been assembled in this church. The cathedral and town stand upon a little hill, about three miles in circumference, raised up, as it were, for the purpose, amidst the rich fen land by which the hill is surrounded, and I dare say that the town formerly consisted of houses built over a great part of this hill, and of probably from fifty to a hundred thousand people. The people do not now exceed above four thousand, including the bed-ridden and the babies.

Having no place provided for lecturing, and knowing no single soul in the place, I was thrown upon my own resources. The first thing I did was to walk up through the market, which contained much more than an audience sufficient for me; but leaving the market people to carry on their affairs, I picked up a sort of labouring man, asked him if he recollected when the local militia-men were flogged under the guard of the Germans; and receiving an answer in the affirmative, I asked him to go and show me the spot, which he did; he showed me a little common along which the men had been marched, and into a piece of pasture-land, where he put his foot upon the identical spot where the flogging had been executed. On that spot I told him what I had suffered for expressing my indignation at that flogging. I told him that a large sum of English money was now every year sent abroad to furnish half pay and allowances to the officers of those German troops, and to maintain the widows and children of such of them as were dead; and I added, "You have to work to help to pay that money; part of the taxes which you pay on your malt, hops, beer, leather, soap, candles, tobacco, tea, sugar, and everything else, goes abroad every year to pay these people: it has thus been going abroad ever since the peace; and it will thus go abroad for the rest of your life, if this system of managing the nation's affairs continue; and I told him that about one million seven hundred thousand pounds had been sent abroad on this account *since the peace*.

When I opened I found that this man was willing to open too; and he uttered sentiments that would have convinced me, if I had not before been convinced of the fact, that there are very few, even amongst the labourers, who do not clearly understand the cause of their ruin. I discovered that there were two Ely men flogged upon that occasion, and that one of them was still alive and residing near the town. I sent for this man, who came to me in the evening when he had done his work, and who told me that he had lived seven years with the same master when he was flogged, and was bailiff or head man to his master. He has now a wife and several children; is a very nice-looking, and appears to be a hard-working, man, and to bear an excellent character.

But how was I to harangue? For I was determined not to quit Ely without something of that sort. I told this labouring man who showed me the flogging spot my name, which seemed to surprise him very much, for he had heard of me before. After I had returned to my inn I walked back again through the market amongst the farmers; then went to an inn that looked out upon the market-place, went into an upstairs room, threw up the sash, and sat down at the window, and looked out upon the market. Little groups soon collected to survey me while I sat in a very unconcerned attitude. The farmers had dined, or I should have found out the most numerous assemblage, and have dined with them. The next best thing was to go and sit down in the room where they usually dropped into drink after dinner; and as they nearly all smoke, to take a pipe with them. This, therefore, I did; and after a time we began to talk.

The room was too small to contain a twentieth part of the people that would have come in if they could. It was hot to suffocation; but, nevertheless, I related to them the account of the flogging, and of my persecution on that account; and I related to them the account above stated with regard to the English money now sent to the Germans, at which they appeared to be utterly astonished. I had not time sufficient for a lecture, but I explained to them briefly the real cause of the distress which prevailed; I warned the farmers particularly against the consequences of hoping that this distress would remove itself. I portrayed to them the effects of the taxes; and showed them that we owe this enormous burden to the want of being fairly represented in the parliament. Above all things, I did that which I never fail to do, showed them the absurdity of grumbling at the six millions a year given in relief to the poor, while they were silent and seemed to think nothing of the sixty millions of taxes collected by the government at London, and I asked them how any man of property could have the impudence to call upon the labouring man to serve in the militia, and to deny that that labouring man had, in case of need, a clear right to a share of the produce of the land. I explained to them how the poor were originally relieved; told them that the revenues of the livings, which had their foundation in *charity*, were divided amongst the poor. The demands for repair of the churches and the clergy themselves; I explained to them how church-rates and poor-rates came to be introduced; how the burden of maintaining the poor came to be thrown upon the people at large; how the nation had sunk by degrees ever since the event called the Reformation; and pointing towards the cathedral I said, "Can you believe, gentlemen, that when that magnificent pile was reared, and when all the fine monasteries, hospitals, schools, and other resorts of piety and charity existed in this town and neighbourhood; can you believe that Ely was the miserable little place that it now is; and that that England which had never heard of the name of *pauper* contained the crowds of miserable creatures that it now contains, some starving at stone-cracking by the way-side, and others drawing loaded waggons on that way?"

A young man in the room (I having come to a pause) said, "But, sir, were there no poor in Catholic times?" "Yes," said I, "to be sure there were. The Scripture says that the poor shall never cease out of the land; and there are five hundred texts of Scripture enjoining on all men to be good and kind to the poor. It is necessary to the existence of civil society that there should be poor. Men have two motives to industry and care in all the walks of life: one to acquire wealth; but the other and stronger to avoid poverty. If there were no poverty, there would be no industry, no enterprise. But this poverty is not to be made a punishment unjustly severe. Idleness, extravagance, are offences against morality; but they are not offences of that heinous nature to justify the infliction of starvation by way of punishment. It is, therefore, the duty of every man that is able; it is particularly the duty of every government, and it was a duty faithfully executed by the Catholic church, to take care that no human being should perish for want in a land of plenty; and to take care, too, that no one should be deficient of a sufficiency of food and raiment, not only to sustain life, but also to sustain health." The young man said: "I thank you, sir; I am answered."

I strongly advised the farmers to be well with their work-people; for that, unless their flocks were as safe in their fields as their bodies were in their beds, their lives must be lives of misery; that if their stacks and barns were not places of as safe deposit for their corn as their drawers were for their money, the life of the farmer was the most wretched upon earth, in place of being the most pleasant, as it ought to be.

BOSTON,
Friday, 9 April 1830.

Quitting Cambridge and Dr. Chafy and Serjeant Frere on Monday, the 29th of March, I arrived at St. Ives, in Huntingdon-shire, about one o'clock in the day. In the evening I harangued to about 200 persons, principally farmers, in a wheelwright's shop, that being the only *safe* place in the town of sufficient dimensions and sufficiently strong. It was market-day; and this is a great cattle-market. As I was not to be at Stamford in Lincolnshire till the 31st, I went from St. Ives to my friend Mr. Wells's, near Huntingdon, and remained there till the 31st in the morning, employing the evening of the 30th in going to Chatteris, in the Isle of Ely, and there addressing a good large company of farmers.

On the 31st I went to Stamford, and in the evening spoke to about 200 farmers and others, in a large room in a very fine and excellent inn, called Standwell's Hotel, which is, with few exceptions, the nicest inn that I have ever been in. On the 1st of April I harangued here again, and had amongst my auditors some most agreeable, intelligent, and public-spirited yeomen from the little county of Rutland, who made, respecting the *seat in parliament*, the details of the purport of which I communicated to my readers in the last Register.

On the 2nd of April I met my audience in the playhouse at Peterborough; and though it had snowed all day, and was very wet and sloppy, I had a good large audience; and I did not let this opportunity pass without telling my hearers of the part that their *good* neighbour, Lord Fitzwilliam, had acted with regard to the *French war*, with regard to *Burke and his pension ;* with regard to the *dungeoning law*, which drove me across the Atlantic in 1817, and with regard to the putting into the present parliament, aye, and for that very town, that very Lawyer Scarlett whose state prosecutions are now become so famous. " Never," said I, " did I say that behind a man's back that I would not say to his face. I wish I had his face before me: but I am here as near to it as I can get: I am before the face of his friends: here, therefore, I will say what I think of him." When I had described his conduct and given my opinion on it, many applauded, and not one expressed disapprobation.

On the 3rd, I speechified at Wisbeach, in the playhouse, to about 220 people, I think it was; and that same night went to sleep at a friend's (a total stranger to me, however) at St. Edmund's, in the heart of the Fens. I stayed there on the 4th (Sunday), the morning of which brought a hard frost: ice an inch thick, and the total destruction of the apricot blossoms.

After passing Sunday and the greater part of Monday (the 5th) at St. Edmund's, where my daughters and myself received the greatest kindness and attention, we went, on Monday afternoon, to Crowland, where we were most kindly lodged and entertained at the houses of two gentlemen, to whom also we were personally perfect strangers; and in the evening I addressed a very large assemblage of most respectable farmers and others, in this once famous town. There was another hard frost on the Monday morning; just, as it were, to *finish* the apricot bloom.

On the 6th I went to Lynn, and on that evening and on the evening of the 7th, I spoke to about 300 people in the playhouse. And here there was more *interruption* than I have ever met with at any other place. This town, though containing as good and kind friends as I have met with in any other; and though the people are generally as good, contains also, apparently, a large proportion of *dead weight,* the offspring, most likely, of the *rottenness of the borough.* Two or three, or even *one* man, may, if not tossed out at once, disturb and interrupt everything in a case where constant attention to *fact* and *argument* is requisite to insure utility to the meeting. There were but *three* here; and though they were finally silenced, it was not without great loss of time, great noise and hubbub. Two, I was told, were *dead-weight* men, and one a sort of *higgling merchant.*

On the 8th I went to Holbeach, in this noble county of Lincoln; and gracious God! what a *contrast* with the scene at Lynn! I knew not a soul in the place. Mr. Fields, a bookseller and printer, had invited me by letter, and had, in the nicest and most unostentatious manner, made all the preparations. Holbeach lies in the midst of some of the richest land in the world; a small market-town, but a parish more than twenty miles across, larger, I believe, than the county of Rutland, produced an audience (in a very nice room, with seats prepared) of 178, apparently all wealthy farmers, and men in that rank of life; and an audience so *deeply* attentive to the dry matters on which I had to address it I have very seldom met with. I was delighted with Holbeach; a neat little town; a most beautiful church with a spire, like that of " the man of Ross, pointing to the skies;" gardens very pretty; fruit-trees in abundance, with blossom-buds ready to burst; and land dark in colour, and as fine in substance as flour, as fine as if sifted through one of the sieves with which we get the dust out of the clover seed; and when cut deep down into with a spade, precisely as to substance like a piece of hard butter; yet nowhere is the *distress* greater than here. I walked on from Holbeach, six miles, towards Boston; and seeing the fatness of the land, and the fine grass and the never-ending sheep lying about like *fat hogs* stretched in the sun, and seeing the abject state of the labouring people, I could not help exclaiming, " God has given us the best country in the world; our brave and wise and virtuous fathers, who built all these magnificent churches, gave us the best government in the world, and we, their cowardly and foolish and profligate sons, have made this once-paradise what we now behold!"

I arrived at Boston (where I am now writing) to-day (Friday, 9th April) about ten o'clock. I must arrive at Louth before I can say *precisely* what my future route will be. There is an immense fair at Lincoln next week; and a friend has been *here* to point out the proper days to be there; as, however, this Register will not come from the press until after I shall have had an opportunity of writing something at Louth, time enough to be inserted in it, I will here go back, and speak of the country that I have travelled over since I left Cambridge on the 29th of March.

From Cambridge to St. Ives the land is generally in open unfenced fields, and some common fields; generally stiff land, and some of it not very good, and wheat in many places looking rather thin. From St. Ives to Chatteris (which last is in the Isle of Ely) the land is better, particularly as you approach the latter place. From Chatteris I came back to Huntingdon, and once more saw its beautiful meadows, of which I spoke when I went thither in 1823. From Huntingdon, through Stilton, to Stamford (the two last in Lincolnshire), is a country of rich arable land and grass fields, and of beautiful meadows. The enclosures are very large, the soil red, with a whitish stone below; very much like the soil at and near Ross in Herefordshire, and like that near Coventry and Warwick. Here, as all over this country, everlasting fine sheep. The houses all along here are built of the stone of the country: you seldom see brick. The churches are large, lofty, and fine, and give proof that the country was formerly much more populous than it is now, and that the people had a vast deal more of wealth in their hands and at their own disposal. There are three beautiful churches at Stamford, not less, I dare say, than three [*quære*] hundred years old; but two of them (I did not go to the other) are as perfect as when just finished, except as to the *images*, most of which have been destroyed by the ungrateful Protestant barbarians, of different sorts, but some of which (*out of the reach* of their ruthless hands) are still in the niches.

From Stamford to Peterborough is a country of the same description, with the additional beauty of *woods* here and there, and with meadows just like those at Huntingdon, and not surpassed by those on the Severn near Worcester nor by those on the Avon at Tewkesbury. The cathedral at Peterborough is exquisitely beautiful, and I have great pleasure in saying that, contrary to the *more magnificent* pile at Ely, it is kept in good order; the bishop (Herbert March) residing a good deal on the spot; and though he *did* write a pamphlet to justify and urge on the war, the ruinous war, and though he *did* get a *pension* for it, he is, they told me, very good to the poor people. My daughters had a great desire to see, and I had a great desire they should see, the burial-place of that ill-used, that savagely treated woman, and that honour to woman-kind, Catherine.

queen of the ferocious tyrant, Henry VIII. To the infamy of that ruffian and the shame of after ages, there is no *monument* to record her virtues and her sufferings; and the remains of this daughter of the wise Ferdinand and of the generous Isabella, who sold her jewels to enable Columbus to discover the new world, lie under the floor of the cathedral, commemorated by a short inscription on a plate of brass. All men, Protestants or not Protestants, feel as I feel upon this subject; search the *hearts* of the bishop and of his dean and chapter, and these feelings are there; but to do *justice* to the memory of this illustrious victim of tyranny would be to cast a reflection on that event, to which they owe their rich possessions, and at the same time to suggest ideas not very favourable to the descendants of those who divided amongst them the plunder of the people arising out of that event, and which descendants are their patrons, and give them what they possess. From this cause, and no other, it is that the memory of the virtuous Catherine is unblazoned, while that of the tyrannical, the cruel, and the immoral Elizabeth is recorded with all possible veneration, and all possible varnishing-over of her disgusting amours and endless crimes.

They relate at Peterborough that the same sexton who buried Queen Catherine, also buried here Mary, Queen of Scots. The remains of the latter, of very questionable virtue, or rather of unquestionable vice, were removed to Westminster Abbey by her son, James I.; but those of the virtuous queen were suffered to remain unhonoured! Good God! what injustice, what a want of principle, what hostility to all virtuous feeling, has not been the fruit of this Protestant Reformation; what plunder, what disgrace to England, what shame, what misery, has that event not produced! There is nothing that I address to my hearers with more visible effect than a statement of *the manner in which the poor-rates and the church-rates came.* This, of course, includes an account of *how the poor were relieved in Catholic times.* To the far greater part of people this is information *wholly new;* they are *deeply interested* in it; and the impression is very great. Always before we part, Tom Cranmer's church receives a considerable blow.

There is in the cathedral a very ancient monument, made to commemorate, they say, the murder of the abbot and his monks by the Danes. Its date is the year 870. Almost all the cathedrals were, it appears, originally churches of monasteries. That of Winchester and several others certainly were. There has lately died in the garden of the bishop's palace a tortoise that had been *there* more, they say, than two hundred years; a fact very likely to be known; because, at the end of thirty or forty, people would begin to talk about it as something remarkable; and thus the record would be handed down from father to son.

From Peterborough to Wisbeach the road, for the most part, lies through the *Fens*, and here we passed through the village of Thorney where there was a famous abbey, which, together with its valuable domain, was given by the savage tyrant Henry VIII. to John Lord Russell (made a lord by that tyrant), the founder of the family of that name. This man got also the abbey and estate at Woburn; the priory and its estate at Tavistock; and in the next reign he got Covent Garden and other parts adjoining; together with other things, all then *public property*. A history, a *true history* of this family (which I hope I shall find time to write) would be a most valuable thing. It would be a nice little specimen of the way in which these families became possessed of a great part of their estates. It would show how the poor-rates and the church-rates came. It would set the whole nation *right* at once. Some years ago I had a set of the *Encyclopædia Britannica* (Scotch), which contained an account of every other *great family* in the kingdom; but I could find in it no account of *this* family, either under the word Russell or the word Bedford. I got into a passion with the book because it contained no account of the mode of raising the birch-tree; and it was sold to *a son* (as I was told) of Mr. Alderman Heygate; and if that gentleman look into the book, he will find what I say to be true; but if I should be in error about this, perhaps he will have the goodness to let me know it. I shall be obliged to any one to point me out any printed account of this family; and particularly to tell me where I can get an old folio, containing (amongst other things) Bulstrode's argument and narrative in justification of the sentence and execution of Lord William Russell in the reign of Charles II. It is impossible to look at the now miserable village of Thorney and to think of its once splendid abbey; it is impossible to look at the *twenty thousand acres* of land around, covered with fat sheep, or bearing six quarters of wheat or ten of oats to the acre, without any manure; it is impossible to think of these without feeling a desire that the whole nation should know all about the *surprising merits* of the possessors.

Wisbeach, lying further up the arm of the sea than Lynn, is, like the latter, a little town of commerce, chiefly engaged in exporting to the south *the corn* that grows in this productive country. It is a good solid town, though not handsome, and has a large market, particularly for corn.

To Crowland I went, as before stated, from Wisbeach, staying two nights at St. Edmund's. Here I was in the heart of the Fens. The whole country as *level* as the table on which I am now writing. The horizon like the sea in a dead calm: you see the morning sun come up just as at sea; and see it go down over the rim in just the same way as at sea in a calm. The land covered with beautiful grass, with sheep lying about upon it as fat as hogs stretched out sleeping in a stye. The kind and polite friends with whom we were lodged had a very neat garden and fine young orchard. Everything grows well here: earth without a stone so big as a pin's head; grass as thick as it can grow on the ground; immense bowling-greens separated by ditches; and not the sign of dock or thistle or other weed to be seen. What a contrast between these and the heath-covered sand-hills of Surrey, amongst which I was born! Yet the labourers, who spuddle about the ground in the little *dips* between those sand-hills, are better off than those that exist in this fat of the land. *Here* the grasping system takes *all* away, because it has the means of coming at the value of all: *there*, the poor man enjoys *something*, because he is thought too poor to have anything: he is there allowed to have what is deemed *worth nothing ;* but here, where every inch is valuable, not one inch is he permitted to enjoy.

At Crowland also (still in the Fens) was a great and rich *abbey*, a good part of the magnificent ruins of the church of which are still standing, one corner or part of it being used as the *parish church*, by the worms, which have crept out of the dead bodies of those who lived in the days of the founders;

> " And wond'ring man could want the larger pile,
> Exult, and claim the corner with a smile."

They tell you that all the country at and near Crowland was a mere swamp, a mere bog, *bearing nothing*, bearing nothing worth naming, until the *modern drainings* took place! The thing called the " Reformation " has lied common sense out of men's minds. So *likely* a thing to choose a barren swamp whereon, or wherein, to make the site of an abbey, and of a Benedictine abbey too! It has been always observed that the monks took care to choose for their places of abode pleasant spots, surrounded by productive land. The likeliest thing in the world for these monks to choose a swamp for their dwelling-place, surrounded by land that produced nothing good! The thing gives the lie to itself: and it is impossible to reject the belief that these Fens were as productive of corn and meat a thousand years ago, and more so, than they are at this hour. There is a curious triangular bridge here, on one part of which stands the statue of one of the ancient kings. It is all of great age; and everything shows that Crowland was a place of importance in the earliest times.

From Crowland to Lynn, through Thorney and Wisbeach, is all Fens, well besprinkled, formerly with monasteries of various descriptions, and still well set with magnificent churches. From Lynn to Holbeach you get out of the real Fens and into the land that I attempted to describe when a few pages back I was speaking of Holbeach. I say attempted; for I defy tongue or pen to make the description adequate to the matter: to know what the thing is you must *see* it. The same land continues all the way on to Boston: endless grass and endless fat sheep: not a stone, not a weed.

BOSTON,
Sunday, 11 *April,* 1830.

Last night I made a speech at the play-house to an audience whose appearance was sufficient to fill me with pride. I had given notice that I should perform *on Friday,* overlooking the circumstance that it was Good Friday. In apologising for this inadvertence, I took occasion to observe that, even if I had persevered, the clergy of the church could have nothing to object, seeing that they were now silent while a bill was passing in parliament to put *Jews* on a level with *Christians;* to enable Jews, the blasphemers of the Redeemer, to sit on the bench, to sit in both Houses of Parliament, to sit in council with the king, and to be kings of England, if entitled to the crown, which, by possibility, they might become, if this bill were to pass; that to this bill *the clergy had offered no opposition :* and that, therefore, how could they hold sacred the anniversary appointed to commemorate the crucifixion of Christ by the hands of the blaspheming and bloody Jews? That, at any rate, if this bill passed; if those who called Jesus Christ an *impostor* were thus declared to be *as good* as those who adored him, there was not, I hoped, a man in the kingdom who would pretend that it would be just to compel the people to pay tithes, and fees, and offerings to men for *teaching Christianity.* This was a *clincher ;* and as such it was received.

This morning I went out at six, looked at the town, walked three miles on the road to Spilsby, and back to breakfast at nine. Boston (*bos* is Latin for *ox*) though not above a fourth or fifth part of the size of its *daughter* in New England, which got its name, I dare say, from some persecuted native of this place, who had quitted England and all her wealth and all her glories to preserve that *freedom* which was still more dear to him; though not a town like New Boston, and though little to what it formerly was, when agricultural produce was the great staple of the kingdom and the great subject of foreign exchange, is, nevertheless, a very fine town; good houses, good shops, pretty gardens about it, a fine open place, nearly equal to that of Nottingham, in the middle of it a river and a canal passing through it, each crossed by a handsome and substantial bridge, a fine market for sheep, cattle, and pigs, and another for meat, butter, and fish; and being, like Lynn, a great place for the export of corn and flour, and having many fine mills, it is altogether a town of very considerable importance; and, which is not to be overlooked, inhabited by people none of whom appear to be in misery.

The great pride and glory of the Bostonians is *their church* which is, I think, 400 feet long, 90 feet wide, and has a towei (or steeple, as they call it) 300 feet high, which is both a landmark and a sea-mark. To describe the richness, the magnificence, the symmetry, the exquisite beauty of this pile is wholly out of my power. It is impossible to look at it without feeling, first, admiration and reverence and gratitude to the memory of our fathers who reared it; and next, indignation at those who affect to believe, and contempt for those who do believe, that when this pile was reared the age was *dark*, the people rude and ignorant, and the country *destitute of wealth* and *thinly peopled*. Look at this church, then look at the heaps of white rubbish that the parsons have lately stuck up under the "*New-church Act*," and which, after having been built with money forced from the nation by odious taxes, they have stuffed full of *locked-up pens*, called *pews*, which they let for money, as cattle and sheep and pig-pens are let at fairs and markets; nay, after having looked at this work of the "*dark* ages," look at that great, heavy, ugly, unmeaning mass of stone called St. Paul's, which an American friend of mine, who came to London from Falmouth and had seen the cathedrals at Exeter and Salisbury, swore to me that, when he first saw it, he was at a loss to guess whether it were a *court-house* or a *gaol*:

after looking at Boston church, go and look at that great, gloomy lump, created by a Protestant Parliament, and by taxes wrung by force from the whole nation; and then say which is the age really meriting the epithet *dark*.

St. Botolph, to whom this church is dedicated, while he (if saints see and hear what is passing on earth) must lament that the piety-inspiring mass has been, in this noble edifice, supplanted by the monotonous hummings of an oaken hutch, has not the mortification to see his church treated in a manner as if the new possessors sighed for the hour of its destruction. It is taken great care of; and though it has cruelly suffered from *Protestant repairs;* though the images are gone and the stained glass; and though the glazing is now in squares instead of lozenges; though the nave is stuffed with *pens* called pews; and though other changes have taken place detracting from the beauty of the edifice, great care is taken of it as it now is, and the inside is not disfigured and disgraced by a *gallery*, that great and characteristic mark of Protestant taste, which, as nearly as may be, makes a church like a play-house. Saint Botolph (on the supposition before mentioned) has the satisfaction to see that the base of his celebrated church is surrounded by an iron fence, to keep from it all offensive and corroding matter, which is so disgusting to the sight round the magnificent piles at Norwich, Ely and other places; that the churchyard, and all appertaining to it, are kept in the neatest and most respectable state; that no money has been spared for these purposes; that here the eye tells the heart that gratitude towards the fathers of the Bostonians is not extinguished in the breasts of their sons; and this the saint will know that he owes to the circumstances that the parish is a poor vicarage, and that the care of his church is in the hands of *the industrious people*, and not in those of a fat and luxurious dean and chapter, wallowing in wealth derived from the people's labour.

HORNCASTLE,
12 *April*.

A fine, soft, showery morning saw us out of Boston, carrying with us the most pleasing reflections as to our reception and treatment there by numerous persons, none of whom we had ever seen before. The face of the country, for about half the way, the soil, the grass, the endless sheep, the thickly-scattered and magnificent churches, continue as on the other side of Boston; but after that we got out of the low and level land.

At Sibsey, a pretty village five miles from Boston, we saw for the first time since we left Peterborough land rising above the level of the horizon; and, not having seen such a thing for so long, it had struck my daughters, who overtook me on the road (I having walked on from Boston), that the sight had an affect like that produced by the first *sight of land* after a voyage across the Atlantic.

We now soon got into a country of hedges and dry land and gravel and clay and stones; the land not bad, however; pretty much like that of Sussex, lying between the forest part and the South Downs. A good proportion of woodland also; and just before we got to Horncastle we passed the park of that Mr. Dymock who is called the " Champion of England," and to whom it is said hereabouts that we pay out of the taxes eight thousand pounds a year! This never can be, to be sure; but if we pay him only a hundred a year, I will lay down my *glove* against that of the " Champion," that we do not pay him even *that* for five years longer.

It is curious that the moment you get out of the *rich land* the churches become *smaller, mean*, and with scarcely anything in the way of *tower* or *steeple*. This town is seated in the middle of a large valley, not, however, remarkable for anything of peculiar value or beauty; a purely agricultural town; well built, and not mean in any part of it. It is a great rendezvous for horses and cattle and sheep-dealers, and for those who sell these; and, accordingly, it suffers severely from the loss of the small paper-money.

HORNCASTLE,
13 *April, Morning.*

I made a speech last evening to from 130 to 150, almost all farmers, and most men of apparent wealth to a certain extent. I have seldom been better pleased with my audience. It is not the clapping and huzzaing that I value so much as the *silent attention*, the *earnest look* at me from *all eyes* at once, and then when the point is concluded, the *look and nod at each other*, as if the parties were saying, " *Think of that !* " And of these I had a great deal at Horncastle. They say that there are *a hundred parish churches within six miles of this town.* I dare say that there was one farmer from almost every one of these parishes. This is sowing the seeds of truth in a very sure manner: it is not scattering broad-cast; it is really *drilling the country.*

There is one deficiency, and that, with me, a great one, throughout this country of corn and grass and oxen and sheep, that I have come over during the last three weeks; namely, the want of *singing birds*. We are now just in that season when they sing most. Here, in all this country, I have seen and heard only about four sky-larks, and not one other singing bird of any description, and of the small birds that do not sing I have seen only one *yellowhammer*, and it was perched on the rail of a pound between Boston and Sibsey. Oh! the thousands of linnets all singing together on one tree in the sand-hills of Surrey! Oh! the carolling in the coppices and the dingles of Hampshire and Sussex and Kent! At this moment (5 o'clock in the morning) the groves at Barn-Elm are echoing with the warblings of thousands upon thousands of birds. The *thrush* begins a little before it is light; next the *blackbird*; next the *larks* begin to rise; all the rest begin the moment the sun gives the signal; and from the hedges, the bushes, from the middle and the topmost twigs of the trees, comes the singing of endless variety; from the long dead grass comes the sound of the sweet and soft voice of the *white-throat* or *nettle-tom*, while the loud and merry song of the *lark* (the songster himself out of sight) seems to descend from the skies. Milton, in his description of paradise, has not omitted the " song of earliest birds." However, everything taken together, here, in Lincolnshire, are more good things than man could have had the conscience to *ask* of God.

And now, if I had time and room to describe the state of *men's affairs* in the country through which I have passed, I should show that the people at Westminster would have known how to turn paradise itself into hell. I must, however, defer this until my next, when I shall have been at Hull and Lincoln, and have had a view of the whole of this rich and fine country. In the meanwhile, however, I cannot help congratulating that *sensible* fellow, Wilmot Horton, and his co-operator, Burdett, that emigration is going on at a swimming rate. Thousands are going, and that, too, *without mortgaging the poor-rates*. But, *sensible* fellows! it is not the *aged*, the *halt*, the *ailing*; it is not the *paupers* that are going; but men with from £200 to £2000 in their pocket! This very year, from two to five millions of pounds sterling will actually be carried *from England* to the United States. The Scotch, who have money to pay their passages, go to New York; those who have none get carried to Canada, that they may thence get into the United States. I will inquire, one of these days, what *right* Burdett has to live in England more than those whom he proposes to send away.

Here we are at the end of a pretty decent trip since we left Boston. The next place on our way to Hull was Horncastle, where I preached politics, in the playhouse, to a most respectable body of farmers, who had come in the wet to meet me. Mr. John Peniston, who had invited me to stop there, behaved in a very obliging manner, and made all things very pleasant.

The country *from* Boston continued, as I said before, flat for about half the way to Horncastle, and we then began to see the high land. From Horncastle I set off two hours before the carriage, and going through a very pretty village called Ashby, got to another at the foot of a hill, which, they say, forms part of the *wolds ;* that is, a ridge of hills. This second village is called Scamblesby. The vale in which it lies is very fine land. A hazel mould, rich and light too. I saw a man here ploughing for barley, after turnips, with *one horse :* the horse did not seem to work hard, and the man was *singing :* I need not say that he was young; and I dare say he had the good sense to keep his legs under another man's table, and to stretch his body on another man's bed.

This is a very fine *corn country :* chalk at bottom: stony near the surface in some places: here and there a chalk-pit in the hills: the shape of the ground somewhat like that of the broadest valleys in Wiltshire; but the fields not without fences as they are there: fields from fifteen to forty acres: the hills not downs, as in Wiltshire; but cultivated all over. The houses white and thatched, as they are in all chalk countries. The valley at Scamblesby has a little rivulet running down it, just as in all the chalk countries. The land continues nearly the same to Louth, which lies in a deep dell, with beautiful pastures on the surrounding hills, like those that I once admired at Shaftesbury, in Dorsetshire, and like that near St. Austle, in Cornwall, which I described in 1808.

At Louth the wise corporation had *refused* to let us have the play-house; but my friends had prepared a very good place; and I had an opportunity of addressing crowded audiences two nights running. At no place have I been better pleased than at Louth. Mr. Paddison, solicitor, a young gentleman whom I had the honour to know slightly before, and to know whom, whether

I estimate by character or by talent, would be an honour to any man, was particularly attentive to us. Mr. Naull, ironmonger, who had had the battle to fight for me for twenty years, expressed his exultation at my triumph, in a manner that showed that he justly participated with me. I breakfasted, at Mr. Naull's, with a gentleman 88 or 89 years of age, whose joy at shaking me by the hand was excessive. "Ah!" said he, "where are *now* those savages who, at Hull, threatened to kill me for raising my voice against this system?" This is a very fine town, and has a beautiful church, nearly equal to that at Boston.

We left Louth on the morning of Thursday the 15th, and got to Barton-on-the-Humber by about noon, over a very fine country, large fields, fine pastures, flocks of those great sheep, of from 200 to 1000 in a flock; and here at Barton we arrived at the northern point of this noble county, having never seen one single acre of waste land, and not one acre that would be called bad land in the south of England. The *wolds*, or highlands, lie away to our right from Horncastle to near Barton; and on the other side of the wolds lie the *marshes of Lincolnshire*, which extend along the coast, from Boston to the mouth of the Humber, on the bank of which we were at Barton, Hull being on the opposite side of the river, which is here about five miles wide, and which we had to cross in a steam-boat.

But let me not forget Great Grimsby, at which we changed horses, and breakfasted, in our way from Louth to Barton. "What the devil!" the reader will say, "should you want to recollect *that* place for? Why do you want not to forget that sink of corruption? What could you find there to be snatched from everlasting oblivion, except for the purpose of being execrated?" I did, however, find something there worthy of being made known not only to every man in England but to every man in the world; and not to mention it here would be to be guilty of the greatest injustice.

To my surprise I found a good many people assembled at the inn-door, evidently expecting my arrival. While breakfast was preparing, I wished to speak to the bookseller of the place, if there were one, and to give him a list of my books and writings, that he might place it in his shop. When he came I was surprised to find that he had it already, and that he, occasionally, sold my books. Upon my asking him how he got it, he said that it was brought down from London and given to him by a Mr. Plaskitt, who, he said, had all my writings, and who, he said, he was sure would be very glad to see me; but that he lived above a mile from the town. A messenger, however, had gone off to carry the news, and Mr. Plaskitt arrived before we had done breakfast, bringing with him a son and a daughter. And from the lips of this gentleman, a man of as kind and benevolent appearance and manners as I ever beheld in my life, I had the following facts; namely, "that one of his sons sailed for New York some years ago; that the ship was cast away on the shores of Long Island; that the captain, crew, and passengers all perished; that the wrecked vessel was taken possession of by people on the coast; that his son had a watch in his trunk, or chest, a purse with fourteen shillings in it, and divers articles of wearing apparel; that the Americans, who searched the wreck, *sent all these articles safely to England to him;*" "and," said he, "I keep the purse and the money at home, and *here is the watch in my pocket!*"

It would have been worth the expense of coming from London to Grimsby if for nothing but to learn this fact, which I record, not only in justice to the free people of America, and particularly in justice to my late neighbours in Long Island, but in justice to the character of mankind. I publish it as something to counter-balance the conduct of the atrocious monsters who plunder the wrecks on the coast of Cornwall, and, as I am told, on the coasts here in the east of the island.

Away go, then, all the accusations upon the character of the Yankees. People may call them *sharp, cunning, over-reaching;* and when they have exhausted the vocabulary of their abuse, the answer is found in this one fact, stated by Mr. Joshua Plaskitt, of Great Grimsby, in Lincolnshire, Old England. The person who sent the things to Mr. Plaskitt was named Jones. It did not occur to me to ask his Christian name, nor to inquire what was the particular place where he lived in Long Island. I request Mr. Plaskitt to contrive to let me know these particulars; as I should like to communicate them to friends that I have on the north side of that island. However, it would excite no surprise there that one of their countrymen had acted this part; for every man of them, having the same opportunity, would do the same. Their forefathers carried to New England the nature and character of the people of Old England, before national debts, paper-money, septennial bills, standing armies, dead weights, and jubilees had beggared and corrupted the people.

At Hull I *lectured* (I laugh at the word) to about seven hundred persons, on the same evening that I arrived from Louth, which was on Thursday the 15th. We had what they call the summer theatre, which was crowded in every part except on the stage, and the evening next the stage was crowded too. The third evening was merely accidental, no previous notice having been given of it. On the Saturday, I went in the middle of the day to Beverley; saw there the beautiful minster, and some of the fine horses which they show there at this season of the year; dined with about fifty farmers; made a speech to them and about a hundred more, perhaps; and got back to Hull time enough to go to the theatre there.

The country round Hull appears to exceed even that of Lincolnshire. The three mornings that I was at Hull I walked out in three different directions, and found the country everywhere fine. To the east lies the Holderness country. I used to wonder that Yorkshire, to which I, from some false impression in my youth, had always attached the idea of *sterility*, should send us of the south those beautiful cattle with short horns and straight and deep bodies. You have only to see the country to cease to wonder at this. It lies on the north side of the mouth of the Humber; is as flat and fat as the land between Holbeach and Boston, without, as they tell me, the necessity of such numerous ditches. The appellation " Yorkshire *bite ;* " the acute sayings ascribed to Yorkshiremen; and their quick manner I remember in the army. When speaking of what country a man was, one used to say, in defence of the party, " York, but honest." Another saying was, that it was a bare common that a Yorkshireman would go over without taking a bite. Every one knows the story of the gentleman who, upon finding that a boot-cleaner in the south was a Yorkshireman, and expressing his surprise that he was not become master of the inn, received for answer, " Ah, sir, but master is York too! " And that of the Yorkshire boy who, seeing a gentleman eating some eggs, asked the cook to give him a little *salt ;* and upon being asked what he could want with salt, he said, " perhaps that gentleman may give me an egg presently."

It is surprising what effect sayings like these produce upon the mind. From one end to the other of the kingdom Yorkshiremen are looked upon as being keener than other people; more eager in pursuit of their own interests; more sharp and more selfish. For my part, I was cured with regard to the *people* long before I saw Yorkshire. In the army, where we see men of all counties, I always found Yorkshiremen distinguished for their frank manners and generous disposition. In the United States, my kind and generous friends of Pennsylvania were the children and descendants of Yorkshire parents; and, in truth, I long ago made up my mind that this hardness and sharpness ascribed to Yorkshiremen arose from the sort of envy excited by that quickness, that activity, that buoyancy of spirits, which bears them up through adverse circumstances, and their consequent success in all the situations of life. They, like the people of Lancashire, are just the very reverse of being *cunning* and *selfish ;* be they farmers, or be they what they may, you get at the bottom of their hearts in a minute. Everything they think soon gets to the tongue, and out it comes, heads and tails, as fast as they can pour it. Fine materials for Oliver to work on! If he had been sent to the *west* instead of the north, he would have found people there on whom he would have exercised his powers in vain. You are not to have every valuable quality in the same man and the same people: you are not to have prudent caution united with quickness and volubility.

But though, as to the character of the *people*, I, having known so many hundreds of Yorkshiremen, was perfectly enlightened, and had quite got the better of all prejudices many years ago, I still, in spite of the matchless horses and matchless cattle, had a general impression that Yorkshire was a *sterile* county, compared with the counties in the south and the west; and this notion was confirmed in some measure by my seeing the moory and rocky parts in the West Riding last winter. It was necessary for me to come and see the country on the banks of the Humber. I have seen the vale of Honiton, in Devonshire, that of Taunton and of Glastonbury, in Somersetshire: I have seen the vales of Gloucester and Worcester, and the banks of the Severn and the Avon: I have seen the vale of Berkshire, that of Aylesbury, in Buckinghamshire: I have seen the beautiful vales of Wiltshire; and the banks of the Medway, from Tunbridge to Maidstone, called the Garden of Eden: I was born at one end of Arthur Young's "finest ten miles in England:" I have ridden my horse across the Thames at its two sources; and I have been along every inch of its banks, from its sources to Gravesend, whence I have sailed out of it into the channel; and having seen and had ability to judge of the goodness of the land in all these places, I declare that I have never seen any to be compared with the land on the banks of the Humber, from the Holderness country included, and with the exception of the land from Wisbeach to Holbeach, and Holbeach to Boston. Really, the single parish of Holbeach, or a patch of the same size in the

Holderness country, seems to be equal in value to the whole of the county of Surrey, if we leave out the little plot of hop-garden at Farnham.

Nor is the town of Hull itself to be overlooked. It is a little city of London: streets, shops, everything like it; clean as the best parts of London, and the people as bustling and attentive. The town of Hull is *surrounded* with commodious docks for shipping. These docks are separated, in three or four places, by draw-bridges, so that, as you walk round the town, you walk by the side of the docks and the ships. The town on the outside of the docks is pretty considerable, and the walks from it into the country beautiful. I went about a good deal and I nowhere saw marks of beggary or filth, even in the outskirts: none of those nasty, shabby, thief-looking sheds that you see in the approaches to London: none of those off-scourings of pernicious and insolent luxury. I hate commercial towns in general: there is generally something so loathsome in the look, and so stern and unfeeling in the manners of sea-faring people, that I have always, from my very youth, disliked sea-ports; but really, the sight of this nice town, the manners of its people, the civil and kind and cordial reception that I met with, and the clean streets, and especially the pretty gardens in every direction, as you walk into the country, has made Hull, though a sea-port, a place that I shall always look back to with delight.

Beverley, which was formerly a very considerable city, with three or four gates, one of which is yet standing, had a great college, built in the year 700 by the Archbishop of York. It had three famous hospitals and two friaries. There is one church, a very fine one, and the minster still left; of which a bookseller in the town was so good as to give me copper-plate representations. It is still a very pretty town; the market large; the land all round the country good; and it is particularly famous for horses; those for speed being shown off here on the market-days at this time of the year. The farmers and gentlemen assemble in a very wide street, on the outside of the western gate of the town; and at a certain time of the day, the grooms come from their different stables to show off their beautiful horses; blood horses, coach horses, hunters, and cart horses; sometimes, they tell me, forty or fifty in number. The day that I was there (being late in the season) there were only seven or eight, or ten at the most. When I was asked at the inn to go and see " *the horses*," I had no curiosity, thinking it was such a parcel of horses as we see at a market in the south; but I found it a sight worth going to see; for, besides the beauty of the horses, there were the adroitness, the agility, and the boldness of the grooms, each running alongside of his horse, with the latter trotting at the rate of ten or twelve miles an hour, and then swinging him round, and showing him off to the best advantage. In short, I was exceedingly gratified by the trip to Beverley: the day was fair and mild; we went by one road and came back by another, and I have very seldom passed a pleasanter day in my life.

I found, very much to my surprise, that at Hull I was very nearly as far north as at Leeds, and at Beverley a little farther north. Of all things in the world I wanted to speak to Mr. Foster, of the *Leeds Patriot;* but was not aware of the relative situation till it was too late to write to him. Boats go up the Humber and the Ouse to within a few miles of Leeds. The Holderness country is that piece of land which lies between Hull and the sea: it appears to be a perfect flat; and is said to be, and I dare say is, one of the very finest spots in the whole kingdom. I had a very kind invitation to go into it; but I could not stay longer on that side of the Humber without neglecting some duty or other. In quitting Hull, I left behind me but one thing, the sight of which had not pleased me; namely, a fine gilded equestrian statue of the Dutch " *Deliverer,*" who gave to England the national debt, that fruitful mother of mischief and misery. Until this statue be replaced by that of Andrew Marvell, that real honour of this town, England will never be what it ought to be.

We came back to Barton by the steam-boat on Sunday, in the afternoon of the 18th, and in the evening reached this place, which is an inn, with three or four houses near it, at the distance of ten miles from Lincoln, to which we are going on Wednesday, the 21st. Between this place and Barton we passed through a delightfully pretty town, called Brigg. The land in this, which is called the high part of Lincolnshire, has generally stone, a solid bed of stone of great depth, at different distances from the surface. In some parts, this stone is of a yellowish colour and in the form of very thick slate; and in these parts the soil is not so good; but, generally speaking, the land is excellent; easily tilled; no surface water; the fields very large; not many trees; but what there are, particularly the ash, very fine, and of free growth; and innumerable flocks of those big, long-woolled sheep from one hundred to a thousand in a flock, each having from eight to ten pounds of wool upon his body. One of the finest sights in the world is one of these thirty or forty acre fields, with four or five or six hundred ewes, each with her one or two lambs skipping about upon grass, the most beautiful that can be conceived, and on lands as level as a bowling-green. I do not recollect having seen a mole-hill or an ant-hill since I came into the country; and not one acre of waste land, though I have gone the whole length of the country one way, and am now got nearly halfway back another way.

Having seen this country, and having had a glimpse at the Holderness country, which lies on the banks of the sea, and to the east and north-east of Hull, can I cease to wonder that those devils, the Danes, found their way hither so often. There were the fat sheep then, just as there are now, depend upon it; and these numbers of noble churches, and these magnificent minsters were reared, because the wealth of the country remained *in the country*, and was not carried away to the south, to keep swarms of devouring tax-eaters, to cram the maws of wasteful idlers, and to be transferred to the grasp of luxurious and blaspheming Jews.

You always perceive that the churches are large and fine and lofty in proportion to the richness of the soil and the extent of the parish. In many places, where there are *now* but a very few houses, and those comparatively miserable, there are churches that look like cathedrals. It is quite curious to observe the difference in the style of the churches of Suffolk and Norfolk, and those of Lincolnshire and of the other bank of the Humber. In the former two counties the churches are good, large, and with a good, plain, and pretty lofty tower. And in a few instances, particularly at Ipswich and Long Melford, you find magnificence in these buildings; but in Lincolnshire the magnificence of the churches is surprising. These churches are the indubitable proof of great and solid wealth, and formerly of great population. From everything that I have heard the *Netherlands* is a country very much resembling Lincolnshire; and they say that the church at Antwerp is like that at Boston; but my opinion is that Lincolnshire alone contains more of these fine buildings than the whole of the continent of Europe.

Still, however, there is the almost total want of the *singing birds*. There had been a shower a little while before we arrived at this place; it was about six o'clock in the evening; and there is a thick wood, together with the orchards and gardens, very near to the inn. We heard a little twittering from one thrush; but, at that very moment, if we had been as near to just such a wood in Surrey, or Hampshire, or Sussex, or Kent, we should have heard ten thousand birds singing altogether; and the thrushes continuing their song till twenty minutes after sunset. When I was at Ipswich, the gardens and plantations round that beautiful town began in the morning to ring with the voices of the different birds. The nightingale is, I believe, *never heard* anywhere on the eastern side of Lincolnshire; though it is sometimes heard in the same latitude in the dells of Yorkshire. How ridiculous it is to suppose that these frail birds, with their slender wings and proportionately heavy bodies, *cross the sea* and come back again! I have not yet heard more than half a dozen skylarks; and I have, only last year, heard ten at a time make the air ring over one of my fields at Barn-Elm. This is a great drawback from the pleasure of viewing this fine country.

It is time for me now, withdrawing myself from these objects visible to the eye, to speak of the state of *the people*, and of the manner in which their affairs are affected by the workings of the system. With regard to the labourers, they are, everywhere, miserable. The wages for those who are employed on the land are, through all the counties that I have come, twelve shillings a week for married men, and less for single ones; but a large part of them are not even at this season employed on the land. The farmers, for want of means of profitable employment, suffer the men to fall upon the parish; and they are employed in digging and breaking stone for the roads; so that the roads are nice and smooth for the sheep and cattle to walk on in their way to the all-devouring jaws of the Jews and other tax-eaters in London and its vicinity. None of the best meat, except by mere accident, is consumed here. To-day (the 20th of April), we have seen hundreds upon hundreds of sheep, as fat as hogs, go by this inn door, their toes, like those of the foot marks at the entrance of the lion's den, all pointing towards the Wen; and the landlord gave us for dinner a little skinny, hard leg of old ewe mutton! Where the man got it, I cannot imagine. Thus it is: every good thing is literally driven or carried away out of the country. In walking out yesterday, I saw three poor fellows digging stone for the roads, who told me that they never had anything but bread to eat, and water to wash it down. One of them was a widower with three children; and his pay was eighteenpence a day; that is to say, about three pounds of bread a day each, for six days in the week; nothing for Sunday, and nothing for lodging, washing, clothing, candle light, or fuel! Just such was the state of things in France at the eve of the Revolution! Precisely such; and precisely the same were the *causes*. Whether the effect will be the same, I do not take upon myself positively to determine. Just on the other side of the hedge, while I was talking to these men, I saw about two hundred fat sheep in a rich pasture. I did not tell them what I might have told them; but I explained to them why the farmers were unable to give them a sufficiency of wages. They listened with great attention; and said that they did believe that the farmers were in great distress themselves.

With regard to the farmers, it is said here that the far greater part, if sold up, would be found to be insolvent. The tradesmen in country towns are, and must be, in but little better state. They all tell you they do not sell half so many goods as they used to sell; and, of course, the manufacturers must suffer in the like degree. There is a diminution and deterioration, every one says, in the stocks upon the farms. *Sheep-washing* is a sort of business in this country; and I heard at Boston that the sheep-washers say that there is a gradual falling off in point of the numbers of sheep washed.

The farmers are all gradually sinking in point of property. The very rich ones do not feel that ruin is absolutely approaching; but they are all alarmed; and as to the poorer ones, they are fast falling into the rank of paupers. When I was at Ely a gentleman who appeared to be a great farmer told me in presence of fifty farmers, at the White Hart Inn, that he had seen that morning *three men* cracking stones on the road as paupers of the parish of Wilbarton; and that all these men had been *overseers of the poor of that same parish within the last seven years*. Wheat keeps up in price to about an average of seven shillings a bushel; which is owing to our two successive bad harvests; but fat beef and pork are at a very low price, and mutton not much better. The beef was selling at Lynn for five shillings the stone of fourteen pounds, and the pork at four and sixpence. The wool (one of the great articles of produce in these countries) selling for less than half of its former price.

And here let me stop to observe that I was well informed before I left London that merchants were exporting our long wool to France, where it paid *thirty per cent. duty*. Well, say the landowners, but we have to thank Huskisson for this, at any rate; and that is true enough; for the law was most rigid against the export of wool; but what will the *manufacturers* say? Thus the collective goes on, smashing one class and then another; and, resolved to adhere to the taxes, it knocks away, one after another, the props of the system itself. By every measure that it adopts for the sake of obtaining security, or of affording relief to the people, it does some act of crying injustice. To save itself from the natural effects of its own measures, it knocked down the country bankers, in direct violation of the law in 1822. It is now about to lay its heavy hand on the big brewers and the publicans, in order to pacify the call for a reduction of taxes, and with the hope of preventing such reduction in reality. It is making a trifling attempt to save the West Indians from total ruin, and the West India colonies from revolt; but by that same attempt it reflects injury on the British distillers, and on the growers of barley. Thus it cannot do justice without doing injustice; it cannot do good without doing evil; and thus it must continue to do, until it take off, in reality, more than one half of the taxes.

One of the great signs of the poverty of people in the middle rank of life is the falling off of the audiences at the playhouses. There is a playhouse in almost every country town, where the players used to act occasionally; and in large towns almost always. In some places they have of late abandoned acting altogether. In others they have acted, very frequently, to not more than *ten or twelve persons*. At Norwich the playhouse had been shut up for a long time. I heard of one manager who has become a porter to a warehouse, and his company dispersed. In most places the insides of the buildings seem to be tumbling to pieces; and the curtains and scenes that they let down seem to be abandoned to the damp and the cobwebs. *My* appearance on the boards seemed to give new life to the drama. I was, until the birth of my third son, a constant haunter of the playhouse, in which I took great delight; but when *he* came into the world, I said, " Now, Nancy, it is time for us to leave off going to the play." It is really melancholy to look at things now, and to think of things then. I feel great sorrow on account of these poor players; for though they are made the tools of the government and the corporations and the parsons, it is not their fault, and they have uniformly, whenever I have come in contact with them, been very civil to me. I am not sorry that they are left out of the list of vagrants in the new act; but in this case, as in so many others, the men have to be grateful to the *women ;* for who believes that this merciful omission would have taken place if so many of the peers had not contracted matrimonial alliances with players; if so many playeresses had not become peeresses. We may thank God for disposing the hearts of our law-makers to be guilty of the same sins and foibles as ourselves; for when a lord had been sentenced to the pillory, the use of that ancient mode of punishing offences was abolished: when a lord (Castlereagh), who was also a minister of state, had cut his own throat, the degrading punishment of burial in cross-roads was abolished; and now, when so many peers and great men have taken to wife play-actresses, which the law termed *vagrants*, that term, as applied to the children of Melpomene and Thalia, is abolished! Laud we the gods that our rulers cannot, after all, divest themselves of flesh and blood! For the Lord have mercy on us, if their great souls were once to soar above that tenement!

Lord Stanhope cautioned his brother peers, a little while ago, against the angry feeling which was *rising up in the poor against the rich*. His lordship is a wise and humane man, and this is evident from all his conduct. Nor is this angry feeling confined to the counties in the south, where the rage of the people, from the very nature of the local circumstances, is more formidable; woods and coppices and dingles and by-lanes and sticks and stones ever at hand, being resources unknown in counties like this. When I was at St. Ives, in Huntingdonshire, an open country, I sat with the farmers, and smoked a pipe by way of preparation for evening service, which I performed on a carpenter's bench in a wheelwright's shop; my friends, the players, never having gained any regular settlement in that grand mart for four-legged fat meat, coming from the Fens, and bound to the Wen. While we were sitting, a hand-bill was handed round the table, advertising *farming stock* for sale; and amongst the implements of husbandry " an *excellent fire-engine, several steel traps, and spring guns !*" And that is the life, is it, of an English *farmer ?* I walked on about six miles of the road from Holbeach to Boston. I have before observed upon the inexhaustible riches of this land. At the end of about five miles and three quarters I came to a public-house, and thought I would get some breakfast; but the poor woman, with a tribe of children about her, had not a morsel of either meat or bread! At a house called an inn, a little further on, the landlord had no meat except a little bit of chine of bacon; and though there were a good many houses near the spot, the landlord told me that the people were become so poor that the butchers had left off killing meat in the neighbourhood. Just the state of things that existed in France on the eve of the Revolution. On that very spot I looked round me and counted more than two thousand fat sheep in the pastures! How long, how long, good God! is this state of

things to last? How long will these people starve in the midst
of plenty? How long will fire-engines, steel traps, and spring
guns be, in such a state of things, a protection to property?
When I was at Beverley, a gentleman told me, it was Mr.
Dawson of that place, that some time before a farmer had been
sold up by his landlord; and that, in a few weeks afterwards, the
farm-house was on fire, and that when the servants of the
landlord arrived to put it out, they found the handle of the pump
taken away and that the homestead was totally destroyed.
This was told me in the presence of several gentlemen, who all
spoke of it as a fact of perfect notoriety.

Another respect in which our situation so exactly resembles
that of France on the eve of the Revolution is the *fleeing from
the country* in every direction. When I was in Norfolk there
were four hundred persons, generally young men, labourers,
carpenters, wheelwrights, millwrights, smiths, and bricklayers;
most of them with some money, and some farmers and others
with good round sums. These people were going to Quebec, in
timber-ships, and from Quebec by land into the United States.
They had been told that they would not be suffered to land in
the United States from on board of ship. The roguish villains
had deceived them: but no matter; they will get into the
United States; and going through Canada will do them good,
for it will teach them to detest everything belonging to it.
From Boston two great barge loads had just gone off by canal
to Liverpool, most of them farmers; all carrying some money,
and some as much as two thousand pounds each. From the
North and West Riding of Yorkshire numerous waggons have
gone, carrying people to the canals leading to Liverpool; and a
gentleman whom I saw at Peterboro' told me that he saw some
of them; and that the men all appeared to be respectable
farmers. At Hull the scene would delight the eyes of the wise
Burdett; for here the emigration is going on in the " old Roman
plan." Ten large ships have gone this spring, laden with these
fugitives from the fangs of taxation; some bound direct to the
ports of the United States; others, like those at Yarmouth, for
Quebec. Those that have most money go direct to the United
States. The single men, who are taken for a mere trifle in the
Canada ships, go that way, have nothing but their carcasses to
carry over the rocks and swamps, and through the myriads of
place-men and pensioners in that miserable region; there are
about fifteen more ships going from this one port this spring.
The ships are fitted up with berths as transports for the carrying

of troops. I went on board one morning, and saw the people putting their things on board and stowing them away. Seeing a nice young woman, with a little baby in her arms, I told her that she was going to a country where she would be sure that her children would never want victuals; where she might make her own malt, soap, and candles, without being half put to death for it, and where the blaspheming Jews would not have a mortgage on the life's labour of her children.

There is at Hull one farmer going who is seventy years of age, but who takes out five sons and fifteen hundred pounds! Brave and sensible old man! and good and affectionate father! He is performing a truly parental and sacred duty; and he will die with the blessing of his sons on his head, for having rescued them from this scene of slavery, misery, cruelty, and crime. Come, then, Wilmot Horton, with your sensible associates, Burdett and Poulett Thomson; come into Lincolnshire, Norfolk, and Yorkshire; come and bring Parson Malthus along with you; regale your sight with this delightful " stream of emigration "; congratulate the " greatest captain of the age," and your brethren of the Collective: congratulate the " noblest assembly of free men," on these the happy effects of their measures. Oh! no, Wilmot! Oh! no, generous and sensible Burdett, it is not the aged, the infirm, the halt, the blind, and the idiots that go: it is the youth, the strength, the wealth, and the spirit that will no longer brook hunger and thirst, in order that the maws of tax-eaters and Jews may be crammed. You want the Irish to go, and so they will *at our expense*, and all the bad of them, to be kept at our expense on the rocks and swamps of Nova Scotia and Canada. You have no money to send them away with: the tax-eaters want it all; and thanks to the " improvements of the age," the steam-boats will continue to bring them in shoals in pursuit of the orts of the food that their taskmasters have taken away from them.

After evening lecture, at Horncastle, a very decent farmer came to me and asked me about America, telling me that he was resolved to go, for that if he stayed much longer, he should not have a shilling to go with. I promised to send him a letter from Louth to a friend at New York, who might be useful to him there, and give him good advice. I forgot it at Louth; but I will do it before I go to bed. From the Thames, and from the several ports down the Channel, about two thousand have gone this spring. All the flower of the labourers of the east of Sussex and west of Kent will be culled out and sent off in a short time.

From Glasgow the sensible Scotch are pouring out amain. Those that are poor and cannot pay their passages, or can rake together only a trifle, are going to a rascally heap of sand and rock and swamp, called Prince Edward's Island, in the horrible Gulf of St. Lawrence; but when the American vessels come over with Indian corn and flour and pork and beef and poultry and eggs and butter and cabbages and green pease and asparagus for the soldier-officers and other tax-eaters that we support upon that lump of worthlessness; for the lump itself bears nothing but potatoes; when these vessels come, which they are continually doing, winter and summer; towards the fall, with apples and pears and melons and cucumbers; and, in short, everlastingly coming and taking away the amount of taxes raised in England; when these vessels return, the sensible Scotch will go back in them for a dollar a head, till at last not a man of them will be left but the bed-ridden. Those villainous colonies are held for no earthly purpose but that of furnishing a pretence of giving money to the relations and dependents of the aristocracy; and they are the nicest channels in the world through which to send English taxes to enrich and strengthen the United States. Withdraw the English taxes, and, except in a small part in Canada, the whole of those horrible regions would be left to the bears and the savages in the course of a year.

This emigration is a famous blow given to the borough-mongers. The way to New York is now as well known and as easy and as little expensive as from old York to London. First the Sussex parishes sent their paupers; they invited over others that were not paupers; they invited over people of some property; then persons of greater property; now substantial farmers are going; men of considerable fortune will follow. It is the letters written across the Atlantic that do the business. Men of fortune will soon discover that, to secure to their families their fortunes, and to take these out of the grasp of the inexorable tax-gatherer, they must get away. Every one that goes will take twenty after him; and thus it will go on. There can be no interruption but *war* : and war the Thing dares not have. As to France or the Netherlands, or any part of that hell called Germany, Englishmen can never settle there. The United States form another England without its unbearable taxes, its insolent game laws, its intolerable dead-weight, and its tread-mills.

EASTERN TOUR ENDED, MIDLAND TOUR BEGUN

FROM the inn at Spittal we came to this famous ancient Roman station, and afterwards grand scene of Saxon and Gothic splendour, on the 21st. It was the third or fourth day of the *Spring fair*, which is one of the greatest in the kingdom, and which lasts for a whole week. Horses begin the fair; then come sheep; and to-day the horned cattle. It is supposed that there were about 50,000 sheep, and I think the whole of the space in the various roads and streets, covered by the cattle, must have amounted to ten acres of ground, or more. Some say that they were as numerous as the sheep. The number of horses I did not hear; but they say that there were 1500 fewer in number than last year. The sheep sold 5s. a head, on an average, lower than last year; and the cattle in the same proportion. High-priced horses sold well; but the horses which are called tradesmen's horses were very low. This is the natural march of the Thing: those who live on the taxes have money to throw away; but those who *pay* them are ruined, and have, of course, no money to lay out on horses.

The country from Spittal to Lincoln continued to be much about the same as from Barton to Spittal. Large fields, rather light loam at top, stone under, about half corn-land and the rest grass. Not so many sheep as in the richer lands, but a great many still. As you get on towards Lincoln, the ground gradually rises, and you go on the road made by the Romans. When you come to the city, you find the ancient castle and the magnificent cathedral on the *brow* of a sort of ridge which ends here; for you look all of a sudden down into a deep valley, where the greater part of the remaining city lies. It once had *fifty-two churches ;* it has now only eight, and only about 9000 inhabitants! The cathedral is, I believe, the *finest building in the whole world.* All the others that I have seen (and I have seen all in England except Chester, York, Carlisle, and Durham) are little things compared with this. To the task of describing a thousandth part of its striking beauties I am inadequate; it surpasses greatly all that I had anticipated; and oh! how loudly it gives the lie to those brazen Scotch historians who would have us believe that England was formerly *a poor* country! The whole revenue raised from Lincolnshire, even by this present system of taxation, would not rear such another pile in two hundred years. Some of the city gates are down; but there is one standing, the arch of which is said to be two thousand years old; and a most curious thing it is. The sight of the cathedral fills the mind alternately with wonder, admiration, melancholy, and rage: wonder at its grandeur and magnificence; admiration of the zeal and dis-interestedness of those who here devoted to the honour of God those immense means which they might have applied to their own enjoyments; melancholy at its present neglected state; and indignation against those who now enjoy the revenues belonging to it, and who creep about it merely as a pretext for devouring a part of the fruit of the people's labour. There are no men in England who ought to wish for *reform* so anxiously as the working clergy of the church of England; we are all oppressed; but they are oppressed and insulted more than any men that ever lived in the world. The clergy in America; I mean in free America, not in our beggarly colonies, where clerical insolence and partiality prevail still more than here; I mean in the United States, where every man gives what he pleases, and no more: the clergy of the episcopal church are a hundred times better off than the working clergy are here. They are, also, much more respected, because their *order* has not to bear the blame of enormous exactions; which exactions here are swallowed up by the aristocracy and their dependents; but which swallowings are imputed to every one bearing the name of parson. Throughout the whole country I have maintained the necessity and the justice of resuming the church property; but I have never failed to say that I know of no more meritorious and ill-used men than the working clergy of the established church.

Leicester,
26 April 1830.

At the famous ancient city of Lincoln I had crowded audiences, principally consisting of farmers, on the 21st and 22nd; exceedingly well-behaved audiences; and great impression produced. One of the evenings, in pointing out to them the wisdom of explaining to their labourers the cause of their distress, in order to ward off the effects of the resentment which the labourers now feel everywhere against the farmers, I related to them what my labourers at Barn-Elm had been doing since I left home: and I repeated to them the complaints that my labourers made, stating to them, from memory, the following parts of that spirited petition:

"That your petitioners have recently observed that many great sums of the money, part of which we pay, have been voted to be given to persons who render no services to the country; some of which sums we will mention here; that the sum £94,900 has been voted for disbanded *foreign* officers, their *widows* and *children;* that your petitioners know that ever since the peace this charge has been annually made; that it has been on an average, £110,000 a year, and that, of course, this band of foreigners have actually taken away out of England, since the peace, one million and seven hundred thousand pounds; partly taken from the fruit of our labour; and if our dinners were actually taken from our table and carried over to Hanover, the process could not be to our eyes more visible than it now is; and we are astonished that those who fear that we, who make the land bring forth crops, and who make the clothing and the houses, shall swallow up the rental, appear to think nothing at all of the swallowings of these Hanoverian men, women, and children, who may continue thus to swallow for half a century to come.

"That the advocates of the project for sending us out of our country to the rocks and snows of Nova Scotia, and the swamps and wilds of Canada, have insisted on the necessity of *checking marriages* amongst us, in order to cause a decrease in our numbers; that, however, while this is insisted on in your honourable House, we perceive a part of our own earnings voted away to encourage marriage amongst those who do no work, and who live at our expense; and that to your petitioners it does seem most wonderful that there should be persons to fear that we, the labourers, shall, on account of our numbers, swallow up the rental while they actually vote away our food and raiment to increase the numbers of those who never have produced, and who never will produce, anything useful to man.

"That your petitioners know that more than one-half of the whole of their wages is taken from them by the taxes; that these taxes go chiefly into the hands of idlers; that your petitioners are the bees, and that the tax-receivers are the drones; and they know, further, that while there is a project for sending the bees out of the country, no one proposes to send away the drones; but that your petitioners hope to see the day when the checking of the increase of the drones, and not of the bees, will be the object of an English parliament.

"That, in consequence of taxes, your petitioners pay sixpence for a pot of worse beer than they could make for one penny; that they pay ten shillings for a pair of shoes that they could have for five shillings; that they pay sevenpence for a pound of soap or candles that they could have for threepence; that they pay sevenpence for a pound of sugar that they could have for threepence; that they pay six shillings for a pound of tea that they could have for two shillings; that they pay double for their bread and meat, of what they would have to pay if there were no idlers to be kept out of the taxes; that, therefore, it is the taxes that make their wages insufficient for their support, and that compel them to apply for aid to the poor-rates; that, knowing these things, they feel indignant at hearing themselves described as *paupers*, while so many thousands of idlers, for whose support they pay taxes, are called *noble Lords* and *Ladies*, *honourable Gentlemen*, *Masters*, and *Misses*; that they feel indignant at hearing themselves described as a nuisance to be got rid of, while the idlers who live upon their earnings are upheld, caressed and cherished, as if they were the sole support of the country."

Having repeated to them these passages, I proceeded: "My workmen were induced thus to petition, in consequence of the information which I, their master, had communicated to them; and, gentlemen, why should not your labourers petition in the same strain? Why should you suffer them to remain in a state of ignorance, relative to the cause of their misery? The eye sweeps over in this county more riches in one moment than are contained in the whole county in which I was born, and in which the petitioners live. Between Holbeach and Boston, even at a public-house, neither bread nor meat was to be found; and while the landlord was telling me that the people were become so poor that the butchers killed no meat in the neighbourhood, I counted more than two thousand fat sheep lying about in the pastures in that richest spot in the whole world. Starvation in the midst of plenty; the land covered with food, and the working people without victuals: everything taken away by the tax-eaters of various descriptions: and yet you take no measures for redress; and your miserable labourers seem to be doomed to expire with hunger, without an effort to obtain relief. What! cannot you point out to them the real cause of their sufferings; cannot you take a piece of paper and write out a petition for them; cannot your labourers petition as well as mine; are God's blessings bestowed on you without any spirit to preserve them; is the fatness of the land, is the earth teeming with food for the body and raiment for the back, to be an apology for the want of that courage for which your fathers were so famous; is the abundance which God has put into your hands to be the excuse for your resigning yourselves to starvation? My God! is there no spirit left in England except in the miserable sand-hills of Surrey?" These words were not uttered without effect, I can assure the reader. The assemblage was of that stamp in which thought goes before expression; but the effect of this example of my men in Surrey will, I am sure, be greater than anything that has been done in the petitioning way for a long time past.

We left Lincoln on the 23rd about noon, and got to Newark, in Nottinghamshire, in the evening, where I gave a lecture at the theatre to about three hundred persons. Newark is a very fine town, and the Castle Inn, where we stopped, extraordinarily good and pleasantly situated. Here I was met by a parcel of the printed petitions of the labourers at Barn-Elm.

I shall continue to *sow these* as I proceed on my way. It should have been stated at the head of the printed petition that it was presented to the House of Lords by his Grace the Duke of Richmond, and by Mr. Pallmer to the House of Commons.

The country from Lincoln to Newark (sixteen miles) is by no means so fine as that which we have been in for so many weeks. The land is clayey in many parts. A pleasant country; a variety of hill and valley; but not that richness which we had so long had under our eye: fields smaller; fewer sheep, and those not so large and so manifestly loaded with flesh. The roads always good. Newark is a town very much like Nottingham, having a very fine and spacious market-place; the buildings everywhere good; but it is in the villages that you find the depth of misery.

Having appointed positively to be at Leicester in the evening of Saturday, the 24th, we could not stop either at Grantham or at Melton Mowbray, not even long enough to view their fine old magnificent churches. In going from Newark to Grantham we got again into Lincolnshire, in which last county Grantham is. From Newark nearly to Melton Mowbray the country is about the same as between Lincoln and Newark; by no means bad land, but not so rich as that of Lincolnshire in the middle and eastern part; not approaching to the Holderness country in point of riches; a large part arable land, well tilled; but not such large homesteads, such numerous great stacks of wheat, and such endless flocks of lazy sheep.

Before we got to Melton Mowbray, the beautiful pastures of this little verdant county of Leicester began to appear. Meadows and green fields, with here and there a corn field, all of smaller dimensions than those of Lincolnshire, but all very beautiful; with gentle hills and woods too; not beautiful woods, like those of Hampshire and of the wilds of Surrey, Sussex and Kent, but very pretty, all the country round being so rich. At Mowbray we began to get amongst the Leicestershire sheep, those fat creatures which we see the butchers' boys battering about so unmercifully in the streets and the outskirts of the Wen. The land is warmer here than in Lincolnshire; the grass more forward, and the wheat, between Mowbray and Leicester, six inches high, and generally looking exceedingly well. In Lincolnshire and Nottinghamshire I found the wheat in general rather thin, and frequently sickly; nothing like so promising as in Suffolk and Norfolk.

We got to Leicester on the 24th at about half-after five o'clock; and the time appointed for the lecture was six. Leicester is a very fine town; spacious streets, fine inns, fine shops, and containing, they say, thirty or forty thousand people. It is well stocked with gaols, of which a new one, in addition to the rest, has just been built, covering three acres of ground! And, as if *proud* of it, the grand portal has little turrets in the castle style, with *embrasures* in miniature on the caps of the turrets. Nothing speaks the want of reflection in the people so much as the self-gratulation which they appear to feel in these edifices in their several towns. Instead of expressing shame at these indubitable proofs of the horrible increase of misery and of crime, they really boast of these "improvements," as they call them. Our forefathers built abbeys and priories and churches, and they made such use of them that gaols were nearly unnecessary. We, their sons, have knocked down the abbeys and priories; suffered half the parsonage-houses and churches to pretty nearly tumble down, and make such uses of the remainder that gaols and treadmills and dungeons have now become the most striking edifices in every county in the kingdom.

Yesterday morning (Sunday, the 25th) I walked out to the village of Knighton, two miles on the Bosworth road, where I breakfasted, and then walked back. This morning I walked out to Hailstone, nearly three miles on the Lutterworth road, and got my breakfast there. You have nothing to do but to walk through these villages to see the cause of the increase of the gaols. Standing on the hill at Knighton, you see the three ancient and lofty and beautiful spires rising up at Leicester; you see the river winding down through a broad bed of the most beautiful meadows that man ever set his eyes on; you see the bright verdure covering all the land, even to the tops of the hills, with here and there a little wood, as if made by God to give variety to the beauty of the scene, for the river brings the coal in abundance, for fuel, and the earth gives the brick and the tile in abundance. But go down into the villages; invited by the spires, rising up amongst the trees in the dells, at scarcely ever more than a mile or two apart; invited by these spires, go down into these villages, view the large, and once the most beautiful, churches; see the parson's house, large, and in the midst of pleasure-gardens; and then look at the miserable sheds in which the labourers reside! Look at these hovels, made of mud and of straw; bits of glass, or of old off-cast windows, without frames or hinges frequently, but merely stuck in the mud wall. Enter them, and look at the bits of chairs or stools; the wretched boards tacked together to serve for a table; the floor of pebble, broken brick, or of the bare ground; look at the thing called a bed; and survey the rags on the backs of the wretched inhabitants; and then wonder if you can that the gaols and dungeons and treadmills increase, and that a standing army and barracks are become the favourite establishments of England!

At the village of Hailstone, I got into the purlieu, as they call it in Hampshire, of a person well known in the Wen; namely, the Reverend Beresford, rector of that fat affair, St. Andrew's, Holborn! In walking through the village, and surveying its deplorable dwellings, so much worse than the cow-sheds of the cottagers on the skirts of the forests in Hampshire, my attention was attracted by the surprising contrast between them and the house of their religious teacher. I met a labouring man. Country people *know everything*. If you have ever made a *faux-pas* of any sort of description; if you have anything about you of which you do not want all the world to know, never retire to a village, keep in some great town; but the Wen, for your life, for there the next-door neighbour will not know even your name; and the vicinage will judge of you solely by the quantity of money that you have to spend. This labourer seemed not to be in a very great hurry. He was digging in his garden; and I, looking over a low hedge, *pitched him up* for a gossip, commencing by asking him whether that was the parson's house. Having answered in the affirmative, and I having asked the parson's name, he proceeded thus: "His name is Beresford; but though he lives there, he has not this living now, he has got the living of St. Andrew's, Holborn; and they say it is worth a great many thousands a year. He could not, they say, keep this living and have that too, because they were so far apart. And so this living was given to Mr. Brown, who is the rector of Hobey, about seven miles off." "Well," said I, "but *how comes Beresford to live here now*, if the living be given to another man?" "Why, sir," said he, "this Beresford married a daughter of Brown; and so, you know (smiling and looking very archly), Brown comes and takes the payment for the tithes, and pays a curate that lives in that house there in the field; and Beresford lives at that fine house still, just as he used to do." I asked him what the living was worth, and he answered twelve hundred pounds a year. It is a rectory, I find, and of course the parson has great tithes as well as small.

The people of this village know a great deal more about Beresford than the people of St. Andrew's, Holborn, know about him. In short, the country people know all about the whole thing. They will be long before they act; but they will make no noise as a signal for action. They will be moved by nothing but actual want of food. This the Thing seems to be aware of; and hence all the innumerable schemes for keeping them quiet: hence the endless gaols and all the terrors of hardened law: hence the schemes for coaxing them by letting them have bits of land: hence the everlasting bills and discussions of committees about the state of the poor, and the state of the poor-laws: all of which will fail; and at last, unless reduction of taxation speedily take place, the schemers will find what the consequences are of reducing millions to the verge of starvation.

The labourers here who are in need of parochial relief are formed into what are called *roundsmen ;* that is to say, they are sent round from one farmer to another, each maintaining a certain number for a certain length of time; and thus they go round from one to the other. If the farmers did not pay three shillings in taxes out of every six shillings that they give in the shape of wages, they could afford to give the men four and sixpence in wages, which would be better to the men than the six. But as long as this burden of taxes shall continue, so long the misery will last, and it will go on increasing with accelerated pace. The march of circumstances is precisely what it was in France just previous to the French Revolution. If the aristocracy were wise they would put a stop to that march. The middle class are fast sinking down to the state of the lower class. *A community of feeling* between these classes, and that feeling an angry one, is what the aristocracy has to dread. As far as the higher clergy are concerned, this community of feeling is already complete. A short time will extend the feeling to every other branch; and then the hideous consequences make their appearance. Reform; a radical reform of the parliament; this reform *in time ;* this reform, which would reconcile the middle class to the aristocracy, and give renovation to that which has now become a mass of decay and disgust; this reform, given with a good grace, and not taken by force, is the only refuge for the aristocracy of this kingdom. Just as it was in France. All the tricks of financiers have been tried in vain; and by and by some trick more pompous and foolish than the rest; Sir Henry Parnell's trick, perhaps, or something equally foolish, would blow the whole concern into the air.

WORCESTER,

18 *May* 1830.

In tracing myself from Leicester to this place, I begin at Lutterworth, in Leicestershire, one of the prettiest country towns that I ever saw; that is to say, prettiest *situated*. At this place they have, in the church (they say), the identical *pulpit* from which Wickliffe preached! This was not his birthplace; but he was, it seems, priest of this parish.

I set off from Lutterworth early on the 29th of April, stopped to breakfast at Birmingham, got to Wolverhampton by two o'clock (a distance altogether of about 50 miles), and lectured at six in the evening. I repeated, or rather continued, the lecturing on the 30th and on the 3rd of May. On the 6th of May went to Dudley, and lectured there: on the 10th of May, at Birmingham; on the 12th and 13th, at Shrewsbury; and on the 14th came here.

Thus have I come through countries of corn and meat and iron and coal; and from the banks of the Humber to those of the Severn I find all the people who do not share in the taxes in a state of distress, greater or less; *mortgagers* all frightened out of their wits; *fathers* trembling for the fate of their children; and *working people* in the most miserable state, and, as they ought to be, in the *worst of temper*. These will, I am afraid, be the *state-doctors* at last! The farmers are cowed down: the poorer they get the more cowardly they are. Every one of them sees the cause of his suffering, and sees general ruin at hand; but every one hopes that by some trick, some act of meanness, some contrivance, *he shall escape*. So that there is no hope of any change for the better but from the *working people*. The farmers will sink to a very low state; and thus the Thing (barring *accidents*) may go on, until neither farmer nor tradesman will see a joint of meat on his table once in a quarter of a year. It appears likely to be precisely as it was in France: it is now just what France was at the close of the reign of Louis XV. It has been the fashion to ascribe the *French Revolution* to the writings of Voltaire, Rousseau, Diderot, and others. These writings had *nothing at all* to do with the matter: no, *nothing at all*. The *Revolution* was produced by *taxes*, which at last became unbearable; by debts of the state; but, in fact, by the despair of the people, produced by the weight of the taxes.

It is curious to observe how ready the supporters of tyranny and taxation are to ascribe rebellions and revolutions to disaffected leaders; and particularly to writers; and as these supporters of tyranny and taxation have had the press at their command; have had generally the absolute command of it, they have caused this belief to go down from generation to generation. It will not do for them to ascribe revolutions and rebellions to the true cause; because then the rebellions and revolutions would be justified; and it is their object to cause them to be condemned. Infinite delusion has prevailed in this country in consequence of the efforts of which I am now speaking. Voltaire was just as much a cause of the French Revolution as I have been the cause of imposing these sixty millions of taxes. The French Revolution was produced by the grindings of taxation; and this I will take an opportunity very soon of proving, to the conviction of every man in the kingdom who chooses to read.

In the iron country, of which Wolverhampton seems to be a sort of central point, and where thousands, and perhaps two or three hundred thousand people, are assembled together, the *truck* or *tommy* system generally prevails; and this is a very remarkable feature in the state of this country. I have made inquiries with regard to the origin, or etymology, of this word *tommy*, and could find no one to furnish me with the information. It is certainly, like so many other good things, to be ascribed to *the army*; for when I was a recruit at Chatham barracks, in the year 1783, we had brown bread served out to us twice in the week. And, for what reason God knows, we used to call it *tommy*. And the sergeants, when they called us out to get our bread, used to tell us to come and get our *tommy*. Even the officers used to call it tommy. Any one that could get white bread called it bread; but the brown stuff that we got in lieu of part of our pay was called *tommy* : and so we used to call it when we got abroad. When the soldiers came to have bread served out to them in the several towns in England, the name of " tommy " went down by tradition; and, doubtless, it was taken up and adapted to the truck system in Staffordshire and elsewhere.

Now, there is nothing wrong, nothing *essentially* wrong, in this system of barter. Barter is in practice in some of the happiest communities in the world. In the new settled parts of the United States of America, to which money has scarcely found its way, to which articles of wearing apparel are brought from a great distance, where the great and almost sole occupations are the rearing of food, the building of houses, and the making of clothes, barter is the rule and money payment the exception. And this is attended with no injury and with very little inconvenience. The bargains are made, and the accounts kept *in money ;* but the payments are made in produce or in goods, the price of these being previously settled on. The store-keeper (which we call shop-keeper) receives the produce in exchange for his goods, and exchanges that produce for more goods; and thus the concerns of the community go on, every one living in abundance, and the sound of misery never heard.

But when this tommy system; this system of barter; when this makes its appearance where money has for ages been the medium of exchange and of payments for labour; when this system makes its appearance in such a state of society, there is something wrong; things are out of joint; and it becomes us to inquire into the real cause of its being resorted to; and it does not become us to join in an outcry against the employers who resort to it until we be perfectly satisfied that those employers are guilty of oppression.

The manner of carrying on the tommy system is this: suppose there to be a master who employs a hundred men. That hundred men, let us suppose, to earn a pound a week each. This is not the case in the iron-works; but no matter, we can illustrate our meaning by one sum as well as by another. These men lay out weekly the whole of the hundred pounds in victuals, drink, clothing, bedding, fuel, and house-rent. Now, the master finding the profits of his trade fall off very much, and being at the same time in want of money to pay the hundred pounds weekly, and perceiving that these hundred pounds are carried away at once, and given to shopkeepers of various descriptions; to butchers, bakers, drapers, hatters, shoemakers, and the rest; and knowing that, on an average, these shop-keepers must all have a profit of thirty *per cent.*, or more, he determines to *keep this thirty per cent. to himself ;* and this is thirty pounds a week gained as a shop-keeper, which amounts to £1560 a year. He, therefore, sets up a tommy shop; a long place containing every commodity that the workman can want, liquor and house-room excepted. Here the workman takes out his pound's worth; and his house-rent he pays in truck, if he do not rent of his master; and if he will have liquor, beer, or gin, or anything else, he must get it by trucking with the goods that he has got at the tommy shop.

Now, there is nothing essentially unjust in this. There is a little inconvenience as far as the house-rent goes; but not much. The tommy is easily turned into money; and if the single saving man does experience some trouble in the sale of his goods, that is compensated for in the more important case of the married man, whose wife and children generally experience the benefit of this payment in kind. It is, to be sure, a sorrowful reflection that such a check upon the drinking propensities of the fathers should be necessary; but *the necessity exists*; and, however sorrowful the fact, the fact, I am assured, is that thousands upon thousands of mothers have to bless this system, though it arises from a loss of trade and the poverty of the masters.

I have often had to observe on the cruel effects of the suppression of markets and fairs, and on the consequent power of extortion possessed by the country shop-keepers. And what a thing it is to reflect on, that these shop-keepers have the whole of the labouring men of England constantly in their debt; have, on an average, a mortgage on their wages to the amount of five or six weeks, and make them pay any price that they choose to extort. So that, in fact, there is a tommy system in every village, the difference being that the shop-keeper is the tommy man instead of the farmer.

The only question is, in this case of the manufacturing tommy work, whether the master charges a higher price than the shop-keepers would charge; and, while I have not heard that the masters do this, I think it improbable that they should. They must desire to avoid the charge of such extortion; and they have little temptation to it; because they buy at best hand and in large quantities; because they are sure of their customers, and know to a certainty the quantity that they want; and because the distribution of the goods is a matter of such perfect regularity and attended with so little expense, compared with the expenses of the shop-keeper. Any farmer who has a parcel of married men working for him might supply them with meat for four-pence the pound, when the butcher must charge them seven-pence, or lose by his trade; and to me it has always appeared astonishing that farmers (where they happen to have the power completely in their hands) do not compel their married labourers to have a sufficiency of bread and meat for their wives and children. What would be more easy than to reckon what would be necessary for house-rent, fuel, and clothing; to pay that in money once a month, or something of that sort, and to pay the rest in meat, flour and malt? I may never occupy a farm again; but if I were to do it, to any extent, the East and West Indies, nor big brewer, nor distiller, should ever have one farthing out of the produce of my farm, except he got it through the throats of those who made the wearing apparel. If I had a village at my command, not a tea-kettle should sing in that village: there should be no extortioner under the name of country shop-keeper, and no straight-backed, bloated fellow, with red eyes, unshaven face, and slip-shod till noon, called a publican, and generally worthy of the name of *sinner*. Well-covered backs and well-lined bellies would be my delight; and as to talking about controlling and compelling, what a control-ling and compelling are there now! It is everlasting control and compulsion. My bargain should be so much in money, and so much in bread, meat, and malt.

And what is the bargain, I want to know, *with yearly servants ?* Why, so much in money and the rest in bread, meat, beer, lodging and fuel. And does any one affect to say that this is wrong? Does any one say that it is wrong to exercise control and com-pulsion over these servants; such control and compulsion is not only the master's right, but they are included in his bounden *duties*. It is his duty to make them rise early, keep good hours, be industrious and careful, be cleanly in their persons and habits, be civil in their language. These are amongst the uses of the means which God has put into his hands; and are these means to be neglected towards married servants any more than towards single ones?

Even in the well-cultivated and thickly-settled parts of the United States of America, it is the general custom, and a very good custom it is, to pay the wages of labour *partly in money and partly in kind ;* and this practice is extended to carpenters, bricklayers, and other workmen about buildings, and even to tailors, shoemakers, and weavers, who go (a most excellent custom) to farm-houses to work. The bargain is so much money *and found ;* that is to say, found in food and drink, and sometimes in lodging. The money then used to be, for a common labourer, in Long Island, at common work (not haying or harvesting), three York shillings a day and found; that is to say, three times sevenpence halfpenny of our money; and three times sevenpence halfpenny a day, which is eleven shillings and threepence a week, and found. This was the wages of the commonest labourer at the commonest work. And the wages of a good labourer now, in Worcestershire, *is eight shillings a week and not found.* Accordingly they are miserably poor and degraded.

Therefore, there is in this mode of payment nothing *essentially* degrading; but the tommy system of Staffordshire, and elsewhere, though not unjust in itself, indirectly inflicts great injustice on the whole race of shop-keepers, who are necessary for the distribution of commodities in great towns, and whose property is taken away from them by this species of monopoly, which the employers of great numbers of men have been compelled to adopt for their own safety. It is not the fault of the masters, who can have no pleasure in making profit in this way: it is the fault of the taxes, which, by lowering the price of their goods, have compelled them to resort to this means of diminishing their expenses, or to quit their business altogether, which a great part of them cannot do without being left without a penny; and if a law could be passed and enforced (which it cannot) to put an end to the tommy system, the consequence would be that instead of a fourth part of the furnaces being let out of blast in this neighbourhood, one-half would be let out of blast, and additional thousands of poor creatures would be left solely dependent on parochial relief.

A view of the situation of things at Shrewsbury will lead us in a minute to the real cause of the tommy system. Shrewsbury is one of the most interesting spots that man ever beheld. It is the capital of the county of Salop, and Salop appears to have been the original name of the town itself. It is curiously enclosed by the river Severn, which is here large and fine, and which, in the form of a *horse-shoe*, completely surrounds it, leaving of the whole of the two miles round only one little place whereon to pass in and out on land. There are two bridges, one on the east and the other on the west; the former called the English and the other the Welsh bridge. The environs of this town, especially on the Welsh side, are the most beautiful that can be conceived. The town lies in the midst of a fine agricultural country, of which it is the great and almost only mart. Hither come the farmers to sell their produce, and hence they take, in exchange, their groceries, their clothing, and all the materials for their implements and the domestic conveniences. It was fair-day when I arrived at Shrewsbury. Everything was on the decline. Cheese, which four years ago sold at sixty shillings the six-score pounds, would not bring forty. I took particular pains to ascertain the fact with regard to the cheese, which is a great article here. I was assured that shop-keepers in general did not now sell half the quantity of goods in a month that they did in that space of time four or five years ago. The *ironmongers* were not selling a fourth-part of what they used to sell five years ago.

Now it is impossible to believe that a somewhat similar falling off in the sale of iron must not have taken place all over the kingdom; and need we then wonder that the iron in Staffordshire has fallen, within these five years, from thirteen pounds to five pounds a ton, or perhaps a great deal more; and need we wonder that the *iron-masters*, who have the same rent and taxes to pay that they had to pay before, have resorted to the tommy system, in order to assist in saving themselves from ruin! Here is the real cause of the tommy system; and if Mr. Littleton really wishes to put an end to it, let him prevail upon the parliament to take off taxes to the amount of forty millions a year.

Another article had experienced a still greater falling off at Shrewsbury; I mean the article of corn-sacks, of which there has been a falling off of *five-sixths*. The sacks are made by weavers in the north; and need we wonder, then, at the low wages of those industrious people, whom I used to see weaving sacks in the miserable cellars at Preston!

Here is the true cause of the tommy system, and of all the other evils which disturb and afflict the country. It is a great country; an immense mass of industry and resources of all sorts *breaking up ;* a prodigious mass of enterprise and capital diminishing and dispersing. The enormous taxes co-operating with the Corn Bill, which those taxes have engendered, are driving skill and wealth out of the country in all directions; are causing iron-masters to make France, and particularly Belgium, blaze with furnaces, in the lieu of those which have been extinguished here; and that have established furnaces and cotton-mills in abundance. These same taxes and this same Corn Bill are sending the long wool from Lincolnshire to France, there to be made into those blankets which, for ages, were to be obtained nowhere but in England.

This is the true state of the country, and here are the true causes of that state; and all that the corrupt writers and speakers say about over-population and poor-laws, and about all the rest of their shuffling excuses, is a heap of nonsense and of lies.

I cannot quit Shrewsbury without expressing the great satisfaction that I derived from my visit to that place. It is the only town into which I have gone, in all England, without knowing beforehand something of some person in it. I could find out no person that took the *Register;* and could discover but one person who took the *Advice to Young Men.* The number of my auditors was expected to be so small that I doubled the price of admission, in order to pay the expense of the room. To my great surprise I had a room full of gentlemen, at the request of some of whom I repeated the dose the next night; and if my audience were as well pleased with me as I was with them, their pleasure must have been great indeed. I saw not one single person in the place that I had ever seen before; yet I never had more cordial shakes by the hand; in proportion to their numbers, not more at Manchester, Oldham, Rochdale, Halifax, Leeds, or Nottingham, or even Hull. I was particularly pleased with the conduct of the *young* gentlemen at Shrewsbury, and especially when I asked them whether they were prepared to act upon the insolent doctrine of Huskisson, and quietly submit to this state of things "*during the present generation.*"

TOUR IN THE WEST

3 July 1830.

JUST as I was closing my third lecture (on Saturday night) at Bristol, to a numerous and most respectable audience, the news of the above event [the death of George IV.] arrived. I had advertised and made all the preparations for lecturing at Bath on Monday, Tuesday, and Wednesday; but under the circumstances, I thought it would not be proper to proceed thither, for that purpose, until after the burial of the king. When that has taken place I shall, as soon as may be, return to Bath, taking Hertfordshire and Buckinghamshire in my way; from Bath, through Somerset, Devon, and into Cornwall; and back through Dorset, South Wilts, Hants, Sussex, Kent, and then go into Essex, and, last of all, into my native county of Surrey. I shall then have seen all England with my own eyes, except Rutland, Westmoreland, Durham, Cumberland, and Northumberland; and these, if I have life and health till next spring, I shall see in my way to Scotland. But never shall I see another place to interest me, and so pleasing to me, as Bristol and its environs, taking the whole together. A good and solid and wealthy city: a people of plain and good manners; private virtue and public spirit united; no empty noise, no insolence, no flattery; men very much like the Yorkers and Lancastrians. And as to the seat of the city and its environs, it surpasses all that I ever saw. A great commercial city in the midst of corn-fields, meadows and woods, and the ships coming into the centre of it, miles from anything like sea, up a narrow river, and passing between two clefts of a rock probably a hundred feet high; so that from the top of these clefts you *look down* upon the main-topgallant masts of lofty ships that are gliding along!

PROGRESS IN THE NORTH

NEWCASTLE-UPON-TYNE,
23 September 1832.

FROM Bolton, in Lancashire, I came through Bury and Rochdale to Todmorden, on the evening of Tuesday, the 18th September. I have formerly described the valley of Todmorden as the most curious and romantic that was ever seen, and where the water and the coal seemed to be engaged in a struggle for getting foremost in point of utility to man. On the 19th I stayed all day at Todmorden to write and to sleep. On the 20th I set off for Leeds by the stage coach, through Halifax and Bradford; and as to *agriculture*, certainly the poorest country that I have ever set my eyes on, except that miserable *Nova Scotia*, where there are the townships of Horton and of Wilmot, and whither the sensible suckling statesman, Lord Howick, is wanting to send English country girls, lest they should breed if they stay in England! This country, from Todmorden to Leeds, is, however, covered over with population, and the two towns of Halifax and Bradford are exceedingly populous. There appears to be nothing produced by the earth but the natural grass of the country, which, however, is not bad. The soil is a sort of yellow-looking, stiffish stuff, lying about a foot thick, upon a bed of rocky stone, lying upon solid rock beneath. The grass does not seem to burn here; nor is it bad in quality; and all the grass appears to be wanted to rear milk for this immense population that absolutely covers the whole face of the country. The only grain crops that I saw were those of very miserable oats; some of which were cut and carried; some standing in *shock*, the sheaves not being more than about a foot and a half long; some still standing, and some yet *nearly green*. The land is very high from Halifax to Bradford, and proportionably cold. Here are some of those " Yorkshire Hills " that they see from Lancashire and Cheshire.

I got to Leeds about four o'clock, and went to bed at eight precisely. At five in the morning of the 21st I came off by the coach to Newcastle, through Harrowgate, Ripon, Darlington, and Durham. As I never was in this part of the country before, and can, therefore, never have described it upon any former occasion, I shall say rather more about it now than I otherwise should do. Having heard and read so much about the "Northern Harvest," about the " Durham ploughs," and the " Northumberland system of husbandry," what was my surprise at finding, which I verily believe to be the fact, that there is not as much corn grown in the North Riding of Yorkshire, which begins at Ripon, and in the whole county of Durham, as is grown in the Isle of Wight alone. A very small part, comparatively speaking, is *arable* land; and all the outward appearances show that that which is arable was formerly pasture. Between Durham and Newcastle there is a pretty general division of the land into grass fields and corn fields; but even here the absence of *homesteads*, the absence of barns, and of labourers' cottages, clearly show that agriculture is a sort of novelty; and that nearly all was pasturage not many years ago, or, at any rate, only so much of the land was cultivated as was necessary to furnish straw for the horses kept for other purposes than those of agriculture, and oats for those horses, and bread corn sufficient for the graziers and their people. All along the road from Leeds to Durham I saw hardly any wheat at all, or any wheat stubble, no barley, the chief crops being oats and beans mixed with peas. These everywhere appeared to be what we should deem most miserable crops. The oats, tied up in sheaves, or yet uncut, were scarcely ever more than two feet and a half long, the beans were about the same height, and in both cases the land so full of grass as to appear to be *a pasture*, after the oats and the beans were cut.

The land appears to be divided into very extensive farms. The corn, when cut, you see put up into little stacks of a circular form, each containing about *three* of our southern waggon-loads of sheaves, which stacks are put up round about the stone house and the buildings of the farmer. How they thrash them out I do not know, for I could see nothing resembling a barn or a barn's door. By the corn being put into such small stacks, I should suppose the thrashing places to be very small, and capable of holding only one stack at a time. I have many times seen one single rick containing a greater quantity of sheaves than fifteen or twenty of these stacks; and I have seen more than twenty stacks, each containing a number of sheaves equal to at least fifteen of these stacks; I have seen more than twenty of these large stacks standing at one and the same time in one single homestead in Wiltshire. I should not at all wonder if

Tom Baring's farmers at Micheldever had a greater bulk of wheat-stacks standing now than any one would be able to find of that grain, especially, in the whole of the North Riding of Yorkshire, and in one half of Durham.

But this by no means implies that these are beggarly counties, even exclusive of their waters, coals, and mines. They are not *agricultural* counties; they are not counties for the producing of bread, but they are counties made for the express purpose of producing meat; in which respect they excel the southern counties in a degree beyond all comparison. I have just spoken of the *beds of grass* that are everywhere seen after the oats and the beans have been cut. Grass is the natural produce of this land, which seems to have been made on purpose to produce it; and we are not to call land *poor* because it will produce nothing but meat. The size and shape of the fields, the sort of fences, the absence of all homesteads and labourers' cottages, the thinness of the country churches, everything shows that this was always a country purely of pasturage. It is curious that, belonging to every farm, there appears to be a large quantity of turnips. They are sowed in drills, cultivated between, beautifully clean, very large in the bulb even now, and apparently having been sowed early in June, if not in May. They are generally the white globe turnip, here and there a field of the swedish kind. These turnips are not fed off by sheep and followed by crops of barley and clover, as in the south, but are raised, I suppose, for the purpose of being carried in and used in the feeding of oxen, which have come off the grass lands in October and November. These turnip lands seem to take all the manure of the farm; and as the reader will perceive, they are merely an adjunct to the pasturage, serving during the winter instead of hay, wherewith to feed the cattle of various descriptions.

This, then, is not a country of farmers, but a country of graziers; a country of pasture, and not a country of the plough; and those who formerly managed the land here were not husbandmen, but herdsmen. Fortescue was, I dare say, a native of this country; for he describes England as a country of shepherds and of herdsmen, not working so very hard as the people of France did, having more leisure for contemplation, and therefore more likely to form a just estimate of their rights and duties: and he describes them as having, at all times, in their houses, plenty of flesh to eat and plenty of woollen to wear. St. Augustine, in writing to the pope an account of the character and conduct of his converts in England, told him that he found the English an exceedingly good and generous people; but they had one fault, their fondness for flesh-meat was so great, and their resolution to have it so determined, that he could not get them to abstain from it, even on the fast-days; and that he was greatly afraid that they would return to their state of horrible heathenism rather than submit to the discipline of the church in this respect. The pope, who had more sense than the greater part of bishops have ever had, wrote for answer: "Keep them within the pale of the church at any rate, even if they slaughter their oxen in the churchyards: let them make shambles of the churches rather than suffer the devil to carry away their souls." The taste of our fathers was by no means for the potato; for the "nice *mealy* potato." The pope himself would not have been able to induce them to carry "cold potatoes in their bags" to the plough-field, as was, in evidence before the special commissions, proved to have been the common practice in Hampshire and Wiltshire, and which had been before proved by evidence taken by unfeeling committees of the boroughmonger House of Commons. Faith! these old papas of ours would have burnt up not only the stacks but the ground itself, rather than have lived upon miserable roots, while those who raised none of the food were eating up all the bread and the meat.

Brougham and Birkbeck, and the rest of the Malthusian crew, are constantly at work preaching *content to the hungry and naked*. To be sure, they themselves, however, are not content to be hungry and naked. Amongst other things, they tell the working people that the working-folks, especially in the north, used to have no bread, except such as was made of oats and of barley. That was better than potatoes, even the "nice mealy ones;" especially when carried cold to the field in a bag. But these literary impostors, these deluders, as far as they are able to delude; these vagabond authors, who thus write and publish for the purpose of persuading the working-people to be quiet, while they sack luxuries and riches out of the fruit of their toil; these literary impostors take care not to tell the people that these oat-cakes and this barley-bread were always associated with great lumps of flesh-meat; they forget to tell them this, or rather these half-mad, perverse, and perverting literary impostors suppress the facts, for reasons far too manifest to need stating.

The cattle here are the most beautiful by far that I ever saw.

The sheep are very handsome; but the horned cattle are the prettiest creatures that my eyes ever beheld. My sons will recollect that when they were little boys I took them to see the " Durham Ox," of which they drew the picture, I dare say, a hundred times. That was upon a large scale, to be sure, the model of all these beautiful cattle: short horns, straight back, a taper neck, very small in proportion where it joins on the small and handsome head, deep dewlap, small-boned in the legs, hoop-ribbed, square-hipped, tail slender. A great part of them are white, or approaching very nearly to white: they all appear to be half fat, cows and oxen and all; and the meat from them is said to be, and I believe it is, as fine as that from Lincolnshire, Herefordshire, Romney Marsh, or Pevensey Level, and I am ready, at any time, to swear, if need be, that one pound of it fed upon this grass is worth more, to me at least, than any ten pounds or twenty pounds fed upon oil-cake, or the stinking stuff of distilleries; aye, or even upon turnips. This is all *grass-land*, even from Staffordshire to this point. In its very nature it produces grass that fattens. The little producing-land that there is even in Lancashire and the West Riding of Yorkshire produces grass that would fatten an ox, though the land be upon the tops of hills. Everywhere, where there is a sufficiency of grass, it will fatten an ox; and well do we southern people know that, except in mere vales and meadows, we have no land that will do this; we know that we might put an ox up to his eyes in our grass, and that it would only just keep him from growing worse: we know that we are obliged to have turnips and meal and cabbages and parsnips and potatoes, and then with some of our hungry hay for them to *pick their teeth with* we make shift to put fat upon an ox.

Yet, so much are we like the beasts which, in the fable, came before Jupiter to ask him to endow them with faculties incompatible with their divers frames and divers degrees of strength, that we, in this age of " *waust improvements, ma'am*," are always hankering after laying fields down in pasture in the south, while these fellows in the north, as if resolved to rival us in " improvement " and perverseness, must needs break up their pasture-lands, and proclaim defiance to the will of Providence, and instead of rich pasture, present to the eye of the traveller half-green starveling oats and peas, some of them in blossom in the last week of September. The land itself, the earth, of its own accord, as if resolved to vindicate the decrees of its Maker, sends up grass under these miserable crops, as if to punish them for their intrusion; and when the crops are off there comes a pasture, at any rate, in which the grass, like that of Herefordshire and Lincolnshire, is not (as it is in our southern countries), mixed with weeds; but, standing upon the ground as thick as the earth can bear it, and fattening everything that eats of it, it forbids the perverse occupier to tear it to pieces. Such is the land of this country; all to the north of Cheshire, at any rate, leaving out the East Riding of Yorkshire and Lincolnshire, which are adapted for corn in some spots and for cattle in others.

These Yorkshire and Durham cows are to be seen in great numbers in and about London, where they are used for the purpose of giving milk, of which I suppose they give great quantities; but it is always an observation that, if you have these cows you must *keep them exceedingly well ;* and this is very true; for upon the food which does very well for the common cows of Hampshire and Surrey they would dwindle away directly and be good for nothing at all; and these sheep, which are as beautiful as even imagination could make them, so round and so loaded with flesh, would actually perish upon those downs and in those folds where our innumerable flocks not only live but fatten so well, and with such facility are made to produce us such quantities of fine mutton and such bales of fine wool. There seems to be something in the soil and climate, and particularly in the soil, to create everywhere a sort of cattle and of sheep fitted to it; Dorsetshire and Somersetshire have sheep different from all others, and the nature of which it is to have their lambs in the fall instead of having them in the spring. I remember when I was amongst the villages on the Cotswold Hills, in Gloucestershire, they showed me their sheep in several places which are a stout big-boned sheep. They told me that many attempts had been made to cross them with the small-boned Leicester breed, but that it had never succeeded, and that the race always got back to the Cotswold breed immediately.

Before closing these rural remarks, I cannot help calling to the mind of the reader an observation of Lord John Scott Eldon, who, at a time when there was a great complaint about " agricultural distress " and about the fearful increase of the poor-rates, said, " that there was no such distress *in Northumberland,* and no such increase of the poor-rates: " and so said my dignitary, Dr. Black, at the same time: and this, this wise lord, and this not less wise dignitary of mine, ascribed to " the bad practice of the farmers o' the sooth paying the labourers their wages out of the poor-rates, which was not the practice in the north." I thought that they were telling what the children call *stories;* but I now find that these observations of theirs arose purely from that want of knowledge of the country which was, and is, common to them both. Why, Lord John, there are no such persons here as we call farmers, and no such persons as we call farm-labourers. From Cheshire to Newcastle I have never seen *one single labourer's cottage by the side of the road!* Oh, Lord! if the good people of this country could but see the endless strings of vine-covered cottages and flower-gardens of the labourers of Kent, Sussex, Surrey, and Hampshire; if they could go down the vale of the Avon in Wiltshire, from Marlborough Forest to the city of Salisbury, and there see *thirty* parish churches in a distance of thirty miles; if they could go up from that city of Salisbury up the valley of Wylly to Warminster, and there see one-and-thirty churches in the space of twenty-seven miles; if they could go upon the top of the down, as I did, not far (I think it was) from St. Mary Cotford, and there have under the eye, in the valley below, *ten parish churches within the distance of eight miles,* see the downs covered with innumerable flocks of sheep, water meadows running down the middle of the valley, while the sides rising from it were covered with corn, sometimes a hundred acres of wheat in one single piece, while the stack-yards were still well stored from the previous harvest; if John Scott Eldon's countrymen could behold these things, their quick-sightedness would soon discover why poor-rates should have increased in the south and not in the north; and though their liberality would suggest an apology for my dignitary, Dr. Black, who was freighted to London in a smack, and has ever since been impounded in the Strand, relieved now and then by an excursion to Blackheath or Clapham Common; to find an apology for their countryman, Lord John, would be putting their liberality to an uncommonly severe test; for he, be it known to them, has chosen his country abode, not in the Strand like my less-informed dignitary, Dr. Black, nor in his native regions in the north; but has in the beautiful county of Dorset, amidst valleys and downs precisely like those of Wiltshire, got as near to the sun as he could possibly get, and there from the top of his mansion he can see a score of churches, and from his lofty and evergreen downs, and from his fat valleys beneath, he annually sends his flocks of long-tailed ewes to Appleshaw fair, thence to be sold to all the southern parts of the kingdom, having L. E. marked upon their beautiful wool; and, like the two factions at Maidstone, all tarred with the same brush. It is curious, too, notwithstanding the old maxim that we all try to get as nearly as possible in our old age to the spot whence we first sprang. Lord John's brother William (who has some title that I have forgotten) has taken up his quarters on the healthy and I say beautiful Cotswold of Gloucestershire, where, in going in a post-chaise from Stowe-in-the-Wold to Cirencester, I thought I should never get by the wall of his park; and I exclaimed to Mr. Dean, who was along with me, " Curse this Northumbrian ship-broker's son, he has got one half of the county; " and then all the way to Cirencester I was explaining to Mr. Dean *how the man had got his money*, at which Dean, who is a Roman Catholic, seemed to me to be ready to cross himself several times.

No, there is no apology for Lord John's observations on the difference between the poor-rates of the south and the north. To go from London to his country-houses he must go across Surrey and Hampshire, along one of the vales of Wiltshire and one of the vales of Dorsetshire, in which latter county he has many a time seen in one single large field *a hundred wind-rows* (stacks made in the field in order that the corn may get quite dry before it be put into great stacks); he has many a time seen, on one farm, two or three hundred of these, each of which was very nearly as big as the stacks which you see in the stack-yards of the North Riding of Yorkshire and of Durham, where a large farm seldom produces more than ten or a dozen of these stacks, and where the farmer's property consists of his cattle and sheep, and where little, very little, agricultural labour is wanted. Lord John ought to have known the cause of the great difference, and not to have suffered such nonsense to come out of a head covered with so very large a wig.

I looked with particular care on the sides of the road all the way through Yorkshire and Durham. The distance, altogether, from Oldham in Lancashire to Newcastle-upon-Tyne, is about a hundred and fifty miles; and, leaving out the *great* towns, I did not see so many churches as are to be seen in any twenty miles of any of the valleys of Wiltshire. All these things prove that these are by nature counties of pasturage, and that they were formerly used solely for that purpose. It is curious that there are none of those lands here which we call " meadows." The rivers run in *deep beds*, and have generally very steep sides; no little rivulets and occasional overflowings that make the meadows in the south, which are so very beautiful, but the grass in which is not of the rich nature that the grass is in these counties in the north; it will produce milk enough, but it will not produce beef. It is hard to say which part of the country is the most valuable gift of God; but every one must see how perverse and injurious it is to endeavour to produce in the one that which nature has intended to confine to the other. After all the unnatural efforts that have been made here to ape the farming of Norfolk and Suffolk, it is only *playing at farming,* as stupid and " loyal " parents used to set their children *to play at soldiers during the last war.*

If any of these sensible men of Newcastle were to see the farming in the South Downs, and to see, as I saw in the month of July last, four teams of large oxen, six in a team, all ploughing in one field in preparation for wheat, and several pairs of horses, in the same field, dragging, harrowing, and rolling, and had seen on the other side of the road from five to six quarters of wheat standing upon the acre, and from nine to ten quarters of oats standing along side of it, each of the two fields from fifty to a hundred statute acres; if any of these sensible men of Newcastle could see these things, they would laugh at the childish work that they see going on here under the name of farming; the very sight would make them feel how imperious is the duty on the law-giver to prevent distress from visiting the fields, and to take care that those whose labour produced all the food and all the raiment, shall not be fed upon potatoes and covered with rags; contemplating the important effects of their labour, each man of them could say as I said when this mean and savage faction had me at my trial, " I would see all these labourers hanged, and be hanged along with them, rather than see them live upon potatoes."

Newcastle-upon-Tyne,
24 September 1832.

Since writing the above I have had an opportunity of receiving information from a very intelligent gentleman of this county, who tells me that in Northumberland there are some lands which bear very heavy crops of wheat; that the agriculture in this county is a great deal better than it is farther south; that, however, it was a most lamentable thing that the paper-money price of corn tempted so many men to break up these fine pastures; that the turf thus destroyed cannot be restored probably in a whole century; that the land does not now, with present prices, yield a clear profit, anything like what it would have yielded in the pasture; and that thus was destroyed the *goose with the golden eggs.* Just so was it with regard to the *downs* in the south and the west of England, where there are hundreds of thousands of acres where the turf was the finest in the world, broken up for the sake of the paper-money prices, but now left to be *downs again ;* and which will not be *downs* for more than a century to come. Thus did this accursed paper-money cause even the fruitful qualities of the earth to be anticipated, and thus was the soil made *worth less* than it was before the accursed invention appeared! This gentleman told me that this breaking up of the pasture land in this country had made the land, though covered again with artificial grasses, unhealthy for sheep; and he gave as an instance the facts that three farmers purchased a hundred and fifty sheep each out of the same flock; that two of them, who put their sheep upon these recently broken-up lands, lost their whole flocks by the rot, with the exception of four in the one case and four in the other, out of the three hundred: and that the third farmer, who put his sheep upon the old pastures, and kept them there, lost not a single sheep out of the hundred and fifty! These, ever accursed paper-money, are amongst thy destructive effects!

I shall now, laying aside for the present these rural affairs, turn to the politics of this fine, opulent, solid, beautiful, and important town; but as this would compel me to speak of particular transactions and particular persons, and as this *Register* will come back to Newcastle before I am likely to quit it, the reader will see reasons quite sufficient for my refraining to go into matters of this sort until the next *Register*, which will in all probability be dated from Edinburgh.

While at Manchester I received an invitation to lodge while here at the house of a friend, of whom I shall have to speak more fully hereafter; but every demonstration of respect and kindness met me at the door of the coach in which I came from Leeds, on Friday, the 21st September. In the early part of Saturday, the 22nd, a deputation waited upon me with *an address.* Let the readers in my native county and parish remember that I am now at the end of thirty years of calumnies poured out incessantly upon me from the poisonous mouths and pens of three hundred mercenary villains, called newspaper editors and reporters; that I have written and published more than a hundred volumes in those thirty years; and that more than a thousand volumes (chiefly paid for out of the taxes) have been written and published for the sole purpose of impeding the progress of those truths that dropped from my pen; that my whole life has been a life of sobriety and labour; that I have invariably shown that I loved and honoured my country, and that I preferred its greatness and happiness far beyond my own; that, at four distinct periods, I might have rolled in wealth derived from the public money, which I always refused on any account to touch; that for having thwarted this government in its wastefulness of the public resources, and particularly for my endeavours to produce that reform of the parliament which the government itself has at last been compelled to resort to; that for having acted this zealous and virtuous part I have been twice stripped of all my earnings by the acts of this government, once lodged in a felon's gaol for two years, and once driven into exile for two years and a half; and that, after all, here I am on a spot within a hundred miles of which I never was before in my life; and here I am receiving the unsolicited applause of men amongst the most intelligent in the whole kingdom, and the names of some of whom have been pronounced accompanied with admiration, even to the southernmost edge of the kingdom.

HEXHAM,

1 *Oct.* 1832.

I left Morpeth this morning pretty early to come to this town, which lies on the banks of the Tyne, at thirty-four miles distant from Morpeth, and at twenty distant from Newcastle. Morpeth is a great market-town, for cattle especially. It is a solid old town; but it has the disgrace of seeing an enormous new gaol rising up in it. From cathedrals and monasteries we are come to be proud of our gaols, which are built in the grandest style, and seemingly as if to imitate the Gothic architecture.

From Morpeth to within about four miles of Hexham the land is but very indifferent; the farms of an enormous extent. I saw in one place more than a hundred corn-stacks in one yard, each having from six to seven Surrey waggon-loads of sheaves in a stack; and not another house to be seen within a mile or two of the farm-house. There appears to be no such thing as barns, but merely a place to take in a stack at a time, and thrash it out by a machine. The country seems to be almost wholly destitute of people. Immense tracks of corn-land, but neither cottages nor churches. There is here and there a spot of good land, just as in the deep valleys that I crossed; but, generally speaking, the country is poor; and its bleakness is proved by the almost total absence of the oak tree, of which we see scarcely one all the way from Morpeth to Hexham. Very few trees of any sort, except in the bottom of the warm valleys; what there are, are chiefly the *ash*, which is a very hardy tree, and will live and thrive where the *oak* will not grow at all, which is very curious, seeing that it comes out into leaf so late in the spring, and sheds its foliage so early in the fall. The trees which stand next in point of hardiness are the *sycamore*, the *beech*, and the *birch*, which are all seen here; but none of them fine. The *ash* is the most common tree, and even it flinches upon the hills, which it never does in the south. It has generally become yellow in the leaf already; and many of the trees are now bare of leaf before any frost has made its appearance.

The cattle all along here are of a coarse kind; the cows swag-backed and badly shaped; Kiloe oxen, except in the dips of good land by the sides of the bourns which I crossed. Never-theless, even here, the fields of turnips of both sorts are very fine. Great pains seem to be taken in raising the crops of these turnips: they are cultivated in rows, are kept exceedingly clean, and they are carried in as winter food for all the animals of a farm, the horses excepted.

As I approached Hexham, which, as the reader knows, was formerly the seat of a famous abbey, and the scene of a not less famous battle, and was indeed at one time the *see* of a bishop, and which has now churches of great antiquity and cathedral-like architecture; as I approached this town, along a valley down which runs a small river that soon after empties itself into the Tyne, the land became good, the ash-trees more lofty, and green as in June; the other trees proportionably large and fine; and when I got down into the vale of Hexham itself, there I found the *oak-tree*, certain proof of a milder atmosphere; for the *oak*, though amongst the hardest *woods*, is amongst the tenderest of plants known as natives of our country. Here everything assumes a different appearance. The Tyne, the southern and northern branches of which meet a few miles above Hexham, runs close by this ancient and celebrated town, all round which the ground rises gradually away towards the hills, crowned here and there with the remains of those castles which were formerly found necessary for the defence of this rich and valuable valley, which, from tip of hill to tip of hill, varies, perhaps, from four to seven miles wide, and which contains as fine corn-fields as those of Wiltshire, and fields of turnips, of both kinds, the largest, finest, and best cultivated that my eyes ever beheld. As a proof of the goodness of the land and the mildness of the climate here, there is, in the grounds of the gentleman who had the kindness to receive and to entertain me (and that in a manner which will prevent me from ever forgetting either him or his most amiable wife); there is, standing in his ground, *about an acre of my corn*, which will ripen perfectly well; and in the same grounds, which, together with the kitchen-garden and all the appurtenances belonging to a house, and the house itself, are laid out, arranged and contrived in a manner so judicious, and to me so original, as to render them objects of great interest, though in general I set very little value on the things which appertain merely to the enjoyments of the rich. In these same grounds (to come back again to the climate) I perceived that the rather tender evergreens not only lived but throve perfectly well, and (a criterion infallible) the *biennial stocks* stand the winter without any covering or any pains taken to shelter them; which, as every one knows, is by no means always the case even at Kensington and Fulham.

At night I gave a lecture at an inn, at Hexham, in the midst of the domains of that impudent and stupid man, Mr. Beaumont, who not many days before, in what he called a speech, I suppose, made at Newcastle, thought proper, as was reported in the newspapers, to utter the following words with regard to me, never having in his life received the slightest provocation for so doing. " The liberty of the press had nothing to fear from the government. It was the duty of the administration to be upon their guard to prevent extremes. There was a crouching servility on the one hand, and an excitement to disorganisation and to licentiousness on the other, which ought to be discountenanced. The company, he believed, as much disapproved of that political traveller who was now going through the country—he meant Cobbett—as they detested the servile effusions of the Tories." Beaumont, in addition to his native stupidity and imbecility, might have been drunk when he said this, but the servile wretch who published it was not drunk; and, at any rate, Beaumont was my mark, it not being my custom to snap at the stick, but at the cowardly hand that wields it.

Such a fellow cannot be an object of what is properly called *vengeance* with any man who is worth a straw; but I say, with Swift, " If a *flea* or a *bug* bite me, I will kill it if I can; " and, acting upon that principle, I, being at Hexham, put my foot upon this contemptible creeping thing, who is offering himself as a candidate for the southern division of the county, being so eminently fitted to be a maker of the laws!

The newspapers have told the whole country that Mr. John Ridley, who is a tradesman at Hexham, and occupies some land close by, has made a stand against the demand for tithes; and that the tithe-owner recently broke open, in the night, the gate of his field, and carried away what he deemed to be the tithe; that Mr. Ridley applied to the magistrates, who could only refer him to a court of law to recover damages for the trespass. When I arrived at Hexham, I found this to be the case. I further found that Beaumont, that impudent, silly and slanderous Beaumont, is the *lay-owner* of the tithes in and round about Hexham; he being, in a right line, doubtless, the heir or successor of the abbot and monks of the Abbey of Hexham; or the heir of the donor, Egfrid, *king of Northumberland*. I found that Beaumont had leased out his tithes to *middle men*, as is the laudable custom with the pious bishops and clergy of the law-church in Ireland.

NORTH SHIELDS,
2 Oct. 1832.

These sides of the Tyne are very fine: corn-fields, woods, pastures, villages; a church every four miles, or thereabouts; cows and sheep beautiful; oak-trees, though none very large; and, in short, a fertile and beautiful country, wanting only the gardens and the vine-covered cottages that so beautify the counties in the south and the west. All the buildings are of stone. Here are coal-works and railways every now and then. The working people seem to be very well off; their dwellings solid and clean, and their furniture good; but the little gardens and orchards are wanting. The farms are all large; and the people who work on them either live in the farm-house, or in buildings appertaining to the farm-house; and they are all well fed, and have no temptation to acts like those which sprang up out of the ill-treament of the labourers in the south. Besides, the mere country people are so few in number, the state of society is altogether so different, that a man that has lived here all his life-time can form no judgment at all with regard to the situation, the wants, and the treatment of the working people in the counties of the south.

They have begun to make a railway from Carlisle to Newcastle; and I saw them at work at it as I came along. There are great *lead mines* not far from Hexham; and I saw a great number of little one-horse carts bringing down the *pigs of lead* to the point where the Tyne becomes navigable to Newcastle; and sometimes I saw loads of these *pigs* lying by the road-side, as you see parcels of timber lying in Kent and Sussex, and other timber counties. No fear of their being stolen: their weight is their security, together with their value compared with that of the labour of carrying. Hearing that Beaumont was, somehow or other, connected with this lead-work, I had got it into my head that he was a pig of lead himself, and half expected to meet with him amongst these groups of his fellow-creatures; but, upon inquiry, I found that some of the lead-mines belonged to him; descending, probably, in that same right line in *which the tithes descended to him ;* and, as the Bishop of Durham is said to be the owner of great lead-mines, Beaumont and the bishop may possibly be in the *same boat* with regard to the subterranean estate as well as that upon the surface; and, if this should be the case, it will, I verily believe, require all the piety of the bishop, and all the wisdom of Beaumont, to keep the boat above water for another five years.

NORTH SHIELDS,
3 Oct. 1832.

I lectured at South Shields last evening, and here this evening. I came over the river from South Shields about eleven o'clock last night, and made a very firm bargain with myself never to do the like again. This evening, after my lecture was over, some gentlemen presented an address to me upon the stage, before the audience, accompanied with the valuable and honourable present of the late Mr. Eneas Mackenzie's *History of the County of Northumberland ;* a very. interesting work, worthy of every library in the kingdom.

From Newcastle to Morpeth; from Morpeth to Hexham; and then all the way down the Tyne; though everywhere such abundance of fine turnips, and in some cases of mangel-wurzel, you see scarcely any *potatoes ;* a certain sign that the working people do not live like hogs. This root is raised in Northumberland and Durham to be used merely as garden stuff; and used in that way it is very good; the contrary of which I never thought, much less did I ever say it. It is the using of it as a *substitute* for bread and for meat that I have deprecated it; and when the Irish poet, Dr. Drennen, called it " the lazy root, and the root of misery," he gave it its true character. Sir Charles Wolseley, who has travelled a great deal in France, Germany and Italy, and who, though Scott-Eldon scratched him out of the commission of the peace, and though the sincere patriot

Brougham will not put him in again, is a very great and accurate observer as to these interesting matters, has assured me that, in whatever proportion the cultivation of potatoes prevails in those countries, in that same proportion the working-people are wretched.

From this degrading curse; from sitting round a dirty board, with potatoes trundled out upon it, as the Irish do; from going to the field with cold potatoes in their bags, as the working-people of Hampshire and Wiltshire *did*, but which they have not done since the appearance of certain *coruscations* which, to spare the feelings of the " Lambs, the Broughams, the Greys, and the Russells," and their dirty bill-of-indictment-drawer Denman, I will not describe, much less will I eulogise; from this degrading curse the county of Northumberland is yet happily free!

SUNDERLAND,
4 *Oct.* 1832.

This morning I left North Shields in a post-chaise, in order to come hither through Newcastle and Gateshead, this affording me the only opportunity that I was likely to have of seeing a plantation of Mr. Annorer Donkin, close in the neighbourhood of Newcastle; which plantation had been made according to the method prescribed in my book called the *Woodlands;* and to see which plantation I previously communicated a request to Mr. Donkin. That gentleman received me in a manner which will want no describing to those who have had the good luck to visit Newcastle. The plantation is most advantageously circumstanced to furnish proof of the excellence of my instructions as to planting. The predecessor of Mr. Donkin also made plantations upon the same spot, and consisting precisely of the same sort of trees. The two plantations are separated from each other merely by a road going through them. Those of the predecessor have been made *six-and-twenty years;* those of Mr. Donkin *six years:* and incredible as it may appear, the trees in the latter are full as lofty as those in the former; and besides the equal loftiness, are vastly superior in point of shape, and, which is very curious, retain all their freshness at this season of the year, while the old plantations are brownish and many of the leaves falling off the trees, though the sort of trees is precisely the same. As a sort of reward for having thus contributed to this very rational source of his pleasure, Mr. Donkin was good enough to give me an elegant copy of the fables of the celebrated Bewick, who was once a native of Newcastle and an honour to the town, and whose books I had had from the time that my children began to look at books, until taken from me by that sort of rapine which I had to experience at the time of my memorable flight across the Atlantic, in order to secure the use of that long arm which I caused to reach them from Long Island to London.

In Mr. Donkin's kitchen-garden (my eyes being never closed in such a scene), I saw what I had never seen before in any kitchen-garden, and which it may be very useful to some of my readers to have described to them. *Wall-fruit* is, when destroyed in the spring, never destroyed by *dry-cold;* but ninety-nine times out of a hundred by wet-frosts, which descend always perpendicularly, and which are generally fatal if they come between the expansion of the blossom and the setting of the fruit; that is to say, if they come after the bloom is quite open, and before it has disentangled itself from the fruit. The great thing, therefore, in getting *wall-fruit,* is to keep off these frosts. The French make use of boards, in the neighbourhood of Paris, projecting from the tops of the walls and supported by poles; and some persons contrive to have curtains to come over the whole tree at night and to be drawn up in the morning. Mr. Donkin's walls have a top of stone; and this top, or cap, projects about eight inches beyond the face of the wall, which is quite sufficient to guard against the wet-frosts which always fall perpendicularly. This is a country of stone to be sure; but those who can afford to build walls for the purpose of having wall-fruit can afford to cap them in this manner: to rear the wall, plant the trees, and then to save the expense of the cap, is really like the old proverbial absurdity, " of losing the ship for the sake of saving a pennyworth of tar."

At Mr. Donkin's I saw a portrait of Bewick, which is said to be a great likeness, and which, though imagination goes a great way in such a case, really bespeaks that simplicity, accompanied with that genius, which distinguished the man. Mr. Wm. Armstrong was kind enough to make me a present of a copy of the last performance of this so justly celebrated man. It is entitled " *Waits for Death,*" exhibiting a poor old horse just about to die, and preceded by an explanatory writing which does as much honour to the heart of Bewick as the whole of his designs put together do to his genius. The sight of the picture, the reading of the preface to it, and the fact that it was the last effort of the man, altogether make it difficult to prevent tears from starting from the eyes of any one not uncommonly steeled with insensibility.

You see nothing here that is pretty; but everything seems to be abundant in value; and one great thing is, the working people live well. Theirs is not a life of ease to be sure, but it is not a life of hunger. The pitmen have twenty-four shillings a week; they live rent-free, their fuel costs them nothing, and their doctor costs them nothing. Their work is terrible, to be sure; and, perhaps, they do not have what they ought to have; but, at any rate, they live well, their houses are good and their furniture good; and though they live not in a beautiful scene, they are in the scene where they were born, and their lives seem to be as good as that of the working part of mankind can reasonably expect. Almost the whole of the country hereabouts is owned by that curious thing called the *Dean and Chapter* of Durham. Almost the whole of South Shields is theirs, granted upon leases with fines at stated periods. This Dean and Chapter are the *lords of the Lords.* Londonderry, with all his huffing and strutting, is but a tenant of the Dean and Chapter of Durham, who souse him so often with their *fines* that it is said that he has had to pay them more than a hundred thousand pounds within the last ten or twelve years. What will Londonderry bet that he is not the *tenant of the public* before this day five years? There would be no difficulty in these cases, but on the contrary a very great convenience; because all these tenants of the Dean and Chapter might then purchase out-and-out, and make that property freehold, which they now hold by a tenure so uncertain and so capricious.

ALNWICK,

7 Oct. 1832.

From Sunderland I came early in the morning of the 5th of October once more (and I hope not for the last time) to Newcastle, there to lecture on the paper-money, which I did in the evening. But before I proceed further, I must record something that I heard at Sunderland respecting that babbling fellow Trevor! My readers will recollect the part which this fellow acted with regard to the " liberal Whig prosecution; " they will recollect that it was he who first mentioned the thing in the House of Commons, and suggested to the wise ministers the propriety of prosecuting me; that Lord Althorp and Denman *hummed* and *ha'd* about it; that the latter had *not read it,* and that the former would offer no opinion upon it; that Trevor came on again, encouraged by the works of the curate of Crowhurst, and by the bloody, bloody old *Times*, whose former editor and now printer is actually a candidate for Berkshire, supported by that unprincipled political prattler, Jepthah Marsh, whom I will call to an account as soon as I get back to the south. My readers will further recollect that the bloody old *Times* then put forth another document as a confession of Goodman, made to Burrell, Tredcroft, and Scawen Blunt, while the culprit was in Horsham gaol with a halter actually about his neck. My readers know the *result* of this affair; but they have yet to learn some circumstances belonging to its progress, which circumstances are not to be stated here. They recollect, however, that from the very first I treated this Trevor with the utmost disdain; and that at the head of the articles which I wrote about him, I put these words, " TREVOR AND POTATOES; " meaning that he hated me because I was resolved, fire or fire not, that working men should not live upon potatoes in my country. Now, mark; now, chopsticks of the south, mark the sagacity, the justice, the promptitude, and the excellent taste of these lads of the north! At the last general election, which took place after the " liberal Whig prosecution " had been begun, Trevor was a candidate for the city of Durham, which is about fourteen miles from this busy town of Sunderland. The freemen of Durham are the voters in that city, and some of these freemen reside at Sunderland. Therefore, this fellow (I wish to God you could *see* him!) went to Sunderland to canvass these freemen residing there; and they pelted him out of the town; and (oh appropriate missiles!) pelted him out with the " accursed root," hallooing and shouting after him—" *Trevor and potatoes!* " Ah! stupid coxcomb! little did he imagine, when he was playing his game with Althorp and Denman, what would be the ultimate effect of that game!

From Newcastle to Morpeth (the country is what I before described it to be). From Morpeth to this place (Alnwick), the country, generally speaking, is very poor as to land, scarcely any trees at all; the farms enormously extensive; only two churches, I think, in the whole of the twenty miles; scarcely anything worthy the name of a tree, and not one single dwelling having the appearance of a labourer's house. Here appears neither hedging nor ditching; no such thing as a sheep-fold or a hurdle to be seen; the cattle and sheep very few in number; the farm servants living in the farm-houses, and very few of them; the thrashing done by machinery and horses; a country without people. This is a pretty country to take a minister from to govern the south of England! A pretty country to take a lord chancellor from to prattle about *Poor Laws* and about *surplus population!* My Lord Grey has, in fact, spent his life here, and Brougham has spent his life in the Inns of Court, or in the botheration of speculative books. How should either of them know anything about the eastern, southern, or western counties? I wish I had my dignitary Dr. Black here; I would soon make him see that he has all these number of years been talking about the bull's horns instead of his tail and his buttocks. Besides the indescribable pleasure of having seen Newcastle, the Shieldses, Sunderland, Durham, and Hexham, I have now discovered the true ground of all the errors of the Scotch *feelosofers* with regard to population, and with regard to poor laws. The two countries are as different as any two things of the same nature can possibly be; that which applies to the one does not at all apply to the other. The agricultural counties are covered all over with parish churches, and with people thinly distributed here and there.

Only look at the two counties of Dorset and Durham. Dorset contains 1005 square miles; Durham contains 1061 square miles. Dorset has 271 *parishes;* Durham has 75 parishes. The population of Dorset is scattered over the whole of the county, there being no town of any magnitude in it. The population of Durham, though larger than that of Dorset, is almost all gathered together at the mouths of the Tyne, the Wear, and the Tees. Northumberland has 1871 square miles; and Suffolk has 1512 square miles. Northumberland has *eighty-eight parishes;* and Suffolk has *five hundred and ten parishes.* So that here is a county one-third part smaller than that of Northumberland with six times as many villages in it! What comparison is there to be made between states of society so essentially different? What rule is there, with regard to population and poor laws, which can apply to both cases? And how is my Lord Howick, born and bred up in Northumberland, to know how to judge of a population suitable to Suffolk? Suffolk is a county teeming with production, as well as with people; and how brutal must that man be who would attempt to reduce the agricultural population of Suffolk to that of the number of Northumberland! The population of Northumberland, larger than Suffolk as it is, does not equal it in total population by nearly one-third, notwithstanding that one half of its whole population have got together on the banks of the Tyne.

And are we to get rid of our people in the south, and supply the places of them by horses and machines? Why not have the people in the fertile counties of the south, where their very existence causes their food and their raiment to come? Blind and thoughtless must that man be who imagines that all but *farms* in the south are unproductive. I much question whether, taking a strip three miles each way from the road coming from Newcastle to Alnwick, an equal quantity of what is called *waste ground*, together with the cottages that skirt it, do not exceed such strip of ground in point of produce. Yes, the cows, pigs, geese, poultry, gardens, bees and fuel that arise from those *wastes* far exceed, even in the capacity of sustaining people, similar breadths of ground, distributed into these large farms in the poorer parts of Northumberland. I have seen not less than ten thousand geese in one tract of common, in about six miles, going from Chobham towards Farnham in Surrey. I believe these geese alone, raised entirely by care and by the common, to be worth more than the clear profit that can be drawn from any similar breadth of land between Morpeth and Alnwick. What folly is it to talk, then, of applying to the counties of the south principles and rules applicable to a country like this!

To-morrow morning I start for " Modern Athens "! My readers will, I dare say, perceive how much my " *antalluct* " has been improved since I crossed the Tyne. What it will get to when I shall have crossed the Tweed God only knows. I wish very much that I could stop a day at Berwick, in order to find some *feelosofer* to ascertain, by some chemical process, the exact degree of the improvement of the " *antalluct*." I am afraid, however, that I shall not be able to manage this; for I must get along; beginning to feel devilishly home-sick since I have left Newcastle.

They tell me that Lord Howick, who is just married by the by, made a speech here the other day, during which he said, " that the Reform was only the means to an end; and that the end was cheap government." Good! stand to that my lord, and, as you are now married, pray let the country fellows and girls marry too: let us have *cheap government*, and I warrant you that there will be room for us all, and plenty for us to eat and drink. It is the drones, and not the bees, that are too numerous; it is the vermin who live upon the taxes, and not those who work to raise them, that we want to get rid of. We are keeping fifty thousand tax-eaters to breed gentlemen and ladies for the industrious and laborious to keep. These are the opinions which I promulgate; and whatever your flatterers may say to the contrary, and whatever *feelosofical* stuff Brougham and his rabble of writers may put forth, these opinions of mine will finally prevail. I repeat my anxious wish (I would call it a hope if I could), that your father's resolution may be equal to his sense, and that he will do that which is demanded by the right which the people have to insist upon measures necessary to restore the greatness and happiness of the country; and, if he show a disposition to do this, I should deem myself the most criminal of all mankind, if I were to make use of any influence that I possess to render his undertaking more difficult than it naturally must be; but if he show not that disposition, it will be my bounden duty to endeavour to drive him from the possession of power; for, be the consequences to individuals what they may, the greatness, the freedom, and the happiness of England must be restored.

NOTES

[*Register*, in the following notes, stands for *Cobbett's Weekly Register*, and *Selections* for *Selections from Cobbett's Political Works*. The numbers at the beginning of paragraphs refer to the pages.]

FORMER VOLUME I

3. *Six Acts.*—Described by Mr. (afterwards Lord Chief Justice) Denman as " Six Bills which went to overthrow all that was valuable in the constitution." *Hansard*, vol. 41, pp. 1072, 1501. Passed in 1819, 60 *Geo.* 3 *and* 1 *Geo.* 4: commonly called the Blasphemous and seditious libels bill, c. 8; Seizure of arms bill, c. 2; Training prevention bill, c. 1; Newspaper stamp duty bill, c. 9; Seditious meetings bill, c. 6; and Misdemeanours bill, c. 4.

4. *The blessings, etc.*—This phrase, touching the national debt, was attributed to the late Sir John Bailey, Bart., one of the Judges of the King's Bench, and afterwards Baron of the Court of Exchequer. *Selections*, v. 5, p. 490.—The first Sir Robert Peel wrote a pamphlet, contending that the national debt was no burthen to the nation, because the people owed it all to themselves.—In a work by a City writer, Mr. Bernard Cohen, *Compendium of Finance, etc.* (1828), the author considered it to be " the generally adopted opinion, that a national debt is indispensable to our independence," p. 197.

6. *Mr. Budd.*—The late Mr. William Budd, for many years Clerk of the Peace for the County of Berks. A Letter from him in *Register*, v. 82, p. 609.—Mr. Cobbett's work, *The Woodlands*, is dedicated to him.

8. *The Report* here referred to, on agricultural distress, is commented upon in *Register* of Nov. 3, 1821, in a *Letter to Landlords*. " In 1790, the nation was in a state of great real prosperity. We heard then of none of these distresses, and these corn bills, and this hole-digging work. We heard then of no emigrations; no overstock of people and overstock of food at the same time; of no persons petitioning to be transported! Of no new jails and ' improved prison discipline;' of no county hospitals for the insane. All these signs of ' prosperity ' have made their appearance while rents were trebling. I, therefore, can see no good reason for the Committee hoping so anxiously that rents will not come back to the old standard. Their reason, however, is this, that, if the rents do come back, it is clear as daylight that the present landlords, if *encumbered*, must lose their estates right speedily; and if not encumbered, the landlords must be *brought down*, and will soon be insignificant creatures compared to the fundlords, who are daily rising over them; and who in a short time will and must have a complete ascendency. . . . It is not all gold that glistens. The gay farm-houses with pianos within were not *improvements*. The pulling down of 200,000 small farm-houses and making the inhabitants paupers was not an *improvement*. The gutting of the cottages of their clocks, and brass kettles, and brewing tackle was no *improvement*. And I ask, where is or where will soon be found the landlord not to wish that his *estate* and *the poor-rates*, independent of all

other taxes, were what they were in 1790?" v. 40, pp. 1031, 1036.—And see *Letter to the Earl of Chichester, Register*, v. 41, p. 129, Jan. 1822.

10. *The Thing*, a term often repeated in this work and in the *Register*, meaning the system of the English government.

18. *Gallon-loaf man.*—"Gallon loaf" refers to a calculated sufficiency for maintenance of labourers. The "man," Mr. John Bennett, M.P. for South Wilts. See *Register*, v. 48, p. 113.

18. *Mr. Blount.*—Mr. Joseph Blount, of the Roman Catholic family of that name. The place, Uphusband, connected with the lowness of wages and misery of the people thereabouts, is frequently mentioned in these *Rides*. About 6 miles from Andover.

28. *Mrs. Westphalin's Grove.*—The estate here named was afterwards purchased by Mr. Henry Baring (the late Lord Ashburton).

29. *"Reverend" gentlemen.*—The late Rev. G. F. Nott, D.D., who is somewhere mentioned by Lord Byron, was Prebendary of Winchester and of Chichester, Rector of Woodchurch in Kent, and of Harrietsham in Kent, and held the advowson of Stoke Canon in Devonshire. While holding all these offices, he was advertised for in the *Morning Herald* of the 12th July, 1831, by a parishioner of Woodchurch, the flock there being anxious to find its shepherd; and it was then ascertained that the Doctor had long been and was residing in Rome.

29. *Public forests.*—The Forests and Crown Lands will be found more minutely treated of further on in this work. Of late, a good deal of stir has been made on the subject. In 1848 a number of charges of "cribbing" timber in the New Forest were preferred against small foresters and minor officials at the Sessions at Winchester: but none were convicted.—There is a Parliamentary *Report of the New and Waltham Forest Commission*, with a *Sub-Report of the Secretary, Mr. J. B. Hume:* 1850.—The gentlemen of the "Financial Reform Association," in their tract on *The Aristocracy and the Public Service*, say—"The Committee of Parliament which inquired into the woods, forests, and land revenues of the Crown, made revelations in the evidence published in 1848 and 1849 about the verderers of Epping Forest, and their clerk, which would have destroyed their reputation for life had the disclosures related to the servants of a private estate."—p. 35.

30. *Monopolising farmer.*—(See p. 300, vol. i.)—The Rev. Mr. Davies, in his work entitled *The Case of the Labourers in Husbandry*, date 1795, complains of the ill effects of engrossing farms; and some of our agricultural publications of the present time, 1853, are asserting that low wages are associated with large rather than with small farms. Mr. Davies says—"Thousands of parishes have not now half the number of farmers which they had formerly; and in proportion as the number of farming families has decreased, the number of poor families has increased." — Mr. Sadler, in his work on *Ireland*, writes strongly in favour of small farms.—Mr. Cobbett's Letter to Mr. Coke (Lord Leicester) on this subject, *Register*, v. 39, p. 505; *Selections*, v. 6, p. 115, and to the Edinburgh Reviewers, v. 52, p. 336.—The *Report* of House of Commons Committee on Allotments of Land to labourers (1843, No. 402) is much in favour of the practice, asserting that it has lessened crime and improved the habits of the poor.—The Rev. J. S. Henslow, Rector of Hitcham, Suffolk, has published (1852) in his *Address to the Parish*, some interesting details, showing the same good results. But he appears to have had to struggle against the large farmers, one of whom says—"I ask what has been the ruin of Ireland but this sub-letting system, and it will be the ruin of this parish if persevered in. . . . I do hereby make this declaration, I will never cart another ton of coals for the poor, so long as this sub-letting system is in existence."— Small holdings, however, should not be confounded with minute subdivisions of property. *The Quarterly Reviewers*, April, 1816, are for the former of these, while, in Dec., 1846, they are, and not inconsistently,

against the latter.—There is a great deal of historical information on this subject in the *Dublin Review*, Nov. 1842.—Earl Stanhope, in his evidence before the Lord's Committee on Poor-Laws, Mar. 1831, says—" I am of opinion that the destruction of small farms, and the formation of large farms, has much diminished the comforts of the people, and injured the prosperity of the country."

36. *Farm of Tull.*—It was by Mr. Budd that Mr. Cobbett was first made acquainted with Mr. Tull's work on Husbandry. See a·lvertisement in *Register*, No. 21, v. 40.—Mr. Loudon speaks of Tull's system as that of an " eccentric " teacher, but says the Scotch were the first to discover its merit. Voltaire says he has tried Mr. Tull's system, and found it " execrable."

36. *Enclosed commons.*—But enclosures have been facilitated by very recent statutes. See 8 and 9 Vict., c. 118; 15 Vict., c. 2.—The *Report* of House of Commons Committee of 1797 states that up to that date there had been 1532 enclosure Bills passed, and 2,804,197 acres enclosed during the reign of George III. In the period from 1792 to 1820, there were 2287 Bills passed, and the number in each session was great in proportion to the dearness of corn at the time.—*Letter to Electors of Berkshire, on the New System for the Management of the Poor*, by the late Mr. John Walter, M.P., 1834.

38. *Consequences of the System.*—See *Register*, addressed to the late Duke of Buckingham, " on his late Speech in the House of Lords, relative to a change in the System." " Does not loss of estate threaten all but the loanmongers and other Jews, etc. ? " v. 60, p. 641 (1826). The present Duke of Buckingham has of late been twitted by our " liberal " press on the fact that it is not his grace, but one of the Barons Rothschild, who is now the greatest man, and who keeps the pack of stag-hounds, in the neighbourhood of Stowe.

40. *The tree planter.*—See preface to *The Woodlands*, on the philosophy of tree-planting.—The gallant Admiral Collingwood in his Correspondence, published in 1829, speaks of the importance of planting oaks.

" What I am most anxious about is the plantation of oak in the country. We shall never cease to be a great people while we have ships, which we cannot have without timber; and that is not planted, because people are unable to play at cards next year with the produce of it. I plant an oak whenever I have a place to put it in, and have some very nice plantations coming on; and not only that, but I have a nursery in my garden, from which I give trees to any gentleman who will plant them, and instruction how to top them at a certain age, to make them spread to knee timber." —(*Letter to Lord Radstock*, dated Ocean, off Cadiz, Feb. 3, 1807.)—" Be kind to old Scott; and when you see him weeding my oaks, give the old man a shilling." (*Letter to his daughters*, dated Queen, at Sea, Feb. 17, 1806.)

43. *The Wen*, a name often applied by the author to London, as a great excrescence on the country. So M. de Sismondi speaks of the city of ancient Rome as a " parasite population." And Mercier, in his *Tableau de Paris*, published at Amsterdam, just before the old French Revolution, calls Paris a *wen*: " Paris is too big; it flourishes at the expense of the whole nation; but there would be more danger now in removing the wen (*loupe*) than in letting it be."—(2nd Edit., 1783, v. 1, chap. 3.)

43. *A penitentiary.*—The Penitentiary at Millbank is said to have been originally suggested by Mr. Jeremy Bentham. *Register*, v. 87, p. 138.

44. " *A sudden transition from war to peace*."—Quoting the language of Lord Liverpool, when accounting for the distress of the country in 1822.

45. *Interest of the debt.*—The *Small Note Bill* was continued soon after this date, viz. in July, 1822.

45. *Pretty little Van.*—Rt. Hon. Nicholas Vansittart, Chancellor of the

Exchequer, afterwards created Lord Bexley. *Register*, v. 30, p. 80; v. 32, p. 57; v. 51, p. 656.

51. *Stern-path-of-duty man, etc.*—These severally, in the order of the text, mean Lord Liverpool, Lord Castlereagh (Londonderry), Mr. Canning, Mr. (the 2nd Sir Robert) Peel, the Barings, and Mr. Ricardo.—" Stern path of duty," in Lord L's. speech of Feb. 24, 1817. " This is the expression always used by Lord Liverpool when he *means* to be firm, and before *circumstances* induce him to swerve." Sir James Graham, *Corn and Currency*, p. 37.

51. *Botley Parson.*—The Rev. Richard Baker, Rector of Botley, the place of the author's residence in Hampshire.

51. *Bawnd* or *baw*, means boy or lad, as *mawther* or *maw* means girl or lass; names in common use in Norfolk, and which Sir Thomas Browne, a Norwich man, derives from the Saxon or Danish.

52. *Provincial Feast of the Gridiron.*—Alluding to what has been called " Cobbett's Gridiron Prophecy," written in Long Island, Sept. 1819 Repeated in several places in *Register*, and the more subsequent repetitions the stronger in terms. V. 35, pp. 165, 170, 179, 364; v. 46, p. 350; v. 48, p. 1; *Selections*, v. 5, pp. 443, 436; v. 6, p. 42.—" Mr. Cobbett foretold, as early as 1818, certainly more distinctly than anybody else at the time, that a gold standard at £3 17s. 10½d. would inevitably reduce the price of wheat to 4s. 6d. or 5s. the bushel on an average, and other commodities in a similar ratio; nor would it have risen upon an average since 1819 but for the different means that were found to prevent the full operation of Peel's Bill. Our statesmen were as little informed as babies of what Mr. Cobbett understood so well, or otherwise fancied they could counteract the effect which that adjustment of the metallic standard would induce." (*Lord Western's Letter to Chelmsford and Essex Agricultural Society*, May, 1835.)—Mr. Matthias Attwood had expressed the same views of the measure, in the House of Commons, as those stated in the *Register*.— Peel's Bill is 59 Geo. 3, c. 4.

59. " *Rags*," bank-notes.

60. *Laws to prevent importation of food.*—Articles on this subject in *Selections*, for which see *Index* thereto.

65. " *Great Man*" and " *Pilot*" refer to the minister Pitt. Bishop Pretyman, Mr. Pitt's tutor.

68. See *Letter* to the Earl of Chichester.—*Register*, v. 41, Jan. 1822. " It appears surprising that the nobility should not endeavour *to conciliate the people*, while they have the means of conciliation in their hands; or, at least, it would appear surprising if one had not witnessed the events of the last thirty years," p. 144. What is said in the same page respecting the little effect of the " writings of philosophers " is exactly repeated by the *Edinburgh Review*, in April, 1838, p. 209.

73. *An act of Sussex farmers.*—The sort of practice here mentioned was afterwards noted by some of the roving Poor-Law Commissioners. And on the motion of the Duke of Richmond, for an inquiry into the state of the country, March 18, 1830, his grace was reported as saying that " he had remonstrated against the putting of men to draught-work like horses, with a man to drive them " (in Sussex).

73. *Kremlin.*—Name of the Russian emperor's palace at Moscow. The Brighton Kremlin is now in the hands of the authorities of the town, and used for public purposes.

85. " *Over-production*," stated by Lord Liverpool, in Parliament, to be a cause of national distress. *Register*, v. 46, pp. 103, 336.

86. " *May makes or mars the wheat.*"—It is also an old saying that " drought never brought dearth into England." And Mr. Cobbett used to say that wheat never wanted a drop of rain from sowing to harvest time.

88. *Potatoes*—One of the author's earlier notices of this root is in an

article entitled *Milton, Shakespear, and Potatoes*, in *Register*, v. 30, p. 82, referring to another in v. 29, p. 193. (1815).—The same subject in v. 46, p. 518 (1823).—During the Irish famine of 1846 the "degrading root" was denounced in the House of Commons (17th April), as being "poor," "watery," etc., and hopes were expressed that the Irish might be "induced to adopt a more generous diet." And the "failure in the potato-crop," as "causing a serious deficiency in the quantity of a material article of food," forms an important topic in the royal speech on the prorogation (August 28, 1846).—The poisonous qualities of the potato have been recently spoken of by several writers, as in the work of Messrs. *Maw and Abercrombie*, 1850, and in Mr. Kemp's *Hand-Book*, 1851. The latter asserts that potatoes, eaten raw, will generally kill a horse.—The prevailing disease in the root appears to have been universal. Mr. Skirving of Liverpool, well known to farmers and gardeners, has found that the plant in its natural state, in Peru, is affected with the disease, which, he also says, has attacked the cultivated potato in the Dargheely Hills in India, a country in which this root has grown unusually well.

94. *Knaves who assembled at the Crown and Anchor.*—These were the "Loyal and Constitutional Association," of which Mr. John Reeves, author of *History of the English Law*, was chairman. Mr. Arthur Young also belonged to this body, and wrote a work against the English reformers entitled *The Example of France a Warning to Britain*.

96. *Grapes.*—William of Malmsbury says that in the 12th century the Vale of Gloucester produced as good wine as many provinces in France. *Domesday Book* gives the number of barrels produced on each estate; and the editor's preface accounts for this cultivation being dropped by citing our treaties with foreign princes to take wine in exchange for our manufactures.

97. *Mr. Birckbeck* was accidentally drowned, in crossing the river Wabash, soon after the date of this *Ride*. Mr. Cobbett's correspondence with him appears in the *Year's Residence in America*. There are several communications from him in the *Register*, in 1815 and 1816.

97. "*As clearly as the sun at noonday.*"—These words refer to speech of Mr. Ponsonby, on Mr. Madock's motion respecting parliamentary seat-selling by ministers, in 1809. "Such things were known to be done by hundreds, and why, therefore, inquire into this transaction. The practice of trafficking in seats had, he admitted, become as glaring as the noonday sun."—*Register*, v. 15, p. 767.

97. "*Dead weight.*"—Name given by the late Lord Castlereagh, "with much more propriety than elegance," to the annual charge of half-pay officers, pensioners, etc.—*Register*, v. 44, p. 36.

99. *Snug corporations.*—Since this date we have not only had Corporation Reform (1835), and other great changes, but our newspapers of October, 1847, were discovering that England is "a poor country," because "in debt for more than she can pay."

99. *Lea.*—The house of the late Mr. John Leech, Member for West Surrey in the first Reform Parliament.

99. *Weald, wald,* or *walt,* a Saxon word, said to mean wood or grove. In some editions of the statutes (23 Eliz., c. 5, and 27 Eliz. c. 19) it is "the *wilds* of Surrey," "the *wilds* of Sussex, Kent," etc.

99. *A worthy old friend's.*—The late Mr. Nicholls, of Odiham, a large holder of lay tithes: one of those to whom the author applied the name of "grey-coated parson."

101. *Education.*—"When I first trudged a field, with my wooden bottle and my satchel swung over my shoulders, I was hardly able to climb the gates and stiles; and, at the close of the day, to reach home was a task of infinite difficulty. My next employment was weeding wheat, and leading a single horse in harrowing barley, etc."—*Porcupine's Works*, v. 4. p. 34. And see *Selections*, v. 1, pp. 132, 214.

102. *A kingly government.*—In Cobbett's *Two-Penny Trash*, No. for May, 1831, p. 252, there is the following passage. The title of this work was adopted from the late Lord Castlereagh (Londonderry) having applied it, in Parliament, to such publications.

"I have observed before, and I beseech you to attend to it, that the words *liberty, freedom, rights,* and the rest of the catalogue, which hypocritical knaves send rolling off the tongue, are worth nothing at all: it is things that we want. Those men who make a fuss about sorts of government, and who tell us about the good things which arise from the republican government of America, deceive themselves, or deceive others. It is not because the government is republican, but because it is cheap; and it is cheap, not because it is republican, but because the people choose those who make the laws and vote the taxes. If the President of America were called King of America, instead of being called President, it would be of no consequence to the people, if the King cost no more than the President now costs. Nothing is worth looking after; nothing is worth talking about but the cost; because it is this that comes and takes the dinner from the labourer, and that takes the coat from his back. We have had, during this last winter, a clear proof that we never can have relief except through the means of a Reform in Parliament. During the winter before, Sir James Graham proved that 113 of the aristocracy of England received out of the taxes six hundred and fifty thousand pounds a year, a sum equal in amount to a year's poor-rates of the five counties of Bedford, Berks, Bucks, Cambridge, and Cumberland!"

It may be observed that the term *republic* had no peculiar terrors in it till of late years. Even in the speeches from the throne, in the reign of James I., we find the phrase "this Republic of England."

103. *Yew-tree.*—Several writers speak of the yew-trees at Fountains Abbey, Yorkshire, as being more than 1000 years old.

106. *Mr. Poulter.*—Rev. Edmund Poulter, Prebendary of Winchester and Rector of Meon Stoke and Soberton.—*Register*, v. 43, p. 711. The "Manifesto" is there, p. 707. This gentleman is mentioned in *History of the Protestant Reformation, Letter* 4.

110, 111. *Peel's Bill.*—A legal tender clause was afterwards enacted in 3 and 4 Wm. 4, c. 98 (August, 1833).

114. *They dare not take the lead in these necessary reforms.*—This passage was afterwards well illustrated in the struggle which eventually occurred at the passing of the Reform Bill.

115. *Population Returns.*—Several writers have pointed out that the Population Returns bear internal evidence of their being erroneous. See the author's speech for repeal of the Malt-Tax.—*Register*, v. 83, p. 705 (1834).—*Selections*, v. 6, p. 781.—The following table is taken from page 3 of the late Mr. John Marshall's *Statistics of the British Empire*, published in 1837. The same table appears in his *Digest of all the Accounts, etc.*, page 3, published in 1833. It strongly supports what Mr. Cobbett says in his speech on the Malt-Tax, and elsewhere, respecting population and employment. the compiler being one of the most able and most faithful dealers with such matters that our country has produced. Numbers of other "statisticians" are borrowers from his book of what suits them, while they strive to hide the disagreeable truths which it contains. He reproached the government of the day with having suppressed a large number, 1250 copies of his work of 1833, which they purchased of him. He was the author of that string of able resolutions proposed to the House of Commons by Mr. Hume in 1826; and the *Tables* of the late Mr. G. R. Porter are founded on the works of this laborious man. Mr. Marshall observes that, "notwithstanding the prevailing notion of manufacturing being the predominant interest of Great Britain, the analysis of the Population Returns shows that *five-sixths* of the whole are dependent on agriculture for subsistence."

OF THE POPULATION OF GREAT BRITAIN

ANALYSIS OF OCCUPATIONS	Number of Families in		Total No. of Persons in 1831
	1821	1831	
1 Agricultural Occupiers . . .	250,000	250,000	1,500,000
2 " Labourers . .	728,956	800,000	4,800,000
3 Mining " . .	110,000	120,000	600,000
4 Millers, Bakers, Butchers . .	160,000	180,000	900,000
5 Artificers, Builders, etc. . .	200,000	230,000	650,000
6 Manufacturers	340,000	400,000	2,400,000
7 Tailors, Shoemakers, & Hatters	150,000	180,000	1,080,000
8 Shopkeepers	310,239	350,000	2,100,000
9 Seamen and Soldiers . .	319,300	277,017	831,000
10 Clerical, Legal, and Medical .	80,000	90,000	450,000
11 Disabled Paupers	100,000	110,000	110,000
12 Proprietors, Annuitants . .	192,888	316,487	1,116,398
Totals	2,941,383	3,303,504	16,537,398

117. *The base accusation of Dundas.*—Viz., " a connection and antici-pation with Mr. Thistlewood and his associates."—*Register*, v. 44, p. 246.

119. *The hanging at Winchester.*—The author shortly afterwards peti-tioned the House of Commons. Petition, presented by Mr. Brougham, is in *Register*, v. 46, p. 386; and in *Hansard*, v. 9, N.S., p. 79. Mr. Thomas Baring is reported as saying, on this occasion, that " half the offenders in Hampshire were committed for poaching."

122. " *Greatest Captain of the Age.*"—A name first given to the Duke of Wellington by the late Sir Francis Burdett.

128. *Whitchurch paper-mills.*—There seems to be good reason for be-lieving that our paper-mills were also once employed, about 1790 or soon after, in making paper for the forgery of French *assignats.* This matter is mentioned in *Paper against Gold, Letter* 14; *Register*, v. 19, p. 1229; and in v. 34, p. 43; v. 35, p. 230; and v. 47, p. 791. The case of *Strongi-tharm v. Lukin*, cited by Mr. Cobbett in the above *Letter*, is reported in 1 Espinasse's Reports, 389; date 1795. Mr. Cobbett sometimes charged Pitt with participation in this business. Lord Kenyon, in the case in Espinasse, impliedly countenances such an act, when done against the enemy, quoting that line of the poet which Dryden translates—" *Let fraud supply the want of force in war.*" It would appear that a part if not the whole of the paper used for these *assignats* was manufactured at Houghton paper-mill, on the North Tyne, a few miles above Hexham, Northumberland.

130. *Kent Petition.*—Sir Moses Manasseh Lopez, M.P., convicted of bribery and corruption. *Register*, v. 49, p. 528.—Joseph Swan: *Register*, v. 50, p. 416.—The speeches on the Kent Petition here mentioned are in *Hansard*, 1822.

131. Lord H. Stuart, son of first Marquis of Bute, was associated with Mr. Robert Liston, English Embassador to America in 1799, and stayed some time with the friends of Mr. Cobbett mentioned in note to p. 248, vol. ii. Lord Henry and Mr. Liston were witnesses for Mr. Cobbett in the case prosecuted by Mr. Perceval.

134. " *Vast improvements, ma'am !* " — This was literally the case around London during the distress of 1825-6.

144. "*The Doctor*," name given by Mr. Canning to Lord Sidmouth.—
"*Long arm*," means the *Register* when written in America and printed in
England. Anecdote of the "long arm," *Register*, v. 32, March 28, 1817.

147. "*Banished*," that is, under the Bill, c. 8, named in note on p. 3.

156. *Sir Charles B——.*—Supposed to refer to Sir Charles Burrell, Bart.,
M.P., who was one of those who attacked the author at the time of the
fires in 1830. He is mentioned in *Register*, v. 84, p. 616, as having a good
Bill before Parliament on the subject of the poor.

158. *Mr. Huskisson's* speech quoted, in *Selections*, v. 6, pp. 229, 445,
and in *Register*, v. 61, p. 339.

164. *They never work.*—The author has elsewhere noticed the difference
to be observed between the Quakers when in trade and those of their sect
engaged in the pursuits of rural life.

167. *Such services as were performed at Manchester.*—Alluding to the
"Manchester Massacre" of 16th August, 1819; vulgarly named *Peterloo*,
having occurred on a spot called Peter's Field.

169. Judge McKean, and Senate, etc.—*Porcupine's Works;* and *Selections*, v. 1, p. 191, contain the particulars of what is here referred to.
Mr. Cobbett, when in America in 1818, memorialised the Pennsylvania
Government at Harrisburgh to obtain compensation in this matter. In
1819 he received a letter from the late Mr. Ambrose Spencer, then Chief
Justice of the Supreme Court of the State of New York, in which that
learned judge (who was personally unknown to Mr. Cobbett) stated his
opinion that the proceedings complained of were illegal, and that compensation ought to have been made by the state's government.

173. *Blanketteers.*—Great numbers of the people in the north who, in the
distress of 1816-17, were said to be on the move towards London, each
carrying his *blanket.*—See *Letters* to, *Register*, vol. 34, pp. 348, 827.

176. *St. Swithin.*—The saint himself was one of our Saxon Lord Chan-
cellors. Is mentioned in Lord Campbell's *Lives.*

179. *How well they are off in the north.*—*Cobbett's Tour in Scotland* on
this subject. It has been several times remarked by the author that the
loud praises bestowed by some on the superior education, morals, well-
being, etc., of the Scotch, were in fact intended to hide from England the
actual state of Scotland, and to reconcile Englishmen to miseries in their
own condition which no people ought to endure. The strongest evidences
we have of the degradation of the poor Scotch have been furnished on
Scotch authorities; and if these tell the truth, one can hardly imagine
anything more shocking than that which is the lot of a large part of the
Scottish nation. "To hold up Scotland as an object of *our imitation* is
to be impudent to a degree worthy of blows." *American Register*, June,
1816.

186. *My road.*—This is the road, 11 miles, from Botley to Winchester,
through Fairoak and Twyford, Hants.

186. *Botley Parson.*—The author of this hoax was an intimate acquaintance of Mr. Cobbett; but the latter in fact knew nothing about the
contrivance at the time when it occurred.

188. *Sentence passed upon me by Ellenborough, etc.*—This was the sentence of two years imprisonment in Newgate and to pay £1000 fine to the
King for a libel published July 1, 1809, in *Register*, v. 15, p. 993. The
libel consists of comments upon the fact of some local militiamen having
been flogged, at Ely, under the guard of German Legion Cavalry. Sir
Vicary Gibbs was the Attorney-General; the defendant was tried on the
15th June, 1810, by a special jury; and received sentence on the 9th July.
—See *Selections*, v. 3, p. 373.—Many have justly remarked that the article
containing this libel is a very inferior piece of the author's writing. See
page 270, vol. i.

215. *A place-hunting lawyer.*—Supposed to refer to the late Mr. F. L.
Holt, afterwards Vice Chancellor of the Duchy of Lancaster. Said to be

a very worthy and benevolent man. Mr. Cobbett somewhere speaks of him as having, when a young man, made a bold stand against Lord Ellenborough in a libel case. He was author of a work on *Libel* (1816), showing a singular leaning towards what are called arbitrary principles.

217. Lord Ellenborough's Act is 43 George 3, c. 58, modified by " Peel's Acts," 4 George 4, c. 48, and 9 George 4, c. 31.—After the date of this *Ride* there was passed the Night-Poaching Act, commonly called " Lord Lansdowne's Act," 9 George 4, c. 69 (1828).

223. *Rewarding Pratt.*—This Lord Camden was grandson of Mr. Pratt, Lord Chief Justice of the King's Bench, and son of Charles, afterwards Lord Camden, who was Lord Chief Justice of the Common Pleas, and then Lord Chancellor.

225. *Mr. Waddington.*—The late Mr. Samuel F. Waddington, whose case is reported in 1 *East*, 153. This matter is spoken of at large in *Cobbett's American Register*, p. 329 (1816).

227. *Joshua Watson.*—Mr. Watson, the same person spoken of in the introductory part of Cobbett's *Hist. of the Protestant Reformation*.

228. *Stocks.*—" It is said that every vill, of common right, is bound to provide a pair of stocks."—*Burns' Justice.*

228. *Police officers from the Wen.*—Since this was written, during the period from 1835 to 1838, we were informed by the government prints of the police being engaged in the work of forcibly separating families among the poor. Also, we have seen the introduction of a newer police, called " rural," which, in some places, have been considered expensive, and of but little use, excepting as gamekeepers.

230. *Shabbily-dressed people do not go to church.*—The same remark has since been made, by some of the clergy, in what they have written on the management of the poor.

242. *Dover fortifications.*—The author is here speaking, not, probably, without a certain share of science, from the study he had formerly given to matters of a military kind. While in his regiment in Nova Scotia and New Brunswick (1785-9: *Selections*, v. 3, p. 251) he mastered English grammar, and wrote a book on arithmetic, in which the rules and sums are stated in a very neat hand, and another book, of equal neatness, setting out the rules of geometry, accompanied by diagrams. He was as particular about his dress, being, it is said, the first in the army to begin wearing the regimental coat buttoned close up. He bore the character of being extremely rigorous in discipline with the soldiers under him. During this time, he made some large plans of military fortifications, drawn with pen-and-ink, most exact in every line, and showing great application. In his *Treatise on Indian Corn*, 1828, par. 183, he mentions a public document which he, while serjeant-major, had drawn up for the commissioners sent out to New Brunswick. This, he says, came into the hands of the late Duke of Kent, when Commander-in-Chief of the Province, who afterwards showed it to Mr. Cobbett, at Halifax, in 1800.—His remarks on the proper discipline for " Volunteers " (at the time of apprehended invasion, 1804, *Register*, v. 5, pp. 32, 54) accord with the recommendations lately published by one of the Generals Napier.

242. *Useless expenditure.*—Twenty years before this date, the writer had been imagined on Shakespeare's Cliff by Mr. Perceval himself, when, as Attorney-General, in 1804, he was prosecuting Mr. Cobbett, before Lord Ellenborough, for the libel written by Mr. Justice Johnson. Borrowing expression for his contempt from the Roman satirist, Mr. P. says—" Who *is* Mr. Cobbett? Is he a man of family in this country? Is he a man writing purely from motives of patriotism? *Quis homo hic est? Quo patre natus?* [Who is this man? what is his origin?] He seems to imagine himself a species of censor, who, elevated to the solemn seat of judgment, is to deal about his decisions for the instruction of mankind. He casts his eye downward, like the character represented by the poet of

nature, from Dover Cliff, and looks upon the inferior world below as pigmies beneath him." 29 *Howell*, S. T. 36.—Mr. Marshall (quoted in note on p. 115) affords striking evidence, if he be correct, of the wildness of "expenditure" at this period. In his note to a table of figures, published in the *Monthly Magazine*, No. 392, year 1824, he says—"The income of the first five years of the war, 1793-7, exceeds, by the enormous sum of about 25 millions, the sum shown to have been expended." And he states another discrepancy as occurring in the public accounts for 1816, "when about 3 millions more is charged for interest than was actually due." In his *Digest*, 1833, he asserts that these matters are still not cleared up.

244. *Our ministers will be crawling and cringing.*—"It is on the warlike spirit of a nation that her honour, security, and happiness must chiefly depend; and this spirit is generally found to exist in an inverse proportion to the magnitude of her purse." *Register*, Dec. 24, 1801; *Selections*, v. 1, p. 221. And in justifying the superiority in fame, over all other men, enjoyed by those engaged in war, the author says—"Much as I abhor cuttings and stabbings, I have a still greater abhorrence of submission to a foreign yoke. Commerce, Opulence, Luxury, Effeminacy, Cowardice, Slavery: these are the stages of national degradation. We are in the fourth; etc." *Register*, August, 1805.—The recent *Declaration of the Merchants, Bankers, Traders, and others, of London*, for " cultivating the arts of peace" with France, was advertised as being signed by 5000 persons, and is in our morning papers of March 29, 1853. Among the leading names there are those of four baronets and of eight commercial members of Parliament. It was carried to the footstool of Napoleon III. by some of the City gentlemen; and to some of these our newspapers imputed motives of the money-making kind. But the Manchester men had long before done this. In 1840, when a warlike spirit was apprehended with Mons. Thiers, the then French minister, there was a meeting of the " Friends of Peace," on a requisition signed by " 60 firms and individuals," at which an address was adopted to their " Friends and Allies," the French nation. This address is in the Manchester papers of Nov. 4, 1840. It was presented at Paris by a deputation, having at their head Dr. Bowring, formerly styled our " commercial agent on the Continent," and now in office at Hong Kong.—The spirit prompting those *Peace Placards*, which were suppressed by Lord Derby's ministry in October, 1852, is thus treated by Mr. Cobbett. " I have told you, as General Washington told a great branch of your combination, that those were not entitled to any of the rights of citizens or subjects, who, under whatever pretence, refused to take up arms in the defence of their country, or of the legal powers of the state, including, in your case, the office and person of the king. I have told you that if we Englishmen were *all* to act upon your principles, the king might be dragged from his throne, and the country torn to pieces, or enslaved by invaders, and that these would be the inevitable results."—*Letter* to Mr. James Tuffnell, the Quaker, *Register*, v. 66, p. 388 (1828).

259. " *Tall soul*," phrase used in Lord John Russell's Tragedy of *Don Carlos*, criticised in *Register*, v. 45, p. 39.

260. *Infamous press caused attacks to be made by the mob upon tradesmen.*—This practice of the press is noticed in the *Letter to the Luddites* (name adopted by the frame-breakers in Nottingham), *Register*, v. 22, p. 10; v. 31, p. 571. *Selections*, " Luddites " in Index.—A similar attack was made, but a short time back, upon the tradesmen of London, who were charged with selling at prices not sufficiently evincing the " benefits of free trade." The character of the American press, as pictured by itself, is given in *Register*, v. 81, p. 732.—With the English, a remarkable instance occurred in the *Courier*, for many years the Tory ministerialist evening organ and advocate of legitimacy. It maintained the cause of the unfortunate Charles X. and Duc D'Angouleme until they were undoubtedly

beaten by the people. But when they were sent to sea, and it was questioned whether they ought to be allowed to land in England, the *Courier* spoke of them as " that couple of vagabonds afloat in the Channel."

262. *Marine of America.*—Something is wanting after " America," which renders the sense incomplete.

262. *Two right honourable youths now gone to the lakes in the north.*—Supposed to refer to Mr. Canning and Mr. Huskisson, who were about this date at a public dinner in Liverpool. *Register*, v. 47, p. 705.

270. The *Sentence* here mentioned: see note to p. 188.—Baron Maseres was a steady advocate of parliamentary reform. He republished a number of valuable tracts, on that and various other subjects, and a large work on Logarithms.

274. *What causes flounders, etc.*—And the same with some other animals. In the south these " fish " are called *flounders* by the country people: in the north, *flukes*, which is another name for flat-fish.

279. *My host.*—The late Mr. John Knowles, of Thursley.

280. *The French War.*—The true cause and circumstances of the war of 1793 are frequently alluded to by the author, as in *Register*, v. 61, p. 37; v. 69, p. 430; *Selections*, v. 5, p. 308; *Register*, v. 70, p. 379. In the latter of these (1830) he says—" In the year 1793, a famous old borough-monger said to Mr. John Nicholls, ' If we suffer this revolution to succeed in France, our order must be overset in this country. We will therefore try to prevent its success. Our *trial* may fail, but if we do not try we *must* be overthrown.' "—See *Recollections and Reflections, etc., during the Reign of George III.*, by John Nicholls, Esq., M.P. in the 15th, 16th, and 18th Parliaments of Great Britain: 2 small 8vo. volumes: 2nd Edit., 1822. This is a work which should be read by every one desiring to understand the matter of the war of 1793, the whole blame of which Mr. Nicholls throws on Mr. Burke, and those whom he describes as " the great Whig families," the leaders of whom were the Duke of Portland, Earl Fitz-william, and Earl Spencer. The author was a barrister, of Lincolns-Inn, and wrote in 1819-20. His book is written in a temperate way, but implies a lasting reproach. " Mr. Burke had sufficient influence over the great Whig families to induce them to concur with the king in clamouring for a crusade against French principles. Mr. Pitt was unable to resist; and that he might retain his situation as minister he was under the necessity of receiving the great Whig families into his cabinet, and of embarking the country in the crusade." v. 2, p. 200. The true character of this war, as respects parties, has been little studied; and recent explanations have done little better than confirm such erroneous notions on the subject as were before prevalent.

283. *General Brown.*—The account of General Brown's performances, in *Register*, v. 30, p. 516.—" Deposing James Madison," an idea attributed to the late Admiral Sir Joseph Yorke, who was also said to have prescribed the " twenty-four hours under water " as the cure for Ireland. The admiral was drowned, near Southampton, from the upsetting of a boat. —*Register*, v. 47, p. 728; v. 53, p. 579, 580.

285. " *London University.*"—The newspapers informed us that Lord Brougham was laughed at, and even " hissed " by the boys of this school, when, in 1848, he was making a speech against boys participating in the revolutionary spirit of the time.

286. *My old hunting scenes.*—The following description of one of these hunting scenes is from his first *Letter to the Hon. John Stuart Wortley*, the present Lord Wharncliffe, on Equitable Adjustment, *Register*, v. 81, p. 514. The author is asserting that Mr. Wortley had been put, by other writers, on a wrong scent as to the value of the currency; and he thus introduces the *Red Herring.*

" When I was a boy, a huntsman, named George Bradley, who was huntsman to Mr. Smither, of Hale, very wantonly gave me a cut with his whip, because I jumped in amongst the dogs, pulled a hare from them, and got her scut, upon a little common, called Seal Common, near Waverly Abbey. I was only about eight years old; but my mind was so strongly imbued with the principles of natural justice that I did not rest satisfied with the mere calling of names, of which, however, I gave Mr. George Bradley a plenty. I sought to inflict a just punishment upon him; and, as I had nɔt the means of proceeding *by force*, I proceeded by *cunning* in the manner that I am presently going to describe. I had not then read the Bible, much less had I read Grotius and Puffendorf: I, therefore, did not know that God and man had declared that it was laudable to combat tyranny by either force or fraud; but, though I did not know what tyranny meant, reason and a sense of justice taught me that Bradley had been guilty of tyranny towards me; and the native resources of my mind, together with my resolution, made me inflict justice on him in the following manner:—Hounds (hare-hounds at least) will follow the trail of a red-herring as eagerly as that of a hare, and rather more so, the scent being stronger and more unbroken. I waited till Bradley and his pack were trailing for a hare in the neighbourhood of that same *Seal Common*. They were pretty sure to find in the space of half an hour and the hare was pretty sure to go up the common and over the hill to the south. I placed myself ready, with a red herring at the end of a string, in a dry field, and near a hard path, along which, or near to which, I was pretty sure the hare would go. I waited a long while; the sun was getting high; the scent bad; but, by and by, I heard the view-halloo and full cry. I squatted down in the fern, and my heart bounded with the prospect of inflicting justice, when I saw my lady come skipping by, going off towards *Pepper Harrow*; that is to say, to the south. In a moment, I clapped down my herring, went off at a right angle towards the west, climbed up a steep bank very soon, where the horsemen, such as they were, could not follow; then on I went over the roughest part of the common that I could find, till I got to the pales of Moor Park, over which I went, there being holes at the bottom for the letting in of the hares. That part of the park was covered with short heath; and I gave some twirls about to amuse Mr. Bradley for half an hour. Then off I went, and down a hanger at last, to the bottom of which no horseman could get without riding round a quarter of a mile. At the bottom of the hanger was an alder-moor, in a swamp. There my herring ceased to perform its service. The river is pretty bad: I tossed it in, that it might go back to the sea, and relate to its brethren the exploits of the land. I washed my hands in the water of the moor; and took a turn, and stood at the top of the hanger to witness the winding-up of the day's sport, which terminated a little before dusk in one of the dark days of November. After overrunning the scent a hundred times; after an hour's puzzling in the dryfield, after all the doubles and all the turns that the seaborn hare had given them, down came the whole *posse* to the swamp; the huntsmen went round a mill-head not far off, and tried the other side of the river: ' *No! d—n her, where can she be ?*' And thus, amidst conjectures, disputations, mutual blamings, and swearings a plenty, they concluded, some of them half leg deep in dirt, and going soaking home at the end of a drizzling day." (*Register*, v. 81, p. 513.)

291. *Doctor Black.*—Mr. John Black, a Scotchman, formerly editor of the *Morning Chronicle*, and often called " Doctor " in the *Register*. Though these two publications were continually warring, on questions of Education, Poor Law, etc., Mr. Black was always a good-humoured opponent. At the hottest of the anti-pauper crusade (1835) his paper held that the New Poor-Law was " the saviour of the landed interest," and " the sheet-anchor of the country," and that " the pauper must be made to feel that poverty is a degradation." Not long afterwards, when the same measure was in odium, Lord Brougham (then cast off by the Whigs) endeavoured

to throw on Lord Melbourne the blame of the New Poor-Law; and then Mr. Black's paper candidly admitted that the great Philippic of Lord B. of 1834, in which he had said that the poor of England were less humane than " the most brutal savages," showed him to have been " ignorant of the subject of his declamation." We find the editor of the *Examiner*, another anti-pauper print, doing the same in 1838. " Lord Brougham has not yet found that he was in error upon the Poor-Law. . . . He designated the statute of Elizabeth as an ' accursed ' act."—When the *History* here named first came out (in numbers, in 1825), there was a publication in answer, made to resemble it, in colour of wrapper, etc., and two or three numbers of this latter were distributed, gratis, to a great many people. The numbers printed of Cobbett's *History* were to the amount of more than 50,000 each, the first edition, and of one No. there were 61,000 sold.

292. *The finest ten miles in England.*—And then, again, for the growth of corn, some say the finest ten miles are those between Worcester and Tewkesbury. But there may be other claimants for a distinction of this kind. There is the vale of Evesham, afterwards noticed in this work.

297. *Humanity Buxton.*—Mr. Buxton here mentioned, the late Sir Thomas Fowell Buxton, Bart. — See article in *Register* (" Aristocratic Quakers "), v. 82, p. 429, on slave-holders, with account of Benjamin Lay, a Quaker, persecuted by Quakers, for endeavouring to free the slaves of Quakers.

298. *The Small-note Bill.*—*Register, To the Ministers,* on this, v. 56, p. 129.

299. *Public credit.*—During the difficulties of 1847, the late Lord Ashburton was reported as saying nearly the same thing to the learned person here named: the latter asking the government to increase the *money* of the country, and the former pointing out to him that there was already more than could be safely used.

300. *Apple felony.*—One of " Peel's Acts," 7 and 8 George 4, c. 42.

303. *Changed the value of money.*—In *Blackstone* there are some interesting passages touching the increase of the precious metals, and the effects resulting; and more especially as respects the custom of *corn rents*, originally invented, he says, for the benefit of the landlord. *Book* 1. *c.* 7. " Lord Treasurer Burleigh, and Sir Thomas Smith, then (time of Elizabeth) Secretary of State, observing how greatly the value of money had sunk, by the quantity of bullion imported, devised this method for upholding the revenues of colleges." *Book* 2, *c.* 20.—The proposed *Resolutions* framed by Col. Thompson, late M.P., during the session of 1852, were in like manner intended to benefit the public creditor in apprehension of his dividend becoming, from the new imports of gold, of less value.

307. *One newspaper says, etc.*—Agreeing with this, and the passage next following it, is the *Letter* to the People of Kent, *Register*, v. 57, p. 614, where the author says that " Nations are essentially enemies of each other. They talk as friends. They make treaties of amity. They make in the most solemn names compacts of perpetual friendship; and, in framing those very treaties, each party has an ultimate eye to war," etc.—Mr. Huskisson's term " *reciprocity*," to which Mr. Cobbett used to add the phrase " *all on one side*," has been succeeded in favour by two other remarkable *dic'a* of leading statesmen. Sir James Graham was reported as declaring, in May, 1846, that " this country can no longer be regarded as an agricultural, but a manufacturing country " (a declaration previously made in No. 30 of the *League Circular*); while Sir Robert Peel, in May, 1842, asserted it to be a principle admitted by all, " that we should buy in the cheapest market, and sell in the dearest." The latter of these is among Lord Chesterfield's very shopkeeper-like *Axioms in Trade*. But it also appears as having been promulgated many hundred years before in Rollin's description of the Carthaginians, where it figures with a more

lively effect. " Traffick," says this historian, " was the predominant inclination and the peculiar characteristic of the Carthaginians; it formed in a manner the basis of the state, the soul of the commonwealth, and the grand spring which gave motion to all their enterprises. The Carthaginians were skilful merchants; employed wholly in traffic; excited strongly by the desire of gain, and esteeming nothing but riches; directing all their talents, and placing their chief glory in amassing them, though, at the same time, they scarce knew the use for which they were designed, or how to use them in a noble or worthy manner. A mountebank had promised to the citizens of Carthage to discover to them their most secret thoughts in case they would come, on a day appointed, to hear him. Being all met, he told them ' they were desirous *to buy cheap and sell dear.*' Every man's conscience pleaded guilty to the charge; and the mountebank was dismissed with applause and laughter."

310. *Universal agricultural bankruptcy.*—A similar state of things was affecting the land about ten years later, when it was resolved to make an onslaught upon the pauper, in 1834.

315. *Repeal of Corn Bill.*—Wheat, in the calculation of Sir Robert Peel, was expected, after repeal of the corn-law, to range from 52s. to 56s. the quarter. It has of late, 1850 to 1853, been down to from 37s. to 45s.

318. *Poor Sir Glory.*—" *Westminster's Pride,*" etc., a name once applied to the late Sir Francis Burdett, by his admirers of Westminster.

320. *The wise barn-orator.*—The " *barn-orator* " is Mr. Edmund Wodehouse, one of the members for Norfolk, from whom Mr. Cobbett adopted the phrase " *equitable adjustment.*" A phrase, however, which had long before been employed, as with the financiers of Louis XIV.—The Norfolk Petition, drawn up by Mr. Cobbett; *Register*, v. 45, p. 78; v. 56, p. 717.

FORMER VOLUME II

10. *Modern system of education.*—" It is only deceiving the poor, and preparing for them a wretched existence, to call them from the plough and the hammer to the school-bench, with a promise that the latter is the way to fortune. . . . If you reduced the number of the labouring class to a fourth or fifth of what they now are, you need dispense also with three-fourths or four-fifths of the clergy, the lawyers, and other professional men. Get rid of *all* the working people, and then you may do without the rest of mankind. . . . It is among those who cultivate the soil that an increase in numbers is attended by the least danger."—*Sismondi's Etudes*, v. 3, pp. 261, 267.

22. " *A mistaken notion.*"—Mr. Locke, on Education, expresses almost exactly the same views of the subject. And we find the same also in writers of the United States, with reference to the condition of their own country, as affected, for good or for evil, by mere book learning.

25. *A breaking merchant . . . will naturally blame the bank.*—This blaming of the bank was afterwards more remarkable when, in 1838-9, the " Manchester Chamber of Commerce " reproached the Bank of England with that confusion and misery which were just then occasioned, in fact, by the joint-stock banks.—A similar error has again appeared now (1853) in the assertion of some, that the influx of gold has done nothing towards the present rise in prices and briskness in trade. Between November, 1851, and July, 1852, the bank received an addition to her gold of about £7,000,000. During the same period, her paper issues increased from £19,355,220 to £23,748,735. An increase of notes to this amount has never yet failed to revive trade and manufactures. It is reported also that the banks of our customers in America have greatly increased their paper, on the strength of the gold lately brought in to the United States.

30. *It is a great error, etc.*—" The modern labourer enjoys a novel and almost magical facility of locomotion. . . . He is whirled along with a velocity, ease, and comfort which would have excited the envy and wonder of ancient civilisation or feudal magnificence." *Lecture* of Professor Rickards, p. 76.—It is certain that it has been the habit of the country people to call those of a neighbouring parish by the name of " foreigner."—In the *Reports* of the " Criminal Statistics " of the north, some of the writers have represented the character of the people in the form of a map, the several districts being marked in a lighter or darker shade, according to the greater or smaller amount of crime. The more thickly populated and manufacturing places are by far the darker.—The gentlemen of the " League " are represented as having said, in some of their speeches, that the immorality of these dark spots is owing to the bad example of those who have come to them from the " dark parishes " (*i.e. ignorant* parishes) of agriculture. Yet it is said, in the *Report on Health of Towns*, and in various other publications, that the infant children of many of the manufacturing people are tended throughout the day somewhat after the manner of rearing house-lambs, but having a very inferior kind of sustenance. One old woman has the care of a lot of these, while the mothers are gone from home to the factory, keeping them quiet by giving them doses of " Godfrey's cordial," " mother's quietness," " infants' cordial," " soothing-syrup," etc. A small work entitled *Public Nurseries*, published by Parker, West Strand, 1850, and in which are quoted a great number of authorities on this subject, says—" In Ashton, 15 druggists sold on an average about 6 gallons per week of these preparations. In Preston 21 druggists sold in one week 68lbs. of narcotics, of which but a very small quantity is said to have been for the use of adults. ' Godfrey ' contains 1½ ounce of pure laudanum to the quart. ' Infants' cordial ' is stronger." Page 11.—General Sir John Elley, in debate on the Factory Bill of 1836 (May 10), said that a " recruiting officer would reject five out of ten of those who offered themselves for the army in the manufacturing districts, whereas he would not reject one in ten in the rural."

33. *Nicholas Grimshaw.*—Mr. Grimshaw, Mayor of Preston, in 1826. " Ditches " refers to passages made for the bringing up of voters at the election in that year. *Register*, v. 58, p. 777.

50. There are passages in the *Etudes* of M. de Sismondi, vol. 3, pp. 235, 237 (1838), which are all but literally the same as what the author here says in pages 48 to 50.—" The problem which it is the business of political economy to solve is—how to produce the most with the least labour." *Westminster Review*, 1827, quoted *Register*, v. 64, p. 245.

52. *Diabolical assertion of Malthus.*—The dismal doctrines on " excessive population " were carried to such a pitch that, in 1838, there was a plan, gravely recommended in a work of 73 octavo pages, for murdering infant children, by means of what the author calls " painless extinction," to facilitate which he gives directions most scientific and minute. This work, brought out in a rather expensive form, is entitled " *On the Possibility of Limiting Populousness*. By MARCUS." It was sold by respectable publishers, Messrs. Sherwood and Co., and bears internal evidence, in its language, of having been written by a Scotchman. The Hon. and Rev. Mr. Baptist Noel, the seceder, in one of his anti corn-law tracts, cast the infamy of this publication upon the poor, alleging that he had found it in the shop of a " chartist " bookseller: the fact being that the little bookseller had republished the work by way of exposing the author and his teaching to what they merited.—" It might be objectionable, on many grounds, to withhold relief from the future issue of marriages already contracted; but why may not such relief be refused to the children born of marriages to be contracted after a certain period? " Lord Brougham, quoting Mr. Malthus, on *Agricultural Distress*, in House of Commons, April 9, 1816 (Speech republished by himself, in 1838).

59. *Rennell and Sturges.*—This refers to the date (1800) of the controversy between Dr. Sturges, Prebendary of Winchester, and the late Dr. Milner, Roman Catholic Bishop, and author of the *Letters to a Prebendary.*

62. *The late Order in Council.*—Order, of Sept. 1, 1826, for admitting certain grain at low duties.—*Register*, v. 59, p. 677.

64. *Gourlay's farm.*—The bank here referred to was one of those which afterwards broke in the unfortunate time of 1847, about December.— *Scotch Farming.* On one of the " League " tracts of 1843, there is a picture representing two Englishmen with a wheeled plough, and having five horses all in tandem; and beneath it a clever ploughman of the Lothians, holding a swing-plough, and two horses, with reins, abreast. But the Scotch borrowed the latter mode of ploughing from England. It is mentioned in Mr. Young's *Southern Tour*, 80 years back, as practised in several counties, Norfolk, Suffolk, Essex, etc. Mr. Cobbett had swing-ploughs, to work with two horses, from Suffolk, in 1811. The practice was certainly used in Surrey as early as 1813; but perhaps long before.— There are some persons, however, who write on these subjects without seeming to be aware that a horse, and even an ox, will not bear the same toil and privation as a human being.

68. *Ottiwell Wood.*—Father of Mr. John Wood, who was M.P. for Preston in 1826, and afterwards Chairman of the Board of Taxes.

70. " *Beef, pork, etc.*" quoting the words of Chancellor Fortescue, in his work in praise of the Laws of England.

72. *Bluff manufacturers.*—Lord John Russell reminded the manufacturers in the House of Commons that it was they who had the most frequently sought the aid of troops to keep the people in order.

74. *Licences to beg.*—Licences to beg were granted, by law, in time of Henry VIII., Edward VI., and Elizabeth, as mentioned in *Register*, v. 88, p. 757.

81. *Tithes as a premium for breeding.*—But it was proposed by Pitt, in 1796, to give premiums for large families in the case of labourers; or, rather, this seems to have been acceded to by Mr. Pitt, on the suggestion of Mr. Whitbread. This was in the debate on Mr. Whitbread's Bill for regulating wages. Here we find Mr. Pitt speaking against the law of settlement, and for that " free circulation of labour " so much urged of late. *Cobbett's Debates*, v. 32, p. 708.—In same debate, page 712, Mr. Lechmere states the barley loaf to be at 12½d., and wages 1s. per day.

83. *To prevent the increase of labourers' children.*—Mr. Robert Dale Owen did (in 1836) publish a work for this purpose. He refers to Mr. Mill, the author of *British India*, as having inculcated the same in the article *Colony, Encyclopædia Britannica.*

83. *Manufactories throwing the people back, etc.*—This operation of " *throwing the people back,*" etc., was suggested in 1841-2; when in one of Mr. Robert Hyde Greg's tracts, he warns the landed proprietors of " vast multitudes residing in the manufacturing districts, but who really *belong* to the agricultural ones," being " cast back upon their birth-place, and claiming support from their native parishes."

90. " *Revered and ruptured Ogden.*"—William Ogden, printer, of Manchester. It has been said that Mr. Canning did not in fact utter this expression. But it was asserted, as a matter of complaint, in Mr. Ogden's own account of his sufferings. *Register*, v. 33, p. 565; v. 61, p. 534. And in his petition, *Id.* v. 70, p. 179.

104. " *Patient resignation* " was the compliment paid in Parliament to the degraded Scotch and Irish poor while dying of hunger.

106. *Colchicum.*—The medicinal plant, *colchicum*, is much like a purple crocus, only about two inches taller in the stalk and rather wider in the flower.

106. *This plagiarist's pamphlet.*—This refers to Sir James Graham's

work on *Corn and Currency*, in which the writer says, in speaking of his own class, the landlords—" Substantial justice is on our side; and who are they that are against us?—the Annuitants, the Fundholders, and the Economists; a body which the land owners, if true to themselves, and in concert with the people, cannot fail to defeat. . . . It is not the price of bread alone which is a check to our industry; on the contrary, I am well convinced that its effect is insignificant compared with the weight of taxation; and every notion of free-trade is worse than visionary unless accompanied by a large reduction of taxes and duties."—(1827), 3rd Edition, pp. 64, 101.

108. *To tramp "aboot, mon," with pack licence.*—In the northern counties the popular name for hawker or pedlar is " Scotchman."

109. *Parson Hay.*—Mr. Hay was Vicar of Rochdale, and Chairman of the Lancashire Sessions at Salford.

115. *Lord Somers wrote a pamphlet, etc.*—And Mr. Lambton (the late Lord Durham) at a dinner in Newcastle-on-Tyne, in 1819, was reported as saying, that " the Radical Reformers were bawling, ignorant, and mischievous quacks, whose doctrines and views were exposed to universal derision and abhorrence." *Newcastle Chronicle*, 9th January. The nobility and landed gentry have now a more powerful, but perhaps not a more magnanimous class of men than the humble Radicals to deal with. The Liverpool " Financial Reform " gentlemen, in treating of the *Aristocracy and Public Service*, observe that " the public have not forgotten the desperate battle fought by the Bentinck family and the Duke of Richmond against the nation's bread and industry." They make no ceremony in their attack upon high ladies on the pension-list. And they assert that " no chairman of a board of guardians has more rigorously enforced the poor-law than the Duke of Richmond, chairman of the West Hampnet Union." At a large reform meeting in Manchester, held on the 3rd Dec. 1851, Mr. John Bright, the present member for the borough, after taking a review of the above-mentioned battle, and of circumstances preceding it, exclaimed, with an emphasis on the last word—" and then, the proudest aristocracy in the world *succumbed !* "—Mr. Cobbett, in his *Letter to the Nobility of England*, thus addresses them:—

" You feel, because you must feel, that you are not the men that your grandfathers were; but you have come into your present state by slow degrees, and therefore you cannot tell, even to yourselves, not only how the change has come about, but you cannot tell what sort of change it really is. You may know what it is, however, or, at least, you may form some little notion of the nature of it when you reflect that your grandfathers would as soon thought, aye, and sooner thought of dining with a chimney-sweep than of dining with a Jew, or with any huckstering reptile who had amassed money by watching the turn of the market; that those grandfathers would have thought it no dishonour at all to sit at table with farmers, or even with labourers, but that they would have shunned the usurious tribe of loan-jobbers, and other notorious changers of money, as they would have shunned the whirlwind or the pestilence. These usurers now take precedence of you in many cases, and many of you really live in awe of them. To this you have brought yourselves by your jealousy of those who are justly denominated the people, who are your natural friends, and whose friendship you have lost, and thereby made yourselves the dependants, in some degree, at any rate, of this tribe of loan-jobbing vagabonds whom you despise in your hearts, and whom you compliment in your words and by your looks. Never, every reader of this *Register* will say, were truer words than these put upon paper. . . .

" Every man of sense knows, as well as he knows how to distinguish daylight from dark, that England must continue the greatest naval nation in the world, or be reduced to be one of the most contemptible nations in the world. Burke has said, and though he was a horrible, pensioned old hack, he said it well and truly, 'that a nation, *once become great*, can never sink into a middle state and there remain; that it must continue to be great or sink so low as hardly to be worthy of the name of a nation.' There are many men, and those by no means fools, who think that England will sink down into the last-mentioned state. I am of a different opinion. The whole of the history of my country tells me that that will never be Divers have been the times when England seemed to be torn to pieces, seemed to be incapable of ever recovering; but in every such case, whether from a change of the government; from the destruction of the sovereign; or from some cause or other, such a change has taken place as to put everything to rights, and to make the nation as formidable as ever to its neighbours. It has always been with the people of England the most monstrous of crimes in their rulers to do anything tending to pull down the country; and, if my observation do not deceive me, that spirit is as much alive at this hour as it was in the days of King John or of Edward the Second. But something must suffer; something must go to wreck; somebody or something must be overturned, when the nation recovers itself by means so convulsive. If, then, my lords, somebody or something must go to wreck in consequence of such convulsive movement; and if I should be able to show to you that the dreaded depression, degradation, abasement, must come, without suitable means of prevention, who, or what is it, my lords, that, in such case, would be most likely to go to wreck?" *Register*, v. 61, pp. 133, 135 (1827).

116. *The little-shilling project.*—The author's "*Letter* to Henry James, Esq., of Birmingham, on his project for making a shilling pass for eighteen-pence," in *Register*, v. 34, p. 1051 (1819).—The converse of this proposed now (1852-3) owing to the apprehended excess of gold.

123. *Church lands.*—Mr. Cobbett wrote against the Tithe Commutation Bill (passed in 1836; 6 and 7 Wm. IV. c. 71), saying that it affected to prop that which it would tend to pull down. *Register*, v. 86, pp. 779, 780; v. 88, p. 89.

124. *Sir William Scott,* afterwards Lord Stowell: mentioned again in p. 284, vol. ii.—Lord Campbell, in his *Life of Ld. Chancellor Eldon*, quotes a letter from Lord Eldon to his brother, in which he says how, if he had his way, *he* would deal with such people as "your friend Cobbett."—It was related, some years back, that Lord Stowell on one occasion invited his brother and Lord Liverpool to hear him read an article in the *Register*, in which the two latter happened to be named as follows, Lord Stowell supplying the innuendos as he read: "'*Liverpool-Jenkinson*' (thereby meaning you, my lord) '*and Scott-Eldon*' (thereby meaning you, my lord"), etc.

126. *Kentish Petition,* is in *Register*, v. 42, p. 676.

129. *Cotswold breed.*—A quarter of one of these Cotswold sheep, weighing 63lbs., was exhibited as a curiosity in the market of New York, in January, 1851. It had been sent from Devizes, in Wiltshire. But there have been considerably heavier; from 75lbs. to even 80lbs. the quarter. The Lincolnshire is said to be a still heavier sheep.

130. *Upping-blocks, or horse blocks,* but little known in some parts of the country, are three or four steps, of brick or stone, to assist in getting on horseback.

130. *Loan-mongering robber.*—Lord Byron's sarcasm, in associating the Jew and the Christian as "fellow-Christians," is perhaps no more than justice to the Jew. Raynal asserts that his church makes no compromise with usury, but repudiates it altogether. But it would seem that the Turk, observing the law of his Koran, is after all the most rigid "Christian" in this respect. The Roman Catholic rules of discipline forbid the taking of interest to this day; but those rules are laid aside in practice. Giannone, in his *History of Naples*, says that "the Jews were all expelled from that city in 1540, the nobles having been pillaged by their exactions; and a

public pawn-house was established, in order to avoid the same evil from the Christian lenders of money, for they, allured by the great gains of the business, began to do worse than the Jews had done before them." v. 4, pp. 70, 71.

132. *Written by Shakespeare.*—See the account of the " Shakespeare Forgeries," *Register*, v. 53, p. 278; v. 68, p. 472, 505; v. 88, p. 552.

134. *George.*—Son of the late Mr. William Palmer, of Bollitree, near Ross.

138. " *Counsellor Bric.*"—The " *intense Comedy*," in *Register*, v. 55, p. 769.—Mr. John Bric, a partisan of the late Mr. O'Connell, and after- wards killed in Ireland in a duel.

154. *Judge Blackstone on the Game Code.*—" This unqualified position of the learned commentator must be deemed incorrect." Chitty s *Game Laws*, 3.—" The statutes for preserving the game are many and various, and not a little obscure and intricate; it being remarked that in one statute only, 5 Anne, c. 14, there is false grammar in no fewer than six places, besides other mistakes: the occasion of which, or what denomina- tion of persons were probably the penners of these statutes, I shall not at present inquire." — Blackstone, *Comm.* Book 4, chap. 13.— " The game laws are already sufficiently oppressive, and therefore ought not to be extended by implication. Nothing can be more oppressive than the present system of the game laws. And wherever a law is productive of tyranny, I shall ever give my consent to narrow the construction." —Mr. Justice Willes, in *Jones v. Smart*, 1 T. R. 44.

" This nation exhibits at this time every mark of a sinking state; every mark that the empire of Rome exhibited when it was approaching to its fall. A false and frivolous taste has seized upon the people, as well as upon the government: in dress, in entertainments, in our manner of receiving our friends, in our language, habits, and everything, we have become a hollow and tinsel nation, compared to what our fathers were. Even in the sports of the field we have become frivolous, and effeminate, and senseless. Our lords and gentlemen now do precisely what the old noblesse of France did just before the Revolution. It is not *sporting*, now, the finding of the game being uncertain, and the toil considerable; but it is going to a poultry-pen with people, instead of dogs, to drive out the animals, to preserve which laws, in emulation of those existing in France, have been made and executed in England; and the at once slothful, effeminate, and tyrannical *Sportsmen* (as they call themselves) have even adopted the phraseology and borrowed the terms of the despicable creatures of France, calling a *day's shooting* a *battu !* This is a remark as old as aristocracy itself; hundreds of wise men have repeated this remark, which has been verified in the decline and fall of every state where such profusion existed. Everything solid and plain is despised; the relationships between *master* and *servant* are obliterated along with the names. All is hollow and false; all is affectation and unjust preten- sion: and as for *love of country* and its honour, let the estimate be founded on this damning fact, that the moment the above announcement was made at Lloyd's, the Funds rose, making good the observation of the old Lord Chatham, that that which was calculated to *sink* the character of the country caused the hopes of these muckworms to rise. His miserable son augmented the number of these muckworms a hundred-fold: it is his system which has debased the country; that has broken its spirit, destroyed its ancient and laudable pride, and made it view disgrace with- out shame; and it really now appears to be fast approaching towards that state which I described when I took my leave of England in 1817 to avoid the dungeons of Sidmouth and Castlereagh or to avoid crawling at their feet. I then told my countrymen (*Leave-taking Address, vol.* 32, *March* 28), that, if the system were to go on for any considerable time, ' it is hard to say how very low this country is to be sunk in the scale of nations. It would, in that case, become so humble, so poverty-stricken, so degraded, so feeble, that it would, in a few years, not have the power, even if it had the inclination, to defend itself against any invader. The people would become the most beggarly and slavish of mankind, and nothing would be left of *England* but the mere *name*, and that only as it were for the purpose of reminding the wretched inhabitants of the valour and public spirit of their forefathers.' Greatly do I fear that this prediction will be verified."—*Letter* to the Duke of Wellington, on Foreign Affairs and Lord Aberdeen, *Register*, v. 66, p. 462 (1828).

156. Mr. Cobbett, while at Botley, was for years a strict preserver of game, though no " shot," keeping sometimes from 30 to 40 dogs, greyhounds, pointers, setters, and spaniels. He had a cart's back full of live hares brought from Berkshire, to turn down on his own farms. He prosecuted one poacher, by suing him, as for a trespass (in the year 1816), in the court of *pie-powder*, at Winchester.

158. *The House that Jack Built* (like the *Man in the Moon*) was one of the many publications of attack upon George IV. and his ministers at the time of Queen Caroline's coming to England, in 1820. No less than 28 editions and 140,000 copies of this were stated to have been sold in six weeks. The Rev. Vicesimus Knox, D.D., Fellow of St. John's, Oxford, was the reputed author. The *Parodies* on the Litany and Creed, for which Mr. Hone was prosecuted in 1817, were supposed to have been written by a Socinian minister, who afterwards went to the United States. —It is the late Sir Robert Wilson who is mentioned in this passage: his gallant conduct, while in service, is frequently alluded to in the *Register*. —It was voted that Mr. Horne Tooke could not sit in Parliament because he was in holy orders.

168. *Some poet has said, etc.*—" The quality of mercy: it is twice bless'd, etc." *Merch. of Venice*, act iv.

170. *Committee on Peel's Bill.*—Afterwards were the *Report of H. of C. Committee on renewal of Bank of England Charter* (1833), and *Report of H. of C. Committee on Joint-Stock Banks* (1837).

177. *Neither of them could marry.*—This question of celibacy seems to have been much contested among the Brazilians about the year 1828, when a Roman Catholic bishop published a work on the subject, afterwards republished in the United States:—" *Demonstration of the Necessity of abolishing a Constrained Clerical Celibacy ;—exhibiting the Evils of that Institution and the Remedy. By the Rt. Rev. Diego Antonio Feijo, Senator and Ex-Regent of the Empire of Brazil, Bishop Elect of Marianna, etc. Translated from the Portuguese, by Rev. D. P. Kidder, A.M., Philadelphia:* 1844."

180. " *Greek cause*," *etc.*—*Register*, v. 60, pp. 385, 449, on the *Greek Pie*, or *Paté à la Grec.*—During the revolutionary war in Spain of 1836, there was a meeting of English bond-holders in London, the anticipation expressed at which was, more recently, stated to have been realised in an abundance of confiscations. Mr. R. Thornton was reported as then saying (May 14), that " The resources of Spain would allow of ample justice being done to the holders of Spanish stock. The monastic property was of the value of eighteen millions per annum. The crown lands realised an immense amount, and the Church property was estimated at eleven millions sterling per annum."

180. *New Forest.*—Blackstone's *Law Tracts* treat at large of this foreign tyranny, and of the origin and history of the Forest Charters, etc.

185. And the same author, *Commentaries*, Book 4, c. 33, says that the Conqueror " had always ready at his command an army of 60,000 knights, or *milites*."

187. *Mr. Chamberlayne's estate.*—The late Mr. Chamberlayne is spoken of in one of the *Registers* as being a superior speaker, and a man of great political independence.

189. *County Friendly Society, etc.*—The " allowance-system," or making

up wages out of rates, was condemned by the author many years back as being most pernicious to the labourer. *Register*, v. 14, p. 73 (1808).—It appears, from the reports in the *Farmer's Herald* and other publications, that some of the farmers at their meetings are now, 1852-3, resolving that, to better the condition of the labourer, it is advisable to pay him better wages. — An old farmer in Surrey says — "The oldest farmers that I remember told me that their labourers were not pleased if they, the masters, did not at Whitsuntide go to their cottages to smoke a pipe with them, and tell them which had got the best ale. And two parishes adjoining that where I was born, being in fear of annexation (that is, for a rate in aid) to a parish having a poor's-rate, called a meeting, and invited the labourers to attend, and offered them money as relief. This they refused, saying they did not want it. The farmers adjourned, and called a second meeting, at which they offered the labourers some malt. This they accepted: and by this means the parishes made a small rate. I believe one if not both of these parishes has since been paying 20s. in the pound for poor's-rate." —The fallacy in the notion of a poor man saving for a "bad day" or "rainy day" has been well and completely exposed by Mr. Sadler, in his work on *Ireland* ; and more recently by Mr. John Bowen of Bridgewater, in his *Letter to the King*, in 1835 (published by Hatchard, Piccadilly). This *Letter* of Mr. Bowen, and his other tracts on the Poor-law question, exhibit such knowledge and talent in the writer as are rarely found among statesmen. " Surely," he says, " the noble diffusers of this ' useful knowledge ' should likewise be brought down to the Prussian standard (sleeping on straw, and their food principally grey hog-peas boiled in water). Lord Brougham's official salary would have paid somewhat more than 90 Prussian judges. Even his pension, for four years' services (£5000 a year), is not materially less than all the judicial salaries of one of the 26 provincial governments of the Prussian monarchy." Authors of Philippics and lectures like Lord Brougham should be reminded that those poor whom he has so unmercifully attacked have no opportunities, such as he has enjoyed, of forcing themselves into high places, with enormous pay, by threatening ministers with the loss of their heads.

192. *Heirs ready made.*—In some of the country towns in the United States, where the people were well off and living much at their ease, it was not at all uncommon for married couples to advertise for children to adopt. Thus illustrating Mr. Doubleday's *True Law of Population*. As is found also in some of the old writers. *Steriliora cuncta pinguia, et in maribus, et in fœminis*. Pliny, *lib*, 11, c. 37.

192. The Hampshire Petition here referred to is in *Register*, v. 32, p. 195. —The author was no doubt much influenced, when making some of the remarks on the clergy which appear in these *Rides*, by his recollections of the political conduct of the clergy on this and other occasions. It is right, however, at this day, to bear in mind the very able and independent stand which has more recently been made by the clergy of the Established Church in behalf of the poor. The Rev. H. F. Yeatman, of Dorsetshire, was the first to expose the fallacies of the early *Reports* of the Poor Law Commissioners. His writing is inserted in *Register*, v. 81, pp. 21, 328. Then, during the 10 or 12 years of commotion occasioned by the New Poor-Law, we had, in the same work, the Rev. G. S. Bull, Rev. Wm. Brock, Rev. H. J. Marshall, Hon. and Rev. S. G. Osborne, and many others of the clergy, whose united talents and great exertions produced most important effects for the good of the poor.

196. *Liable to be hanged upon the bare word of these vagabonds.*—Enactments since, in 1828 and 1833, enabling Quakers and Moravians to affirm in place of swearing: 9 Geo. 4, c. 32, and 3 and 4 Wm. 4, c. 49. And again, those who have been, but cease to be of these sects, but "retain their scruples of conscience," have the same privilege, by 1 and 2 Vict., c. 77.

196. *Poor Singleton.*—This man, John Singleton, lived on the skirt of Waltham Chase, and bore the repute of being a great poacher. The cogent evidence against him (on the charge of wounding a mare, the property of a person named Earwaker, by shooting) was asserted to have been a distorted statement of his own, made to a fellow-prisoner, while awaiting his trial. He was transported for life, but permitted to return at the end of 18 years to his old place of residence. And, although he had lost a leg while abroad, being a man of great energy, he had, at the time of his death, in the winter of 1852, managed to acquire some property in land. In 1806-7, when Mr. Windham and Mr. Cobbett were advocating the encouragement of athletic sports, boxing, single-stick, etc., this man was one of a number of countrymen who contended for prizes on the stage for single-stick established at Botley, and was noted for his indomitable courage under the blows of the stick. In a private letter from Mr. Cobbett to Mr. Windham, dated August 2nd, 1805, the writer says: " Before this reaches you, you will have seen that I have written, this week, no article upon the subject of the boxers; and I am glad I have not; because your letter, this day received, throws great light upon the subject; I mean of this particular case. I fear, with you, the disposition of the judges: the *cant* of *humanity* and *gentleness* is the order of the day, especially towards the weakest part of the community. . . . I hope soon to hear from you again, with some suggestions on the subject of the boxers."

213. *The French derided us.*—Spoken at a time when the French were writing of England in a taunting style, as quoted in the Register, v. 68, p. 408 (Sept., 1829).

213. *Bank restriction and small notes.*—Both of these measures were in fact proposed during the time of distress in 1847, in Parliament as well as out.

218. *Sheffield knives.*—Probably the author had in recollection what occurred about 1820, when English goods were almost given away at the auction sales in the United States.

233. *Dr. Chafy,* Vice-Chancellor of Cambridge; and Sergeant Frere, Master of Downing College. The author had asked leave of the former to be permitted to lecture at Cambridge, which was refused. Correspondence between the three, in *Register,* v. 69, p. 425.—Since this date we have the *University Commission.*

248. " *Friends of Pennsylvania,*" with whom the author was staying in 1798, at Bustleton, near Philadelphia. There were two brothers, James and Thomas Paul, Quaker farmers, the son of the first of whom, the present Mr. James Paul, was afterwards a member of the Pennsylvania State Senate.—*Register,* v. 69, p. 462.

253. *Nightingale.*—Several other birds, called *night-warblers,* are occasionally mistaken for the nightingale. Thus it is, in Lancashire and Cheshire, with the bird vulgarly called *pitsparrow,* which is heard late at night, but the note of which is nothing like that of the nightingale.

256. *Lord Stanhope's caution, etc.*—With what is here referred to from Lord Stanhope should also be taken the speech of the Marquis of Salisbury, made shortly after this date (Nov. 29, 1830: in *Register,* v. 70, p. 896). " Clearing estates," and " paying wages out of the poor's-rates," are there treated of. It was confidently predicted, subsequently, particularly by Lord Althorp (the late Earl Spencer), that the New Poor-Law would cause wages to rise. The contrary result has been notorious.

263. *A pot of worse beer.*—The importance to farm-labourers of having beer to drink can be fully known to those only who are aware of the amount of work done by these men, which is perhaps greater than is performed by any other class in the world.—In the debate on Mr. D'Israeli's Budget, 1852, Mr. Cobden is reported as having declared that the labourers did not require any beer or that they would be all the better without it. The same gentleman, in his *England, Ireland, and America,* 1837, attacks the

Marquis of Chandos for having moved against the Malt-Tax: speaks of the " almost fanatical outcry against the Malt-Tax " as tending to cause " the British nation to be declared bankrupt."

268. *Sir Henry Parnell's trick.*—The " trick " here meant is the scheme for the joint-stock banks, whioh, after they got into operation, threatened to break the Bank of England, and did break a great many other people, and, finally, were themselves broken down with much disgrace. *Register*, v. 69, p. 755 (1830), reports the meeting in London, at which the project for these companies was discussed, Sir Henry Parnell (afterwards Lord Congleton) and Mr. Spring Rice (now Lord Monteagle) among the advocates of the proposed experiment.

273. *The tommy system.*—This system of payment was afterwards partially suppressed, in 1831, by the " Truck-Act," 1 and 2 Wm. 4, c. 37.

280. " *Malthusian :* " see note, ii. p. 52.—" *Brougham.*" This personage, as all readers of the *Register* know, was for a long series of years an object of the author's frequent animadversion, being designated by a variety of undignifying names, such as " shallow and noisy man," " bawler," " barker," " bow-wow," " ramper," and " swamper: " the two latter specially applying to those epochs in Lord B.'s history in which he thrust himself into office, and quickly afterwards, by his fierce crusade against the pauper, brought his own associates in government into difficulty. Lord B., though having singular powers and opportunities for retaliating at the moment, has thought right to lie by, and to take his vengeance at a time when there could be no more danger from the adversary's club. Accordingly, in his *Letter to the Marquess of Lansdowne* (published by Ridgway, in 1848) the noble writer brings in the name and the deeds of Mr. Cobbett. Pleading for those whom he used to denounce, without mercy, as " foreign tyrants," and denouncing that " anonymous monster," the Press, which he formerly eulogised, he charges statesmen with having been influenced in their votes by " the dread they felt of Cobbett," and charges a jury of having (in 1831) " refused," from the same unworthy motive, " to convict " Cobbett. He also charges Mr. Cobbett with " direct incitements to the invasion of private property," " to plunderers," " to incendiaries." He had before this, in 1838, in an article against the Press in the *Edinburgh Review*, charged the same man with bribery of the basest possible kind, namely, in taking a money reward for services rendered to Queen Caroline. This latter imputation is answered in *Selections*, vol. 6. And then, again, in the *Letter to Lord Lansdowne*, he intimates that there is still a something more in " his recollection," but which he does not express, connected with the prosecution by Sir Vicary Gibbs, in 1810: a something intended, probably, at some future day, to be divulged posthumously, and by the means of that kind of agency which has given us Mr. Roebuck's defence of Lord Brougham in the form of a *History of the Whigs of* 1830.—No one, in fact, appeared to have more " dread " of the *Register* than Lord Brougham himself. When presenting the petition mentioned in note 119, vol. i. (in 1823) he went somewhat out of his way to describe Mr. Cobbett as of a character the very opposite of that given in the *Letter* above quoted. And three years after, in 1826, he even addressed a communication " to the Editor of the Register," consisting of a tissue of sarcasm and ridicule upon his own political rivals, persons of high rank. But this is only the same treatment as other people have experienced from the same personage; nor is it necessary to refer so far back as to the opprobrious language applied by him to his opponents in the House of Lords. In this same *Letter* to the Noble Marquess (1848) the reader finds Louis Napoleon, the then mere " Paris Deputy " hailed by the noble and learned writer's sneer of contempt. Yet the first announcement in England of the prince becoming emperor (November, 1852) is accompanied by another announcement of a visit from Lord B. to the new potentate. In this *Letter*, Lord B. complains of certain speeches of his on French

matters (probably of a Conservative kind) having been " prevented from being given to the public." The speech by which he made himself chancellor was also on French affairs, and in time of revolution and the greatest excitement, and delivered, in Yorkshire, just at the moment when, principally from measures adopted against the Press, Charles X. was losing his crown. It was the means of a sudden great gain of popularity for the hon. and learned speaker; and (reported as follows in Mr. Hone's *Annals of the Revolution of* 1830) affords an edifying example of how the clever can take advantage of the cat's jump.—" When Mr. Brougham visited Sheffield as a candidate to represent the county of York, the measures of Charles X. and his ministers had just become known. Mr. Brougham's *Opinion* upon the subject was requested, and he said, with a power and energy peculiarly his own—' Alas! the news has reached us that a frantic tyrant (for I can call him nothing else), bent upon mischief, and guided by an ignorant and besotted priesthood—led by the most despicable advisers—forgetful of the obligation he owes to his people, forgetful of the duty he owes to that Providence which restored him to his throne—has in the face of that Providence, and in defiance of that people, declared that he will trample on the liberties of his country, and rule 30,000,000 of its people by the sword. I heartily pray that his advisers will meet with that punishment which they so richly merit. The minister who could give such counsels deserves that his head should be severed from his body and rolled in the dust. If it were possible that any could dare to give such advice to our king, the same punishment ought to be inflicted upon him, and his head should roll in the dust the same day, before sunset, on which he gave that command.' "

285. " *Potatoes:* " see p. 291, vol. ii. and note to p. 88, vol. i.—The trial: that of July 7, 1831, for an alleged libel in *Register*, of Dec. 11, 1830, in an article headed " *Rural War*," v. 70, p. 929. Tried before Lord Tenterden and a special jury. The prosecution by Sir Thomas, now Lord Denman, then Attorney-General. There is a verbatim report of this trial, published at the time, by Mr. William Carpenter. The speech of Mr. Cobbett to the jury, owing to the manner in which he assailed the government, was remarked as being one of the most furious attacks ever made for the purpose of defence.

289. *Mr. Beaumont.*—The author elsewhere writes of two other like receptions while travelling, at Meriden, in 1820, and in Scotland, in 1832. *Register*, v. 36, p. 197: *Tour in Scotland*, p. 228.

295. *Whose former editor and now printer.*—The late Mr. John Walter, afterwards M.P. for Berkshire.—The articles mentioned in this page, " *Trevor and Potatoes*," are in *Register*, v. 70, p. 1099, and v. 71, p. 38.

298. *Large Parishes.*—What the author says of these, p. 296, vol. ii., agrees with the reason recited in 13 and 14 Charles II., c. 112, sec. 21, whereby townships, in Durham and other northern counties, are to maintain their separate poor.—" *These opinions of mine*," etc. It now seems to be formally announced, and, as it were, on public scientific authority, that the doctrine of Mr. Malthus, so much combated in these *Rides* and throughout the *Register*, is to be abandoned as being no more than a great delusion. See *Lectures delivered before the University of Oxford in* 1852, by George K. Rickards, M.A., Professor of Political Economy (Oxford and London: published by J. H. Parker). " It is impossible," says Mr. Rickards, " to construe this doctrine in any other sense than as an impeachment upon the wisdom of those laws by which Providence has regulated both the fecundity of the species and the productiveness of the earth." It is, also, impossible not to observe, in reading these *Lectures*, the large heap of French and Scotch volumes on political economy in which Mr. Rickard buries himself, while he acknowledges nothing on the part of such writers as Mr. Sadler, Mr. Doubleday, Mr. Booth, and Mr. Bowen, who had all long preceded him.

INDEX